P9-DBV-789

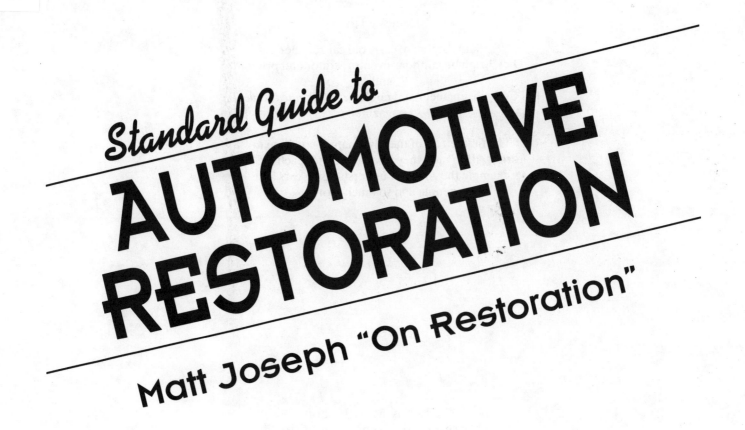

Standard Guide to

AUTOMOTIVE RESTORATION

Matt Joseph "On Restoration"

Dedicated to:

Sam Adelman, early old car recycler
Dick Brigham, author, inventor, editor and printer
and
Bill Cannon, engineer and publisher of *Skinned Knuckles*
magazine

The first letters of their last names combine to
form "ABC," and they have helped to teach me by
example the ABCs of understanding cars and
people and so much more.

Published by

**krause
publications**
700 E State St., Iola, WI 54990-0001

**Library of Congress Catalog Number: 91-77562
ISBN: 0-87341-188-9
Printed in the United States of America**

CONTENTS

Preface 5

Chapter 1: A Place to Begin 7
Restoration and the Restorer 9
To "Restore" 9
Elements of Successful Restoration 11

Chapter 2: Alligator Tactics, Logistics and Timing 16
Tactic: Deploying Others 17
Doing It Yourself 21
Some General Tactical Considerations 22
Logistics and Timing 23

Chapter 3: Good Restorers and Old Engines 25
Characteristics of Old Engines 29
Some Good News About Older Engines 32

Chapter 4: A General Approach to Engine Rebuilding
.... 35
Basic Engine Disassembly 37
Cleaning the Basic Engine Block 38
Crack Detection and Repair 39
Measurement and Inspection of Basic Blocks 41
The Repair of Basic Blocks 42

Chapter 5: Basic Engine Remachining 44
Three Basic Systems to Consider 45
The Valve System 46
Other Parts of the Valve System 52
Rocker Arms 53
The Camshaft 53

Chapter 6: The Crankshaft and Bearing System 55
Bearings and Saddles 61
Crankshaft Installation 63

Chapter 7: Basic Engine Remachining: The Piston System 70
The Head and Deck Surfaces 71
The Cylinder Walls 73
The Importance of Cleanup 78
Pistons 78
Piston Rings 80
Fitting Piston Pins 81
Piston Installation 83

Chapter 8: Engine Lubrication and Cooling Systems
.... 85
The Engine Lubrication System 85
Engine Cooling Systems 90

Chapter 9: Final Engine Assembly Hints 97
Basic Engine Assembly 97
Installing Head Gaskets 98
Some Other Odds and Ends of Engine Assembly 99
Engine Start-up 100

Chapter 10: Old Car Ignition Systems 103
Conventional Ignition Systems: The Basic Theory 105
Oscilloscopes 106
The Actual Practice 107
The Coil 109
Primary Wiring 109

Ignition Points 110
Condensers 112
Other Parts of the Distributor Low Tension
    System 112
The High Tension System 115
Spark Plugs 117
Some Final Thoughts 117

Chapter 11: Starting and Generating Systems 118
Common Physical Elements in Conventional
    Generators and Starters 120
Electrical Tests and Procedures — Starters 128
Electrical Tests and Procedures — Generators 131
Starter Engagement Systems 131
General Regulation Circuits 133
"A" and "B" Circuits in Charging Systems 135
Polarizing Generators 136

Chapter 12: The Truth About Carburetors 137
The Basic Principles of Carburetion 139
The Practice of Carburetion 139
Restoring Carburetors: The Preliminaries 142
Carburetor Restoration: Disassembly 144
Carburetor Rebuilding: Cleaning the Parts 146
Carburetor Restoration: Repair and Reassembly 149
Calibration and Adjustment 152

Chapter 13: Fuel Containment and Delivery Systems
.... 154
The Gas Tank 157
Fuel Lines, Fittings and Filters 159
Vapor Lock 159
Fuel Delivery Systems 160
Camshaft-Driven Mechanical Fuel Pumps 161
Disassembly and Reassembly of Mechanical Fuel Pumps
.... 163
Electric Fuel Pumps 165
Fuel Gauges 166

Chapter 14: Clutches and Transmissions 168
Why They Are Needed 168
Operation of the Conventional Three-Element Clutch
.... 170
Clutches in General 171
Clutch Removal 171
Clutch Inspection and Diagnosis 173
Clutch Installation 174
Other Considerations 176
The "Good News" and the "Bad News" About
    Transmissions 176
The Maintenance of Standard Transmissions 179
Standard Transmission Fault Diagnosis and
    Repair 181
Automatic Transmission Maintenance and Adjustment
.... 181
Automatic Transmission Diagnosis and Repair 184

Chapter 15: Getting the Drive Back to the Wheels 185
Universal Joints 186
Drive Shafts 187

4

Automotive Rear Ends 188
Rear Axle Lubrication 190
Rear End Diagnosis 191
Rear Axle Shafts and Wheel Bearings 191
Rear End Disassembly, Repair and Installation 193

Chapter 16: Front Wheel Bearings and Drum Brake Friction Systems 196
Front Wheel Bearings 197
Front Wheel Bearing Disassembly and Inspection ... 199
Front Wheel Bearing Reassembly 200
Some General Working Considerations 203
Drum Brake Fault Diagnosis 205
Drum and Shoe System Disassembly and Inspection 205
Reconditioning Brake Drums and Shoes 206
Reassembly of Drum Type Brakes 207
"Major" and "Minor" Brake Adjustments 207

Chapter 17: Brake Actuating Systems 209
Mechanical Brakes 212
Hydraulic Brake Operation 212
Hydraulic System Diagnosis 214
Some General Considerations in Hydraulic Brake Service 215
Master and Wheel Cylinder Disassembly and Inspection 216
Master and Wheel Cylinder Assembly 218
Hydraulic Hoses and Tubing 219
A Word(s) About Brake Fluids 220
Bleeding Hydraulic Brake Systems 220
Brake Booster Operation and Service 222

Chapter 18: Chassis, Suspension, and Steering 223
Frames 223
Suspension Springs 227
Suspension Diagnosis and Repair 229
Snubbers, Shock Absorbers and Other Things 230
Chassis Lubrication 232
Refinishing Chassis and Suspension Parts 234

Chapter 19: The Mysteries of Front Ends Made Almost Simple 235
Alignment Factors, Reasons, and Development 236
Problems Requiring Wheel Alignment 239
Camber and King Pin Inclination 240
Caster 241
Toe-In 242
Steering Box Adjustment, Lubrication, and Repair 242

Chapter 20: The Physical Restoration and Refinishing of Collector Car Bodies 244
A Matter of Perception 244
Expectations 246
Body and Refinish Standards Are Higher for Old Cars 247
Old Crafts and New Technologies 248
Goals and Necessities 249
Pitfalls and Worse 251
Specialties 252

Chapter 21: Sheet Metal Basics 253

Sheet Metal: Composition, Fabrication, and Basic Characteristics 255
Acquired Characteristics in Old and Damaged Sheet Metal 260
Impact Repair Approaches 262

Chapter 22: The Repair of Minor Impact Damage ... 266
Strategy for Removing Minor Damage 267
Auto Body Hand Tools and Their Basic Uses 268
Some Final Thoughts on Acquiring Bodywork Skills 276

Chapter 23: Shrinking and Stretching, Welding and Sectioning 281
Shrinking Metal 281
Sectioning: Cutting and Forming 283
Some General Thoughts on Panel Attachment 297
Gas Welding and Brazing 298
Electric Welding 302

Chapter 24: Auto Body Metal Preparation and Filling 310
Concepts in Body Filling 310
Surface Preparation for Fillers 312
The Theory of Lead 314
Tinning for Lead 315
The Practice of Applying Lead 317
Some Body Solder "Don'ts" 320
Finishing Lead 321
Plastic Fillers 323

Chapter 25: Automotive Refinishing, Part I 325
Choosing Restoration Paint 328
The Constituents of Automotive Finishes 328
The Choice of Paint for Restoration 329
The Great "Bare Metal" Debate 330
Primers — The Foundation of Any Refinishing Endeavor 332
Facilities and Equipment 332

Chapter 26: Automotive Refinishing, Part II 337
Various and Assorted Matters of Strategy 337
Sanding 341
Masking 343
Paint Film Thickness 345
Putties — A Matter of a Shady Reputation 346
Spray Guns 348
Spray Guns: Adjustment and Technique 351
Those Dreaded Sand Scratches 355
Special Situations, Problems of Compatibility, and Sealers 356
General Admonitions 357
Tricks of the Trade 360

Chapter 27: Automotive Refinishing, Part III 363
Compounding and Polishing 363
Spot Repair to Damaged Finishes 367
Very Minor (Brush) Repairs 369
Paint Defects — What Went Wrong? 370
Finish Maintenance 375

About the Author 379
About the Photographer 380

PREFACE

This is a book about how to restore old automobiles. Its purpose is to inform owners and restorers about many aspects of car restoration. It is not meant to be comprehensive, and such topics as upholstering, plating, and wiring are not specifically discussed here. What is discussed are all of the major mechanical systems in old automobiles and all major aspects of restoring their bodies.

The approach taken is "generic" so the discussion is of general approaches, principles, strategies, and practices — not of particular cars. Each chapter attempts to inform the reader on the historical development of the item or system under consideration — how it works, how it developed, how it varies on different cars — and then deals with the issues of how to repair and restore it. I hope that there is information in these pages that will be of interest to novice restorers, to intermediate restorers, and even to advanced restorers.

Most old cars never see the services of professional restoration shops. Instead, owners marshal their skills, talents, and resources, or they purchase the skills and talents of others to accomplish their restoration goals. These goals may be very limited — an engine component repair or refinishing a body — or they may sometimes range to a complete body-off-frame restoration. The attempt here is to provide useful information on renovation that addresses the wide variety of goals that are possible in old car restoration pursuits.

Old car owners need all of the restoration help that they can get. What they are doing amounts to grass roots preservation of important historical artifacts. This is an enterprise of tremendous importance, but it is also work that is often difficult and/or expensive to do and to commission. Often it is very satisfying work that results in a tremendous sense of accomplishment. The information in this book is intended to offer aid to restorers at many levels of performing or commissioning this work and across a wide range of topics.

This book grew out of a series of lectures on car restoration — "The Mechanical and Physical Restoration of Old Cars" that I delivered at the University of Wisconsin on several occasions and at several campuses from the late 1970s to the present — and out of about 30 articles

that were published in *Skinned Knuckles* magazine in the early and mid-1980s. Over the years, numerous students and *Skinned Knuckles* readers have suggested that I write a "restoration book." This is that book.

There are so many people whom I would like to thank for helping me with The *Standard Guide to Automotive Restoration* that the list would be as long as any chapter in it. That would make pretty dull reading and might embarrass some of the people who have contributed to my knowledge of car restoration. Let me single out a few people for thanks, whose contributions to this effort were both crucial and extraordinary.

Bill, Terry, and Charlotte Cannon at *Skinned Knuckles* magazine have published my restoration articles on a monthly basis for almost 10 years. Without their support and encouragement over those years, this book would not have been contemplated, much less written. The Cannons represent the very best in every aspect of old car collecting, and their magazine, *Skinned Knuckles,* has been an important beacon of that best for almost two decades.

Joseph W. Jackson III was tireless in taking many of the photographs that appear in this book. By day, Joe is a staff photographer at the *Wisconsin State Journal.* Joe is also an old car enthusiast of long standing. For the last year and a half he has devoted many of his evenings and "days off" to taking the photographs that appear in this book. His photographic artistry is self-evident, and I stand in awe of his talent with a camera and in the darkroom. Joe did more than just take pictures, he designed them and made them beautiful. No matter how late at night we worked, or how many more pictures we had to take late at night, Joe's enthusiasm and talent came through. We never stopped working on a photograph because it was "good enough," we only stopped when it was right. About half of the original photos in this book are Joe's; the rest are mine.

Professor Blake Kellogg of the University of Wisconsin — Extension generously contributed his time and knowledge to the considerable task of getting the typescripts of my original typed material into a computer format. He, too, generously contributed many hours to this task and was available on weekends and at other times that must surely have been inconvenient for him. He offered great encouragement and support to my work on this book.

Pat Klug, head of the Book Division at Krause Publications Inc., had the vision to see that there might be merit in the proposal for this book. She and John Gunnell endorsed the project with enthusiasm, and put the considerable resources of Krause Publications behind it.

Mary Sieber worked skillfully and hard editing my writing and always improving it. She supervised the page designs and layouts for this volume, and the results speak for themselves.

Finally, my wife and children offered enormous support to this project by helping me to find and segregate the time in which to do it. My sons offered many helpful suggestions and worked with me and Joe Jackson on the photographs. My parents offered early support of and encouragement to my interest in old car restoration: my father by nurturing my early interest in this activity and supporting it with his great knowledge of automobiles, and my mother by tolerating and even encouraging her two "car guys" more than any male car collectors had a right to expect from any American lady in the 1950s and 1960s.

My thanks to those named above, and to many other friends who have helped to further my understanding of automotive restoration.

Matt L. Joseph
Martinsville, Wisconsin
April 1992

CHAPTER 1:

A Place to Begin

The most difficult aspect of any complex undertaking is usually finding a place to begin and the self-assurance to do so. This is true of restoring an automobile or commencing a book on how to restore automobiles. Once begun, most projects proceed, either in or out of control, to rewards and catastrophes. It will be the purpose of this book to give readers the benefit of knowledge derived from my many rewards and catastrophes in automobile restoration. *The Standard Guide* is organized by automotive system and topic because the first step in attacking any complex task is to break it down into a series of simpler and less intimidating component tasks.

The knowledge that I have of restoration practices was gained mostly by the expedient of trial and error. There were few helpful books on this topic years ago when I began to gather experience. Often the amount of error in this trial and error was enormous — sometimes it still is. However, as I look back over thirty-five years of restoration endeavors, I am amazed at how uncostly some of my errors were. I remember, for example, a 1923 Pierce-Arrow that my father and I worked on in the late 1950s. Pierce had a really neat system for separating the head from the block of their massive six-cylinder, twenty-four-valve engine. There were two blind bolts threaded into the head and against the block. To unseize the head from its studs, you simply ran these bolts down against the block, and up came the head. It was a refreshingly simple way to accomplish what would otherwise have been a difficult job. However, this system of head removal placed a heavy premium on the mechanic to remember to run the blind bolts back up before reinstalling the head.

You guessed it. In an early restoration effort, we forgot to run the bolts back into the head on one of those massive engines. As we tightened the head nuts there was an ominous cracking sound. I suggested that we stop and find the cause, but a gnarled, old mechanic who was assisting us that evening acidly responded to my timidity, "Aw, it's just the head settlin' in." It wasn't, but I have often marveled at that improbable explanation. It was offered so spontaneously and with such commanding authority as if everyone knew the sound of a "head settlin' in." Finally, the cracking sound reached crescendo levels and, after the gnarled, old mechanic had excused himself from the premises — I think that he sensed a catastrophe was occurring — we found the cause of the sound. And, of course, the block was almost hopelessly cracked and distorted.

Well, in those days this was a catastrophe, but one of minor dimensions. A call to Sam Adelman, the major parts guru in the Northeast in those days, and another block was on the way from Mount Vernon, New York to Bennington, Vermont. The replacement block cost $65, plus $15 for Railway Express. Crating was included in the $65. Then, of course, the new block had to be cleaned, checked for cracks, deck ground, and painted. The cylinders had to be honed and the valves and guides dealt with. The point is, the whole miserable misadventure cost, maybe, $250. Unpleasant, but not devastating.

That same error today would probably run you twenty times what it cost us in the late 1950s. The cost of making mistakes has gone up radically. Twenty-five years ago, if you had a car painted and the paint checked, you were out a few hundred dollars. Today, it can amount to thousands. And mistakes do happen.

The gracious teacher that I had to assist me in my early learning about working on old machinery, trial and error, has become a very expensive mistress. Somehow, when she was cheap, her capricious nature didn't prevent her from seeming a gracious teacher. Now that she is expensive, her erratic excesses class her as a mistress. By way of introduction, it is the intention of this book to try to help readers avoid what are by now costly mistakes.

A caveat is in order. Restoration is a vast and varied field. It includes many obscure specialties, and there is a good deal of controversy at every juncture of decision. Also, things change. New techniques and new technologies come "on line" and change the ways that we approach restoration problems and procedures. The caveat is this: I guarantee the accuracy of what I write to "about" plus-or-minus fifteen percent for ninety days. Inevitably, there will be errors in these pages. Since the material in this book appeared first as a series of thirty-one articles in *Skinned Knuckles* magazine, it has had the benefit of inspection by the very informed readership of that magazine. Many comments and corrections were incorporated into the text of this *Standard Guide* that should reduce the incidence of error here, but a few may slip through. By the way, when you consume any restora-

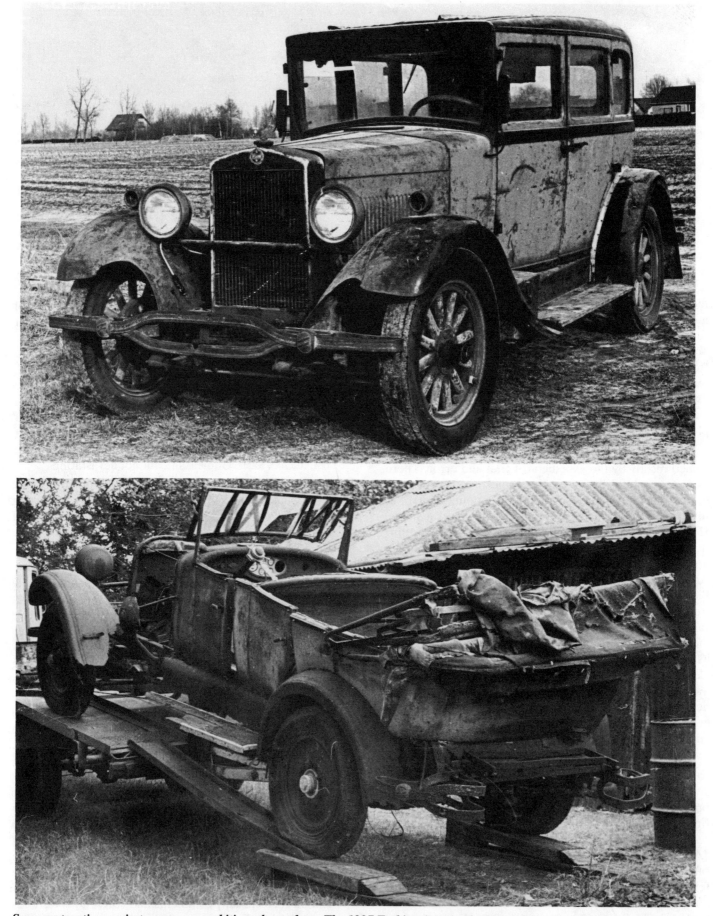

Some restoration projects are more ambitious than others. The 1927 Erskine (top) and 1925 or 1926 Studebaker (bottom) shown here would challenge the abilities of the most capable restorer. Cars that are as deteriorated as these don't offer a choice of strategies; they require complete restoration. (Photos courtesy of The Antique Studebaker Club.)

tion product, supply, or service, insist on a better guarantee of precision than plus-or-minus fifteen percent for ninety days.

Restoration and the Restorer

Restoration is probably the most ultimate and intimate involvement of human being and automobile. It can be an almost endless involvement; the only limits on the tasks that you can accomplish will be imposed by time and by your aptitudes. For some, just organizing a restoration can be a thrill. For most of us economic constraints and the nature of our enjoyment dictate an involvement beyond simple check writing. I often think that the checkbook restorers miss most of the fun and all of the sense of accomplishment that are available in our hobby. They rarely know much about their cars beyond the superficial, and they exist in a perpetual state of dependency on others to keep their machinery functioning and tidy.

True restorers are a breed apart. You see them congregate at meets and other gatherings. Because there are many kinds of cars and many valid approaches to restoring them, restorers are basically a varied lot. Yet some things can be said about them in general. Good restorers are characterized by their massive patience, their certain knowledge of many fields, their tenacity in the face of adversity, their innate curiosity and incisive research capabilities, their mastery of impeccable manual skills and good work habits, their perfect judgment, and, finally, their uncommon ability to make water run uphill. It is a fraternity of dedication, talent, and of accomplishment.

To "Restore"

Clearly, "restore" means different things to different people. To the neophyte it usually means shiny paint. For some, a deluxe run through the local car wash is considered tantamount to restoration. In fact, the definition of restoration is dynamic. It is a different proposition for different cars. Standards of restoration vary over time and from place to place and club to club. Restoration is always a matter of degree, the degree that must relate the purpose of owning a car to the work done on it. Regarding this point, restorers must be exceedingly clearheaded. They must relate the work done on their cars to their purposes for owning them.

Most cars are owned for one or a combination of the following three purposes: fun and driving, competitive showing, or investment. The reason(s) for owning a car dictate what type and degree of restoration work is rational and called for. Clearly, the three different reasons for owning any old car will suggest different kinds of emphasis in restoration work.

Even when the purpose(s) for engaging in restoration work are known, it is hardly obvious what the work should be or how it will be best accomplished. The fact is, there is no one standard of restoration. It would be nice if restoration simply meant to exactly duplicate original condition. Unfortunately, such a simple approach is not possible. Even if it were, it would rarely be practical or economically feasible. Take, for example, the business of refinishing a car. It is possible to refinish cars in authentic materials — varnishes, Japanning lacquers, nitrocellulose lacquers, and synthetic enamels. While such authentic finishes have unique and, to me, highly desirable appearances, it is simply not practical to use them on cars that are going to be driven or stored in less than ideal conditions. The old finishes are too fragile for cars that are intended to be driven, and some of them are too difficult to apply and repair. By today's standards, all of the old finishes oxidize and deteriorate quickly. Although these finishes are still available and can exactly duplicate the original condition of most old cars, they are not practical to use for the purposes of many people who own these cars. For some they are. For most, the durability of modern acrylic finishes is an economic necessity.

Inevitably, when the purpose(s) for undertaking a restoration are squared with the possibilities of restoration, a series of compromises results. These are compromises between some perfect ideal and some affordable, practical reality. Yet, having said that there must be compromises between the ideal, perfect duplication of original condition and some possible, achievable reality, I would quickly add that the ideal is easily stated and should never be very far from work that is actually done.

The ideal is to authentically preserve and maintain, and to improve. This ideal can, and should, become an obsession for every restorer. No action should ever violate it. Temporary fixes have their place, but there is no place for damage. "Do no harm" is a primary tenet of the Hippocratic Oath taken by medical doctors, and it should be an article of faith for those who would restore cars. This may sound obvious, but I have seen cases of cars that were destroyed in the processes of their restorations. In fact, restoration damage is very prevalent. Sometimes it is the work of a quick-buck artist trying to unload a car. More often it is the result of ignorance and/or impatience on the part of a well-meaning owner who got in "over his head" trying to restore a car.

I cannot overemphasize the importance of avoiding restoration damage. As the causes of deterioration of an automobile are reviewed and accounted for — wear, corrosion, impact damage, and the like — restoration damage and maintenance damage often emerge to pose the most serious problems for restorers. I have seen cars taken from restorable condition to scrap condition by well-intentioned owners and their minions. Sometimes the damage is gross, like pop rivet and Bondo repairs lurking under shiny paint. Sometimes it is less obvious, like the skillful but improper conversion of Packard touring cars into dual cowl phaetons that occurred at a rapid pace in the 1970s. Sometimes it is downright subtle and is discovered only after an extended period of ownership. In this last category, I once owned a '37 Dodge that had been owned by a plumber for thirty-five years. After he sold it, the car changed hands every couple of months.

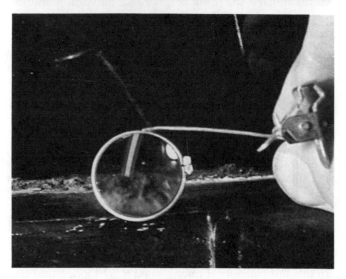

This 1931 Chevrolet looks great from a distance because there is no major body damage visible, and everything looks sound and authentic. Closer inspection reveals local areas of deterioration. To really judge the damage to the beaded area at the bottom of the hood's side panel, you will need a magnifying glass, and even that won't reveal everything. Some things you only find when you get there. The fabricoid top on this car looks rough from a distance, and very rough when you get up close to it. Damage to the top joists is a distinct possibility that may lurk under the covering.

For all I know, after I sold it, it has continued to run the buy-sell cycle six times a year. The problem that caused love to turn to hate so quickly for those who succeeded the original owner was that he had converted almost every possible thread on the car to a pipe thread. In some covered areas he had used modified plumbing fittings for nuts and bolts. I class this as subtle damage because the car was inevitably bought and sold at low prices. The buyers' enthusiasm always seemed to prevent them from noticing the subtle but substantial defect in the car's assembly.

I would suggest here that if those engaging in the restoration of automobiles would adopt the simple rationale for restoration stated above — to preserve, to maintain, and to improve — restoration damage would almost never occur. If any action taken in restoration does not square with that rationale, then damage will probably occur. There is often an enormous temptation to do something, sometimes anything, to make an old car look better or run for a while. It is a temptation that should be resisted if it does not result in maintenance or improvement of the vehicle in question. Most restorers would far rather deal with the ravages of time and wear than with the quick and dirty fixes of previous owners/restorers and their mercenaries.

The question is a simple one — whether a restorer wants to join that nameless, faceless legion of people who have defiled a national historic heritage, or the informed elite who are actively preserving our grass-roots history. I strongly suspect that if you have read this far you are, or aspire to be, part of the latter group.

Elements of Successful Restoration

Once you adopt your own rationale for restoration, you can look at the actual process as a small war against wear, corrosion, and the sins of previous owners. In this war you will need to employ strategy, tactics, logistics, and timing. Strategy is the grand plan for the restoration. It includes what you want to accomplish and, in broad outline, how you will proceed. Tactics involve the use of personnel, the details of sequences, the utilization of outside resources, and specific methods. Logistics involve such things as efficiently purchasing necessary parts and services. Finally, timing is the element of having it all come together at one time. If these aspects of restoration planning are not accounted for, needless expense and delay will result.

It is pretty clear that anyone can restore a car — given endless amounts of time and limitless money to spend. The point is, most of us don't have unlimited resources and must work with what we do have. Besides, the challenge of the thing is not just to restore a car by throwing vast amounts of money at it; that takes no talent at all. The proper object should be to accomplish what must be done at an acceptable level of expense and in a reasonable amount of time. I have seen restorations reputed to have taken ten years or more. Frequently such cars weren't in particularly bad condition when these marathon restorations began. Usually, the element of timing was ignored in these nearly endless endeavors. First one task was completed, say the body restoration, then its result was laid aside and another task was undertaken, say the drive line. At any point in this sequence, a delay in one area would stop the whole project, sometimes for weeks or months. A more useful approach would seem to be to account for timing and to attack several components at once. If restoration timing is worked out properly, a delay in one area will allow progress in others, as money and time are shifted to them. Rescheduling or minor schedule adjustments will then allow the various aspects of the project to reach completion at about the same time.

Or take the matter of logistics. I knew a man who erected a prefab spray booth to paint one car. He was only restoring one car, but he insisted on completing all work on-premises. Since he was a perfectionist and an equipment-freak, he built an expensive spray booth to paint one car. Certainly the job of painting the car was accomplished under very good conditions. Logistically the decision to build a spray booth to paint one car was incredibly inefficient or worse.

The first element in waging the war of restoration is the element of strategy. If that and the other elements, tactics, logistics, and timing, are worked out properly, "the enemy" will be deprived of most of the potential for surprise counterattacks. There are two basic, overall strategies that can be utilized in automobile restoration. They are the "ground-up" and "component" approaches. One involves the total restoration of a car at one time. The other proceeds, component by component, with the car being operable between bouts of restoration. The choice between these two strategies involves such variables as the reason(s) for attempting a restoration, the resources available, and the specific capabilities of the restorer.

If total restoration to a very high standard is the objective, the component approach will inevitably be more expensive and will yield a lesser result than an all-at-once approach. This is because component-by-component restoration involves more time, and its overall results lack the crispness of a restoration completed at one time. Another difficulty with the component approach is that what should be restoration often lapses into repair. The difference is that restoration involves the best and most authentic reconditioning that can be done, while repair only contemplates overhaul that will last the expected life span of the repaired vehicle.

Yet, having said all of that, the component approach to restoration definitely has its place. Component-by-component restoration can yield excellent results and it is generally far more susceptible to owner efforts than is ground-up restoration. It reduces the risk of creating a "basket case," and is economically more convenient because it spreads what might otherwise represent a huge financial outlay over a time frame that can include periods of economic recuperation.

The choice of one of these two major strategies ulti-

Authentic restoration means bringing a car back as close as possible to its original condition, with some exceptions. The use of original finishes is technically possible, but in the case of older cars they are far less durable than modern finishes. Some modern finishes, like acrylic lacquers and enamels, look very much like the original finishes that were applied in nitrocellulose lacquer and synthetic enamel. However, very modern urethane and polyurethane finishes do not look original on old cars and should not be used.

Restoration can involve some very radical procedures. This fender will require "sectioning" in its side/bead area to remove a rusted-through section and replace it with sound metal. The worker shown here is exercising one of the most important restoration strategies — looking over a job very carefully and planning his approach to its details before he begins.

mately relates to your purpose, your resources and the condition of your car. If your purpose is to produce a show car and you have the money and/or skills that are required, the ground-up approach is probably your ticket. If your main purpose is to have fun owning and driving your car, and if the minor deterioration of one component that may occur before you can attack the next component doesn't bother you, then you would probably be best advised to stick with restoring components and systems, one at a time. This is particularly true when postwar cars are involved. This is because they are complex compared to prewar cars, and there is always the chance of getting in over your head. It usually seems easier to disassemble a car than to reassemble it. In many cases, the choice of an overall restoration strategy will be out of your hands because the condition of the car will dictate the best strategy to be adopted.

The actual strategy underlying the component approach is far simpler than for the ground-up approach. The issues mostly revolve around the sequence in which components will be restored. Say, for example, the engine in a car is in need of a complete rebuild. It is logical to go through the clutch and transmission while they are out and to install a wiring harness at the same time. It also makes good sense to paint the engine bay and the firewall at this time. The reasonable sequence is, therefore, to deal first with the deteriorated components that are most likely to cause damage to themselves, and to deal with the components that are easy to get at when the first class of components are being dealt with. A knocking rod says "...deal with me and my environment before you send the chrome plating out." If all of this seems obvious, that is because it simply restates the basic rationale for restoration — to maintain, to preserve, to improve. However, restorers frequently do not deal first with the components that most need attention. Often they deal with the components that are most visibly in need of attention. Thus, a bad engine is left on self-destruct mode, while shiny paint is applied to correct a chalking or rub through problem with the finish. This may be a more efficient way of raising the presentability and price of a car, but it does not effectively consider the ultimate good of the car. The engine will have to be dealt with eventually, and it will probably be increasingly expensive to do so as further damage occurs. The nice paint that was applied will undoubtedly be damaged when the engine is removed and replaced — it always is. What we are describing here is a bad strategy and one that doesn't square with the rationale for restoration.

A careful, rational, and flexible plan of component restoration can make the technique workable and efficient. One prejudice that I have in these matters is to leave operable components alone. I am not quite endorsing the "don't fix it if it ain't broke" theory, but I see no reason to disassemble and rebuild or replace components just because they are old. If maintenance will do the job, avoid the mania for throwing overhauls, new old stock (NOS), new old replacement stock (NORS) and reproduction parts at every area of restoration. It's expensive and often pointless or counterproductive to the ultimate preservation of a vehicle.

The "ground-up" approach — when I use this term, I often envision a huge grinder with grated car coming out of the mesh — places extreme requirements on the restorer for a carefully worked out strategy. We've all heard of someone who disassembled a car and restored it, bit by bit, in his living room. Then he had to tear a wall down to get it out of his house. Rather a lack of strategic planning there, I would think. Any strategy of ground-up restoration has to account for the availability of time and

money to complete the job at hand, and for such basic things as living in one place long enough to finish what is usually an undertaking of several years' duration. Before such a project is begun, a worst case scenario has to be formulated for such things as mechanical work, electrical work, and structural and cosmetic body restoration. Suppliers of parts and services have to be identified and the relevant costs and lead times determined. Only then can the other elements of planning a ground-up restoration — tactics, logistics, and timing — be nailed down. Restoration is one of those areas of endeavor where a few hours spent in initial planning can result in weeks or months saved in completing a project.

I know a man who restores cars and plots his projects' progress, or lack thereof, with pins stuck in a four-foot-long chart on his garage wall. He creates a timeline chart for every restoration that he undertakes. Each component or service is represented by a horizontal line. The chart goes from left to right with the weeks plotted vertically. Each task done in-house or out is begun at a time that is selected to assure completion when it will be needed for some stage of sub or final assembly of the vehicle. The interlocking nature of individual tasks is perfectly accounted for. Suppliers who fall behind are represented by pins to the left of the actual calendar week. Frequently there are expletives and uncomplimentary

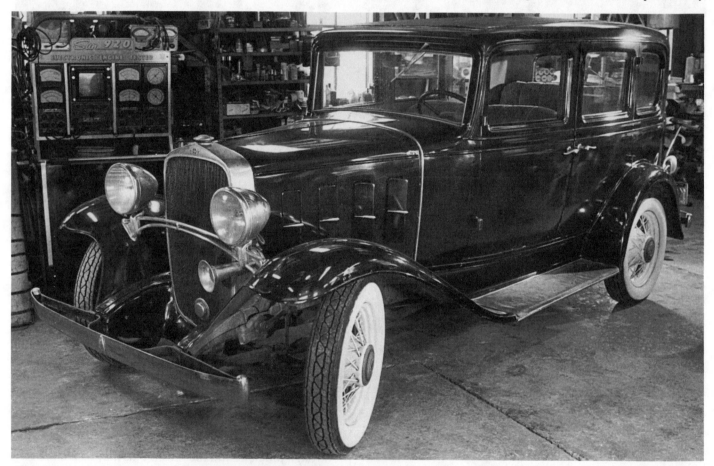

One element of strategy and tactics that you should nail down early in any restoration project is a good place to do your restoration work. The car shown here is also shown in "the great outdoors" on page 10. In that setting it looks small. Move it inside, and it looks much bigger. You should figure that an area a minimum of three times the area occupied by a car will be needed to do a body-off restoration or complete disassembly of a unibody car. That is the minimum. An area five times the size of the car will be more comfortable for this work.

suggestions about their ancestry written above their lines.

This elaborate technique for scheduling and coordination may be overkill, but it sure beats having a car completely restored but unusable because an intake manifold or water pump that was missing, hopelessly damaged, or assigned to a subcontractor was let go until everything else was done and isn't available now. Maybe someday there will be computer software to organize ground-up restorations, but for the present it is incumbent on any restorer using this approach to do a careful inventory of what he has and what he needs. He can then carefully formulate a plan that will result in a uniformly completed project in a reasonable time frame. I think that if would-be ground-up restorers did this planning every time, and realized the probable expenditure of time and money involved in a contemplated project, many projects that ultimately fail would never be attempted. You know how these failures are announced, "...for sale, reasonable, disassembled for restoration, body in primer, ninety percent complete, easy restoration...."

CHAPTER 2:

Alligator Tactics, Logistics, and Timing

A friend of mine who collects and restores the strange little cars built by Powell Crosley has a profound sign on one of his garage walls. It's one of those eight-by-ten-inch cardboard ditties with jagged edges and a grotesquely unreal wood grain background. There's a silhouette of an alligator on the left side and the text next to it reads, "When you're up to your ass in alligators, it is difficult to remember that your primary objective was to drain the swamp." For anyone involved in restoration endeavors, this must strike a resonant chord.

These photos show the kinds of places where major restoration problems can lurk, waiting to derail your most carefully thought-out restoration plans and strategies. Days spent inspecting the insides and hidden spaces in an old car and planning a restoration strategy to confront what you find is the key to staying on budget and on schedule in these projects.

We've all had "those days." The plater calls to inform you that an inexperienced forklift operator ran down your radiator shell. He's very sorry. You finally reach the man in New Jersey who said he had the magneto that you need. Now he says that he doesn't — you think that he sold it to someone else for a few bucks more more than you offered him for it. The pistons came in from the Coast, but they're the wrong ones. The machine shop called to tell you that the head that you left for Magnafluxing is almost hopelessly cracked. Finally, an "expert" in Kansas writes to tell you that the pictures you sent him indicate that the body you have just finished restoring is three years earlier than the chassis that you removed it from and are now restoring. Enough?

The point of this account of imaginary disaster is that some of the approaches to restoration mentioned in the last chapter — strategy, tactics, logistics, and timing — can help you to avoid the kind of cascading disasters detailed above. In Chapter 1 we looked at restoration strategy in some detail. Now we will concentrate on tactics, logistics, and timing. Certainly the application of these approaches will not eliminate disasters, but, as with the element of strategy discussed in Chapter 1, the adoption of a restoration plan that includes elements of tactics, logistics, and timing will help to minimize the impact of adversity on the trail to restoration.

In the matter of tactics, the first and most important tactic is the deployment of personnel. This consideration often boils down to what tasks you will do yourself and what tasks you will subcontract. The decisions here can be critical. Knowing what you cannot do effectively, and how to choose those who can, will often involve very fine points of judgment. For example, I am a pretty fair "farm welder" with experience in torch, stick, MIG (GMAW) and TIG (GTAW) applications. When it comes to sheet metal and other non-critical welding, I am comfortable doing it myself. But when it comes to critical welds or difficult cast iron repair, I usually leave it to someone with the experience of doing this work all day, every day. Knowing when to quit and what not to attempt can be difficult. On the other hand, some people are unnecessarily intimidated by expertise and will not attempt any new procedures just because they are new. Good tactics involve knowing your limits and working up to them, but not beyond them.

Now if all of this talk of tactics has tended to cast the restorer in the role of a "general," it should be remembered that most of the work to be done is on the level of a "grunt."

The unromantic truth is that car restoration is somewhere between sixty and seventy-five percent cleaning things. I know that restoration has been pictured as some sort of endlessly exciting endeavor in which the restorer will travel to the far coasts of the earth and discourse with quaint and interesting people about complex and engrossing problems that are ultimately resolved with brilliant and stimulating solutions. Bunk! Most of it is cleaning; cleaning old lubricants, varnish, carbon, and corrosion. There is precious little romance to be found here. What can be found is some level of efficiency.

All cleaning is the result of an abrasive process. When the abrasion is on a molecular level, the process is usually classed as a chemical process; occasionally an electrolytic or ultrasonic factor is thrown in with the chemistry. When the abrasion is not chemical, it is mechanical. Then its instruments will be things like wire brushes and sand paper. In either case, some level of mechanization will reduce the amount of unpleasant work. Such techniques as steam cleaning, dip tank immersion, glass beading, reverse plating and the like can greatly reduce the number of hours spent on the dirtiest and most monotonous aspects of restoration. But remember this; when you're out there deploying all of that personnel, most of it may be yourself, and the most exciting things that you are likely to see for several hours at a stretch may be a can of solvent, a putty knife, and a succession of Scotchbrite pads. The funny thing is, you may find this "grunt" work very satisfying to do.

Tactic: Deploying Others

Many people starting out at restoration endeavors begin by subcontracting the most basic cleaning work to dip tank operators. Then they progress to subcontracting just about everything else. In this approach, they become assemblers of assemblies and subassemblies restored by others. There is probably nothing wrong with this, except that it can be needlessly expensive. Sometimes the specialty shops that recondition things like clutches and dashboard instruments have highly specialized skills, tools, and equipment and can simply do their work better than any generalist could hope to. Most clutches, for example, require precise grinding equipment and special parts, fixtures, and assembly tools. For all but the most primitive clutches, it is probably best to have the work done by those who specialize in it. Carburetors, on the other hand, will usually yield restoration perfection to a talented and persevering amateur. Special tools and knowledge are necessary to refurbish some carburetors, but most can be rebuilt effectively without resorting to sending them out. If sending a carburetor out means that it will go to a local electrical and ignition shop, be careful. Many of these shops have suffered a severe decline in repair capability and quality in recent years as rebuilding has gone from the mainline of their business to a distant sideline. I have seen work come out of these shops that is atrocious. Some of the nationally advertised old car carburetor specialists are competent and fair, but at least a couple of them are wildly overpriced and basically not that careful about providing quality in their work. Sending assemblies and subassemblies out for restoration is not always the easiest or best tactics.

We live in an age of specialization and experts. This may be comforting, but if a restorer overdoes it, it can be very expensive. If a job doesn't require specialized and expensive tools and equipment, a restorer should consider doing it himself. Even such seemingly unfathomable mechanisms as automatic transmissions can often be

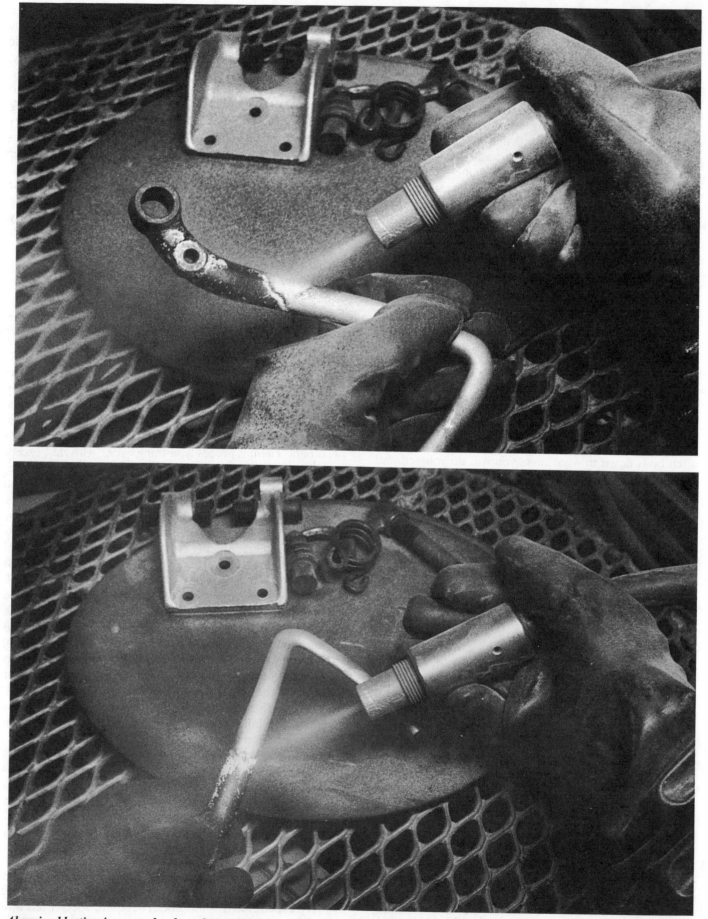

Abrasive blasting is one technology that aids greatly in the seemingly endless job of cleaning small parts. It doesn't work well for light sheet metal parts or for big panels unless you have very highly specialized blasting equipment and supplies, but for cleaning small parts it is just what the restoration doctor ordered.

rebuilt with little more than common hand tools when you know what you are doing.

For those items that have to be sent out for specialized restoration services, there is the difficult business of choosing someone to do the work. In some cases there are so few people who can do a given job that the choice is virtually automatic. In other cases where you may choose to subcontract fairly common tasks like plating, refinishing, engine machine shop work, or upholstery, there are so many potential providers that the choices can become baffling. There is no foolproof way to choose competent and reasonable providers of services, but I do have a short list of suggestions that will increase the odds in your favor when you have make these kinds of tactical choices. Needless to say, most of these suggestions were gained at the expense of bitter experience.

The first tactical rule in choosing providers of restoration services is to demand to see examples of actual work before you commit your job. Don't take a provider's word for his level of workmanship. Everyone wants to get involved in restoration work. It's more interesting than everyday repair, and it reflects great glory on the shops that do it. Body shops that do fair-to-average commercial repair work will often represent themselves to the unsuspecting as providers of exquisite restoration sheet metal work and refinishing. They'll point to examples of their craft on the shop floor and dismiss them with phrases like, "Oh, that's just our commercial work — our restoration work is very different — much better." Don't bet your car on it. My experience suggests that the differences between performing undistinguished work and really terrific work can be very subtle. They generally involve good work habits, fine judgments, and basic attitudes. It's pretty hard to switch these things "on" and "off" from one job to another. In my experience, each shop and each craftsman has just one standard of workmanship — no more. If what you are shown is tacky, commercial work, it is probably what you will get on your job. Many more people talk good restoration work than actually perform it.

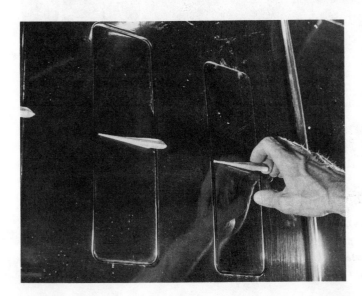

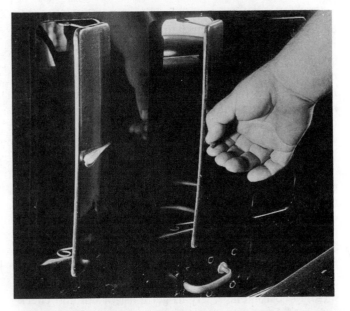

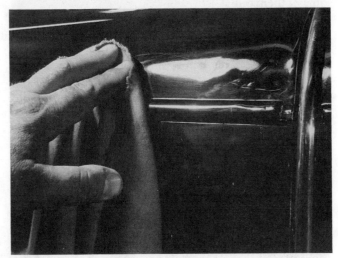

There is just so much about restoration that is different from commercial repair work. In a good restoration, the vent doors on this hood not only have to open and close tightly, but they have to have a crisp and identical feel as they do it. Little details like that are often hard to explain to people who don't deal with them all day, every day.

Restoration involves the use of very special and refined approaches to common tasks, to produce the highest quality work possible. You can see impact damage to the sheet metal in the cowl of this car (visible on the right). The question is, how far to the left does it extend? Feeling the metal with your fingertips through a rag will often answer this question better than your eyes can. Once you eliminate the friction of moisture and oil on your fingers by feeling through a rag, you will be amazed at how sensitive they are to minor variations in sheet metal. Try this little restoration trick. Restoration involves many such tricks.

With some exceptions, it is good restoration practice to avoid large, commercial repair facilities. They are simply not set up for restoration work. Usually they don't understand old cars, and their production schedules are not conducive to learning about them. For example, many nationally franchised transmission shops will try to repair anything that can be driven, towed, or pushed through their doors. The results are almost uniformly disastrous when old cars are involved.

When you choose subcontractors for specialized work, use common sense. Disgustingly messy and cluttered shops are unsafe and will usually produce poor or inconsistent work. Obsessively neat and antiseptic shops are frequently very slow and often overpriced. Any shop should be able and willing to provide references from satisfied customers. You should ask for references and check them out carefully. Anyone can find two or three satisfied customers, so try to get a list of ten and check some of them out.

A basic tactic in commissioning work is to demand a detailed explanation of the work to be done and the price for doing it. Do this before any work commences. If a provider can't explain the work that he proposes to do on your car, it's time to get suspicious. Car restoration is not nuclear physics or brain surgery. Most work can be explained pretty easily. People who can't explain what they are doing, often — not always — don't know what they are doing. If you don't understand the whole explanation of work to be done, evaluate the part that you do understand on the basis of what you do know. If something seems inconsistent or doesn't make any sense, persevere in demanding an explanation until it is clarified. Never let service providers talk you out of authenticity.

The importance of choosing the best subcontractors for specialty work cannot be overemphasized when the tactics of restoration are considered. An incompetent or unreliable provider can mess up everything by butchering or endlessly delaying the repair of a needed component. Unfortunately, there is a theory abroad in the land that everyone who advertises in reputable old car publications can and will do exactly what his advertisement says he can and will do. This is simply not true. At least one of these publications makes little or no attempt to check out the reliability of its advertisers. Another of these publications that does make an effort to police its display advertising will freely admit that it is impossible to do much about even the worst frauds in the old car field until several people have been stung. Recent stories in the old car press have detailed fraudulent ads for parts and restora-

Simple, rugged, and built to be maintained and repaired, that's what the steering and suspension on this 1931 Chevrolet look like. All of that is true, and all of it benefits the restorer. However, the Delco-Morraine lever-action shock absorber (left center) will probably require very specialized care from an expert who has the parts, tools and knowledge to deal with it. About half of the outfits that advertise the repair of these units in the old car press routinely butcher them and return the shocks that were entrusted to them for repair looking pretty but not working. It pays to check out repair sources before you use them.

tion services that have been run by prison inmates using the post office boxes at the prisons where they were/are incarcerated. Unfortunately, not all of the locations of these restoration "businesses" were as easily recognizable as Leavenworth, Kansas, and Statesville, Illinois. "Be careful out there."

A second tactical rule for choosing restoration services involves resisting the temptation to pursue convenience by letting a specialist work in an area that is not his real area of specialty. For example, it may seem convenient to let the transmission people do your engine work, or *vice versa.* This usually ends in trouble. It is far better to let specialists broaden their skills on their own time and machinery than on yours. The cost of their education in working out of their specialties can be greater than wasted money, it can be wrecked machinery. This is not to say that some shops don't have multiple specialties; many do. Just be sure to restrict the shops that you employ to areas in which they have demonstrated successful previous experience.

Some years ago I was visiting a well-known and highly regarded restoration shop that specializes in body restoration. I noticed that they were assembling the engine for a 1933 KB Lincoln for which they had just completed the body restoration. Since this particular shop had no repu-

Rod bearings, like this one from a 1933 KB Lincoln, are among the fussiest and most precise components in any old engine. While most of the sizing done on these bearings is done by machine, it is still a good idea to check them for interference and high spots in their working environment, and to make corrections with a bearing scraper as needed.

tation — good or bad — in mechanical work, I wondered how capable they were in this area. As I looked around, I noticed the main and rod bearings for this engine in a box with a mailing label that indicated the bearing work had been done by a large and very well-known machine shop which advertises nationally. This horrified me because I had just finished making a new set of rod bearing shells for a man with a KB Lincoln who had sent his bearings to this same shop for rebabbitting. They had been returned to him so badly warped and racked that they couldn't be repaired. Sure enough, six weeks later I was making up another set of rod bearings for the body restoration firm that I had visited. The point is that this firm was working well out of its areas of specialization and competence, and was using little or no good judgment in its sourcing. In the process, a remarkably incompetent subcontractor had been chosen to do extremely critical work. If you suspect that your subcontractor is going to use the services of other sub-subcontractors, check out these ultimate providers yourself. Whenever you are in a shop that does work for you, be very observant of things like labels on cartons and advertising calendars.

Doing It Yourself

As you progress in restoration endeavors, the tactic of performing more and more reconditioning tasks for yourself will probably be part of that progress. You will tend to choose this tactic because it gets support from both the economics of the situation and from a basic sense of pride in accomplishment. Another reason for doing your own work is the inherent simplicity of automobiles manufactured in the past. While today's automobiles are estimated to have upwards of 15,000 parts, cars of the 1950s averaged about 5,000, and as you go back to cars built before World War II, all but the most expensive of them are far simpler than that. For some reason, people viewing the under-hood area of a well-restored car will often marvel at how "complicated" it looks. Actually, it doesn't usually look that *complicated,* just shiny and well kept. Furthermore, such devices as carburetors tended to be much simpler, more purposeful, and better built in the past. It was often possible to "eyeball" a carburetor and determine the function of each part and circuit. This made repair far simpler than the repair of, say, an emission-motivated design for some 175+ part Thermo-Quad or Quadra-Jet monstrosity of the 1960s or 1970s. By now, in the age of fuel injection, it is difficult to eyeball much of anything. You scan for codes and replace parts.

There are many different types of work inherent in any restoration. Some of them require something beyond special skills and equipment; they call for a high level of basic aptitude. Most of this becomes possible with experience, but don't expect to do every task in a restoration yourself. Few people can handle everything from mechanical rebuilds to upholstery and painting. More claim they do than actually do.

This six-cylinder overhead valve engine might have looked complicated in comparison to the four-cylinder side-valve engines that dominated the low price field before it. It may even look complicated compared to some modern engines, where most of what you see in the engine bay is plastic covers. However, in terms of number of parts and complexity of operation, this is a very simple engine. Most older engines are relatively simple.

Some General Tactical Considerations

There must be about a hundred general tactical considerations that could be stated regarding approaches to car restoration. A handful of them are far from obvious but still very important.

The first is to evaluate systems and components before you disassemble them. If a car is not running, this can be difficult to do, but it is often still possible. It is a mistake to just tear an automobile apart for restoration without any idea of what areas are malfunctioning. I have seen it done hundreds of times. A new acquisition is dismantled without any consideration of what works and what doesn't. The fact is, it is far easier to repair and restore things if you know which ones are malfunctioning and how. Such knowledge is also a good guide to determining which items should be left alone. If a car is not running when it is acquired, it is often a worthwhile investment of time to get it running and gain some experience with it before beginning major restoration work.

A second tactic that will pay off is to inspect and test each system in a car separately, particularly where systems are closely interrelated. If, for example, a car overheats, it is a bad tactic to simultaneously disassemble and

repair or replace the thermostat, radiator, water pump, ignition system, head gasket(s), and fuel system. You may never find out which system(s) caused the problem. It is, however, a good idea to test and replace or repair, as necessary, the systems listed above, singly, and in roughly the order that they are listed. That way, when the problem is located, you will know where it was and you will avoid the pitfall of inducing other problems that may mask the solution.

A third, and perhaps most important, rule of procedure is to seek simple solutions to problems. This is appropriate because, for the most part, the cars that we are talking about were relatively simple in their design and construction. True, complex solutions are more intriguing, but they are usually unnecessary. I recently worked on a "restored" car that was plagued with violent overheating just after start-up. If the car had been left to stand and cool off for more than a couple of hours after running, it would heat up after it was restarted and boil very soon thereafter. Then, as it ran, it would cool to normal. Changing thermostats hadn't helped. The radiator, hoses, water pump and block had been either rebuilt or replaced in the restoration. The ignition checked out, and the fuel system was delivering the correct mixture, as measured at the tailpipe with infrared equipment. Exotic theories of hose collapse and cooling system suction leaks and cavitation had been proposed. Appropriate remedies for these obscure problems had been applied without success.

Overheating can be one of the most difficult to solve of the common problems afflicting old cars. In cars, as in human beings, overheating can be an indication of almost anything that is wrong. Causes can run the gamut from a slipping clutch or coupling to combustion leaks, or from a simple error in timing to an improperly assembled carburetor or dragging brake shoe. Sometimes overheating results from a combination of two or more causes, which makes it particularly difficult to diagnose.

In the case of this particular car, the cause of the problem turned out to be disarmingly simple. After restoration, the radiator had been filled with antifreeze and with a highly effective sealing additive. Unfortunately, the new thermostat that had been installed had an extremely small air bleed hole. When the overheating had occurred, this thermostat had, in turn, been tested and replaced with an identical unit in an effort to cure the problem. It didn't and no one had bothered to save the original thermostat to see if it was somehow different from the new ones that were used to replace it.

This is what was happening. The sealer in the coolant was sealing the air bleed holes in the thermostats that were installed to replace the original unit. The air bleed holes were so small that this became possible. When the engine cooled off after a run, the heat soak expansion of the coolant drove it out of the head and upper cylinder block areas. When the car cooled off, the plugged bleed hole air-locked the system and prevented coolant from reentering the head. Since there was no water in the head to transmit heat to the thermostat, and thus open it as the engine's temperature rose, when the car was started the engine overheated and boiled. Eventually the extreme heat and pressure in the cooling system allowed some water vapor to reach the thermostat and open it. This established coolant flow. Then the thermostat would open fully and the engine temperature would decline.

Simply drilling the pin size bleed hole in the thermostat plate out to 3/32 inch completely cured the problem. It was almost anticlimactic to tell the owner of this car that a little thought directed towards a simple solution to his car's overheating problem had cured it. I suspect that some of the "mechanics" who had worked on this car were dismayed when it turned out that their exotic theories had been totally irrelevant to actually solving the problem. I sure hope that the car's owner didn't pay them for all that nonsense. Most problems with old cars yield to simple solutions. It's a good idea to give problems some careful observation, analysis, and logical thought before you flail at them with wrenches and tear down machinery in pursuit of improbable obscure or exotic causes of problems.

Logistics and Timing

Logistics and timing in restoration work mean having the whole project come together at about the same time. Proper planning in these areas can save vast amounts of money, time and frustration. Much of this planning involves squaring the resources available with the best sequence in which to proceed. It involves choosing the most appropriate sources of parts and services in terms of cost and availability. For example, if the general strategy for a restoration dictates project completion in eighteen months, it is not necessary to acquire a fully restored magneto in the early stages if the one on the car can be restored at a considerably lower cost over a period of three months. In fact, if you know that a three-month turnaround for repairing the magneto is a certainty, you would probably do well to let it go until four or five months before it is actually needed, and allocate the resources that won't be tied up someplace else where they are needed. On the other hand, if you need a cylinder head and they are scarce, it would be a good logistical move to find one in the early stages of your restoration so that this crucial item isn't the last thing holding up completion.

Two elements of logistics and timing that are especially important are to cultivate reliable sources and not to

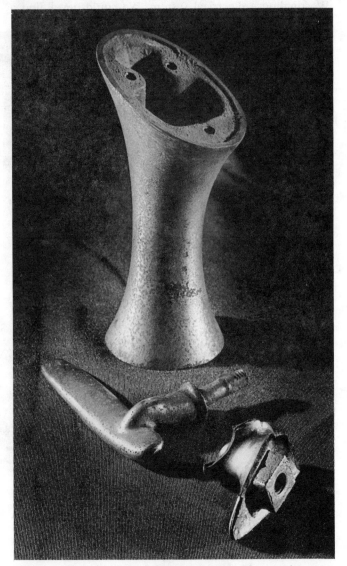

Casting repair is a very difficult business. Zinc castings present the worst problems. When you have items like these repaired and plated you should allow plenty of lead time.

overlook small problems. The basic wisdom in restoration sourcing is that when you find good work at tolerable prices, stay with and cultivate it, and be willing to pay a fair price for it. The temptation to abandon good and proven providers for those who *might* be a bit cheaper or a tad faster often leads to disaster. "Multiple sourcing" is a great strategy for large shops with huge volumes of work to subcontract. It guarantees them fall back suppliers if primary suppliers lose their edge or fail and it allows them to use competition between suppliers of the same item or service to improve quality or reduce price, or both. Great stuff if you manage a million-dollar-a-year-plus restoration budget. I wouldn't suggest trying this strategy if you restore one car every few years or so. You will find it hard enough to gain the attention and loyalty of one supplier of a service like chrome plating at such a low volume of work. As I said, when you find a good source of work, stay with it.

Always remember that seemingly innocuous and simple little things, like dash gauges, can mess up a very well-detailed and thought out restoration plan. I once worked on a 1913 Locomobile with an Adlake-Newbold-Westinghouse electrical system. We could never find a voltage regulator for this car. For years after the restoration was otherwise completed, we had no charging system and had to avoid night driving and rely on battery charges to keep this car running. It took ten years to find a voltage regulator, which turned out to be a beautiful cast aluminum box about three inches high and six-by-eight inches on its sides. It had a neat little window that revealed a dashpot connected by cable to an electromagnet. The cable ran over a cute little brass arm and moved it to switch various resistances in and out of the generator field circuit. A ten-year search for this unit finally yielded an interesting piece of information. The regulator had been built by Adlake for Locomobile and for the Pullman Sleeping Car Company, among others. Pullman cars used these regulators to regulate the output of their axle generators. We finally found one of these gems in a railroad museum and reworked it from forty-eight volts to six. Wonder of wonders, we installed it and it worked. It's good logistics to sort out most of the small unknowns in restoration propositions early in the game. It's also good timing. In this case, knowing more about the electrical system of that Locomobile would have saved us about ten years of looking for something in the wrong place!

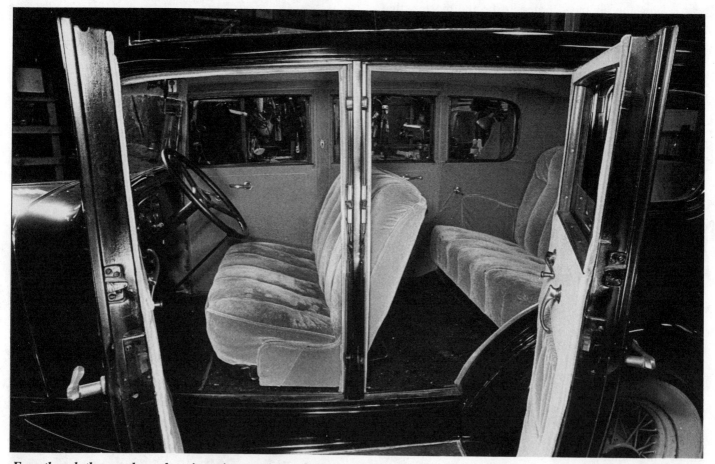

Even though the car shown here is an inexpensive and simple one, it will take a lot of planning to cause its restoration to come together at one time in the "not too distant future." Planning for the most effective strategies, tactics and timing will be the key to making this happen.

CHAPTER 3:

Good Restorers and Old Engines

Let me say at the outset that I don't personally know the individual whom I am about to describe — the "Good Restorer." He is, in fact, a composite of all of the desirable traits of the best that I have known in the restoration field. I doubt if he — or she — exists in reality, but the prototype described here can be a model for the rest of us.

"The Good Restorer" has developed impeccable work habits. I say "habits" because these actions have become unconscious reflexes. While some of us occasionally have to remind ourselves that screwdrivers are not cold chisels and crescent wrenches are not variable metric nut and bolt holders, the "Good Restorer" knows these things instinctively and acts accordingly. Since most disasters have their origins in small mistakes, good work habits are crucially important. Somehow, it is rarely a major lapse of judgment that causes catastrophe, it's more usually some miserable little mistake or a string of them. Good habits go a long way to preventing these mistakes.

For example, several years ago I developed the bad habit of turning sideways to the bench in my shop and working over my lap. This miserable habit meant that if I dropped something, it travelled to the floor, with its impact there related to the distance fallen. Then it could be very hard to find the thing if it was small. Once I realized that I had acquired it, it took me a month to break this habit. That was possible only when I discovered its cause. The light was better in the direction that I was turning to. The reasons for bad habits can be subtle.

The best time to develop good habits is when you are first developing new skills. In refinishing, for example, it is very difficult to break the habit of "arcing" a spray gun — moving it in an arc with respect to the panel that you are painting, rather than parallel to it — once you have acquired this habit. It is far better to learn new skills right in the first place. Then there are no bad habits to break later, and it is easier to fine tune your skills.

The "Good Restorer" cultivates flawless judgment. In the abstract this is easy. When a restoration problem is reviewed at some distance, it is almost always easy to come up with rational and correct solutions to it. But when some miserable press-fitted part won't yield to the persuasions of a decently sized hammer or puller, it is always tempting to get a bigger hammer or puller. This kind of thing can escalate rapidly to the point where a sixteen-ounce hammer gives way to a two-pound persuader and then to an eight-pound sledge. When that doesn't work, the "gas wrench" (torch) comes out with a large bore tip. Somewhere along the line it is easy to forget that the part that you are working to free is living in a fragile grey iron casting, or that the casting may not be yielding the part to your escalating applications of force because of something that you overlooked, like a concealed pin or a threaded collar. In these situations, you should try to resist the bigger-hammer or longer-pipe-over-the-wrench-handle temptation, even in the heat generated by fury. Such success as I have had in applying rational judgment rather than overusing brute force has come from remembering Oliver Cromwell's words to the Theologians. "Gentlemen, I beseech you, from the bowels of the earth, consider the possibility that you may be wrong." It's hard to believe that Cromwell never worked on old cars.

"The Good Restorer" has struck a balance between acquiring adequate knowledge before attempting something new, and not being intimidated by not having perfect knowledge. Just think, for a minute, how difficult it is to explain with words and diagrams the functioning of the differential mechanism in the rear end of an automobile. If a restorer insisted on understanding how this device works before the disassembly of his first rear end, the job might never get done. Yet when a differential setup is disassembled and sitting in front of you, its operation is easily understood from simple examination. Often it is necessary to take something apart that you don't fully understand. This can produce a queasy feeling and the attendant fear that lots of little springs and levers are going to jump out of the thing and make reassembly very difficult. In the cases of a very few devices this is exactly what will happen, but it's unusual. If you can easily find out the details of something before you take it apart, so much the better. However, it is unrealistic to always insist on such

Old engines can benefit from the use of modern equipment to rebuild them. Often, machining can be done that is far more accurate than anything that was available in the repair sector when old engines were new. Despite its massive size and weight, the crankshaft shown in this photograph of a mid-1930s Lincoln engine can be turned with just a few pounds/inch effort, and with the bearing caps fully tightened.

knowledge. Strike a balance that directs a reasonable amount of time to research, but not an all-consuming effort that never allows you to get to the job at hand.

Coupled with a balanced approach to knowledge, "The Good Restorer" has innate curiosity which causes him to always seek a better way to do a job. This is now popularly known as "continuous improvement." Sometimes it involves using a better material or a better understanding of the engineering of something or a better manual technique.

One thing that "The Good Restorer" never counts on is luck. He never hopes a problem "fixes itself" or "will go away maybe." He knows that the sad truth is that there are few, if any, problems in an automobile that will cure themselves on a long-range basis. If a problem is important enough to worry about, it is important enough to do something about. For example, if you hear a knock or a seal is leaking, there is little or no chance for improvement without disassembly intervention of some sort. While we're on this topic, I know of very few products that can be poured, spooned, sprinkled, squeezed, or hammered into any of the filler holes, sumps, orifices, or other entry points of automotive mechanism that will

It takes experience and good judgment to evaluate the condition and restoration potential of a door like this wood-framed item. In this photo the camera has been turned, and you see photographer Joseph W. Jackson III in front of his camera inspecting this door.

cure any real problem. The one exception may be the use of top oil to alleviate the symptoms of sticky valves. Of course, "The Good Restorer" knows all of that instinctively.

"The Good Restorer" has an absolute mania for good record keeping. This takes the form of good hand and typewritten notes, tags, diagrams, photographs, video tapes, and the like. I once knew a man who had a voice activated tape recorder in his shop. It was a neat idea because he could take verbal notes without having to stop working to degrease his hands to write down notes. There were a couple of flaws in this approach. Everytime he dropped a wrench or made any other discernible noise, the tape recorder ran for ten seconds. This resulted in many long, annoying gaps in the tapes. Another problem was more serious. Some of what he said as he worked was in the nature of spontaneously emitted expletives. His children found some of his shop tapes and had a dandy time. Now he uses a tape recorder that is activated by a foot pedal to record his verbal notes. Not a bad idea.

"The Good Restorer" understands the importance of very careful inspection before he disassembles and reassembles old cars and their systems. It is amazing what important information simple visual inspection will yield if it is unhurried by some overpowering desire to get things back together together. When I have put things together that *didn't work,* I have often found obvious faults when they were disassembled the second time. Often I have wondered how I could have missed these obvious problems that caused malfunctions the first time around.

"The Good Restorer" understands the importance of using proper equipment properly. Now, at some unnecessary extreme, this could be construed to mean that you would not consider a carburetor rebuild complete without a flow bench test. Let's stop short of that extreme because using proper equipment is much less subtle than that. It usually involves no more investment than walking across a room to get the right type and size wrench, or avoiding the temptation to make Vise Grips the universal tool. Most of the special tools shown in post-World War II shop manuals are desirable for the work for which they are recommended, but they are usually not absolutely necessary. If a restorer actually had to find all of them to do a job, the job would never get done. Often they can be approximated with homemade special tools or disregarded entirely. The most important thing here is not to insist on using special tools just because a shop manual directs you to. It is better to analyze the reasons for using a special tool, and come up with an alternative that preserves that idea without actually having to find the tool. Still more important is the practice of using very ordinary tools properly and for the purposes that they were intended.

"The Good Restorer" is safety conscious for his person and his work. He pulls wrenches when possible and avoids pushing them. When working with heavy things or

Highly developed and practiced manual skills are crucial in restoration work. In the leading process shown here, you have to use just the right application and manipulation of the torch and paddle to get good results. All of this takes concentration, practice, and dedication.

If you concentrate on what you are doing and think about every action that you take in restoration work, you will discover little tricks like blowing out the lids of paint cans before you pour paint. That eliminates one very obvious source of paint contamination. Eventually, these little tricks become habits, and the kind of thinking and logic that underlies them becomes ingrained and automatic.

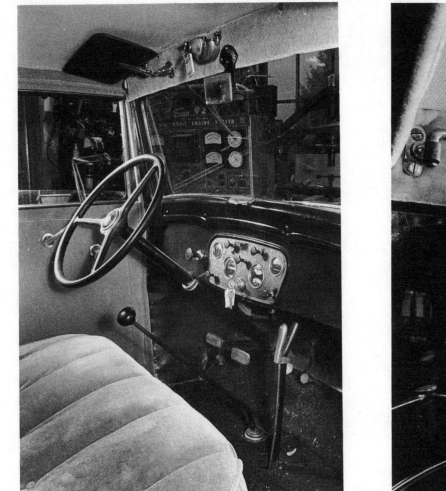

Most restorations involve working with cars that are combinations of authentic original parts, inauthentic parts that were added later, and parts that are borderline in terms of authenticity. All of the hardware in the first picture appears to be authentic. The upholstery material, carpeting, and inside cowl panel are obviously made from inauthentic materials. On closer examination (second photograph), the headliner is clearly made out of a grossly inauthentic embossed vinyl. That will be easy to correct. Note the authentic windshield ventilator knob and visor hardware. Items like these can be hard to find. Luckily these original parts are still with this car.

with parts constrained by great pressure, he knows that it is vitally important to provide an escape route for himself, just in case things get out of control. He constantly considers fire hazards, and is downright obsessive about eye, ear, and lung safety.

Finally, "The Good Restorer" keeps uppermost in his mind the importance of authenticity, and the ideal of restoration that was stated in Chapter 1 — to preserve, to maintain, and to improve. He realizes that restoration is an extreme exercise in detailing. A perfect restoration is an accumulation of all possible perfect details — many of which may seem insignificant when taken singly. When taken together, the resulting totality is the quality of any restoration. In this respect, the quest for a perfect restoration must be unrelenting because any missed or botched detail will be unforgiving. While perfect restoration is not the goal of most restorers, in any restoration work that you do it is best to know which details are not being pursued to perfection and why they are not.

As I said at the outset, I don't claim to know this fellow, "The Good Restorer," but his reflected brilliance has lighted the way for me and I hope for you as well. Out-

side of his restoration work, I suspect that he is an insufferable fuss-budget who probably routinely kicks his cat through his perfect hedge row after a day of working perfectly in his shop.

Characteristics of Old Engines

To varying degrees and with obvious exceptions, progress in automobile engine design and manufacture over the years has involved consistently higher engine speeds, greater compression ratios, and more highly stressed components. This trend continues today in response to performance, fuel economy, and emission control demands. It is made possible by design evolution and by the introduction of new materials and production processes and techniques. What this means for the restorer is that by comparison to modern engines, older engines tend to turn at lower speeds. Due to design and materials limitations, they tend to produce less local heat in critical areas and to be more over-built in terms of component stress. Machining tolerances tend to be less critical in many areas the further back that you go. When you get back to the early part of the century, automobile engines were so over-built that they tended to be amenable to the crude ministrations of blacksmiths, who were often the main source of their repair.

This is not to say that particular components and systems in specific automobiles were not notoriously over-stressed. The front wheel drive Cord L-29 had chronically failure-prone universal joints. Or take the bearings in Ford's trouble-prone small twelve (Lincoln Zephyr and Continental) built from 1936 to 1948. These engines were so over-stressed, and tended to fail so rapidly and repeatedly, that a large percentage of the engines originally fitted in existing examples of these cars have been replaced with various and assorted V-8s. But having cited these exceptions and noting the existence of numerous others, the fact remains that older engines tended to run cooler, slower, and with less component stress than modern units. They also tended to benefit from very adequate engineering, often bordering on over-engineering. Basic component failures and "recalls" are more a fact of modern automobile production than a feature of automotive history. I can think of few examples of engines made after the 1950s that are as chronically weak as the early versions of General Motors 350 (valve guides and other problems) or the General Motors 292 (bent rods).

This fact of generally less stressed engine components in collector car engines has an important payoff for the restorer. It is usually possible to make minor improvements in older engines in the course of rebuilding them. This is done by including modern parts and materials in the rebuild. If done within reason, such improvements, coupled with the enormous improvements in lubricants and fuels over the years, make it possible to produce results in restoration that will far outlive many original constructions. For example, modern Teflon/composite valve stem seals will vastly outperform some of the older natural rubber and Neoprene units. In fact, some of them perform so spectacularly that they will actually deprive valve stems and guides of the lubrication necessary to prevent rapid and premature wear. Care must always be taken when adapting new technology to old machinery. Engines are integrated entities and must have their systems work in concord. Consider this when adapting some new part or material in your restoration, but do not overlook the enormous benefits of new materials and techniques in reviving older engines. The technique of knurling valve guides can be both economical and mechanically desirable. It produces a working surface that can be more durable than the original, and at a fraction of the cost of bushing or replacement. The use of Teflon packings in steam engine cross-head glans has virtually eliminated the routine repacking of these units. Modern friction facing materials have often tripled the life expectancy of older clutches and transmission bands. The application of machine shop knacks, like countersinking crankshaft oil holes and block stud holes, or providing an adequate radius for crankshaft journal fillets has often greatly im-

proved the durability of the engine components involved.

In some cases, I suspect that the use of the new materials and rebuilding procedures enhances restoration only to a degree made necessary by modern conditions. It is doubtful if the cars of the early 1930s and before could be driven on the lubricants that were available when they were made at anything like the continuous high speeds that are characteristic of today's interstate highways. When these cars were new, poor roads tended to limit the exposure of automobiles to sustained high speed operation. Or consider what the exclusive use of modern unleaded fuels means for old cars. Now, the once exotic use of hardened valves and/or hardened valve seats has become an absolute necessity in all restorations.

Usually the only tolerances in older engines that were held to standards approaching modern standards were the bearing specs. Such factors as valve concentricity and cylinder taper were not held to such rigorous dimensions as are those for today's fast-turning, short-stroke engines. Yet in rebuilding older engines, I would advise holding

The people who factory built engines, like this 1934 Lincoln mill, probably had some type of torque limiting wrench that they used for bearing cap installation. However, this equipment was so unusual at that time that no torque specifications were published for critical bolted and nutted assemblies, like rod bearing caps, main bearings caps, and head bolts. You can improve on old repair procedures by figuring out tightening specifications for critical areas of an engine and using a precise torque wrench to apply them.

the tightest specifications possible. In many cases, the interface of modern parts and old engines requires this. Modern pistons, for example, will not tolerate the out-of-round and taper that their predecessors did. If we look at rebuilding a pre-World War I engine that was originally equipped with cast iron pistons, or even a post-World War II General Motors engine fitted with cast steel pistons, it would be good practice to use modern split-skirt aluminum pistons in a rebuild. This would dictate holding modern out-of-round and taper limits. The equipment that is available today in most automotive machine shops makes this easy to do.

While it is easy to improve on many older tolerances and materials, it is a mistake to assume that the basic engineering of older cars was not correct. It is a mistake born of a certain kind of arrogance, and it is sometimes paid for in the currency of broken and twisted engine parts.

Old connecting rods can be very beautiful and fragile castings and forgings. About the last thing that you want to do is grind the I-beam section of a highly machined rod like this one. It is possible to weld on and grind off material from the "pads" on the rod bearing caps for the purposes of achieving balance. These rods were factory balanced and, while you might be able to improve on this balance, it would probably make little difference in the operating smoothness of the very slow turning engine in which this rod lives. Knowing how far to take modern technology and engineering concepts in a restoration and knowing when to quit is a key to doing this work well.

It is one thing to replace an old-fashioned, graphited, braided rope water pump packing with a modern Teflon packing, or to Parkerize a camshaft after a regrind. It is quite another matter to start using exotic items, like sodium filled valves in old engines, with the hope of reducing the running tappet clearances by seventy percent to make things a bit quieter. Solid valve lifters are inherently noisier than their hydraulic counterparts. Either learn to live with this fact or get your hobby ride on an electric street car. A good tappet is one you can hear — that means that the valve probably isn't burning. Trying to modernize old cars by second guessing the people who engineered them is usually a bad bet.

I knew a man many years ago who restored a 1934 Lincoln phaeton. It was a meticulous restoration by the standards of the time. Somewhere along the line he decided to balance the engine. When I heard of his plan I wondered at the necessity of balancing an engine that turned as slowly as this one did, but it seemed, at worst, pointless. Well, in the general category of "he knew just enough to be dangerous," this individual achieved his balance of the connecting rods by grinding material from the edges of the parallel surfaces of the I-beam configured rods. Apparently he thought that the strength of the rods was in the wide central section. In reality, the central section in a connecting rod is there mostly to keep the parallel side sections separated, and contributes little beyond this service to the strength of the rod. This fact was vividly illustrated when, on its post-restoration "maiden voyage," the balanced engine in this Lincoln launched three rods and was basically degraded into mangled junk. In restoration work, overkill can indeed kill.

I keep hearing about exotic improvements that can be made in older engines. Some of them sound okay and have proven out in use. I can buy the idea that a Model A Ford will benefit from the installation of a counterbalanced crankshaft. This makes sense. But when I hear theories that involve halving factory bearing clearances to solve the deficiencies of the problematic small Lincoln V-12s, or doubling the pumping capacity of the oil pumps in these engines by retrofitting a truck oil pump, I become skeptical. The people who engineered cars in the past were no dummies. Their outlooks may have been limited by the materials that they had to work with and the concepts and standards of contemporary engineering, but they didn't often overlook the obvious basics of engineering. To assume that they did and to try to make corrections will usually lead to all kinds of mischief, not to mention inauthentic restorations.

On several occasions I have met some of the people who propound or endorse some of the wilder modifications of old engines. They have seemed a pretty squeaky lot. In most cases, the wildness of their ideas for re-engineering old engines is related to their ignorance of basic engineering. By the way, the people with cockeyed notions and wares for engine modification are not only described in the classified columns of club and hobby magazines. Many of them work in automotive machine shops. Beware.

Although old engines were substantially constructed and carefully engineered, inconsistencies and mistakes did occasionally occur. Whenever you have a highly stressed part, like a camshaft, out of an engine, make the extra effort to check for cracks with the best technology that you have or can buy. This picture shows a wet magnetic particle inspection being performed with a black light. Although the inspection of this four-cylinder BMW camshaft was routine, and there was little expectation of finding crack damage, a surprise was found. The shaft was cracked near one of its bearing journals.

Some Good News About Older Engines

Now, if you have gotten over any disappointment associated with discovering that older engines were pretty well thought out and executed, and are not usually susceptible to being re-engineered by the fellow who operates the valve grinding machine at your local machine shop, I have some good news for you. Older engines were designed with much more consideration of rebuilding than modern mills. For one thing, car bodies were very substantially constructed, and engines had to last longer than they do today to equal the durability of those bodies. Then too, lubricants were vastly inferior to what is commonly available today and for that reason engines wore more rapidly and had to be repaired more often than they do now. If we go back to the 1920s, we find that fuels were so inconsistent that it was the recommendation of many automobile manufacturers that cylinder heads be removed at intervals of six thousand to ten thousand miles, and combustion chambers and piston tops be scraped free of carbon. Can you imagine that sort of maintenance regimen being applied to cars today?

The point is this. Engines were built to be rebuilt and then rebuilt again without any consideration that they were somehow disposable or throwaway units. This meant that adequate material was provided for successive grinding operations on cranks and cylinders, etc. I'm not sure who invented the concept of the disposable or impossible-to-work-on engine, but developments by the 1950s went a long way in that direction.

Take, for example, the "Kettering Engine" that appeared in the late 1940s Cadillac and Oldsmobile lines. It is considered the predecessor of the modern, light, fast-turning, push-rod overhead valve, short-stroke engine. It set the direction for the light, oversquare, high speed engines of the later 1950s and 1960s. It also set the pattern for engines that were difficult to repair and not particularly durable to begin with. A developmental error caused the heads on early versions of these engines to crack easily and extensively. Worse, the rocker arms were not adjustable, and valve rework that took valve actuation part dimensions outside of the limited range of the hydraulic lifters made it necessary to use hard-to-find, nonstandard push rods. Some years after the Kettering engine debuted, Chrysler introduced their infamous "thin wall" block with cylinder bores so close to each other that they could not be bored to the depths usually associated with engine rebuilding. At about that time Chrysler also introduced their "Tufftrided" (nitrided) crankshaft which, while enormously durable, could not be reground without extraordinary measures. There followed such rebuilding nightmares as camshafts that ran without separate bearings (modern practice) and even without detachable bearing caps. Then there were the cylinder heads with integral valve guides. Ugh! All of these developments and others in the direction of throwaway components have made modern engines either difficult or uncommonly expensive to rebuild.

Many of the subsystems used in modern engines are designed with no contemplation of repair or adjustment. After the 1940s, distributor vacuum advance units were built with provision for calibration, and mechanical fuel pumps mostly could not be disassembled for the replacement of inexpensive wear parts. Simple, functional mechanisms, like manifold heat control valves, gave way to absurdities like exhaust restrictors, allegedly because no one maintained the old heat control valves. By the 1990s, computer-controlled fuel injection and distributorless ignition replaced all of the old hardware for controlling fuel flow and ignition. Modern automobiles are designed for a minimum of maintenance and external adjustment. Closed loop computer systems, hooked to arrays of sensors, make nearly instantaneous adjustments hundreds or thousands of times a minute. Most repair involves the use of bolt-on replacements for malfunctioning systems. This makes repair easy, but often unnecessarily and stupidly expensive.

The point of mentioning all of this is that older vehicle engines and related subsystems *are* susceptible to rebuilding and *require* calibration and adjustment. The subsystem parts on older cars tend to be much more individually designed for particular applications, and are not generic items designed for "groups" or "families" of engines as they would probably be today.

It is sometimes hard to find the parts and information necessary to rebuild things like fuel pumps, or to adjust and calibrate devices like voltage regulators. Yet it is often a lot less difficult and less expensive than finding replacement units. There is a mania abroad in the land for mindlessly throwing new old stock (NOS), new old restored stock (NORS), reproduction, and new design parts at old engines. People who engage in this kind of "bolt-on-restoration" have missed most of the point of the design of old engines and their accessories. Sometimes it's comical. I once had a customer argue that he preferred to have me install a thirty+ year old NOS rebuilt fuel pump on his car (cost $65 plus installation) to my suggestion that he rebuild the existing pump on the car (cost $30 plus in stallation). It was his car so we did it his way. The old rebuilt pump that he had found lasted two days in service before its rotted textile diaphragm fractured and the pump quit. Then it had to be removed and rebuilt.

In recent years, people have come up with all sorts of modern parts to replace old ones. Precise modern, solid state voltage regulators can be slipped into the original electromechanical voltage regulator boxes, and diode and laser triggered ignition systems with fully computerized advance/retard controls can be fitted into old distributor cases to provide the benefits of modern ignition. Some of this stuff represents an improvement in performance over what it replaces, and some of it is easier to deal with than the repair or restoration of the original items. None of the modern replacement hardware is authentic, and restorers should consider this point carefully before installing any of it.

If you do a little checking with good equipment and sometimes do a little repair, you can avoid purchasing new or restored assemblies for every component in a car that you restore. The check-and-repair-when-possible approach to restoration work saves a lot of money, and should produce more satisfaction than just bolting on NOS/NORS stuff everywhere.

Mechanical components like this wire wheel are readily available as reproduction parts. Sometimes replacement is necessary when a part is deteriorated to the point of being dangerous, or too time consuming to restore. However, often you can restore an original part or have it restored. This often saves expense and promotes authenticity. It's a judgment call.

CHAPTER 4:

A General Approach to Engine Rebuilding

Ponderous books could be and have been written about engine rebuilding. It isn't a topic that can be covered exhaustively in a few chapters in a general book on restoration. My purpose here in dealing with the topic of engine rebuilding is to touch on some of the high points, and to discuss some of the areas where I have seen people get into trouble — not to mention various problems that *I* have encountered rebuilding old engines over the years.

As for the books, a few stand out in my mind and should be consulted as comprehensive authorities on engine rebuilding techniques and skills. These are *Motor's Auto Engines and Electrical Systems,* various books on this topic by Harold Glenn (published by Chilton) and several pertinent titles published by the American Technical Society. Other readily available and well-written works are Martin Stockel's *Auto Service and Repair* published by Goodhart-Wilcox and several chapters of a book by that publisher titled *Automobile Encyclopedia.* The volumes devoted to engines in Chilton's *Mechanics Handbook* series are also excellent. There are probably several other books that are useful on this topic, but the ones mentioned above are probably the best. Some books that should be avoided are various newsstand hot rod journals and several obsolete works such as A. L. Dyke's "Encyclopedias." The latter contain some useful information and much dangerous misinformation. It's sometimes hard to sort one from the other. Hot rod journals often have useful tips on and techniques for engine rebuilding, but do not hold authenticity as a priority. That makes them an uncertain source for restoration information.

There are many areas of controversy in engine rebuilding, and it is not my purpose here to attempt to settle many of these. It is generally my policy to take a very conservative approach to engine rebuilding. Where controversy exists, I side with the sure thing — even at the cost of not getting on the ultimate cutting edge of potential performance and durability.

There has been, for example, a controversy raging over the use of "chromium" piston rings in old engines. Advocates suggest that these modern rings retain their shapes

There are all kinds of reference books that are useful when you work on old engines. Before the 1930s there weren't many shop manuals for cars. Repair data came from owner's manuals, factory service bulletins, and general books such as the ones shown here.

better, provide more predictable sealing pressure, and resist wear better. It is also claimed that they reduce engine friction. Opponents of the use of these rings in older engines suggest that the metallurgy of pre- World War II engine blocks is inadequate to withstand the wear inflicted by chromium piston rings. I have heard both sides of this argument for many years. Both can be presented persuasively and with numerous and convincing examples. I suspect that there is nothing wrong with using these modern piston rings in old engines. But I am not sure. Until I am, I will continue to order out cast iron rings for my prewar restoration work. They are adequately reliable, and break in quickly. I simply won't take the chance on chrome content rings until I am certain. Cast iron piston rings are much closer to original equipment on old engines and are the "sure thing" in this case.

On the other hand, the arguments that knurling valve guides provides performance and durability equal to or

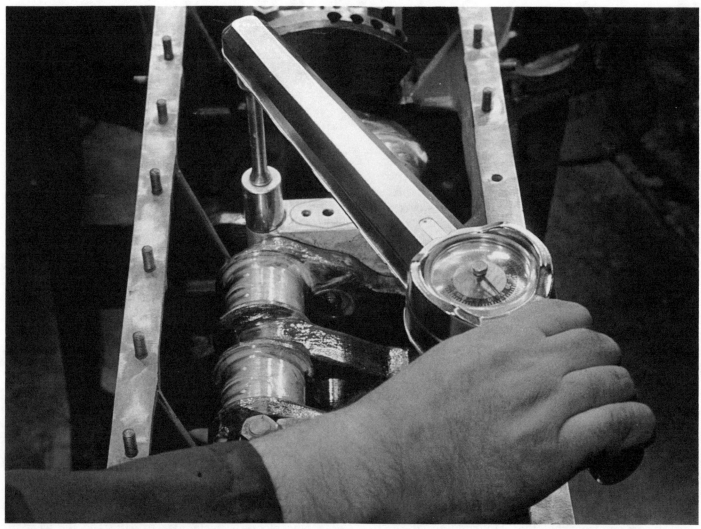

Basic engine block work must be precisely done work.

surpassing replacement, and at much less expense, have convinced me. As long as the knurling technique is not used unrealistically to reduce unreasonable clearances, the technique tends to produce a desirably hard running surface for valve stems, and improved oil retention by creating recesses. This technique is one that I fully endorse and frequently use in my own work.

It is counterproductive to reject all new techniques, materials, and processes just because they are new, and it is equally bad policy to adopt all of them without determining their individual merits. A good basic approach is to adopt those that have proven out over several years and in the experience of several people, and to avoid those where the "jury is still out."

Not all cockeyed theories of engine rebuilding are new. Some of them have been around for years. The first engine that I ever rebuilt was under the direction of a hard-boiled German mechanic. I learned a lot from him about measuring technique and the need for cleanliness in engine rebuilding. When the engine was finally finished and ready to leave his machine shop, he gave me a present, or rather, *he inflicted a present on me.* Without my consent or approval, he poured some of the contents of a rumpled and disreputable looking brown paper bag into the oil sump of my just completed engine. He explained, reassuringly, that this would aid the break-in process. I didn't know any better, so I thanked him. I got to thank him again about 15,000 miles down the road when I burned out a rod bearing in that engine. Somehow, my friend had overlooked the possibility that the flake graphite he poured into my oil was of a particle size that was too large for a colloidal suspension in the oil. Most of it settled harmlessly to the bottom of the oil pan, where I found it when I had to go in after that rod bearing. Some of the rest was quickly trapped in the engine's partial flow oil filter. Unfortunately, the remainder was efficiently centrifuged by the crankshaft until several oil passages to main bearings were blocked. That caused adjacent rod bearings to burn. Bad ideas come in many disguises and formats, in this case out of a rumpled paper bag.

Basic Engine Disassembly

After the accessories have been removed from a basic engine block and head, and their positions adequately recorded and indexed, it is time to disassemble the basic block. This can be done quickly and violently, with little regard for the fine points, or it can be done slowly and carefully. If you choose the first route, you will inevitably find that any time saved in disassembly will be spent tens or hundreds of times again repairing the damage that you have inflicted. I have seen people apply brutal kinds of force removing cylinder heads when some simple observation, analysis, and preparation would have saved them from the damage that resulted from this violence. Basically, any method of prying or wedging a cylinder head from a block will inflict damage. A cold chisel will do

more damage than a .015-inch feeler gauge hammered in sideways. But both of these approaches run an unacceptable risk of doing damage.

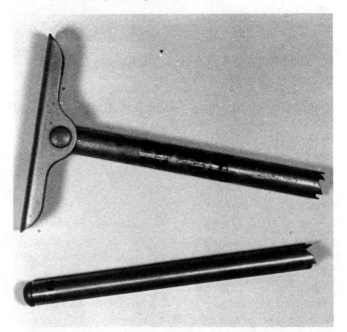

"Undercutting" the studs that secure heads to blocks can be done easily with the homemade cutters shown here. The one on the top is turned by hand, and the one on the bottom is chucked in a drill motor. These cutters are made from tubing with teeth filed in. When you use this kind of cutter, always provide some kind of a depth stop so that you don't cut into the block deck.

Analysis indicates that heads do not seize to blocks, they seize to studs. In the case of aluminum heads, this seizure is electrolytic in nature and achieves a bond that has the tenacity of welding. If the process has had decades to occur, no amount of prying will lift a head off a block in one piece. In fact, any head that cannot be lifted off a block with the compression generated by rotating the engine will need to have the stud to head clearance reestablished. This can be done relatively easily buying thin wall stainless tubing with an i.d. a "smidgeon" larger than the size of the stud. A half a dozen cutting teeth can be ground into the end of the tubing and a visual stop installed to prevent undercutting the block's deck surface. Then this cutting tool can be hand operated or chucked in a drill motor and run down over each stud to the block deck. With the stud to head clearance reestablished, the head can now be removed easily.

In the above example, a little thought and a little fine work can prevent the destruction of an important component. Another example of violent engine disassembly involves the removal of studs themselves. I have seen people go at this with pipe wrenches and with long arm "persuaders," with an abandon that is shocking. The theory seems to be, "what the — if I break 'em off, I'm gunna replace 'em anyway." Maybe, but drilling out studs is one of life's most irksome and unrewarding tasks. True, studs should be replaced during an engine rebuild because the torque characteristics of old studs are suspect, at best.

But breaking them off gets you involved with the likes of "Easyouts," or "wedge-proof screw extractors," or "fluted screw removers," etc. Since this class of tools often fails, escalation to drilling and thread insert remedies is just around the corner. And, of course, there is a jackpot reserved for those who succeed in breaking their choice of screw extractor off in the drilled out stud. Break a stud extractor off and you will usually find that it is made from a steel alloy that is much too hard to drill out. You can go after it with a diamond grinding tool or make a trip to the local die shop for an an expensive bout on an EDM device that will vaporize your broken screw extractor and stud. It's simply easier and more placid to get studs out in one piece the first time around. Everyone will be happier that way, except possibly the manufacturers of screw extractors.

Not to leave you hanging, stud removal can be made relatively easy by cleaning the bases of the studs to be removed, heating them to low temperatures with a very mild flame, such as air-propane or air-acetylene, and blowing a good grade of penetrating oil into the threads with shop air pressure. This last step is most important when you use penetrating oil. I had always used penetrating oil on the theory that it couldn't hurt and it might even help. I discovered by accident several years ago that when penetrating oil is forced into thread interfaces with shop air pressure (150 pounds in my shop) it becomes very effective and always aids in separating threaded fasteners. It's just that when it is squirted out of an aerosol can at half a dozen or so pounds pressure, it's capabilities are marginal.

When you go after a stud that is stuck in a casting, a stud remover is a far better tool than a pipe wrench. If applications of penetrating oil and a stud remover don't do the job, there is a very effective arc welding technique for heating and removing studs. It usually works on extreme, hard cases and should be performed by someone who knows how to do it.

Back to the disassembly of the basic engine block. What's inside an engine seems simple enough. There aren't very many parts, and most of them tend to be big and heavy. It's not at all like a carburetor, with all of those bothersome little parts. Well, not quite. A carburetor usually has only one or two of everything. A basic block may have one, two, three, four, five, six, eight, twelve or sixteen of everything, or, when we get to the valve train, twice those numbers. It is always desirable, and often essential, that everything go back in its own hole and in the direction that it was originally facing. Accomplishing this means producing the usual notes, diagrams, and photographs. It also means labeling parts. Tags are okay, but they can come off or become illegible. My preference is for scribing, stamping, or punching marks on parts that indicate their relative positions and installation orientation. A good habit to avoid is that of filing marks onto internal engine parts. A V-shaped file mark is a wonderful place for a crack to propagate.

Somehow, when you are taking a basic engine block apart, it seems simple, straightforward, and easy to keep track of. This may be true, but remember that six months, or a year, or more may elapse between disassembly and reassembly. In that time, what once seemed simple can create some major questions. If there are enough of these questions, you get to listen very carefully to your finished engine while you wait for some sign of misassembly related failure to occur. Every sound or vibration that cannot easily be explained becomes suspect. This is a situation that can greatly reduce any enjoyment that might be derived from a finished restoration. It is easier to get it right the first time around.

It is a good idea to do all marking and indexing with an engine in the top dead center (TDC or UDC) phase. Then, if you adopt a ground rule that all marks will be made in an up position, it becomes easy to remate things such as the flywheel and crankshaft, flywheel and clutch, timing gears or chains and sprockets, etc. in their correct relative positions. Piston tops should be numbered gently with number stamps, and the numbers should be stamped facing in a consistent direction — say, toward the front of the engine. Connecting rods, rod bearing caps, and main bearing caps should be numbered for sequence and position. Valve lifters, push rods, rocker arms, and valves must be identified as to position. Since these valve parts can be difficult to stamp or punch numbers onto, they should be kept in compartmented containers that clearly indicate their proper sequence. Even if you don't plan to reuse internal engine parts, it is still good practice to note their positions until you have the replacement parts in hand.

Cleaning the Basic Engine Block

When everything has been removed from a basic block, it can be cleaned. Any method of adequately cleaning a block will tend to destroy any components left behind. This means that such items as camshaft bearings, casting core plugs (alias, Welch plugs or "freeze" plugs) and the like should be removed either for their preservation or to enhance cleaning of the block.

There are several exotic methods of cleaning blocks, heads, and other engine parts. Major engine rebuilders and well-equipped machine shops use such techniques as convection oven baking or molten salt baths, followed by cabinet shot peening, tumbling, and jet cabinet washing. These advanced cleaning techniques are usually used due to the economies of scale necessary in production engine rebuilding. Many custom automotive machine shops still use a hot tanking method to clean large engine parts. There are even special hot and "cold tank" solutions available that are compatible with aluminum components. Never allow any aluminum or zinc alloy part to go into a common hot tank. The damage will be severe and almost always irreparable. It is a good idea to avoid the use of abrasive blasting processes on basic engine blocks. Such processes as glass beading, grit blasting, and the like present cleanup problems that are all but impossible to deal with. One stray glass bead or piece of aluminum oxide grit can do enormous damage if it gets to the wrong place in an engine. It isn't worth taking the chance.

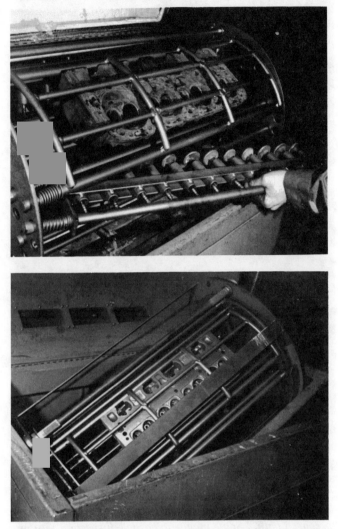

The latest wrinkle in cleaning engine parts involves baking them in an oven and then shot-peening them in a cabinet with airless shot. The shot is generated by one or more high speed bucket wheels at the bottom of the cabinet. After shot-peening, the parts are tumbled to get the shot out of them, and then they are jet washed to remove all cleaning residues.

The only blasting process that has any proper application to basic blocks is the use of air generated or airless steel shot. This cleaning technique is promoted as fast, effective, and clean. It is also sometimes alleged that shot-peening stress-relieves engine castings. This last claim is potentially true but, in practice, shot-peening applications to heavy engine parts are almost never carried out in ways that are controlled enough to achieve any predictable stress-relieving results. One drawback of shot-peening blocks and other heavy engine parts is that the process tends to smear a minutely thin coating of steel on the surfaces of iron parts. This can result in corrosion under the parts' finishes and subsequent paint failure. When you shot-peen engine parts with exposed surfaces that will later be painted, you should always use a conversion coating to etch them, or an etching primer under your engine paint.

Hot tanking a block is still a good way to clean it. It does tend to leave undesirable chemical residues on a block's surface, and this has to be cleaned off. After all machining operations have been completed on a block it should be washed and rinsed with common hand soap and water. This will remove any residual chemicals from the hot tanking or jet washing operation. It also gets rid of any chips and grit left over from machining operations. After this hand bath, the working and sealing surfaces of the block should be completely dried with compressed air and be coated with light oil to prevent rusting prior to reassembly.

Crack Detection and Repair

For a very small cost the basic engine block, head, and internal components of any engine that you restore can be subjected to a Magnaflux inspection for cracks. This step is absolutely essential to proper engine rebuilding. Most engine block cracks will be found in the combustion chambers in the vicinity of the valves. In "L," "T," and "F" head engines this means that they will be in the block, but there are other possibilities. Cracks across the deck of a block, in bearing saddle areas, or in valve chambers are common. We do our own Magnaflux inspection of critical and stressed engine components, then we take the same parts to the machine shop that we use. Whenever I take the parts from an engine that we are working on to the machine shop that we use, a standing joke is activated. I say something like, "Look here, this engine model has a bad reputation for cracks, better give it a particularly careful going over." And one of the machinists always says something like, "Oh, where do they crack?" To which I always answer, "Everywhere, just everywhere."

The people who sell Magnaflux crack detection systems also sell a very abbreviated detection process called "Spotcheck," and a slightly more sophisticated process called "Zyglo." These systems are generally sold through

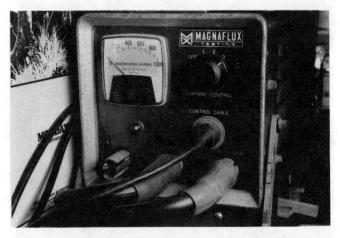

This power unit provides the power to energize various forms of magnetic field that are used for crack inspections of steel and iron parts.

welding supply shops, but have also been offered and misrepresented through advertising in several old car journals. They are reasonably effective in discerning gross cracks, but their usefulness ends there. They are *not* a substitute for Magnaflux or other magnetic particle inspection analysis of blocks, heads, and internal engine parts. They were not intended for that purpose. These and some other dye-penetrant, aerosol crack detection systems simply do not exhibit the sensitivity to cracks that is necessary for the purposes of engine rebuilding. The fact is that very small cracks in engines can open up and become very large when they are repeatedly heated, cooled and mechanically stressed. There are inevitably enough unknowns in rebuilding fifty-year-old engines without adding potential cracks to the list. Magnafluxing isn't particularly expensive, and it comes as close to being foolproof as any materials testing procedure that I know. I recommend it.

In these pictures, various formats and configurations of magnetic flux are used to examine a connecting rod for cracks. Note that a black light is used to make the magnetic particles in the test fluoresce. The particles will line up along a crack and indicate it as a line. Note that the magnetic particles for the test are being applied from an aerosol can in a "prepared bath." Some magnetic particle inspection set-ups use a constant flow bath to apply the particles.

This connecting rod has failed the magnetic particle test. A crack is clearly visible.

Measurement and Inspection of Basic Blocks

Measurement and inspection are critically important in engine rebuilding. This is particularly true of basic engine blocks. Inspection does not end with Magnafluxing. Such matters as the condition of threaded holes and the straightness of manifold mating surfaces are critically important. Part of the inspection process relies on the un-aided eye, as, for example, the evaluation of sealing and running surfaces for porosity and pin-holing. Every working and mating flat surface must be inspected with a straight edge and thickness gauges. The straight edge should be a hefty piece of stabilized and ground steel, and the thickness gauges should be in good condition. As a general rule, if you can find warping in a head or block of more than .002 inch in any six-inch run, it's time to surface grind that surface. This is true of the head, block deck, block bottom, or the manifold surfaces of an engine. Of course, if visual inspection reveals porous, rough, or deeply scratched surfaces, then surface grinding is required even if the .002 inch in six-inch test can be passed.

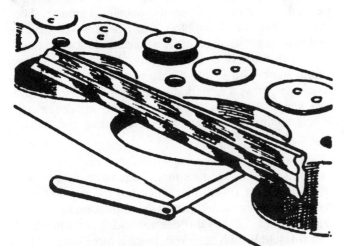

Throughout the inspection and measurement process, remember that old castings can be very capricious in the ways that they choose to distort. Blocks tend to twist and warp in unexpected directions. Wear tends to occur predictably and then, if you let up for a minute in your inspection, unpredictably. I have seen examples of wear that seem inexplicable according to the physical laws that would seem to control such things. I suppose that if all of the variables were known and accounted for, there would be a logical explanation, but at the present state of my knowledge I sometimes just shake my head and think, '...must have happened during a full moon.'

Well, whenever it happened, you will have to look for weird wear patterns and distortions to find them. My basic rule is to make every possible measurement that I can. Assume that the engine that you are working on was assembled by an incompetent apprentice and maintained by lunatics. Proceed from there and measure the alignment of the main bearing saddles for straightness and with the cylinder bores, the alignment of the camshaft bearing bores, the straightness of the cylinder bores, etc. Bore straightness is an interesting example of the subtleties of measurement. Cylinder wall wear patterns should tip you off to a crooked cylinder, but they don't always do that for you. If you attempt to surface a cylinder wall with a simple hone, or even with a sophisticated dwell-hone, you will perpetuate any deflection in the cylinder wall from straight. The only way to cure this problem is with a boring bar. But what could cause a cylinder to be non-perpendicular to the crank centerline? A lot of things could, but the condition, when it is found, is often there because the block left the factory that way. In other words, the inspection and measurement process is not just to account for wear and casting distortion after manufacture, it also has to account for manufacturing error, and there is a surprising amount of that error in older engines.

The business of measuring block dimensions and deviations is not terribly complex or hard to learn, but it does require some experience. The use of feeler (thick-

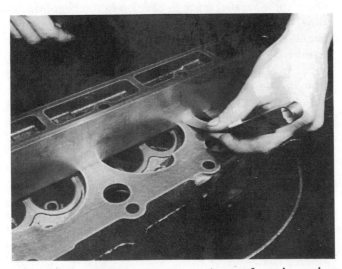

Block decks, heads, and other mating surfaces in engines should be checked for flatness with a straight edge and feeler gauge.

A feeler gauge and straight edge can also be used to check such alignments as that of the main bearing saddles.

A cylinder bore gauge is the best way to check cylinders for wear, distortion, out-of-round, and taper. Always carefully record the measurements that you make and indicate exactly where they were taken.

ness) gauges, micrometers, bore gauges, etc. requires a sense of feel that takes some time to develop. Conventional measuring tools are easily capable of vernier measurement to .0001 inch. This level of precision is highly desirable in areas such as bearing clearance. To achieve this accuracy requires not only a feel for the measuring instruments involved, but also the ability to calibrate these devices, and extreme attention to cleanliness. A new generation of electronic/digital readout instruments is making precise measurements easier to obtain, but it would be a mistake to attempt any precision measurements with any kind of precision measuring equipment without proper instruction and, at least, some experience.

Another critical aspect of measuring technique involves knowing and understanding measurement terminology, cold. It is surprising how many people engaging in engine rebuilding cannot handle the basic use of the decimal system. They will say, "three thousandths," but write ".0003 inch" (which is really three ten thousandths). The results can be disastrous. Terminology confusion goes beyond the use of the decimal system. Take, for example, the conventions surrounding the specification of bearing clearances. These clearances are specified as the difference between the diameter of bearing bore and shaft diameter. Yet some people think that this specification denotes the space on each side of a shaft centered in a bearing. If someone operating under this misconception orders a crankshaft grind or a new set of bearings, and the error is not caught, he will end up with twice the specified running clearance. It sounds ridiculous, but it happens everyday. If you have any questions about measurement terminology or convention, don't be embarrassed to ask. Errors in this area are always more embarrassing than honest questions.

When dealing with old engine blocks and their innards, try to get the particular data that applies to the engine that you are rebuilding. While most main and rod bearings run in the clearance range of .0015 inch to .002 inch,

some do not. It pays to find the right specifications for any engine that you are working on and adhere to them throughout the rebuilding process. Splash lubricated systems, for example, have different clearance requirements than full pressure systems.

The Repair of Basic Blocks

There are basically two major classes of defect that occur in old engine castings; these are cracks and rust-throughs. This is not to say that there are not other possibilities. Burn-out defects are occasionally encountered and extraordinary wear, such as bearing spin-out damage, can erode the metal of a basic block. But cracks and rust-outs account for about ninety percent of the block defects that require repair.

Cracks are commonly repaired by drilling the crack ends to stop propagation, and either welding, peening, or pinning and peening. The pinning and peening approach involves drilling either adjacent or overlapping holes in a crack and forcing threaded or tapered pins into the holes. The heads of the pins are then cut off and the stubs peened over with a pneumatic peening hammer. Then the whole inside of the block's or head's water jacket is sealed by internally coating it with ceramic sealant that is flowed through it under pressure. This technique may sound haphazard in my description of it, but the technique has proven remarkably successful in use for over fifty years. A crucial aspect of this, or any other crack repair technique, involves pressure testing the finished repair.

Welding cracks in castings is another highly successful method of repair, but requires extreme skill to produce reliable results. Cast iron, particularly the gray and nodular castings that sometimes show up in automobile block engine blocks, is very difficult to weld. Even when a successful weld bead is achieved, there is a considerable tendency for a parallel crack to develop in the heat-affected zone adjacent to the weld. Specific measures, such as peening, preheating, slow heat reduction, and the like are required to circumvent this tendency. I know enough about welding stressed castings to pretty much stay away from it. This is one of those areas of skill best left to people who do it all day, every day. Several specialty welding shops produce great results when welding engine block and head cracks. There are also several companies that specialize in repairing cracked diesel heads for the trucking industry. These providers are a particularly good bet because they routinely deal with castings that are stressed way beyond almost anything encountered in old car engines. Water jacket cracks are susceptible to brazing, but are still best left to people who can accurately assess the movement and stress of castings under the application of welding heat.

The choice of crack repair technique ultimately depends on the metallurgical composition of the block in question, and the location of the crack(s). In some cases, the economics of crack repair will dictate the replacement of a block. This is particularly true of freeze cracked blocks, where the cracks, combined with block distortion, make any contemplated repair very expensive.

One thing should be obvious from all of this. Never put an engine together that has any cracks or suspected cracks. I have seen this done because some poor person has assumed that he could beat the cost of crack repair by pouring some magic fluid into the cooling system after the engine is together and, thus, cure the problem. Such a cure will be temporary at best, and the crack will just get bigger after the engine has been bolted together and run for a while. ("Nature always sides with the hidden defect.") I realize that the crack repair fluids and solids that are sold for addition to cooling systems often have intriguing names and come in some really great-looking containers. Often these substances have wonderful appearances of bronze, copper, or aluminum flakes. A few even look like rejected props from the sci fi movie, "The Blob." Whatever the appearance or product name, whether it's high tech sounding or just folksy, such remedies won't work for long. I've heard all of the stories about sodium silicate and I don't believe any of them. The ultimate cost of trying to live with cracks is, at best, running problems. At worst it's the twisted and ruined parts caused by "hydrolock." That's when a pressurized cooling system has filled a cylinder with coolant by leaking into it overnight, and a subsequent attempt to start the car brings the torque of a one horsepower starting motor against a connecting rod through a 25:1 gear ratio on the flywheel. Since the cylinder has filled with a relatively incompressible fluid, the piston has no place to go. That's right, something has to give, usually the rod. If you're old enough to be rebuilding engines, you already know the part of the sad truth. There's no tooth fairy, just generous parents. Here's part two — there isn't a block genie that can be poured out of a bottle or plastic tube.

A final class of block repair that is often necessary is the repair of the threads in a block. We have already discussed the desirability of removing all threaded block fasteners intact. When this cannot be done, or when threaded holes have rusted through into an engine's water jacket, it is time to use a rethreading technique. The best solution is to carefully center drill the damaged hole to a larger thread size and run a regular tap in, followed by a blind tap. If this cannot be done, due to lack of wall material, an inserted thread technique must be used. Although the spring-like Heli-coil is probably the best known and most popular such repair, I find the threaded sleeve type of rethreading insert, such as the Slimsert, to be more satisfactory. Its most obvious advantage is that because it is a solid piece, it has a sealing capability and strength that a Heli-coil does not have. I have also found torque readings in Heli-coil threaded holes to be erratic. It should be stressed that if simply "chasing" threads or retapping them will do the job, this is far preferable to any of the thread insert repair techniques. In any thread repair that involves drilling, take extreme care to center the hole that you drill in the old fastener, and keep the new hole parallel to it. If it isn't, you will have a real problem; one that may be worse than the one that you set out to solve.

The tops of threaded holes in blocks should be counterbored to the depth of one thread. This prevents a tightened fastener from raising the top thread in a hole above the deck surface and having it interfere with surface mating.

One last word of caution about block fasteners and the holes that they live in. There is no better way to strip threads and warp and distort castings than to try to torque down a fastener that is too long for the hole that it is in. Lubricated threads give enormous mechanical advantage, and the fasteners in them can exert fantastic pressures when they are tightened. Take extreme care in disassembly to note any differences in fastener length, and relate them to reassembly in the proper holes.

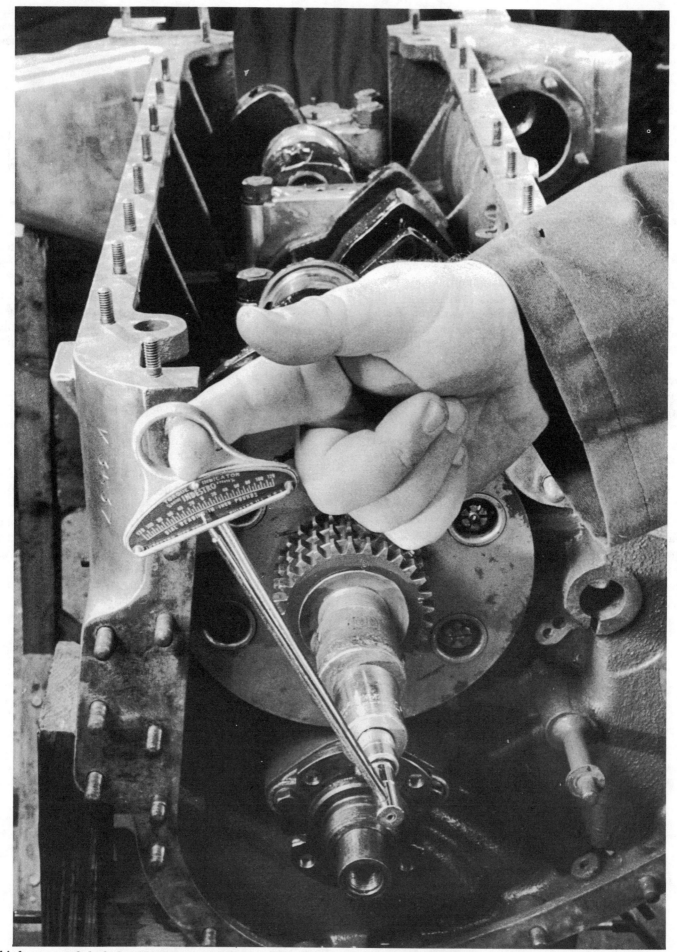

This heavy crankshaft should be like a vault door and turn very easily with just a little effort.

CHAPTER 5:

Basic Engine Remachining

Every so often, at an auction or swap meet, I see some of the crude old tools that were used to do basic engine remachining years ago. Sometimes, from the representations that accompany these devices, it is actually suggested that they could be used today for this purpose. A few probably can. I have seen thirty-year-old boring bars that still do credible work, and some well maintained line-boring devices and crankshaft grinders seem to have lives of their own. But the class of devices that I am talking about includes hand-held crankpin reamers, or the devices that were used to grind rod journals with the crank in the engine, and the engine in the car! Most of these "gyp" tools were used by service stations, used car lots, and minor repair shops — outfits which were sometimes involved in major overhauls that they should never have attempted. They are about as appropriate to engine machining as the old cast iron wrenches and sheet metal sockets are to operations that involve hand tools.

Engine machine shop tools have become very precise and very automated, and this is a definite advantage for today's rebuilders and their customers. Such precision and automation were not always the case. While most automakers held reasonably close tolerances in their basic manufacturing processes, these tolerances tended to be degraded in the successive ministrations of repair shops. Grotesque practices were commonplace, like hand filing bearing caps to remove the thickness of a non-existent shim. In fact, most, if not all of the practices that are presently considered substandard, were described in great detail in popular "how-to" books, such as A. L. Dykes' *Automobile Encyclopedia*. They were presented in the old manuals as standard and acceptable shop technique and practice.

Occasionally you meet an old-time mechanic who can't understand why anyone would repour and remachine a thick shell babbitt bearing, when a few swaths with a file, and alternately hitting the bearing shell's outside radius with a hammer and compressing it in a vise will do the same thing. Of course, it *won't* accomplish the same thing, or anything else that is likely to work. While it is

not necessary to build the precision of a Cosworth racing engine into a 1949 Hudson power plant, it is a good idea to use contemporary standards of precision rather than those of 1949 or 1916. I know of no engine failure that occurred because relevant specifications were adhered to too precisely.

The automotive machine shop is simply one place where we can be very happy that they don't "[re]build 'em like they used to." I wouldn't trade a modern wet valve facer for one of the old dry ones, or a new Sunnen rod honing machine for a 1930s vintage bearing sizing machine for all of the lock washers at the Ford Motor Company in Dearborn.

Three Basic Systems to Consider

When considering machine shop operations on conventional engines, there are three basic systems that must be accounted for. These are the valve system, the crankshaft system, and the cylinder/piston system. The valve system in its simplest form is comprised of a camshaft and its bearings and side-play system, the tappets and tappet bores, the valves and their seats, and assorted valve springs and their retainers, keepers and rotators. On overhead valve (OHV) engines that are not overhead cam, you can add push rods and one or more sets of rocker arms and shafts, or studs and buckets, to this inventory. The crankshaft area includes the shaft itself, counterweights (integral or attached), and the rod and main bearings. Finally, the cylinder/piston system is comprised of pistons, rings, wrist pins and their retainers and bearings, rods, and the cylinder walls, or in some cases, sleeves. There are other areas and surfaces, such as the timing system and head and block deck surfaces, which may require attention in the machine shop, but the basic division outlined above is a reasonable framework in which to consider basic engine work.

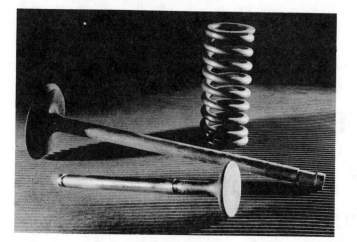

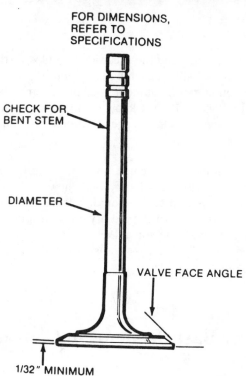

FOR DIMENSIONS, REFER TO SPECIFICATIONS

CHECK FOR BENT STEM

DIAMETER

VALVE FACE ANGLE

1/32" MINIMUM

Engine valves and springs come in many sizes and configurations. Poppet valves are the weakest link in most engines and require extreme care when engines are rebuilt. There aren't too many factors to account for in valve work, but you have to be deadly accurate with the factors that must be accounted for.

The Valve System

The environment in which automotive valves operate is not quite impossible, but it comes close. Valves are far and away the most stressed parts of the average engine. They run at temperatures that often cause them to turn cherry red and they open and slam shut a couple of thousand times for every mile driven in most postwar cars. For every mile that you drive, each valve will travel over a hundred feet in increments of one third of an inch. If all

of this weren't bad enough, the valves in an automobile engine are constantly surrounded by incredibly corrosive gases and are subject to occasional attacks by nasty squadrons of carbon and other particles that are the by-products of combustion, or at least find their ways into the valve seat area. Add to all of this the fact that valves are virtually impossible to lubricate where they need it most, and you have a component that has good reasons for being the weakest link in an engine system. Cam lobes are a distant second on the list of engine self-destruct components.

I freely admit that it is the purpose of this brief tribute to the largely unheralded tribulations of the common engine valve to try to gain sympathy for its plight and to translate that sympathy into attention and consideration in the rebuilding process. Valves need all of the help that we can give them.

Almost anything that is wrong in a valve train will cause disaster in fairly short order. Burned valves will never cure themselves, and valves that are set too "tight" can be ruined in a matter of a few hours, or in extreme cases, in a few minutes. Outside of engine bearings, valves require the greatest accuracy in engine rebuilding, but they don't always get it. Valve work, whether it is a minor refacing or a major insert installation, should be done by people who know exactly what they are doing.

In valve work, problems can be encountered that are difficult but never impossible to solve. One of my favorites is the set of problems that can be encountered when an engine (early postwar GM V-8s and others) with push rods and hydraulic lifters is being rebuilt and there is no provision for adjusting valve clearances. Getting the hydraulic lifters acceptably positioned (centered) can involve grinding the valve stem ends and keepers, shimming the rocker shaft supports, converting to adjustable push rods, or rocker arms, etc. Again, this is work for professionals who know their equipment, your situation, and the available options.

Because there are several valid approaches to valve work, and many different kinds of equipment on which to accomplish the basic machining operations of valve system reconditioning, I will deal only with some of the general considerations. In the area of valve seats and valve guides, the main consideration is that valve guides be absolutely straight and uniform in bore, and perfectly concentric to their valve seats; and that they provide the proper clearance to valve stems. They must also be installed at the correct heights and be correct with regard to undercut. Valve seats must be cut to exactly correct widths, and they must meet valve faces at the prescribed angles and be absolutely concentric with respect to their valve guides. Valve faces must sit in their seats in heads or blocks at correct depths and the seats must contact the middle of the valve faces.

Operationally, all of this means that proper valve work cannot be accomplished by lapping valves and seats with grinding compound, as was done years ago. This is not an accurate enough procedure to produce usable results because it does not produce an acceptably accurate or smooth finish. Proper valve work involves the use of precise pilots and accurately faced grinding stones or carbide cutters to produce the necessary three valve seat angles that provide for proper seat width and position. The old hand-turned metal cutters that were used in conjunction with a final lapping operation produced pretty dismal results. Another type of equipment that should not be used is the old, dry valve facer. This device tended to heat check valve faces in the grinding process. The quality of some of the valves on the market today is questionable enough without adding the problems caused by using substandard grinding processes.

Not every valve can be saved by refacing, though some rebuilders seem to try to accomplish this. When you replace valves, you can use exhaust valves of comparable dimensions in intake applications, but not the other way around. Exhaust valves are usually much more durable

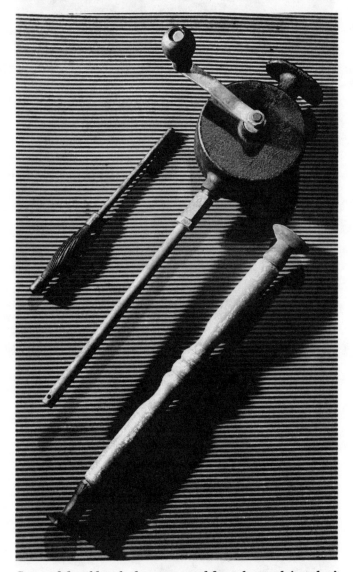

Some of the old tools that were used for valve work just don't meet modern standards. The old style guide cleaner (top) is okay for cleaning guides, but the reciprocating hand valve "grinders" shown below it should not be used to lap valves and seats because valves should be ground on the specially designed machines that have been available for the last forty or more years.

and heat resistant than intakes, they have to be. Since many of us don't have the equipment or experience to do our own valve work, we have it done by commercial machine shops. It is probably best to leave most decisions to the machinists who do the work. There are a few areas where owners and restorers should have input. One is on the question of whether or not use seat inserts. My feeling is that if there is any question about saving a valve seat — if the seat is marginal in any way — an insert should be used. This is particularly true in an era of unleaded gasoline. At this point, I am using seat inserts on almost all exhaust valves that I deal with.

Valve seat recession can occur when old engines (pre-1973) are run on unleaded gasoline. This is because the metallic additive, lead, that cushioned the impact of valve faces on their seats is no longer added to gasoline, or is added in such small quantities as to be useless for the purpose of protecting valve seats from recession. The threshold for protection is 0.5 grams/gallon tetraethyl lead added to gasoline. What little "leaded" gasoline is available today contains a maximum of 0.1 grams/ gallon; way below that threshold. Valve seat recession can be dealt with by using non-lead gasoline additives, but it is best to deal with it when you rebuild an engine. Using stainless steel valves, hardening valve faces with a welded or metal sprayed coating, or using hardened seats will do the job. You can also solve the recession problem by using hardened valve seats. This is an either/or proposition. You don't have to use hard valves *and* hard seats, either one will do. This is because the valve seat recession problem involves hard particles that embed in valve faces and grind valve seats away on impact. If you harden the valve, the particles will not embed, and if you install hard seats, the particles will not grind them away. Of course, all of this applies only to exhaust valves. Intake valves are cooled by the incoming air/fuel mixture and do not require measures to combat the valve seat recession that is a problem when you use unleaded gasoline in older engines.

Another "hot" issue is the issue of seat width. The wider the contact area of a valve face and seat is, the more opportunity there is for heat transfer and cooling during valve closure, but there is also increased opportunity for particles to lodge between valves and seats and hold valves slightly open. Also, as seat width increases, the pounds per square inch of available sealing pressure declines proportionally. I have found that a seat width of 3/32 inch, or slightly less, is an almost ideal specification for most engines, but check particular specifications for any engine that you work on.

Some engines require an interference angle between valve faces and seats. This means that a valve face and seat are ground to slightly different angles, usually by 1°. Some machinists will attempt to grind an interference angle into every valve and seat that they do. I tend to use interference angles only where they are called for by engine manufacturers, as this approach requires certain characteristics in the metallurgy of valves and their seats. One procedure that used to be fairly commonplace, but is now, thank goodness, dying out, is the practice of doing a

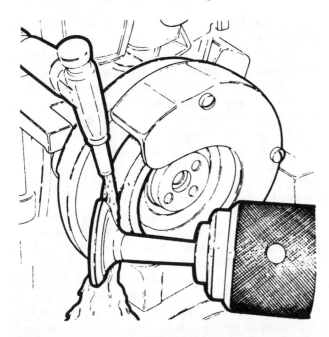

Modern "wet" valve grinding machines are deadly accurate, and they don't heat check the valve faces as the older "dry" machines sometimes did.

It is good practice to face the end of a valve stem when you grind it.

final check on valves and seats with fine lapping compound. This practice is an interesting study in the persistence of obsolescence. When modern valve facing equipment arrived on the scene fifty or more years ago, automotive machinists did not trust this equipment, or, perhaps, their use of it. To check the ground surfaces of freshly ground valves and seats, they would place some very fine grinding compound between a valve and its seat and gently lap the surfaces together. If the grind was correct, they would see the contact area as a dull gray band, uniformly distributed on the highly polished surfaces of the valve and seat, "Ah, a good seal." Unfortunately, this

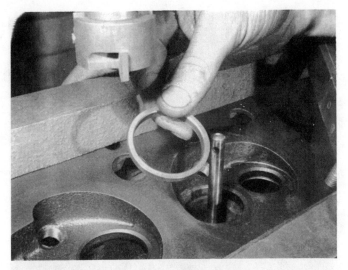

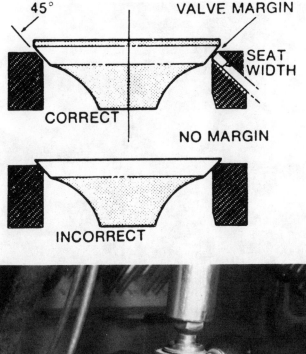

Valve seat inserts for exhaust valves are one sure way to provide for the use of unleaded gasoline in older engines that were not designed for this fuel. These seats can also be used to repair badly damaged valve seats when there isn't enough material left in a head or block to grind a new seat into it.

practice destroys the dimensional accuracy of grinding procedures and replaces it with a random approximation of that accuracy. It also produces a vastly inferior finish. If there is need to check the contact area of a valve and seat, Prussian blue will do a very adequate job.

Valve guide wear is probably the main predictable cause of valve seat failure. Because the hot ends of valve guides receive little or no lubrication, these ends tend to wear in a bell-mouth shape. Eventually, they will fail to provide adequate location to the closing valves. The result is run out, or too much clearance between valve stems and guides. This causes rapid deterioration of valve seats. In older engines, valve guides could be replaced easily, and this was standard practice in engine rebuilding. Presently, many engines are being built without removable valve guides. In these engines, excessive guide to stem clearance has to be dealt with by knurling the guide surface, or by using valves with oversize stems, and reaming the guide surfaces to size. The knurling process tends to produce a very hard working surface in the valve guide and has the added advantage of creating pockets or recesses that hold oil. I prefer knurling to guide replacement, if a guide is still in the range of successful knurling. When guide replacement is necessary, it is often possible to find bronze guides, or to have them made. These are far superior to the usual cast iron guides and eliminate some of the vulnerability of a potentially weak engine component. With the advent integral valve guides in engines, there are also bronze and iron guide liners that can be used when a guide is worn beyond the limits of knurling.

Since the 1950s the automobile industry has developed increasingly effective valve stem seals. On the old "L" and "T" head (valve-in-block) engines, sealing valve stems was hardly a problem. In fact, the downward position of the stems in relatively dry valve chambers meant that they were usually deprived of adequate lubrication. Often they had to run more on good will and oil fumes

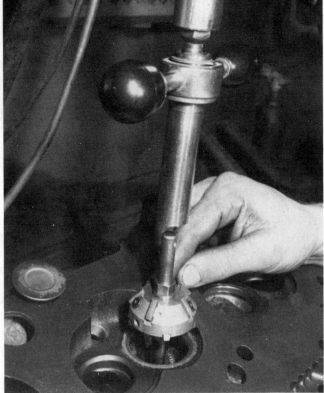

Correct valve seat width is critical to valve survival. Modern practice is to grind three angles into a valve seat so that the contact width can be adjusted exactly. Old cars often used only one angle in their valve seats because the cutters used to machine the seats weren't precise enough to cut a throat and deck angle in addition to the seat angle. Modern carbide cutters, such as the one shown here, give restorers this good option.

than on real lubrication. Many owners used top oils — also called upper cylinder lubricants — so at least some lubrication was provided to the critical upper ends of the valve stems and guides. Using top oil in side valve engines is still a very good idea. With the complete conversion of American engines to OHV engines in the early 1950s, the problems of dry valve stems disappeared. In these engines the valves are inclined downward and the

Valve guides can be reamed to either accommodate valves with oversized stems or they can be sleeved. Note the guide sleeve in the foreground of this photo. After the guide is reamed, the sleeve will be pressed into it.

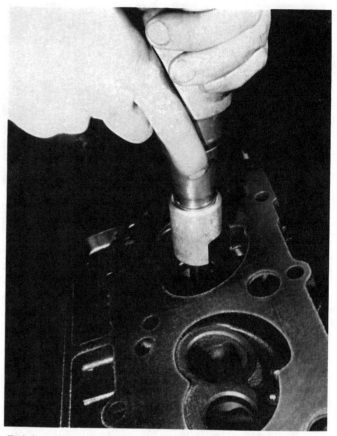

Driving old valve guides in and out of heads and blocks is easy. Be sure to use a correctly sized pilot and drive it with a hammer or zip gun.

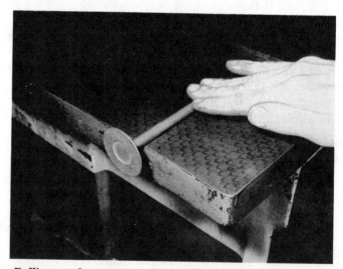

Rolling a valve stem on a flat surface will quickly tell you if it is warped.

upper ends of the stems and guides run in a virtual oil bath. Now the problem became sealing the top ends of valve guides and stems from an overabundant oil supply. Two basic types of seal were developed. One was a stem seal, which is an 0-ring fitted to the upper end of the valve guide for the purpose of sealing the stem to guide clearance. The other type of stem seal is the bucket, or "umbrella" type, which sits in the valve spring and over the end of the guide. It sheds most of the oil sprayed by the rocker arms. Both types of seal prevent oil from running down the guide, a situation which would result in high oil consumption and engine smoking. It is relatively easy to retrofit either or both types of seals to early OHV engines, and it is usually an exceedingly *bad* idea. Unless an engine was designed for these seals, their use can deprive the valve stems and guides of adequate lubrication and cause rapid and premature wear. However, some of the modern materials used in bucket seals have far better durability than those in early versions of these items. I routinely throw away the bucket seals that come in gasket sets and opt for some of the higher quality aftermarket versions of this item. The best practice is not to retrofit stem seals to engines that didn't have them, and to upgrade the quality of the seals that you use on engines that did have them.

Another area of the basic valve assembly that requires critical attention is valve springs. Old springs should never be reused without thorough evaluation, and new springs should also be checked before they are installed. Automotive machine shops have equipment for checking the relationship of spring height to various loadings. Valve springs must match the compression-pressure-at-height specifications given for them. Special spring seat washers can be used, as necessary, to exactly achieve correct and uniform installed height specifications. It is vitally important to check new valve springs as thoroughly as you would check old ones. The use of over-aggressive springs will pound valves and seats to oblivion in short order. Weaker than specified springs will usually cause

---

compression leakage that rapidly worsens as valve faces and seats are eroded by leaking gases. It should be noted that some aftermarket springs do not physically resemble the springs that they replace, and in some cases double springs are used to replace single springs. This is not a problem, as long as the replacements are engineered to achieve the necessary characteristics for the application in which they are being used.

Check valve spring installed height:

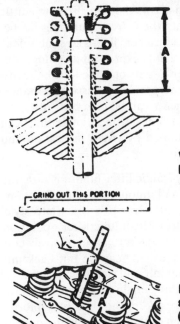

Valve spring installed height (A)

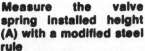

Measure the valve spring installed height (A) with a modified steel rule

Check the valve springs:

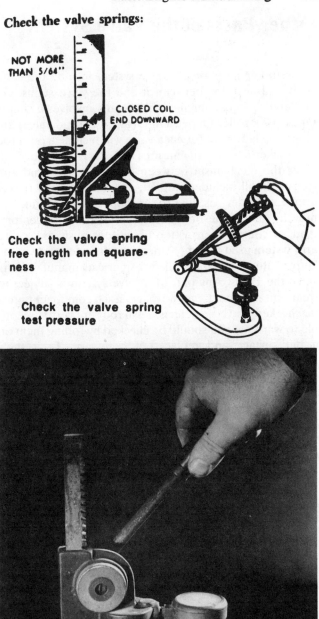

Check the valve spring free length and square-ness

Check the valve spring test pressure

It is very important to check every measurable aspect of valve spring condition. Height, installed height, and compression loading are critical. A weak or overly aggressive valve spring will lead to valve failure in short order. There are many kinds of equipment for checking valve spring condition. Some of it is general, such as a carpenter's square. Other spring testing equipment is dedicated and very precise — such as spring compression testers.

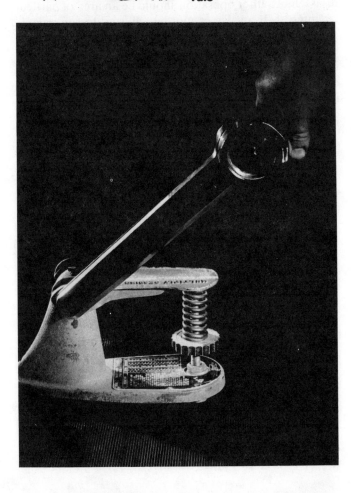

Other Parts of the Valve System

The other parts of the valve system include the camshaft and anything between it and the valve stems. On "L" and "T" head engines this usually involves a simple tappet or a roller tappet. On OHV (overhead valve) engines, the hardware for each valve will include a push rod and rocker arm setup, and for OHC (overhead cam) engines the mechanism between the valve stem end and camshaft will include a tappet, and sometimes a rocker arm. Exotic devices, like roller tappets, are not uncommon in cars of the first forty years of the 20th century. And, of course, there is the ubiquitous push rod/rocker arm system used in some American cars since early in the 20th century, and favored by American manufacturers since the 1950s. Any part of a valve system is subject to wear, misalignment, and warpage. Each component must be checked for these defects. Push rods are very susceptible to warping, and should be checked by rolling them on a flat surface and replaced if necessary. Their ends should also be checked for wear. Tappets should be checked for pitting and scoring on their cam following surfaces and ground, as necessary, to correct these defects. Many tappets have a small angle ground into their lower surfaces to cause them to rotate as cam lobes contact them. This, in turn, promotes valve rotation, and this tappet base angle must be preserved in any resurfacing

operation. Tappet bore clearance should be checked, and if it is found to be excessive, it should be corrected by the use of oversize tappets or other means. This consideration is particularly critical for engines with hydraulic lifters (tappets), since excessive bore clearance can result in inadequate oil pressure to operate hydraulic zero lash systems.

Hydraulic lifters require particular attention. They are built to exceedingly close tolerances and include a factor called "leak down," which allows them to circulate a little oil internally and prevents them from pumping up beyond correct clearances. However, if this desirable leak down characteristic — which is expressed as plunger-to-bore clearance in the lifter — gets out of control, the lifters will tend to collapse and provide excessive clearance. This critical leak-down factor can be checked with a set of lifter pliers or a leak-down tester in an oil bath. It can also be pretty well ascertained by visual inspection and measurement of the lifter parts.

The main reason for hydraulic lifter failure is dirt, varnish, and sludge. Very small amounts of these contaminants can clog the ball (early style) or disk (late style) valves that are at the heart of hydraulic lifter operation. Unless lifters have been subjected to an excessively contaminated oil supply, they usually can be put back into service after simple disassembly and cleaning. It is critical that hydraulic lifters from any engine be returned to the bores from which they were taken, and that their internal parts never be mixed. When evaluating an engine prior to disassembly, lifter operation should be an area of particular interest. If a valve cannot be adjusted to run quietly, or will not hold an adjustment, the lifter and other parts in the valve train become suspect and should be examined especially carefully during engine disassembly and evaluation. If a camshaft has been replaced or reground, it is absolutely essential that lifter operating faces be ground or the lifters replaced. Failure to do this will almost invariably cause the camshaft to chip out in a matter of minutes after engine startup.

Hydraulic valve lifters usually work well if they are kept clean. Never mix lifter parts, and always return lifters to their original bores.

Hydraulic lifter testers, such as this one, allow you to get a very good reading on lifter condition and performance.

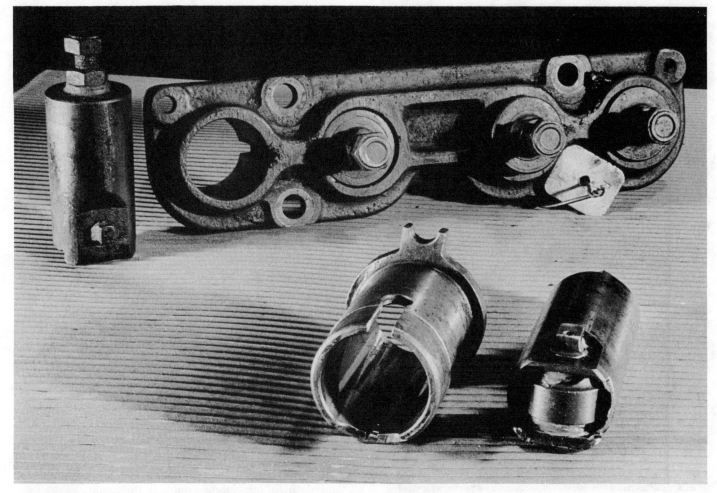

Old roller tappets, such as those shown here, can be very difficult to rebuild because they are often swaged or welded together and have to be disassembled to replace the needle bearings or bushings on which the rollers run.

Rocker Arms

In some engines, rocker arms and their shafts can have wear problems. Some engines are notoriously under-oiled in this area — Buicks of the late 1950s and early l960s — and their rocker arms and shafts tend to wear severely. Some rocker arms are susceptible to being re-bushed and others have to be replaced. In any case, excessive clearance at this point in the valve system is not tolerable as it will lead to erratic valve clearances. A complete automotive machine shop will have a tappet grinder and a device for resurfacing the valve contacting ends of rocker arms.

Ideally, there would be few parts between camshafts and valves. One of the advantages of OHC engines is that they can achieve this ideal almost completely — that is, those that don't have rocker arms. In engines that interpose items like rocker arms and push rods between tappets and valve stems, it is the rebuilder's objective to keep any unspecified motion, such as rocker arm-on-shaft play, to a minimum. It is possible to eliminate the problems of reciprocating weight and heat expansion in push rods and rocker arms, and therefore it is never possible to attain the valve accuracy in push rod engines that is inherent in simpler OHC designs. Yet, every attempt

should be made in that direction. Any worn or bent valve actuating parts that get by a rebuilder will inevitably cause performance problems.

The Camshaft

Most camshaft bearings are replaceable. On many recent engines and a few older ones, the camshafts run on integral bearings in the cylinder head or the block. Camshaft bearings run at relatively wide clearances and are seldom badly worn at the time of engine rebuilding. However, because any method of adequately cleaning a block will destroy them, they must be removed during a total engine rebuild. Unfortunately, it is inadvisable to reinstall camshaft bearings because the damage that is inevitably inflicted on them in the removal process means that they have to be replaced (thin shell type) or rebabbitted and align bored (thick shell type) once they have been removed.

By the late 1930s, in most cases, camshaft bearings were of the thin babbitt type and replacements can be installed without any other consideration than checking the bore saddles for alignment, out-of-round, and smoothness. However, earlier engines used a thick bab-

Next to valves, camshafts probably take the worst beating in any engine. Any good rebuild will include camshaft regrinding. Badly damaged cams can be welded up and ground. Cams should always be Parkerized (hardened) before they are put back into service.

bitt (thick shell) cam bearing design that requires line boring the installed camshaft bearings. In cases where the camshaft has been resurfaced and the bearing journals have been reduced in diameter, the newly poured bearings can accommodate the reduced shaft journal diameter, and the camshaft does not have to be built back

up in these areas. Whenever you install any type of camshaft bearing, always see that all holes line up with holes in the bearing saddle. Failure to do this is not uncommon and causes problems quickly. If a particular bearing has two oil holes, both must line up with holes in the block or head in which it resides.

The camshaft itself is probably the most neglected component in most engine rebuilds. Cams and camshaft bearing journals do wear, and this is not always obvious from visually reading them for pitting, grooving, and galling. I consider it essential to regrind cams and tappet bottoms in any serious engine rebuild. This work should be done by a very large general machine shop or by one that specializes in cams. The grinding process for cams uses master blanks to achieve lobe format. A few shops have an historical collection of these blanks and can grind cams from them. Try to find such a shop. In the cases of particularly obscure engines, there will probably be no master blanks available for the grind, and all that can be done is to select the best cam lobe on a shaft and grind the others from its format. This is a compromise, but it is, at least, far preferable to no grind at all. Any serious wear in cam lobes — this usually occurs in the ramp area — can be repaired by welding, as can damage to camshaft bearing journals. A final step in reworking camshafts is to Parkerize them. This is a surface treatment process that will enhance the wear characteristics of the lobes and journals. It is not worth bothering to rework a camshaft if it is not Parkerized afterward.

In my experience, the cost of camshaft work is not particularly high, but the difference in the quality of the job is terrific. A reground camshaft silences all kinds of little vibrations and noises that would otherwise be heard and felt if this work was not done. I would not consider an engine rebuild complete without grinding the cam any more than I would consider it complete if an old, stretched timing chain was reinstalled.

When working on valves and their actuating mechanisms, it should be realized that there isn't much safety factor or margin built into their design. Mistakes are rarely made without serious consequences, and the variant of Murphy's Law which states that "Nature always sides with the hidden defect" seems to be in control.

CHAPTER 6:

The Crankshaft and Bearing System

The basic concept of friction bearings goes back to the beginnings of mechanical times. The specific application of hard metal on soft metal friction bearings was patented in roughly its present form in 1839. The use of this type of bearing as the crankshaft bearing in reciprocating internal combustion hydrocarbon engines (that is, conventional automobile engines) was an obvious extension of the pump, locomotive, stationary engine, and machinery practices of the late 19th century. Although various attempts have been made to use alternative bearings (usually anti-friction bearings of a ball or roller configuration), in this application, these alternatives have not met with notable success. In this connection, one thinks of Lozier at the beginning of the automobile era and, more recently, Porsche. Although conventional hard metal on soft metal bearings are an improbable sounding proposition, the fact is that they work. Amazingly, they work remarkably well if their operating conditions do not differ too radically from their design capabilities. The trouble is that when these factors do differ significantly, say for example when there is oil deprivation, friction bearings do fail, and they tend to fail fast and violently.

The basic proposition in crankshaft and rod bearings is that the crankshaft will be somewhere between hard and extremely hard — the latter in the cases of crankshafts treated with a nitrate process or "nitrided" — and that it will run in metallic bearings that are very soft. These bearings can be made up of one of several alloys. The choices include alloys based on tin, lead, copper, aluminum, zinc, etc. Most of the alloys that will be encountered in old car engine rebuilding fall under the label "babbitt," which encompasses alloys based primarily in tin and lead.

The actual composition of babbitt (named after its American patent holder, Isaac Babbitt) is both complex and varied according to application. In the rebuilding field there are presently available about four grades of babbitt and almost everyone who is involved with this material has nothing but complaints about its present quality.

Until the mid-1930s, and in a few cases much later, babbitt crankshaft and rod bearings were poured extremely thick in rigid bronze shells. An eighth of an inch thickness of babbitt was not uncommon. The babbitt in these "thick shell" applications was then bored to size and finished by honing it. On some connecting rods the babbitt was poured directly into the steel rod saddle, without a separate bronze shell. Chevrolet, for example, persisted in this practice into the 1950s. For the most part, after World War II, most rod and main bearings had gone to the thin shell ("insert" type") design that we use today. This involves a relatively thin layer of babbitt plated over other metals that have been plated or sprayed onto relatively flexible steel backings. These bearings typically use copper plate below the babbitt and include in their design a factor called "crush." Crush means that the bearing shell is actually a few thousandths larger than its saddle, and when the saddle is cinched together, the protruding ends of the bearing halves are crushed into the saddle by some small factor. This forces the bearing into conformity with the saddle and guarantees a degree of surface contact with the saddle that promotes correct bearing shape and enhances heat transfer from the bearing to the crankcase's metal. Insert bearings work better than thick shell bearings because their vastly thinner babbitt layers don't trap as much heat as do the thick babbett type running surfaces.

Whether the bearing under consideration is the old bronze backed, rigid, thick shell babbitt type, or a modern thin shell, crush type, the concept of the bearing surface is the same. This concept is that the soft babbitt acts in several specific ways to handle its job. The major requirements of the babbitt surface are that it: 1) produce a low friction running surface, 2) handle the loads and pounding thrusts to which it is subjected, 3) transfer heat away from the bearing/shaft inter face, 4) retain oil and maintain an oil film to protect bearing surfaces from direct contact with crankshafts, 5) provide some degree of plastic conformability to crankshaft bearing journals, and 6) embed a certain number of small particles that may enter the bearing environment with lubricating oil, and prevent them from damaging crankshaft journals. There are more things that babbitt friction bearings have to do,

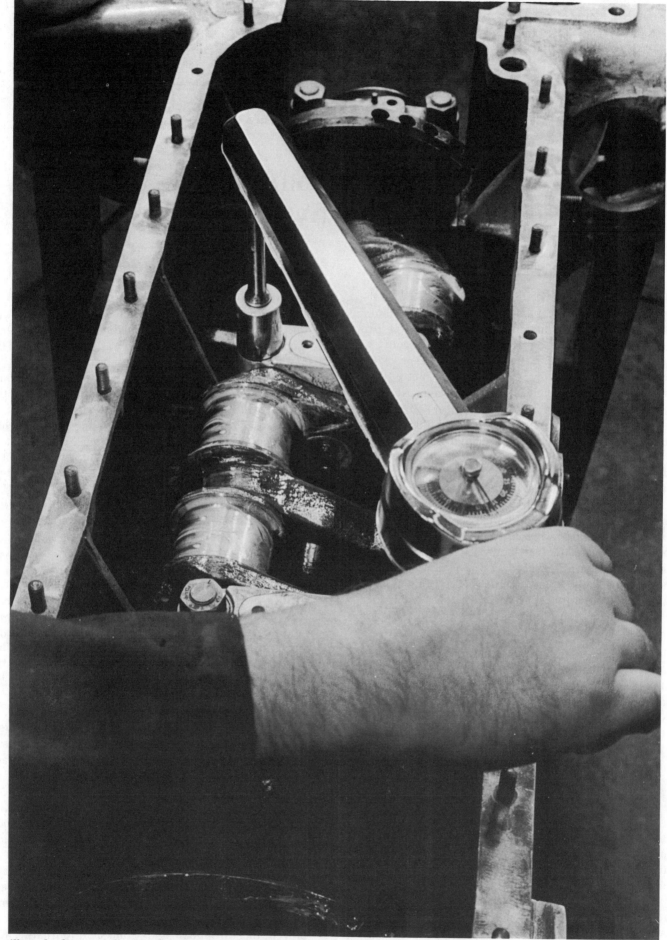

You'll need a few specialized and very accurate tools to install a crankshaft.

Babbitt bearings are asked to do a lot in an engine. In the case of the crankcase shown here, only three main bearings support a massive crankshaft that is driven by an almost 600 cubic inch engine. However, the center bearing in this mill is over six inches long.

but these are the major ones — and it is quite a list. When you stop and think that the babbitt bearings in an automobile engine have to survive tens of thousands of miles of high temperature transit by the crankshaft under very adverse conditions, and that the material involved, babbitt, is soft enough to mark handily with your fingernail, you have to gain a certain respect for babbitt bearings. This respect, or even admiration, survives, despite the connotation that Sinclair Lewis stamped almost indelibly on the name "Babbitt."

The operating requirements of an automobile engine are quite varied. Engines must run and start at temperatures as low as -30° f. and continue to run at underhood temperatures that can approach 300° f. Internal temperatures at some critical points can run intermittently as high as 1750° f. Engines have to operate at a few hundred rpm and at several thousand, and all of this under widely varying loads. A lot of the beating for these conditions is taken up by the rod and main bearings, and they will take it until some basic condition of their welfare is breached. Then they will fail rapidly. Because the surfaces of babbitt bearings are slowly consumed, and because of the

varied and adverse conditions that they are subjected to, almost any engine that you may have occasion to rebuild will reveal bearings that are progressing towards failure in one way or another.

The first step in dealing with engine bearings in a rebuild is to determine what sort of failure they were progressing towards, and how quickly they were headed there. Almost all automotive engine rebuilding textbooks and repair manuals contain a section on bearing failure, complete with autopsy pictures and captions. It is well worth the effort to compare what you find in an engine with this printed material. If one particular bearing is failing due to unevenly distributed thrust, or oil deprivation, or some other discreet factor, it will tell you what to look for as you proceed. In the above examples, a bent or offset rod for the first condition and a plugged oil passage for the second. I emphasize that even if the reason that finally dictated an engine rebuild had nothing to do with bearings, it still pays to analyze their condition and correct any problems that the analysis reveals.

It would be impossible to cover all, or even most, considerations in bearing work here, but there are a few gen-

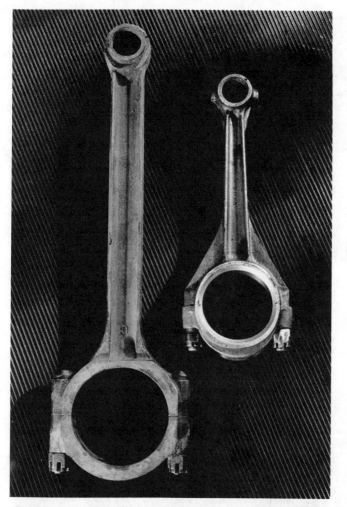

Connecting rod bearings are usually made out of babbitt, although aluminum, white metal, and copper bronze have also been used, as have anti-friction needle and ball bearings.

eralities that are worth looking at. The first is that bearing work must be very clean and accurate work. This is one of those places where things have to fit very accurately and precisely. The inadvertent inclusion of a particle of grit with a 0.002 inch diameter between a crush bearing and its saddle will do all kinds of damage because it can deform the crush fit in three or four places. Another critical generality is that bearing work tends to have a set of "rebuilder's standards" for such things as allowable bearing taper, out-of-round, and surface scoring. These should not be confused with restoration standards. For example, undersize replacement bearings are typically available in undersizes of 0.001 inch and 0.002 inch, before you get into the standard grind sizes of 0.010 inch, 0.020 inch, 0.030 inch, and 0.040 inch. This is because it is generally considered okay to tolerate 0.0015 inch or even 0.002 inch of out-of-round in a crankshaft before a regrind is mandated. That is, garage practice is to fit a 0.002 inch undersize bearing to a shaft journal that is worn out-of-round from standard by 0.0015 inch or 0.002 inch. To all of which I say, when you are restoring an engine, do not tolerate any measurable deviation in out-of-round, taper, or surface finish. The object here is not just to throw an engine together so that it will outlast a rapidly

deteriorating car body. That may be a valid repair proposition and it may fit well within repair economics. The restoration point is to build an engine that is as permanent as possible and that has no avoidable weak links.

When you restore an engine that doesn't have one of the miracle hardened crankshafts, the overwhelming probability is that you will have to grind the shaft. Certainly, if you are doing a total mechanical restoration, and the crankshaft is out of specification or finish, it should be ground. It usually will need grinding because the part of the rod journal that encounters the force transmitted by the rod on combustion strokes will almost always wear more than the other 320° of the shaft. You can just about figure on grinding cranks to an undersize.

It is vitally important to check old cranks and blocks for warping and distortion. Blocks and shafts do warp. If the bearing centerline in a block isn't checked, it can come back to haunt a restorer in such obscure ways as failing valve guides, caused by inadequate lubrication, caused by low oil pressure, caused by bearing leakage, caused by a warped crank or block. It's just easier to sort these things out when they are apart and visible, rather than to have to work backwards from seemingly unrelated symptoms of malfunction.

If the engine that you are restoring uses modern, thin shell bearings, the shaft can be ground in increments of 0.010 inch to undersizes of up to 0.040 inch, and bearings can usually be found for these grinds. Ordinarily, this will represent a satisfactory approach to repairing any shaft wear that is found, even if the shaft has been ground before. In the case of thick shell bearings, you can still grind as necessary to an 0.040 inch undersize, and even a bit beyond that, as long as you don't weaken the shaft or produce an unacceptably small bearing surface; and then bore the repoured bearings to the new crank journal size. Occasionally, extreme wear or physical damage to a crankshaft is so great that it has to be built up before it is reground. Over the years several buildup techniques have been tried and have enjoyed popularity. Until recently, the most popular of these was GNAW welding (more commonly called "MIG" or "wire" welding). This has proven very satisfactory for all but nitrided crankshafts, and nitrided crankshafts rarely require much attention, anyway. In the last few years, submerged arc crank welding machines have come into use and these provide the very best approach to repairing and building up worn or damaged crankshafts. The superiority of submerged arc repairs is chiefly seen in the uniformity of the added material and in its lack of any porosity. Other techniques have been used and are still used to build up shafts, and these include metal spray and chrome plating. Both of these latter techniques have notable drawbacks, and a restorer should stick with GMAW and submerged arc welding to build up worn cranks.

There are several common pitfalls that should be avoided when crankshafts are ground. One is the use of oddball equipment. Make sure that your provider of this service is using modern and well-maintained equipment. There are a lot of pretty shoddy operations doing crank

Some of the old thick shell bearings had an eighth of an inch of babbitt poured into bronze shells. Babbitt that thick tends to pound out when it is on the receiving end of large radial loads. Thick babbitt also tends to hold heat and fail for that reason. Modern practice is to plate just a few thousandths of babbitt on insert type bearing shells.

grinding these days. Make sure that your shaft is ground with wheels that are in good shape and properly dressed. Crank grinding wheels are very expensive and some fast buck operators who quote terrific prices tend to economize on wheels. It is also important that your provider have a wheel or wheels for putting the correct radius on the crank shaft fillets (right angle journal-to-cheek interfaces). Some grinders use small auxiliary wheels for this purpose. In any case, it is not unusual to get a crank back from an "economy grinder" with no radius on the fillets. Since sharp fillets are a great place for cracks to propagate, this defect is bad news for any crank, but particularly for one that is old and stressed.

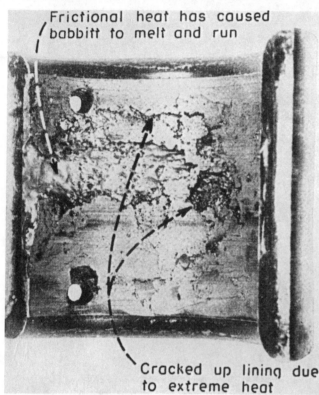

This thick shell babbitt bearing failed from overheating — a fairly common reason for bearing failure in older cars. Usually the overheating is related to inadequate oil flow, or to badly contaminated oil.

Another all-to-common pitfall is to order one of the garbage crankshafts that are supplied "ready to install" by unscrupulous mail order purveyors. A friend recently told me that several years ago when he was purchasing some parts at the home office of a very large and well-known mail order auto parts supplier, he was accidently allowed to see the "inner sanctum," where they reconditioned crankshafts. He had accompanied a counterman to the basement of a building to find a part, and he noticed men busily mounting cranks on an ancient shaft grinder and surfacing them with a finishing belt. No attempt was being made to measure them or grind them accurately to dimension. When he made inquiry regarding this amazing sight, the door that he was looking through was slammed shut, and he was emphatically told, "Don't ask about that." I have personal knowledge of at least three cranks that were ordered from this supplier

and that failed a few thousand miles after their installations. It is best to know the outfit that regrinds your crankshaft and to get one that is fresh and undamaged by poor storage or in shipping. It's amazing but true, a mighty crankshaft will often warp significantly if it is stored on its side for a few days without the support of bearings. When you store a crankshaft, stand it up on end and secure it to some vertical feature of the available architecture.

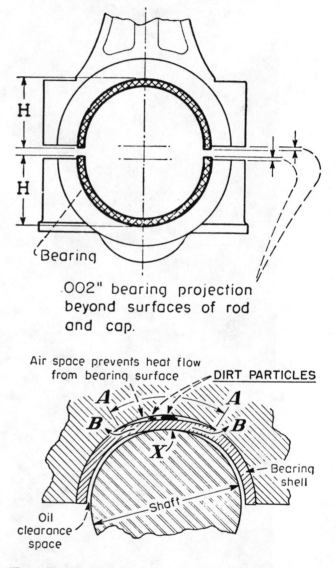

"Insert" or "crush" type bearings rely on the clamping pressure of the cap to press them into their saddles. This promotes a close contact of the bearing outer surface and saddle, and that helps to transfer heat away from the bearing and to give it its shape. Unfortunately, crush type bearings will not tolerate any dirt or particles between the bearing shell and saddle. Any contamination there will badly deform this type of bearing.

You can do a simple check for bore alignment of insert type main bearings, and most times it will show good alignment. Thick shell babbitt mains, like these, always have to be line bored after they are poured.

Crankshafts look rugged, but they are really very delicate. Always store crankshafts standing up to protect them from warping and to protect their bearing journal surfaces from impact and corrosion.

Bearings and Saddles

Main bearing saddles usually require very little attention when you rebuild an engine. They should always be checked for roundness, alignment, and any kind of gross physical damage, but you will usually encounter few problems in this area. Almost any problem that does occur in main bearing saddles can be corrected by line boring the saddles, or by welding them up and line boring them.

Rods are another story. Rods are often afflicted to some degree by two common maladies. One is bending and twisting, and the other is saddle elongation. Bent and twisted rods can be fixed by a process of jigging them and applying force to straighten them. Rod saddle elongation is most often a malady of high speed engines of the 1950s and after. It occurs when saddles get out-of-round, and is corrected by milling the parting surfaces of rods and their caps and honing or boring back to roundness. This process of reconditioning rod bores is a common operation in most automotive machine shops. In fact, the technicians at the machine shop that I use always have an attitude of

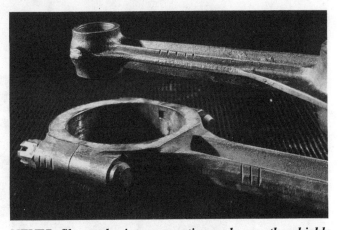

NEVER file marks into connecting rods or other highly stressed engine parts. It's necessary to keep track of rods with regard to what cylinder they came from, but this can be done with prick punch marks or stamped numbers. The file marks shown here would probably cause these rods to fracture in service.

incredulity when I bring in rods from something fifty years old with 150,000 miles on it, and the rod saddles are still perfectly round. Old engines didn't subject their connecting rods to the same kinds of stress that are routine in modern engines. I think that they called that "over engineering." It sure was appreciated.

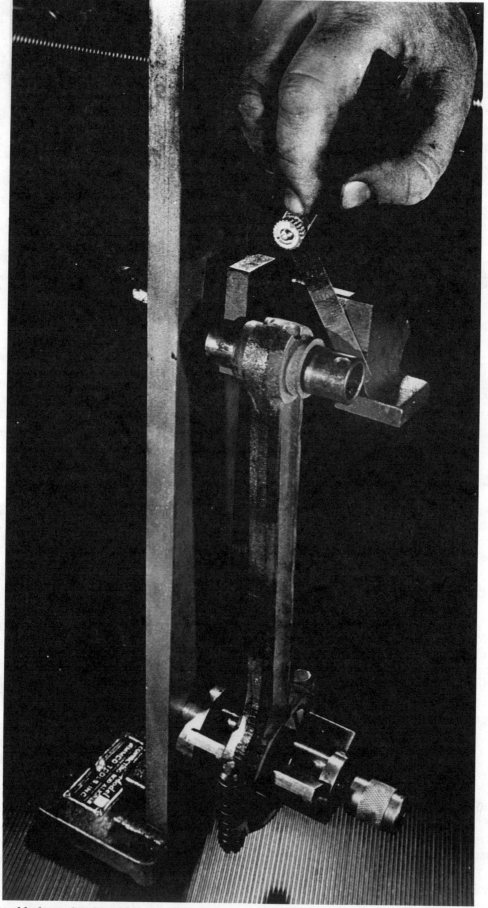

Connecting rods should always be checked in a jig for straightness. Forged rods can be straightened in a jig if they are warped, twisted, or out of parallel. Cast rods should be replaced if they are not straight.

Crankshaft Installation

The first and last steps in restoring a crankshaft both involve cleaning. Before a crankshaft is straightened and ground, it should be cleaned thoroughly. You can do this in a hot tank, but there are other, more satisfactory methods that involve oven baking, shot-peening, tumbling, and jet spray washing. Whatever method of cleaning a crankshaft you use, it should be followed by rodding the shaft's oil passages with spiral wire gun brushes and then blowing them clean with compressed air. It is critically important that the oil passages in crankshafts be carefully cleaned, since the shaft's operation will have centrifuged contaminants from the oil into solid masses in these passages. Crankshafts should be cleaned thoroughly before machine shop work is performed on them. Then, when a finished crankshaft is returned from a machine shop, it should again be cleaned meticulously to remove any abrasive residues or chips from machining that might foul new bearings. I use Ivory soap and lots of water to rewash crankshafts that I get back from grinding. Then I thoroughly dry them and coat them with a water displacing penetrating oil to preserve them until they are installed. The same soap and water and drying regimen should be applied to crankcases after they are cleaned and ma-

A spiral wire brush ("rifle brush") is ideal for cleaning out oil passages in crankshafts and blocks. This is a step that you don't want to omit because all sorts of stuff will come out of these passages when you clean them. If you don't clean them, it will come out into your freshly rebuilt engine bearings.

chined, and prior to crankshaft installation. Oil or grease should be applied to crankcase surfaces after washing and drying to protect them.

The object of torquing main and rod bearings is to get even and correct torque. Be sure to thoroughly lubricate bearing fasteners and then torque them in a correct pattern and in at least three stages. A high-quality and recently calibrated torque wrench is a real plus in this work.

It would be impossible to overemphasize the importance of cleanliness when crankshafts are installed. Bearing saddle tops and caps should be blown off with compressed air and then finger wiped to remove any lurking particles. Bearing shells should be carefully wiped down and gently persuaded into saddles and caps with light hand pressure. A final finger wipe of bearing surfaces should then be performed. Never blow on a bearing surface with compressed air because it can embed particles in them. Just before you install a crankshaft, all bearing and shaft working surfaces should be wiped liberally with a good assembly lubricant. I use Lubriplate 105 for this purpose because I have an almost religious faith in it.

After all seals and bearings are in place, the crankshaft should be lowered gently into its bearings, and the caps should be quickly put in place to keep out contamination. Every good practice in bolting things together should be used when main and rod bearing caps are tightened. Anti-seize lubricant should be used on fastener threads, and on the nut or bolt head undersides of the fasteners that are used. All parts should be reassembled in the order and orientation that existed when they were removed. If a cap was removed that was out of order or backwards, it should be reinstalled that way, if it is dimensionally correct and if basic corrective machining was not done with it installed properly. An accurate torque wrench must be used on main and rod cap fasteners, and correct figures for torque should be found or derived. The object here is not just to get even torque on fasten-

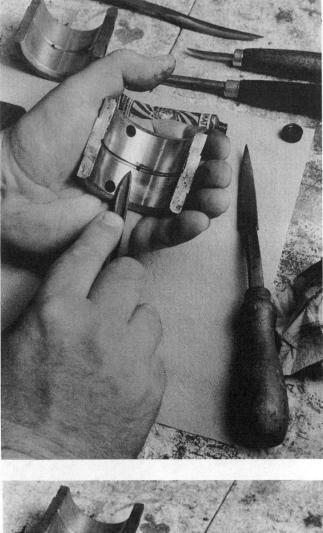

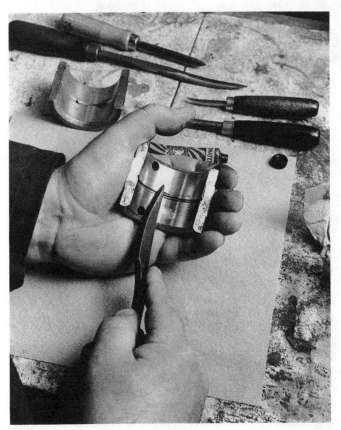

Scraping bearings is an obscure but useful technique for removing high spots. Due to the potential for distortion in thick bronze bearing shells when they are clamped in their saddles, high spots sometimes appear on bearing surfaces. Indicating them with Prussian blue and gently scraping them away will improve bearing contact and avoid local bearing overheating. Three scraping tools are shown in these photographs: a scraping knife, a machinist's knife, and a burnishing tool.

When you torque castellated nuts, it is sometimes necessary to file or grind their bottom faces so that they will come into correct readings with the cotter key ports lined up. This is a fussy business, but it is sometimes necessary. It is best to pretorque castellated nuts and get the values right before you try to install them in an engine. After you grind or file a castellated nut, be sure to deburr it, and be sure that all grinding residue and chips are removed from the the nut's threads.

ers, but to get correct numerical values on them as well. Torque should be applied in reasonable alternating sequences and in at least three stages. Inconsistent torque applications can distort crankcases and even cylinder walls. If rod nuts or main bearing cap nuts were restrained by special lock washers, these must be replaced with exact duplicates. If castellated nuts were used, it is sometimes necessary to file or grind their bottoms to get cotter key alignment to coincide with correct torque readings. If this is done, the filing should be followed by careful deburring and removal of all chips or abrasive grit from these parts.

A final Platigage check of main bearings is a good idea. I prefer this approach to taking the chance of scratching the bearings' delicate working surfaces with an inside micrometer, telescope gauge, or bore gauge. The practice of checking bearing clearance by inserting various brass shim stocks between the bearing and shaft until they jam is both archaic and barbaric. Don't do it. The reason for a final check of bearing clearances is that new bearings are infrequently mislabeled and this is the best way to catch that error before it becomes a disaster. It is unnecessary to check main bearings and crankshaft journals for contact with Prussian blue if the bearings are insert type, or if they have been line bored and the crankshaft has been checked for straightness and/or ground. However, it is always a good idea to check thick shell rod bearings for shaft contact with Prussian blue, even though their journals have been ground and the bearings sized and finished on a precise honing machine. Every so often, such a

check will reveal one or more high spots caused by rod saddle distortion that may occur when a rod cap is tightened onto its bearing. Such high spots can be scraped down with a bearing scraper. If you are not thoroughly familiar with the techniques of scraping bearings, do not attempt this work without some instruction and practice — it's easy to do more harm than good.

The final step in installing crankshaft main and rod bearings is to leak test the whole system. This test accomplishes two desirable tasks. It offers proof positive that the work that you have completed contains no errors, and it prelubricates the whole engine oiling system for the critical start-up period. What is involved is finding a leak detector tank, or fabricating one. Such a tank must be clean and it must be capable of withstanding at least 50 pounds of pressure. It must have a filler cap to pour oil in, an input for compressed air at the top, and an output for pressurized oil at the bottom. It's a good idea to have a filter for the output oil and a valve to turn the thing on and off. A pressure gauge on the tester is a nice feature.

In practice, the leak detector is filled with SAE 20 oil and pressurized to about 15 pounds. Its oil output is hooked up to the main oil galley of the engine through an external plug, or through the oil pump output connection, if the oil pump has not yet been installed. I prefer this latter connection because you don't have to stopper the oil pump pickup. If you pressurize the system through a galley plug, you will have to close off the oil pump pickup to prevent oil from flowing back through the pump and out of the system. Don't forget to put a large pan under the engine for this test. With the engine right-side-up and the oil pressure from the leak detector valved on, the engine should be slowly turned by its front pulley nut or rear flange with a wrench. Oil leakage should now

You can easily run an oil leak test on the lubrication system of any engine that you rebuild. A homemade tester is shown on the left, and a professional version on the right. The homemade leak detector was made out of a fire extinguisher shell, but despite this humble origin, it has served admirably for many years.

When bearing and crankshaft work are done correctly, it should take very little pressure to turn even a massive crank. It's the same theory that governs opening a fine safe door.

be observed. At this point, any place that oil leaks will be evident. If a bearing is improperly fitted or an oil galley connection is defective, it will show as a steady squirt of oil or as a drip where there shouldn't be one. Half a dozen or so drops per minute should escape from each bearing, with the pressure and oil viscosity stated above, if the test is run at an average room temperature. If a bearing spews out a stream of oil, or if one or more bearings fail to drip at all, there is something wrong that must be corrected. I realize that this is a messy test that wastes oil, but its results are important. Take the time to use a good light source and verify everything in a pressure lubrication system for adequate flow, but not excessive flow. If you have access to a "black light" you can add a fluorescing dye to the oil that you use in this test and then use the black light to examine the test oil as it comes out of the engine. The light will cause the oil drops to glow and will make the inspection much easier to perform. Such problems as inadequate lubrication of timing chains or gears will be evident with an oil leak test. Most engines that are rebuilt and later experience bearing system failure could probably have avoided this outcome if an oil leak test had been run before they were started. This test will pinpoint the causes of lubrication failure before they destroy a rebuilt engine.

After an engine is assembled and started, it is important to watch the oil pressure. Many older cars have external pressure settings and these should be set to factory specification. Excessively high oil pressure is not desir-

Here's a nice touch when you grind a crankshaft. Chamfer its oil holes. That will prevent a sharp edge or burr from sculpting the babbitt in its bearing. You should cut the chamfer before you grind or polish the shaft.

able because it can damage oil plumbing and seals. Of course, low oil pressure endangers bearings and cylinder walls. Anything that causes a rapid decline in oil pressure, and particularly one that is accompanied by pulsations, should be investigated immediately because it forewarns of progressing failure of the bearing system. Watch that oil pressure gauge!

Pistons and their associated parts, wrist pins and rings, do the front line work in an engine, and they take quite a beating in the process. The piston on the left has partially disintegrated in service.

CHAPTER 7:

Basic Engine Remachining: The Piston System

Modern piston systems and the types of equipment available to recondition them are complex and precise. This follows from the fact that modern engines are lighter and run at higher speeds and compression pressures than their predecessors did. The result is more stressed piston system components than those in older engines.

Although the application of modern rebuilding equipment to pistons and piston pins usually represents overkill for old engines, it is a situation that will not harm restoration work, and in most cases this overkill will actually improve results. However, it is important that the close tolerances that are possible with modern reconditioning equipment not be used to reduce some of the critical dimensional tolerances used in older engines. The key is the application of appropriate technology, which involves understanding which tolerances are dictated by engine design and which result from the nature or limitations of the equipment used in rebuilding. This distinction will be evident in the discussion of wrist pin fitting later in this chapter.

The piston system in any conventional automobile engine includes the cylinder walls, or sleeves, the pistons, the piston pins and their bearing surfaces, and the piston rings. Although the dimensional requirements for most of this system (not including the critical pin fit) are not as precise as for systems like engine bearings, they do require a high degree of accuracy and cleanliness when this work is performed. Almost any contemplated rebuild of the "bottom end" of an engine — everything below the head(s), but not including the valves on "L" and "T" head engines — should include consideration of the piston system. That is to say, if an engine is being rebuilt because of bearing failure, camshaft failure, or the like, this is a good time to recondition the components of the piston system. Usually, an engine will be rebuilt for ring failure, and this kind of rebuild should always include a complete reconditioning of the piston system. The repair practice of simply cleaning pistons, replacing rings, and breaking the glaze on cylinder walls is a traditional repair

format that has little or no place in engine restoration work. It may be an economical approach to keeping an aging vehicle on the road for a few more months or years, but it is not a reliable enough approach to be considered for the purposes of restoration work.

The Head and Deck Surfaces

On engines with removable heads, the first surfaces encountered in disassembly of the basic block will be the mating surfaces of the block and head(s). These surfaces, and the manifold mating surfaces, should be checked for straightness and resurfaced if deviations from perfect flatness are greater than 0.002 inch in any linear six inches of head or deck; or more than 0.005 inch for the entire length of the surface in question. On "V" type engines, it is necessary to grind the included angle manifold

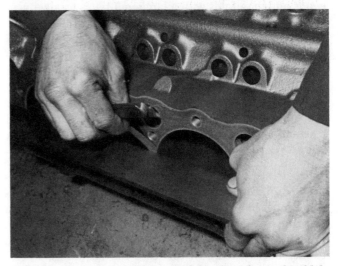

Cylinder block deck surfaces and head surfaces should be checked with a straight edge and feeler gauge to make sure that they are flat enough to seal a head gasket.

Long manifolds, like these V-12 breathers, can easily warp, and should be checked for straightness and ground flat as necessary.

Resurfacing cylinder heads is a routine automotive machine shop job. The best equipment does this job wet, with a grinding coolant, to prevent overheating damage.

Manifolds are ground on surface grinders after they are positioned parallel to the grinding stones.

surfaces of the heads when the major head or deck surfaces have been ground. This maintains alignment of the manifold flanges with their mating surfaces on the heads. The practice of correcting flatness and surface defects of heads and manifolds with a large mill file is totally unacceptable. Included angle manifolds on "V" type engines must be perfectly flat. Straight six and eight manifolds should be held to no more than 0.012 inch deviation — from flat for their entire lengths. In this last case, the possibility of tightening a warped manifold back flat against a head or block has to be considered against the probability of weakening the manifold's flanges and cracking or breaking them if this manhandling approach is used.

Frequently, the limits of head warping will be expressed in a phone call from a machine shop that goes something like this, "Hey Mack, the heads that you brought in are warped about 0.006 inch and 0.008 inch. Do you want us to 'shave' 0.010 inch off 'em? It'll run ya twenty bucks each." In this case the answer is, "Yes," with the proviso that if 0.010 inch won't "clean them up," go to 0.015 inch. On long, flat-head engines, the heads are pretty flexible and *may* conform to the block when

they are cinched down, but it is better to grind them flat. The exception would be when the head or heads in question have been ground before and there is danger of weakening them with further grinding, or producing valve-to-piston interference (OHV and OHC engines), or of raising the compression ratio unacceptably by removing more stock. I get nervous in situations where the total removal of stock from a head goes beyond 0.040 inch from the original dimension.

Engine block decks rarely warp significantly, but when they do, they should be ground back to flatness. If this is necessary, the stock removal must be considered in conjunction with the amount(s) that may have been removed from the head(s), so as not to go too far.

The Cylinder Walls

To understand the appropriate procedures for reconditioning cylinder walls, it is necessary to describe the nature of the wear to which they are subjected. There are basically three kinds of wear that afflict cylinder walls — two of them are inevitable, and the third is sometimes present. From the first rotation of a new engine, the cylinder walls tend to slowly wear out-of-round in a way that enlarges their dimensions disproportionately at right angles to the crankshaft. They also tend to become tapered with the large end of the taper at the top. Actually, most cylinder wear occurs in the top two inches of ring travel, while the bottoms of the cylinder walls remain relatively

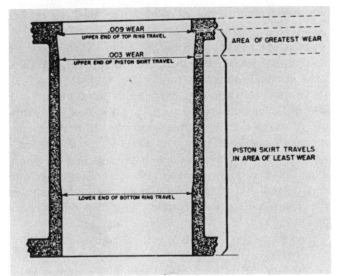

Most cylinder wear occurs at the tops of cylinders and is referred to as "taper." Lower cylinder areas rarely show much measurable wear.

unworn. At the very top of a cylinder there will be a ridge which is an unworn section of the cylinder that exists above the top of the top (compression) ring's travel. A third type of wear that may be present in cylinders is scor-

There are many designs and types of ridge reamers. The two shown here are pretty typical. Basically, ridge reamers are small hand-turned lathes.

ing, which almost always results from stuck or broken rings.

As a rebuilding proposition, taper is allowable in amounts of up to 0.010 inch, and out-of-round is tolerated in small amounts, usually less than 0.005 inch. If these conditions are met, and new or resized pistons with so-called, "engineered ring sets," are installed, the results are often serviceable in the short run. In practice, this means that a quick, cheap rebuild uses the above limits and conditions. Cylinders are simply roughed up with a glaze breaker to give them a finish that will allow the new rings to seat. While these conditions may be tolerated in the repair field, they are certainly not acceptable in restoration work.

I would suggest that the proper restoration proposition for engines is **no taper** and **no out-of-round**. If a car's engine is to be restored, it is a very false economy to do anything but return the cylinders to perfect roundness and straightness.

The first step in resizing a cylinder is to remove the ridge that always forms at its top. This procedure involves the use of a "ridge reamer" which is a small hand operated lathe device with a cutter that removes the protruding material on the top half inch or less of the cylinder wall. A ridge reamer should be used prior to piston removal, if pistons are to be removed from the top of an engine. This is because it is almost impossible to get a piston and its rings past a cylinder ridge without damaging the piston's ring lands. Be careful not to overuse a ridge reamer because if you undercut cylinder you may be forced to bore or hone it to a larger oversize than would have otherwise been necessary.

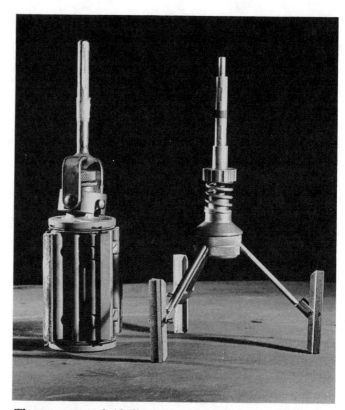

The two manual (drill motor operated) hones shown here have somewhat different purposes. The one on the left is a sizing hone and has a micrometer adjustment to position the stones for dimensional grinding of cylinders to a specific size. The hone on the right is a glaze breaker and is designed only to surface a cylinder, not to dimension it.

When you use a ridge reamer, be careful not to overdo it and cut below a cylinder's bore size.

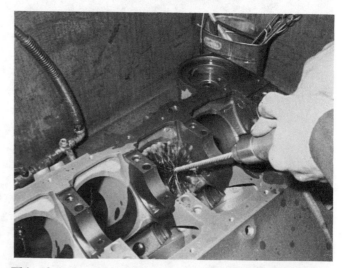

This glaze breaking hone has hundreds of small abrasive stones mounted on wire stems. It surfaces a cylinder with almost no measurable stock removal.

The equipment available for resizing cylinders is varied and highly specialized. Roughly speaking, it falls into two categories: hones (fixed or floating stones) and boring devices (fixed cutters). Hones, which range from drill-motor operated hand tools to huge dwell honing machines, are considered efficient for resizing cylinders where the taper does not exceed 0.008 inch or 0.010 inch for the full length of a cylinder. A new generation of dwell honing machines is designed to "dwell" for most of the up-and-down honing cycle in the bottoms of cylinders and gradually work its way up to the tops on successive strokes. The actual amount of time that a dwell hone spends in any part of a cylinder is determined by the cur-

rent draw of the motor that runs it or, more recently, by a computer program that uses out-of-round and taper measurements to calculate the hone action that will produce a round, straight cylinder bore. This type of automation makes it possible to efficiently hone to depths somewhat beyond the 0.008 inch to 0.010 inch rule-of-thumb standard that prevailed in the past. Manual "sizing" hones (adjustable fixed stones) that are operated with an electric drill motor are not really efficient enough or accurate enough to use beyond the above limit. The problem with any type of hone is that if there is any deviation in the center line of the cylinder with regard to the crankshaft center line (this should always be 90°, but factory error in this area is surprisingly common), the error will be perpetuated in the honing operation.

Cylinder boring devices may differ significantly in type. The newer ones tend to take their position from the crankshaft bearing saddles directly, and not, as the older ones did, from the deck surface(s) of the block. Boring

relative to the crankshaft centerline is far preferable to boring from the block deck(s). Since boring machines use rigidly positioned cutters to remove stock, they leave a surface that is too rough for piston rings to seat properly. Therefore, boring is always followed by a honing operation that ideally achieves about a 20 micron finish on the cylinders with a crosshatch pattern of 40° to 60°.

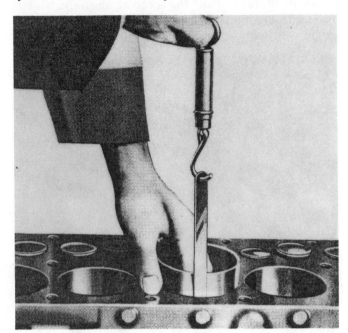

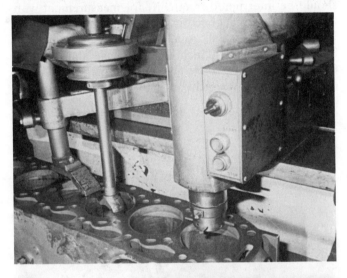

When a lot of stock has to be removed from a cylinder, or when its bore has to be straightened out, honing will not do the job and a boring bar must be used. The boring bar shown here takes its position off the crankshaft main bearing saddles, not off the block deck. This allows it to straighten out crooked bores.

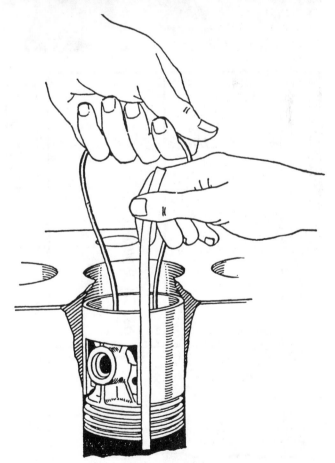

Years ago, piston-to-cylinder clearance was measured with a blade micrometer and a pull scale. This procedure gave a fair indication of piston skirt clearance.

If you are dealing with cylinders that have small taper and out-of-round deviations, it is perfectly permissible to use a drill-motor-operated, expanding hone to remove these deviations and leave a proper cylinder surface. Use of this equipment requires at least a half horsepower drill motor and some practice to achieve the proper final crosshatch pattern. This pattern is important, and depends on drill speed and the speed at which the hone is inserted and withdrawn from the cylinder. In honing, you begin with fairly rough stones (80 to 150 grit for stock

removal and dimensional finishing). This is followed by "medium stones," (280 grit) used with lubrication for the final surfacing. The main trick to manual honing is to spend most of your time at the bottom of the cylinder. This is because this is the area with the least wear and it will require the most stock removal to eliminate taper. As you work progressively higher in the cylinder, taper is eliminated, and the lower, less worn part of the cylinder acts as a guide for the hone stones as they reach the worn areas of the cylinder near its top. The process of honing should be interrupted frequently for measurement with bore gauges, inside micrometers, or telescope gauges. Honing operations will usually aim at oversizes of 0.010 inch, 0.020 inch, 0.030 inch, or 0.040 inch, and frequent checks of size will insure that you don't go beyond these oversizes before you achieve a final finish. Remember

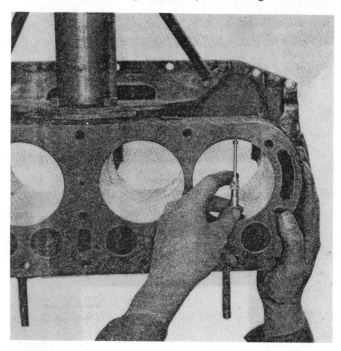

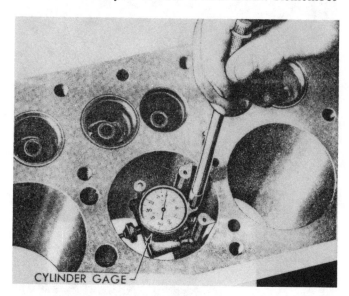

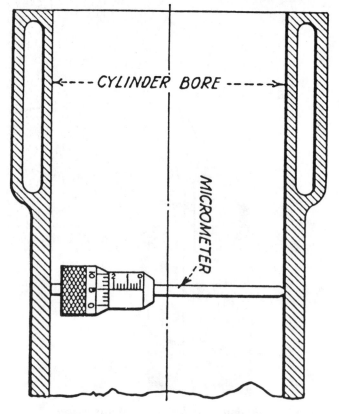

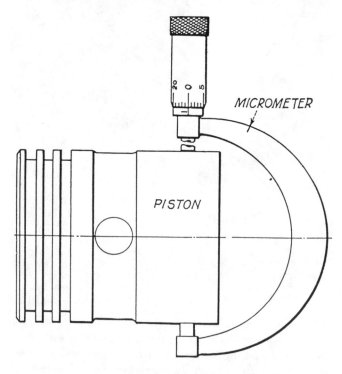

Modern practice is to use measuring instruments to determine the dimensions of pistons and cylinders. Inside micrometers and bore gauges (shown here) can be used, as can micrometers and telescope gauges. Pistons are measured with micrometers.

that cylinder/piston clearance is almost always a function of piston size. Cylinder sizes and their oversizes tend to be very standard and recognizable figures.

Some engines are built with cylinder sleeves. These sleeves are either "dry" (seated against the block's metal for their entire lengths) or "wet" (seated in the block at the top and bottom, but exposed directly to coolant for most of their lengths). Factory sleeved engines can be treated as non-sleeved engines and honing and boring procedures can be applied to them. However, frequently it is easier to replace worn sleeve assemblies with new ones. These are often supplied with fitted pistons, rings, and piston pins. Occasionally, cylinder damage, usually scoring, is so severe that a sleeve must be inserted into the cylinder of an engine that was not built with sleeves originally. This is a specialized process that is outwardly simple, but, in reality, it involves a lot of knowhow to make it work. Sleeving, which involves boring a cylinder to an oversize and forcing a sleeve into the oversize hole, should be left to shops and individuals who have considerable experience in this area. Amateur sleeve installations sometimes result in the sleeve(s) working loose in its bore and doing enormous damage to block(s).

Although some older engines actually left the factory with differently sized cylinders in the same block, and although it was not unusual for this situation to be created in rebuilding years ago, it is desirable that all cylinders in a restored engine be the same size. Sometimes, a badly scored cylinder requires sleeving, because it is easier and/or better to sleeve one cylinder and bore it to stan-

dard size than it would be to bore every other cylinder to an enormous oversize to duplicate the oversize that would be necessary to repair deep scores in one damaged cylinder.

Badly damaged cylinders sometimes have to be bored to an oversize and sleeved. Boring to oversize and sleeve installation are shown here.

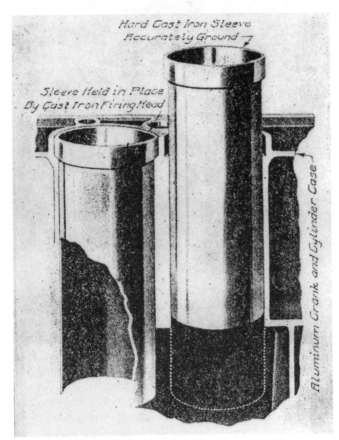

Some engines were manufactured with sleeves in them, such as this aluminum alloy block engine.

The Importance of Cleanup

There are lots of tricks and shop kinks that are acquired in years of resizing cylinders. Some mechanics swear by kerosene as the ideal lubricant for final hone-surfacing cylinders, and others use engine oil or machine oil. Opinion varies widely on the exact point at which it is more economical or better to bore than to hone, and answering the question of the speed at which a hone should be run can take on the complexity and passion of a theological debate. One point on which all good mechanics and automotive machinists tend to agree, and which many do not pursue in practice, is the importance of washing up with soap and water after any honing operation. That's right, the stuff Mother wanted you to use behind your ears. I have seen people use exotic solvents like methylene chloride, and dangerous ones, like gasoline, to clean up the abrasives and debris left by boring and honing operations. The fact is that these solvents will not do the job that soap and water will. Good old Ivory and a garden hose will float abrasive particles out of the pores of metal in a way that petroleum solvents won't. Wash liberally after honing because any particles that you leave behind will, at best, cause severe wear to rings and cylinders and, at worst, they will end up embedded in bearings.

While we're on this, it should be mentioned that abrasives are a necessary evil in engine rebuilding. They are used at many points because they are necessary, but their residues are deadly to an engine's health. A while back one of the major OEM diesel engine manufacturers sent a directive to its authorized repair facilities stating that in the future, no glass bead process was to be used in any phase of rebuilding their engines. This was because their warranty people found glass beads embedded in the main bearings of three engines that had been disassembled for inspection when they failed after being rebuilt, but while under warranty. While I believe that it is both possible and practical to remove glass bead or grinding residues from heads, valves, pistons, etc. to a degree that these contaminants should not be a problem, you should always remember what can happen if you are careless with abrasives or blast particles. You can't do too good a job removing machine shop residues from engine parts, so try to work in that direction.

Pistons

For some unexplained reason, years ago when pistons were relatively cheap, there was all kinds of equipment around to salvage them. Now that they are excruciatingly expensive, it is hard to find a shop that has piston resizing equipment.

There were various types of equipment that accomplished piston resizing, and all of it dealt with the piston skirt, which tends to collapse as a result of contact with its cylinder wall. For split skirt pistons, there were nasty expander springs that were installed inside the pistons and stayed there (one hoped) to spread the piston's skirt. There were other systems that hammer peened piston skirts back to original dimensions and retempered them. Yet others knurled piston skirt faces, to selectively increase their dimensions.

In my opinion, the only piston skirt reconditioning proposition that is valid is the knurling proposition, and even this becomes problematical when dealing with cam ground (elliptical) piston skirts. In spite of the expense, when an engine is being rebuilt and the pistons have collapsed skirts, or cylinders have been honed more than a few thousandths oversize to regain proper roundness and straightness, the pistons should be replaced. The expense will be considerable because the days of less-than-$25 pistons have mostly succumbed to the days of $50-$250 pistons. Yet this expense may be worth it to avoid the uncertainty of mucking around with the archaic arts of piston resizing. Of course, there are shops that are good at this operation and that can produce a good resized piston at a fraction of the cost of a new one. If you know of such a shop, great. If you don't, I wouldn't spend a lot of time looking for one; the results could be disappointing.

Knurling piston skirts raises metal and restores proper clearance to cylinder walls. This is the one piston reconditioning process that I know of that works well.

If pistons are dimensionally correct, and are being put back into an engine in which only slight deviations in cylinder format have been corrected, then they should be cleaned, checked for cracks and for ring groove depth and width, and for pin fit, and reinstalled if they pass these checks. The best method for manually cleaning pistons is to use an application of fine glass bead. This will clean them without changing their dimensions appreciably. Piston ring grooves may be cleaned with one of numerous devices made for this purpose, and if they do not clean up in factory ring dimensions, they should be resized for wider rings and fitted with such rings.

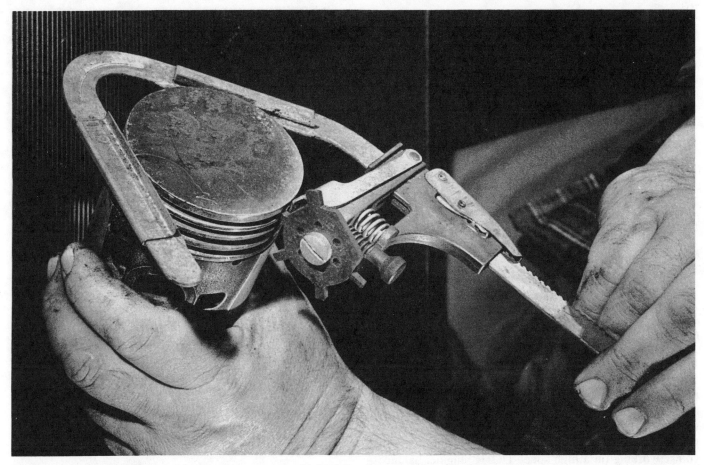

Ring regrooving tools, such as this one, do a pretty good job of cleaning up piston ring grooves.

Ring side clearance should never exceed .0015 inch and back clearance should be to the ring manufacturer's specifications. Many ring sets include a cardboard gauge for measuring this factor. These measurements are not particularly complex, but they are critical and it is easy to get them wrong. This is yet another reason that when pistons are involved, I tend to forsake my usual prejudice against automatically ordering new parts, and spring for a set of new pistons. A piston, at its widest point, should provide about 0.001 inch to 0.003 inch clearance to the cylinder. Check the piston manufacturer's data for an exact figure. Special rings and skirt expansion can be used to fit original pistons to slightly oversized cylinders, but I doubt if it is worth the chance. Most pistons are pretty delicate and hard-working members of the engine team, and sending in relievers is not an unreasonable call in the rebuild game.

Not all pistons are created equal. Some outfits that custom make pistons don't really have the engineering depth or sophisticated equipment to properly manufacture them. I have seen some really atrocious pistons from well-known sources; pistons that I wouldn't put in an engine. The OEM (Original Equipment Manufacturer) piston companies, like TRW, Perfect Circle, and Sealed Power tend to sell highly engineered pistons which are often cheaper than some of the low quality stuff sold to old car enthusiasts by the specialty houses.

Balancing pistons is a good idea, up to a point. I have a suspicion that balancing components in old, low speed, long stroke engines is often a fruitless gesture. I have seen people go to enormous lengths to achieve better-than-factory balance in engines where I am sure that it wouldn't make any discernible difference. Recently, I had the occasion to examine an engine that had failed a couple of thousand miles after being rebuilt. The rebuilder had spent a lot of time and effort balancing the crankshaft, rods, and pistons. In this process he had destroyed the rods by grinding the support veins out of the caps. This was all done for balance and in the name of making the engine run smoothly. I noticed that he hadn't reground the camshaft — an area that would have made a considerable difference in the smoothness of the engine — but he had gone hog wild on balancing. What all of this leads up to is this: Under no circumstances should substantial amounts of material be removed from or added to pistons to achieve balance in old engines. Pistons should be weighed and their weights compared prior to installation to prevent the possibility of gross error.

If a large discrepancy exists between pistons, it should be eliminated by selecting other pistons that have reasonably matched weights. But the business of trying to get exact piston balance on an engine that will never turn more than 2,000 or 3,000 rpm is silly. I have seen pistons that disintegrated because of the ministrations of some balancing freak, and every time that I see it, I wonder what was being attempted and why. I've heard all of the stories about how smoothly balanced engines run versus their unbalanced poor relations, and it's mostly eye wash.

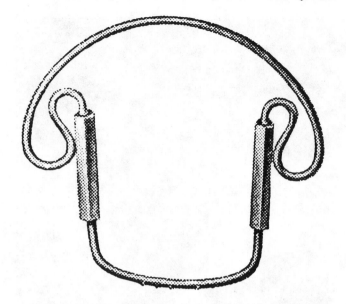

There used to be numerous devices on the market that you could install in pistons to expand collapsed skirts. Don't bother with this stuff; it never really worked very well.

Most older engines weren't designed with exact static balance in mind, much less dynamic balance. The elimination of vibration can be more fruitfully pursued in about half a dozen other areas. Don't mess around trying to exactly balance pistons for use in low performance engines; they have enough problems without that. Now if you're working on a high speed DOHC engine, balance can be critical and should be attended to.

When cast steel or cast iron pistons are encountered in an old engine, it is usually best to thank them for the years of faithful service that they may have rendered, and then put them in a nice, clean cardboard box and store them until you can find the emotional resources to throw them away. Modern aluminum alloy pistons have infinitely better heat dissipation characteristics and are almost always lighter than old ferrous pistons. They are invariably tough enough to withstand any service conditions that they will encounter, and lighter pistons mean more power, so don't hesitate to make the replacement.

Piston Rings

For something that looks relatively simple, piston rings turn out to be complex and tricky products. Mechanics used to have to purchase them separately for each of the three or four grooves in a piston, and a whole body of arcane knowledge and theory was developed to support this purpose.

Presently, rings are supplied in sets specific to particular pistons, but several distinctions remain. For example, there are "factory" rings for use in perfectly straight and round cylinder bores and there are "engineered" rings for bores with a lot of taper. There are "chrome" rings, which are actually chrome plated, and "moly" or molybdenum rings, which are plated, and cast iron rings, which

Ring side clearance is critical and it is easy to measure. All you need is a "feeler," or thickness gauge.

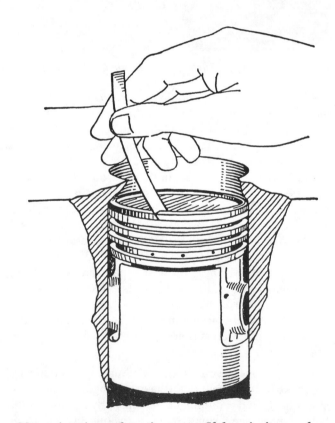

Measuring ring end gap is a must. If there isn't enough gap, ring ends can lock when the rings get hot and expand. This can seize up an engine.

aren't plated but which have a thin coating of iron oxide to assist in break-in. Ring design varies from those with expander springs to those without them, and there are even a few old sets of wrap around rings being sold by someone out there.

The latest wrinkle in the field is very narrow, low pressure rings (4 or 5 psi instead of 25 or more psi). These "low friction" rings definitely have no place in old cars. My prejudice in all of this is to order new pistons and the rings that their manufacturer supplies with them or recommends for them. That is another problem with resizing old pistons — you have to enter the thicket of choosing rings, and it can be very confusing.

Good piston rings are relatively expensive, or seem so for what you get. There are lots of economy or "gyp" rings out there and these should be avoided. Good rings are very precisely made and involve some pretty sophisticated engineering, machining, heat treating, coating, and testing. It is unlikely that the machine shops that make "gyp" rings have the resources to do all of this.

One of the great debates that rages among restorers in choosing piston rings has to do with the use of chrome plated rings in older engines. Supporters of these rings claim that they do a better job of sealing and break-in better with less distortion. It is also claimed that they can reduce cylinder wall friction. The other side of this controversy has horror stories about blocks allegedly shaved to oblivion by these rings, which they claim are too hard for the metallurgy of old blocks. I've never seen evidence of this shaving effect, but I stay away from chrome rings for old engines out of caution and because I have found that they break-in more slowly than do simple iron oxide coated rings.

In any case, the performance of non-chrome rings is more than adequate for prewar engines. Modern versions of "cast iron" rings from reputable suppliers are definitely better engineered and manufactured than the

OEM rings that were originally specified for prewar engines. I also prefer the simplest rings available and will happily forgo such neat innovations as rings with expander springs and double side rails. Modern rings are designed to control compression pressures that are as much as twice those developed by engines fifty years ago. They do this at rates of piston travel (Piston Feet Per Minute, "PFPM") that are two or three times what they were then. The complicated rings developed for modern engines are definitely unnecessary in older engines, and are mostly a nuisance to install.

Piston ring installation or "fitting" is one of those manual tasks that looks simple, but is easy to foul up. Piston rings are delicate and easy to break or distort. It is imperative that a good ring expander be used to get them into piston grooves and that they not be overexpanded and distorted in this process. In ring sets that have expander springs, side rails and the like, it is imperative that everything be installed in the right order, in the right place, and in the right orientation.

Before installing any new ring set, be sure to check the groove side clearance (never more than 0.0015 inch), depth clearance, and end gap. This last factor is critical, as an engine will overheat and even seize up if it has rings installed without adequate end gaps. End gap is measured by placing each ring in the cylinder and pushing it down the bore about half way with an unringed piston. Thickness gauges are then used to measure the gap between its ends. You should file or mill ring ends to provide at least 0.004 inch for each inch of cylinder bore. After cutting ring ends to produce the correct end gap dimension, always deburr them. Manufacturers usually give a specific figure for this crucial dimension and it should be followed rigorously. Even rings with diagonal or notched ends have to be dealt with in this regard. Just because a few rings in a set check out okay for end gap, don't forgo checking all of the rings in the set. There can be some surprises. In initial ring installation, be sure that ring ends are placed at 90° to each other, to prevent early scoring and rotational lockup.

Fitting Piston Pins

Piston pin fits used to be achieved by reaming rod bushings or piston pin bushings or both, depending on the pin's designed flotation. Weird phrases like "thumb fit" and "palm fit" emerged to describe the proper feel of a particular fit. Presently, there is honing equipment available for pin fitting, and fits are specified in ten thousandths of an inch. Because honing is much more accurate than reaming, the pin fits specified when this work is done on honing machines are much tighter than were the old, reamed, "feel" fits. The old reamed bushings and bosses were so rough that they were initially fitted quite tightly and allowed to wear into proper fits.

Modern pin fit specifications, for modern pistons, take into account equipment that provides smoother piston

You can file ring end gap to specification with the ring in a vise with lined jaws and a file. You can also use a special fixture designed for this purpose. However you do the job, be sure to deburr the ring ends after you have dimensioned them.

boss surfaces and allows fits with less clearance than was used in the past. Good pin fitting equipment will heat the pin and its bushings or bosses to simulate to some degree the temperature in a working engine. It is my practice to have an automotive machine shop install and burnish new pin bushings, where they are used, and hone fit them to fit the pins. I always specify that the pins be fitted "a bit loose" because I am deathly afraid of the seizure that can result from too tight a pin fit. If you go much too loose, a pin will make a hollow, wrapping noise, but it takes a lot of looseness to get this, and it is diagnosable by its sound. A pin that is fitted too tight doesn't give any warnings until it wears loose, or the piston fails in the boss area or in its skirt. Those failures tend to be sudden and violent.

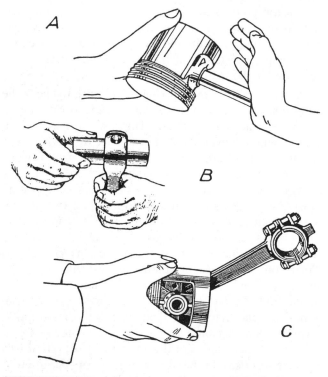

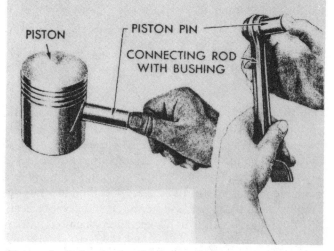

Piston pin fitting in the old days relied mostly on the feel of the fit. "Palm" and "thumb" fits were terms that meant something to old time mechanics.

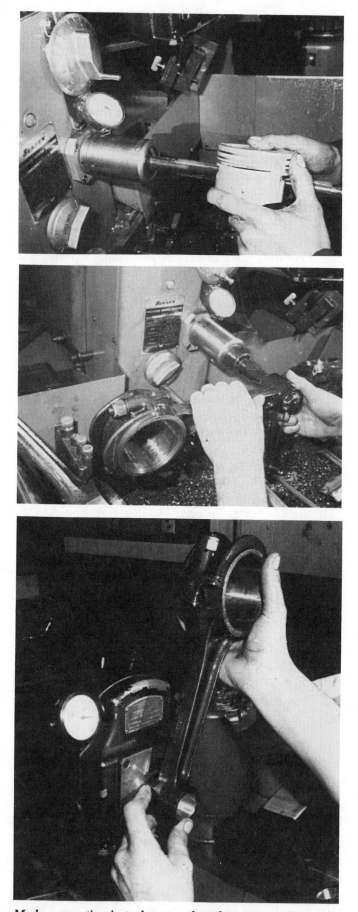

Modern practice is to hone, rather than ream, piston pin bosses and rod bushings. Very accurate measuring fixtures are used so that honing is done to exact dimensions. These dimensions are measured to ten-thousandths of an inch.

Piston Installation

Piston installation is almost always accomplished from the top of an engine, except on engines with non-removable heads. Bottom installation uses a chamfer in a cylinder to enter the rings, but this is a difficult installation and is risky for rings. On a few engines that are designed for bottom piston installation, the bottom ends of the rods won't clear through the cylinders, seemingly mandating installation from the bottom. You can beat this wrap by pushing the rods up from the bottom and then inserting the piston pins with the pistons above the deck. I like this installation in preference to installing pistons from the bottom of an engine.

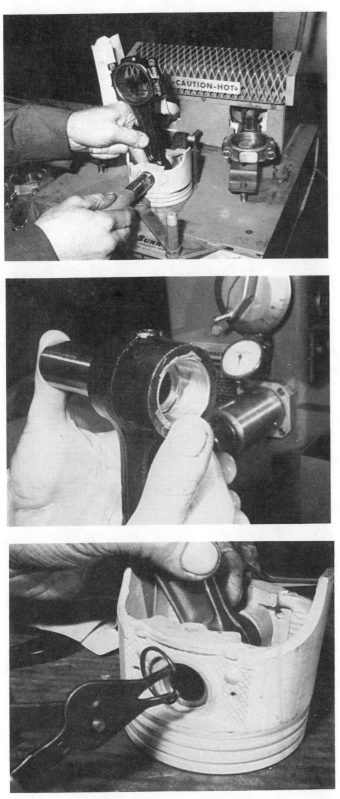

Final piston pin fitting is done with the pins, rod ends, and piston bosses heated to operating temperatures. With all that, the pins should still be checked for a feel fit as a final insurance. A good machinist will know the right feel of a rod rocking on its pin, with the pin retaining hardware installed.

A good ring expander is a must when you install piston rings. Installing rings with your bare hands is dangerous to rings' health!

When entering pistons and rings into cylinders, use lots of oil on everything in sight, and use a minimum of force to push the pistons and rings through your ring sleeve. A rag taped over the end of a hammer handle makes a nice tamper to push pistons and rings down through an installing sleeve and into cylinders. Always put tightly fitting protectors (plastic or rubber hose lengths) over any protruding rod bolts or rod end surfaces so that they won't damage a crankshaft as rods descend into the crankcase during piston installation. The crank throw for each cylinder in which you are installing a piston should be well out of the way.

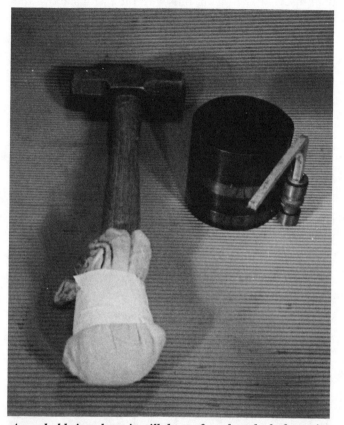

A good old ring sleeve is still the preferred method of entering ringed pistons into cylinders. A hammer handle with a rag taped to it works very well to drive the pistons home in their cylinders.

CHAPTER 8:

Engine Lubrication and Cooling Systems

The Engine Lubrication System

One of the early purveyors of parts, knowledge, and humanity to the old car hobby was a Russian immigrant by the name of Sam Adelman. From the 1930s through the 1960s, Sam ran an exclusive salvage business in Mount Vernon, New York. He humorously referred to his establishment as "the Emporium."

From a set of almost unbelievably dilapidated old buildings, he catered to the owners of Lincolns, Packards, Pierce-Arrows, Deusenbergs, and Rolls-Royce vehicles. Most people who collected these cars in that period knew of Sam, and many were helped by him. As a young man, I was astounded by the knowledge that he had acquired as a result of disassembling hundreds, or perhaps thousands, of classic automobiles. It was Sam's contention that as long as an engine had an uninterrupted supply of high grade, clean, relatively cool oil, it would run forever. He impressed this theory on me so completely that it has become an article of faith with me, known as "Sam's Rule." Of course, the impact of Sam's Rule is that if an engine is deprived of this oil supply for any appreciable amount of time, things will begin to fail.

Since most people who restore collector car engines work with a high degree of care, it is unusual for them to make big mistakes. For example, major misassembly is rarely encountered. However, in restoration work, small mistakes can to be deadly. There are few places that are less tolerant of small mistakes than the lubrication systems of old engines. I recently heard of a 12-cylinder Lincoln engine that was seriously damaged because one of the solder joints in the oil pickup plumbing failed. The reason for the failure was apparently that some soldering flux had been inadvertently trapped in the joint at the time that it was manufactured. The failure took almost 50 years to occur, but when it did, major engine damage resulted.

Although modern lubricants are infinitely superior to those available before the 1960s, they still must be supplied to critical lubrication points in adequate amounts and pressures for engine systems to work. Modern lubricants are wonders of chemical complexity. In addition to basic lubrication, they have been buffered against thinning out, and fortified to prevent oxidation, foaming, and corrosiveness to a degree undreamed of 40 years ago. They have a level of detergency that makes them capable of cleaning up varnish and harmlessly suspending all kinds of garbage — up to a pound in five quarts of oil — that the older lubricants used to routinely deposit in engines. The huge oil capacities of some older engines — my 1932 Lincoln holds 12 quarts, plus two for the filter — were in large part necessary because the viscosity of the oils that were available when this car was manufactured were so inherently unstable as to require huge reserves for cooling purposes. The point is, advances in lubricant technology are on the restorer's side, but he must still work to be certain that lubricants are supplied to engines in a clean, cool, and uninterrupted manner.

Oiling systems range from the very simple splash and drip systems of the early automobile age to the more complex pressure, shot, and dry sump systems that had evolved by the 1930s. Many older lubrication systems are marginal, at best. Even with the advantages of modern lubricants, they must perform very well to avoid failure of the bearings, timing chains or gears, and other vulnerable engine components. Always remember Sam's Rule.

The most basic element in working on lubrication systems is that you understand them. That may sound obvious, but some of these system are difficult to puzzle out. I remember a 1910 Maxwell that I once owned that had a wonderfully simple, but intriguing system. This car had a two-cylinder, opposed ("pancake") engine. When both cylinders fired, the incoming pistons momentarily pressurized the crankcase. This pressure was conducted to the top of a small tank, mounted on the firewall and filled with oil. This tank was sealed with a gasketed screw-on cap, and the pressure put in it by the pistons was maintained there by a check valve. From this tank, oil was piped to three drip oilers on the dash board. The drips were visible through sight glasses and adjustable with needle valves. One drip oiler fed a trough that, in turn,

Before there were water pumps, such as this one, cooling systems circulated water by thermosyphon action. It's based on the idea that heat rises, and it was supposed to provide a self-regulating cooling system for automobiles. Water pumps, and later thermostats, made for great improvements in automotive cooling systems.

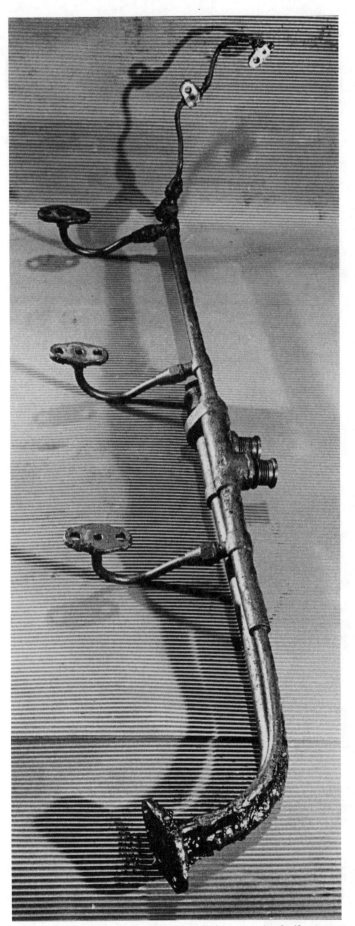

This hand-soldered oil galley supplies pressurized oil to most of the critical lubrication points in the engine that it serves. If it leaks, the car's engine will self-destruct.

fed the rear main bearing. Each of the others was plumbed to a hole midway down, and drilled through the upside of each cylinder — remember, this was a horizontal, opposed engine. The drops of oil would flow to the cylinders and lay on the sides of the pistons' crowns or skirts until the pistons' movement caused the drops to align with the wrist pins. At that point, the oil would drip into the partially drilled wrist pins and lubricate their bearings. From there the oil ran down the wrist pin and exited the rod bushings through holes drilled in them, and ran down the horizontal troughs in the I-beam rods. At the rod crankshaft journals, it entered holes drilled into the rod bearings and oiled them.

Since this was not a recirculating system, any oil left after this long trip fell to the bottom of the crankcase where it was splashed around by the crankshaft and lubricated the front main bearing via a trough, the cylinder walls, and the camshafts. It was a wonderfully simple system that pushed any reasonable concept of adequate lubrication to the limits of the possible. Apparently it worked.

Other lubricating designs, such as Franklin's positive displacement shot system, are wonders of uncompromising engineering. Whatever the system is that you are working on, it must be understood and it must be put in good clean working order. On engines where the crankshaft is pressurized, the enemy is frequently the centrifuging capability of the crankshaft as it spins. Any oiling system requires that passages, galleys, and plumbing be in perfect order — free of dirt and obstructions and tightly and durably connected.

Some older "V" type engines had "fork & blade" or "yoked" connecting rods. This, coupled with the use of very thick babbitt in the bearings, often produced a situation where the ability of the small gear oil pumps that were used was questionable. These rod configurations require enormous amounts of oil for adequate lubrication, and any decline in output from the pumps is usually fatal. Modern lubrication systems are less marginal, particularly those that employ rotor type pumps. The mandate here is to always rebuild older oil pumps to factory specification with regard to side and gear tooth or rotor clearance, and to test them thoroughly before installation.

Pressure lubricated engines vary from those that run at very low pressures of 15 to 20 psi, to those that run as high as 75 psi. Many older systems are combinations of pressure and splash feeds. Again, each aspect of such systems must be analyzed as to function and put into working order in every particular. Splash lubricated bearings depend on simple laws of nature, such as those governing the surface tension of liquids and gravity. About all that can be done for them is to make sure that they are physically intact, absolutely clean and unobstructed, and that they have bearings adjusted to the correct clearances. Pressure systems, on the other hand, require all of the above, but also depend on properly functioning pumps, sound plumbing, functioning pressure relief valves, and clean pickups and filters (if used). These last items are vitally important, and are sometimes overlooked.

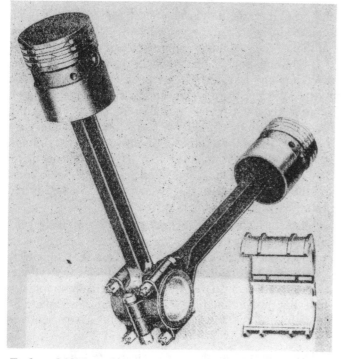

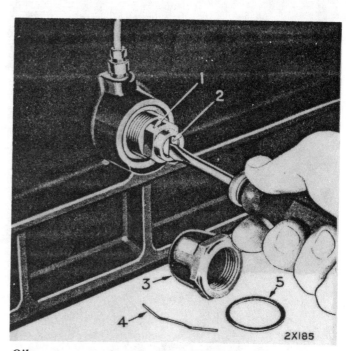

Fork and blade rod setups, such as this one, require a lot of lubrication, and the oil pumps in many engines that used this rod design were marginal at best. When you work on an engine with this type of rods, you have to get everything right in the lubrication system to avoid bearing failure.

Oil pressure regulators usually require thorough cleaning and careful adjustment to work. Be careful of the springs in these units, and never stretch them or substitute other springs.

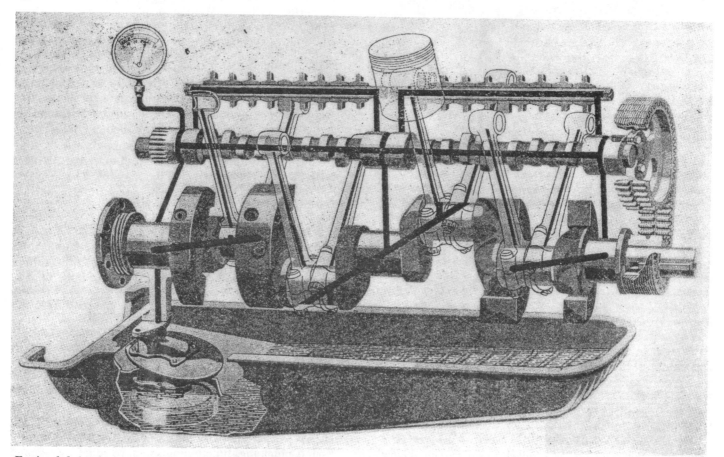

Engine lubrication systems vary in design. This one is pretty straightforward; many lubrication systems are much more complex. Be sure that you understand the principles and fine details of the lubrication system in any engine that you restore.

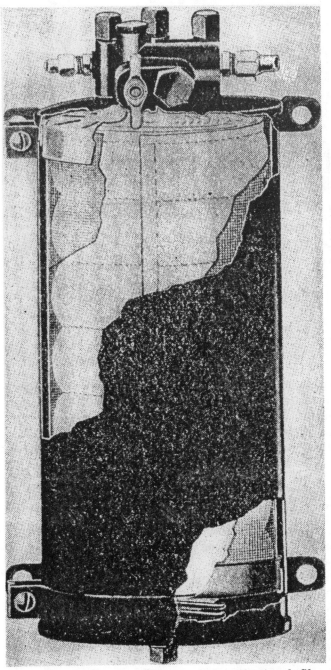

This old partial flow filter is physically large but it only filters 15 percent to 20 percent of the oil being circulated by an engine at any time.

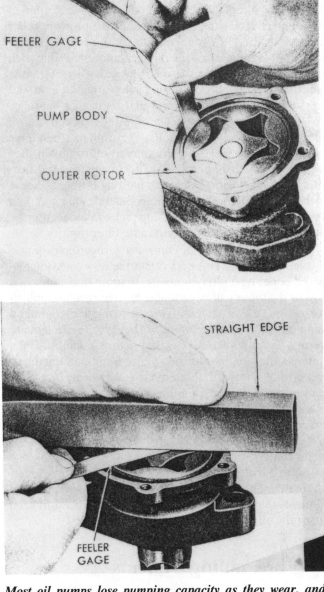

Most oil pumps lose pumping capacity as they wear, and their internal clearances increase. Gear and rotor type pumps can usually be checked for dimensional integrity and for pumping capacity. These are checks that are well worth making.

Pressure lubrication systems invariably have some provision for limiting oil pressure to account for bearing wear and oil viscosity changes. These are either simple or compound spring-loaded pressure relief valves in combination with fixed or adjustable orifices. The orifices usually regulate oil pressure at low engine speeds, and the spring-loaded valves regulate oil pressure at higher engine speeds. All parts of regulators must be clean and free to move, and orifice dimensions should never be changed from original. The springs in oil pressure regulators should never be stretched or replaced with other than original type springs. Some regulator systems are resident in oil pumps, and others are mounted outside of engines. When you are dealing with an adjustable oil pressure regulator, and the normal range of adjustment

to tension a spring or open and close an orifice will not produce adequate oil pressure at hot idle, or limit the maximum oil pressure to a safe level with cold oil at road speeds, either the regulator or something else in the system is defective. Any problems in this area must be found and fixed quickly since damage to the engine is almost inevitable if they are not.

Oil pickup devices are either stationary or floating, and it is imperative that they not leak, as air entering the system at this point will raise havoc with proper oil pressure and lubrication. This happens because air entering on the vacuum side of an oil pump will foam as it goes through the pump, and this will deprive the cylinder walls of proper lubrication. Always check oil pickups very carefully for cracks, joint defects, and other problems that could cause leaks.

Oil filters are either of the partial flow or full flow type. Partial flow filters take a portion of an engine's pumped oil, usually the oil which is bypassed by the pressure relief valve, and filter it. Frequently this is no more than 15 percent or 20 percent of the oil in circulation. While such filtration helps cleanse the oil, it provides no guarantee against contamination entering and circulating in the pressurized part of the system and damaging bearings. Full flow systems interpose an oil filter between the oil pump and all lubrication points. These filters often have a bypass feature that allows unfiltered oil to flow if they are plugged. It is imperative that canister type full flow filters be loaded with the correct filtering elements. Some of the older glued cartridge filters must be changed on a time basis as well as on a mileage schedule because the glue seams can deteriorate and cause filter rupture.

There is a great deal of controversy regarding the use of thick "dense" filter media versus the now common resinated paper type filter elements. In some cases, only one type or the other will be available for a particular application. If there is a choice, I would strongly recommend using pleated paper type filters. They give very adequate control (a four micron pass, that's four millionths of a meter, is the standard for one major filter manufacturer) and do not absorb the detergent additives in the oil as readily as the dense type filters do. Remember, drain oil that is dirty is an indication that the additive package is doing its job and suspending contamination. Drain oil that is clean after use does not necessarily indicate a superior filter. It may indicate that the inevitable crankcase refuse that hydrocarbon engines produce is sitting somewhere in the engine because the detergents and other oil additives that should be suspending it have been filtered out of the oil by the oil filter.

Engine Cooling Systems

In the 18th century, Count Rumsford concluded that heat is energy and *vice versa*. Yet even before he came to this then startling conclusion, tinkerers had been trying to effect an efficient conversion of heat to mechanical energy for centuries. The reciprocating hydrocarbon internal combustion engine that we all know and love (mostly) is the result of more than a century of intensive human effort to get the best possible conversion of heat to energy. It operates within the limits of our design imagination and the limitations of the materials that are available to construct, fuel, lubricate, and cool it. In common use, this engine succeeds in converting only 15 percent to 30 percent of the energy (heat) that is available in the fuel that it burns into useful mechanical energy. One of the things that Rumsford didn't realize, and that modern combustion engineers must account for, is the fact that to produce mechanical energy from heat, there must be a "gradient." Put most concisely, this means that something has to be hotter than something else. The necessity for this gradient means, in practice, that some considerable proportion of the heat that is generated in

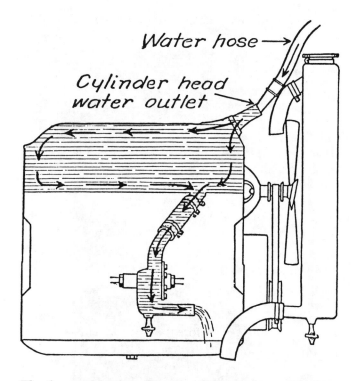

The theory of most cooling systems is simple enough. Water is circulated through an engine's water jacket and picks up heat. It is pumped or thermosyphoned through a radiator and transfers that heat to the air going through the radiator. A radiator fan is usually incorporated into the system to insure air flow through the radiator and around the engine.

any engine design will have to be rejected into the environment for the system to work.

This brings us to automotive cooling systems. While it is difficult to become enthusiastic about anything as seemingly incongruous as efficiency in rejecting heat from an engine, this efficiency is necessary and must be provided for in the restoration process. While engineering journals report on the wonders of adiabatic and LHR (low heat rejection) engine designs and prototypes, we must realize that the power plants in our beloved old cars are, for the most part, comparatively inefficient in the business of power production. They need the maximum possible efficiency that their design makes available in the matter of cooling system operation. Okay, the cooling system may well be the most theoretically unlovely part of an automobile, but it still has to work, and work well.

The statistics on automotive cooling systems are impressive, even if the theory isn't. Some postwar systems operate under pressures of up to 18 pounds and circulate as much as 10,000 gallons of coolant an hour. Any one of these systems rejects enough engine heat to provide winter warmth for a small house. Automotive cooling systems have to maintain a very narrow range of coolant temperatures despite widely varying ambient temperatures and incredibly varied engine heat inputs. This is necessary because engines running at water jacket temperatures much below 160° to 200° Fahrenheit tend to produce vastly increased quantities of sludge in their lubricants. Engines running much hotter than 240° to 250°

Fahrenheit (in highly pressurized systems) will tend toward destructive pre-ignition and boil-over.

Most of the maladies that afflict automotive cooling systems fall into two general classes: leaks and inefficiencies. Every major component in a cooling system is capable of generating leaks or inefficiencies — sometimes both. These include: the block (internally and externally), the hoses and pipes, the radiator, the water pump, the thermostat, and the fan. The performance of each of these components can deteriorate faster than almost any other component in an engine system. In some cases the integrity of cooling systems depends on thousands of fragile brass or copper cartridges that are held together by delicate and fragile solder joints.

In all cases, cooling systems require meticulous restoration and exacting maintenance if they are not to become a weak link in an entire engine system. Mostly, cooling systems are dealt with by adding an array of chemicals, alone or in combination, to cure defects or to ward them off shortly before their symptoms become evident. Flushes, sealants, pump lubricants, corrosion inhibitors, etc. are manufactured in thousands of varieties to keep cooling systems operating at high enough levels of efficiency to keep vehicles on the road. While each of these nostrums may have a place in automotive maintenance, the best restoration policy is prevention, which involves the careful evaluation and rebuilding of cooling system components. The importance of cleaning blocks and insuring the integrity of the coolant diverter tubes that sometimes lurk in them is paramount. Proper installation of core plugs and head gaskets is also critical and is covered under the rubric of "Engine Final Assembly" in the next chapter.

Every other part and subsystem in a cooling system deserves minute attention. Hoses must be in good shape — not old, hard, and cracked, or soft and mushy. Bottom hoses frequently have internal springs to prevent collapse

There are hundreds of cooling system chemicals on the market and most of them only put off rebuilding, rather than preventing it. It is a good idea to use a good anti-rust water pump lubricant in the cooling systems of older cars with packing style water pumps.

Block diverter tubes direct coolant from the radiator to the block water jacket in a way that cools potential hot spots and promotes a smooth, even flow of coolant. These tubes sometimes rust out and are often overlooked when engines are restored.

during coolant surges. These springs must be replaced when new hoses are installed. Hoses that are very stiff can literally tear a radiator inlet or outlet off a radiator as an engine vibrates on its mounts. It is sometimes hard to find replacements for old molded hoses and there is a temptation to replace them with modern flex hoses. Usually this subjects the radiator to unwanted and destructive stress. If you sort through enough bins of old hoses at truck dealerships, you can usually find something that will work in your application.

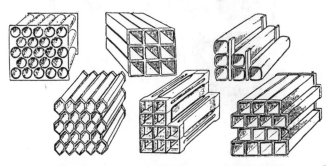

Cartridge core or cellular radiators are built from thousands of horizontally placed copper or brass cartridges that are soldered together. These radiators have tremendous cooling capacity for their size, but have a tendency to leak, and cannot be rodded as conventional tubular radiators.

Radiator repair has been the subject of many books, and the construction of radiators is so varied that it would be impossible to cover it here in any detail. Suffice it to say that radiators from the 1930s on are mostly of the tubular type and are relatively easy for experienced restorers or radiator repair shops to deal with. The older, cellular or cartridge type radiators are another story. Very recent radiators are often constructed with plastic tanks that are O-ringed to aluminum cores, and these are so difficult to repair that replacement is usually the best strategy. Restoration of any type of radiator, other than the plastic tank variety, should include thorough cleaning in a radiator hot tank and rodding if the core is tubular type and needs it. Before installation, a radiator should be flow tested for capacity and pressure and visually inspected for weak walls and joints. Any deficiencies that are found must be corrected. A marginal radiator will not work and may mess up other aspects of a restoration. Sometimes, recoring (or should I say, "core transplanting") is the only solution. In the case of cartridge type radiators, this work will be very expensive. One often overlooked aspect of radiator repair is thorough cleaning of the outside fins or passages. Any external dirt, paint, or corrosion will vastly reduce cooling efficiency. When radiator cores and tanks are painted, special paints are available for this purpose that won't interfere unduly with cooling.

Water pump packings dry out in service and have to be replaced. You can still buy braided packings like these at pump specialty stores. The packings in the foreground are pre-cut and formed. The packing material in the center of the picture is a modern Teflon type. Teflon packings have replaced many of the older asbestos packings.

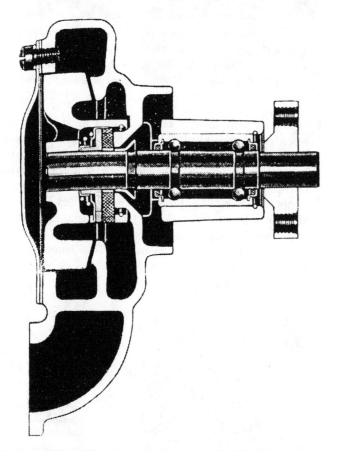

By the mid-1930s most water pumps looked like this and ran on ball bearings with carbon seals. Older pumps were often driven by an engine's timing chains or gears, and used a stuffing box type packing system to seal them.

Water pumps vary in design, from simple front mounted cavity covers with impellers to magnificent bronze castings with complex seal and bearing arrangements. What they all have in common is perishable bearings, seals and gaskets. Modern pumps use spring loaded graphite or composition seals that rarely give trouble and are not susceptible to periodic adjustment or maintenance. Older pumps used oiled, graphited, braided textile packings that require external lubrication (grease) and some adjustments. On most water pumps of the older variety, I have found that Teflon packings some-

times work. Teflon type packings certainly reduce the potential for damage to the seal areas on shafts but many of them tend to ooze out as you tighten glan nuts down on them. If you use the old textile type packings, you will find that square packing material almost always works better than the round type. Excessive glan nut pressure will burn packings and dry out textile packings very quickly. It is important that packings, and the shafts that run in them, get a good initial dose of waterproof lubricant and that they be greased sparingly but regularly if grease cups or fittings are provided. Use a good grade of waterproof grease, such as Lubriplate 1200-2, for this application. Most packing troubles in old water pumps are not caused by simple wear and age; they are caused by failure to provide adequate lubrication. Sometimes packings spin out because they have been installed incorrectly. The cure for this common malady is to install packing coils counter to the rotation of their pump shaft, and to stake the bottom of the packing box slightly with a punch. It doesn't hurt to level the ends of packings with a razor blade after their correct length and format have been determined.

If a pump shaft is pitted or galled, no packing will provide a satisfactory seal for very long. Such shaft defects and shaft warping must be corrected by getting the shaft back into condition. Either a new shaft can be fabricated (use stainless, if possible) or the old shaft will have to be trued and plated, welded, or metal sprayed and ground back to dimension. Sometimes it is possible to sleeve the seal area of a pitted shaft with one of the special sleeves that are sold by some automotive stores and bearing suppliers.

Water pump impellers can rust or erode to the point that they are ineffective in moving the necessary quantities of coolant. Postwar, curved vein impellers have to be

There aren't many parts in most water pumps. The parts that are there have to fit perfectly and be in top condition if the pump is to do its job without leaking.

in perfect shape because they are designed for high speed pumping and are relatively inefficient at idle speeds. Any wear on them will cause overheating at idle. Pump bearings are either sleeve or anti-friction types, but in either case they will have to be in proper alignment and in top condition if pump seals are to function without leaking. Water pump cases should be examined for warping and cracking because, like seals, they not only have to keep water from leaking out, they also have to prevent air from leaking in on the suction sides of pumps.

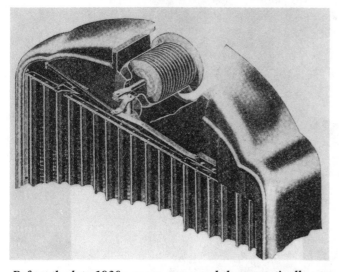

Before the late 1930s, many cars used thermostatically controlled air restriction to regulate engine temperature. The system shown here uses an ether-filled sylphon bellows to control radiator shutters. Hood louvres were also often controlled by ether-filled coils.

Most cooling systems use some type of mechanical thermostat to regulate coolant temperature by restricting either the water flow in an engine or the air flow around it. Very early automobiles did not enjoy the benefits of thermostatic temperature regulation, and some of them employed self-regulating thermosyphon water circulation instead of pumped coolant flow. Air restriction systems were used as late as World War II because many motorists persisted in using methanol- and ethanol-based antifreezes and these could, under certain circumstances, freeze in car radiators if coolant flow restriction was attempted. After the war the almost complete conversion to ethylene glycol-based antifreezes produced the uniform adoption by manufacturers of coolant flow restriction thermostats.

Air flow restriction was accomplished with thermostat controlled radiator shutters and/or hood louvres. These air control devices were operated by ether filled sylphon bellows and tended to be quite troublesome. Most of the trouble was caused by bent or poorly lubricated linkage, and restorers should be careful to insure the freest possible operation of these parts. The sylphon bellows themselves often failed due to pinholing and fatigue cracking, and the subsequent escape of the ether. There are still several companies that repair sylphon bellows canisters and coils. It is important to specify the desired opening and closing temperatures to anyone who attempts to re-

pair an ether-filled thermostat for you. New sylphon units are also available for some applications.

Contemporary water flow restriction thermostats are of the wax pellet type and should be tested and replaced if they malfunction. Older water restriction thermostats used bellows activation or, in some rare cases, bimetallic element activation. In most cases, the superior, modern pellet types can be substituted. Be sure to always install thermostats with the activation element facing towards the block and away from the radiator.

Early water flow control thermostats were of the bellows type, but these were quickly replaced with wax pellet type thermostats.

Automotive fans are used to pull air through radiators. This is necessary for cooling purposes at low and moderate vehicle speeds. At high speeds, fans are mostly useless because vehicle movement produces enough air flow for cooling purposes, except, of course, in air cooled engines. At road speeds, cooling fans not only don't do any good, they consume considerable engine power and produce noise and vibration. Enter the clutch fans of 1930s origins. By the 1960s, these devices had become ubiquitous in American automobiles. At about that time, the sophistication of viscous silicone drives and bimetallic calibration had been added to them. Clutch fans are susceptible to internal wear and leakage. They should be checked for proper operation before an engine is disassembled for restoration. With a cold, stopped engine, you should feel very little resistance when you try to turn a clutched fan by hand. After the engine reaches operating temperature and the underhood temperature reaches the point at which the clutch should engage the fan, the engine is stopped and the blades of the fan are turned by hand to sense drag. If there is no drag, the fan clutch is defective. It is impossible to test these fans if they can't be run on an engine, so it is best to do this before you disassemble an engine.

The fan blades on any fan should be checked for cracks, deformities, and blade attachment integrity. Since fans spin faster than crankshaft speed, their integrity must be perfect or they are a real hazard. Many fans from the 1930s on are asymmetrical. This design is supposed to break up harmonic vibrations. Whether symmetrical or not, fans must be balanced because their great operating speed and large diameters mean that small imbalances can become large radial loads that will shake a whole vehicle. The threaded fasteners that hold fan blades to hubs should be replaced routinely with grade 5 or better fasteners. If rivets are used to make this attachment, they should be checked for tightness. Fan hub bearings should be cleaned and lubricated if this is possible.

Fan belts must be correctly sized and correctly tensioned. If they run too loose, overheating will result, and if they are overtightened, water pump or generator bearing failures can result. Old, cracked fan belts should be replaced, and if the old-style link belts are encountered, they should be discarded and replaced with modern one piece fabric/rubber belts.

Coolant recovery systems, or "expansion tanks," date back to the 1920s and should be put in absolutely tight condition, as should the plumbing connecting them to radiators. Another system that contains coolant in many cars is the interior heater. These units should be checked for leaks and cleanliness during restoration and repaired in much the same ways that radiators are dealt with.

Coolant expansion tanks were one of those new ideas in the 1960s and 1970s that really went back to the 1920s or earlier. These systems allow radiator water expansion to be recovered when a cooling system cools off after a run.

The coolant used in any automobile should be a 50 percent mixture of water and ethylene glycol-based antifreeze. Propylene glycol antifreezes are advocated by some because they are less abrasive than ethylene glycol antifreezes if they mix with oil and attack bearings. This advantage is offset by the fact that propylene glycol antifreezes have a relatively low flash point and are a fire hazard if they seep or leak out of the coolant containment in an engine. Since the lime contained in "hard"

water has a bad effect on radiators and other cooling system surfaces, it is best to use demineralized water. In systems that contain aluminum parts, the use of distilled water is not recommended because this liquid tends to be "mineral hungry" and may have an etching effect on aluminum. It is also *not* a good idea to increase the antifreeze proportion of a coolant mix to more than the recommended 50 percent (34° below zero Fahrenheit protection), and concentrations above 66 percent will actually cause the freezing point of the mixture to rise. Many commercial antifreezes contain additives to deal with corrosion, and some contain water pump lubricant. I always add a water pump lubricant-anti-corrosion additive to antifreeze to protect these parts of the cooling system. In practice, this additive is simply a water soluble oil that coats the internal surfaces of a cooling system. For pressurized systems, it is often recommended that a sealant be added to coolant to seal very small leaks and voids. I don't endorse this practice because you should be able to get the system air tight without relying on sealants, and the sealants that I have seen on the market all have the potential for reducing cooling efficiency.

After a restored vehicle has been started and run for a while, the cooling system should be checked. If the system is a pressure system, it should be pumped up and tested for leak down. On non-pressure systems, it is sometimes possible to apply mild pressure for a leak down test, or you may have to satisfy yourself with physically inspecting for visible damp spots at vulnerable points. The most troublesome leaks are air leaks on the vacuum side of a water pump. These leaks allow air to get into the coolant and cause foaming and bubbling. This "aeration" destroys antifreeze solutions, rapidly rusts system components, and interferes with cooling by insulating the block and radiator from the coolant. The smallest leak that water will work through is very easy for air to pass through, so any small leak that is visible must be closed.

A second class of leaks that can cause severe problems involves combustion leakage through head gaskets, blocks or heads. Combustion gases are highly corrosive and tend to acidify coolant to the point where it can damage the delicate brass, copper (or aluminum), and solder surfaces used in radiator construction. Like suction leaks, combustion leaks cause bubbles that act to insulate a block or head, and make it difficult for proper heat transfer to the coolant to occur. They also insulate the radiator core and make it difficult for the coolant there to transfer heat to the core and thence to the air. It's a good idea to check for combustion leaks in any restored engine with either the bubble test or by a chemical test. In the bubble test, the top radiator hose, thermostat housing, thermostat, and fan belt are removed. The engine is then run up to temperature. This will occur quickly, with the fan belt removed (or water pump drive coupling removed, in the case of engines with direct driven water pumps). The thermostat cavity or top hose outlet is now examined for bubbles. With the water circulating system disabled, there shouldn't be any bubbles with the engine idling or accelerating. If there are, a combustion leak or

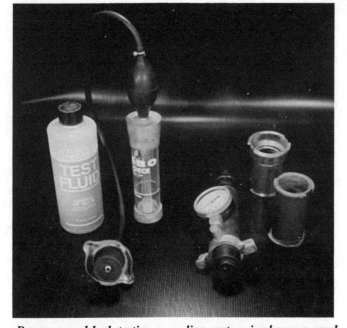

Pressure and leak testing a cooling system is always a good idea. The tester on the left is a monoxide detection system. Air on the top of the radiator is pumped and bubbled through an indicator fluid. If combustion leakage is occurring, carbon monoxide gas in the cooling system will cause the indicator fluid to change color. The tester on the right is a cooling system pressure tester. It allows you to pump air pressure into a cooling system and see if it holds or leaks out. You can also test the release pressure of a radiator cap with this tester.

hot spot in the system is indicated and must be corrected. A suction leak will also cause bubbles.

A more sophisticated test of combustion leakage involves bubbling the air on top of the cooling system through a special indicator fluid that will change color in the presence of carbon monoxide. This type of test is very sensitive, and is marketed by several companies under various brand names. For meaningful results, a monoxide test should be performed with the engine both cold and hot, and under several different speed and load conditions.

Not all overheating problems have their origins in cooling systems. Their causes are frequently found in ignition systems, in fuel delivery and carburation systems, or in some entirely unlikely areas, such as dragging brakes or a slipping clutch. On many cars, the cooling system is designed with little margin, and minor defects in other systems will cause the symptoms of overheating. Because of the multiplicity of possible causes for overheating, it is important to have cooling systems in top notch condition so that if overheating symptoms do appear, the cooling system itself can be eliminated as a likely cause.

CHAPTER 9:

Final Engine Assembly Hints, Start-up Procedures and Considerations

Basic Engine Assembly

Earlier chapters in this book have covered the specific assembly of major engine subsystems. Here, I would like to look at some other areas of assembly and at some general considerations in bolting up old engines.

A general rule is that everything in engine assembly must be right and must make sense. Don't trust anything to luck. If a threaded hole for a head stud or bolt looks weak, it will probably pull out after the head is partially bolted down and the head gasket has been ruined. Whenever and wherever engines are bolted up, Murphy is there, making sure that his law gets enforced.

Core plugs are a particular problem. Some of them are very hard to get at when an engine is in a car, so install them with sealant or Loctite and install them carefully. This is particularly true of the core plugs used at the back ends of some engines to seal the ends of camshafts. Various threaded pipe plugs are used to seal oil and water galleys and their manufacturing drill access holes. These should be reinstalled meticulously. Sometimes these plugs can be threaded in far enough to obstruct connecting right-angle passages. This must be avoided. For the plugs themselves, I prefer brass, and a Teflon (PTFE or TFE) paste sealant for the threads. One caution here. Teflon sealants are wonderful lubricants and it is very easy to over-tighten a plug that has been sealed with them. If you don't use caution here, it's easy to exert enough pressure to crack castings. This sealant works very well at low tightening torques.

Main bearing seals should be bolted on if they are that type, or seated in their saddles with a sealant (I prefer high temperature silicone rubber for this purpose) if they are the one-piece molded type. For the more common rope kind, a good, self-lubricating packing of the right size should be rolled into the groove provided for it with a round bar, or forced in with a special tool. The ends

should be trimmed almost flush to the block but with a bit of stand up. They should be doped with a dab of sealant. If the upper rear main bearing assembly used wooden strips for side sealing, I have found that a fine packing string, smeared with silicone rubber, can be pounded into the recess with a small punch with good results. The original wooden strips can be hard to find, hard to install, and uncertain as to sealing.

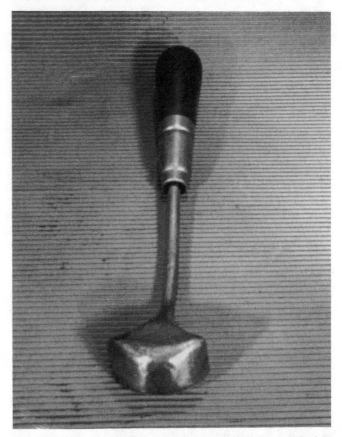

This special tool is used to tamp main bearing seals into their grooves. You can roll them in with any bar if you don't have one of these tools.

Timing gears or chains must be installed with their markings correctly oriented or, on some older engines, with the valves set and timed to specification. I have pulled a surprising number of engines apart in which the valve timing was slightly off, and this makes a big difference in performance. Be sure camshaft end play is correctly adjusted with shims or by whatever other method is specified. Timing gears or sprockets must be aligned in the same plane, and they must be pre-lubricated with oil or assembly lubricant prior to start-up. The timing cases on most engines are the last places to get lubricated by pressure or splash.

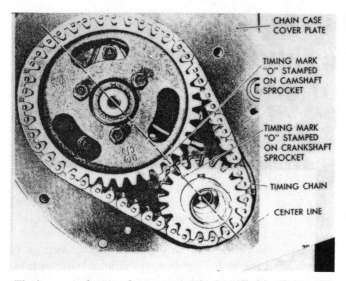

Timing sprockets and gears must be installed in the correct relationship, or valve timing will be off. Many different marking systems have been used over the years for timing alignment. Be sure that you understand this relationship and the marking system in any engine that you restore.

Modern oil pans often require a baffling array of stamped and molded gaskets to make them seal. These, and the mercifully simpler gaskets for older pans, should be coated with a good sealant prior to installation. Where several different pieces are used in a pan seal system, it is important to use sealant liberally where they meet. Oil pans should be tightened with a torque wrench and in a reasonable cross pattern sequence. This will help to prevent gasket distortion and leakage. There is a trick to prevent oil pan leakage. Place the end of a one-inch by two-inch piece of hardwood in a vise with about six or eight inches above the vise jaws. With the pan upside down, the bottoms of the pan bolt holes should then be centered on the piece of wood, one-by-one, and the material around the holes pounded down flat against the wood. If this is not done, and the pan is distorted (cupped) around the bolt holes, new gaskets will tend to squeeze out around the bolts when they are tightened.

The attachment of flywheels is a critical juncture of engine rebuilding. This is because failure to achieve specified and invariably high tightening values on the flywheel to crankshaft fasteners can lead to extreme disaster. I was once in a car when the flywheel sheared its fasteners and escaped. It is not an experience that I would like to repeat, but it did give me a lifelong perspective on what a

nuclear war might be like if one were unlucky enough to be at ground zero when a detonation occurred. In both cases, there is a lot of uncontrolled energy around.

Installing Head Gaskets

Head gaskets usually work for a long time if their basic installation is correctly attended to. Most older car engines used copper sheathed asbestos head gaskets, with a few applications of "shim" type steel gaskets showing up by the late 1930s. Modern gaskets are usually of the "composition" type, with "fire ring" protection (steel or tin crimp rings) around the cylinders. Some air cooled engines used solid copper sealing rings and there are a few other obscure gasket types for sealing heads to blocks.

The first step in installing head gaskets is to get the correct gasket. If the old gasket was working, without any overheating or leaking problems, the new one should match it for type, and hole-for-hole, binder ring-for-binder ring. If some of the holes in the old gasket are not duplicated in the new one, or *vice versa,* this may be an acceptable variation of later or earlier design origins. In any case, make sure that you know what the differences are between the gasket that you took out and the one that you are installing, and if differences do exist, be sure that you have some plausible explanation for them.

Never attempt to reuse old head gaskets. It's a false economy that never works in the long run. There are wonderfully quaint procedures offered for resealing old gaskets with various compounds, and there is a great deal of folklore about soaking them in various brews in bathtubs with claw feet — and that only during full phases of the moon. If you happen to believe that the earth is flat, then maybe you will believe that a used head gasket will clamp flat enough to seal, otherwise spend a few bucks and get a new gasket or gaskets.

Make sure that you install head gaskets right-side-up and correctly end-for-end. On engines that don't have alignment pins for gasket installation, it is handy to buy or make a set. These pins sit in the threaded fastener holes of the block and can be drawn out with special probe tool after the head is on. On bolted heads, if just the cap screws align the gasket, it can end up being misaligned and interfere with coolant flow and cylinder sealing. Always be sure that the head and block are absolutely flat and clean before head installation. Be certain that there isn't a lurking glass bead or machining chip that will fall out of the head and lodge between it and its gasket when you go to mount it. A very small particle can cause a very big leak in a head gasket.

Heads should be torqued down with an accurate torque measuring device, and this should be done in stages and in the factory prescribed pattern. If no pattern is available for the engine that you are working on, use a spiraling sequence that includes all fasteners and radiates from the middle of the head to its ends. It is essential that a good anti-seize compound be used on the fastener threads and fastener head undersides. The fasteners should be in good condition, pitted or stretched. My preference is to replace head fasteners when this is practical. The penalties for an inconsistently torqued head can be simple coolant leakage, oil leakage, or distortion of the block which can lead to excessive oil consumption. I once knew a man who styled himself the "Human Torque Wrench." He claimed that he could come to within two pounds/feet on any fastener, without the benefit of a torque wrench. Sad to tell, he left a trail of broken and distorted castings in his wake. I hope that none like him shall ever pass this way again.

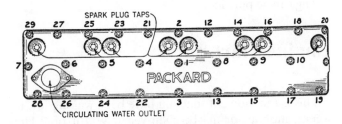

Head bolts or nuts should always be torqued to the right pounds/feet value in at least three stages. They should also be tightened in the pattern suggested by the manufacturer. If you can't find a pattern for the engine that you are working on, tighten these fasteners in a spiral that radiates from the center of the head and includes all fasteners.

Some gasket companies that cater to the old car trade supply some pretty wretched gaskets to replace the original copper sheathed items. These reproductions are typically made out of materials such as Victor Corbestos, which is a fine product when it is used for its intended purpose — which is not making head gaskets. Sometimes they are copper/asbestos sandwich gaskets, but lack binder rings for cylinders and coolant passages. Often these gaskets will fail, and they should be avoided when N.O.S. (New Old Stock) originals in good condition or good reproductions can be found.

Modern fire ring/composition gaskets and older shim gaskets do not need retorquing if they are installed properly. Retorquing may produce a 20 percent or 30 percent additional compression of gasket material, and that endangers the integrity of the fire ring seal. It takes much over-torquing to break these delicate seals. Unless a gasket manufacturer or engine manufacturer specifically calls for it, applying sealant to head gaskets will do little good, and may do harm. It is definitely not recommended for shim type gaskets — these already have an anti-cold flow coating — or for modern siliconized composition gaskets. Copper/asbestos sandwich gaskets may benefit from applications of sealant, and from retorquing with the engines hot. A lot of failures that are blamed on head gaskets have their real origins in poor installation technique or the use of worn or substandard fasteners.

Roughly the same considerations that apply to head gaskets apply to manifold gaskets. However, I generally find it advisable to use sealer on manifold gaskets, particularly when you have to deal with the one-piece manifolds that are sometimes used on long engines such as straight eights. If manifolds are attached with studs and nuts, it is a nice touch to use brass nuts, as this will give you a chance of removing the manifolds at some later date without breaking the studs. Where heat boxes are used between the exhaust and intake manifolds, it is good practice to first tighten the manifolds to the block, and then tighten them together. This will produce more satisfactory conformance of manifolds to blocks, and will reduce the chance of breaking a flange or cracking a manifold.

Some Other Odds and Ends of Engine Assembly

It is undesirable to adjust valves "cold," unless an engine is constructed in a way that precludes "hot" adjustment. My beloved Lincolns are constructed in a way that makes it necessary to remove the manifolds to adjust the valves. Clearly this makes a hot, or "running," adjustment impossible. On most engines it is possible to do a final adjustment of the valves with the engine hot and running, and this should be done. Some of these require you to work through a little access panel in the inner fender, and your ministrations will require manipulating three

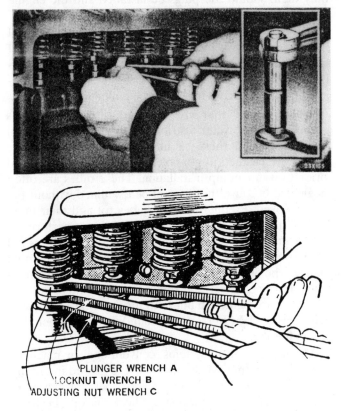

These illustrations show the two-wrench and three-wrench manipulations to set the valves in some "L" head engines. If ever there was a real need for a third hand, this has to be it. This adjustment is particularly fun when it is performed on a hot, running engine. The lifters are jumping up and down, and you often have to work through a small access panel in a car's inner fender. Fortunately, once valves of this type are adjusted, they usually hold the adjustment for a long time.

wrenches with one hand and a feeler gauge with the other. This is not an easy or pleasant task, but a lot depends on doing it right. For the preliminary valve clearance settings that you make when assembling an engine, always go a few thousandths wider than the specified hot setting because valve stems, lifters, and push rods tend to expand as they get hot and they therefore tend to close up the clearances that you allow. I always tend to go a bit wide on the final settings because a "happy" valve is one that closes fully and doesn't get held open a crack so that it can burn. The solution is, as I say, to readjust the valves hot, if possible.

Before an engine that has been rebuilt is started, the oil pump must be primed with engine oil by pressurizing it externally, pouring oil into it, packing it, or spinning it with a drill motor. Some people pack oil pumps with Vaseline for this purpose, but I find this unnecessary if the engine oil system has been pre-pressurized with a leak detector (See Chapter 8 on lubricating systems). It is very good practice to fill oil filters or filter canisters with engine oil when they have been emptied, and before engines are started. This eliminates the "dry" time that would occur while the oil pump filled them. To be absolutely sure of immediate oil pressure, always spin a rebuilt engine with a crank or starter motor with the plugs out until you get an indication of oil pressure. Then, and only then, should the plugs be installed and the engine started.

Before mounting clutches on flywheels, mount a dial indicator on a convenient flywheel bolt and check the bell housing for lateral run-out (concentricity) and parallelism. Some older engines have to be shimmed and adjusted with eccentrics to achieve alignment in this regard.

Water pumps that are mounted directly to blocks sometimes have water distribution tubes behind them in the blocks, and these should be removed before the blocks are cleaned, if possible, and repaired or replaced prior to water pump installation. These tubes are often neglected because they cannot be examined without being removed. Frequently these tubes rot and their function of directing the coolant in a block is not performed. This can lead to localized overheating and hard-to-find "hot spots" that cause boiling. Take care in tightening flange-type water pumps because they are often machined from relatively low quality castings and break easily if they are tightened unevenly, or if they are held away from the block by burrs or by rebuilding debris when they are tightened.

Mounting ignition systems, conventional or magneto, can be frustrating. Most magnetos are geared internally, and alignment of the timing marks does not guarantee that they are in the right phase. Check this out. Distributors have to be "dead timed" for initial start up. This involves mounting the distributor so that whatever its drive engagement system is, it engages with the cam gear or oil pump "T" drive with its rotor in the right orientation. In some designs, the oil pump will have to be jogged a little with a long screw driver before everything engages in the correct manner. I always start with the crankshaft timing marks at Top Dead Center for number 1 cylinder (usu-

ally designated "TDC" or "UDC") and engage the distributor drive so that the rotor is pointing to the number 1 distributor cap terminal. I then rotate the distributor body to a position where, if the engine were moved in its direction of rotation, the points would open. This is done visually by observing the points and the distributor cam. After this point has been found, roughly, it can be ascertained more precisely by connecting a continuity tester or magneto timing light across the points and moving the distributor body slightly to the exact point where the light is turned on and off. This procedure is no substitute for timing an engine with a strobe light, but it will always be accurate enough to get an engine started so that dynamic timing can be pursued.

Engine Start-up

This is the moment that you have been waiting for, for weeks, months, or maybe even years. Will it run? How will it sound? Will all that effort pay off?

These are good questions, but there is another equally important consideration. Because the start-up for a restored engine is the most critical period in its normal life, you should ask, "Am I doing anything that will damage this engine?" Remember, when you first turn that engine over with fuel and spark, and it begins to run, many of its working surfaces will be fitting rather poorly. Rings, for example, will not seat completely for several thousand miles. There is the potential in initial engine start-up to do damage that will equal tens of thousands of miles of normal driving wear, or worse.

The first rules of proper engine start up have to do with creating a proper environment. The main elements are to have at least one good fire extinguisher (preferably the Halon type) handy and very good ventilation. The great law giver, Murphy, makes a point of attending all engine start-ups — with a vengeance. He delights in things like dripping fuel line connections and leaking manifold gaskets. Be ready for him.

The most critical aspect of a start-up is lubrication. It must be immediate and of adequate pressure. To insure this, a reliable oil pressure gauge should be plumbed into the oiling system, in addition to the dashboard gauge or warning light. Engine bearings, cam lobes, timing chains or gears, lifters, etc. should have been coated with assembly lubricant at the times of their installations. The whole oiling system should have been pressurized externally with an oil leak detector. Finally, the engine should be free spun with the starter or crank until oil pressure registers on the gauges, and only then should the plugs be installed and start-up attempted. The oil used for start-up should be the same as will be run in regular use or one grade thinner (say 5-30 when 10-30 will be used). In no case should start-up oil be thicker than the intended running oil.

It is imperative that the initial start up of a restored engine be accomplished quickly, and not preceded by

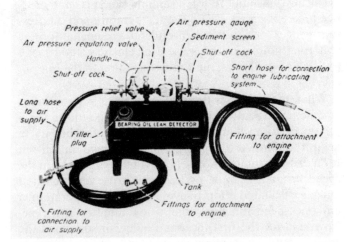

An oil leak detector can be used to pre-lubricate an engine before it is started for the first time after rebuilding. This procedure guarantees oil to critical bearing surfaces as soon as an engine fires.

misadventures, such as flooding the carburetor or running the battery down by "grinding" the starter. Extended periods of attempted starting will tend to wash the cylinder walls clean of lubricant with unburned gasoline. Then scraping damage from unseated rings can easily occur. To the end of insuring a quick initial start, use a very good battery in top condition of charge. This is no time to drag an old relic of a battery out of some dark corner of the garage, "just to get the thing started."

Another trick for getting a quick initial start-up is to prime the fuel system in whatever way its construction allows. In the case of an air pressure fuel system, this is done with a primer valve. Vacuum tank systems should be filled manually. On gravity systems, all that you can do is make sure that the car is right side up! On fuel pump systems, I always suck a little gas past the pump and out of the carburetor feed pipe. In the cases of all of these systems, it's a good idea to fill the carburetor float bowl by running a little gas into it with a gravity tank and a rubber hose. I always add half a smidgeon of top oil to the gas used to prime a carburetor for start-up, just to get some ring lubrication into action immediately.

The practice of priming an engine by pouring a bit of gas down the carburetor throat is to be discouraged unless you know what you are doing and have strong nerves. It's usually safer and more effective to prime the carburetor internally, or by pumping the accelerator pump if there is one. Once, many years ago, a friend and I were starting an engine after a lengthy rebuild. Since we were young, ignorant, and enthusiastic, we broke every one of the above rules and defied common sense in several other ways. Our final insult to safety and common sense was to have my friend stand poised over the carburetor with a Campbell's Soup can full of gasoline, and pour it down the carburetor, as I turned the engine over. Murphy was there. He must have been. First we succeeded in flooding the engine so that it wouldn't start. Then, when it did, it backfired violently and the remains of the can of gasoline, which were by now burning explo-

sively, left my friend's hand headed for the ceiling of the garage. Somehow he wasn't injured, and we got the resulting conflagration out by beating it down with coats and rags — no sissy fire extinguishers for us guys. If there hadn't been quite a few people around to help us with damage control, Standard Oil would have been out one three-bay service station. Unfortunately, one of those helpers was the station's manager/franchisee, and my friend and I were required to relocate our automotive activities abruptly and forever that night. From that point on, I began to take safety considerations very personally.

If an engine doesn't start within ten or so rotations, take the plugs out and go back and check the spark quality, timing, and the availability of gas in the carburetor.

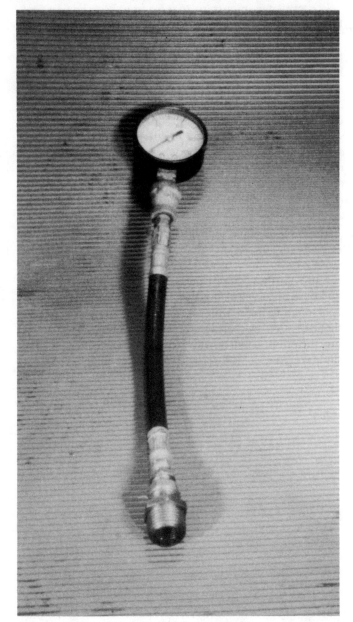

It's a good idea to use a pressure gauge of known accuracy to doublecheck the oil pressure on an engine when it is first started after restoration. You can usually plumb such a gauge into an engine's oil galley through a drill passage. If this is not possible, it can be piped to pressure via a "T" fitting that is screwed into an engine's oil output tap for its pressure gauge or warning light.

This last check can be made by either pumping the throttle and listening or watching for output from the accelerator pump, or, on engines without accelerator pumps, watching the carburetor jets for flow while the engine is turned over with the plugs in. Note: If you watch the jets, do so from a distance and with full face protection in place if the ignition is operative at this point.

After all this is sorted out, the engine should start, and, if everything is roughly right, it should run passably well. It isn't going to run wonderfully at this point because too many things like valve settings, ignition timing, and carburetor settings are still only approximate, and there is too much internal engine friction for really smooth running. At this point, don't try to attend to these details.

It is critically important that when a fresh engine first fires, it be run at 1200 to 1500 rpm immediately and for about 20 or 30 minutes. This figure applies to engines of the 1930s and after. Earlier engines should be run at lower speeds, but at speeds sufficient to cause the crankshaft to throw oil up onto the cylinders. What is not recommended is to let a fresh engine sit and idle for half an hour or so at the time of initial start-up. This practice, which was once common in repair shops, will cause substantial damage to the cylinder walls because there will not be enough oil thrown up on them to meet the increased lubrication requirements of the relatively rough rings and cylinder walls. Local overheating and scoring can very easily result.

It is a good idea, during the first 20 or 30 minutes of engine start-up, to vary the engine speed up and down a couple of hundred rpm to avoid the creation of ridges at the tops of the cylinders. It is a very bad idea to run the engine with a water hose in the radiator and the drain cock open to break it in "cold." This practice was recommended years ago, along with its sister practice of removing the thermostat during break-in. Both are very bad things to do.

During this initial 20- or 30-minute run, it is good practice to keep a close eye on the temperature and oil pressure gauges, and to listen carefully to the engine for any abnormal noises. I always use a mechanic's stethoscope to listen to the lifters, the timing case, and to the bottom end.

When the engine is thoroughly warm, it's a good idea to time it and set the idle mixture. This will require dropping back to an idle for a couple of minutes, but try to keep it to that. At this point, I generally take the car out for a drive for an hour or so. During this drive I keep the speed around 45 mph, or less, and drive very gently. I make a calculated effort to avoid continuous operation at any one speed for more than a few minutes at a time. Now, and for the first thousand miles, or so, I load the engine gently by accelerating steadily, and then going on back-throttle by coasting down or descending hills. This last practice tends to suck oil up into the rings and that assists in break-in. It's not a good idea to use top oil in gasoline during break-in, or to use synthetic oils in the crankcase at this time, since the superior lubrication that both of these practices provide will retard the break-in process.

The rest of engine break-in mostly involves common sense. Avoid runs at constant speeds for a while, and drive gently. I always change oil and filter at 1,000 miles, 1500 miles, and every 2,000-2,500 miles thereafter. At 3500 miles I begin adding top oil to the gasoline, and do so from then on. This is a particularly good practice on side valve engines where valve stem and guide lubrication is, at best, marginal. While all of this may sound finicky, I have had occasion to work on engines that were literally ruined during break-in by driving off at high speed while things were still new and tight. It is astounding how much damage can be inflicted on an engine if the proper conditions for its break-in period are not respected.

CHAPTER 10:

Old Car Ignition Systems; Making Sparks

From the 1920s, generally and in some cases much earlier, to the 1970s, almost all automotive ignition systems were of the point/condenser variety. This type of engine ignition was easy to understand, easy to troubleshoot, simple to repair, and responsible for about 90 percent of all engine malfunction. The substantial reduction in the ratio of mechanics to automobiles that has occurred in the last decade — from about 1:600 to roughly 1:1100 — is largely traceable to the almost universal adoption of more reliable electronic and distributorless ignition systems on cars built after the 1970s.

By now, the wonderfully simple point/condenser ignition system has become almost an oddity in the service sector. Invented by Charles F. "Boss" Kettering at General Motors' DELCO subsidiary in the second decade of this century, the point condenser ignition was a vast improvement on what preceded it. Now it is history, and mostly of interest to car restorers. That's us.

Ignition systems of the pre-1920 era were often complex and cumbersome. The Model T Ford system, for example, included a heavy flywheel magneto, four trouble-prone buzzer coils, and a finicky cam driven timer (distributor). After the Model T, sanity prevailed at Ford for a few years, and the Model A was blessed with a very conventional ignition system. However, that was then abandoned for the needlessly awkward complicated system used on most Ford products for many years after 1932. This was allegedly done to avoid having to produce costly distributor drive gears because Henry preferred to drive his ignition systems directly from the camshaft. For other reasons, most of the few remaining modern distributor applications are driven directly from camshafts, but most modern ignition systems are fully electronic and have no distributor, other than a timing signal trigger on a camshaft or crankshaft gear.

Other early ignition systems, with generic names like "heat tube," or "make and break," or "low tension" and "high tension" magneto were developed and used variously because the marvelously simple idea of the point/condenser ignition hadn't been developed. As I said, the credit for this system — along with some controversy regarding that credit — goes to Charles Kettering and his Dayton Engineering Laboratories Company (DELCO) subsidiary of GM. With the introduction of this system before World War I, the older electric ignition systems tended to disappear from newly manufactured automobiles.

Most early ignition systems, after the primitive heat tube and make and break monstrosities, were magneto based. First there were the low tension systems that used individual "trembler" (buzzer) coils to build up the voltage of the feeble, timed magneto output. These were followed by "dual ignition" systems, hybrids that employed high tension magnetos to supply spark quality voltage without further external buildup but that also retained a single buzzer coil system for starting. The dual ignition involved in these hybrids was made necessary by their basic unreliability, and from the fact that magnetos tend to be very inadequate to the low-rpm-high-output requirements of engine starting, while buzzer coil ignitions are fine for starting but can't supply adequate spark voltage at the higher engine rpms needed to operate a car at speed. If you combine these two systems, and switch from battery to magneto after starting, you have something that works reasonably well for starting and running an automobile. Better still, if one system fails, you can usually fall back on the other, because the only important shared component of the two systems is a common magneto timer.

Magnetos, themselves, are simply self-contained units which generate, time, and distribute either small or large voltage impulses. The ones that produce low voltage (low tension) require an external coil system to intensify that voltage. The high tension type have internal induction coils wound onto their armatures or elsewhere, and emit spark quality voltages without external coils. There is nothing terribly mysterious about magneto ignition systems, but the parts in them tend to be highly specialized — magneto points usually don't look like distributor points, and their care, feeding, and adjustment tends to

The old point/condenser ignition systems aren't that complex or difficult to understand, but almost any defect in them would cause problems. A visual inspection of the condition of this early 1930s Chevrolet ignition reveals room for improvement. Instrumented testing will tell the whole story. Note the manual spark advance feature on the distributor (lower right).

be specialized as well.

For many years the reigning magneto repair specialist in this country was a man by the name of Louis Volmer. He lived in Longmeadow, Massachusetts, until his death in the 1960s, and was a disciple of *the* Robert Bosch. Louis was a "crackerjack" magneto mechanic, but he had a way of describing his work that made it, and the magneto itself, seem incomprehensible. I remember standing in awe, and some legitimate fear of life and limb, as Louis — also called "Windinger" because he spoke with a thick German accent and could rewind magneto armatures — presided over three or four magnetos on the test benches in his cellar workshop — each producing from one to six quarter-inch sparks on gap plates. It was the kind of atmosphere where one expected Igor, Frankenstein, or at least Bela Lugosi to materialize in air at any moment. I liked Louis, but I remember feeling a sense of relief when it was time to leave his magneto enclave. Given the option, I preferred to deal with him by mail.

Years later, I discovered that magnetos were not quite as mysterious as Louis seemed to imply, and that I could often repair them by replacing their bearings, cleaning and adjusting their points, or clarifying the wires and switches that control and feed them. The problems that can stop me on magnetos are: 1) lack of parts, 2) bad windings, or 3) lack of specifications for adjustment. In these cases, it is useful to seek out the aid of a magneto specialist, and you can do no better than the reigning specialist in the field, George Pounden of Sebastopol, California. I hasten to add that magnetos are sufficiently unreliable to make it a good idea to always have a spare on hand for any car that you own that uses one.

Conventional Ignition Systems: The Basic Theory

For the most part, restorers will find themselves working on conventional point/condenser ignition systems because these still represent the vast majority of all ignitions ever manufactured. There are some small variations here, as, for example, between single and dual point systems, but the theory behind these spark producers is engagingly simple, and their hardware is refreshingly uncomplicated. There are, however, some repair strategies and techniques that deserve notice and attention.

What Kettering and his colleagues at DELCO "discovered," or at least popularized, was the fact that a set of timing points could control the flow of electricity through the primary windings of an induction coil, and thus the resulting secondary spark output of that coil, by making and breaking contact in sequence with each cylinder's need for a spark. This timed low voltage signal across the primary windings would, then, induce a voltage rise in a set of secondary windings in the coil case. The level of voltage induced into these secondary windings depends on the initial voltage in the primary windings and on the

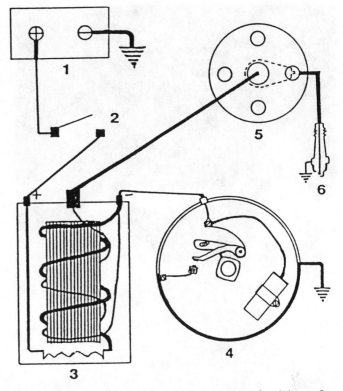

This schematic shows the components and wiring of a point/condenser ignition system. The low tension or primary current is supplied by the (1) battery and flows to an (2) ignition switch. When the switch is closed it goes to and through the primary windings on the (3) coil, and from there to the (4) primary section of the distributor. The arrangement and connections for the points and condenser are shown inside the distributor. Note that the distributor case is grounded, and this ultimately grounds the current flowing through the points when they are closed. High tension voltage, induced into the secondary windings of the (3) coil goes from the coil tower to the center terminal in the distributor cap, which is part of the ignition (5) secondary system. Shown in this system are the rotor and cap. From the center terminal of the distributor cap, the high voltage secondary electricity travels via the rotor to the correct spark plug terminal on the cap and from there by wires to the spark plugs.

ratio of primary to secondary winding turns. In practice, ignition voltages of 15,000 to 30,000 can be created from a starting point of six or twelve volts. One problem that Kettering and other early ignition researchers encountered was the fact that it was difficult to get their timing points to break cleanly. In particular, the points tended to arc during their opening (break) cycle. The solution to this problem was the inclusion of a condenser (properly called a capacitor in electric terminology), wired parallel to the points. A condenser is nothing more than two conductors of relatively enormous surface area that are confined in a small physical space. The condenser in an ignition system gives the electricity available at the points a place to go when they open and break the circuit. This greatly reduces arcing across the points, as they open to initiate the collapse of the primary magnetic field in the coil that induces spark voltages in the coil's secondary windings.

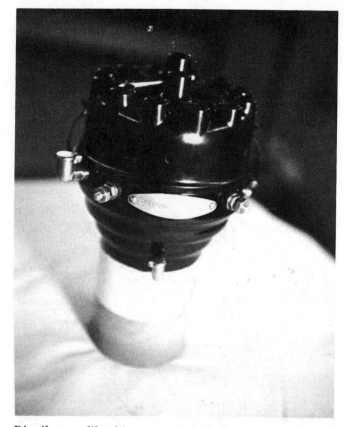

Distributors, like this one, contain both primary point and condenser systems and secondary distributor systems. The primary ignition components are mounted under the cap on the distributor plate, and the cap and rotor are the secondary system.

That was it. Gone were cumbersome buzzer coils and finicky magnetos. A few simple components did the whole job: a point set, a condenser, a simple induction coil, with some wire to connect these components and some insulators to isolate them, as necessary.

Of course, in practice, there were a few other items necessary to make the system work. There had to be a rotor and distributor cap to get the spark voltages to the correct cylinders in the right sequence. There had to be wires to conduct spark voltage to the spark plugs. Later, there had to be one or more systems for advancing and retarding the timing of the spark, with reference to changing engine rpm, or manifold vacuum, or both. Later still, there had to be a method of suppressing the emission of radio frequency signals that could interfere with aviation radar, car radios, or home television reception.

Oscilloscopes

One of the best ways to understand a point/condenser ignition system is in terms of the graphic representation of this system on an automotive oscilloscope. By the 1950s, oscilloscopic instrumentation ("ignition scopes") had come into use in many repair shops. These devices made it possible to visually represent the electric action going on in automotive ignition systems. Scopes accom-

plish this by plotting the voltage in an ignition system (either the low "primary" voltage, or the "secondary" spark voltage) against time, and representing these cycles on a CRT (cathode ray tube or VDT — video display terminal — in computer talk). The use of ignition scopes, coupled with knowledge of basic ignition theory, makes it possible for a professional mechanic or talented amateur to tune old ignition systems to performance levels that will, in many cases, exceed what was originally intended in their design.

For example, before the era of scopes, it was thought proper practice to run spark plug wires from the distributor to the spark plugs, with the wires laying parallel for long distances. Often, these wires were confined in conduits that held them in close proximity for two or more feet. When ignition scopes became available and such systems were displayed on them, it was immediately clear that something called "sympathetic sparks" or "ghost firing" was occurring. This happens because as a spark plug wire conducts spark voltage to its plug, it builds up an induction field that exceeds the wire's insulation. When the spark stops, this field collapses, and if it does so across an adjacent wire for any considerable length, it can induce voltage into that wire. Given sufficient length exposure, this induced voltage can be high enough (3,000 to 5,000 volts) to fire the plug connected to the other wire. In practice, this can translate into a six-cylinder system having eight, or perhaps ten, sparks in its two-revolution cycle instead of the expected six. Of course, if these sympathetic sparks occur at inopportune times — such as during the compression stroke in a cylinder — they can raise havoc with a car's performance and economy by prematurely firing a cylinder. Some very new cars have parallel secondary wires, but these have been subjected to a careful analysis and positioned so that any sympathetic firing that occurs happens only between wires at times where and when it will not cause running problems.

Other problems, such as arcing in the distributor cap or points that resonate (bounce) can be found easily with an

Modern engines sometimes have adjacent spark plug wires, but on old engines this can be trouble. A scope analysis of ignition firing will tell you if parallel wires are causing "sympathetic spark" problems on your car.

ignition scope. In fact, oscilloscopic analysis of ignition systems is the only quick and reliable method of determining whether or not they are performing properly. I suggest that any of the considerations in ignition work can and should be checked with a scope *before* an ignition system is "passed," and certainly before it is dismantled.

The basic scope pattern for a functioning ignition plots voltage against time. Time is represented on a left-to-right continuum and voltage increases are shown as upward vertical changes. Any scope pattern of secondary ignition voltage (high voltage as opposed to the voltage in the ignition point circuit) should have the following features — with some variation in the actual representation, depending on the vintage and brand of the scope that is being used: A POINT OPEN signal indicating when and how the points break, A SPARK VOLTAGE spike indicating how much voltage is needed to ionize the air gap between a spark plug's electrodes to initiate a spark, A SPARK LINE, indicating the lower voltage necessary to maintain the spark for its duration, INTERMEDIATE OSCILLATIONS, indicating coil/condenser action that dissipates energy after spark firing is completed,

a downward line indicating POINT CLOSURE several SMALL OSCILLATIONS representing the buildup of magnetic field in the coil and then a straight, slightly upward HORIZONTAL LINE, indicating energy flowing into the coil, and finally, another SPARK LINE, indicating point opening and the beginning of the next firing cycle. The section of the line from the point close signal to the firing line for the next cycle represents the "dwell" section of the pattern and is also a representation of the dwell angle of the points. That is the number of rotational degrees in one firing cycle that the points remain closed. Reference to the diagram of a basic scope pattern will help you understand the ignition pattern and sequence.

The Actual Practice

It is always a good idea to completely evaluate an ignition system before attempting to repair or restore it. Timing should be checked with a good timing light and, if

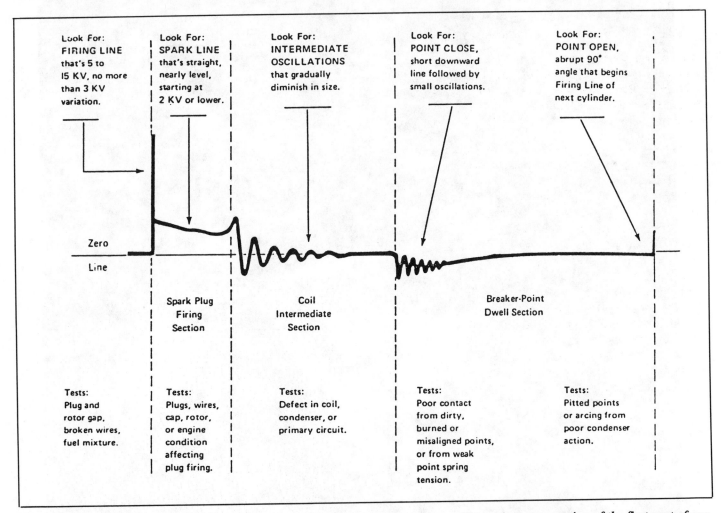

The the basic secondary point/condenser ignition system scope pattern and an oscilloscopic representation of the first part of one cylinder's secondary firing sequence are shown here in this photograph and schematic diagram. There may be minor differences in how different equipment represents these patterns, but most will be pretty close to the one shown here. For the basic ignition pattern, additional formats, like all cylinders spread out, stacked cylinders (raster), and all cylinders superimposed, are also available on many scopes. Some scopes also allow display of primary ignition electrical action.

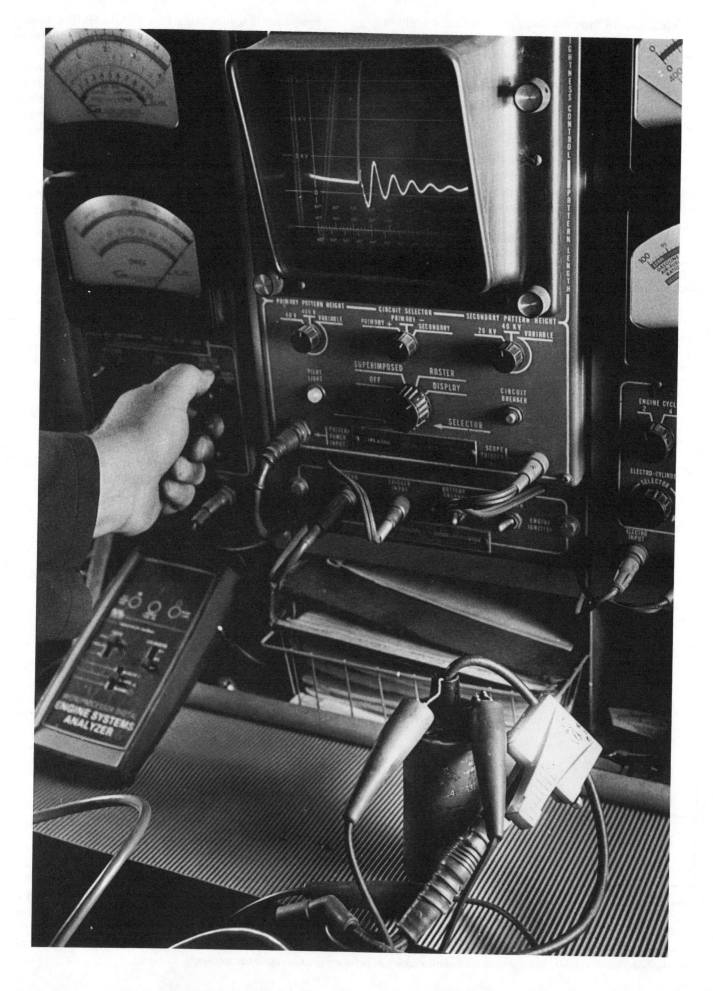

possible, the system should be "scoped" for secondary voltage pattern. These two test operations will provide a complete guide to the system's operation, but there are, of course, other ways to get the same information. If a scope is not available, it is a good idea to check voltages in the assembled system at every point that it is possible to do this. Six volt systems supply full voltage to the coil. Their voltage readings should be taken on both sides of the coil and at the points. These readings should then be compared with the specifications given by the system's manufacturer but voltage drops of more than a few tenths of a volt are suspect. On twelve-volt ignitions, there will be either an external block resistor, primary resistance wire that will increase resistance with engine compartment temperature, or (very rarely) a resistor in the coil case. In any twelve-volt ignition system, the actual voltage delivered to the coil windings for normal operation will be about six to eight volts, and this should be verified. Failure of the resistance circuit to limit voltage in a twelve-volt system will result in rapid deterioration of the points or coil or both.

The most troublesome part in any conventional ignition system is probably the condenser. Happily, it is also about the cheapest part in the system. Condensers fail unpredictably and are very susceptible to failure related to age, use, and dampness. They can be superficially checked for leakage with an ohmmeter, but any meaningful test must involve loading and unloading them, and checking for capacitance and leakage under substantial loads.

Coil tower spark leakage is a fairly common problem in old coils. Repairs are sometimes possible.

Coils can also be checked for insulation breakdown and discontinuity with an ohmmeter, as can plug wires and distributor caps and rotors. In each case, it is far better to do all of this checking with an ignition scope under actual running conditions, or to get someone who has one and knows how to use it to do this for you. This last point needs emphasis. Using older scopes requires knowledge of ignition theory that goes beyond just knowing how to hook them up. I am told by the sales people who sell the newer, computerized instruments that they can be run by idiots — and often are. Just because someone has equipment for ignition analysis does not mean that he knows how to use it. Some of the worst work comes out of shops with the best equipment. Ignition analysis is no exception.

When you have gathered sufficient information regarding the operation of an ignition system, it is time to separate it into its component parts and deal with them separately. Let's look at these component parts individually.

The Coil

Malfunction in coils is best identified under operating conditions with a scope or with a console unit that can simulate hard operating conditions in a coil test. Coils rarely fail suddenly; they usually succumb to partial shorts and "opens" before completely failing. Coils can be statically tested with an ohmmeter. Specific values vary for different coils, but generally you will be looking for very little resistance across a coil's primary (low voltage) terminals and several thousand ohms from the primaries to the secondary (high voltage) terminal. An ohmmeter can also be used to spot the sites of arcing around a coil's high tension tower.

That is what can be determined with an ohmmeter about a coil's condition, but it is no substitute for scope analysis and, in the long run, will tell you little of value about a coil's long-range prospects. Of course, obvious physical defects in a coil, such as a burned high tension connector or cracks in the tower will need to be corrected by replacing the coil or by repairing cracks by grooving them and filling in the groves with a high dialectric epoxy. Replacement is the best bet, unless you are dealing with a very rare coil that is difficult or very expensive to replace.

Primary Wiring

It is essential that coils and distributors get the full voltage on which they were designed to operate. All switches, primary wiring, and resistance units in that wiring should be checked with a volt meter. In practice, this means taking readings at the coil positive terminal (often designated as the "ign." or "bat." terminal) and at the coil's distributor terminal (almost always marked with a minus sign on negative ground cars) and at the points. These readings vary from system to system, but must be in the correct range as stated in a shop or general repair manual. If there is no resistance wire or block resistor, these readings should be near actual battery voltage.

Ignition Points

The physical condition and adjustment of ignition points is critical. This includes: point alignment, rubbing block condition, contact surface condition, dwell adjustment, spring tension, bearing condition, ground quality, and synchronization in dual point systems. Let's look at these individually. Remember, those little devils that we call "points" and their accomplices, condensers, account for the majority of the problems that stop engines.

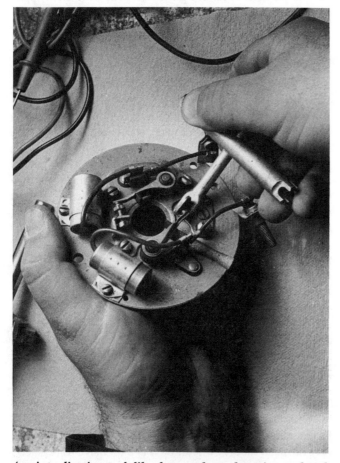

A point adjusting tool, like the one shown here, is very handy for aligning ignition points when this is necessary. Although this tool has a fixture for bending the movable point, it is almost always a bad idea to bend anything but the fixed point.

When points are installed, they should be aligned. This involves bending the fixed point — almost never the movable or "arm" point — with a special point adjusting tool until the point faces meet squarely and in the same plane. If this is not done, rapid point wear will result, and point adjustment will be quickly lost. Point cams and rubbing blocks should also be checked for wear, and lubricated with a smear of point grease. A dab of this special grease

should be applied to the recess in the rubbing block that sits toward the direction of cam rotation. Be careful to use a grease that is designed for this purpose, and to use it sparingly. Some point systems have lubricating wheels or pads that contact the distributor cam. These may also need replacement or sparing lubrication.

The spring tension that closes points is adjustable, and if it is too light, the points will tend to bounce and give very poor performance. If this tension is too great, rapid rubbing block wear will result and possibly cam damage. Almost all points operate on between 19 and 22 ounces of pressure, as measured from the contact end of the movable point.

This push-pull spring tension gauge is used to check the closing pressure on a movable point. Low pressure can cause point bounce and may result in erratic spark. Pressure that is too high will cause rapid rubbing block wear and possibly damage to the distributor cam. This is an easy test to perform, and well worth the effort.

The appearance of properly functioning point contacts will be a dull gray. If the point contact surfaces are burned and black, it probably indicates that grease or oil has gotten on them. If they are severely pitted and show a pit-and-crater configuration, it indicates that the ignition condenser is incorrectly sized. There is a cute little rule for correcting this defect, but since ignition condensers that are labelled in microfarads are necessary to apply this rule usefully, the rule — the "minus-minus-minus" rule — is more of a curiosity than anything else these days.

If you can find automotive condensers that are labelled for capacitance, the pertinent rule states that if the negative point (first minus) is missing material (second minus) then the condenser lacks capacitance (third minus). If you change any one of these conditions (example, the positive point loses material or the negative point accumulates material) then the result is opposite and the condenser has too much capacitance. If you change any two conditions, the result is the same.

The movable ignition point runs on a bushing which can be checked for looseness by applying finger pressure to its sides and checking for lateral motion. A drop of light oil on this bushing at the time of its installation should preserve it for the duration of the electrical life of the points.

Point adjustment is given either as an electrical fact, "degrees of dwell" (also called "cam angle") or as a physical approximation of that fact, called "gap." It is always better to set point dwell with an accurate dwell meter than to gap points with a thickness gauge, gap gauge, or dial indicator. The dwell angle for a given application is the number of degrees in one distributor cam segment that the points remain closed. Assuming a correct operating voltage, this is the main operative fact in coil saturation. Gapping points by physical means only approximates "dwell" and is an inferior way to adjust them. For pre-World War II engines, specifications for dwell settings are often not available so a point gap setting must be used. If this latter method is employed, then the best way to set points is with a dial indicator, but a thickness gauge will work if you have the right feel for it.

Unfortunately, cheap and uncalibrated dwell meters abound in the land. It is a sad reality of life that you can-

not purchase a good, new dwell meter for $29.95, unless you intend to marry one of the offspring of the manufacturer. Digital dwell meters are very accurate and often very hard to use. They tend to scan rather than average indicated dwell. This means that if there is any dwell variation, a digital gauge will produce a bewildering array of readings. If these readings vary by more than two or three integers, it is probably an indication of significant dwell variation, but there can be other causes. Such variation may indicate an electrical fault, or possibly point bounce, or distributor cam wear, or even a slightly bent distributor shaft. Distributor cam wear is usually evident from physical inspection, but it is a good idea to check for it by comparing the specified gap measurement for a set of points with the actual gap that produces the correct dwell angle reading. If these two measurements differ substantially, you are probably dealing with a worn distributor cam. When gap data is used to set ignition ponts, and a range of gap is given, points should be set to the widest opening in the range. This is because as a point rubbing block wears, the gap will decrease towards the lower figure in the range.

Setting points with a thickness ("feeler") gauge is the old way to do the job. The new way is better. However, if the points are new or filed flat, you can use a thickness gauge to set them. The gauge should give you just a faint feel of drag as you pull it through the points, with the rubbing block on a high point of the cam. It takes some practice to get the technique of this measurement right.

Note that these points are being adjusted with an eccentric screw and locking screws. Other types of adjustment involve slots, gear wheels, threaded adjusters, and many other configurations.

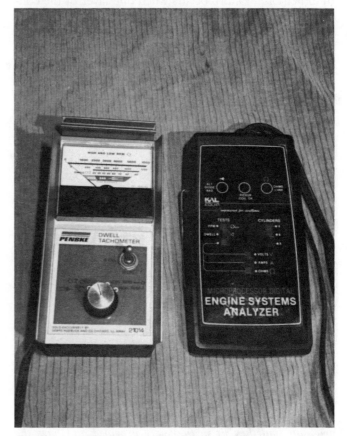

Dwell meters like these are the best way to adjust points if you have the specifications for a dwell setting. The meter on the left uses a pointer and the one on the right has a digital readout.

An often overlooked aspect of point operation that is essential to good performance is the grounding of the fixed point. This is often provided for by a "pigtail" wire in the distributor that grounds the point subassembly or fixed point to the distributor plate. Sometimes a second pigtail wire carries the plate grounding to the distributor body. These pigtails should be checked for physical condition, and an ohmmeter should be used to insure that there is virtually no measurable resistance in the point ground circuit.

Some distributors employ dual points in conjunction with either single or dual coils. When dual points are used, it is essential that they are synchronized. On some engines, this can be done with a timing light and the markings provided on the flywheel or vibration damper for this purpose. On other engines, a special point synchronizing degree wheel tool or a stroboscopic distributor tester must be used to synchronize dual points.

Condensers

Early automotive condensers were oil-filled units. Modern condensers are not. The oil-filled type had small plates separated by an oil insulating medium. The modern type use two layers of foil separated by a nonconducting goo and wrapped in a jelly roll configuration. In either case, failure occurs when one layer of the condenser penetrates its insulating medium and touches the next layer. Sometimes this doesn't involve actual contact but a very low resistance barrier between two layers. Both of these situations produce a condition of "leakage," and result in some level of condenser failure. The other common reason for condenser failure is a discontinuity in the input wiring to the condenser.

The condensers shown here are shaped differently from the originals, but they fit in the space provided and have the right microfarad rating for this application. I'll go with them.

Most modern condensers are calibrated to about .26 MFD, but some use other values. Older condensers were not that standardized. There are also many different mounting configurations for condensers and interchangeability for substitution has to be worked out carefully. For example, the old, flat Northeast condensers, used in some 1920s DELCO distributors, are almost im-

possible to find, and there is no modern automotive condenser that will fit inside those distributors in the narrow space that was allowed for the original units. Usual restoration practice in this case has been to mount modern oil filled condensers outside of the distributor.

There are inexpensive condenser testers on the market, but they can only test leakage at very low ranges of capacitance. They do not simulate actual operating conditions. A good condenser tester loads the condenser with substantial current and then unloads it. These testers are usually part of larger tune up consoles, but some freestanding units are available. The simplest way to test a condenser, if specialized equipment is not available, is to disconnect its isolated lead and temporarily wire in a condenser that is known to be good. If this substitution improves performance, then the original condenser is defective. The substitute condenser that you use for this test does not have to be the correct unit in size or configuration. An incorrectly sized condenser will perform adequately for the short duration of the test. Over long periods, it would cause a progressive metal transfer from one ignition point to the other; so be sure to replace the test condenser with a correct unit if the test indicates a problem.

Other Parts of the Distributor Low Tension System

The initial timing check of an engine that I recommended you perform before any ignition system disassembly will disclose any timing variation. This variation appears as a floating or moving timing mark when a timing light is aimed at the timing pointer and marks. Such movement can occur because of looseness or "slop" anywhere in the distributor drive system. Worn timing gears or worn sprockets and/or chains can cause it, as can very worn distributor/camshaft drive gears. A more usual cause, however, is a worn distributor plate bearing or centrifugal advance system.

Most post-World War II distributors have two timing control systems to match the occurrence of sparks to the load and speed realities of engine operation. Centrifugal advance systems go back to the 1920s, and before, and use governor type weights to advance ignition timing with in creasing engine speed. These devices vary in design but are usually housed near the base of a distributor, under the distributor plate. Generally, they have two pivoting weights and two matched or differing restraining springs. As the distributor shaft spins, the weights move against their springs and advance a sleeve (distributor stubshaft) over the distributor mainshaft that carries the distributor cam. The cam is thus advanced, and this, in turn, advances the spark timing in relation to crankshaft rotation and engine piston movement. This whole system is marginally lubricated in most distributors, and the weight pivot points and base plate bearing surfaces are

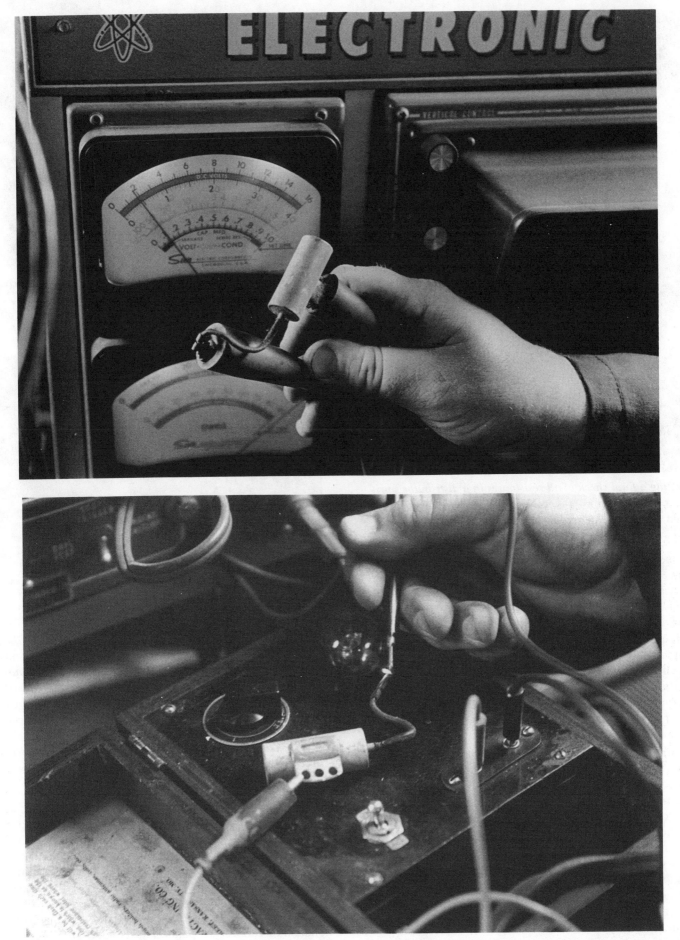

Old console ignition testers, like the one shown here, can be used to test condensers for leakage and capacity, but the old "discharge" testers (also shown) will produce a much more rigorous and better test of condenser condition.

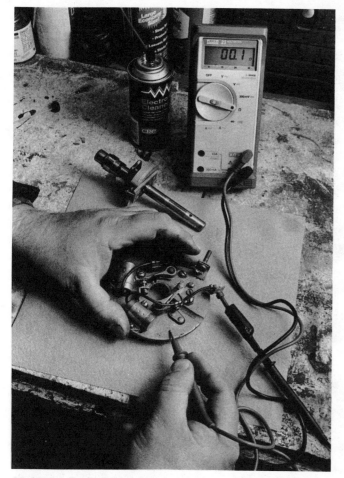

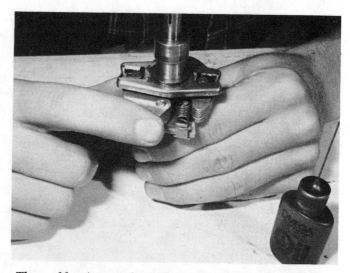

These old point synchronizing tools are surprisingly accurate, and will synchronize points to within a half degree, or so. They are particularly useful when distributors that cannot be mounted on a distributor tester have to be dealt with.

Making a final check of all resistances in a distributor's primary ignition is always a good idea before you assemble it. A good digital ohmmeter, like the one shown here, will also let you watch a condenser "load up" on an ohms test.

prone to wear that introduces bind or slack into the system. The advance springs are even more vulnerable, as they can easily stretch and lose their ability to hold the cam tightly in its unadvanced position. The key to diagnosing all of this is that if, with the engine stopped, you can move the distributor rotor forward without its being immediately and crisply pulled back to the farthest point at which it will rest, there is wear or looseness somewhere in the drive system and probably in the advance system. Before you make this check, be sure that the distributor rotor sits tightly on its shaft as looseness there will give false indications of drive sloppiness.

Repairing distributor advance systems involves installing new parts or, if they are not available, bushing and machining the old ones. While timing variation of a degree or two is marginally tolerable in many engines, if the flutter is more than that, its cause or causes must be found and the underlying faults repaired. Be sure to lubricate the moving parts in the centrifugal advance system when a distributor is apart for service. This should also be an item of routine maintenance and is accomplished by oiling the wick in a distributor stubshaft, under the rotor, or through holes provided in the plates on many distributors.

Most post-World War II automobiles have a vacuum advance unit in addition to their centrifugal advance sys-

Most centrifugal advance systems look something like this. The weights shown at the bottom of the picture pivot out and drive the subplate and stubshaft to advance the point timing cam and distributor rotor. This advances the ignition spark. All parts in a centrifugal advance system have to be snug to work well. This means tight bushings and unstretched springs. Always keep centrifugal advance systems well lubricated when you install them, and maintain this lubrication in service.

tem. These units are round, flat, cadmium-plated devices that are mounted on the sides of distributors and that act to match spark advance to engine load, as indicated by manifold vacuum. Engine vacuum from the carburetor is piped to the vacuum advance unit and applied against a spring-loaded diaphragm to pull the main distributor plate in the direction that advances timing. The pulling is done by a small arm that extends from the center of the diaphragm into the distributor case and attaches to the plate that carries the points and condenser. There is a small bushing where the arm joins the plate.

There are three main considerations in working with

vacuum advance units: the integrity of the diaphragm, the condition of the bearing that allows the distributor plate to rotate, and in some cases, the calibration of the spring that restrains diaphragm movement. There are also some oddball variations on this system, such as one used by Chevrolet that allowed the vacuum advance system to rotate the whole distributor, and not just an internal plate. Such variations are not often encountered.

The simplest way to check the operation of this system in a gross sense is to attach a small hose to the vacuum advance unit's port and pull vacuum on it. This should produce visible movement of the distributor plate. If it does not, it is likely that the plate bearing is frozen or the advance unit diaphragm is ruptured. If the diaphragm is ruptured, you will be able to suck air through it. If it is not, no air will pass by it and your problem is excessive resistance to movement in the distributor plate bearing. These bearings fail by either freezing or wearing out. If a plate bearing is frozen, cleaning and lubrication will often correct the problem. If it is worn out, it will tend to become very sloppy and can be moved in several directions with finger pressure. Such a condition will provide erratic advance, and possibly dwell variation. In the last decades of distributors, plate bearings tended to use nylon bushings instead of the older practice of using ball bearings. The ball bearings often froze, but rarely wore to the point of sloppiness, the new type bearings frequently wear badly.

If the problem with a vacuum advance system is in the rubber diaphragm in the advance unit, the whole unit will probably have to be replaced. These diaphragms are made from neoprene or natural rubber and succumb to a combination of age, heat, fumes, and cyclical failure. They can be a real toothache of a problem because some of the more obscure ones are getting awfully difficult to find and none are constructed in a way that allows easy rebuilding. Often new old stock units will fail shortly after installation, because the diaphragm material has dried and become so brittle that the normal flexing imposed by service ruptures it. I have accumulated hours, mounting on days, trying to find these units for cars that I was working on. The only hope that I can offer is that my efforts have always been rewarded with success. Sometimes, as in the case of locating some early Lucas vacuum advance units, success has been painfully expensive. In recent years, a service has been advertised for opening old advance units and replacing their diaphragms with new material. I have not tried this service yet, but it sounds like a good idea.

Some vacuum advance units are susceptible to calibration. This is usually accomplished by removing a threaded plug at the vacuum inlet port and adding or subtracting small calibration spacers to increase or decrease the tension on the calibration spring. On most advance units this can he done with a vacuum gauge and metered vacuum on a distributor testing machine. In some cases, it can also be done on a car with an advance timing light and measured vacuum. The former method is preferable. A few cars, notably Ford products after World War II, use a "vacuum brake" device that operates on such small increments of vacuum (literally tenths of an inch of mercury) that manometers (viscous barometer devices) must be used to calibrate them.

A distributor testing machine, like this one, is the best way to synchronize distributors with dual points. It can also be used to check centrifugal and vacuum advance systems with great accuracy.

If you do not have the knowledge or equipment to calibrate vacuum units, it is best to leave them to those who do. If you are dealing with the completely sealed type which cannot be calibrated, simple replacement of a defective unit is the only way to do the job.

When a distributor is being checked for operation, another cause of timing flutter is a damaged distributor mainshaft or loose bearings or both. Mainshaft warping is best checked on a scope with a superimposed pattern, or on a distributor tester. Bearings or bushings can be inspected visually and by feel. Bad distributor bushings can cause very serious problems beyond simple ignition malfunction. At the extreme, they can cause a distributor shaft to seize and strip the camshaft drive gears. It is essential that these bearings be inspected, lubricated, and adjusted for end play. Loose, sloppy or rough running bearings or bushings must be replaced.

The High Tension System

All electric ignition systems for engines of more than one cylinder have some method of distributing and conveying spark quality voltage from the coil to the spark plugs. Commonly, this will involve wires from the coil(s) to a distributing device. This device will include some form of rotor(s) and cap(s) and will have insulated leads to the spark plugs. While the placement and configuration of high tension systems varies greatly, the considerations in inspecting and repairing them are pretty standard.

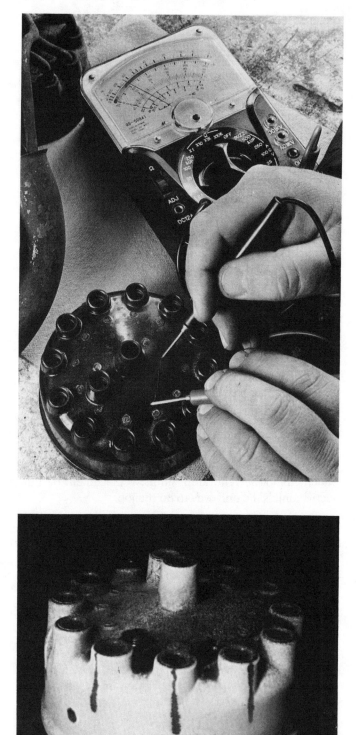

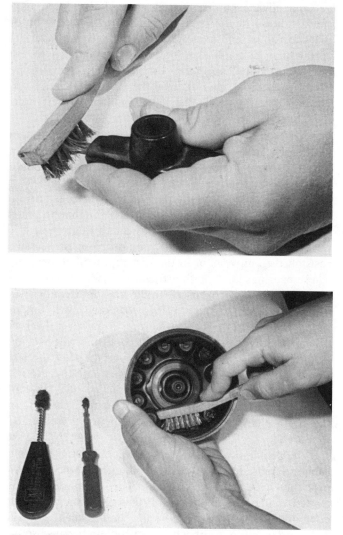

Clean all secondary ignition contacts with an electrical solvent and a fine wire brush. The round brushes shown in the second photograph are used to clean out the distributor cap spark plug wire terminals.

Spark leakage and arcing can occur on surfaces like coil towers and distributor caps. Feeling around this cap with ohmmeter probes revealed electrical continuity where there shouldn't have been any. A dye penetrant inspection of this cap shows the reason for the conductivity — the plug wire towers were all cracked, and the cracks had filled with carbon. This made perfect tracks for electrical leakage.

High tension wire is either cored with conductive metals like copper, stainless steel, or tinned copper, or it is cored with a high resistance conductive material like carbon impregnated glass fibres. Nonmetallic conductors are used to promote radio frequency suppression and for reasons of manufacturing economy. They are found mostly in cars of the 1960s and after. This type of wire should not be used in older cars because the other parts of the secondary ignition system are not designed for the higher resistances inherent in them. Some carbon/fibre glass ignition wire has a monel metal shield for radio frequency suppression, but this is not metal conductor wire, since the metal shield is grounded and is not used to convey spark voltage. This type of wire should not be used in older systems. All secondary wire has thick insulation because it carries very high voltage that tends to leak, particularly as the insulation ages and deteriorates. This deterioration is greatly accelerated by the fact that as these wires conduct spark voltages, they also produce a "corona" that promotes the formation of ozone. Ozone causes the rapid deterioration of rubber insulation. The best high tension ignition wires are either insulated with silicone rubber, or with natural rubber sheathed in a synthetic shield, like Hyphalon. Both types resist the attack of ozone. For early cars that used high tension wire with textile (cambric) insulation, modern spark plug wire with a rubber/synthetic layer of insulation under an authentic appearing textile sheath is available. The sheath used to cover this wire usually includes a mildew retardant, and this greatly prolongs its life. High tension wiring must have tight, clean terminal connections. My preference is for soldering these connections when possible.

Distributor caps and rotors are prone to the same kind of attack and deterioration that afflicts wires, and also to the formation of carbon tracks that promote arcing. These parts should be cleaned with a good electrical solvent, and inspected for cracks and pitting of their conductors and insulators. This is particularly important for rotor and cap brushes (contactors) that rub against metal or carbon contacts or tracks. This wiping contact or track design was common in older distributor cap/rotor systems designed for dual ignition. Pits in distributor caps and rotors can be filed and filled with a high dielectric epoxy. These parts can also be coated with a dielectric lacquer or enamel to fill surface porosity.

Spark Plugs

Automotive spark plugs vary enormously in type and construction. Generally, they must be correct for their applications, clean, undamaged, and correctly gapped. There is also the issue of quality. Over the years, a lot of junk plugs have been sold. Swap meets abound with such "off-brands" as the infamous "Leonard Air Cooled Plug" and the like. Some of these, like the Leonard, look great, but are almost useless when you attempt to use them as spark plugs. Older plugs tended to be rebuildable. They employed packings that could dry out and shrink, creating combustion leaks around their porcelain insulators.

Spark plugs are also very susceptible to having their porcelain insulators crack. This kind of damage will destroy engine performance. Modern resistor plugs platinum, and air gap plugs are unnecessary for older applications and represent overkill. Stick with standard brand spark plugs in recommended types and heat ranges.

The gap adjustment for spark plugs is critical. Engine manufacturers' recommendations should be adhered to rigorously. It is very easy to accidentally break the porcelain insulator on a spark plug by prying against the center electrode when the plug is being gapped. Avoid this common mistake.

Final Thought

I have stressed the importance of scope testing in this discussion of ignition systems because this was the best practice in the repair sector when our collector cars were new, or at least younger, and it is the best approach to restoring their ignition systems today. While it is theoretically possible to get the same information from other tests, such tests are time-consuming and often difficult to perform. A good ignition scope test will not only test the older point/condenser systems but also the more modern capacitive discharge and solid state systems. The very modern, fully computerized ignition systems require very specialized scopes and scan tools.

Since a properly functioning ignition system is absolutely essential to good automobile performance, restoration efforts directed toward ignition systems definitely should include a final scope test. This will locate most existing minor problems before they become serious enough to detract from engine performance. If you don't want to invest the time and money involved in purchasing and operating this equipment, seek out the aid of someone who has the necessary equipment and skills.

This old generator is pretty straightforward and easy to repair.

CHAPTER 11:

Starting and Generating Systems

Except for carburetion, starting and generating systems probably encompass more complex variation and detail than any other systems in automobiles. Unlike carburetion, a theoretical understanding of these electrical system components requires mastery of a substantial body of scientific and engineering material. It's the sort of stuff that can make your head hurt if you aren't accustomed to it. Happily, a great deal of testing and repair can be accomplished without a sophisticated understanding of the theoretical and engineering considerations involved in electrical systems and their components.

Some years ago I came into possession of a more or less complete set of generator and starter test and repair tools — it was a complex trade involving a Hillman, a Zenith Trans-Oceanic radio, and the repair of an ignition switch. There was a growler, testing meters, a commutator undercutting and regrooving tool, special pullers, etc. There were many items for which I never did quite figure out a use. The whole mess completely occupied the cargo area of a van. Well, in the year after this great acquisition, I had occasion to use my newly acquired capability two or three times. Gradually the paraphernalia was moved into an unheated storage area to join such other

nonessential items as my brake arc grinder, my 400,000 BTU gas-fired tempering furnace, and an absolutely hideous vase owned by my late maternal grandmother and unmercifully converted into a lamp. Believe me, only a grandmother could love that vase.

Starters and generators have very similar layouts, in terms of their basic internal electrical components.

On the two or three occasions that I did use all of that electrical repair stuff, it involved the kind of situation where three manuals were open at once and confusion abounded. Eventually, I determined that I could, with great effort, successfully test and repair starters, generators, and regulators. Having met that challenge, I had very little continuing desire to engage in my newfound proficiency. For one thing, there is so much variation in these units that to understand each one, and then to apply the correct tests and repair procedures to it, is almost impossible on an occasional basis. It wouldn't be so bad to work on just shunt wound units, or just interpole devices, or only bucking coil generators, etc. But when you

This venerable armature lathe and commutator grooving device was one of the pieces of equipment that I acquired in my "great" electrical service tools trade.

have to sort between an almost endless variety of equipment types, specifications, and repair procedures, you quickly come to the conclusion that any serious work on generating systems, and to a lesser degree, starting systems, should be left to those who do this work all day, every day. A second, more practical problem with homespun electrical repair is that proper repair requires specialized parts, like brushes, springs, and insulators. These parts have, in most cases, been obsolete for years and they now reside mostly in the parts shelving, cabinets, and drawers of large electrical repair specialty shops.

The general theory that governs the operation of starting motors and generators has to do with the movement of electrons through conductors and with the number of electrons (amps), the pressure at which they are moved (volts), and the tendency of the conductor that they move in to resist their movement (resistance measured in ohms). It also has to do with the phenomenon that occurs when there is movement of a conductor relative to a magnetic field, or *vice versa*. Such movement induces electron flow in the conductor when the lines of force of the magnetic field are cut by the conductor. In the case of a generator, the electron flow that is induced into the conductor(s) ultimately becomes the generated current. In the case of a starter, the magnetic fields are produced in an arrangement that allows the attraction and repulsion characteristics of the magnets to force mechanical rotation of a shaft carrying one of the magnet clusters (the armature).

If you understood all of that before you read it here, it should still be perfectly clear to you now. If you didn't, I doubt if what I wrote in the preceding paragraph put you in the picture. Sorry. The problem is that the theory of these things is somewhat complex and has the layered characteristics of an onion. The important point is that the use of a wound armature that can be rotated on bearings through the field of other stationary magnets makes it possible to convert mechanical energy into electrical energy (as in a generator) or the other way around (as in a starter). It is the arrangement of these magnetic and conducting elements, and the nature of the connections between them, that creates most of the variation in starters and generators.

Common Physical Elements in Conventional Generators and Starters

Outwardly, starters and conventional generators (as opposed to alternators) are remarkably similar in appearance. Of course, starters end in some sort of driving arrangement and generators end in a pulley, sprocket, or gear drive. In both units, the field coils, armatures, brushes, and bearings are very similar, as are the outer casings.

This similarity is so great that over the years, several manufacturers have combined both units into a "starter-generator" device (aka "starter-genny") that uses one ro-

Careful note-taking, sketching, etc. are important when you rebuild any unfamiliar generator (shown here) or starter.

The first step in generator rebuilding is to remove the cover band and see what lies below.

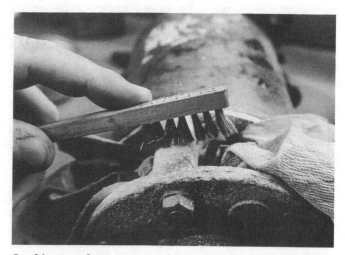

In this case there was massive corrosion of the aluminum brush holder/end assembly. A little wire brushing cleaned it up.

tating element and case instead of two. The object of producing these combined units has been to save weight, space, and expense. In these regards they have not been notably successful, and reliability has often suffered. There is also similarity in the things that can go wrong with the armatures and field coils of starters and generators. Perhaps the most vulnerable parts in both units are the bearings. These are particularly vulnerable in starters, due to the great forces imposed by these high torque motors. It should be remembered that a large part of the invention of the "self-starter" had nothing to do with the practical considerations of how to wind a sufficiently high torque motor, or how to couple and uncouple it from an engine. While these questions were crucial, much of the development of the self-starter had to do with overcoming the then prevalent concepts of the integrity of motors.

What Charles Kettering and the other inventors of self-starting devices came to understand was that to produce an acceptably light and small starting motor, they had to disregard the known rules of motor cooling and bearing support. They came to understand that the motors that they were developing for starting automobile engines had to run for only a matter of seconds, and did not have to have the integrity of motors that were used in continuous service. If they had followed the normal rules of utility motor construction, they would have ended up with starting motors half as heavy as the engines they were designed to start. It is interesting to note that Kettering was influenced by his work for National Cash Register, where he had been involved in the development of small high torque motors to open cash register drawers — certainly an intermittent duty motor application. The conceptual breakthrough that allowed the design of light, intermittent duty motors gave us usable electric starting systems, but it also gave us motors that were very overstressed and very prone to many types of failure, particularly bearing failure.

The bearings in generators, and particularly those in starters, must receive meticulous attention in restoration. Whether ball or sleeve bearings are encountered, they must be checked for wear and for corrosion damage and

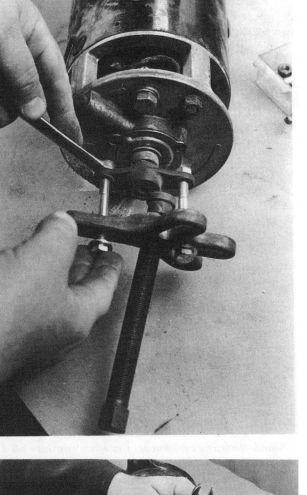

You have to improvise in this work. The first attempt to remove this generator's water pump drive coupling with a battery terminal puller ended in failure, and a heavier-duty harmonic balancer puller was "pressed" into service. That worked.

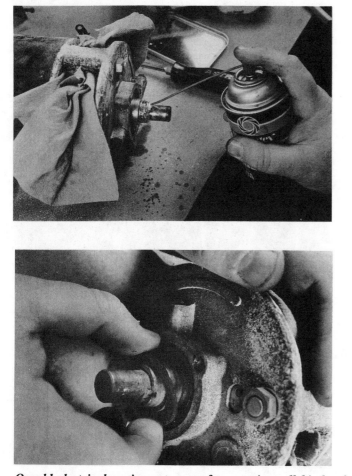

On old electrical equipment, you often run into all kinds of odd fittings, threads, and fastener configurations. This threaded bearing retainer looked like it would be trouble. First it was softened with some penetrating oil. Then the outer bearing retainer was removed, and the spacers and lubricating felt washer under the outside retaining plate were noted for position.

replaced if damage is found. If they are found to be sound, these bearings should be cleaned and properly lubricated with grease when they are installed. Their installation must be such that they are retained securely and cannot spin out. They should be installed in their retainers in ways that do not cause damage to the bearings. Where bearings have spun out of their retainers, it may be necessary to weld and remachine the retainer areas. A relatively new product from Loctite, called "Quick Metal," will fill the gaps from spun-out bearings, up to about 0.005 inch, and retain new bearings. I've used this product for about eight years and my initial skepticism about it has turned into complete approval. It works.

Many of the older ball bearing starter motors and generators, and all of the sleeve bearing applications, have provisions for periodic lubrication. This should be performed according to the recommended schedule with non-detergent oil of about SAE 20 viscosity. Many electric motor shops sell special motor bearing oils for ball and sleeve bearings. These are particularly good because they do not leave the residues that some engine oils tend to. Never over oil a starter or generator; it will cause as much trouble as failing to oil it. Although post-assembly maintenance lubrication of starter motors and generators will have to be done with oil, the initial lubrication at the time of assembly will properly use a light grease designed

for ball bearings or Oilite bushings. It is important to remember that bearing deterioration in starters and generators will inevitably — and sometimes very quickly — lead to the destruction of other parts, like armatures or field coils. Bearing problems are usually easily discovered by looking for play in armature bearings, or by listening for unusual howls, moans, or screeches when generators and starters are working. Any bearing problems that are observed should be attended to immediately before more serious damage occurs. Certainly, when a car is undergoing restoration, its starter and generator should be disassembled and dealt with.

A second common element of starters and conventional generators is a brush/commutator setup. Most operational problems that don't have their origins in bearings begin here. In addition to the friction of the brushes against their commutator segments, and wear of both, there is always an element of arcing and the possibility of abrasive contamination. In the cases of both starters and generators, the brushes are used to switch the rotating magnetic or conducting elements in and out of the working circuit. In starters, this is done to align the attracting and repelling forces of the stationary and rotating magnets in a way that rotates the armature with the greatest force. In the case of generators, the brushes switch the armature conductors to provide direct current.

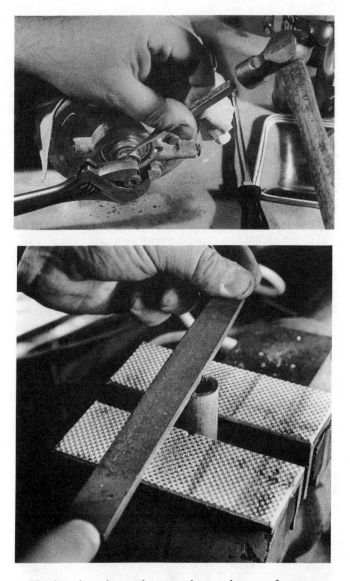

It was back to trying to remove the inner bearing retainer by gently hitting it with a punch. It soon became clear that this approach would not work without damaging this part, so a wrench tool was made from an old piece of pipe. This approach did work.

The brushes themselves can be made out of many materials, but a high percentage of carbon is common to almost all of them. To work properly, brushes have to be positioned so that they can move in and out and bear against their commutators without excessive sideways deflection. This in-and-out movement may occur in a sleeve-like holder, or the whole brush holder may pivot to provide brush contact with the commutator. In either case, a spring arrangement will provide the necessary pressure. Wear or deformation of the brush holder, pivot point, or tensioning springs will lead to a lack of pressure and/or misalignment. This will cause arcing and overall malfunction. Brushes should be replaced if they have worn anywhere near half of their original length. Brush holders that are deformed in any way should also be replaced. Brush springs should be checked with a spring gauge or by dimension, and be replaced if they deviate from manufacturers' specifications.

Armatures should be cleaned in a perchloride vapor bath or with special solvents before they are worked on. All carbon, oil, and grease should be removed from them and the condition of their insulators and insulating varnish should be checked and repaired as necessary.

Worn, arced out, or dirty commutators will tend to de-

teriorate quickly and should be turned and regrooved if they are even slightly damaged or dirty. This will prevent major arcing damage from occurring. Turning commutators to dress them can be accomplished on a conventional lathe, or on a special commutator cutting device. In either case, remove as little material as is necessary to clean the commutator, and don't undercut the inboard shoulder of the commutator where the bar connections to the armature coils are made. These connections should be electrically tested, and physically inspected, as well. Particularly note any solder that has been thrown off this shoulder area because it indicates armature overheating and probable problems with the bar connectors.

The insulating material (mica on older cars, plastic on newer ones) that separates the segments of commutators on generators must be undercut by about 1/32 inch from the copper segments. While this is not absolutely necessary on many starters, undercutting is almost always desirable. Sometimes people attempt to perform this operation crudely, with a hacksaw blade or other "blunt instrument." It is always best that the commutator undercutting operation be done with a jigged tool so that the straightness, width, depth, and uniformity of the undercuts can be accurately controlled. All of this suggests that

When you disassemble starters and generators, it is important to mark their bodies and end plates so that you can get them back together the same way they came apart.

this is work for an electrical shop with the proper equipment.

After a commutator has been cleaned up and regrooved, it is good practice to conform new brushes to it. If this is not done, there will be very little contact between the flat brush ends and the round commutator. This lack of contact will promote arcing and can quickly ruin the work that you have just done. The usual way to conform brushes to a commutator is to wrap a strip of triple aught (000) silica or flint sandpaper around the commutator and run it against the brushes for several rotations. Never use emery cloth for this purpose, as the aluminum oxide abrasive in it will embed in the brushes and cause arcing and rapid deterioration.

While it is tempting to lubricate moving brush holders or brush sides, avoid this temptation. Oil and grease are deadly enemies of commutators, brushes, and insulated coils, and must be used sparingly in generator and starter environments. This also applies to the end bearings and front bearings of generators and starters. Sliding brushes shouldn't bind in their holders because there is enough graphite in their composition to lubricate them. Spring pivot type brush holders are designed not to need lubrication at their pivot points.

The reassembly of generators and starters is pretty straightforward. It is essential that end plates be reassembled in the same orientation to the motor or generator body that they were in at the time of disassembly. This will be easy because you should have marked or diagramed these components before you disassembled them. The major assembly problem that you are likely to en-

The aluminum brush holder section of this generator had become seized to its iron body. The first attempt to separate these two parts was with a small hammer and a block of wood. Gentle strikes were used around the circumference of the brush holder/end plate assembly to avoid cocking it and breaking it. This approach was not successful.

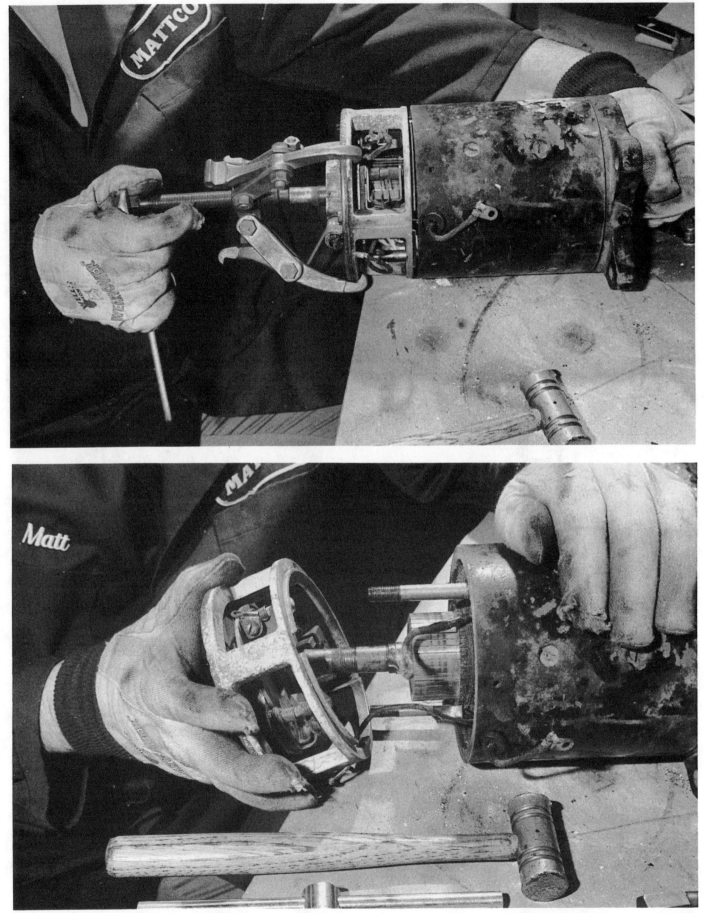

A threaded puller was then tried, and it did separate these two parts. The brass hammer in the foreground of the picture was used to apply shock to the brush holder/end plate assembly as pressure was applied with the puller. Success at last. Patience has its rewards.

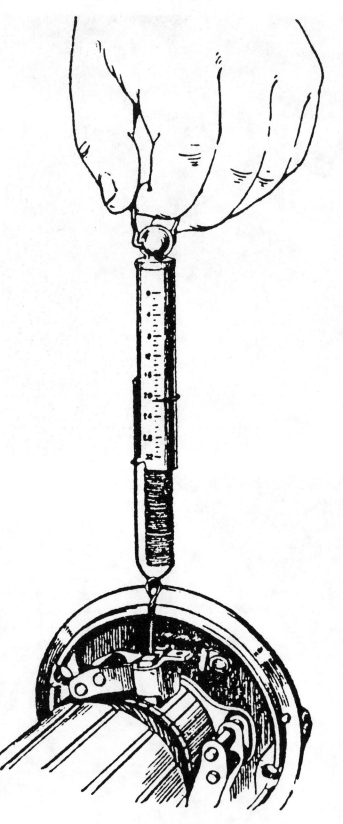

The brush holder assembly was taken apart so that it could be cleaned properly. The fiber parts in these assemblies will not survive the chemical and abrasive assaults that are needed to clean the metal parts.

FINGER RAISES BRUSH WHEN
PAPER IS SLID FORWARD
FINGER HOLDS BRUSH DOWN
WHEN PAPER IS PULLED OUT

SANDED SIDE OF SANDPAPER

USE STRIP OF SAND PAPER ¾ X 8 IN

PULL PAPER AROUND COMMUTATOR
SO THAT EDGE OF BRUSH
IS NOT SANDED OFF

If possible, you should check brush spring pressure against the commutator, and replace brush springs if they are not performing within manufacturers' specifications.

When you install new brushes and/or turn a starter or generator commutator down to true or dress it, always use a strip of sandpaper to conform the brushes and commutator, as shown here.

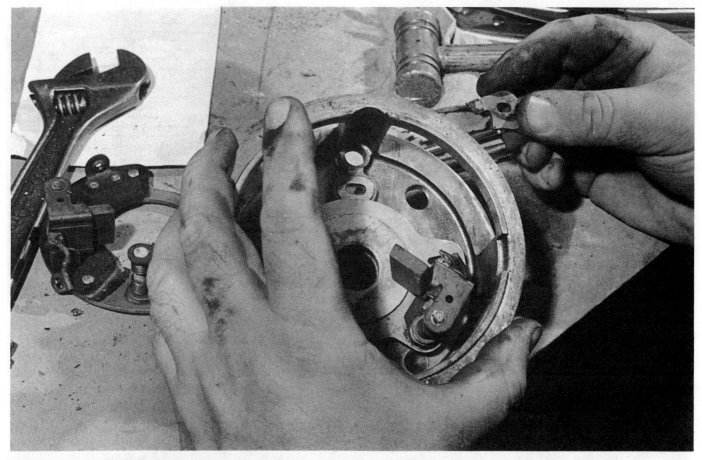

The little item in the author's right hand in this picture is part of the third brush adjusting assembly. You will have to know where and how all the little parts go to reassemble a unit like this one. The best idea is to take lots of notes and to draw pictures.

counter is keeping the brushes away from the commutator as it is slipped past them, and the end bearing is seated. On many starters and generators this is most easily done by keeping the brush springs off the brush holders when you slip the end of the armature into its end plate bearing, and pushing them into place through outer ends of their holders, after the end bearing is seated. Pivoting brush holders can usually be wired out of the way, or have their springs disabled, to facilitate armature installation. In other cases special holding tools may aid in assembly.

In generator and starter work, you will often have to use a small screw or arbor press to remove bearings from shafts. In this photograph, the armature is below the bearing holder platform on a press, and screw pressure is being applied to the drive end of the armature to remove the bearing from it.

There are lots of little parts in an old generator, so it pays to work on these items in an orderly way.

Electrical Tests and Procedures — Starters

The simplest on-car test of any starting system involves ascertaining that the battery is producing and delivering ample starting current, that the switching and engaging devices (solenoids and Bendix or other starter drives) are working, and that the engine to be started can, in fact, be turned over without extraordinary effort. The terminals and conductors that carry battery energy to the starter motor have to be in good condition, and should be checked with an inductive amperage draw meter to prove that they are delivering sufficient amperage to the starter motor. If all of these conditions prevail, and the starter still will not turn over an engine at a reasonable rate of speed, it is in need of repair. If this is the case, the starter should be removed and disassembled, and its parts should be cleaned with an electrical solvent. The armature, field coils, and brushes should be wiped with a very light application of a solvent designed specifically for this purpose. They should never be immersed in any solvent. In no case should a petroleum-based solvent be used on any insulated internal part of a starter or generator.

The field coils should be visually inspected and tested with an ohmmeter for isolation from the starter frame. They should also be tested for continuity and resistance.

Any time you have an armature out of a generator or starter, you should turn the commutator down just enough to get a true, smooth surface. Remove as little material as is needed to do this job. Then smooth the commutator with a backed strip of sandpaper after it has been trued with a lathe tool.

Commutator continuity and shorting can be easily checked with a test light.

Armature coil shorting is tested with a "growler." Shorts will be indicated by the metal strip — a hacksaw blade in this case — vibrating when a shorted armature coil is encountered and tested.

A portable commutator grooving tool, like the one pictured here, will do credible work undercutting the mica that separates commutator segments. A motorized cutting tool does an even better job.

Ordinarily, you will not have to remove the field coils and pole shoes from a generator or starter when you refurbish it, but this is what those components look like. It is best to leave them in place unless testing indicates that they are defective.

This is done by taking an ohmmeter reading from the solenoid input terminal to the field brushes. The resistance should be negligible.

The armature of a starter motor should be checked for two faults, shorts and grounding. Shorts are checked with a specialized piece of equipment called a "growler." If you don't have one, take the armature to an an automotive electric or electric motor repair shop and they can run this test in about a minute. Armature grounding can be tested by touching one lead of an ohmmeter to any part of the armature's laminated steel core and the other lead to the commutator segments, one by one. There must be no continuity here. Finally, check the commutator segments for continuity with the connector bars that go from them into the armature coils. An ohmmeter should show good continuity here, but be sure to apply light finger pressure to the bars while running the test to detect any discontinuity resulting from looseness. If an armature is shorted or grounded, it will have to be repaired or replaced. Commutator to connector bar defects can often be easily repaired by resoldering. Any time that a starter is reconditioned, it should be checked on appropriate bench equipment to determine its torque output capability.

Usually, when a starter is disassembled for reconditioning without any history of malfunction, it can be reassembled with little more than cleaning, lubrication, and brush and/or spring replacement.

Electrical Tests and Procedures — Generators

Electrical testing of conventional generators is more difficult than for starters due to the variety of circuits and windings used in generators. The disassembly and cleaning procedures are about the same as those for starters. As with starters, the field coils must be tested for continuity and for isolation from the generator's frame. The connecting terminals and insulated brush holder must also be checked for isolation from the frame. Testing generator field coils for internal insulation is also a good idea, but it requires a good ammeter to determine the current draw of the coils for comparison to factory specifications. The armature tests for generators are basically the same as those outlined above for starter motors, except that the growler test for shorts may be misleading for some generator armatures that utilize special winding patterns. A refurbished generator should definitely be output tested on a test bench. The old folk test of "motoring" the generator as a final test should never be seriously confused with a proper output test. Reassembly of generators follows the basic procedure outlined for starter motors.

The simplest regulation of a generator is done by a cutout relay such as the one pictured here. This is a feature of all automobile generating systems — you have to uncouple the generator or alternator when its output drops near, to, or below battery voltage. Otherwise, the battery would discharge through the generator.

Starter Engagement Systems

There are two basic methods of coupling and uncoupling starter motors from the engines that they operate. One involves a physical or magnetic (either by solenoid or field coil) engagement of the motor gear with engine flywheel teeth. In this method, an overrunning (one-way) clutch is used to affect the attachment of the motor gear to its shaft, and when the engine starts, the gear is run backwards on the clutch because the speed of the flywheel teeth with the engine running is much greater than the speed of the driven starter motor gear teeth. Final uncoupling of the two units occurs when they are physically released or magnetically released by the operator taking his foot off the starter pedal or allowing the starter key switch or button to return to its unconnected position. The other common method of engaging starters is via an inertial device known as "Bendix." Bendix drives are engaged by the forces of inertia (their engagers spin *out* but not *with* the shafts that drive them) and are easily understood from inspection, or from a good set of pictures of their sequential operation. Explaining how they work with words is likely to be as successful as explaining with only words how to tie a shoe lace.

Overrunning clutch starter drives usually work until the starter end bearings fail, their gear teeth break, the overrunning clutch rollers seize or fail to hold, or the shifting fork bends or breaks. They can also fail due to broken cushion springs, or, of course, defective engagement solenoids. When starters are restored, it is a good idea to

The Bendix drive is the "Old Faithful" of starter drives. It's simple, compact, and works amazingly well.

The drive spring in a Bendix absorbs shock when the drive engages its flywheel. Sometimes there is too much shock and torque and the spring bends or breaks.

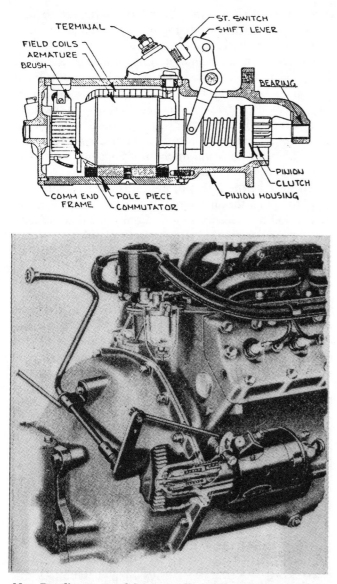

Non-Bendix starter drives usually involve some sort of mechanical engagement and an overrunning clutch, like the system shown here. A toe pedal in the car sequentially engages the drive and closes the starter motor's switch. It's simple and it works.

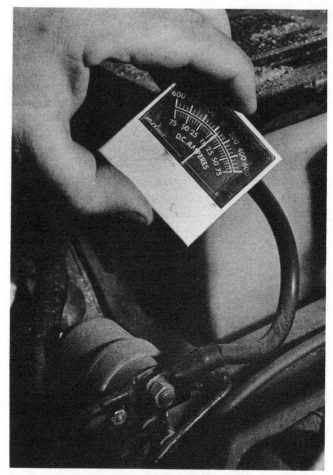

A current draw test of a starter is performed with an inductive ammeter. You hold the ammeter against a straight portion of the hot battery cable and see how much current the starter draws. That will tell you if "juice" is getting to the starter, or if too little is getting there, or if too much is being drawn.

replace any worn drive parts, and to pay particular attention to the their end bearings — where troubles often begin with these units. Overrunning clutch drives, sometimes called "positive engagement" drives, are usually activated by a solenoid mounted directly on a starter motor. It both engages the drive and switches current to the starter motor. Less often they are engaged directly by linkage from a starter pedal, or by a lever activated by the magnetism in one of the field coils (late model Ford).

Bendix-engaged starter drives use massive springs to transmit starting torque and ease the shock of engagement. This "Bendix spring" is often deformed by that shock and becomes a source of malfunction. Other problems with this type of drive are wear of the engagement gear or of the large threads that drive it into contact with the flywheel gear. And, of course, end bearings are vulnerable, as are the drive latch teeth. Physical inspection

of a Bendix will quickly show any worn or defective parts. These must be replaced.

Another wrinkle in starter drives is the use of gear reduction motors — particularly on large displacement applications. These miserable starters were created primarily to save space or money or both. The gears used to be fabricated from aluminum (in modern practice they are steel) and they fail with an amazing regularity. Chrysler used these units extensively in the days of high compression/big displacement engines. You can expect the older gear reduction starters to deliver about half of the working life or less of direct drive units. Also in the miserable idea department was a spate of GM starters some years ago that required starter motors to be shimmed against bell housings for alignment with flywheel ring gears. Whenever shims are removed from a starter motor to bell housing interface, make sure that they are reinstalled, or that a proper measuring and installation procedure for starter alignment is followed.

Generator Regulation Circuits

Starters and generators amaze me. When these devices first appeared on the scene, they both used control systems that were complex and cumbersome. Many starters used physical engagement systems, and generators used magnetically activated regulators that inserted resistances into their field coil circuits. As time went by, most manufacturers adopted the simple Bendix drives for their starters and simple third brush/cut out regulation for their generators. These systems were easy to understand, easy to repair, and comparatively inexpensive to construct. Yet, by the late 1930s, the original complex systems were coming back, albeit in improved forms.

Among the most finicky parts of any electrical system is the voltage regulator. The old third brush regulated generators of the 1920s and 1930s don't have "regulators" as such, and achieve self-regulation of voltage and current by energizing the field coils directly from an adjustable third brush. The effect is that of self-regulation because you can arrange things so that internal magnetic phenomenon in a generator will cause voltage output to fall off with increases in shaft speed, after a specific charging rate is reached. It isn't a very accurate system of regulation — remember how people used to go down the highway with their headlights on during the day when they went on long trips, to prevent battery overcharging? — but it did work. It was also easy to increase or decrease the charging rates by adjusting the third brush's position on the armature relative to the other brushes. Of course, third brush regulation was only usable with relatively simple electrical systems, and better voltage regulation was

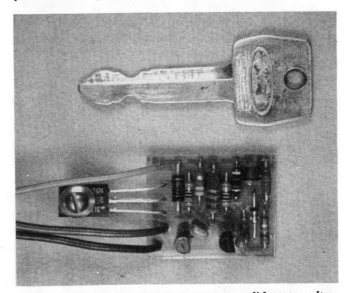

Some restorers are using little custom solid state voltage regulators, such as the one shown here, to improve on the performance and durability of third brush and vibrating point regulated generating systems. You can hide one of these little masterpieces in a generator frame or in a voltage regulator box, and "only your mechanic will know for sure" — except that your ammeter should show much better than factory voltage regulation taking place.

necessitated by the increasing array of electrical doodads that became standard and optional on automobiles after the late 1930s.

One part of the old, third brush system that was common to the later "voltage regulator" equipped systems was the use of a set of cutout points. This was simply a magnetically driven set of contact points that closed when increasing engine speed and generator voltage output reached a predetermined level. When the generator voltage output fell below that level, the points opened and disconnected the generator from the system, thus preventing the flow of current from the battery back to ground through the generator's brushes. At an idle, or when an engine was turned off, the points remained open and prevented electrical back flow. A cutout device remained an essential element of the later vibrating point regulators, and it has a solid state analog in the diodes in modern alternators.

The theory of vibrating point regulators is simple enough. The repair and adjustment procedures that pertain to them can be maddeningly complex and varied. Avoiding the variations for the moment, the basic theory is this. In automotive generators, several conductors are rotated through two or more magnetic fields and are energized as a result. This is the basis of any practical automotive electrical generating system. While it is possible to use permanent magnets to supply the necessary magnetic fields — future generators may well do just this with special, high tech magnets — such magnets would have to have been very large and heavy, given the magnetic materials available in the past. Permanent magnet generators would have been impractical to use. Instead, electromagnets were (and are) used in generators, and these were energized by the flow of electricity through coils of wire wrapped around iron pole shoes. The more electricity that is carried through these "field" magnets, the more output there will be from the conductors on the armature that is passed through the field magnets' magnetic fields. A voltage regulator controls the current that runs through a generator's field coils and, by doing so, it controls the level of magnetism in the coils, and thus the voltage in the armature. A voltage regulator does not directly control generator output. It indirectly controls that output by regulating that portion of the output that is passed back through the field coils. By doing this, of course, it achieves control of the overall output.

In addition to the cutout and voltage regulating features that I have described, a voltage regulator may have an additional section, a current regulator. Both of the voltage regulating and current regulating units in a voltage regulator use electromagnetically controlled points to open and close contacts which insert resistance into a generator's field circuit. This diminishes the strength of the magnetic field surrounding the armature, thus controlling generator output. Both units work by cycling or vibrating, and they never work at the same time. This is because when a generator is meeting large current demands, its voltage output will be low and the voltage regulator contacts will not be working. When the current demands are not so large, the current relay will not be

The two-unit (left) and three-unit (right) vibrating point voltage regulators in this photograph are about average for cars from the late 1930s through the early 1960s. The two-unit device is for small electrical systems and has only voltage regulation. The three-unit regulator is a heavier-duty unit, and will support more electrical accessories on its system. It has both voltage and current regulation capabilities.

working, but voltage output will increase and the voltage points and coil will activate to control it.

Voltage regulators are almost impossible to repair if the nature of their problems involves burned coils, badly burned points, broken or distorted springs, or burned-out resistance units. Otherwise, it is possible to clean and adjust them. To do this, you must know what you are doing in general, and what particular specifications apply to the unit that you are working on.

Adjustment of regulators is accomplished by adjusting screws in some cases, and by bending positioning arms in others. On many regulators, the temperature of the regulator is one of the major specifications of adjustment. The condition of a car's battery is always a factor in regulator adjustment. A lot of mechanics and tinkerers will go into voltage regulators — it's easy to get their covers off — with a screwdriver and a set of needle nose pliers and bend and adjust things randomly until they seem to work. This approach *may* work in the very short run, to increase or decrease a charging rate, but in the long run it will almost always fail.

My experience has been that unless the time is taken to

fully adjust all aspects of a regulator to factory specifications of point air gap and dimension, and gauge measured output, an almost endless series of subsequent adjustments will have to be undertaken. These are usually indicated by the frequent discovery of a boiling or dead battery. If you have the equipment, manuals, and understanding to work on voltage regulators, or if you are working with a regulator that is hard to find or expensive, by all means either have it adjusted or make the adjustments yourself. In the cases of common regulators, I usually opt to buy a replacement when one fails. I always save the old regulator for some future date, when I may not have easy access to a replacement. By now, I have quite a shelf full of the things.

If you go the route of cleaning and adjusting, you will need a good set of meters, a variable resistor, a clip-on thermometer, a tang bending tool, and feeler gauges. The specific information contained in a *Chilton's* or *Motor's* manual that covers the year of manufacture for the system that you are working on will provide adequate step-by-step adjusting procedure data. Try refurbishing a couple of junk regulators, and decide if the cost of a new regulator, at $10 to $60, isn't worth the investment.

Temperature is very important in setting voltage regulators. This clip-on thermal correction gauge actually indicates what voltage outputs should be at specific regulator operating temperatures.

"A" and "B" Circuits in Charging Systems

Of the many internal differences in voltage regulator designs, the distinction between "A" and "B" circuits is the one that anyone working on generating systems must be familiar with. Understanding and accounting for this distinction is necessary to do preliminary on-car tests to determine whether it is a voltage regulator or a generator that is not working when a charging system ceases to function properly. It is also necessary to know "A" circuits from "B" circuits to reconnect generators and voltage regulators any time either, or both, have been disconnected from their wiring for any reason.

The "A" circuit was used on Delco Remy and Autolite

"standard duty" systems, which amounts to almost all of the passenger car systems produced by these manufacturers. In the "A" circuit, the field coils are grounded through the regulator. The "B" circuit was sometimes used by Ford, especially on some "heavy-duty" Autolite applications, and to a lesser degree on heavy-duty Delco Remy applications. It grounds the field internally in the generator.

There are two ways to tell "A" from "B" circuits, aside from the safe assumption that Delco and Autolite car systems will be "A'" and Ford applications will be "B." One way is to disconnect the field wire (marked "F" or "FLD") from the generator field terminal and connect a voltmeter from the generator field terminal to ground. With the engine running at moderate speed, an "A" circuit system will give you a voltage reading, but a "B" circuit setup won't. When running this test, be sure to protect the disconnected field wire from contacting ground — it can ruin the regulator if it grounds. The other way to distinguish "A" from "B" charging circuits is to examine the generator brush connections. If the field coil lead in the generator is connected to the insulated brush, you are dealing with an "A" circuit, if it is connected to the grounded brush, you have a "B" circuit.

Armed with this wonderful distinction between the two common grounding systems for field coils, you are now ready to perform an important on-car test, and to install voltage regulators and generators. First the test. When a charging system fails to provide an adequate charging rate, it's important to determine whether it is the regulator or the generator that is not working. On "A" circuit systems (This pertains only to single contact regulator systems and not to double contact units used on some air conditioned cars in, and after the late 1950's.) make sure that the regulator base is grounded and connect a jumper wire from the regulator field terminal to a good ground. Some older regulators have a ground terminal and, if this is the case, make your jumper connection from the regulator field terminal to this ground terminal. Now, run the engine at about 1500 RPM and check for a carge. If the ammeter shows a charge, or if the headlights brighten as engine speed is increased from 1000 to 1500 RPM, the problem is probably in your regulator. What this test does is to take the regulator out of the charging system and allow the field coils to get full energy. With the regulator eliminated, if there is a charge of adequate size, then the fault is probably in the regulator. Remember, when you run this test, the generator is running unregulated. Avoid running the engine faster than fifteen hundred RPM, as you can burn out any circuit that is connected, as well as the generator, itself. Never attempt to drive a car with the regulator bypassed.

To apply the test described above to "B," or Ford circuits, connect a jumper wire from the "A" or "ARM" terminal on the generator to the "F" or "FLD" terminal on the generator. Again, what this accomplishes for these internally grounded systems is to eliminate the voltage regulator from the circuit. With the above cautions about engine speed in mind, a charge indicates that the regulator is the problem and the absence of a charge indicates that the generator is at fault. Of course, in either "A" or "B" circuit tests, the regulator to generator wiring can always be defective and should be checked prior to re-

moving either of these components for further testing. These tests also require that the battery be capable of accepting a charge.

There is one other system that requires a special hookup for this isolation test. This is the Delco Remy double-contact regulator system. This was used on air conditioned cars as early as the 1950s, and is basically an "A" grounding system. If you encounter it, don't ground the generator or regulator field terminals, since instant damage to the voltage regulator will result. The isolation and testing of this system requires special procedures and will not be covered here.

Polarizing Generators

The second important use of the "A" and "B" circuit distinction is in "polarizing" generators after they have been disconnected from their wiring. Polarizing is not optional, it must be done before a car is started when the generator or regulator has been disconnected from its partner. If you do not do it, there is a good chance that damage will occur to the generator or regulator. To polarize the "A" circuit (externally grounded), reconnect all leads to the generator and regulator and momentarily touch (flash) a jumper wire between the "GEN" or "ARM" terminal and "BAT" terminal of the regulator. To polarize the "B" circuit (internally grounded), disconnect the lead from the field ("F" or "FLD") terminal of the regulator and flash it across the connected "BAT" terminal of the regulator. On the double-contact "A" circuit (Delco Remy) systems, used on some air conditioned cars, you should disconnect the field lead from the regulator and ground it. Then flash a jumper from the "BAT" terminal to the "GEN" or "ARM" terminal. Polarizing conforms the residual magnetism in the generator pole shoes to the battery system hook up.

If all of this sounds cumbersome and detailed, that's because it is. After years of fooling around with this stuff, I still need a book open on the fender about half of the time when I have to deal with it. The whole situation reminds me of Stevie Wonder's brilliant observation, "...When you believe in something that you don't understand, you get into trouble."

CHAPTER 12:

The Truth About Carburetors: Understanding Basic Carburetor Principles

In the last twenty years, fuel injection has gone from being an obscure and very expensive fuel delivery system, used mostly on expensive and exotic cars, to being the standard system in almost all modern automobiles. The carburetor, alternately cussed at and beloved by old car collectors and tinkerers, is on the verge of extinction. Fairly soon, the press will announce that the carburetor has gone on to join the immortal ranks of manual key-strike typewriters, bathtubs with legs, and passenger pigeons. To the general public, this passing will will be viewed as automotive progress.

Carburetors were, without doubt, the most unfairly maligned components in automobiles. For the most part they performed their function faithfully and reliably and seldom needed repair or adjustment. However, for almost a hundred years, a succession of unskilled but well-meaning individuals, and collectivities of individuals (called service organizations), have tampered the poor things into malfunction.

It never ceases to amaze me that when I see a car broken down by the side of the road, the hood is invariably raised, and someone is mucking around with the carburetor, if it has one. Frequently this individual is totally without mechanical knowledge or ability, but this never stops him from molesting the carburetor. In this degrading process, every adjustment on the carburetor is boldly turned or bent out of calibration. Every attaching screw is ruthlessly over-tightened, and other liberties are taken and indignities inflicted.

None of this is to say that carburetors don't sometimes fail, or that they are not legitimate objects of repair and adjustment. It is just that in my experience, carburetors are "rebuilt" about three times for every time that they really need it, and adjusted out of calibration about every third time that the hoods over them are raised. Barring defects in a carburetor's environment — bad intake valves or contaminated gasoline, for example — a prop-

erly set-up carburetor will function flawlessly for tens of thousands of miles and years of service. I have no idea from whence the bad reputation of carburetors comes, but I suspect that their vulnerability to unnecessary and harmful tinkering stems largely from the fact that they are usually easy to get at and look like they could cause problems.

It is critically important that the carburetor on any collector car be clean, that all of its systems be functional, and that the integrity of its parts and the calibration of its adjustments be perfect. Then, for goodness sake, leave the poor thing alone to do its job. This job is basically a simple one — to meter and atomize gasoline into an automobile's induction system in the correct concentrations for a variety of running conditions.

Early carburetors performed this function in very simple but usually inadequate ways. Some of these were little more than a crude wick system or a simple jet in a straight tube. The old carbureting wick devices were not like the delicate things in kerosene lanterns, but more like the business end of a mop in the gas tank, with a short wick, resembling a two-inch hemp rope, leading to the intake manifold. By 1900, these crude systems had given way to relatively modern jet-in-venturi systems that had provisions for a choke, and even for multiple metering systems that matched fuel delivery to engine requirements in different modes of operation. From then until the recent past, carburetors became more complex and more responsive to engine needs. Multiple barrels were added, and the early updraft carburetor had, by the 1930s, mostly given way to downdraft carburetion.

After the early 1970s, carburetion became increasingly complex and cumbersome, as first emission, then fuel economy standards were mandated by the federal government and began to have an impact on automobile engine design. By the 1980s, increasingly stringent standards, and the availability of small, reliable, and relatively

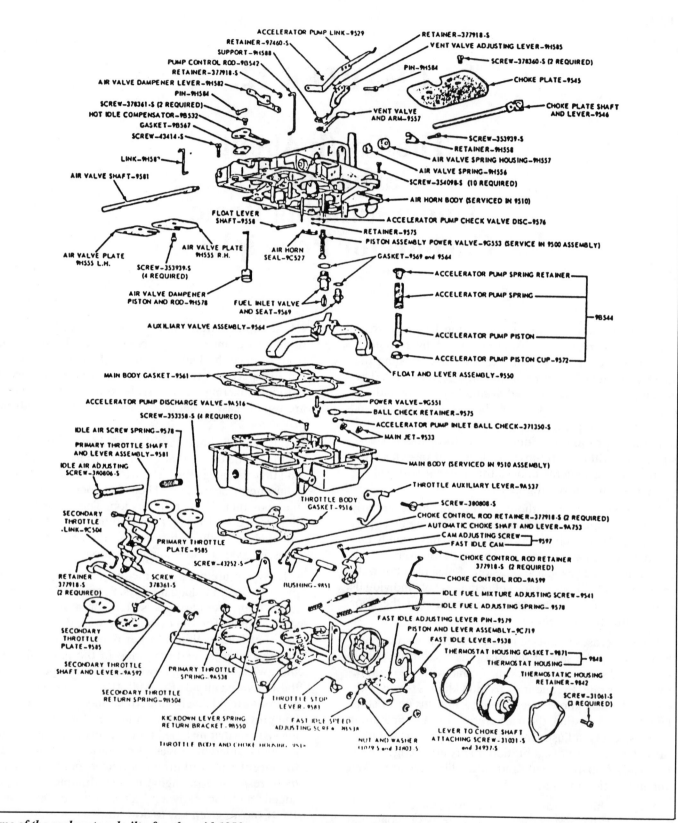

Some of the carburetors built after the mid-1950s get very complicated. The one shown in this parts illustration is pretty tame by comparison to the likes of the Thermo-Quads and Quadra-Jets of the 1970s.

cheap computer controls, had changed the thrust of fuel delivery design to fuel injection. Now, hybrid, pseudo-carburetors — appearing under such catchy names as "throttle body injection" — suggest that the end of the carburetor is at hand. These systems do the job better than carburetors and cost no more to build. By the mid 1990s, it is doubtful that any automobile will be manufactured for the North American market with a carburetor as original equipment. It is hard to believe, but in a couple of decades, the automobiling public will come to regard carburetors as part of the past that includes wooden spoked wheels and deflector vent windows. (Personal note: I think that I can make peace with fuel injection, but I will never stop lamenting the loss of deflector vent windows.)

The Basic Principles of Carburetion

The basic principles of carburetion, and much of the hardware for it, are pretty easy to understand. While a detailed understanding of these principles is not necessary to restore carburetors, it is helpful in analyzing some of the hardware. The basic proposition of carburetion is to mix a liquid (gasoline) with a gas (air, actually a mixture of gasses) in a variety of ratios between 1:12 and 1:18, by weight, with 16.7:1 being the ideal mixture for most driving conditions. This mixing of air and fuel ideally involves complete atomization of the gasoline into a fine mist, but, in reality, usually falls short of this ideal when an engine is cold. The metering function of a carburetor is particularly impressive when you consider that the mix ratio of the volume of gasoline to air is on the order of 1:9000.

The basic principles that allow this mixing function to take place in the device that we call a "carburetor" were elaborated by a Swiss and modeled by an Italian in the 19th and 18th centuries. The Italian, G. B. Venturi, sometimes gets more of the credit than he deserves when, in fact, the Bernoulli effect provides most of the theoretical basis for carburetion. Simply stated, this principle suggests that when a fluid (gas or liquid) flowing through a tube encounters a region of diminishing cross-sectional area, its velocity will increase and its pressure will be reduced. If a fluid at atmospheric pressure is ported into this area of reduced pressure, the fluid at atmospheric pressure will flow into the area of reduced pressure. This explains how a perfume atomizer, a carburetor, and an automatic shutoff gasoline nozzle work, when they work.

For our purposes, the impact of this theoretical framework suggests that if a small jet, or nozzle, containing gasoline at a level slightly below its tip, is placed in an air stream that has been accelerated by being pulled through a tube with a smooth and gradual restriction, gasoline will be pulled from the jet and atomized into the flowing air steam. The jet must be placed in, or just beyond, the

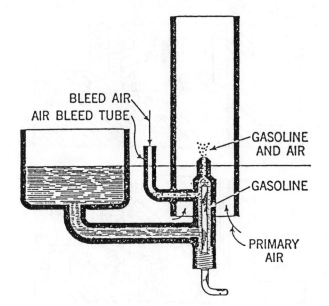

This "basic carburetor" illustrates the most important principles of carburetion. It would need some refinements to work well enough to feed fuel to an automobile engine. Note that this is an "updraft" carburetor, as the air is sucked up into it from its bottom, and exits its top end, on its way into an engine.

location of reduced cross-sectional area and (thus) reduced pressure. The whole thing works something like a perfume atomizer, but more efficiently. It is, by the way, certain that neither Venturi or Bernoulli had the slightest idea that their theoretical explorations would ever have anything to do with the development of engines for self-propelled vehicles. In fact, they were both long extinct before their theories were applied to automotive engineering. I am, however, certain that both of them would have lamented the passing of deflector vent windows if they had lived into the latter part of the 20th century.

The Practice of Carburetion

In practice, a carburetor consists of some sort of "float" device and one, or more, venturi tubes, discharge jets, air bleeds, enrichment and economizer devices, choking devices, and throttle plate system. Let's try to sort all of this hardware out.

Gasoline is supplied to a carburetor by gravity, air pressure, or pump pressure. A float-activated valve in the carburetor controls the amount of gasoline admitted to the carburetor and holds it at a specific level in the float chamber by closing a needle or disc valve when the gasoline attempts to rise above that level. From the float chamber, the gasoline travels, via one or more circuits, to a point of discharge in the carburetor throat. In practice, two or more discharge points may be used, and the choice between them is made on the basis of the position of the throttle plate — a moving plate which restricts air flow through the carburetor and, thus, controls engine speed. The destination and distribution of the gasoline to

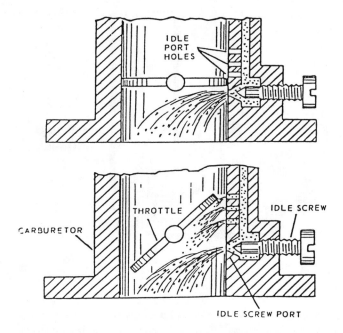

This illustration shows how a carburetor's throttle butterfly uncovers successive idle and low speed jets, as an engine is speeded up from an idle. Further opening the butterfly will disable the idle and low speed discharge jets and convert them to air bleeds for the carburetor's main discharge jet(s).

be discharged can also be determined by a system of internal metering rods or other metering devices. The float level is always set to keep the gasoline just below the level of the tip of the main discharge jet(s), so that it cannot continue to flow out of the jet(s) and into the engine's intake manifold after the engine has been stopped and the air flow and suction created by the downward travel of its pistons ceases. Also, the path to the discharge jet(s) is usually restricted by a main or auxiliary metering jet that acts to limit the amount of gasoline that can reach the discharge jet(s). When I refer to "jets," I am speaking of small calibrated holes that restrict the flow of gasoline in a carburetor.

What has been described above represents the main operating features of a basic carburetor. It would work, in theory, but in practice it would not accommodate the variety of operating conditions — variables of temperature, speed, load, etc. — that are common to an engine in the real world. Let's consider some of the systems in a carburetor that deal with these variables. Not all carburetors use all of these systems, and there are many obscure control systems that I will not detail here. What follows is a description of most of the important modifications of a basic carburetor that you might expect to encounter in any carburetor that you will restore.

MULTIPLE BARRELS AND MULTIPLE CARBURETORS. One way to increase carburetor capacity, and tailor air/fuel mixture to engine needs, is to add more carburetor barrels to the system. These barrels can differ in size, so that smaller barrels provide for low speed operation and larger ones only come into play during acceleration or high speed operation. You can also link several carburetors together, so that specific barrels in each

correspond to and feed air/fuel mixture to one or more cylinders in an engine. While this refinement, multiple carburetors, may increase engine responsiveness and efficiency, it inevitably creates complexity and may produce calibration problems. Early updraft carburetors usually had only one barrel for all cylinders. Later, downdraft carburetors frequently had two or four barrels. By the 1950s, it was not uncommon for a high performance, V-8 engine to have three two-barrel carburetors, or even two four-barrel units. In both of these situations, there is a substantial problem keeping everything synchronized so that carburetor valves and circuits open up at the optimum times in their sequences.

SECOND VENTURIS. Another feature found on some carburetors, particularly performance carburetors, is a second venturi suspended inside the main venturi in the throat of a carburetor. This greatly increases the local vacuum applied to the gasoline extracted from the discharge jet. More important, the speed of the air/fuel mixture entering the engine is also increased. There were even a few triple venturi carburetors.

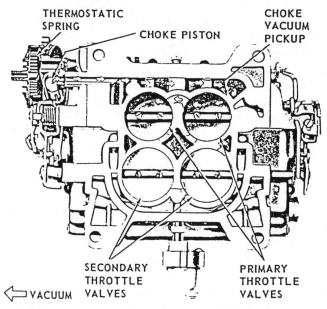

A modern four-barrel carburetor, like this one, can be very complicated.

MIXTURE HEATING DEVICES. One of the problems with the "basic carburetor," described above, is its tendency to ice up. This occurs because as the gasoline entering its venturi system is transformed from a liquid to a vaporized state, it has to give up heat and the resulting mixture's temperature drops. Condensation tends to occur, and ice can form. Various systems have been developed for heating the bases of carburetors with engine coolant or exhaust gases — one of these is common to most carburetion systems. It is also common to use a manifold heat stove to heat the incoming combustion air fed to cold engines. Water-jacketed intake manifolds and exhaust-stove-heated intake manifolds are also present on some engines to help defeat tendencies towards carburetor icing. Some of these systems are non-regulated, or regulated only in the gross sense that they can be turned "on" or "off." Other heating systems, like mani-

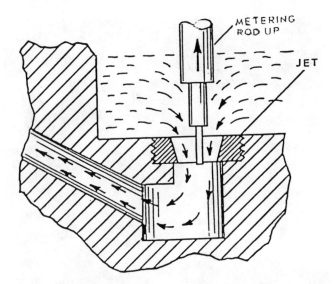

As the metering rod, shown here, works in-and-out of the orifice below it, it restricts and opens the flow of fuel and thus controls running mixture.

fold heat boxes, are often controlled by bimetallic springs that sense engine temperature and engine speed (based on exhaust volume and pressure). These systems are inherently troublesome because they operate in the very corrosive environment of heated exhaust gases. They need frequent maintenance and repair and should be put back into "as new" condition when an engine is restored.

COLD STARTING SYSTEMS: THE CHOKE. Almost all engines have some arrangement for radically increasing the fuel-to-air ratio for cold starting. Such a system is generally called a "choke," even though this term is a misnomer for a whole class of such systems. Almost all American cars use a butterfly valve type choke, placed at the carburetor's air inlet, above the discharge jet(s). By closing this valve partially, or completely, for cold starting, increased suction is created in the carburetor's throat, and a relatively "richer" (more gasoline) gasoline-to-air mixture is created and sucked into the engine than would have been the case if the choke were open and more air could enter with less vacuum.

This type of choke can either be controlled automatically by a thermostatic, bimetallic coil, or manually with a driver-operated control. Often a choke butterfly will incorporate a spring-loaded feature which allows it to partially open automatically, as soon as an engine begins to run, and before an operator would be able to open the choke manually. On automatic choke systems, a combination of engine vacuum and/or air flow automatically provides this initial choke opening. Complete opening of automatic chokes is provided for by a temperature-responsive bimetallic spring which may be electrically heated to hasten full choke opening.

Most variable venturi carburetors (also called constant depression, constant vacuum, or choke type) such as S.U. (Skinner Union) manipulate their main metering jet for starting enrichment purposes. They do not have conventional butterfly chokes.

THROTTLE. All carburetors provide speed control by restricting air flow into their engine's induction systems.

This is done with a butterfly valve located down stream from the venturi and main metering jet(s), or by some exotic tumbler system. When a throttle butterfly is used, as is usually the case, it is controlled by a cable or linkage rods to a hand and/or foot control, or both. It is interesting to note that this method of controlling engine speed is one of the main inefficiencies that is inherent in gasoline engines. Diesels, for all of their faults, at least avoid the expedient of controlling engine speed by the strangulation of their induction systems.

AIR BLEEDS AND ANTI-PERCOLATION CIRCUITS. These are small passages that open into the carburetor throat and allow air to mix with the gasoline, or gases to escape from the gasoline, before the fuel reaches discharge locations. Air bleeds enhance atomization, while anti-percolation ports prevent gasoline from bubbling excessively while in the carburetor's internal passages.

FLOAT VENT. This is a baffled vent that allows atmospheric pressure into the float chamber to prevent vacuum or pressure from forming as gasoline is evacuated from the float chamber. On early carburetors float chambers were usually vented directly to the atmosphere, sometimes via a small filter. After the early 1930s, it was discovered that if a float chamber was vented into the top of the carburetor barrel, just below the air cleaner, a compensating pressure was effectively applied to the gasoline in the float chamber. This made up for any increase in carburetor vacuum due to air cleaner clogging, and maintained correct air/fuel ratios.

DASHPOTS AND FAST IDLE CAMS. Carburetors, after the early 1930s, used a variety of systems to hold a fast idle when the choke was partially or completely closed. This is necessary to keep a choked engine running. On very early cars, this function was usually provided by a hand throttle, but with the disappearance of hand throttles and the advent of automatic chokes, one or more cam devices was incorporated into carburetor design to provide specified throttle openings when a choke was partially or fully closed. Another linkage system was used to open the choke when the throttle was opened widely while the choke was still closed. On some cars, built after the mid-1950s, vacuum operated dashpots and solenoid-operated throttle stops performed these functions.

INTERNAL CARBURETOR CIRCUITRY AND ARCHITECTURE. The most complex aspect of almost any carburetor is the internal circuitry that acts to change the metering of fuel to meet engine needs. (The obvious exception is constant depression carburetors which avoid most such circuitry.) The variety and complexity of this type of control system can be mind-boggling. The main features include a system that switches fuel feed from an idle port to a low speed system, and then to the main discharge or cruising circuit. These changes are usually accomplished by uncovering successively larger ports as the throttle butterfly plate as it is opened. Ultimately, a high speed circuit begins to operate and disables the first two systems by converting them to air bleeds for the main discharge system.

In addition to this basic circuitry, most carburetors have either vacuum- or linkage-operated metering rods that allow more or less gas to pass through the metering jets, depending on engine requirements and the need for economy or power in a given situation. Some of these systems do not even use physical metering devices, but depend on the principles of hydraulics and fluidics to achieve their switching. The basic condition that these metering systems respond to is the need for a relatively lean mixture at cruising speeds, compared to idle and low speeds, and the need for substantial air/fuel enrichment when heavy acceleration is demanded. Such terms as "economizer valve" or "acceleration circuits" are often employed to describe the features of this kind of system.

ACCELERATION PUMP OR WELL: Most carburetors employ some sort of system to provide an extra shot of gasoline, instantly, when the throttle is opened rapidly. For this purpose, early carburetors tended to use a well filled with gasoline that was rapidly drawn empty when the throttle butterfly was suddenly opened. Later carburetors, of the downdraft type, tended to use a little pump with check valves and separate discharge jets to put an extra squirt of gas into the system. The pump systems are also useful in starting a cold engine because a couple of down strokes on the accelerator pedal will cause the discharge of raw gas into the intake manifold, which aids in starting. Too many such strokes will, of course, flood the engine.

IDLE MIXTURE SCREWS: Until several years ago, all carburetors featured accessible idle mixture screws for each low speed (primary) barrel. These were used to set the air/fuel ratio at idle speeds. The idle mixture screws, recognizable because they are usually brass or brass colored and have springs on their shanks and serrations around their heads, are among the most misunderstood of all carburetor parts. They regulate the air/fuel mixture entering the carburetor barrel for idling purposes, only. Usually, they will lean the idle mixture when they are screwed in, and enrich it when they are screwed out. Idle mixture screws have no effect on the running mixture supplied by the high speed discharge jet(s). I emphasize this because many people attempt to set a carburetor's running mixture by adjusting the idle mixture screws and, of course, fail to achieve that end. To further confuse things, a few carburetors use idle mixture screws that control the air flow into the idle circuit and, in this case, turning these screws in enriches the mixture and turning them out leans it — the opposite of the other, more common, type of adjustment. You have to know which type you are working with.

The hardware for the systems described above is most of what is likely to be found inside, and hung outside, the majority of carburetors that a restorer will encounter. There is a whole range of other stuff that has been used over the years, and if you come across any of it, you should try to understand what it is and what it is supposed to do. *Chilton* and *Motor* manuals from the 1930s through the 1980s do a pretty good job describing the details of the carburetor systems used in the cars for the years that they cover. Shop manuals are another good

This SU (Skinner Union) H-6 carburetor is of the "variable venturi" or "constant depression" type. It operates very simple hardware on very simple principles. Restorers should not be afraid to tackle carburetors, like this one, that are different from the mainstream.

source of repair information. On very early cars, the owners' manuals are often the best sources of operating descriptions, adjustment specifications, and repair procedures for carburetors. Finally, major carburetor companies like Stromberg, Zenith, Marvel, Carter B&B, Holly, Schebler, Rayfield, etc. put out parts and service books that contain a wealth of information that is useful in carburetor repair and calibration.

Restoring Carburetors: The Preliminaries

There are some important preliminaries before you undertake carburetor disassembly. The first is to make sure that you have enough information about the carburetor that you are working on to effect a reasonable rebuild. You should try to know what malfunctions were occurring in the car that the carburetor was mounted on that could be traceable to the carburetor. For example, if the car tended to stall whenever you rounded a corner, you should look for a fault in the float system. While there is a good chance that a complete cleaning, inspection, and adjustment of any carburetor will cure all of its problems, it is always better to identify problems beforehand, and then look for specific causes and remedy them when you rebuild a carburetor.

A second preliminary that can be important is to have a carburetor kit in hand before attempting disassembly. A good kit will include all of the gaskets and many of the wear parts that you will need to reassemble the carbure-

more complete than contemporary "zip" or "jiffy" kits. However, kits that have sat around for years often contain parts that have dried out beyond usefulness. All kits include some form of instructions and diagrams for assembly and calibration. In some cases these instructions are pretty general, and pretty skimpy on exact details of assembly and calibration of any particular carburetor in the "family" that they cover. In these cases, you will do better with one of the other information sources mentioned above. Some older carburetors require kits that are no longer available, and you will have to secure the parts that you need from open stock and cut your own gaskets. In some cases, reproduction carburetor kits are available from carburetor specialists and from marque specialists. These can be located by checking relevant advertising in major old car publications, marque publications, and various old car business and supplier directories.

It is usually easier to take something apart than to put it back together — and carburetors may be the best example of this rule. Make sure that before you disassem-

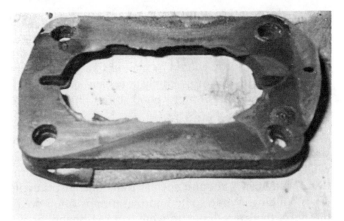

Always consider the operating environment of any carburetor that you restore. If not replaced, this deteriorated base gasket would cause problems with the operation of any carburetor mounted on it.

Part of the job of restoring a carburetor is to return it to a "like new" appearance. These "before and after" photos indicate what is possible.

tor. The most prominent of these will be bowl and base gaskets, ball checks, an accelerator pump plunger, metering rods and springs (if used), a float valve, and various other wear and sealing parts applicable to the carburetor that you are working on. Some older kits tend to be much

Always get the gasoline out of any carburetor that you work on before you bring it inside to your work area.

It is best to carefully read the instructions (left) from and look over the parts in (right bottom) any carburetor that you are going to restore. You should do this before you begin disassembly,

A good step to take before disassembling any carburetor is to wash its exterior in shop solvent. This makes it easier to disassemble, and saves some of the life of your more expensive carburetor solvent.

ble one, you have adequate pictures or keep good enough notes and sketches to put it together correctly. Since some former rebuilder may have misassembled the thing, it is best to be guided by manuals and logic of operation, as well as by disassembly notes and sketches. After a while, you will get pretty good at knowing how carbs fit together.

A final preliminary to carburetor rebuilding is to make sure that you have any special tools or instruments that will be required for disassembly, reassembly, and calibration. Many carbs require special tools and instruments for rebuilding. While some improvisation is often possible here, there are limits to what can reasonably be accomplished with a pair of needle nose pliers and a bent screwdriver. I have often seen delicate parts, like jets, ruined by rough handling in previous rebuilds. If you don't have the necessary tools to rebuild a carburetor, send it to someone who does. I receive butchered carburetors for rebuilding about once a month, and it can be a very expensive proposition to rectify previous mistakes.

Carburetor Restoration: Disassembly

If you are rebuilding a carburetor that is particularly grimy and varnish-coated on the outside, it is a good idea to do what you can to clean up its outside with a petroleum-based solvent before you disassemble it. Having done this, remove external linkage and cam parts and lay them out in a logical sequence. There will be lots of little parts by the time that disassembly is finished, so be sure to work on a clean, uncluttered surface, and avoid working on a surface that will allow little parts to roll around on their way to the floor.

Some linkage parts cannot be removed before the carb base, intermediate section, and top are separated. Pay attention to these linkage parts because they will have to be reengaged before the carburetor castings are reassembled and tightened. The float will usually come out of its chamber easily, but note how it is retained, and see if what you find is logical, or the result of previous misassembly. In the disassembly process, anything that can be unscrewed should be removed carefully with the appropriate wrench or screwdriver. When you work on slotted jets, remember that they will distort easily if your tool slips, or if excessive force is applied to them. Pay particular attention to which removable parts have gaskets, metal sealing rings, or 0-rings under them, and determine if those that don't, should. Generally, parts with tapered shanks or parts that fit into tapered seats will require no gasketing, but parts with flat flange areas will.

It is a good idea to keep all internal gaskets segregated with the parts that they are removed from, and to take notes as to which parts require gasketing. The concept of using the parts and gaskets in a rebuild kit until they are all gone, and hoping that this will put everything in the right place, is a charming but not a very effective way to insure success in carburetor rebuilding. Most rebuild kits are pretty general in content, and will contain some parts and gaskets that you don't need for your particular application, or lack things that you do need, or both.

One of the most difficult disassembly propositions, even for an experienced carburetor technician, is knowing when to stop. For example, some carburetors have external copper, lead, or brass friction plugs that must be removed for proper internal cleaning. Others have pressed-in jets that must *not* be removed unless replacements are available. If you understand the internal circuitry in a carburetor, you will know what lurks behind various pressed-in and threaded parts, and whether they must be removed, or even can be removed for proper cleaning during disassembly. One certainty is that all plastic or fiber parts have to come out of a carburetor prior to cleaning it in carburetor solvent. Any good carburetor solvent will quickly destroy these parts.

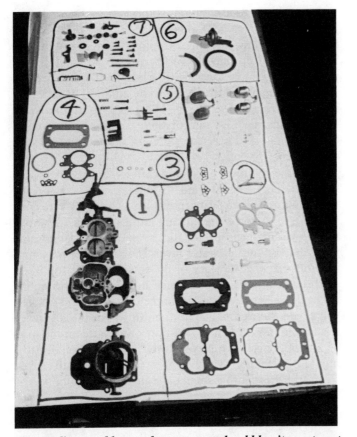

As you disassemble a carburetor, you should lay its parts out in an orderly manner. This helps to keep things simple during reassembly. Note that the disassembled parts shown here have been organized by type and function.

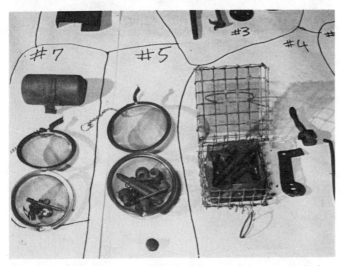

Very small parts should be put in mesh containers before they are chemically cleaned in carburetor solvent.

When you disassemble a carburetor, it is important that you keep its body right-side-up until all removable parts have been taken out. Many carburetors have two, or more, check balls that are different sizes. These tend to reside in wells, where they are hard to see. If they are not removed with tweezers or a magnet, they can end up on the floor before you can note their proper locations. Then you get to wonder how many there were and which wells they go in. The kit or book diagram that you are using may help, but just as likely, it will not. As I said, kits

After you remove the bowl cover from a carburetor, be sure that you remove all small parts lurking under the cover, before you turn the carburetor base over. Otherwise, things can fall out and get lost. In this picture, a magnet is being used to remove a ball check from its well.

and their diagrams tend to be pretty general, and may deviate significantly from what you are working on; even though they are supposed to cover it.

Springs and screw-in jets with similar appearances can also cause confusion at the time of carburetor reassembly. Usually the jets, tubes, and other screw in parts in a carburetor have different sized threads that preclude misassembly, but don't count on it. Springs must be identified by the number of coils in them, so that they can be replaced with new springs from a kit, or reinstalled in the correct locations.

An area of particular concern inside carburetors is the metering rods (if used). Metering rods must be free of wear, free of warping, and free of burrs. Their seats must be smooth, round, and unworn. Any linkage or springs involved in their movement must be free and capable of smooth operation. All metering rod adjustments must be made correctly and precisely.

Carburetor float level is a critical setting. Be sure that you understand the method of measuring the float level for each different carburetor that you work on. Typically, setting a float involves a measurement from the top of the float to the top of the carburetor bowl or lid surface. Sometimes the measurement includes the thickness of the bowl gasket, sometimes it does not. Be sure that you know which is the case. Float settings are achieved either by turning an external screw, or by bending an internal arm and/or tang. Be careful not to exert pressure on the float valve when making any adjustment. If the float adjustment is a bending adjustment, support the float arm while bending it. When you find a screw plug in the side of a float chamber, this is the gasoline level sight-line for the proper float setting. Thank the carburetor manufacturer for providing this final positive check of float level, and curse other manufacturers for omitting it. Remember that float settings are critical to a carburetor's proper air/fuel mixture in all modes of engine operation. These levels are sometimes given in 32nds, and even 64ths of an inch. They are that critical. In a few carburetors, multiple floats are used, and they are almost always set to different levels.

Carburetor Rebuilding: Cleaning the Parts

There are several commercial carburetor cleaning solvents on the market. They vary in speed and quality. Of the readily available ones, I would recommend: Delco, Speedclean, Metalclean, Thyme, and Gunk. There are probably several others that are as good as these. My personal preference is Speedclean. This product was introduced by Bendix many years ago, but is presently sold by a company that bought the rights to the name and formulation from Bendix. All of the carburetor cleaners mentioned above are "hydroseal" formulations. This means that they are layered solutions with water as the top layer. The water acts as a seal to keep the volatile solvents and detergents below it from escaping from the solution. Most of these products have "boosters" available to replenish their active ingredients when they are depleted, and all of them require the periodic addition of water to keep their volatiles sealed in. The best carburetor cleaning products have, as one of their top layers, a sealant that will coat and seal the pores of aluminum and pot metal parts.

The time required to clean a carburetor in solvent will depend on the cleaner used, its temperature, its age, and the condition of the carburetor parts. Overexposure can, in some cases, produce etching and cavitation, so watch out. Never let a carburetor part stick out of cleaning solvent, or even into its water layer. If you do, the part may be etched at the interface of the water and the top layer of the cleaning solution's active ingredients. This could destroy the part! Agitating parts in carburetor cleaner will speed the cleaning action, but it will also tend to release volatiles from the solution and cause premature ageing of the cleaner. Never throw a bunch of small parts into a big cleaner drum, as they will be difficult to retrieve. Always confine small parts in mesh containers.

How long you dunk dirty carburetor parts in carburetor cleaner depends mostly on their condition, and on the condition and temperature of the cleaner. After dunking, parts should be rinsed and rerinsed in clean water.

ALWAYS WEAR EYE AND HAND PROTECTION WHEN WORKING WITH CARBURETOR CLEANERS. They are very caustic and will burn your skin, or destroy your eyesight in a second, if you substitute *bravado* for common sense.

When the carburetor that you are working on is in the "soup" (solvent), let things take their course and don't try to rush the process. Some stubborn stains can take overnight, or even longer, to remove. With sufficient time, any good carburetor solvent should remove all carbon and varnish from the inside and outside of a carburetor. No carburetor cleaner will remove rust or other corrosion, so don't wait for that to happen.

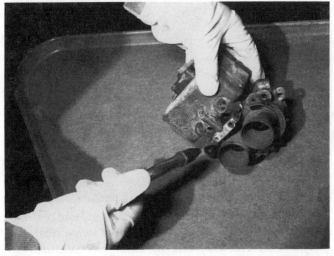

After a thorough rinsing, solvent cleaned carburetor parts should be blown dry with compressed air. Be sure to blow out all internal passages, and be certain to wear good eye protection while you are doing this.

When your carburetor castings and associated parts have been completely cleaned by solvent action, they should be double rinsed in clean water and blown dry with compressed air. Be sure to blow out every internal passage at least twice. You will probably need straight and right-angle blow guns to accomplish this. Not to harp on this point, but, again, PLEASE WEAR GOOD EYE PROTECTION WHEN USING A BLOW GUN ON A CARBURETOR. Many of the passages that you will be blowing out make connections that may cause the air to exit them right into your face, even though you are applying the air at right angles to the area you are facing. If you were to succeed in blowing an internal passage of a carburetor out so that its contents exited into your face, you would be exposing yourself to a blast of particles and harsh chemical residues, traveling at speeds up to a hundred miles an hour. You can imagine what chance your unprotected eyes would have against this assault. No carburetor repair is worth the risk of serious eye injury, so don't put yourself in the position of risking one for the other.

At this point, the carburetor should be clean internally. The out side may not look great, but the working parts of the carburetor should be clean. If the basic material of the carb is brass or bronze, it will probably look pretty

good. If it is aluminum or pot metal, it may look good or it may have areas showing white chalky deposits. If it is cast iron, it may show rust deposits. Some restorers will now use a light application of fine glass beads to remove chalky deposits or rust, and get down to good metal. They will follow this blast application with a clear epoxy sealant, a zinc tincture coating, or dichromate plating of the major carburetor castings and visible linkage pieces.

For the sake of appearance, I usually bead blast and clear coat carburetor castings. If you decide to do this, be sure to carefully mask the carburetor castings so that the glass beads are kept out of their internal areas. If a bead lodges there, and later enters an engine's induction system, it can do enormous damage. If you don't have blast cleaning equipment, scrubbing with a very fine stainless wire brush, followed by a brass wire brush, will get most of the chalky oxides off pot metal and aluminum parts.

After cleaning the parts of this carburetor in chemical solvent, they still look grungy. Carburetor cleaner will not remove the rust and oxides that tend to attack the outside surfaces of carburetors.

The major parts of this carburetor were abrasively blasted with very fine glass beads to remove surface deposits and get down to clean metal.

You can see what a difference bead blasting made. The parts are now shiny and clean.

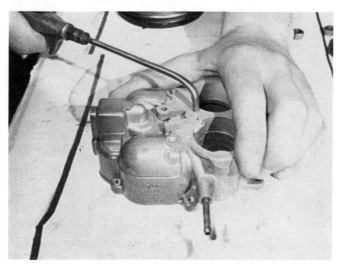

It is critically important to blow all glass beads and beading residues out of every nook and cranny of any carburetor that you have cleaned this way.

Note the use of a curved-end blow gun to get at passages that are cast or drilled into this carburetor bowl.

After blasting and blow-off, these cast pot metal and cast iron carburetor parts were masked and sprayed with a clear, flat epoxy varnish. This will protect the metal from corrosion.

Small parts that don't come clean in chemical cleaners can be tumbled in abrasive media in a small rock tumbler or vibratory cleaner.

Carburetor Restoration: Repair and Reassembly

At this point, all worn parts should be replaced or repaired, and the carburetor reassembled. A carburetor repair kit usually contains most of the parts that will require replacement. Accelerator pump and economizer valve seals should be replaced routinely in carburetor rebuilding and restoration. Usually carburetor kits contain whole plunger assemblies to replace these seals. Float needle valves should always be replaced in a carburetor rebuild or restoration. In some cases, Viton tipped float needle valves are available to replace needles that were originally made from brass or steel. The soft tipped needle valves are always a better bet than the solid metal kind.

If you don't replace a carburetor float when you rebuild it, you can at least check it for leaks by boiling it in water and looking for escaping air bubbles. Bubbles mean leaks, and leaks must be soldered shut. Some modern floats are made out of plastic or plastic foam. These should always be replaced when a carburetor is rebuilt. Metal floats should also be replaced if you can get a replacement.

The float, itself, should be checked for leaks by placing it in a pan of boiling water and submerging it. Then inspect it for bubbles. If these are found to escape from inside the float, it should be boiled until all liquids and gasses are expelled. It should then be allowed to cool, before it is resealed by carefully soldering the points from which bubbles were observed to exit the float. You can tell when all gasoline has been expelled from a float by shaking it and listening for sloshing sounds. It is important that float resoldering be done in a way that adds little or no weight to the float.

Throttle and choke shafts should be checked for clearance in their bearing surfaces. If either is found to be sloppy, a new, oversize shaft must fitted, or the carburetor body will have to be bushed and reamed so that the shaft fits in it with no more than .002 inch (two thousandths of an inch) clearance between it and its bearing surfaces. When replacing or refitting butterfly valves mounted to flat or split shafts, always close the butterfly plate(s) gently with firm finger pressure before the attaching screws are tightened. This seats the butterfly plate(s) squarely in the carb throat(s). Then the butterfly attaching screws should be tightened and secured with a good thread locking compound. It is a good idea to spread or "bugger" the protruding threads of these screws, so that there is no possibility of their vibrating loose and entering an engine's induction system.

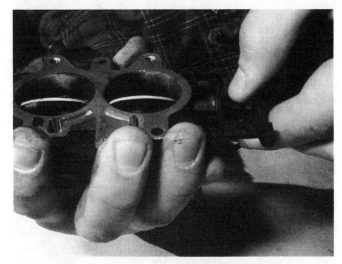

If a throttle shaft feels loose in its bearings, it will have to be replaced with an oversized shaft, and the bearing surfaces in the casting will have to be reamed to the new, oversize dimension.

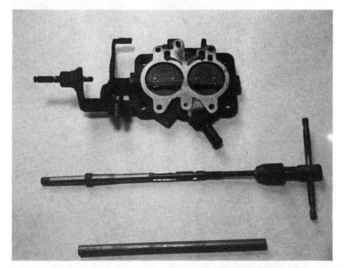

If an oversize shaft is not available, and if the old shaft is not badly worn, it is possible to to bush the bearing surfaces in the casting and ream the bushings to the proper diameter for the shaft. A hand reamer, used for this purpose, and an oversize throttle shaft are shown in the foreground of this picture.

Internal carburetor parts should have been cleaned in the same solvent as the major parts, and blown dry. If you have access to an ultrasonic cleaner, this is certainly a premium way to do a final cleansing of small carburetor parts. If not, use a very fine brass bristled brush on them. Jet orifices can be rodded with a broom straw or soft cop-

Delicate internal carburetor surfaces and parts can be cleaned with a brass brush if an ultrasonic cleaner is not available. Nothing hard, sharp, or abrasive should be used on these surfaces.

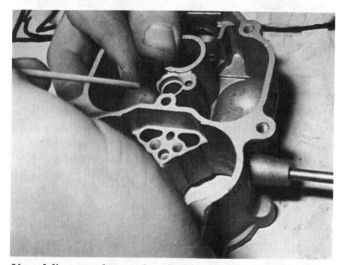

Very delicate gaskets and seals, like this one, should be handled very carefully. Here, a wooden stick is being used to install a small fibre seal. A metal tool might scratch the delicate pot metal bore that this seal resides in.

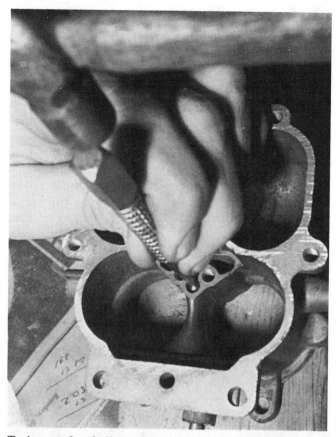

To insure that ball checks seat properly, it is sometimes a good idea to take the old ball that you removed and tap it gently against its seat with a hollow tip punch and hammer. Then remove the ball and install its new replacement. Tapping the old ball shapes the seat for the new one.

Before you install new, nonmetallic gaskets and seals in a carburetor, they should be soaked in kerosene or penetrating oil for half an hour. This helps them to comply to the surfaces that they will be clamped between. Accelerator pump flanges that are made out of leather should be slightly "flared" with a soft, smooth tool just prior to installation.

per bell wire, but should never be probed with anything hard or sharp. Threaded parts should be gently screwed into their proper holes and tightened so that their seats contact, or their gaskets are compressed and seal. They should never be over-tightened, as they can easily be distorted. This is particularly true of screw-in jets. Make sure that the jets that you install have the right sizing numbers for your application. It is surprising how often incorrect jets have been installed by previous rebuilders or restorers. Make sure that all carburetor restoration is done in a clean work environment — almost "medical" — because even a human hair in the wrong place can mess up a carburetor's operation. Lots of small parts are used in carburetors, and you should adopt an organized approach to this work, so that you can get things back where they belong.

When installing carburetor ring gaskets, pump or economizer valve leathers, or bowl gaskets, it is a good practice to soak them in a dish of kerosene for at least

one hour prior to installation. They should then be slightly flared just prior to installation. Carburetor bowls and bowl covers should be checked for flatness and cleaned with a brass brush on their mating surfaces. Any warping of a cover, or damage to a bowl sealing surface will have to be repaired if a seal is to be achieved. The final attachment of a carb cover and base can only occur after every internal part, and some linkage parts, are in place. If you screw a bowl cover down, and later have to go back in, you will have to use a new bowl cover gasket, or you will have leaks. It is best to be sure before you tighten a bowl cover down.

About half of the pre-1970 carburetors out there seem to have warped covers. This often occurs because the cover attaching screws have previously been over-tightened, or tightened unevenly. If you begin with a cover that is warped, and you don't straighten it out, you will have dangerous and unsightly gasoline leakage very soon after you put the carburetor back into service.

Warped bowl covers can be gently hammered straight and filed until their sealing surfaces are flat enough to seal. If you have to hammer them, use a very small brass hammer and back the casting up with a flat piece of hard wood. Oven heating a warped bowl cover to about 350 degrees Fahrenheit for 30 minutes will make it easier to straighten it. Whether you heat it or not, it is very easy to crack or break a carburetor bowl cover in the act of straightening it. Go easy.

Soaking a bowl cover gasket in kerosene, before installation, swells it and helps it to conform to sealing surfaces, and thus to achieve a working seal. Finally, tightening carburetor sections together must be done in stages, and in a pattern that works across the carburetor in a reasonable sequence. Be sure to lubricate the cover screws on their threads and under their heads. Initial or subsequent over-tightening of the cover screws will not

Straightening bowl covers is best accomplished after they have been oven heated to 350 degrees Fahrenheit for about half an hour.

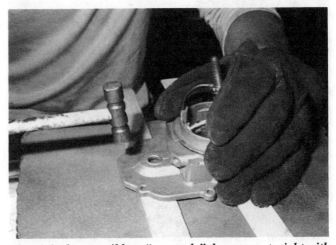

Then it is then possible to "persuade" the covers straight with a small brass hammer.

Warped bowl covers are a real problem on many old carburetors. When you rebuild a carburetor, always check the flatness of its major sealing surfaces, and make necessary repairs and adjustments. The best way to check is with a straightedge and a .002 inch feeler gauge. If you can get the feeler gauge under the straightedge at any position that the straightedge is held across component sealing surfaces, you will need to straighten or flatten the bowl cover.

Different hitting and backing approaches may be required to accomplish the desired straightening.

Final flattening of this bowl cover was accomplished by carefully filing it. As you file, look for low spots and address them, but be sure to maintain overall cover flatness.

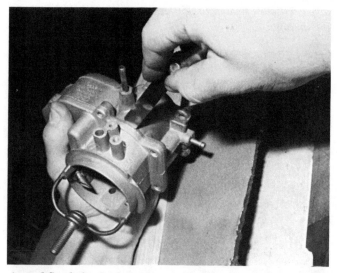

A good final check of carburetor flange sealing is to assemble the cover to the bowl section, and see if you can get a .002 inch feeler gauge through the interface at any point. If you can't, the cover should seal.

cure leaks for long, but will ultimately make them worse. It is best to use a torque indicating screwdriver for cover tightening, and to start with very low values. Final tightening values should be no more than 12 to 24 pounds/inch. You can always tighten things up later, but once you have warped a carb bowl cover, you have a much more serious problem than looseness. Some carburetor tops have attaching screws that are pretty well hidden in their throats, or that come up from below. It is important to consider these in any tightening sequence.

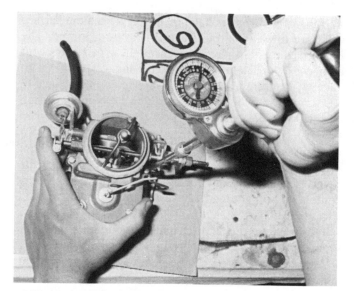

When you tighten the bowl cover down on a carburetor, be sure to tighten the screws that secure it in even stages. It is best to use a torque indicating screwdriver for this purpose. Be sure to alternately tighten screws on opposite sides of the cover. This avoids distorting the cover by applying too much tightening force in one place.

Calibration and Adjustment

The final calibration and adjustment of a rebuilt carburetor is very important. It will not suffice to simply set things the way that they were before the rebuild. They may well have been wrong. Almost all of the adjustments that you will encounter are given dimensionally or physically. Some require special jigs and tools, but some are

Carburetor calibration tools are either general, like these dimensional gages, or very specific, like the special tools issued by the carburetor companies for a variety of disassembly / assembly and calibration purposes. You can sometimes improvise both the general tools and the specific ones. Sometimes you can't. Note the carburetor float level gauge that is shown in the front left of this picture. This is a very handy "general" tool to have around if you plan to rebuild many carburetors.

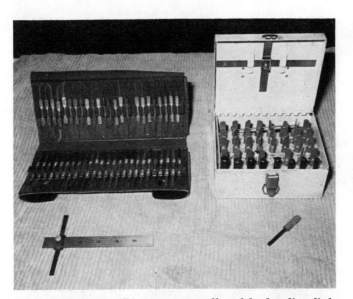

Many carburetor adjustments are effected by bending linkage pieces to specified dimensions or gauge points. Be sure that you know what you are doing before you attempt this kind of adjustment.

very generic measurements or physical directions — "turn the mixture screws out three-quarters of a turn for initial setting," or "place the accelerator pump link in the middle lever hole," for example. Many carburetor calibration jigs can be fabricated from things like cardboard or bent wire. Some general purpose tools are available for procedures like float level settings. Some settings, however, like the famous Carter pump-travel-setting, require the use of correct factory tools. Unfortunately, when this situation is encountered, guessing will usually fail to provide an appropriate adjustment. You should find someone who has the right tool.

On later carburetors, adjustments are frequently effected by the expedient of bending linkage pieces. If you find that a great deal of bending seems to be indicated, go back and check your directions and assembly — there is probably a mistake laying in wait to laugh at you after you have bent some poor linkage rod beyond the possibility of rehabilitation. I speak from bitter experience.

Many carburetor calibrations will not work when they are set "by the book" when you bench rebuild a carb. These calibrations are given only as starting points, and are used as initial settings when a carburetor has been disassembled and is rebuilt. Such settings as choke, idle mixture, choke unloader, and the like, may require further running adjustments on a warm engine. A good manual and some experience will give you the method, sequence, and values for making running adjustments after a carburetor is installed.

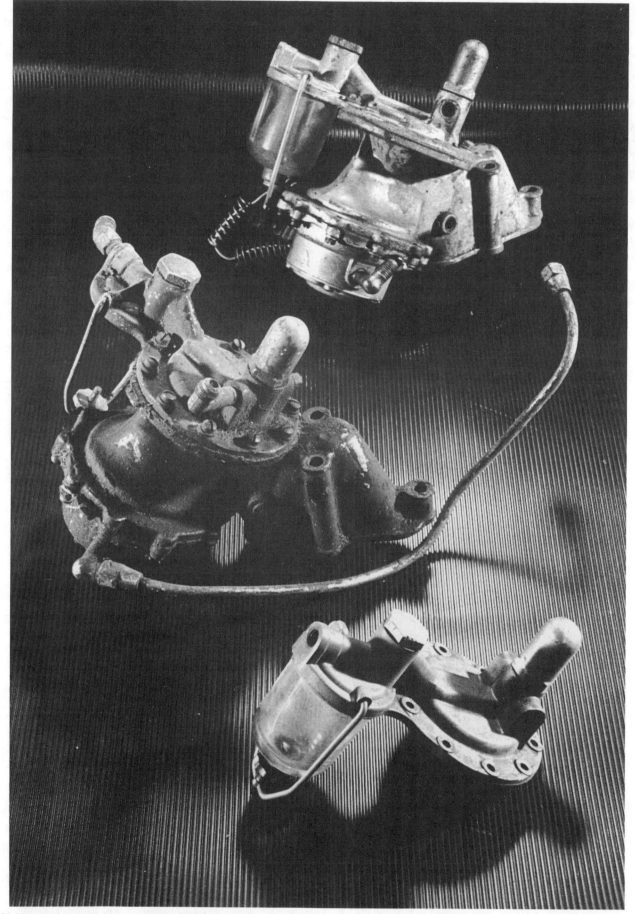

Old fuel pumps and their parts are just unreliable enough so that you should always carry a spare and know how to install it or repair the one on your collector car.

CHAPTER 13:

Fuel Containment and Delivery Systems

It's really quite extraordinary when you think about it. Gasoline, which fuels most automobiles, contains more BTUs of energy than dynamite, by weight or by volume. It is relatively easy to ignite when it is mixed with air, and burns violently, even at atmospheric pressure. When it is subjected to higher pressures, or wicked, it can burn explosively. Yet, for all of the potential hazards in the storage and delivery of gasoline in automobiles, relatively few mishaps occur. This, despite the fact that the vast majority of automobile operators, and even technicians, have little or no respect for gasoline and its hazards.

In the very early days of motoring, when the mighty Standard Oil of New Jersey was a monopoly that dealt primarily in lamp oil, gasoline was a by-product of the refining process, and existed mostly in paint stores for various obscure purposes. Hiram Percy Maxim, an early American automobile innovator, recounts that after purchasing gasoline at a paint store several times for his automotive experiments, he was regarded with suspician by the store's proprietor, and finally warned by him that anyone who fooled around with gasoline regularly would ultimately blow himself up. This was before the turn of the century.

At that time it would have astounded any reasonable person to contemplate that in twenty years gasoline would be dispensed and purchased routinely, and in gross quantities that made it the basis of one of the largest industries in the world. The very hazards associated with this substance would have made such a *scenario* incomprehensible to most people in 1900. Keep that in mind the next time you hear a discussion of hydrogen as the automobile fuel medium of the future.

The delivery of fuel to automobile engines has evolved greatly over the years. Many storage configurations and delivery systems have been tried. There are certain common elements to all of them, such as a basic gas tank, plumbing, and some sort of differential pressure system to convey gasoline from the tank to the engine. In part, the nature of the delivery system will dictate the type of tank that is used and its location in an automobile. At the extreme, a few early motorcars placed the fuel tank above the car and conveyed fuel to the engine via a wick. More practical early systems used gravity, but this made

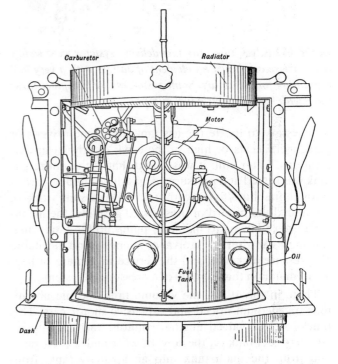

The first practical fuel delivery systems were gravity driven. They worked, but they delivered very little fuel pressure and often required dangerous and inconvenient gas tank locations.

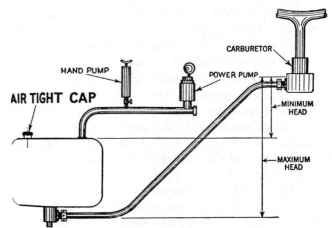

Pressure fuel feed systems allowed location of the gas tank at the back of a car, but they were still dangerous and very difficult to maintain.

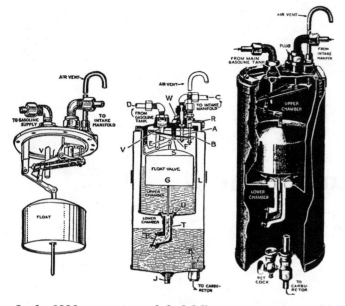

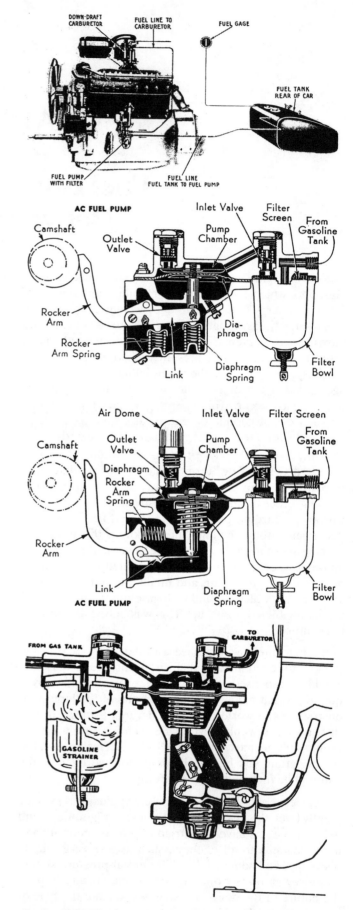

In the 1920s, vacuum tank fuel delivery systems were widely used. These combined an element of danger with a very bad reputation for reliability. Some restorers like to replace these units with hidden electric fuel pumps.

it necessary to locate the gas tank under the driver's or passengers' seats or high in the cowl; clearly hazardous locations. Later still, it was found that if the entire gas tank was sealed and pressurized, gasoline could be forced through fuel lines to the carburetor. This system worked, but added the hazard of pressurized gasoline, the inconvenience of having to manually pump up the tank when starting a car after an interval of idleness (and inevitable air pressure leakage), and the service nightmare of having to maintain the integrity of a pressurized system.

Then, in the 1920s, the vacuum tank became ubiquitous on medium-priced and expensive motor cars. This finicky device valved engine manifold vacuum into an auxiliary fuel tank on the cowl of a car and sucked gasoline from the main tank into an auxiliary tank, from whence it ran, by gravity, to the carburetor. In principle it was a good idea, but in fact it involved the hazard of storage of as much as two gallons of gasoline in the cowl. The system was also prone to numerous gremlins, like vacuum leaks and valving failures. This system required a very well-balanced carburetor float system because its final gravity feed to the carburetor provided only miniscule fuel pressure to activate a float.

By the late 1920s, camshaft driven mechanical fuel pumps began to appear on American cars, and these remained the standard of fuel delivery systems into the 1970s. Today mechanical fuel pumps have all but disappeared and been replaced by electric fuel pumps that feed fuel injectors via "fuel rails." Not many cars are being restored that have electric fuel pumps feeding carburetors or fuel injection systems. Not yet, at least. A restorer can expect to encounter any of the variations in fuel delivery systems mentioned above.

By the 1930s, most medium-priced to expensive cars had fuel pump systems that were compact and reliable. At the time, everyone raved about the new AC fuel pumps as a "technological breakthrough!"

The Gas Tank

Gasoline tanks are almost always made out of steel with welded or crimped and soldered seams. If they are located under car seats or in the cowl (gravity systems), they are protected from most road hazards. If they are located at a car's rear (pressure, vacuum tank, and pump systems), they are very vulnerable to things that go "thump" from underneath. In any location, they are vulnerable to attack by corrosion from inside and outside. Corrosion and leaking seams are the main defects that restorers will find in gas tanks. Corrosion damage is most prevalent at the bottoms of tanks because that is where water condensation settles. On pressurized tanks, it is common to find pin holes almost anywhere in the tanks. Loose tank baffles are also a common result of internal tank corrosion.

If the structural integrity of a gas tank is breached, it must be repaired. Some damage is susceptible to soldering, as for example, damage to the connection of the tank filler neck and main tank body or leakage around one of the crimped side seams or top seam. These joints are either riveted, crimped, or pressure welded for structural strength, and their sealing can usually be reestablished by soldering. The easiest way to find all of the leaks in a gas tank is to wash it out, seal its openings, and put from three to five pounds of air pressure in it. If it is then submerged in water, one surface at a time, any leaks will be indicated by escaping air bubbles. Never run this test near any source of ignition and wear full face and body protection when you do it. *Unless a tank has been completely cleaned with steam or by hot tanking, and completely filled with water or inert gas, it is extremely hazardous to solder it, particularly with an open flame.* This is because as a fuel tank is heated, volatiles trapped in the pores of its metal can be released by the heat. If there is in the vicinity an open flame, spark source, or surface hotter than the flash point of these volatiles, the results can be disastrous. An electric wire brush can also provide ignition, and should not be used for fuel tank work unless special cautions are observed.

The best way to solder a gas tank is to clean it thoroughly with chemicals. Then use a metal-bristled hand brush on the areas that will be soldered. Then blow these areas dry with compressed air, and treat them with a noncorrosive flux. During the tinning and soldering operations the tank should be filled with water or an inert gas such as CO_2 or argon. The area to be soldered should be tinned and soldered with a 40/60 or 50/50 tin/lead solder. Soldering should be done with large soldering coppers (at least 1-1/2 pounds) and the furnace used to heat the coppers should be kept well away from the tank.

The first step, tinning, involves applying solder to the metal in the repair area after it has been heated with the soldering copper, and then wiping it with steel wool or a rag. This removes excess solder and flux. Solder can then be flowed into the repair area using heat from the coppers. This type of repair will work well for sweated and crimped joints, but should not be used to repair large open tears or rust-throughs. If sweating more than a small patch on a tank won't seal it, welding will be required. Be sure that when you weld or solder gas tanks you have adequate ventilation in your work area and that all possible precautions are taken against igniting latent fumes in the tank. I prefer to do this work outside when weather permits.

Welding patches on gas tanks is dangerous work. Over the years, a lot of people have failed to reach the full promise of their personhoods because they were unaware of the hazards of gas tank repair, or failed to heed them. In many cases, these were people who tended to talk when they should have been listening, but their loss is felt, nonetheless. Don't join them. When you heat a seemingly clean gas tank to welding temperatures, it will emit flammable fumes which the welding or brazing process can ignite. An explosion will follow. Before any welding on a tank is attempted, the tank must be steam cleaned or hot tanked, rinsed with water and detergent, thoroughly filled with water or inert gas, and then dealt with like a live bomb. The key to welding or brazing is to almost completely fill the tank with water, leaving only the area where you are working clear of the water, or to fill the tank with an inert gas. This deprives the heated area of the oxygen that supports combustion. Even with these precautions, it is necessary to wear full face protection and body protection when you weld old gas tanks.

I know that there are people out there who have been soldering and welding gas tanks for years with little regard for the above cautions. As with many hazardous activities, you can get away with this until the conditions are just right. In the case of gas tank explosions, the penalty is extreme. Don't fool around with welding or soldering gas tanks. If you have any doubts, find a welding shop to do it for you.

Soldering fuel tanks is a dangerous business if you aren't very careful. Large soldering coppers, like these, are preferred for this work. The furnace that you heat the coppers in should be about 50 feet away from the tank that you are working on, and this work should be done outside, never in a building.

Dent removal on gas tanks can frequently be accomplished by filling a tank with water and applying five to ten pounds of air pressure to the sealed tank. This will pop out many large creaseless dents. More stubborn dents that are locked into the sheet metal by creases will have to be forced out with prying tools through the available entry holes in the tank, such as the filler neck and sending unit holes.

Corrosion that has not yet perforated a gas tank is another main area of concern for restorers. Almost all tanks were tinned or plated at the time of manufacture, and as long as this barrier to corrosion stands up, there are no problems. When it breaks down, pinholing, followed by rust-out, will occur. When you look inside a tank through its filler neck or sending unit hole, you can see if corrosion has started, and how far it has advanced. If it hasn't gone too far, you can slow it down by routinely adding alcohol (methanol and ethanol are commonly available as gasline dryers) to your gasoline. This causes the small quantities of water that may be present in the tank to combine with the alcohol and the gasoline. This prevents the water from promoting further corrosion.

If a more permanent and certain solution is desired, the use of one of the commercially available PVC/zinc chromate gas tank sloshing compounds may be appropriate. These are poly vinyl chloride (PVC) based compounds with zinc chromate rust inhibitors. They are widely advertised in old car specialty publications and they really do work if they are applied correctly. The idea behind these sloshing compounds is to coat the inside of a gas tank in a way that seals it and protects it from further deterioration. The PVC remains somewhat resilient after it hardens, so the sloshing treatment amounts to installing a bladder in a gas tank. These non-hardening sloshing compounds are applied by pouring them into a gas tank and sloshing them around until every surface has been coated. The excess is then drained out of the tank and the tank is air dried until the compound cures into a thin bladder-like coating, adhering to all inside surfaces of the tank. These compounds are absolutely impervious to gasoline and have terrific adhesion to the tank's metal, even if it is slightly rusty. However, some of the early sloshing compounds were somewhat soluble in some alcohols, and tanks sloshed with these compounds must not be exposed to much alcohol. Later sloshing compounds were formulated in a way that avoids this problem. Keep this in mind when adding gasline dryer to your car, purchasing a gasahol concoction, or purchasing gas tank sloshing compound. Be sure to use only sloshing compounds that are compatible with alcohol.

I must admit that when I first heard of sloshing compounds, I was skeptical. It all sounded like one of those "pie in the sky" quick fixes that you pour in and get to scrape out when it doesn't work. Later, I found out that some of these coatings were certified by the CAB or FAA for use in aircraft gas tanks. Instant credibility! You don't park a stalled, single-engine airplane by the side of the road when the fuel system fails in flight. In the twenty-five years that I have been using sloshing compounds, I have had only one failure, and that was due to improper

You can clean a gas tank by hot tanking it or by filling it with a buffered, diluted acid solution, and rocking it back and forth on a saw horse or log.

application.

Although various distributors of sloshing compounds sometimes claim that you don't need to clean a gas tank thoroughly before applying the compound, the truth is that you do. This can be accomplished by taking the tank that you are going to treat to a radiator shop and having it boiled out in caustic radiator solvents. Steam cleaning or an overnight dip in the hot tank at an automotive machine shop will accomplish about the same thing. You can also get a tank clean for sloshing by taking it to a "dip strip" outfit and having it cleaned in their immersion tanks.

If you want to clean and etch the tank yourself, this can be done with a solution of 20° inhibited hydrochloric acid (denoted chemically as "HCL," and frequently called "muriatic" acid) diluted with water in a starting ratio of one part acid to five parts water, and with some liquid soap, such as dishwashing detergent, added. This solution is poured into the tank and allowed to stand, or gently agitated, for from fifteen minutes to half an hour. The initial 1:5 mix is followed by one of 1:10, again with the addition of some liquid soap. The tank is then thoroughly rinsed with water. It will take at least fifteen minutes with a garden hose to effect a complete rinse. Then, a gallon of methanol or isopropryl alcohol should be sloshed around in the tank. You should then drain the tank and allow it to dry in in a warm environment, such as sunlight, for several hours. Throughout this cleaning and etching procedure you have to wear face and body protection to prevent the possibility of acid burns. Gauntlet style rubber gloves are a must. If you choose to agitate the tank that you are etching, one good way to accomplish this is to balance it on a saw horse and gently rock it back and forth.

Once the tank has been thoroughly dried, the sloshing compound should be poured in, sloshed around onto every internal surface, and drained. Most of the sloshing compound that you pour in will drain back out and can be used on other tanks if it doesn't look too badly contaminated. It's important that the tank be cool when it is sloshed and that it be dried in a cool place and left open to drain at its lowest point. If you place the tank in the sun to speed up the drying/curing time, you can get blisters in the sloshing compound. These will eventually rupture and allow gasoline to run outside the bladder, where it can leak out of the tank. If you fail to drain the sloshed tank thoroughly, you will get a thick clot of sloshing compound at the bottom. This lump will skin over, but it will never cure all the way through. It's good practice to apply two or three coats of sloshing compound to a tank, and these should be applied at least two days apart to allow each layer to dry thoroughly and cure.

A few tanks, like Chrysler tanks on some postwar models, have an internal gasoline filter and pickup line that cannot be removed without cutting the tank apart. Clearly, if the pickup unit in a tank cannot be removed or plugged through an access opening without cutting into the tank, sloshing compound cannot be used because it will plug the pickup. Of course, any tank that is sloshed must have the gas gauge sending unit removed. Any dent removal, soldering, brazing, or welding must be completed before a tank is sloshed.

Gas tank exteriors should be cleaned to bare metal, primed with an etching type primer, and painted with a good enamel. Any good engine enamel or hardened acrylic enamel will give the tank a tough and attractive finish. If the tank is secured to the chassis with metal straps, these should be lined with composition cork or synthetic rubber strips to prevent chafing and rub-through of the tank's surface coating. Tanks are very prone to rusting under their securing straps. Always be sure that any gas tank that you install is grounded to the chassis. It is good practice to provide redundant grounds to accomplish this. Any rubber hoses that connect a fuel tank to a car filler or to tank vents must be checked for deterioration, and clamped securely in place to prevent leakage. Drain cocks and other fittings and connections should be adequately tight, and a good gas resistant sealer such as Permatex #1 should be used on their threads. Gasoline leaks are extremely hazardous because gasoline fumes are heavier than air and will pool on a floor and traverse it. If they seep and roll far enough to find a source of ignition, the result will probably be catastrophic. Keep this in mind when you make any connection that will contain gasoline.

Fuel Lines, Fittings, and Filters

Unless you are working on a very early automobile that used copper fuel lines and must be restored with them for the sake of appearance, it is a good idea to use modern double flared brake lines for fuel system lines. The best practice is to purchase the line in the correct diameter in the bulk 25-foot or 50-foot coils that are readily available in diameters from 3/16 of an inch to 3/8 of an

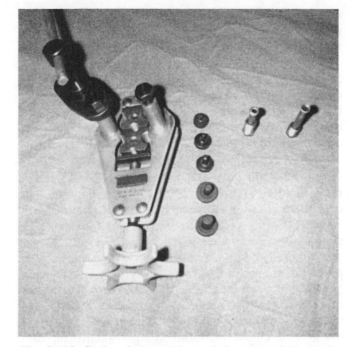

The double flaring device and mandrels, shown here, is designed for brake line work, but it's your best bet for making gas line terminations that use the double flare style fitting.

inch. Then bend the lines that you need to the right shapes and cut them to length. Fuel line terminations vary greatly. Compression fittings should be avoided, and if flared ends are used, they should be made with a double flaring tool. Copper lines are a bad idea because they have a tendency to work harden and crack if they are subjected to much vibration. And fuel lines do vibrate as a car goes down the road. Single flaring does not produce an adequate seal for fuel, and should be avoided. The best bet is a double flared mild steel line with as few couplings as possible and good attachment to the chassis, wherever possible.

Because most engines after the early 1930s are mounted on flexible rubber cushioning mounts, they are able to rock and vibrate independently of the chassis. This means that the final connection from a fuel pump to its chasssis fuel line should be a flexible line that allows for this movement. Various kinds of reinforced rubber and plastic have been used for this purpose, and it is important that a good quality flexible line be fitted in this application. The old flex lines, and the new ones used to replace them, must be able to sustain both suction and flexing without collapsing. When high pressure flexible fuel lines are used on the pressure side of a fuel pump, they must be in perfect condition. These should be replaced as a matter of routine in restoration work.

Vapor Lock

Fuel lines that run in an engine compartment are susceptible to the dreaded vapor lock. This is a condition that results from gasoline in the fuel delivery system boiling. This starves the engine, and sputtering and stalling result. The usual reason for gas boiling in fuel lines is not that the ambient under-hood temperature is sufficient to cause this, but that radiant heat from an exhaust manifold is overheating a gas line, filter, or fuel pump. The easiest fix is to locate gas lines and filters away from surfaces in the engine that radiate high heat, insofar as this is possible. When the geography of the engine compartment makes this impossible, some heat shielding will usually cure the problem.

Many old-time Ford V-8 drivers and dabblers tell stories of cutting grapefruits in half and stuffing one half over the fuel sediment bowls on the tops of early Ford V-8 fuel pumps. It is alleged that this cure for vapor lock worked, but modern restoration tries to avoid that degree of authenticity in restoration work. Vapor lock problems are becoming increasingly worse as refiners have added more and more "high ends" to their products. Such gasoline components as butane tend to boil out of gasoline at relatively low temperatures and raise havoc with engine performance, particularly on cars equipped with vacuum tanks. Since modern fuel systems involve relatively high fuel pressure (about thirty pounds) in the fuel rails, vapor lock is not a problem, and refiners have not been terribly concerned with the vapor pressures of their products. At this point, the federal government has begun to look at this problem as a pollution issue, and the Environmental Protection Agency has propounded a standard to control the volatility of gasoline that is sold. Keep all of this in mind when you replace fuel lines and filters and can easily change their routing for better protection from radiated heat.

Fuel filters are constructed from materials ranging from sintered bronze and ceramic to expanded and resinated paper. Older systems frequently made do with a sediment bowl on the fuel pump and a fine brass gauze screen. Except for this last type, fuel filters are meant to be replaced and cannot be effectively cleaned. Attempts to blow out sintered bronze and expanded paper filters will prove fruitless. It is equally fruitless to attempt to check the condition of a fuel filter by blowing air through it, though I have seen this tried many times. Air can easily be blown through barriers that would never let gasoline through. The only meaningful test of a fuel filter is to let the fuel delivery system try to force fuel through it. If it can't do this easily, replace the filter. On older systems that depend on a gauze screen and sediment bowl for fuel filtration, it's a good idea to add a modern resinated paper filter to the system. Such filters are compact and effective and will pass much cleaner gasoline than the gauze type. If you decide to add one of these, the decision of where to locate it should take into account the possibility of vapor lock in the filter case if it is overheated by radiant heat. You should also consider the aesthetics of the situation. Always locate add-on filters on the pressure side of the fuel pump, never on the vacuum side.

Fuel Delivery Systems

The earliest practical fuel delivery systems were based on gravity. Aside from keeping the fuel lines tight and in clean condition, and the carburetor float and needle in top condition, there isn't much that needs special attention in these systems. Operators of cars equipped with them will quickly discover that fuel tanks should be kept at least one quarter full at all times, if they intend to ascend any kind of hill.

Pressure systems that force air pressure into a gas tank are simple in concept, but may require extensive repair and maintenance. In these systems, every part has to be capable of holding air pressure. This includes the fuel gauge, the filler cap, the fuel tank, and all of the lines to the engine and air pressure components. These systems usually rely on a hand pump to generate initial pressure, and a small engine-driven piston pump to maintain pressure. A blow-off keeps the pressure from exceeding a few pounds. Those who own cars with this type of system are generally condemned to spending considerable time, usually at incredibly inconvenient moments, finding and repairing leaks. Whenever a car with a pressure system is shut off, it is a very good idea to manually bleed the pressure out of the system at the hand pump, if it has a provision for this, and at the filler cap if it doesn't.

The tribulations of the owners of pressurized fuel system-equipped cars may be easily matched or exceeded by those with cars that employ the notorious vacuum tank devices to deliver fuel. About 90 percent of these systems seem to have been built by Stewart-Warner. At the time of their manufacture they were considered to be quite an advance in fuel system design. "That was then, this is now." Aside from natural deterioration and wear that occurs in these devices, a whole new range of problems is posed by contemporary fuels, with lots of high fractions and volatile gases as components, and a tremendous tendency to vapor lock. There are so many things that can go wrong with vacuum tanks that I hesitate to select the leading causes of malfunction for fear of omission.

It would seem that the spring-loaded, float-operated valving devices on early vacuum tanks would be the source of most problems with them. These fussy looking devices valve vacuum to a tank inside the main vacuum tank and draw fuel into it from the car's rear-mounted storage tank. The incoming fuel raises a float in the auxiliary tank and when it is full, the float releases the gas in the inner tank so that it flows into the outer tanks and closes the valve between them. Then it reapplies engine vacuum to the inner tank and repeats the cycle. Strangely, the fussy looking float-valving system is not usually the source of vacuum tank problems. Things aren't always what they seem.

The innocuous looking flapper valve on the discharge port between the inner and outer tanks can cause plenty of trouble. It must not stick to its seat — where it likes to bind — and it must be able to seal against its seat. If this seal is the cause of problems, the valve face should be

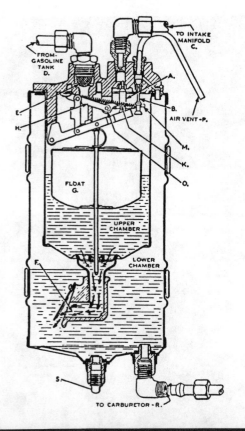

No doubt about it, vacuum tanks are finicky. The flapper valve below the inside tank can be a particular problem; it often sticks or leaks.

lapped onto its seat with a very fine abrasive. The inner tank itself is very prone to pinholing and internal leakage. It should be checked and resealed by soldering, if this is the problem. Then, every threaded connection and the top tank gaskets have to be perfect for the thing to work. Any accumulation of varnish or corrosion on the valve mechanism can cause malfunction. See why vacuum tanks are so beloved by restorers?

When a vacuum tank is restored, my preference is for etching the inner and outer tanks and having them retinned by someone with a tin pot. Almost any other coating will cause problems later. In fact, problems later are what vacuum tanks are all about. Don't feel badly if you restore one and find it failing every so often after that. If the flapper valve sticks, or the top gasket leaks about every third time that you want to use the car, you have arrived at the average for these units. Meticulous attention to the fine points may produce a vacuum tank that is almost reliable.

Camshaft-Driven Mechanical Fuel Pumps

From the 1930s on, mechanical fuel pumps came to dominate fuel delivery system design in this country. Most of these pumps were first manufactured by the AC division of General Motors, but later there were other manufacturers. The earliest pumps were pretty simple and tended to incorporate pull rod actuation with a straightforward diaphragm pump. By the mid-1930s, compound pumps with vacuum booster diaphragms began to appear. The purpose of the second pumping diaphragm was to provide adequate vacuum for windshield wipers during periods of low manifold vacuum (acceleration and low speed operation). By the 1950s, many pumps included a second, passive diaphragm in the fuel section to help damp out the pulsations that are inherent in any diaphragm pump.

Unfortunately, as fuel pumps became more complex and sophisticated, it has become more difficult to repair them. Early pumps tended to have their valving retained by large hex fittings that were easy to remove and replace. Later designs had the valving pressed in behind flimsy retainers that are often hard to remove and difficult to resecure, if they have been staked badly in a previous repair. By the time you get to some of the compound pumps, the valving and rebound springing can be pretty complex because there can be a lot of it.

Finally, in the march to make fuel pumps more difficult to repair, ultimate success was achieved with the development of the sealed (crimped together) disposable fuel pumps of the 1970s and after. These maddening units will fail for want of a 50¢ diaphragm or a 25¢ valve, and there is absolutely nothing that can be done to repair them. *I know, I know,* the labor to repair them would cost more than replacement, and this is the best approach. It's progress. Somehow that sounds good in the abstract, but can be a bit too theoretical when you have to pop for a $30 fuel pump that could have been repairable with less than a buck's worth of parts and half an hour of labor.

Mechanical fuel pump restoration is, in many ways, similar to carburetor restoration. The parts tend to be made out of the same materials, and such procedures as cleaning and flange straightening are basically the same for both of these fuel system components. Please refer to

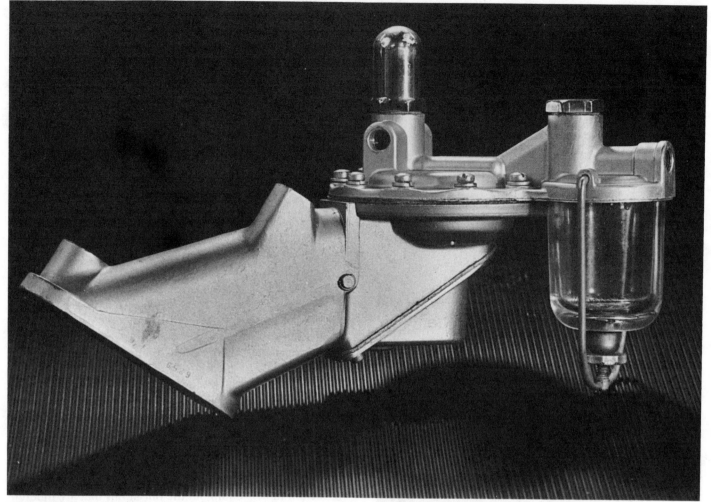

When camshaft driven fuel pumps first became popular, in the late 1920s, almost everyone agreed that this was a better way to deliver fuel.

the chapter on carburetor restoration for this background.

Aside from the obvious need for tight, leakproof connections and assemblies, there are several special considerations in fuel pump repair. The first is testing. Fuel pumps can be tested easily on a car by checking their output pressure, input suction, and delivery volume. Output pressure is tested with a low pressure gauge with the engine running for several seconds on the gas in the carburetor bowel. The gauge is held at about the level of the carburetor and connected to the carburetor input line fitting. From three to seven psi is about average for most pumps' output pressures, but check the specifications given by the manufacturer for exact values. Unfortunately, just because a pump can generate adequate pressure does not mean that it can also produce adequate fuel volume. Sometimes a fuel or air bubble, trapped between layers of an old diaphragm, will fill the pumping cavity to cause a pump to produce inadequate fuel volume, while maintaining adequate output pressure. An air leak on the vacuum side of the pump can cause the same result. To check pump delivery, run a hose from the pumps output line into a container with the end submerged at the bottom in gasoline. The pump should produce roughly a quart per minute at 500 engine rpm, and

there should be no air bubbles. Bubbles indicate an air leak somewhere in the pump, or in its supply lines. The vacuum side of the pump should indicate about 10 inches of Hg at the above engine rpm. If the pump is equipped with a booster vacuum pump (compound type), it should generate about eight inches of Hg from that section.

One of the laments that restorers experience with fuel pumps involves "N.O.S." units. Frequently when these pumps, or pumps that were rebuilt long ago, are put into service, they fail very quickly. This occurs because the diaphragm material has hardened. Although it will work for a short while, it soon cracks and leaks. The older diaphragm materials were tarred canvas, textile reinforced rubber, and primitive rubber substitutes. Later practice was to use textile reinforced synthetics like Neoprene. This was a vast improvement. The best diaphragm material that I know of for use today is nylon reinforced Nitrile. It is almost completely impervious to anything in gasoline and seems to resist hardening wonderfully. It is readily available in several thicknesses from any good gasket and packing supply house. In any case, if you are contemplating the use of an N.O.S. pump, or an older rebuild, consider making a new diaphragm for it before you install the pump in a car.

For the most part, cam driven fuel pumps are reliable. When they fail, it is usually because little items, like their valves (shown on the fingertips in this photo) or valve springs (shown between the fingers in the photo) have deteriorated. The valve disc on the left is worn badly enough to leak; the one on the right is new. Correcting fuel pump problems can be that subtle.

Most automotive vacuum gauges, like this one, have a pressure side to indicate fuel pump pressure. This is a good test to run on any fuel pump, but even if a pump delivers adequate pressure, be sure to check it for delivery volume. That can still be substandard and cause running problems.

Old fuel pump diaphragms are made from layered textile materials and get very hard as they age. Diaphragms cut from the Nylon reinforced Nitrile material, shown here, will last almost forever in fuel pump service. You can buy this material from most packing and gasket supply houses.

Disassembly and Reassembly of Mechanical Fuel Pumps

Before disassembling a fuel pump, always mark its major parts for phase, so that they can be reinstalled in the right orientation to each other. Barring such unusual problems as cracked or broken castings, almost all problems will be found in the mechanical linkage, inlet and outlet valves, diaphragm(s), or pull rod(s) and their seal(s). Any rebuild should deal with all of these areas.

Mechanical linkage and actuating and tensioning springs should be checked for corrosion, distortion, and breakage. Pivot points must be tight, and if they are not, rebushing them is necessary. The pump's cam follower has to be smooth and flat in the plane of the cam, and if a push rod is used, it has to be straight and undamaged by pitting or wear. Fuel pump valves have to be flat and smooth. It is always a good idea to replace them and their springs if these have been removed. Some valve seats are replaceable and others have to be lapped in the pump. In either case, it is a good idea to recondition the valves and their seats and check their performance with mild air pressure and suction. Valves are often held in place by staking the pump body over their retainer parts. Do this carefully, but securely. The pull rod seal is important and should be replaced in any rebuild. Any good kit will contain a new pull rod seal. The installation of this seal can be difficult. Check the illustration of proper and improper installation in the instructions that accompany your rebuild kit.

You'll need open stock parts like these, or a kit, to rebuild any fuel pump.

These fuel pump kit parts are pretty much what you will need to do a minor rebuild of most fuel pumps. Most fuel pump kits are made for more than one application, so there will usually be extra pieces when your rebuild is complete.

This is about what an average compound fuel pump will look like when its parts are all separated and laid out.

When you install a new diaphragm in a fuel pump pull rod, put a little dab of silicone rubber on the area where the pull rod goes through the diaphragm material. This will help to seal it. In this photo, note that the vise jaws holding the pull rod have been lined with wood to protect it. Fuel pump work is careful work.

Of course, main diaphragms and pulsation diaphragms (if so equipped) cause most of the problems in fuel pumps. Most of the older diaphragms have flanges nutted to the pull rod and are easy to replace. You simply buy or cut a new diaphragm piece and reattach the flanges. Be sure to save or duplicate any fiber spacers or cushions included in the diaphragm and flange assembly originally. Use a good thread-locking compound to lock the nut threads, and deform the nut slightly to prevent loosening. Go easy on this because someone, someday will have to rebuild the pump again, and he will need threads that are usable. Where the diaphragm and flanges are secured to the pull rod by swaging, it is usually possible to grind or file enough of the swage away to allow for disassembly and subsequent reassembly and reswaging. Sometimes swaged pull rods can be threaded and reassembled with a nut or a screw instead of a swage.

If you can't remove a valve seat from a pump body, or if it is only slightly eroded, you can often face it with the flat end of a wooden dowel and some very fine valve grinding compound. You do this in a drill press.

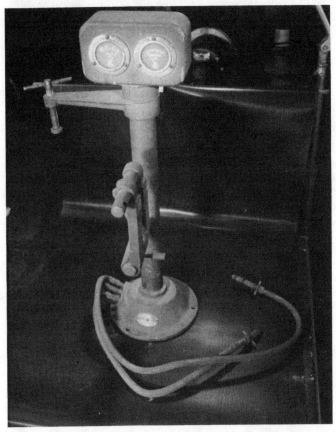

They used to test rebuilt fuel pumps on a tester like this one. By now, most mechanical fuel pumps are tested on a car.

This, of course, makes subsequent rebuilding easier. Whatever the method of securing a fuel pump's diaphragm and flanges to its pull rod is, it is a good idea to use just a smear of silicone rubber RTV compound to seal this joint.

Final assembly of mechanical pumps is relatively easy. Make sure that the valves are installed correctly — there is a logic to their position, *vis á vis* the pumping action, which is inescapable. Lubricate all linkage pivot points,

and be sure to put a dab of grease on the cam follower or push rod end. Give the diaphragm flanges a final tightening that is both even and sequenced across their diameter.

About the only thing that you can do wrong in installing a fuel pump is to get the cam follower on the wrong side of the cam. This sounds innocent, but the results can be disastrous. Be sure that you know which side of the follower goes against the cam, and that it is seated there. Installation is much easier if the engine is turned over until the flat side of the cam drive lobe is positioned against the cam follower during installation. Tighten the pump body to the crankcase securely and evenly against a fresh cork or composition gasket.

Electric Fuel Pumps

Electric fuel pumps were born partly in the fight against vapor lock and start-up starvation due to percolation. That sorry sequence occurs when an engine compartment heat soaks after a car engine is shut down and air no longer removes heat from the under-hood area. The high under-hood heat that results causes the gasoline in a carburetor bowl to percolate (boil), and when you go to start the car there is no gas in the carburetor. It takes many engine rotations with the starter to get gas to displace the air in the system. However, electric pumps start when a key is turned and do not require starter engine rotation to supply fuel pressure and force air out of the system. The pumping sections of most electrics are exactly the same as those in mechanical pumps. The difference is that an electromagnet is used to impulse them in most designs. This magnet is activated by a set of contact points which sense the position of the diaphragm and, thus, the need for another pump stroke.

This electric fuel pump can be inconspicuously installed in a frame rail, or elsewhere, to either assist or replace a mechanical fuel pump. This particular pump has a pressure regulator built into its top. Be careful not to let too much pressure get at a carburetor float when you install an electric fuel pump replacement or helper.

Most of the trouble with electrics is not diaphragm or valve related, it is simple pitting of their contact points. These can be dressed in some cases, and in other cases they have to be replaced. There are a few submersible electric pumps that have been used, but this design is mostly a recent application and involves rotary turbine/impeller type pumps. Very few British cars, such as Jaguar and Rolls-Royce, used electric rotary impeller type pumps that allowed the crisp ticking of the dashboard clock to be heard over what would otherwise have been the din created by fuel pump operation. These wonderful pumps delivered fuel with very little pulsation but, sadly, with very little reliability as well.

It is not unusual for the owners of old cars to replace vacuum tanks and mechanical fuel pumps with electric units. This has its advantages in helping to eliminate vapor lock and percolation related problems, but it also can have some drawbacks. In the case of vacuum tanks, the final feed to the carburetor is by gravity, so the float is designed to be operated by very low fuel pressures. On the other hand, most electric pumps deliver 6+ pounds, and this is too much for the float systems on vacuum tank-equipped cars. The float valves can't handle pressures like this. Even on cars with conventional mechanical pumps, replacement electric pumps frequently deliver twice the pressure that the system was designed for. Whenever an electric pump is used to replace an original non-electric delivery system, a pressure regulator should be added to the system to bring fuel delivery pressure into the range of what was originally provided for in the carburetor float valve design. One brand of inexpensive electric fuel pump has an adjustable pressure regulator built into it, but this regulator is between useless and worthless. If you use that pump, add another adjustable pressure regulator to the system.

Fuel Gauges

The earliest fuel gauges were foolproof. They were dead accurate, completely reliable, and cheap to construct. They did lack a certain elegance, not to say convenience. They were, of course, strips of wood resembling half of a yardstick with calibrations marked on them. One had but to remove a car's front seat, the tank cover, the tank cap, and stick the "gauge" into the gasoline. It instantly registered the fuel's exact level, no foolin' around.

By the teens, various mechanical gauges based on shellacked cork or soldered brass floats had come into use. In practice, the float level was translated through gearing onto the face of a rotary gauge. Usually the gauge was mounted directly on the tank and had to be read at the back of the car. In the case of the Ford Model A, a float system mounted in the gas tank, which was in the cowl, allowed for a dashboard gauge. Lincolns, for a few years in the mid-1920s, actually carried the mechanical motion of a gas tank float by cable linkage up to the dashboard where it was indicated on a geared rotary gauge.

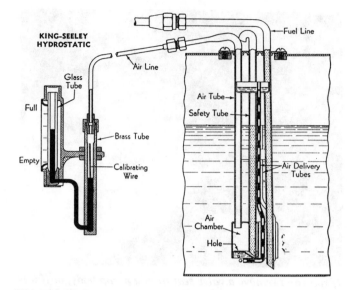

The King-Seeley hydrostatic fuel gauge was a great advance in its day, but it is a great headache today for many restorers. The capillary line that leads from the tank to the dash gauge has to be air tight and with out any crimps, and its solder and cement joints have to be perfect.

By the late 1920s, many cars used the King-Seeley hydrostatic gauge. This troublesome device used differential air pressure conducted from the tank, via a capillary tube, to a viscous tube indicator glass on the dash. These systems are a nightmare to maintain because their delicate capillary tubing is prone to damage, and the various soldered and cemented joints are frequently in a failure mode. The indicator fluid — many different fluids were used, with acetylene tetrabromide being the best of them — is frequently quite corrosive and is also susceptible to contamination damage, evaporation, and coagulation.

Electric fuel gauges are usually driven magnetically or by a heater and bimetallic element. There are a few oddball designs out there, like the King-Seeley bimetallic-heater-interrupter system that was used by Ford, Hudson, Nash, and a few others just before and just after World War II. Common heater and magnetic type electric fuel gauges use a gas tank float linked by a pivot-and-arm to a wound resistance coil and contacts that rub across it. This amounts to a rheostat which increases or decreases resistance as the float moves from "full" to "empty." In the magnetic type indicator (AC), the resistance in the tank sending unit increases as the tank is filled and the float rises. A single wire connects the dash gauge to the sending unit. Two balancing coils mounted at 90° to each other in the gauge pull the needle toward "full" and "empty," respectively. The coils are connected in series and grounded through the tank rheostat, with the coil on the "full" side having greater internal resistance than the coil on the "empty" side. As the resistance in the circuit increases, the coil on the "full" side will produce proportionally greater attraction for the needle. A variation on the magnetic system that was used by Autolite had a permanently energized magnetic coil on the "empty" side and a potentially stronger magnetic coil on the "full" side. In this system, an increase in fuel level in the tank produces a corresponding reduction resistance in the tank rheostat, and thus a stronger pull toward "full" on the gauge.

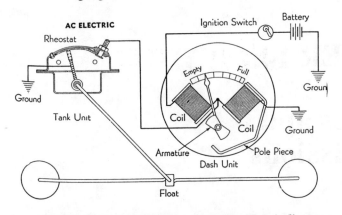

Electric fuel gauges are simple and reliable. They indicate on the basis of rheostat varied voltage that moves a bimetallic or a magnetic needle drive.

This universal replacement sending unit fits many applications. The float is slid on the drive arm and the arm is bent to duplicate an original sending unit. Then the float is secured to the arm. The reason that the rheostats in gas gauge sending units don't cause gas tank explosions is because they are designed with overlapping rheostat contacts that can't spark, and also because the mixture in a fuel tank is supposed to be too rich to ignite.

The heater type gauge, associated with Auto-lite and others, used a heater coil and bimetallic element to indicate fuel level. In this system, when a tank is full, the gauge wire is effectively grounded and the heater in the gauge receives the full voltage in the system. This, in turn, heats the bimetallic element and deflects a needle linked to it to the maximum degree, indicating "full." Less fuel in the tank means more grounding resistance and therefore less heat and less deflection of the bimetallic element and, thus, a lower gauge reading. The heater type gauges usually have a secondary heater that is designed to correct for ambient temperatures, such as occur on very hot or very cold days that would otherwise influence gauge readings.

Beyond cleaning the tank rheostat contacts and coil and dealing with any mechanical or electrical defects in the dash gauge units, none of these electric systems is particularly susceptible to rebuilding. Sending unit coil failure is a frequent problem, as is float failure. Heat type fuel gauge systems can be tested. The simplest way to accomplish this is to substitute a good tank sending unit for the one in the tank and determine by moving its float manually if the system fault lies in the sending unit, the gauge, or the wiring. In magnetic systems, grounding the sending unit and gas tank to the chassis is critical.

CHAPTER 14:

Clutches and Transmissions

Why They Are Needed

In the beginning of the age of self-propelled vehicles, it looked as if there wouldn't be any need for clutches or transmissions. That was just as well because there weren't any units "on the shelf" that could have been adopted readily to the needs of automobiles. The reason there was no need to couple and uncouple the engine of a vehicle from some cumbersome variable gearing device was that steam and electricity provided motive power for most of the earliest automobiles. In both cases, with some small allowances for rotary momentum, the "torque curves" of these propulsion units are virtually flat. Take steam, for example; the combustion is external to the engine and its speed has no effect on the pressure of the steam being applied to an engine's pistons. If you have, say, 100 psi of steam and supply it to a particular steam engine, the horsepower will be a function of that pressure and the dimensions and valving efficiency of the engine — with some allowance for friction, momentum, and other minor losses. The same applies to electricity as a source of motive power. Supply a certain level of power and you will generate a corresponding torque. This is true if the motor is turning over at 1 rpm or 1000 rpm — with some allowance for momentum.

Alas, the internal combustion, reciprocating engine has anything but a flat torque curve. In fact, its torque curve is so "peaky" that there is only a narrow band of rpms at which its power can be tapped for the business of driving a motor vehicle. Whereas a gearbox is a fine point on steam cars, for the esoteric purpose of limiting rpm to reduce engine wear, on internal combustion powered automobiles, it is a necessity. While the device (transmission) used to perform the function of changing drive ratios may appear in widely varying forms, its purpose is always the same, to mate the engine to the driving wheels at a rotational speed that falls within the range in which the engine produces sufficient torque to move the vehicle.

The variety of automotive mechanisms to gear and to couple and uncouple gearing devices is monumental. The human ingenuity applied to the design of this hardware over the years is astounding. Several different clutch materials and configurations have enjoyed popularity. Early clutches used such available friction facing materials as leather, cork inserts, and woven compositions of textile. Clutch configurations varied from cones to multiple wet and dry discs to single and compound three-element disc systems. The simplicity and compactness of the modern clutch was not possible until major advances in friction facing materials had occurred in the 1920s. By the 1930s, manufacturers like Borg and Beck and Long had pretty much standardized the format and materials of the modern clutch. After that, the evolution of clutches involved continued improvements in materials. This allowed ever lighter and more durable clutches to be produced. A few manufacturers, like Hudson, persisted in producing cars with distinctive clutches which utilized archaic facing materials such as cork. As well, some experimentation with configurations like diaphragm springing and carbon release bearings continued.

Early transmissions tended to divide between planetary gear (epicyclic) systems and sliding gear types. With the exception of the Model T Ford — Henry Ford could be a stubborn man — the planetary systems had pretty much given way to sliding gear units by the end of the first decade of the 20th century. By the 1930s, constant mesh, synchronized gearing began to appear on American cars. In the years after World War II, synchromesh-type systems became standard, and synchronization was applied to all gears, not just the top two ratios.

The other major thrust in automotive gearing devices was the development of the hydraulically operated planetary transmission — "automatic transmission" — just before and after World War II. Over the years, automatic transmissions became the most popular shifters. In the next few years, it is probable that steel belt driven CVTs (continuously variable transmissions), pioneered by Van Doorne in Holland on the DAF, and presently offered by Subaru as an option on their Justy, will come into common use.

These are the main trends in clutch and transmission design. There were also some wonderful "odd ball" de-

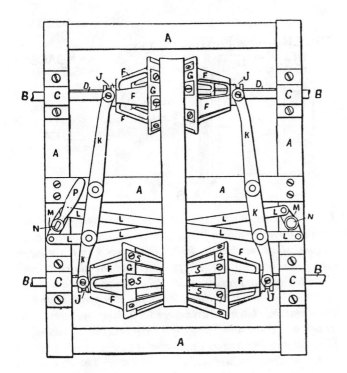

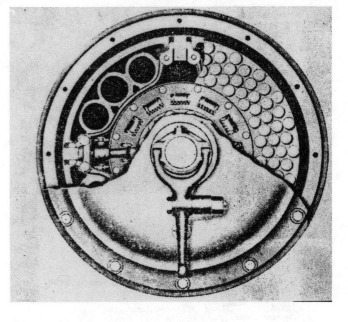

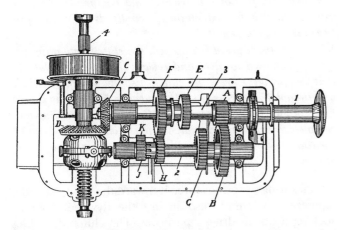

Over the years many different configurations and formats for clutches and transmissions have been used on automobiles. The first illustration shows a variable pulley-and-belt system that is remarkably similar in principle and layout to the ultra modern CVT (continuously variable transmission) systems that are just now coming into production.

If you thought that transaxles were something new, from Europe or Japan, have a look at this early 20th century transaxle unit used in a rear-wheel drive automobile. Note that this is a sliding gear design.

Hudson's famous cork insert clutch was used from almost the beginning on this company's cars to almost the end. It was a cumbersome system, but it worked.

Modern clutch design and materials had pretty much evolved by the 1930s and resulted in a very compact and efficient system. Note the horizontal central springs in the unit shown here. The splined hub drives the outer friction disc through these springs. This cushions the drive. These springs are called "clutch torsion springs," and if they are broken or deformed, a rough, jerky clutch disengagement may result.

signs, like Metz's and Cartercar's intriguing application of friction transmissions, or the fabulous Owen Magnetic's Entz drive, or the early mechanical/planetary transmission used on the mid-1930s Reo Royale. Some hybrid transmissions, like Chrysler's Vacamatic or the European Cotal and Wilson controls, predicted parts of the future. The variations are intriguing and almost endless.

The majority of collector cars are equipped with clutch/constant mesh gear change units, or with hydraulic/epicyclic automatics. Even within these two sys-

tem headings there is enormous variation in design and fabrication. Many of the automatically shifted units of both types are enormously complex. Clutch and transmission rebuilding is generally best left to specialists, but restorers should know how to remove and replace these units, how to diagnose their maladies, and how to provide for their maintenance. The thrust of this chapter on clutches and transmissions will be to these points.

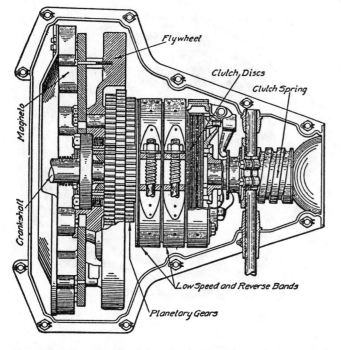

Henry Ford's epicyclic (planetary) gear transmission wasn't the latest item in transmission design in 1908 when the Model T was introduced, and it was certainly a dinosaur in 1927, when the venerable T was discontinued. However, for all of the quirks of its design, it was a compact and reasonably rugged gearing device for its time. It was certainly no more difficult to operate than the sliding gear transmissions that were its contemporaries in the early days of the Model T. Maybe Henry got the last laugh. With only a few exceptions, modern automatic transmissions get their gearing through epicyclic gear sets. However, the addition of torque converters and hydraulically controlled shifting is really what made Henry's beloved planetary gear clusters work.

Operation of the Conventional Three-Element Clutch

All friction clutches operate by squeezing a part or parts attached to the transmission between parts attached to the engine crankshaft. This squeezing is effected by spring pressure, and when a clutch is fully released (pedal out), the pressure is great enough to produce an almost total lockup of its members. When the clutch is uncoupled ("disengaged," or pedal down) the activating springs are compressed through the application of foot or other pressure applied through various linkage pieces. This uncouples the engine from the transmission by allowing the parts of the clutch assembly attached to the engine to spin free of the part or parts attached to the transmission.

In practice, a housing containing the pressure plate is bolted to an engine's flywheel, with a disc between the flywheel and pressure plate. This disc is completely free of attachment to the flywheel or pressure plate, except that when the pressure plate assembly is bolted up, the

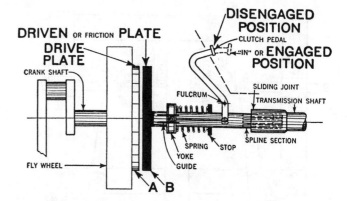

This schematic illustrates the action of a simple clutch. The "driven plate" or clutch "disc," which is splined to the transmission shaft, or "input shaft," is squeezed by a spring or springs between an engine's flywheel and the clutch "plate" or "intermediate pressure plate." The latter is in a housing that is bolted to the flywheel. When the foot pedal is pressed down and the clutch is "disengaged," linkage operates a "release" or "throw-out" bearing. This bearing is caused to press on pivoting fingers that withdraw the clutch's pressure plate from the flywheel and the clutch disc. The clutch disk can now spin free of the flywheel and engine. This allows transmission shaft to which the clutch disc is splined to spin free of the engine as well.

When the clutch pedal is released, the clutch actuating fingers are allowed to pivot and release the pressure plate so that its spring(s) press the clutch disc against the flywheel and immobilize the disc in this sandwich. The engine is now fully coupled to the transmission. Between full coupling and complete uncoupling, the clutch is partly engaged and can be used to smoothly couple or uncouple the engine and transmission.

clutch spring or springs force it toward the flywheel and it squeezes the clutch disc against the flywheel, thereby locking it up for driving purposes. The clutch disc rides on splines on the transmission input shaft. Therefore, when the flywheel and clutch assembly turn, with the clutch disc squeezed between them, the disc turns and turns the transmission input shaft as well.

When the clutch is disengaged its linkage withdraws the pressure plate a very small distance from the flywheel. This is usually done through levers which pivot in the clutch housing and move the pressure plate back a very small distance away from the flywheel. The moment the spring pressure on the pressure plate is mitigated by these levers, the clutch disc begins to slip. When the pressure plate has been moved back a half inch or so, the flywheel and clutch pressure plate will have no contact with the clutch disc and the engine will spin independently of the disc and transmission input shaft. When the clutch is partially released, the disc will drag on the pressure plate and flywheel, producing partial clutch engagement. This condition is used in breaking the momentum of a stationary vehicle and, to a lesser degree, in changing gears in a moving automobile.

The variations on the basic clutch described above mostly involve the use of multiple friction units. Instead

Clutches in General

Conventional three-element clutches are small, relatively inexpensive, and very efficient units. They can also cause more problems than would seem possible. For one thing, you usually can't see them operate or malfunction. Clutch work is very exacting work and an assembly misstep, or improperly placed greasy thumb print, can ruin the whole job. I have probably more failure after installation among clutches than with any other single major system in a car. When you get into wet clutches and multiple disc units, the attendant problems become even worse than with simple clutches.

I generally go through a clutch completely any time that I have it out for any reason. Clutches also become the objects of repair when they grab, judder, or slip. These maladies usually result from wear or distortion of the driven and driving parts of the clutch, but there are other possibilities, such as binding linkage or friction surface glazing due to leaking oil seals. One of the realities of clutch malfunction is that defects always get worse, and usually do so rapidly. For example, a leaking rear main bearing seal that sprays just a little oil onto the upper bell housing will cause clutch problems beyond what one might expect. When the oil drips down and gets onto the clutch facings, it will cause them to slip. If they slip, they will glaze to a point that causes juddering and further slipping. Further slipping will cause further overheating and warping, scoring, or heat checking of the three elements in the unit. So it goes; any defect that causes a clutch to slip or judder will quickly create other damage that will quickly render the clutch inoperative.

It's human nature to wait for improvement, and hope and pray that mysterious knocks, wraps, and other symptoms of problems in an automobile will go away. If they do, the remission is temporary at best. In the case of clutches, there will probably be no remission, and if repairs are not made soon after the onset of problems, further damage will occur. A juddering or slipping clutch has no good place to go without repair.

Clutch Removal

Removing a clutch is usually not difficult, but if the clutch is a big one, or lives in a one-piece transmission and bell housing, the job can be a clumsy business. It is important to accomplish it carefully, precisely, and with a certain degree of advance planning. Failure to plan clutch removal can result in stupidly watching a transmission dangle from its input shaft as it destroys the clutch disc and transmission input shaft.

The removal of most clutches requires that the transmission and bell housing be removed from the engine. A few can be removed with the bell housing in place through an access plate on top or bottom. In any case, the first order of business is to remove the transmission or

This "compound" clutch from the early 1930s employs two clutch discs and double pressure plates. This design was used to increase the amount of friction area in a clutch and thus prevent overheating and glazing. As facing materials improved, the need for this kind of cumbersome design evaporated, and single friction element clutches became the standard.

In the 1920s, some clutches were really elaborate, like this multiple element unit. Here more than fifteen interleavened plates and discs are alternately coupled by "saw teeth" to internal and external driving and driven members. Often, multiple disc clutches of this type ran in an oil bath.

of one pressure plate, there can be two or more used to squeeze two or more driving discs. In some clutches ten or more interleavened discs and plates are used to achieve smooth engagement and release. In almost all cases, the basic sandwich of driving and driven members described above is used.

transmission/bell housing unit. To do this, the clutch operating linkage is first removed in the simplest possible way. Some clutch linkage is complex, like Chrysler's "over-center" compensating linkage. In such cases, do not throw the linkage out of adjustment when you remove it because the special jigs required to readjust it are no longer available and you will spend a long time trying to get it right. Minor adjustment of complex linkage is much easier than having to start from scratch with it.

After removing clutch operating linkage, the next step is to unbolt one of the drive shaft U-joints and remove the drive shaft. Be sure to mark the relative positions of the U-joints flanges, yokes, or splines so that they can be reassembled in the same phase that they were in when they were taken apart. Now, position a good transmission jack under the transmission and adjust its tilt to cradle the transmission firmly. Strap the transmission securely to the jack and raise the jack to just contact the bottom of the transmission.

At this point, if you are removing a transmission from a bell housing, remove the two uppermost attaching bolts and install two guide pins. These pins can be purchased or easily fabricated by sawing the heads off two unhardened bolts that are the same size and thread as the transmission attaching bolts. The pins should have no more threads than can be engaged in the transmission bolt holes, and it is best to saw screw slots in their beheaded ends so that their installation and removal will be possible with a screwdriver. These guide pins should be about four or five inches long. Install them with the bolt holes on top of the transmission and remove the bottom fasteners. The transmission can now be slid back on the guide pins with the jack supporting its weight. If the transmission and bell housing are one piece, use the same procedure, with the guide pins on either side and near the top of the bell housing and threaded into the back of the engine block. The use of guide pins virtually

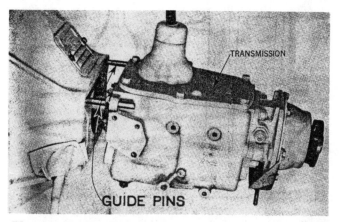

The use of guide pins, like the ones shown here, will greatly aid in the safety and ease of clutch removal and reattachment. You can make your own guide pins for this purpose by sawing the heads of soft bolts and sawing screw drive slots in their outer ends.

Guide pins help to prevent the terrible error of allowing a transmission to dangle on the end of its input shaft during the removal or reattachment process. That little goof can bend the shaft or bend the clutch disc.

eliminates the chance of having the transmission slip off the jack and hang on its input shaft.

Sometimes a transmission or transmission/bell housing gets frozen on an assembly rim or on locating pins that project from the surface it mates to. Then it is difficult to separate the two assemblies. If this happens, some prying force can be applied to the side of the transmission, but avoid trying to wedge anything into the sticking joint. It's tempting, but don't do it. In extreme cases, I have had great success in separating transmissions and transmission/bell housings from their mating members with a little rearward pull applied to the transmission case with a cable-come-along. The come-along is attached to the transmission case and rear axle. A few smart raps with a brass hammer in the area of seizure will usually do the trick, and a little heat may help, too. Remember that the area of separation is always a locating surface, and on wet clutches it is also a gasket surface. Treat it with respect.

Some older bell housings were assembled to their engines with shims, or used cam screws to achieve alignment of the transmission input shaft with the crankshaft. If there are any shims in a unit that you are disassembling, be sure to note their thickness and location so that they can be reassembled as they were taken apart. This will save you a lot of time and fuss later. Cam screws should be left alone.

Having removed the transmission and bell housing, you will have the clutch release fork and throw out bearing out as well. You will now have access to the clutch. Before you do anything else, note that there is a brown-gray dust covering the clutch housing and parts of the clutch. This stuff contains asbestos and is potentially deadly. Insofar as possible, avoid inhaling or touching it. It is best to dampen it with water and wipe it away. Avoid vacuuming it with a shop vacuum cleaner as it will go through the filter and into the air that you and others are breathing. There are special vacuum cleaners available for this purpose. NEVER blow this stuff around with compressed air.

You are now ready to remove the clutch from the flywheel. Since the existing balance of the rotating crankshaft system may have been achieved by balancing the shaft, flywheel, and clutch together, it is good practice to reinstall everything in the position that it was in at the time of disassembly. Of course, if a new or rebuilt clutch unit is being substituted for the one that was in service, this will be impossible. If you are not going to rebuild and reuse the original clutch, it is best to rebalance the crankshaft system with the clutch mounted. In any case, mark the clutch housing relative to the flywheel for reassembly. I always bring the engine to top dead center (TDC) and number stamp mark the clutch housing, the flywheel, and the crankshaft flange at their twelve o'clock positions. This makes reassembly easy. Use number stamps rather than punch marks for this for phase indication because previous mechanics are likely to already have used prick punch marks for this purpose and more punch marks will only confuse things.

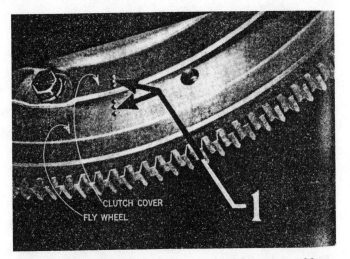

Over the years, the clutches were removed from most old cars for repair or replacement, and mechanics left behind punch marks, like these. Often there are enough marks to be very confusing when you go to reassemble a clutch to a flywheel. The best practice is to use a number stamp that cannot be confused with previous punch marks.

Removal of a clutch from a flywheel will require either blocking the clutch fingers open with one or more blocks of wood or removing the clutch housing to flywheel fasteners, half a turn at a time, and working across the housing for each loosening. Any other procedure will apply the clutch springs unevenly against the pressure plate and very probably bend the housing. When all clutch fasteners have been loosened to the stage of finger tight, you can remove them the rest of the way without worrying about this. At this point, a clutch aligning arbor or other rod of the right diameter should be inserted through the clutch disc hub and into the pilot bearing so that when the clutch housing fasteners are taken out of the flywheel, the clutch disc doesn't drop out. You can then finish undoing the housing fasteners and remove the housing and clutch disc. Be sure to note whether the disc hub is facing forward or backward with respect to the flywheel. In a very few cases, there is no difference, and in most others the disc will only install one way. There are some cases where it will seem to install either way, but will not work properly the wrong way. It's better to note its correct installation position at this point than to have to experiment with it later.

Clutch Inspection and Diagnosis

The environment in which a clutch operates is often the culprit in causing its failure. Be sure to check the rear main bearing seal for oil leakage, and the transmission input seal, if so equipped. It is pointless to replace a clutch if there is any possibility of it becoming oil soaked again soon after replacement.

Clutch discs should be checked for wear (thickness) and replaced if they are beyond manufacturers' recommended limits. If you don't have specifications, you should strongly consider replacement of an old clutch disc with a rebuilt unit when the disc surfaces are worn to within a tenth of an inch of the attaching rivet heads. This pertains if there are no other problems with a disc. If a disc is glazed, oil soaked, or checked, or if there is any evidence of warping, it should be replaced. If the torsion springs clustered around a clutch's hub are loose, or if the splines are sloppy on the transmission input shaft, hub replacement is necessary. The only defect in a clutch that can be dealt with without replacement is mild glazing. This condition can sometimes be cured by block sanding with 240 grit open-coat sandpaper to break the glaze. If you choose to do this, remember that you are sanding asbestos and there are considerable health hazards involved.

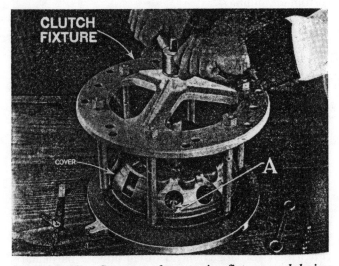

Special holding fixtures and measuring fixtures and devices are necessary to properly disassemble and reassemble clutch pressure plate assemblies. This is work best left to professionals.

The iron friction surfaces of the clutch system — flywheel face and pressure plate — are also susceptible to a whole inventory of defects. Most of these, warping, glazing, superficial cracks, hard spots, and scoring, can be dealt with by grinding. In the case of the pressure plate or plates, this procedure is accomplished during the rebuilding process. If you have this work done, or use an exchange clutch unit, you will still have to deal with the flywheel surface. Flywheels should always be ground when clutch work is done, and the grinding is best done on a special flywheel grinding machine. If reasonable grinding does not remove all defects, the flywheel will have to be replaced. Never install a flywheel with cracks in the clutch facing area. If cracks cannot be ground out at a reasonable depth, replace the flywheel. Flywheels with cracks are dangerous, and besides, the metal in the area of the crack is likely to be harder than the surrounding material and will quickly cause clutch judder in the "repaired" unit.

The pressure plate/clutch assembly can often be adjusted if it has finger actuation as opposed to actuation by a diaphragm spring. Beyond this, work on clutches requires specialized fixtures, measuring devices, and parts.

While it is possible for generalists to repair these units, I vastly prefer enlisting the aid of clutch specialists. Virtually every major industrial city has one or more clutch specialty houses. These people can reface your disc(s) with appropriate materials and gauge the overall setup of your clutch. The older houses often have specification books for clutches that reach back into the early 20th century. Armed with this knowledge, they are able to replace springs, cups, pins, levers, and other parts that will bring the repaired clutch back to its original tolerances and loading figures. Since many manufacturers did not change their clutches for runs of several years, there are still many exchange units available in rebuilder stocks for older cars. Check this out before you have a clutch rebuilt because an exchange will probably be less expensive than custom rebuilding.

A note of caution is in order regarding exchange clutches. It is not unusual for several clutch applications to share common housings. This means that you can get an exchange housing that bolts correctly to your flywheel but has the wrong number of clutch springs, or the wrong specification springs, or incorrect lever ratios. When you install an exchange clutch, make sure that the number of springs matches that in the original, and if you have any doubts about it, take it to a clutch house and have its loading measured. Another problem with exchange clutches is that some of them are rebuilt late at night at Joe's Saloon, Bar-B-Que, and Automotive Component Rebuilding Facility. They must be because I have seen exchange clutches that are as bad as some of the carburetors that they do at Joe's. Always eyeball any exchange clutch that you are going to install and be particularly careful to note that the fingers are adjusted correctly. This means that they should all be at the same altitude as measured from the housing top, flywheel face, or whatever other measurement method is specified for the particular clutch that you are working on. On some older clutches, the spring tension of the pressure plate can be adjusted for each spring, and it is good practice to leave this adjustment alone unless you are going to rebuild the clutch completely and understand the method for setting and equalizing spring pressure.

For a clutch to operate properly, the transmission input shaft that supports the clutch disc must run true. This means that it must be checked for straightness. The pilot bearing that supports it in the crankshaft and the transmission bearing that supports its rear end must both be in good condition. Always remove and replace pilot bushings when doing clutch work. If the pilot bearing is a ball bearing, it should be inspected and carefully cleaned and lightly lubricated before reinstallation. The splines on the transmission input shaft must be unworn and free of burrs, distortion and other defects. They must mate with the clutch disc hub freely and smoothly.

Sometimes clutch problems are caused by problems in the attachment of a flywheel to a crankshaft. Dirt at this interface, or a warped flange or bent flywheel, or any burrs will cause malfunction. It is always a good idea to check the flywheel for horizontal run-out with a dial indicator after it is ground and installed. It is also a good

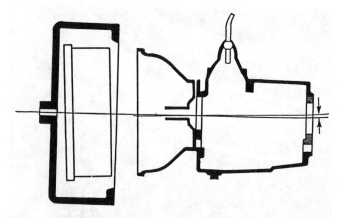

Inspection of this graphic will indicate several possibilities of clutch misalignment. The one shown here is flywheel misalignment, but it could as easily be bell housing or transmission misalignment. No matter what the cause of misalignment in a clutch/transmission system, the result will always be the same, rapid clutch failure.
One way to check for misalignment is with a dial indicator attached to and centered on the clutch housing. Indications from the bell housing surface that mates to the transmission will allow you to check for lateral and in-and-out deviations from concentricity and true.

practice to use a dial indicator to check the back face of the clutch housing for run-out which would indicate a warped clutch housing.

The inspection and diagnosis of clutches will be more fruitful if you know the initial problem with the unit. Then you can try to remedy it in the rebuilding or restoration process. Simply rebuilding in the hope that the problem will somehow be eliminated will often prove futile. Problems that involve warping and distortion of clutch components, or related components, must be tracked down specifically and corrected on that basis.

Clutch Installation

The installation of simple clutches is not particularly difficult, but it has to be done carefully to avoid ruining the job. It is essential that the clutch facings, pressure plate, and flywheel surfaces be kept clean of all oil and grease. It is a good idea to spray them and wipe them down with a non-petroleum, evaporating cleaner (a good aerosol brake cleaner is perfect for the job) and blow them off prior to assembly. This will remove any minor traces of oil or grease that may have accidentally gotten on them when they were handled prior to installation. Any grit left from grinding or deglazing must also be removed at this point.

The first order of business in installing a clutch is to install the pilot bearing in the end of the crankshaft. Pilot bearing spin-out is not uncommon, so make sure that the pilot bearing fits snugly into its bore. Stake it in with a punch if necessary. Treatment with one of the less aggressive anaerobic retaining compounds (Loctite, Fel-

Pro, etc.) will help with steel backed bushings and bearings, but is of questionable value on the more common Oilite (sintered bronze) type. Ball bearing-type pilot bearings require a sparing application of high temperature grease in the ball/race area. Bushing type pilot bearings should be lightly coated in their bores with a high temperature grease. This is also a good time to lightly grease the throw-out bearing and install it on the transmission input shaft sleeve. The sleeve and the grease recess in the bearing carrier should be lightly greased, as should the splines on the clutch hub and transmission input shaft where it rides. All of these areas should be greased for the clutch to work smoothly, but most of them rotate and can throw grease off onto the clutch friction surfaces if it is applied to them in excess. It is essential that any grease applied to these areas is kept to a thin layer. I usually paint it on with a solder tinning brush.

At this point, a clutch aligning arbor with the correct pilot adapter should be inserted through the clutch disc and into the pilot bearing. Be sure that the disc hub is facing the same way that it was at the time of disassembly. Matching the phase markings that you made at the time of disassembly, bring the pressure plate and clutch housing up to the flywheel. Secure the clutch housing loosely to the flywheel with a few symmetrically placed fasteners. Be sure to use graded fasteners and be sure that they are free of cracks and that the threads are in good shape. Clutch fasteners can break or come undone, and this causes a real hazard. Worn or stretched fasteners are dangerous, so replace old fasteners with new ones if you have any doubts about their integrity. Whatever system was used to retain the clutch housing-to-flywheel fastener heads — bend-tabs, wire, cotter keys, lock washers, star washers, etc. — must be reinstalled in good condition. This is no place to economize by reusing old lock washers.

When all of the fasteners have been tightened finger tight, they should be snugged down half a turn at a time in a pattern that works across the clutch housing until they are evenly tightened to the correct torque. The clutch aligning tool can now be pulled out of the pilot bearing in the crankshaft.

If the clutch that you are working on has a bell housing that separates from its transmission, the bell housing should be installed and a dial indicator should be set up on the flywheel to check for concentricity and parallelism of the bell housing-transmission mating surface and the clutch and flywheel. Some bell housings have eccentric locating cams that can be used to achieve concentricity. Sometimes shims will have to be used to achieve parallelism. This may all sound finicky, but it is not all that unusual to find misalignment in bell housings. If a clutch was in trouble before a rebuild and no other cause of the malfunction has been found, alignment is a good possibility.

Using the guide pins that were employed for clutch removal, the transmission should now be installed with a transmission jack. On some smaller transmissions, it is possible to wrestle the tranny up and into place without a

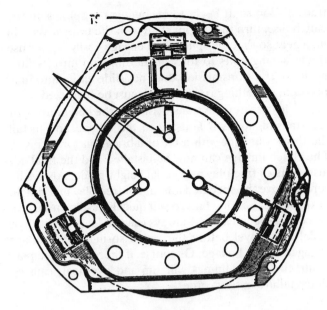

The three (more for some clutches) actuating fingers shown in this graphic have to contact the clutch release bearing at exactly the same time for a clutch to work properly. If one finger hits before or after the others, the clutch will judder. Always check this factor with a thickness ("feeler") gauge before you put a clutch back into service.

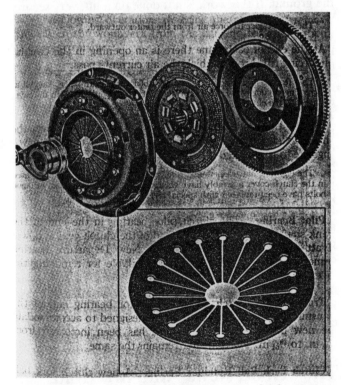

"Diaphragm spring" type clutches are one fairly common variation on the basic clutch theme. In this design, used on many Chevrolets in the late 1940s, a plate spring is pivoted off of holes near its outer edge and made to drive a clutch intermediate plate in-and-out as the spring's inner fingers are pushed in and released by the throw-out bearing.

jack, but don't try this with heavy transmissions. In any case, avoid letting the weight of the transmission hang off its input shaft — guide pins should be used to preclude this — or you will bend the shaft. As the splines on the transmission shaft begin to encounter the splines on the clutch disc, turn the output shaft with the transmission in high gear so that the splines can engage easily. Never use the attaching bolts to force a transmission into its final position. If a transmission does not slide easily into final position, something is wrong and must be corrected.

Finish attaching the transmission to the bell housing or the transmission/bell housing to the engine and install the throw-out fork with a bit of lubrication for its pivot. The clutch linkage can now be installed and the final adjustments of free play and pedal height made. Always be sure to leave the specified amount of free play in a clutch, or throw out bearing failure will quickly result. In the absence of a specification, I always leave at least one inch of pedal free travel before the clutch spring or levers are engaged by the linkage. Of course, if there is no free play at all, the clutch linings will slip and overheat, causing clutch failure in short order.

Other Considerations

Throughout the clutch removal and installation procedures, a car will have to be elevated a foot or more from the ground. If this work is not done on a lift, very secure wheel stands or jack stands should be used. Be sure that any car that you work on is secure because some of the loosening and tightening operations in this work will tend to push it laterally.

The above description of clutch work pertains to the simplest form of clutch which had its origins before the 1920s, became common in the 1930s, and is still in use today. There were many other types of clutches and some of them can be pretty hairy to work on. It is always necessary to have data on repair and adjustment to recondition the more complex clutches. There are certain logical propositions which should also be taken for guidance. For example, all clutches need to have even springing and, if levers are used, some method of equalizing spring pressure is necessary. All propositions in clutch work come from the simple logic of what clutches do, but some of the materials and configurations used in clutches can be difficult to dope out. If you work on complex clutches, be sure that you completely understand how things operate before you disassemble them.

The "Good News" and the "Bad News" About Transmissions

The good news about transmissions is that many of them are capable of going 200,000 miles, or more, without repair, as long as the minimum amenities of maintenance are observed. The bad news is that some of them are inherently trouble prone — particularly early automatics — and bad maintenance can cause even the best of them to fail before their times.

In the normal course of owning old cars, you are likely to have to rebuild five or ten engines for every transmission that you have to take apart. Even then, frequently transmission problems, like broken detente springs on standard transmissions, will yield to repair with very little disassembly. Even some of the more complex automatics can often be repaired with very little disassembly. Take, for example, the notorious Buick Dynaflow "no reverse" syndrome that has afflicted almost all Buicks made from 1948 to 1964. The problem was caused by a broken reverse band holding strut and the fix could be made by simply removing the pan, filter, and valve body, and installing an aftermarket strut kit.

When you do have to go into a transmission, you may find what seem to be handfulls of little parts that come apart far more easily than they go back together. This does not pertain to early sliding gear transmissions, but to modern automatics and modern synchronized four- and five-speed units. These are marvels of complexity and the tendency to assemble a lot of little parts into small spaces.

I think that my most unpleasant transmission rebuilding experience was with a Saburu 360 (the so-called "Japanese Beetle") which had a five-speed synchronized transmission that was assembled in a casting that parted as halves of the crankcase. The whole integrated engine/transaxle unit was about the size of a hat box. Items like that little monster should make anyone a fan of a relatively simple Ford or Chevrolet three-speed. Some automatics are nightmarish in their complexity, and I don't claim competence in their diagnosis or repair. Early Hydramatics fall into this category, as do Packard Ultramatics. Of the automatics, Chrysler's early Torqueflite units are my favorites and are among the easiest automatics to work on. They are also so well designed and constructed that they need about half of the attention that some of the more complex units require.

It is interesting to note that when workshop manuals came into common use to supplant owners' manuals as sources of repair information — this was in the late 1920s and early 1930s for many automakers — they usually had relatively brief sections devoted to transmission fault diagnosis, removal, and repair. Such sections were about the same length as the chapters on wheels and tires or suspensions. With the advent of synchronized gearing, and the attendant complexity of these systems, the transmission sections of shop manuals grew to equal the sections devoted to electrical data. Then, when General Motors introduced hydraulically controlled automatic planetary gearing in the late 1930s (Hydramatic), the transmission sections of the shop manuals that covered these cars grew to nearly half of the bulk of the manuals, or had to be issued as separate books. From then on, it was a good bet that any shop manual covering cars with automatic transmissions would devote half of its pages to this topic, and that half of the special tools that were recommended for servicing these cars would pertain to their automatic transmissions.

Of course, the development of the hydraulically controlled automatic transmission after World War II was one of the automotive wonders of the age. Europeans, with their Cotal and Wilson units, had nothing that came close in convenience or reliability. Car producers like Rolls-Royce and Mercedes-Benz used American automatics from manufacturers like General Motors and Borg Warner because there was nothing produced in Europe to match them. It is only recently that several Japanese and European companies have come up with world class automatic transmissions.

One of the reasons that the development of the automatic transmission was so long in coming and spreading is that the manufacturing technology involved necessitates a level of precision that is well beyond the toler-

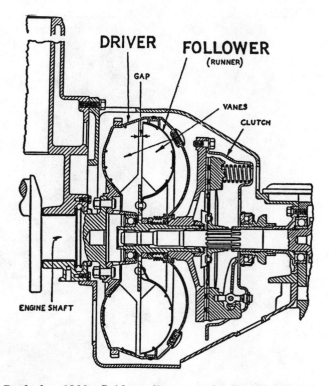

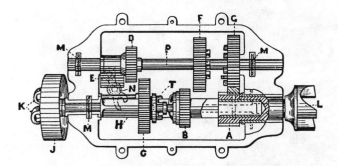

The earliest geared automobile transmissions (a) were sliding gear types. The teeth of the gears in these units were slid in and out of engagement on square or splined shafts. These transmissions had to have large, rugged gears, due to the wear and tear of engagement on the teeth.

By the late 1930s, fluid couplings were developed by Chrysler and others. The unit shown here is coupled to a conventional clutch and a conventional, semi-automatically shifted, synchronized transmission. This semi-automatic two-speed unit had to be clutched into first gear when a car was first put into motion, but then shifted automatically.

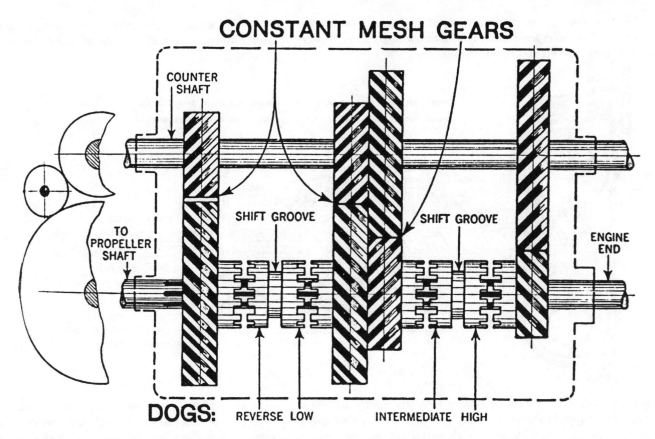

Later, constant mesh transmissions (b) replaced the sliding gear types. In the constant mesh units, the driving and driven gears are all always in mesh. Power is directed to the desired gear set by couplers that lock them to the appropriate shafts.

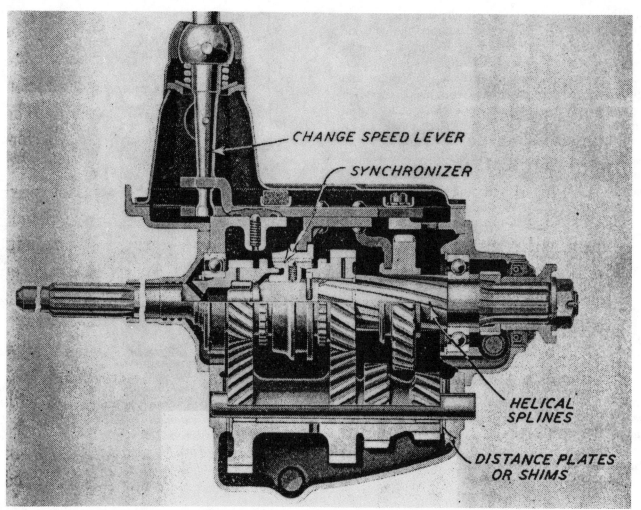

By the 1930s, various forms of gear synchronizing devices (now almost universally called "Synchromesh") were developed to prevent the shaft engagers from clashing with the engagers on their gears. Compact transmissions, like the one pictured here, were still possible, even with the synchronizing hardware.

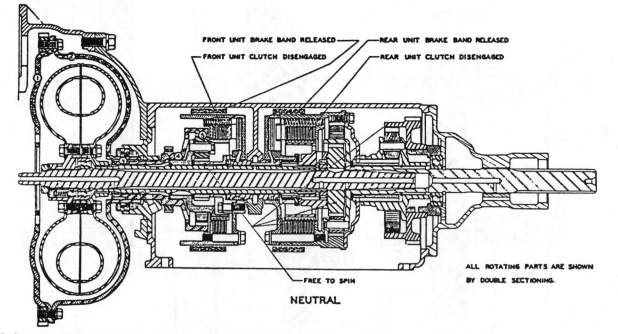

Just before World War II, General Motors developed a fully automatic transmission (Hydramatic) which utilized a torque converter and hydraulically shifted planetary gear sets. In this arrangement, the torque converter has a "stator" with variable pitch blades. This makes it possible to multiply engine torque and provide the effect of small gearing changes. Larger changes are achieved by coupling and uncoupling different ratio planetary gear sets by applying hydraulic pressure to tighten or loosen bands applied over the planet drums.

ances of other systems in most automobiles. Automatic transmissions require the mass production of components that in some cases have to be held to specifications of dimension and finish as tight as those for jet aircraft engines. Yet, as late as the World War II era, Chrysler astounded the technical world with the "Superfinish" process (actually a liquid honing procedure) that was used on the brass sealing components of their fluid drive clutches. We've come a long way since then.

This discussion of the restoration aspects of transmissions must, necessarily, be very general in scope. Actual repair procedures are so varied and specific in nature that it would take a library of books to cover them adequately. Every distinctive transmission, automatic or manual, comes apart differently and needs specific procedures to effect adjustments and repairs. Some of this is best left to experienced transmission mechanics with the requisite special tools and knowledge. The simpler transmissions, early planetary, sliding gear, constant mesh, and automatically shifted constant mesh will yield to amateur repair in some cases. Some generalities regarding these units will be covered here. Fault diagnosis and maintenance will also be discussed.

The Maintenance of Standard Transmissions

Standard transmissions are usually trouble free for long periods and great distances, if they are operated properly and if they receive good lubrication. If, on the other hand, they are regularly shifted in a violent manner, or operated with a dragging clutch, or need, but don't have, a working clutch brake (sliding gear type) they will suffer severe damage. If they run dry, or their lubricant is contaminated with water, debris or dirt, they will inevitably suffer failure. Transmissions are difficult enough and expensive enough to rebuild to make it good sense to attend to their maintenance. There are numerous "quick fixes" for specific transmission faults — all of them evade the real issues, though some of them will work for a while. Who among us has not owned a car with a synchronized transmission that someone treated for synchro failure with a handful of sawdust? The old handful-of-sawdust or rosin trick will work to fix a malfunctioning gear synchronizer in the short run. In the medium run it will severely damage a transmission that may have only needed minor repair before this kind of shoddy fix was attempted.

Likewise, a transmission that regularly slips out of second gear is often dealt with by the expedient of tying a short loop of rope to the dashboard so that it can be used to restrain the shifter in second. This evades the problem of a worn fork or rail, or a broken detente spring, or even a bad clutch pilot bearing. The repair of these items is so easy that it is a waste of good rope to go the Neanderthal route. Besides, alert judges always deduct points for rope. If you have mechanical problems with a transmis-

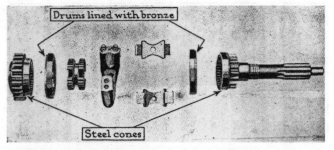

These are parts that are typical of the synchronizer setups in old manual transmissions. Early synchronizers were not terribly complex or durable and they do usually come apart and reassemble fairly easily.

sion, diagnose and repair them.

The routine maintenance of standard transmissions mostly involves keeping their linkages adjusted, keeping them filled to the correct level with the right specification of good quality lubricant, and keeping any venting devices clear of clogging. It is a good idea to periodically flush standard transmissions with a good solvent and then thoroughly dry them before refilling them with lubricant. This should be done about once or twice every decade, depending on storage and use.

On transmissions that are linked to their shifters externally (column shift), there is usually a provision for linkage adjustment. In most cases this is a simple matter of centering the linkage on the fork levers. Sometimes stay slots or pin slots are provided to get the linkage into the correct position before locking it to the shift levers on the transmission. If you have any questions about linkage adjustment procedures, consult an appropriate data source (shop manual or general car repair manual). The worst linkage problem that you are likely to encounter is worn or bent linkage in column shifts. There is no quick fix for this problem and bushings or levers and rods will have to be replaced to restore the operation of this shift linkage.

Modern manual transmissions often run in multi-grade motor oils or ATF (automatic transmission fluid). I don't like that idea because some of the additives in such fluids are inappropriate to lubricating transmissions, but that's what Honda and General Motors, among others, specify. Older transmissions run on anything from 600W boiler grease to mineral oil to modern EP (extreme pressure) lubricants. Some of the older lubricant designations, like "110 F.W.," can be troublesome to correlate to modern lubricant nomenclature. In this case, "F.W." stood for "Free Wheeling" and the numbers in that scale run a bit higher than the SAE (Society of Automotive Engineers) Gear Oil numbers that are currently in use. These SAE gear oil numbers that most of us are familiar with do not correlate to the SAE numbers used for motor oils. SAE 50 motor oil, in fact, has the same viscosity as SAE 90 gear oil. To make matters worse (or better, depending on your point of view), a new system, "ISO-VG" is probably about to descend on us and introduce a whole new cause for confusion (or clarification, again, depending on your point of view). The accompanying chart of oil viscosity relationships should help you keep some of this sorted out.

SAE MOTOR OIL	SAE GEAR
--	--
--	--
--	--
10	75
10	--
20	80
30	--
40	85
50	90
--	--
--	140
--	--

It is a little known fact that the SAE specifications for gear oils and motor oils involve two completely different scales. Reference to the accompanying "viscosity cross reference chart" will indicate that an SAE 50 weight motor oil is the same viscosity as an SAE 90 weight gear oil.

To a point it makes sense to use a slightly heavier lubricant than was specified when lubricating a slightly worn transmission. However, if you are going to drive in the winter, this can make shifting hard, and in very cold climates the thicker oils, like SAE 140 gear oil, will tend to channel and damage a transmission. I keep a mixture of SAE 90 and 140 gear oil around for older cars that spec-

ify 110 F.W. or any SAE viscosity from 75 to 90. A mix of equal quantities of 90 and 140 produces an actual viscosity of around 105 — when you mix oils of differing viscosities the results will tend toward the lower number by some very complex factor.

Almost all modern gear oils are of the EP (extreme pressure) type. The designations "hypoid" and "multipurpose" or "APG" ("all purpose gear") mean the same thing as EP. These oils were developed to combat the gear face pressures generated by hypoid rear end gears — introduced by Chrysler in 1934 on the Airflow for the sole purpose of lowering the floor line — and the resulting heat. They have phosphorus and sulfur based additives that tend to combine at a glacially slow rate with the steel in gear faces and thus achieve a coating action that simple viscosity could not achieve at elevated running temperatures. The trouble is that gears that run in these lubricants have to be made of specially formulated steel alloys. These alloys only came into use after the introduction of hypoid gearing and hypoid lubricants. Hypoid lubricants can be very corrosive and can etch bronze and brass and, given enough time — usually decades — they can also pit, and even weld, gears through electrolytic reaction. Of course, this damage occurs to gears in cars that were designed before hypoid gearing appeared on the scene, and before EP gear oils became the universally available gear lubricants.

Since transmission gears do not produce the kinds of face pressures or oil temperatures that require EP lubricants, and since these lubricants can be very bad for such things as planetary overdrive units, I avoid using them in transmissions. This is a fine point, but fine points are what restoration is all about. Some of the manufacturers of EP/MultiPurpose/APG/hypoid lubricants claim that the extreme pressure additives in their formulations are not activated until they reach elevated temperatures, but I have my doubts about this.

Okay, if you are *not* to going to continue to use the ubiquitous yellow squeeze bottles of Penzoil 80-90 EP gear oil, what are you going to use? With a little effort you could probably lay your hands on some straight mineral oil in the right viscosity range and that would be pretty close to what a 1920s or 1930s car originally used in its rear end or transmission. But lubricant technology has come a long way since then. Modern gear lubricants have all kinds of neat anti-scuff, anti-corrosion, antifoam, etc. additive packages. You want that stuff. Fiske Brothers, the makers of the Lubriplate line, still manufacture 90 and 140 weight lubricants that have all of the good additives except the EP package. These are designated as products #4, #8, and SPO series gear oils. For my money they are the highest quality non-EP quality lubricants available anywhere. They are optimum for use in any transmission and in any non-hypoid rear end. Never use them in hypoid rear ends because disaster will soon follow.

There is, of course, the possibility of using synthetic, non-EP lubricants in standard transmissions made after the mid 1930s, and this is a very attractive possibility due to the superior lubricating and viscosity stability characteristics inherent in these formulations. The trouble is that some of what is sold as "synthetic" lubricant is snake oil — beware of the guys who go door-to-door with this stuff. Even the good synthetics will rapidly eat Neoprene and some other seal compounds that are found in the transmissions of older cars. That's why they should never be used in pre 1970s cars. A final and often overlooked aspect of routine transmission maintenance is to make sure that if an air vent is provided for your transmission, it is clear. Failure to do this can get you involved in seal replacement before it would otherwise be necessary.

Standard Transmission Fault Diagnosis and Repair

If it works, leave it alone. Clean the outside of the case, flush the inside, but don't disassemble a transmission if there is no indication of fault. It's a waste of time, and you may regret such a venture when it comes time to put the thing back together. If you encounter a problem, such as worn shift rails, a broken detente spring, or a leaking seal, satisfy yourself with repairing just the offending part or system. Resist the temptation to get out the spanners and pullers for a total disassembly. Once you remove the access plate(s) and clean things up inside a bit, you should be able to inspect a transmission completely to determine the presence of problems like chipped teeth, worn shafts, or rough or sloppy bearings or bushings.

Almost all transmission problems will manifest themselves in four simple types of symptoms: noise and vibration, gear clash when shifting, jumping out of gear, and lubricant leaks. Except for the last symptom, any one of these can be caused by a transmission problem or a clutch defect. Over the years, untold numbers of transmissions have been ripped out and torn down to correct problems that had their causes in clutch malfunctions. Clutches are usually easier to repair than transmissions, and much more likely to cause problems. Be sure to eliminate clutch problems before proceeding with a transmission rebuild.

If diagnosis and inspection have revealed a true transmission fault, remove the transmission as outlined in the clutch section of this chapter and look for the fault. Clean things up and inspect gears, shafts, synchronizer cones, springs, bearings, retainers, and engager teeth. All of these should be smooth and within reasonable wear limits. If you find a broken gear, or any other broken or badly deformed part, you should Magnaflux every stressed component in the transmission, including the case.

Since the same people who design transmissions are also the authors of the more advanced jigsaw puzzles, you had best have "the book" available before you attempt transmission disassembly and repair. You will need disassembly/assembly procedures and the specifications for shaft end play and shimming and adjustment, among other things, for any complex unit. A shop manual will

Some transmission specifications are easy to check, like this simple clearance dimension, but others require specialized gauging devices.

also speed disassembly and may prevent catastrophic mistakes. Transmission disassembly sometimes requires force, but usually very little, and always in the right places. Two-pound hammers and nine-pound slide hammers are a bad idea.

If you do have the gear clusters and shafts out of a transmission, look at the bearings very critically and if they are at all deteriorated, replace them with exact duplicates. Always use new snap rings if this method is used to retain parts. If wiring is used for this purpose, be sure to replace it in an effective and correct manner. New plugs and gaskets should also be used. On later synchronized transmissions, there are lots of little parts, and sometimes special fixtures are needed to reassemble the clusters. Again, a good shop or general repair manual is invaluable in this work if you are inexperienced at it.

Automatic Transmission Maintenance and Adjustment

Modern automatic transmissions — World War II era and after — are comprised of three basic systems: one or more fluid couplings or torque converters, one or more planetary gearsets, and a hydraulic or hydraulic/vacuum or hydraulic/electric control system. If this sounds complicated, that is because it is. The repair of these units can be a complex proposition and is usually best left to specialists. I have often said that automobile repair and restoration is not nuclear physics and can be understood by most people. Automatic transmission repair may well be the exception to this.

There are not too many things that a driver can do to damage an automatic transmission without trying, but there are a few. Shifts from "park" or "neutral" into a driving range at high rpm, or into park at speed can damage a transmission. The shift into park shouldn't be a problem, but if the pawl locking device malfunctions, great damage can occur. A more subtle way to damage some automatics is to tow a car without disconnecting the drive shaft, or to push start a car for substantial distances. Some automatics can take this and some can't. It depends on whether or not they have a rear oil pump and whether rear and front pump output are needed for lubrication and drive. Consult the appropriate owner's manual or motor manual to determine if a particular automatic is susceptible to push starting or towing.

The maintenance of automatics consists of some minor adjustments on some units, checking some parts for function on some units, and maintaining the hydraulic fluid on all units. First the fluid. Its nomenclature can be confusing. Such terms as "Type A, Suffix A" or "Type F" or or "Type M" or "Dexron" and "Dexron II" compound this confusion.

Then there are some unknown quantities, like "Chrysler Fluid Coupling Fluid." The owner's manuals on fluid coupling equipped Chryslers suggested that light engine oil could be used in emergencies, as long as it was flushed out later. You wouldn't believe how many owners of these cars filled them with SAE 10 weight engine oil when they couldn't find "Chrysler Fluid Coupling Fluid." As if all of that weren't bad enough, the actual gear boxes on these cars ran in SAE 10 engine oil because they had a hydraulic plunger shifting device. On some later Chryslers and DeSotos with hydraulically shifted constant mesh gears they actually circulated the engine oil through the fluid couplings. That didn't work, but it did surprise a lot of service station attendants when these early 1950s V-8s absorbed 13 quarts in an oil change.

Such engineering insanity was not, by the way, confined to Americans. The French and British had their strange ideas about transmission lubrication, too. On the early transverse engine cars that Alex Issigonis inspired, such as the Austin America and MG 1100, and the FWD French Simcas of the 1970s, a shared common sump was used for the engine and gear box. The effect using common lubricant in engines and transmissions was disastrous. The engines and transmissions didn't last long. A few years after the last of these cars were imported, they were hard to find on streets and highways but very common in salvage yards.

Generally, engine oil should not be used in older transmissions except in a few very specific cases like the gearbox sections of Underdrive Chryslers. Even there, a good mineral oil of the right weight is probably a better bet because it more closely resembles the old engine oils than do modern engine oils.

Older automatics (Hydramatics, Torqueflites, Fordomatics, and Flashomatics) run on ATF Type A, Suffix A, Dexron, or Dexron II, depending on their age. Dexron II can be substituted for the now obsolete Dexron. The latter was obsoleted because its formulation used a friction reducer derived from whale blubber, and that material became unavailable as whaling was outlawed. Dexron II should probably not be used in cars specified for ATF Type A, Suffix A fluid unless the transmission involved has been completely rebuilt. This is because the Dexron II fluids contain detergents in their additive packages that are so vigorous that they will sometimes loosen scale in a torque converter or fluid coupling that has been run for years on Type A, Suffix A. The scale then plugs things up. In fact, the detergents in Dexron ATFs are so aggressive that they are often added to motor oils by mechanics to free sticking valve lifters. The designation "AQ-ATF" is obsolete, but applied to fluid for Powerglide transmissions and some others. The ATF Type A, Suffix A to Dexron range of fluids will substitute here, depending on whether the unit in question has been rebuilt.

Early Ford automatics used Type A, Suffix A fluids and more recent Ford transmissions use the Dexron II fluids. For some years, in the 1970s, Ford transmissions used "Type F" fluid, which included a unique friction modifier to enhance clutch engagement. These units must get Type F, or their clutches will slip and engage roughly and at the wrong times. Some rebuild kits, it is claimed, include clutch disks that are made out of Dexron compatible materials. This wrinkle further complicates servicing Ford transmissions because even though a transmission might normally use Type F fluid, a rebuild may have converted it to Dexron II. Due to the nature of the friction enhancers in Type F fluid, it should never be used in units which specify any of the other fluids types. The Allison "C" series fluids should not be used in passenger car automatics, and the mysterious and illusive "type B" fluid was actually an early version of Dexron and, if specified, can be replaced with Dexron II.

Having gotten that out of the way, the question remains, when should transmission fluid be changed? It is my suggestion that on a new or rebuilt transmission, the fluid should be changed every two years or 25,000 miles. At present, manufacturers do not recommend this routine change if a car is used in "normal service," whatever that is, and have not provided drain plugs in their torque converters or transmission pans for many years. In the case of older automatics, the fluid should be evaluated for color and odor. Most transmission fluids start out with red dye in them and if they become brown or foggy it indicates that burning or water contamination has occurred, and they must be changed and the cause of the problem discovered. If transmission fluid smells burned, it must be replaced. A note of caution here. When you sniff a dip stick for the purpose of evaluating transmission fluid, try to do it when no one is looking. While this is a perfectly valid evaluation procedure, it can be difficult to explain to bystanders and you will, invariably, look dumb doing it.

In the opinion of many transmission technicians, an oil and filter change is not a good idea if a transmission has gone for decades without one. This is because the detergents in transmission oil — unlike motor oil — are very vicious and they can loosen scale when fresh fluid is used to replace fluid with depleted detergents. If you buy a car

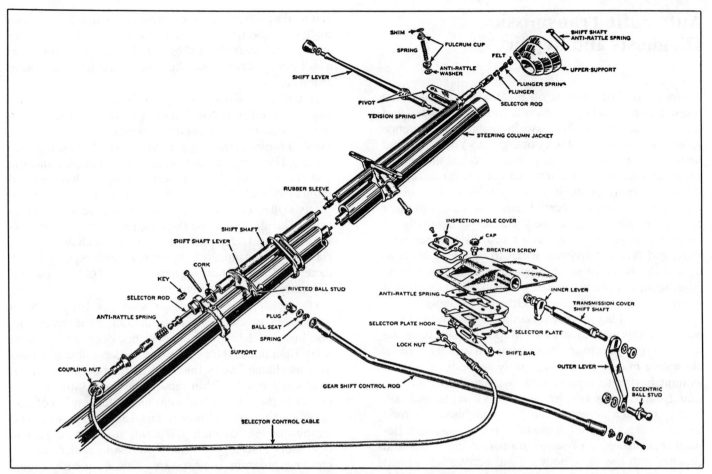

Steering column-mounted shift linkage on older cars can always be a problem in terms of wear and proper adjustment. The worst of it applies to standard transmission linkage, like that pictured here, but automatic linkage can also become worn and get out of adjustment. Note the use of both a cable and linkage rods in the unit pictured here.

with a thirty- or forty-year-old automatic and you have reason to believe that the fluid has not been changed for decades, and the fluid looks and smells okay, I suggest that you leave it alone. Some people will disagree with this recommendation, but it has the support of three of the four best transmission techs whom I know. In particular, the Dexron series fluids are fortified with aggressive detergents, so be careful with them in old, potentially scaled, units. All of this boils down to a gamble and, while I don't like to throw the dice in any aspect of automotive maintenance, that kind of risk seems built into the fluid change decision with old automatics.

Another important aspect of transmission maintenance is that the fluid must be kept at the correct level. You can severely damage the bearings and seals in a transmission by overfilling it because the fluid will tend to foam as the transmission operates. Underfilling will also cause problems, but not as quickly or dramatically, unless several quarts are involved. The trick is to follow instructions and to allow for the expansion of the fluid that will occur as it heats in operation, and for the amount of fluid retained in the transmission's servo plungers as the car is shifted through its ranges. All of this is covered in shop manuals and general repair manuals.

A lot of automatic transmission problems turn out to really be engine problems. If an automatic does not get adequate torque from its engine in roughly the amount

that it was designed for, it will appear to malfunction. If an engine has weak vacuum for any of several possible reasons, a vacuum modulated automatic attached to it will not shift correctly. Before any diagnosis of an automatic transmission is attempted, be sure that the engine that runs it is in good working order and performing up to specifications. Many automatics have been treated for problems that were really engine problems. Avoid this mistake.

Proper adjustment of automatic transmission shift and T.V. linkage (if used) are essential and must be done by the book. Some of these adjustments are complex and require the use of jigs or gauging rods and points. Get a book that covers the unit that you are working on and follow it rigorously. Vacuum modulators are easy to replace, inexpensive, and often defective. Isn't that nice? Beyond that, it is usually possible to externally adjust bands on transmissions that have them. These adjustments are sometimes based on torque, sometimes on dimensions, and sometimes on oil pressure. You have to go by the book on this one, too.

Any time that you deal with an automatic tranny, either from the bottom, through the pan, or just to add fluid to the top, it is essential to keep things almost medically clean. Automatic transmissions are close tolerance units and have very little tolerance for contamination of any kind.

Automatic Transmission Diagnosis and Repair

Any good shop manual on a car with an automatic transmission has a large section devoted to diagnosis and repair of the tranny. This usually includes a sequence schematic and a troubleshooting guide. You may need both because there are numerous maladies that afflict automatics and cause them to run hot, or vibrate, or fail to shift smoothly, or slip in gear, etc. Each of these maladies has one or more potential causes, and some of them can be definitively diagnosed without disassembly. If there are no gross defects in a transmission's performance, and the only problem seems to be a lack of crispness in the shifts, or some slippage in the shifts, a band adjustment will often cure the problem, providing that it is a band shifted transmission. Other "good news" maladies are such things as case leaks due to porosity — these will frequently yield to an external epoxy repair. Even the trouble-prone governors on many automatics are accessible with a minimum of disassembly and can be treated without having to remove and disassemble a transmission. Neutral safety switches are always external and easy to get at. Much diagnosis can be accomplished by road testing, stall testing, or the use of oil pressure gauges. Beyond that, using air pressure to operate the bands and clutches with the valve body off will accomplish a great deal towards analysis of a malfunctioning unit. All of this is very specific to each transmission type, and you must go by the book.

Some transmission problems involve a scaled converter or a cooler that causes transmission fluid to mix with radiator coolant. These problems can sometimes be dealt with without disassembly of the transmission. A scaled converter will have to be replaced or can sometimes be flushed on a converter flushing machine. Leaking coolers can usually be repaired.

Most other problems will require transmission disassembly. This, and the converter flushing routine mentioned above, require transmission removal. Again, go by the book. One important hint regarding automatic transmission removal is that the flex plate that connects most torque converters or fluid couplings to their engines' flywheels is fragile and should not be pried against. Never turn an automatic over by prying the starter teeth or flex plate damage can occur. The best bet on most of these transmissions is to pry against the nuts where the flex plate mounts to the converter, or to use the starter motor to turn the transmission over. When you remove an automatic, remember that the converter is not held on its shaft once the transmission is pulled back from the engine. It must be restrained by a chain, bar, or strap so that it will not go "thunk" on the floor as the transmission is removed.

Actual disassembly and repair of automatics is something best left to professionals. This can be a real problem because there are probably more crooks in the transmission business than in any other aspect of automotive repair. The inherent complexity of automatics and the fact that the majority of general mechanics have no real familiarity with them creates a situation where some pretty skilled con men have established lucrative operations. The abuses can be flagrant, and I am not just talking about local felons. One major national chain that specializes in transmission repair has been repeatedly indicted by local authorities and by the FTC for a pattern of grossly fraudulent activities.

Here's a classic example of what can happen. Most automatics produce a certain amount of clutch, band, and bushing debris and deposit this, over time, in their pans, right under their filters. A knowledgeable transmission mechanic knows this, and if the amount of debris found in a pan is within reasonable limits, attributes its existence there to normal wear and deterioration of frictional components. However, crooked transmission service outfits will routinely point this stuff out to gullible customers and suggest that a thousand dollar-plus rebuilding program is necessary. This frequently occurs when a customer only came in for a fluid and filter change. If this bit of deception doesn't get them well into a customer's wallet, they have been known to overfill a transmission knowing that it will blow out its seals after a few miles. That's right, the people who are supposed to repair transmissions have been known to sabotage them. Of course, when a customer has his car towed back, after this sequence of events, the gents at the transmission shop shake their heads wisely and remind him of their predictions of impending disaster. The evidence of what they did is spread out on the road and can no longer be discovered.

So there is a dilemma. Special knowledge, special tools, and some real hazards in the form of very compressed clutch springs tend to make automatic transmission repair something beyond the competence of the novice to intermediate restorer. Larceny makes many repair shops an almost equally uncertain option. The best advice that I can give for dealing with automatic transmissions that need repair or restoration is to shop carefully for an experienced repairer and demand a reasonable guarantee for the work that you have done.

CHAPTER 15:

Getting the Drive Back to the Wheels

Very early motorized vehicles either drove their wheels directly, as was the case with electrics, or through some cumbersome arrangement of belts, sprocket chains, or friction disks. There were really two problems that had to be solved in designing the "drive lines" for these cars. One was to transmit the drive the distance from the engine to the rear wheels — very few collector cars are front-wheel drive. The other major problem was to provide some basis for the drive wheels to turn at different speeds while engaged to an engine. This was necessary because when a car rounds a corner, the outboard wheel must turn farther and faster than the inboard wheel. In addition to these major problems, the development of final drives also encompassed a gear reduction of roughly three or four to one, and the connection of the engine to the driving axles in a way that allows the engine to be mounted for-and-aft in the front of the car, with the drive wheels placed at the back of the car facing fore-and-aft. A right angle gearing mechanism (rear end) is necessary to accomplish power delivery with this layout.

All of this involved a great deal of hardware that had to be developed and refined before we could have the

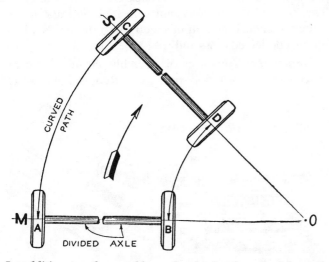

In addition to other problems that had to be solved in early automobiles, there was the need to adapt some sort of device that would allow the outboard wheel to turn farther and faster than the inboard wheel, when a car rounded a turn. The answer was the "differential."

Hotchkiss drive/live axle system that has been used in most rear-wheel drive cars from the first decade of the 20th century until recent times. Of course, pioneer cars tended to have their engines mounted in the rear, or midship, and the distance to the driving axles was only a matter of a few feet or less. Then, too, the power output of early engines was so limited that the drive hardware didn't have to withstand the extreme stress and friction associated with these parts in later stages of automotive development. Yet, by the end of the first decade of the 20th century, monsters like the Simplex 90 and several upper echelon Mercedes used massive one- or two-stage sprocket chain systems to transmit their driving power to the rear wheels, and to reduce their drive gear ratios. Such systems were dangerous, noisy, inefficient, trouble-prone, and messy. Other than that, they were fine. What was clearly needed was some form of drive system that was compact, quiet, efficient, and easy to maintain.

Enter the Hotchkiss and the torque tube drive systems. Both systems use a rigid drive shaft connected by one or more universal joints to a rear ring and pinion gear device. The rear end arrangement associated with these drive systems uses an internal differential gearing system, bolted or riveted to the ring gear, which transmits drive to the drive axles through differential side and pinion gears. The whole system runs in an oil bath, and is contained in a heavy casing that is bolted directly to an automobile's springs. This is the "conventional" drive system that until recently has dominated automobile construction since early in this century. It is a marvel of simplicity and durability — particularly when you consider what preceded it.

The torque tube drive system, which was primarily used on medium priced and expensive cars, was very common in the 1920s and died out in the 1960s — when Buick finally abandoned it. This system uses a solid drive shaft casing which bolts firmly to the rear axle housing and to a floating ball socket at the back of the transmission. In this system, only one universal joint is used, and this is at the front end of the shaft. The rear axle uses a ring and pinion gear with a differential case and gears bolted directly to the ring gear. The axles are driven by differential side gears in the differential case. The torque tube system is very strong and prevents axle windup during acceleration or movement from a standstill. However, it is a heavy and expensive system to build, and this construction necessitates removal of the entire rear axle for U-joint service or transmission or clutch removal.

Hotchkiss drive, favored by car builders from the 1930s on, is similar to torque tube drive, except that the drive shaft is in the open and two or more universal joints are used to account for the deflection of the drive line angle that occurs as the rear axle moves up and down on its springs. This system was used very early in the century, but was avoided by many manufacturers due to its inherent tendencies towards axle windup when power is applied. On non-leaf spring applications some addition of trailing or leading arms, or other devices, is used in conjunction with Hotchkiss drive to locate the axle and to overcome its windup tendencies.

There are, of course, many substantial variations on these themes, as for example, the worm gear rear ends favored by Ford on their trucks for many years, or the three-universal-joint open-drive-shafts-with-center-support-bearings used on trucks, limousines, and in other applications where very long drive shaft distances dictated this design. Even within the standard Hotchkiss and torque tube designs, there is enormous variation in axle construction and universal joint type. Before any disassembly and repair or restoration work is attempted, it is best to understand what you are dealing with and what the appropriate renovation procedure will be. In many cases, special tools and measuring devices are necessary to repair components of the drive line. Such things as pinion depth gauges and companion flange holders are sometimes difficult to "fudge." Other tools, like rear end spreaders, can be fabricated from the scrap steel bin if you know what you are doing.

Universal Joints

Most universal joints in rear-wheel drive cars are simple and very perishable parts. Newer cross and yoke type joints often do not allow for maintenance lubrication, and seem to fail predictably at the end of their "design lives." Older U-joints of this type either run in an oil bath (some torque tube installations), or are greasable through zerk or needle fittings, or are filled with heavy gear oil through a small filler plug.

For some older U-joints that are greasable there are replacement joints that are not greasable. This is a normal situation and you should not be alarmed if a new joint that replaces an old greasable joint has no provision for greasing. I prefer the greasable types because they seem to last longer if they are maintained. When greasing the greasable type joints, it is not necessary to use the hard-to-find short fiber and sodium soap greases that were originally specified for this application. A good quality general purpose lithium or aluminum complex grease, like Lubriplate 1200-2, will work well. It is impor-

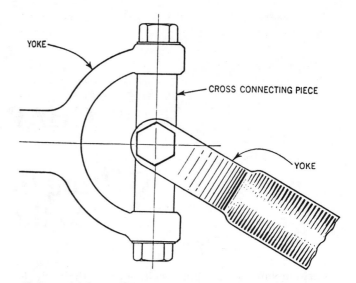

Universal joints of the yoke type are easily understood from visual inspection. They allow drive to be transmitted through an angle — but not too large an angle!

tant that these joints, and the drive shaft slip joints that are frequently located next to front U-joints, be greased carefully or with a pressure limiting gun. Don't overgrease these joints, and don't pump them up quickly with a conventional grease gun (10,000-20,000 psi) because you will blow the seals out of them and hasten joint failure. Blown seals will quickly produce a grease slick six inches wide down the bottom of a car in the area of the joint. As with any greasing operation, wipe off the fittings before and after injecting grease.

For many years Chrysler used a special roller and trunion U-joint that is a bit more complex than the conventional cross and yoke type. Follow the instructions in a shop manual or other information source when dealing with one of these, and be sure to get the roller pin centered when you reassemble this type of joint. Another odd variation on the normal cross and yoke type U-joint is one formed by two back-to-back cross and yoke units. This is a "C.V." or "constant velocity" joint and is designed to cancel the output speed variation that is inherent in a deflected cross and yoke type joint.

U-joint repair involves disassembly, cleaning, and replacement of worn or suspect parts. Removal of most U-

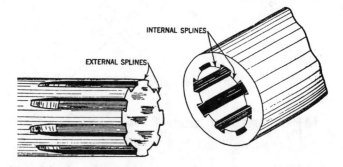

On rear wheel drive cars, as the axle bounces up and down, the drive shaft length has to change slightly to accommodate these changes in distance from the transmission output shaft to the rear end input shaft. A splined slip joint, such as the one shown here, is how this is accomplished.

joints is accomplished by unbolting the rear joint from the rear end pinion companion flange and removing the drive shaft, front U-joint, and slip joint from the car. Always tape or rubber band the bearing caps of an unattached joint so that you will not have to chase the teeny-weeny little needle bearings that can fall out of the cap all over the garage floor. Also, be sure when you unbolt rear U-joint caps or straps that the drive shaft doesn't fall on your anatomy or on the floor. One will damage you and the other can damage the joint or, possibly, the drive shaft.

Further disassembly of U-joints usually involves removing bolts, locking flat clips, or snap rings. The latter are removed with needle nose pliers or snap ring pliers. The joint's caps can then be forced out of their yokes in a joint press or vise. If you use a vise, place a small socket against one U-joint cap and use a larger socket outside of the yoke to receive the opposite cap. Now close the vise jaws to press the U-joint caps and spider out of the yoke. Now you can pull the spider out of its caps and push the other cap out.

A dedicated U-joint removing tool, such as the one shown here, is very handy for removing U-joint spiders and caps from their yokes, but you can do the same job in a shop vise with some assorted sockets if you are careful.

This procedure is crude but effective. Never hammer on a U-joint to remove it, and never use a pneumatic "zip" gun. Either of these approaches will usually remove the joint, but only at the expense of a bent yoke or damaged cap seat — if you slip. Never grasp a drive shaft in a bench vise with anything but minimum pressure and soft jaws, and be sure to support the opposite end of a shaft when you are working on a U-joint yoke. Never hold a drive shaft yoke in a common bench vise, since the vise has enough mechanical advantage to bend a yoke or deform a drive shaft tube.

Universal joints need repair when they emit noise or rumble, or when you can sense that the joint has play in it when hand pressure is applied. When U-joint failure occurs, you will find worn or corroded needle bearings and

worn bearing caps and/or cross shafts. On most joints, repair of these parts is futile and replacement is necessary. Some very early joints use bushings that can be replaced, and some later joints allow the replacement of parts of the cross and yoke system. Total replacement is always best. Bad seals that allow lubricant to leak out and water to get in are a main cause of U-joint failure. A certain amount of care is necessary to avoid seal damage when installing a new U-joint. It is also critical that the yoke surfaces are free of burrs and other defects if the joint is to work properly.

When reinstalling U-joints, be sure that they are "phased" correctly (the yokes are almost always set in the same plane and never at 90° to each other) and don't over-tighten the bolts or straps that secure the rear U-joint to its companion flange. If lock washers or other locking devices are used to secure the bearing caps or straps, be sure to continue the tradition. Many joints are susceptible to incorrect phasing by misassembling the U-joint slip joint behind the front U-joint. Some have arrows or other markings stamped on the parts to make correct phasing easy.

The most intriguing U-joint that I ever saw had two yokes bolted at 90° to opposite sides of a piece of one-half inch thick rubberized fabric. This was on an MG "M" from the early 1930s. I think that it was "factory." Other designs go in the other direction, towards complexity, with double cardan joints and center support bearings. All of them require precision and considerate handling if they are to move power to the rear end of a car without failure.

Drive Shafts

Most drive shafts are relatively simple and crude looking things that appear to be innocent of any charges that could be leveled at them. This is not the case. For one thing, drive shafts and their universals are very bad at transmitting power if they are asked to drive through angles that are beyond their design limits. Then, too, drive shafts are susceptible to warping, denting, and imbalance — all of which will produce a rumble under your feet and premature failure of other drive line components. As rugged as they look, drive shafts are surprisingly delicate, and must be maintained within very close dimensional and balance limits if they are to operate without creating a simulation of the San Andreas fault zone during an earthquake.

The first thing to check on a drive shaft is the integrity of its slip joint. The splines should be tight and free to allow drive shaft length variations as the rear springs compress and release, which causes the shaft distance to shorten and lengthen. The slip joint will be found in front of or behind the front universal joint on Hotchkiss drive cars, and near the rear axle or torque ball on torque tube drive cars. The second thing to check is drive shaft straightness and balance. Straightness is initially checked by rotating one rear wheel with the other blocked and the transmission in neutral. Any movement of the shaft surface laterally by more than a tenth of an inch or so *may* indicate a bent shaft. This can most accurately be checked in a lathe. Drive shaft imbalance is also a common problem that usually occurs because something got added to the shaft (like undercoating) or something got subtracted from it (like a welded balance weight). Again, this has to be checked in a lathe with a balancing attachment, or in a specially designed balancing machine. Unbalanced drive shafts can be fixed by rebalancing, but warped or bent shafts should be replaced entirely or have their yokes rewelded to a new shaft tube. This may sound extreme, but my experience with "straightened" drive shafts has been uniformly unsatisfactory.

One little trick that mechanics often use when shaft imbalance is suspected is trial and error balancing with a screw type hose clamp applied to various locations and at various radial positions on the suspect drive shaft. If the vibration situation can be improved this way, diagnosis of an out-of-balance shaft is confirmed. This "little trick" should never be considered a final repair, as it is not precise enough for that purpose.

Long, two-piece drive shafts with center support bearings frequently are defective in the center support bearing, or the rubber cushion that locates that bearing. Always check this on cars equipped with center support bearing drive shafts.

Some drive shafts have external vibration damper systems that are easy to find and sometimes require replacement. A sneakier system was one used by Chrysler that located a rubber damper *inside* the shaft itself. These can go bad and result in permanent imbalance of the shaft.

One thing that Hotchkiss drive systems do badly is to drive through excessive angles. When a car is restored, and removal of the engine or rear axle has occurred, it is a good idea to check the drive shaft angle with a spirit level/protractor and compare the drive-shaft-to-rear-axle-angular-deviation with that allowed by the manufacturer. If this angle is in excess, it is unlikely that the U-joints will be able to perform their function without audible complaint and rapid wear. Angular correction is accomplished by shimming either the transmission on its rear mounting surface, or the rear axle housing where it attaches to the springs. If you find any shims in these areas at the time of disassembly, keep track of them, or your reassembly will probably fail.

Automotive Rear Ends

If they are properly set up and reasonably maintained, most automobile rear ends will outlast several engines. They are one of the most trouble free aspects of most automobiles. There are, of course, some exceptions, such as certain E-type Jaguars and a few other cars. That's the "good news." The "bad news" is that when a rear end needs repair, beyond something simple like a pinion shaft

seal replacement or a wheel bearing replacement, it can be pretty tough going. There are usually some special tools, fixtures, and measuring devices associated with rear end disassembly and setup, and the need for precision is enormous. However, rear end repair is something that a talented amateur can handle if he has access to the necessary tools, equipment, and information.

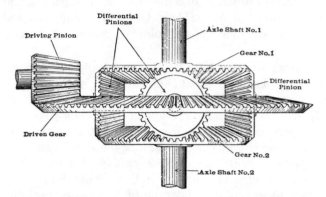

Differential gearing is easy enough to understand if you have a unit in your hands and can watch it work. Try staring at this nice diagram of a ring and pinion gear and a differential gear set, and see if the notion of the operation of the thing doesn't just "fly into your head."

With all of this in mind, and given the rarity of the need for major rear end repairs, it is usually preferable to substitute a functioning rear end for one that is damaged, unless, of course, the damaged unit is very rare and/or expensive. In terms of labor, probable service life, and cost of repair, a rear end transplant almost always comes out ahead of "going in." When you do go in, what you will find is a device that is very tough in some respects and very delicate in others. Always, there is need for great precision in rear end work. Worn or broken differential parts are unusual because differentials are only activated when a car rounds a corner or spins one wheel. Bent and broken axles and leaking seals are common but can usually be repaired without resorting to major rear end disassembly. Worn or chipped out ring and pinion gears are the most usual cause of serious rear end problems.

Axle nomenclature is important because the type of axle that you are dealing with will determine, in large part, the correct repair procedure. In broad terms, gear-driven rear axles and their parts are described by the following terms.

LIMITED SLIP or "POSI TRACTION." These units, available from around the 1960s on, use clutching devices to overcome some of the tendency of differential gear setups to allow the wheel with the least traction to spin. A posi equipped car will climb the side of a barn in a sleet storm, but it can be difficult to repair these units. It is almost always easier and cheaper to transplant a whole rear end assembly when axles of this type go bad. When you add lubricant to them, be sure to use the special lubricants that they require to keep their clutches holding.

INTEGRAL, REMOVABLE CARRIER, AND BANJO axles. These terms describe the basic construc-

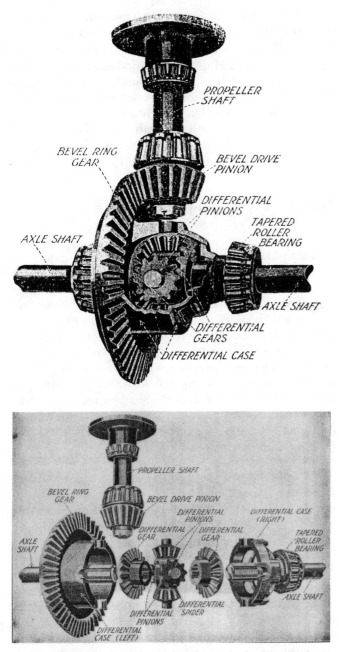

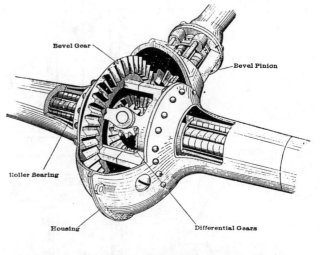

These banjo style axles can be hard to set up because they usually don't allow much inspection of meshed gears. The Ford setup, on top, doesn't have a center section; its halves bolt directly together. The axle shown in the bottom photo has banjo casings that bolt to a central carrier section.

Here's what actual rear end hardware looks like, both assembled and spread out.

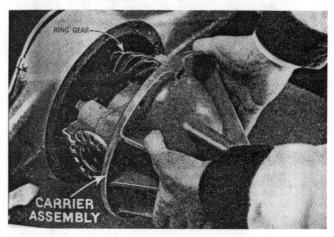

Integral type rear axles are very easy to work on because you can remove their working guts and doctor them on your bench. In this photo you can see the left side adjuster for setting ring gear lateral position.

tion of an axle. The most common one in collector cars is the integral axle, which has the guts of its ring and pinion set and their bearings bolted to the major housing that includes the axle tubes. On these units, you will find a cover plate at the back of the axle housing that allows access to the gears and bearings. It is usually better to service integral setups with the axle removed from a car. Removable carrier type axles are set up so that the ring, pinion, and differential gears and their bearings can be removed from the axle housing in one assembly. This makes them easy to work on, as you can pull the "pumpkin" and leave the cumbersome axle housing under the car. This construction has no removable back plate. The banjo type axle is constructed in two lateral halves that bolt to a central casting, or to each other, or both. Banjo axles are unnerving to work on because about the only final adjustment that you can make on them with cer-

tainty is ring and pinion backlash; and that leaves a great deal of uncertainty.

FLOATING AND SEMI-FLOATING AXLES. These terms apply to axle outer end bearing construction. The semi-floating construction (there is also a "three-quarter floating") has the axle end bearings inside the axle tubes so that the axle shaft ends both bear a car's weight and transmit drive power. In the full floating design — still used on most trucks, heavy-duty three-quarter-ton capacity and over — the bearings that support the wheel hubs are mounted on the outsides of the axle tubes, and the axle shafts bear none of the car's weight. In a full floating

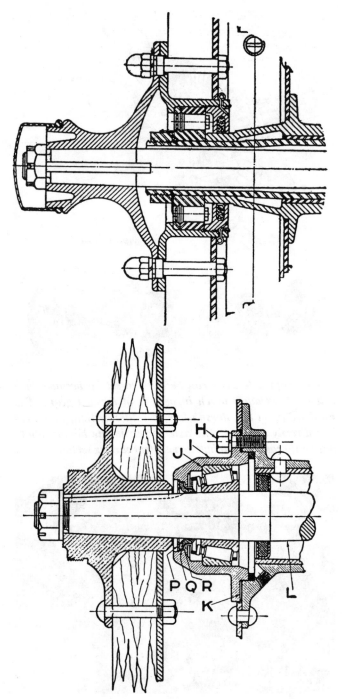

In the "semi-floating" axle, shown in the drawing on the left, the axle's wheel bearing bears the weight of the car and transmits drive to the wheel. The "full floating" axle, shown on the right, puts the car's weight on the outside aspect of the axle tube, and the axle shaft only transmits power.

axle, the axle shafts are usually retained by a snap wire, and can be removed with the wheels and hubs left behind on the car.

FLANGED AND REMOVABLE-HUB AXLE SHAFTS. Older axles were made in two pieces with a straight shaft and a splined or keyed hub nutted to it. After World War II through the 1960s, manufacturers switched to a one-piece axle construction, with the flange/hub and shaft forged as one unit. On a very few of the removable hub type axles, the hub has unfinished splines that are conformed by nutting the hub to the axle

shaft. On this type, the hubs are not reusable and must be discarded after separation from their axle shafts.

OTHER AXLE DISTINCTIONS. There are some other axle types and distinctions out there, such as the worm drive assemblies favored by Ford on their early trucks, and a few obscure planetary differential units. The two-speed Columbia unit, fitted primarily to Ford products, is another interesting variation. Yet, 98 percent or more of all axles ever built will conform to one or more of the descriptive terms outlined above.

Rear Axle Lubrication

Many of the important distinctions regarding the gear lubricants used in rear axles were covered in the previous chapter on transmissions. Please refer to that chapter for details. In general, there are three types of lubricants that you should be aware of: EP (extreme pressure), non-EP, and posi. In modern hypoid gear axles, that is, axles with the pinion gear entering the ring gear below its center line, you must use a hypoid type lubricant. Lubricants in this class counter the extremely high face pressures and wiping actions of hypoid configured gear teeth. The correct lubricants for this application are designated as EP (Extreme Pressure) hypoid, multipurpose, APG (All Purpose Gear), or multipurpose.

For axles that are not hypoid type, you should probably use a non-hypoid lubricant of the correct weight. Lubriplate still makes 90 and 140 weight lubricants that have all of the additives that good gear oils should have (anti-scuff, anti-foam, anti-corrosion, etc.) but none of the corrosive EP additives (phosphorous and sulfur-based things) that can hurt non-hypoid gears. The metallurgy of pre-hypoid units, in some cases, may not be able to withstand the assault of hypoid additives over long periods. Etching of brass and bronze by these lubricants is a certainty, and pitting and welding of the gear teeth can also result.

Positraction type axles require the use of lubricants with friction modifying additives to insure that their clutches will grip. This class of lubricants must be used in these units but should never be used in non-locking type axles. Basically, hypoid gear oils are a compromise and are not very good lubricants for general purposes. That is probably one of the reasons that this type of axle has a comparatively high failure rate.

Rear axles run in gear oil, generally SAE 90 to 140 on the gear oil scale. The older ones used 140, and the newer ones use 90 or even 75W-90. I have seen people try to use the old, original specification 600W boiler grease to quiet a noisy rear end or to compensate for excessive ring and pinion backlash. This will not work, and unless a very early car specifies this kind of heavy grease, its use should be avoided. SAE 140 gear oils are the same viscosity and are much better lubricants. I have run a good grade of 140 in rear ends that did specify 600W with good results.

Rear End Diagnosis

Rear end symptoms divide into two classes: noises and leaks. Beyond dealing with those symptoms and making a simple check for gear backlash or for a bent or broken axle, there is not too much that can be determined without disassembly. That is probably why about half of the rear ends that are disassembled suffer this fate for no valid reason. Unfortunately, it is not unusual for a mechanic with more enthusiasm for wrench work than analytical ability to disassemble a rear axle to seek the source of a noise that is, in reality, being generated by an entirely different aspect of a car — such as tires or front wheel bearings. Before you go down this glory path, remember this. Rear axles don't often malfunction. They are very durable, and are good candidates to be left alone. Car noises, such as leaks in a house roof, seldom originate where they seem to come from. If you do take a rear end apart for no good reason — such as a noise that really has its origins elsewhere— it is more likely to fail than if you had shown the restraint to leave it alone. This is because it will be virtually impossible to get the bearing preloads and unit dimensions to exactly what they were before disassembly, and what they were when the parts wore in. "For goo'ness sake, if it ain't broke, don't fix it."

The adjusting system shown here, with threaded side adjusters, is pretty standard for many ring gears. First the bearing caps are loosened, and then the ring gear lateral position is adjusted. Then the bearing caps are retightened.

Rear axle leaks are usually simple to correct. Leaking gaskets may yield to some careful and even tightening or they may need replacement. Pinion seals and axle seals are relatively easy to replace.

Noises and vibrations are more complex to analyze. Books could be, and probably have been, written about them. Here, a few paragraphs will have to do. Rear end noise symptoms are best heard from the back seat of a car with the rear windows open. These noises can have timbres varying from a rumble, to a scream, to a clicking, to a roar. Be sure that you eliminate common symptomatic noises, often mistaken for rear end noises, before you tear into a rear end. Tire noises should disappear when the tires are overinflated, at least the pitch of their

noises will change. U-joint and seal noises can be confirmed by close inspection. True rear end noises will almost always change radically as you go from acceleration, to coast, to back throttle. If the noise that you are hearing doesn't do this, it is probably a tire noise or a transmission noise. Clicking noises that are heard as you round a corner are very likely to be differential related. In any case, before disassembling a rear end to correct a noise or vibration problem, get someone with rear end experience to listen and render an opinion.

Rear Axle Shafts and Wheel Bearings

Most axle work involves the axle shafts, their outer bearings, and their oil or grease seals. Such work usually does not involve the center section of the axle housing, and is accomplished entirely from the ends of the housing. The exception to this is some General Motors products from the 1930s and long after, which required removal of "C" washers from the inner ends of the axle shafts for shaft removal. Chevrolet was famous for this system.

Flanged axles are removed by loosening the nuts or bolts that secure the retaining plates just behind their flanges. Usually there is a hole in the flange to allow access to the retainer fastener heads by rotating the axle around them. Once the retaining plate and seal behind it are free, the axle should slide out with its bearing. A little persuasion with an axle slide hammer may be necessary. Removable hub type axles usually don't allow easy access to the fasteners securing their bearing/seal retaining plates, and their hubs usually have to be removed to permit retainer and bearing removal. The removal of splined or keyed hubs from axles is one of life's little annoyances because they frequently don't want to seem to separate with persuasion of less magnitude than a small nuclear detonation.

The first attempts to remove hubs, after the securing cotter keys and axle end nuts have been removed, should involve using a threaded puller. If this fails, it is common procedure to escalate things to the use of a barbaric device called a "striking hub puller." This is a puller that is struck to generate enormous force and substantial shock on its ram threads. It is capable of doing enormous damage by warping the hub or splitting the end of an axle, without actually accomplishing removal of the hub from the axle shaft. The alternative to this kind of brute force is disarmingly simple. Loosen the axle hub retaining nuts about half to three-quarters of a turn from finger-tight and replace their cotter keys. Now drive the car a mile or two on a bumpy road. Usually the hubs will come off in your hands when the nuts are backed off the rest of the way. Of course, if the car isn't running, this won't work and you may have to use pullers and even mild heat on the hubs to remove them. If heat is used, it should be kept under 350° Fahrenheit to avoid changing the metallurgy of the axle and hub. It helps to strike the hub with a

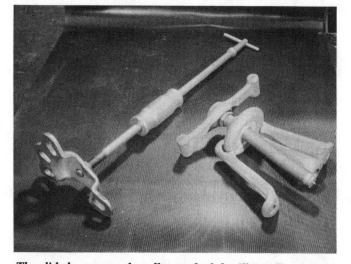

The slide hammer axle puller on the left will usually get out a stuck axle. It bolts to the hub and delivers impact. The striking hub puller on the right is designed to remove hubs from axles, and should be used gently. Pounding the ram screw striking arm delivers enormous force and shock to the hub and axle end, enough to endanger both.

brass hammer while applying force and heat.

When separated, the axle's tapered end and hub hole should be inspected for damage to the keyways or splines. Axle shafts and their bearings are removed by hand, or with a puller, after the retaining plate and seal are removed.

Chevrolet, and a few other GM cars, used "C" washers to hold their axles in as well as retainer plates. This is like wearing a belt and suspenders, but as long as you know about it, it shouldn't be a problem. These axles are removed as above, except that the rear end case cover has to be removed and the differential pinion shaft locking screw loosened, and the pinion shaft removed. Then the axle ends can be pushed in from their recesses in the differential side gears and the "C" lock washers that retain them can be removed with a magnet.

Chrysler had a nasty little trick in the 1960s of drilling holes in the inner ends of their axles and inserting a flanged pin-spacer-doohicky, with the pin ends entered into each axle end. Be careful not to lose the pin in the soup when you remove this type of axle shaft. It is particularly easy to do this if you are using a slide hammer to remove an axle on one of these installations.

Broken axles are in a department all by themselves because removing the inner ends can be a study in frustration. Magnets sometimes do the trick, and there are many types of stub removers made to deal with this situation. Some of them may even work.

Any time an axle is removed, it should be checked for twisting and straightness. Twisting can usually be seen on the surface of the axle shaft, and straightness can be determined by putting the machined ends of an axle on V-blocks or in a big lathe. The axle splines, squares, or hexes that engage the differential side gears should be inspected for chipping, cracking, or other damage, and axle seal bosses should be looked at for erosion. Bent

axles can, theoretically, be straightened, but if they are twisted, there is little that can be done to prevent their failure. Damaged seal areas can be spray- or wire-welded and remachined, or a sleeve, such as Chicago Rawhide's "Speedi-Sleeve" product, can be found for many shaft diameters and easily and cheaply installed. It is always a good idea to Magnaflux axles and hubs when they are out for any reason.

Axle outer bearings are driven or pressed off their shafts. Considerable force is usually required to do this. If an axle bearing is retained by a small, ringlike piece driven against its side, this collar can be removed by supporting its bottom and striking it hard in three places on its circumference with a hammered cold chisel. It should then slide off its axle boss easily. Never try to drive an axle bearing and one of these ring retainers off an axle at the same time. The best way to remove press fit axle bearings is to use a press. Whatever method you use, protect the splined ends of axles from damage, and protect the threaded ends of removable hub type axles. Also, be sure to protect the oil seal surfaces on axles from accidental damage when you are removing bearings and their retainers.

Some axles have their bearings located so close to their bearing seal retaining plates that there isn't room for a bearing pulling cage behind them. On these, the outer races have to be ground away until individual rollers can be removed and then the whole outer race. This will allow the inboard edge of the inner race to be held for the purpose of pulling it off the shaft.

Never attempt to reuse a bearing that has been removed from an axle. This can be tempting when the object of the repair is to replace a $2.50 seal, but you have to destroy a $26 axle bearing to get to it. Resist the temptation. Axle bearings can be expensive, but they are not reusable after removal. Also, be sure to mark the right and left axles if both are removed. It's easy to forget to do this, but important to get it right.

When reassembling an axle shaft, its seals, retainer plate, bearing, and bearing retainer ring, be sure to get the parts in the right sequence and orientation. It is surprisingly easy to put a roller bearing in backwards, or to forget a seal until the bearing is on the axle. When ring retainers are used to secure bearings to an axle, never drive them on in the same operation as the bearings. First drive or press the bearings home, and then drive the retainers against the bearings.

When pressing or driving bearings and retainers on, it is essential that they be supported over most of their circumferences. Don't try to drive a bearing on with a cold chisel. Bearings can only be driven or pressed on shafts by their inner races. Force applied to the outer race of a bearing will destroy it. When installing or removing bearings and their retainers from axle shafts, it is very good practice to use some kind of protective sleeve to prevent damage to adjacent seal riding surfaces.

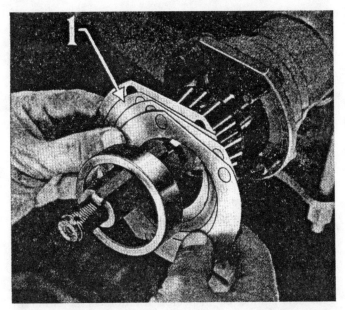

When you remove shims like these from an axle tube end, be sure that you replace them when you reassemble the axle shafts in their housing. If you have installed a new wheel bearing, you may have to readjust the shim pack to accommodate it.

Always wear good eye protection when working with bearing press fits on axles. Flying chips are a very real possibility. Bearing races can "explode" when they are forced off or into place.

When an axle, its bearing, seal(s), and retainer have been assembled together, it's time to install the axle in its housing. There are several points to note here. If shims are used behind the retainer to provide for axle shaft end float, these should be reinstalled as they were originally and the end float checked with a dial indicator. The shims can then be adjusted to provide for the correct combined axle end float. On some axle designs, a threaded adjuster is used to control end float. In either case, this factor has to be attended to, or the wheel bearings can be destroyed. Always use new gaskets behind axle retainer plates, and be sure that they are made from material that will compress to roughly the same thickness as the original gaskets when they were compressed. Be sure that if retainer plates can be installed in more than one position on their bolts, they are installed with their drain holes down to allow the escape of any axle lubricant that gets past the seals and would otherwise threaten the brakes. Be sure that when you slip axles into their tubes, oil seals in the tubes (if used) are not contacted by or cut by the axles' end splines. If such seals exist, they should always be changed when axles are removed. These seals are pressed into the axle housing ends and should be coated on their outer diameters with a non-hardening sealer before they are installed. Their lips should be greased lightly before the axles are inserted through them.

With the axles and retainers installed, the retainers can be tightened. Always be sure that whatever method was used to secure the retainer fasteners is reestablished — cotter keys, wire, aircraft nuts, bend tabs, and the like.

Tightening the retainer is an acceptable method of seating the axle bearing outer race in the axle tube as long as excessive force is not applied.

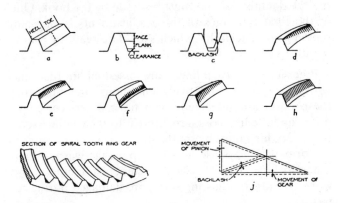

The ring and pinion gear tooth pattern can be read in white or red lead. This gives a good indication of ring and pinion mesh. Many manufacturers provided data on correct mesh patterns in their shop manuals.

On removable hub-type axles, the hub inner surfaces and the axles' tapered mating surfaces should be cleaned and deburred. The hubs can then be installed on the shafts with a very light coating of grease on both surfaces. The hub nuts are then tightened to the correct torque. The hubs should then be rapped with a brass hummer a couple of times and the end nuts retorqued and advanced to the first available cotter key hole. Never slacken this nut to make a cotter key hole work. A final check of axle end float should then be made and compared to the manufacturer's specification. The axle case can then be topped with the correct lubricant and the axle can be put into service. Always make sure that axle venting ports are clear so that pressure does not build up in the housing and blow lubricant past the seals.

Rear End Disassembly, Repair, and Installation: When You Have To Go In

Only the foolhardy would consider going into an engine without some bare minimum of knowledge of repair procedure and specification information. Ring/pinion/differential assemblies represent a similar situation. These are highly evolved units that require exact and precise set up. You can't just feel your way around in there and hope for the best with any realistic expectation of success. Rear end inner bearings, unlike wheel bearings, usually operate on the principle of preload. This means that two bearings work in opposition to each other with a small but specific loading on the shaft between them. In most rear ends, preload is used on the shaft that carries the pinion gear, and on the bearing set that supports the ring gear/differential assembly. Preload involves a critical adjustment and allows for no "fudge" factor. Similarly, the ring and pinion relationship is susceptible to four types of adjustment movement: pinion depth (pinion in and out) and ring gear position (to one side or the other). These adjustments use shims or threaded adjusters, and must be made by the book. One of the final outcomes of these adjustments is ring and pinion gear "backlash," which should be read for confirmation of what has been done.

Precision and cleanliness are essential in rear end work. Due to the relatively enormous pressures that these parts are subjected to in normal service, chips, burrs, and the like pose a real threat to the whole assembly. Everything must be spotlessly clean when this work is performed. Always use new keys, pins, tab washers, and other locking devices. Check fasteners for cracks and worn threads. If adjusting shims are damaged during removal, replace them.

The first step when you go into a rear end is to drain the lubricant and remove the axle shafts, as outlined above. If you are working on a removable carrier unit, the "pumpkin" can then be removed from the axle housing and installed in a holding fixture on your bench. For integral axle types, you will have to work on the whole case. Banjo axles are separated either before or after removing the pinion gear carrier, depending on construction.

It is always a good idea to get any measurements and mesh indications that are possible before you change the relationships in an axle by disassembly. On banjo axles this will mean determining gear backlash before any disassembly occurs. On integral and removable carrier type axles, it is a good idea to measure backlash, pinion depth, preload, and tooth contact pattern (explained later) before disassembly. This will give you data for comparison purposes after your reassembly is complete.

All load bearing parts in a rear end should be Magnafluxed and checked for burrs, chips, warping, run-out, pitting, and any other defects that you can think of. Gear teeth should be checked for excessive scuffing and wear. Bearings must be in perfect condition, and any scoring, spalling, or indications of burning or pitting will mandate their replacement.

Ring gear and differential case removal is accomplished with the axle shafts out, and by removing the bolts holding the bearing caps on the differential side bearings. These caps should be labeled for location and orientation. The ring gear and differential unit can now be removed, but it may take a special slide hammer or pry bars to persuade it out. Sometimes an axle case spreader has to be used to free a ring gear and differential case from an axle housing. If this type of device is used, it must be used with restraint, and never for more than a 0.020 inch spread of the axle case. If shims are the method of adjustment for the ring gear gear set position, they should be saved and noted for location.

Differential cases are bolted or riveted to the ring gears. The manner of this attachment is extremely important. Special hardened, shouldered bolts or rivets are used to precisely locate these parts. Differential cases themselves should be labeled for position in ring gears,

and the relative positions of the cases' halves must also be labeled so that reassembly will be the same as original.

Pinion gears are usually removed from axle housings or carriers by holding their companion flanges or yokes with special holding fixtures and removing the nuts securing the flanges or yokes to their pinion gear shafts. The flanges or yokes are then removed with special pullers. Then pinion gears and shafts can be removed by pressing them into the axle housing after their ring gears have been removed. Some pinion shafts are secured to the axle housing on separate carriers that can be removed as units. On some rear ends, a collapsible pinion spacer/preload bushing is used. This part is designed to achieve a specified preload by deforming as the flange holding nut is tightened. Never try to reuse one of these spacers. They must be replaced.

The gears in ring and pinion sets and the differential gear sets should be inspected for defects. If either of these sets have defective gears, the complete sets will have to be replaced. You can never replace either just a ring or just a pinion gear, or one gear in a differential set. While differential gears and shafts rarely wear, if you do find worn shafts, these and their gears must be replaced. Rear ends are one of the places where a bad or mismatched part will quickly ruin the other parts that it works with. Half measures don't work here.

When everything is spotlessly clean, and all defective parts have been replaced, a rear end can be reassembled and set up. As suggested earlier, a manual and the wisdom to follow it are a must at this point. It is also essential that any new gears that are used be in matched sets, and bearings be the correct grade for this application. Just finding a bearing or pinion gear that "sort of" fits will not effect a repair. Most ring and pinion gears are numbered to indicate the status of twins in a common heritage. They are also frequently marked for pinion depth setting. Some are marked for tooth mesh point, particularly those without a hunting tooth (pinion tooth number can be evenly divided into ring gear tooth number). Rear end bearings should be matched by number and by application and not by dimension only. Extreme care should be taken in installing rear end bearings on their shafts and in their seats. Pressing a well supported bearing is correct; hammering a bearing is a definite "no no."

Differential cases should be bolted to their ring gears at the right torque and with their halves in the correct relationship to each other and to their ring gears. All parts that assemble should be checked for burrs and other defects, and these must be corrected before installation. Shims should be installed as they were removed, with final shimming left for later. Threaded adjusters that locate ring gear bearings should be put in their original positions and the bearing caps tightened to the correct torques. At this point, the manual must be followed for correct pinion gear depth and preload, and for correct ring gear lateral position and preload. In some cases, special measuring jigs will be needed to measure the critical pinion depth dimension, and in others dial indicators and other fairly common tools will suffice for rear end setup work.

While I have the greatest admiration for people who improvise tools and measuring jigs, rear ends are one place where this kind of endeavor is often inappropriate. There is a rumor abroad in the land that if a pinion gear has its outer edge brought exactly flush with the inner edge of its ring gear, it will be in adjustment. This rumor is false and dangerous. Many pinions are marked for depth over-standard and under-standard, so simply bringing a pinion flush with the inner edge of a mating ring gear will not work except in a few 1930s cars that specified this primitive form of adjustment. Whatever adjustment technique is used, there are two sources of information about ring and pinion mesh that are always available and should be compared to known specifications.

The first is backlash. When all dimensional adjustments have been made, backlash must be within specification or something is wrong. The second general indication is gear tooth contact pattern. Some manufacturers used gear tooth contact pattern as the primary specification for the entire rear end setup, and did not rely on dimensional data. Gear tooth contact pattern is read by painting the ring gear with white or red lead paste. White lead is better, but red lead is easier to find and cheaper.

The ring gear is then turned by rotating the pinion gear. A little drag should be applied to the ring gear as it is turned by applying the hand brake, or by pressing a pry bar against the edge of the ring gear. A clear mesh pattern will appear on the lead paste on the ring gear teeth. Each rear end application will have a slightly different "ideal" contact pattern, but the accompanying chart shows generally what the deviations and corrections are. A final check of tooth contact pattern with lead paste is so important that no matter what primary adjustment technique was used, this method should be used for confirmation of the setup. When lead paste is used, remember that red lead residue must be cleaned up because it degrades rear end lubricant. White lead, on the other hand, should be left on the ring and pinion because it tends to improve the performance of rear end lubricants. Until the early 1980s, when the EPA banned lead additives in gear oils, many of them contained a sulphur-lead-chlorine ("SLC") additive package, or a lead napthanate additive, to improve gear oil performance.

When all of this work is completed and a new pinion shaft seal is installed, and the carrier or access cover bolted back on, you can refill the rear end with lubricant and put it into service. It's a good idea to listen to a freshly rebuilt rear end for a while, or at least to listen for it. If you are inclined toward prayer, this might be a good place to apply some.

Brakes have come a long way since systems such as the external contracting system, shown here, was used to stop cars (1908).

Most brake environments end up looking pretty sad by the time you restore a car. The brake shoes in this photo are obviously badly contaminated with grease.

Front wheel bearings are pretty simple items, but they have to work right or they will scream, howl, or rumble. Many people don't realize that the inner race of a wheel bearing marches slowly around the spindle that it is mounted on as the wheel turns mostly on the bearing itself.

CHAPTER 16:

Front Wheel Bearings and Drum Brake Friction Systems

Front Wheel Bearings

Automotive front wheel bearings have changed less and are subject to less design variation than just about any other complex stress laden system in automobiles. Even the advent of disc brakes and front-wheel drive in recent years has made little significant difference in the principles and practices of front wheel bearing design.

All front wheel bearing systems that I am familiar with utilize anti-friction bearings of either tapered roller or ball configuration. Most of the differences in design involve details such as grease seal placement or provisions for external greasing. The big distinction is between systems using tapered roller bearings and ball bearings. Both of these approaches use two thrust bearings working in opposition to each other to support a car's weight and align its wheels. The tapered roller type, which has pretty much dominated the field since the beginning, runs with a small but essential amount of side play to allow for bearing expansion, and to let the inner bearing races "creep" or march around their spindles. The ball bearing type, which involves an annular thrust design, usually operates under a small amount of preload.

If wheel bearings are set up correctly, and if their seals

Spindles with tapered roller bearings, such as the one shown here, will go a long way if they are kept dry and clean and have adequate lubricant packed in them.

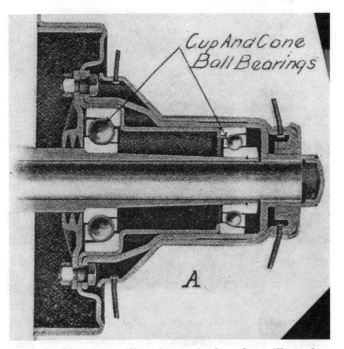

Bad wheel bearings will produce noise but often will not show symptoms of failure if you just spin the wheels that run on them with your hand in an unloaded condition.

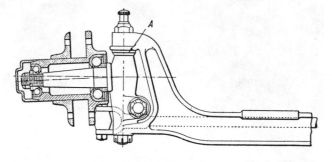

The front wheel bearing setups on rear wheel drive cars hasn't changed much since this king pin front end was manufactured early in the century. Most modern applications use tapered roller bearings instead of the annular ball bearings shown on this spindle.

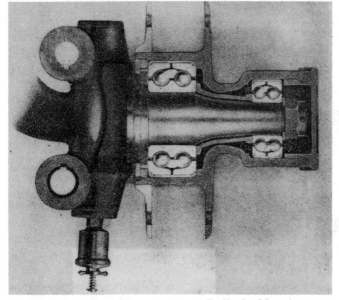

On some cars you will encounter oddball wheel bearing configurations, such as this double row ball bearing setup.

perform adequately to keep grease in and water out, they will require very little attention. Under most conditions, good wheel bearing grease will last the better part of a decade, and inspection and repacking can safely be left to intervals of 25,000 miles or more. When these bearings are disassembled and repacked, they become vulnerable to misadjustment and subsequent failure. I have probably seen more front wheel bearings fail shortly after repacking than at any other time. I think that this is due to improper installation or adjustment.

Front wheel bearings probably are victimized by receiving more attention than they merit. While they do not often fail, they are easy to inspect, and their failure symptoms (mostly noises) are easily confused with those of

other, less accessible parts of cars, such as transmissions and rear ends. They can also affect the performance of other systems, such as steering and braking — resulting in false diagnoses and unnecessary disassembly of those systems, when it is really wheel bearings that are at fault. Try to avoid this pitfall. Remember, too, that just jacking up a car and rotating a wheel will almost never result in detection of a bad front wheel bearing. Faults are usually only evident with load applied.

Front wheel bearing failure is relatively easy to diagnose. Like rear wheel bearings, front wheel bearings indicate failure by emitting noises anywhere from howls to screams to rumbles. Like their partners on back axles, front wheel bearings will change the tone of their com-

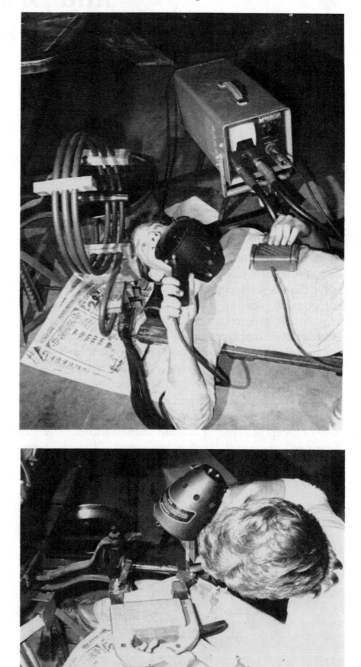

The 85-year-old spindle shown here is suspect for cracks. A magnetic particle inspection showed possible cracks, and a more sensitive wet magnetic particle inspection was performed with a black light.

plaints as a car takes a curve. This is because the load on and speed of the bearing changes differently, side-to-side, in a curve. The noise produced by a defective front wheel bearing will be different or absent in a left or right turn. So far, all of these indications of trouble are the same for front and for rear wheel bearings. The diagnostic difference between them is that a defective rear wheel bearing will change its tonal output as the operation of a car is changed from power to back-throttle (coast). This change in operation should not affect the noises made by bad front wheel bearings.

Disassembly and reassembly of front wheel bearings is simple but exacting work. Whether disassembly is being pursued to correct a diagnosed defect or for time-and-mileage maintenance considerations, careful inspection of the system's parts is essential. These are safety related systems, and their integrity can be a matter of life and death. The 40- or 50-year-old metal found in the front spindles of collector cars is always suspect and can fail suddenly, with catastrophic results. These parts should always be checked with a crack detection system like Zyglo or Spotcheck when they are exposed by any work in this area. If the parts are off a car, or if there is any reason to doubt their integrity, a full magnetic particle inspection regimen should be applied to them.

Front Wheel Bearing Disassembly and Inspection

Front wheel bearing work should always be done with tires and wheels removed from their hubs. If a brake disc or drum can be separated easily from its hub, this should be done before the hub is removed. First, the hub dust cap is gently screwed or pried off the hub, in the latter case by working around its circumference. Once a hub grease cap is pried or tapped out enough to loosen it, a pair of large slip-joint pliers can be used to complete its removal. From here on, it's important that you note the relative positions and orientations of parts that you take off the spindle. It's surprisingly easy to install a bearing cup backwards on some cars, and the results will be disastrous. It is also important to keep the parts from one side of the car unmixed with those from the other.

With the front axle cap off, you will encounter a cotter key or, sometimes, a bend-tab washer. Remove and discard these locking devices; never try to reuse them. When one considers the pain and suffering that has afflicted humankind since the advent of the automobile age because some people have tried to reuse cotter keys rather than spend a few cents for new ones, you sometimes wonder how we have survived. After the cotter key, you will sometimes find a nut retainer and always a spindle nut. Remove these. Under this there is a nibbed thrust washer which can be removed easily with a hooked wire. At this point, pull the hub out an inch or so, and then push it back while supporting its outer aspect. Now the outer wheel bearing's inner race, cage, and balls or rollers can

This self-locking wheel bearing nut required a special wrench because a regular socket was too thick to fit in the hub where it lived. A wrench was made by welding some angle iron and a nut to a flat piece of scrap steel. Note the chisel marks on this nut. They were made by someone who tried to remove it with a chisel.

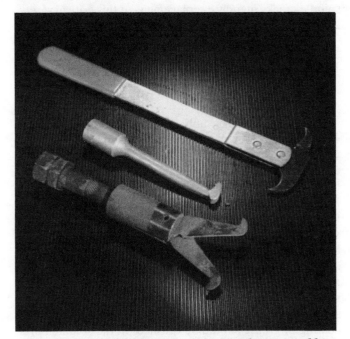

Tools like these will make it easy to remove the most stubborn wheel bearing grease seal. The tool on top is used to pry seals out, and the ones on the bottom attach to a slide hammer and whack seals out with impact. No matter how you remove wheel bearing seals, never try to reuse them.

be removed with one hand, while the other supports and centers the hub assembly. Now, with both hands, withdraw the hub assembly from the spindle. The inside wheel bearing and its seal will come out with the hub. The grease seal can now be removed from the hub by prying — preferably with a tool like the inexpensive but wonderfully effective tool that is pictured. With the seal out, the inside bearing can be removed.

At this point, all of the parts that you have removed should be washed in solvent and completely cleansed of old grease. If, in this process, the brake drum or disc rotor is contaminated with solvent or grease, it should be rewashed in alcohol or in one of the chlorinated solvents designed for cleaning brake parts, or in one of the new biodegradable detergent type solvents that are being sold for this purpose.

Inspect the bearings for rust, pitting, galling, and cracks. If any one of the bearing components is bad, the whole bearing will have to be replaced. To remove the bearing races from a hub, you can use a special puller or press attachment, or you can use a soft steel drift punch. In all cases, wear eye protection while performing outer bearing race removal procedures, and if a punch is used, be sure to use it evenly around the circumference of the bearing race that you are working on. Never allow the race to become cocked or tipped in its bore during removal as this will damage the hub bore. The same considerations apply to the installation of wheel bearing races.

The spindle should now be cleaned thoroughly and inspected for cracks, burrs, and other defects. Since the inner races of wheel bearings are designed to "creep" slowly around their spindles, to distribute the wear evenly over their surfaces, any roughness on spindles must be removed or the spindles must be replaced. Of course, any spindle cracks mandate replacement of this critical safety component.

Front Wheel Bearing Reassembly

When the bearings, hub, and spindle are thoroughly clean and dry, they should be repacked and reassembled. Older practice was to use a short fiber grease, but modern high temperature greases without fibre are a better bet. Never mix greases or add grease to existing lubricant, if its type is unknown. The three grease types available for wheel bearing applications, lithium, sodium soap, and synthetic, are not compatible. Each bearing should be lubricated by smearing its outer race with grease and using a needle fitting or pressure cone to lubricate the inner races and balls or rollers. Packing by hand rubbing is possible but messy and slow. The grease recess in the hub should be filled flush with the sides of the hub, and a thin coating of grease should be brushed on the spindle parts and on the inside of the axle dust cap. Do not over-fill the hub or pack it solid, as this can result in seal leakage and possible damage to brakes.

After the inside bearing inner race, cage, and rollers have been inserted in the hub, the grease retaining seal can be installed. Its outer press fit surface should be coated with a non-hardening sealer, like Permatex High Tack, and it should be inserted with a seal driver only. Do not try to install any grease seal with a punch as you will probably warp the seal and render it useless. Always install grease seals with their lips facing toward the lubricant reserve, and always coat the seal lips with a little

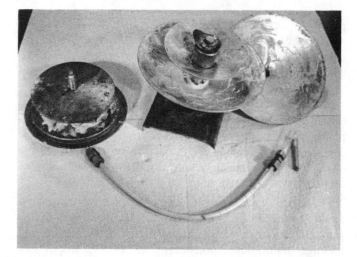

You can rub grease into wheel bearing cups, rollers and outer races, but it's a messy job. The two grease cones pictured here make this a much neater job. The needle greaser, shown in front of the grease cones, can be used with a grease gun to inject grease between wheel bearing rollers or balls.

This seal driver has just enough adapters to drive almost any wheel bearing seal that a restorer will ever encounter. If you don't have a seal driver in a needed size, it is easy enough to make one.

grease. If seals are made of leather or felt, they should be soaked in heavy oil for at least 30 minutes prior to installation. Always check seal mating surfaces for burrs, scratches, or other defects, and remove these with a file and sandpaper, or solve the problem by replacing the spindle. Coat seal wiping surfaces with a smear of grease. Some installations utilize a removable hub spacer; be sure to include this in reassembly if it is used.

Being very careful not to damage the seal lip on the spindle threads, the hub can now be lifted and placed back on the spindle, and the seal engaged with its mating surface. While supporting the outer end of the hub with one hand, insert the outside bearing inner race and rollers (or balls) and place the bearing thrust washer, spindle nut, and spindle nut lock (if used) in position. Much older installations use a second nut and lock plate here. The wheel bearings can now be "adjusted" for preload or end play. Never forget to install the cotter key after adjustment.

Ball bearing front wheel bearings either use some specified preload or zero clearance. Preload is set with a torque wrench to manufacturers' specifications. If it is specified, zero clearance is best checked with a dial indicator attached to some convenient part of the hub and indicated off the spindle's end. Generally, the specified clearance for older cars will be in the 0.002 inch to 0.005 inch range for tapered roller bearings, and about 0.001 inch for cars equipped with disc brakes. These clearances are best determined by using a torque wrench to tighten the spindle nut, as the hub is turned in the direction of its forward rotation. A torque of 10 or 15 pounds will seat the wheel bearings. The spindle nut is then backed off and retightened, finger tight. It is then backed off a specified number of nut castellations — usually from one to three — and secured with the cotter key. Do not overtighten the spindle nut during the initial seating procedure as the small points of contact of the bearing races and balls or rollers make damage to them a very real possibility. Do not put too much faith in the dial indicator method of checking clearance as the grease in the bearings will tend to interfere with any precise measurement of end play. Always check the final assembly of a wheel bearing for play by shaking the wheel with your hands, but be sure not to confuse ball joint or king pin play with wheel bearing play. With the wheel and tire on, you should feel barely perceptible wheel bearing play in roller bearing equipped front spindles.

While too much play will damage the bearing components and possibly cause a steering shimmy or brake vibration, wheel bearings that are too tight will quickly overheat, score or spawl, and self-destruct. Remember, there must be room for roller bearing parts to expand as they get hot, and the inner races must be loose enough to be able to creep around their spindles. After you have done enough of them, you get a feel for front wheel bearings that allows you to affect proper adjustments. The final step in wheel bearing replacement or packing is to coat the sealing edge of the axle cap with a non-hardening sealer and tap it evenly into place. If the cap has a funny copper wafer spring in it that is part of the car's radio static suppression system, it   should be stretched enough so that it contacts the end of the spindle and reinstalled.

Drum Brake Friction Systems

My first recollection of brakes dates from the early 1950s, when the kids in my town were all deeply involved in the soap box derby. The year that I began to notice such things, the "brakes" on these kids' gravity carts consisted of a pedal which, when pushed by the operator, rubbed directly on the road's surface; thus breaking the cart's momentum-derived speed. It was primitive, but it worked. I remember wondering why automobiles didn't use the same kind of apparatus to stop. Shortly thereafter, the official soap box derby rules changed and required brakes that bore directly on the vehicles' "tires." This system consisted of a board that was positioned on a pivot and moved by cables and pulleys. When the brakes were operated, the snubber board rubbed against the front surfaces of the rear wheels and slowed the racing cart. Of course, this was a much more difficult system to construct than the road snubber that it replaced, and there was a good deal of grumbling about that. But it did stop the carts more certainly and with less sideways deviation than the old system. I remember thinking that this was the height of engineering sophistication — the ultimate in vehicle braking. Again, I wondered why automobiles didn't operate their brakes with similar hardware. While I now understand the drawbacks of these two types of braking system, I still find their simplicity alluring — particularly when I find myself involved in repairing one of the more complex modern hydraulic drum or disc systems.

Of course what all braking systems have in common, whether they are soap box derby style or the latest four-wheel floating caliper disc setups, is the function of exchanging mechanical motion for friction. The engine of an automobile burns gasoline or other fuel to produce heat — which is energy. This energy, through the medium of expanding air, or water vapor, drives pistons or rotors that are linked in some fashion to the vehicle's wheels to produce mechanical motion. Braking reverses this process by using mechanical pressure to create massive friction to counter a car's forward or rearward momentum. This applied friction produces sudden and massive heat buildup, which the braking system must then dissipate into the environment. When you stop and think that the average city-driven car in these United States has its brakes applied more than 50,000 times a year, and exchanges roughly 30 percent of its kinetic energy for the heat resulting from braking, it all seems awfully wasteful. In fact, it is so wasteful that generations of inventors and tinkerers have tried to capture some of the energy extravagantly dissipated in braking and store it in media such as compressed air or electricity so that it can be put to purposeful use. To date these efforts have failed due to the logistics of the situation and the weight and complexity of the hardware that is proposed to effect recapture of this energy.

Braking design, then, is the business of finding ways to create friction and dissipate the resulting heat in compact, reliable, and convenient packages. Early automobile innovators were more concerned with making their machinery go than with stopping it, and they initially followed carriage practice with "spoon" brakes or levers that acted directly on hard tires much like the *improved* soap box derby design mentioned previously. By the time of the epochal 1885 Benz, a crude transmission brake had become popular among the then nascent automobile builders of the world, and this system remained popular as late as the 1920s, as evidenced by the Model T Ford. Other popular early braking systems included drive shaft brakes that brought contracting brake shoes to bear against a drum mounted on a car's drive shaft, and rim brakes that acted on the wheel rims, much as modern bicycle hand brakes do. There were oddball variants of these primitive systems, like cable brakes that wrapped around wheel drums, and the delightful system used on early Lanchesters (always different) that activated a braking cone opposed to the clutch cone to brake the car's motion when the clutch was depressed beyond disengagement.

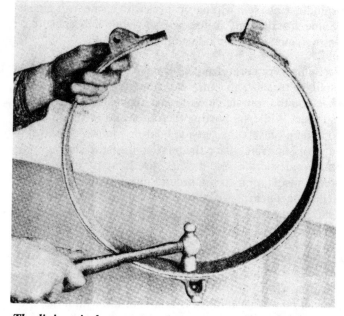

The linings in large external contracting brakes have to be smoothed out with a hammer as they are riveted to their shoes.

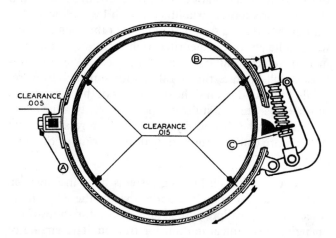

You can eyeball external contracting brakes and figure out how they work and how they are adjusted. Their advantages end there.

After 1900, the convention of a rear drum brake had been adopted by most manufacturers, although transmission brakes continued to be popular on cars with planetary (epicyclic) gearsets. These drum brakes were usually external contracting systems. Sometimes external contracting bands were combined on the same drums as internal expanding shoe systems to provide separate foot and hand brakes. Compared to what had gone before, these systems were very effective, reliable, and compact.

By 1920, internal expanding drum brakes had become the convention, and by the middle of that decade, hydraulic activation was beginning to appear. The self-servo principle, which uses the rotary motion of a wheel to transfer a small part of a car's kinetic energy to one or both ("single servo" or "dual servo") brake shoes, and thus assist the operator's foot-applied braking effort, was being perfected; as were better lining materials and better brake drum constructions. The 1930s saw the continued evolution of the hardware for self-servo brakes, the common use of vacuum power assist units on heavier

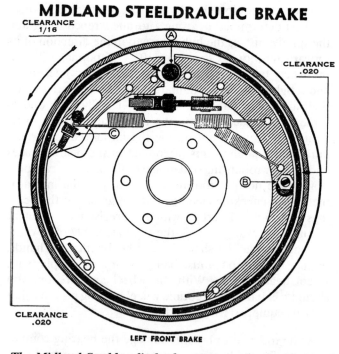

MIDLAND STEELDRAULIC BRAKE

The Midland Steeldrualic brake was a mechanical internal expanding brake that was favored by Ford long after the competition had gone to hydraulic brakes.

cars, and the universal acceptance of hydraulic brakes. (Ford was, of course, the last major manufacturer to adopt hydraulic activation systems. Seems Henry didn't like things that he couldn't understand.)

From the late 1930s until the introduction of full disc brakes by Chrysler in the early 1950s brake design, and even actual brake hardware, changed little from the late 1930s. There was continuous improvement in friction materials for shoes, but design advances encompassed mostly short-lived, minor innovations like pressed steel brake drums and aluminum-lined-iron brake drums, and miscellaneous hardware to make brakes "self-adjusting." Gradually, the aircraft derived caliper disc brake system evolved from Chrysler's wonderful but cumbersome full disc system of the early 1950s. Caliper disc brakes then evolved into the now common floating ("slider") caliper systems that grace the front axles of almost every car made today, and the axle of many.

Some General Working Considerations

The balance of this chapter will deal with the internal expanding drum brake systems that have dominated the field from the 1920s until the 1970s when disc brakes began to replace them, at least in front. External contracting brakes and transmission or drive shaft brakes were so specialized to each manufacturer that they are best dealt with using specific manufacturers' instructions and data. Disc brakes are not covered here because modern repair information that is readily available deals with them, and few collector cars use them anyway.

The first consideration in brake work is that these are precise systems that must operate under very demanding conditions. Brake temperatures of 300° Fahrenheit to 400° Fahrenheit are common, and sporadic temperatures of 600° Fahrenheit to even 700° Fahrenheit can occur in heavy braking situations. On the average car in heavy braking, forces involving literally hundreds of horsepower may come into play. All of this means that the parts of a brake system are highly stressed and require the most exacting work in repair and restoration. If, for example, grease is allowed to get on brake friction parts, it will modify their friction characteristics to the point of rendering the brakes useless.

Brake work should be backed up with good, specific information regarding the system that you are working on. Shop manuals, *Motor's* and *Chilton* manuals, and other sources of information should be used extensively. You should understand the function and environment of every part in a system that you are restoring. Raybestos Manhattan prints a particularly good general manual on braking systems that has specific information on current and older cars. Brake component manuals go back to the 1930s, under various authorship and sponsorship, and are prime sources of brake restoration information. Older automobile owners' manuals usually contain extensive information on brake adjustment procedures; many of them even deal with relining procedures. Automobile shop manuals always contain extensive data on the braking systems for the cars that they cover.

When you work on any aspect of a braking system, it is necessary to consider the whole system. Repairs to friction system parts must always be performed on pairs of brakes, front or back. My preference is to go through every aspect of the hydraulic, mechanical, and friction systems of any braking system that I work on, no matter what the original complaint may have been. It is, for example, dangerous to work on the friction parts of a braking system without inspecting the hydraulic system for bad hoses, leaking cylinders, or deteriorating lines. Or you can have a system that has worn friction parts but a perfectly operating hydraulic system. However, when you install new shoes or pads, the hydraulic pistons are pushed back into an area in their cylinder bores where they have not been working, and where pitting and deposits may cause rapid failure of the piston seals and result in system leaks. In this case, the new shoe facings that were installed will probably be ruined by leaking fluid, and the whole job will have to be redone. Worse, the system will be dangerous after the first repair.

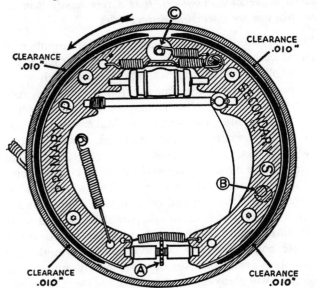

The principle on which "servo" brakes operate is simple enough, but you absolutely have to know which shoe is primary and which is secondary when you rebuild one of these systems. The primary shoe will always be the first shoe from the anchor pin in the direction of rotation of the brake drum.

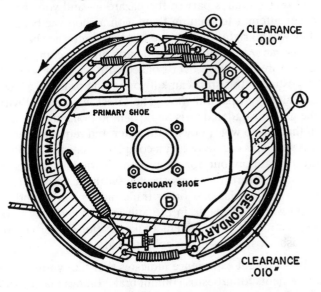

This single acting hydraulic brake is of the servo type and uses a single acting hydraulic piston. By the time you add self-adjusting hardware to a brake like this, it gets pretty complex. This one is manually adjusted and is relatively simple.

As I said, the expense and time involved in renovating *whole braking systems* will pay off in the long run. Complete brake rebuilds produce a degree of certainty that is wholly appropriate to a safety system that is as critical as brakes are. Remember, old hydraulic systems do not have the redundancy that modern systems do (dual hydraulic circuits) so one small area of failure can cause them not to operate.

New grease seals are a must when front brakes are restored. Rear brakes should at least get new outer seals if a two seal system is used, and certainly new seals if a one seal system is provided. You just don't want to sacrifice the time and money involved in brake work — not to mention personal safety — to the probability that a $4 seal that has not been replaced will ruin the job.

Because brake work involves new linings and grinding, cutting, or replacing drums, it will modify drum friction characteristics (coefficient of friction). It is essential, therefore, that brake work encompass *both* brakes at either end of a car. Never work on just one brake, or you will almost inevitably produce a car that swerves in braking. I have seen people take a can of chlorinated solvent and an air gun and "clean up" an oil soaked set of brake linings with the misconception that they have effected a repair. This can become a doubly deadly misconception because in the long run, the asbestos that they blow around will probably get them, and in the short run, the grabbing, uneven brake system that they have created will put their lives at risk and also threaten the innocent people who have to share the roads with them. When seals leak, replace them in axle pairs, and replace the oil soaked linings that they have contaminated.

Virtually all collector car brakes will have shoes made from asbestos compounds that are either molded or woven. This stuff is dangerous and is virtually impossible to handle safely. Asbestos fibers are exceedingly short and thin — that's part of the hazard — and you should never attempt to vacuum them with a shop vac because they will go right through the filter and into the shop air. *Never, never* blow brake system parts off with compressed air before they have been soaked with water or solvent. Exposure to this stuff can kill you in one or more of several slow and painful ways. The safest way to deal with the asbestos-laden debris found behind brake drums, and in them, is to wet it down with water and remove it while it is wet. This certainly isn't a completely satisfactory hazard precaution, but, for the present, it will have to do. In the near future the non-asbestos synthetic brake lining materials (Kevlar and other trade names for aramid fibers) will be available in the aftermarket and may have application as replacement brake friction materials for the asbestos linings in our collector cars.

Some recent experience indicates that the synthetic replacements for asbestos content brake linings may be too abrasive for the metallurgy of some old drums, and it will be difficult or impossible to find molded linings in some diameters for older cars. Worse still, present legislation will soon prohibit commercial stripping of asbestos content linings from brake shoes, and it may be very difficult

to find providers of relined shoes. All of this is stated in the nature of describing present and future problems for those who rebuild the brakes on old cars. It is unclear at this time what the solutions to these problems will be. For those of us who work on older cars, it is essential that we be ever mindful of asbestos hazards. Some recent assessments of these hazards have claimed that the dangers of working with automotive friction surfaces have been overstated because automotive applications of this fiber tend to result in grinding off the "hooks" that bond the fibers to human tissues. This may be true, but I have not seen a scintilla of evidence that suggests that asbestos brake debris is not dangerous to human health. I suggest that if you work regularly, or even occasionally, with old brakes, you treat asbestos debris like "the black death."

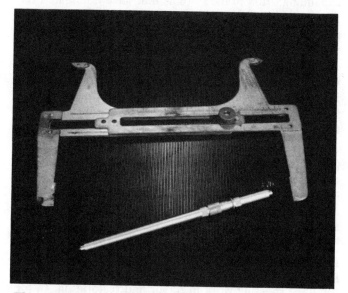

The tubular micrometer in the foreground of this picture allows precise measurements of brake drum diameters. The brake gauge in back of it measures both drum diameters and installed brake shoe diameters. It is a very handy item to have when you are assembling drum brakes.

Drum brake systems can contain a fair number of springs, washers, pins, levers, cables, and other parts that can go "plink" on the floor when brakes are taken apart. This is particularly true in the more complex, self-energizing (servo), self-adjusting brake systems that came into use after the mid-1950s. Make sure that you keep track of where and how parts go, and be sure to draw diagrams, take pictures, or refer to appropriate manuals if you have any doubts. Brakes can be misassembled and will not work properly if "only a little bit" is wrong. When I first worked on brakes, I often found it useful to take one side of an axle pair apart and reassemble it before I did the other side so that the brake on the opposite end of the axle was available as a model for reassembly. Small mistakes of misassembly are easy to make, and will always cause problems, but there are some big mistakes available too.

For example, modern systems of the single, fixed anchor, servo type use a "primary" and a "secondary" shoe system. In this system the primary shoe has a shorter lining and does very little braking. Instead, it uses a little of the kinetic energy that the passing drum surface imparts to it to wrap or pivot the two shoes around the anchor pin and force the secondary shoe into the drum surface. It's a neat trick to use a car's motion to produce an enhancement of braking force to stop the car. The only problem is that since the primary and secondary shoes often differ only in lining length or sometimes only in lining material, it is very easy to mix up these shoes at the time of installation. The result is a braking system that tends to be mostly ineffective, but which also may tend to lock up or grab violently at high speed. In this case, careful notation at the time of disassembly, having an opposite axle for comparison or a good reference manual, or some theoretical knowledge will help. In fact, you should already have the necessary theoretical knowledge from reading the preceding sentences to sort out primary and secondary shoes in a servo brake system. The primary shoe, with the shorter lining, will always be the first one in the direction of forward wheel rotation from the anchor pin. Think about it!

Brake reconditioning tools, like shoe arc grinders and drum lathes and grinders, are complex, expensive and potentially dangerous; so this work will almost certainly have to be sent out. There are a few relatively inexpensive hand tools and gauging devices that are necessary to work on brakes. Good brake pliers, hold-down spring tools, and piston retainers are on the necessary list. A drum/shoe diameter caliper gauge will be very helpful but is not essential.

Drum Brake Fault Diagnosis

The main symptom of brake malfunction is pretty obvious and pretty deadly — a car fails to stop in a straight line in a reasonable distance. Precursors to this symptom can be odd noises and vibrations that occur when the brakes are applied. Any of these symptom clusters will require brake inspection. The causes of the symptoms will *usually* be evident in conditions like leaking fluid or worn, warped, or scored parts. Low brake pedal is usually caused by actuating system faults, but it can also have its origin in the friction system. This is particularly true in disc brake systems where misadjustment of the rear brakes combines with pad wear in the front brakes to produce low pedal. Failure of a drum brake's self-adjusting system can also cause this problem.

Obscure problems such as a loose backing plate or wrong or incorrectly installed parts from a previous rebuild can also cause brake problems. Sometimes brake symptoms have their origins in defects in other, related systems. Bad wheel alignment will frequently be particularly evident under braking conditions, and loose wheel bearings can often do a very good imitation of a defective brake shoe system.

Drum and Shoe System Disassembly and Inspection

Brake drum removal is accomplished by removing wheel nuts or lugs, after which a brake drum can usually be removed. Some rear brakes and many front brakes will require hub removal to get the drums off. This procedure was covered in this chapter, under the front wheel bearing topic, and in the last chapter with regard to rear axle drums.

Always be sure that the parking bake is not engaged when removing rear brake drums, and if the shoes offer any resistance to removal, back off their adjusting mechanism — with particular care to raise the star wheel locking lever on self-adjusting mechanisms — *before* any attempt is made to back the star wheel off. Some drums are pretty well frozen to their hubs, and a drum puller can be used within reason to effect removal. Heat applied around the studs and on the center boss will help, but it must be very moderate heat to avoid damaging these parts.

On particularly stubborn drums that won't yield to heat and mild shock, or to a puller and judicious tapping with a brass hammer, there is a trick. It consists of driving one

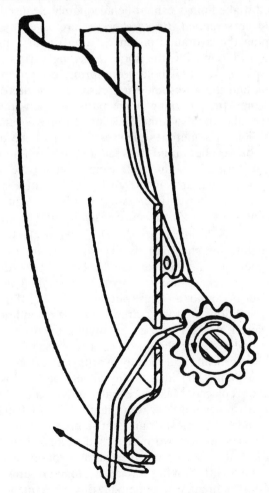

You'll need a special, curved tool to adjust the star wheels on drum brakes. Most of these adjusters have a locking wire that has to be lifted and kept off the wheel while you adjust it.

or more of the wheel studs back into the drum — be careful that the stud isn't forced into any of the brake mechanism — with a hammer, and insinuating the end of a small, *cheap* (78¢ or less) screwdriver between the drum and the hub. A little wedging with the screwdriver and a hammer will free the most recalcitrant, stuck brake drum. You may have to drive several studs in (they are almost always held by friction, but if they aren't, don't use this trick) to get enough positions for this wedging maneuver to work. You will probably have to repair burrs that you raise on the drum and hub, and you will certainly "total" the screwdrivers that you use for this purpose. On the good side, not only does this trick work, but it also provides an appropriate use for the 78¢ (or less) screwdrivers that you see in bins in the middle of supermarket aisles — I know of no other legitimate or illegitimate use for them.

When brake drums have been removed, the debris behind them should be flushed away with water. Oil should be removed with a solvent-saturated rag. Then throw the rag away. Water, alcohol, and chlorinated brake solvents are the only solvents that should ever be used on brake friction surfaces. Petroleum-based solvents must never be used on brake linings or drums. If very minor grease or oil residues must be removed from these parts, this should be done with chlorinated brake solvents. Badly soaked brake linings cannot be adequately cleansed and should be scrapped. Brake shoes are removed by first clamping the hydraulic pistons (if used) with a piston clamp and removing the shoe retracting springs with brake pliers. The shoe hold-down springs can now be removed, and the shoes and their push rods (if used) will then come free. Parking brake parts and self-adjuster parts should now also come free. Spring removal can be a clumsy job. It sometimes involves the use of the pliers end of brake pliers used between a spring end and the lining material. Sometimes the cupped end of the pliers handle is rotated around the anchor pin to lift a spring end off of it. Conventional swear words are legitimate here, but check for the presence of small children.

With all of the hardware off, clean the backing plate thoroughly, and check for damage to it and for its tight attachment to the axle or spindle boss. Brake drums should be checked for cracks, scores, taper ("bell mouthing") out-of-round, and rust pitting or glazing. If any of these conditions are found, drums must be reconditioned or replaced. A good bore gauge, tubular micrometer, or other similar device should be used to measure several positions vertically and radially in drums. If a drum is off by more than 0.005 inch in any dimension, it must be turned or replaced. Make sure that drums are not ground and/or worn beyond their wear limits. This is 0.060 inch over standard for most drums, but some can go to 0.080 inch. Drums that are worn or turned beyond their wear limits lack the rigidity and thermal absorption capabilities to deal with braking forces and temperatures, and can distort or break with potentially dire consequences.

Shoes should be inspected for lining thickness and uneven wear. Glazing, oil contamination, cracking, and lining adhesion to shoe metal should also be checked. Wear within one-sixteenth of an inch of rivet heads on riveted shoes, and less than roughly one-quarter of an inch of lining on metal on bonded shoes, will mandate relining. Metal shoe parts should be inspected for deformation, weld integrity, and worn ends or elongated pivot points. Defective shoe metal means replacement in most cases since repair is usually impractical.

Other brake hardware should be evaluated critically. Hold down and retracting springs are usually easy to get, and cheap. They should be replaced almost routinely. Certainly stretched or distorted springs or springs that are discolored from heat or from rust must be replaced, and it is generally a good idea to replace all springs if one of them is found to be defective. Brake shoe push rods frequently bend or wear, and if this is the case, replace them. Other adjuster parts can wear or acquire burrs. These should either be completely cleaned, deburred and sparingly lubricated, or, if there is any doubt, they should be replaced. While the cost of replacing all of the minor hardware in a brake system adds up, it is frequently a good investment to go this route. A sticking adjuster or stretched retracting spring that is tolerated in a rebuild can cause all sorts of problems later.

Reconditioning Brake Drums and Shoes

Brake drums can be cut or ground on special drum turning equipment. Some people prefer the theoretical precision of drum grinding. Steel drums should only be ground, not cut. Cutting allows the lathe operator to hear the hard spots in a drum (heat hardened areas) and know when he has cut below them. Grinding does not allow this certainty. In any case, be sure not to cut or grind a drum beyond its diametral limit, and if cutting is used, be sure to employ a slightly rounded cutting tool to avoid "threading" or grooving the drum. A turned drum should be deburred with 80 grit sandpaper and washed in soap and water. Since drum friction surfaces will rust very quickly after they are cut or ground, drums should not be reconditioned until the time of installation is at hand, unless they are immediately treated with a special brake friction surface preservative.

Brake shoe linings are either adhesive bonded or riveted to their metal shoes. Modern bonding techniques, which use a baked adhesive, are so wonderfully effective that many restorers now have all of their relined shoes secured by this method. Retaining brake linings to shoes with rivets can be tricky because you never really know how tight they are, and riveted shoes do not provide for the level of heat transfer from linings to metal shoes that bonded shoes do. Rivets can work loose under lining stress conditions, but the newer bonding adhesives seem to perform perfectly. Of course, external contracting shoes and transmission brake shoes require relatively soft friction materials, which have to be riveted in almost all cases. The more common internal expanding brake systems use molded shoes that are compatible with adhesive bonding, whether this was the original attaching technique or not. Some restorers both bond and rivet brake shoes, and that may be a very good idea.

For many years brake shoes were available in oversizes in increments of 0.010 inch, designated X, XX, XXX, and XXXX. Shoes were then matched to drum diameter requirements after drums were turned. The shoes were then "arc ground" ("arced") or cam ground to specification. On non-servo brakes, this grind was from 0.010 inch to as much as 0.025 inch under final drum diameter, which would allow about 0.005 inch clearance between the ends of the shoes and the drum, with the center of the shoe in contact. Servo brakes worked on 0.040 inch or more diametral difference between the shoes and the drums for 0.010 inch or more of shoe end clearance.

Unfortunately, arc grinding shoes — which is the only proper way to replace brake shoes — involved the use of grinders that made little or no provision for dealing with asbestos hazards. People died from operating these machines, and strict regulatory action was taken. The current crop of "safe" arc grinders is so expensive to buy and insure that few concerns do arc grinding anymore. The exacting "cam grinds" that many collector car brake shoes require can be very hard to procure. Yet reconditioning brakes without the benefit of an arc grind is poor practice. Shoe contact can be so slight or so improperly positioned as to glaze and crack shoes very quickly after reconditioning. For the work in this area that I do, I have found a supplier who will bond shoes with new linings of the correct thickness for oversizes or at least shim new linings to the correct dimensions, and arc grind them for a proper drum fit. There are still several regional suppliers who offer this service, and it is well worth seeking them out.

One practice that should be avoided is using metalized linings in applications that originally called for nonmetallic lining materials. Metalized linings should be used where they are provided for in original design, and never used in unauthorized applications. These linings require a rigorous 20 micron drum finish that can be difficult to achieve with some of the drum finishing equipment out there.

Reassembly of Drum Type Brakes

Drum brakes reassemble in the reverse order of their disassembly. The raised riding pads on brake backing plates should be *lightly* smeared with a high temperature grease before remounting shoes. Push rods and shoe engaging ends should get the same treatment, as should the parking brake strut ends and anchor pins. The shoes can now be engaged with the various pieces of hardware of the parking brake and self-adjuster systems, and held in place by installing their hold-down springs. Be sure to sparingly lubricate the self-adjuster parts with a dry lubri-

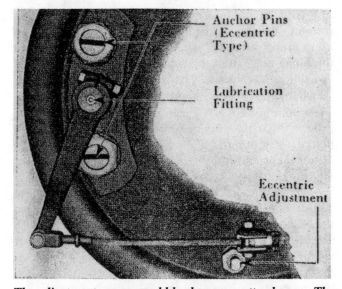

The adjustments on some old brakes are pretty obscure. The mechanical drum setup shown here requires some special attention when you adjust it.

cant, such as graphite, and check to make sure that they are very free to move and to allow for self-adjustment. The retracting springs can now be installed, using either brake pliers hooking ends or the spring anchor installing tool that is formed out of the sharp end of most brake pliers handles. Be careful not to over-stretch the retracting springs during installation, and be sure to use photos, notes, manuals, or the model of the opposite brake to get them in the right places and correct orientations. Some springs that are seemingly identical differ only in tension. These are usually identified by a color code that must be followed, or the brakes won't work properly.

A final check of the common single, fixed anchor pin brake system operation can be made by moving the bottom of the shoe/adjuster assembly fore and aft an inch or so to check for freedom of motion. Throughout brake shoe and hardware installation, try to avoid touching the linings and drum surfaces, and if any contamination has gotten on them, remove it with repeated applications of a chlorinated brake solvent and a very clean rag or towel. The shoe adjuster should now be backed off sufficiently for the drums to be installed and secured in place.

"Major" and "Minor" Brake Adjustments

Drum brake systems that have an adjustable anchor pin or, in the case of dual activation systems, two adjustable anchor pins, must have their shoes centralized on their backing plates after a rebuild has disturbed this relationship. In some cases the adjustment is made by turning an anchor pin cam after its locking nut has been loosened. In other cases, the anchor pin is moved up and down by tapping it with a hammer. In either case, the object of this "major adjustment" is to center the shoes in the drum. Various procedures are specified for this setting, from hit and miss methods to using brake activation to center the shoes. The best method is almost always to use a brake centering gauge, which describes a circle at the lining edge from the spindle. If such a gauge is not available, one can usually be fabricated easily.

"Minor brake adjustments" are often necessitated by wear, but must always be made after relining brakes. It is essential that the parking brake be completely released before attempting either major or minor adjustments. Minor adjustments are typically affected by either turning cam adjusters on the backing plate, or by adjusting a star wheel adjuster behind the drum. The object of these adjustments is to bring brake shoes as close as possible to the brake drums without actually touching them. In both cases, the shoes are brought into hard contact with drums via the adjusting mechanism, and then backed off a specified number of notches or flats (or by dimension) until no contact exists.

The amount of back-off is specified for each type of brake, and must always be the same on all wheel pairs. It is critically important that brake shoes be brought into an initial hard contact with their drums before they are backed off, and that there be no drag when this adjustment is completed. In the case of self-adjusting brakes, a rough adjustment should be made at the time of shoe installation, and the self-adjuster lock lever or wire must be held off the star wheel during adjustment. Failure to do this can damage the self-adjusting mechanism. In the case of cam-adjusted brakes (minor adjustment), be sure that the adjusting nut is locked by friction or a locking nut so that it can't vibrate out of adjustment after the adjustment. You must replace any rubber covers or hole plugs that you remove from brake backing plates to gain access to cam adjusters or to star wheel adjusters. Failure to replace these covers can result in corrosion damage to brakes and poor braking, if the brakes get excessively wet.

After repairing self-adjusting brakes, a car should be driven backward and stopped in reverse several times to allow the self-adjusters to activate. I always make a final check of brake adjustment by making a hard stop in our gravel driveway. During this stop I check to see if the steering wheel pulls to one side or the other, and note any tendency of the car to swerve. I then inspect the driveway for roughly equal length "skid marks" in the gravel. This procedure has saved me thousands of dollars because it has given me a justification for not installing one of the blacktop and asphalt driveways that my neighbors favor. It's also a good place to check out brake adjustments.

This homemade brake adjusting tool allows you to adjust brakes that have to be centered with a gauge. The bearing in the tool fits on a wheel spindle and the gauge arm stop is set to the correct diameter. Then the brake shoes are adjusted until the tool can be swung around them with a consistent clearance from the tool arm stop to the brake linings.

CHAPTER 17:

Brake Actuating Systems

Of course, the most important proposition with the earliest automobiles was to make them go, and little attention was devoted to the business of stopping them. Such crude braking devices as had been used on horse-drawn vehicles more than sufficed to stop cars in the early motoring age. However, these devices were not adequate for the task of slowing and stopping the multi-cylinder automobiles that began to appear at the turn of the century, and various expanding and contracting drum brake devices and combinations came into use.

These drum brakes were, in every case, activated mechanically by the application of levers, cams, rods, cables, and the like. In almost every case, braking was accomplished by slowing the motion of only the rear wheels, either directly via drum brakes mounted on them, or indirectly, via drive shaft or transmission mounted drum brakes. In the case of wheel braked systems, an equalizing bar pivoted off a central point was used — much like the equalizer used on contemporary parking brakes — but even with that addition, these systems were remarkably simple to construct and easy to maintain. The few four-wheel brake systems that appeared in this era, such as were used by Mercedes on some of their powerful behemoths, were cumbersome, complex, and finicky. It was generally assumed at this time that braking the front wheels of an automobile would cause an automobile to flip end-for-end over the axis of its front wheel bearings. Besides, no one had yet devised a practical mechanism for activating front brakes that would maintain independence when the front wheels were turned. In any case, equalizing such a system to the rear brakes was beyond the imagination of most early automobile designers.

By the mid-1920s, and in some cases before that, the increasing power-to-weight ratios of cars made it necessary to find braking systems that were more aggressive than the prevalent two-wheel systems. The earliest of the four-wheel brake systems in this era used complex arrangements of cables and pulleys to activate the drum brakes on front wheels with lots of hardware to allow for steering, equalization, and proportioning of force between the front and rear brakes. This quickly gave way to Perrot rod activation (universal jointed, rod activated devices) which were wonderfully complex and precise, and

Bowden cables which were wonderfully simple, but un-wonderfully prone to binding. The (sheathed) Bowden cable was, at least, simple and inexpensive to construct, and it became the standard of front wheel brake activation until it was replaced by hydraulic activation.

The application of hydraulics to brake activation had its origin before the turn-of-the-century in bicycle brakes, and is still used on some very deluxe bicycle applications. By the teens of the 20th century, some European car makers were experimenting with this form of brake activation. It was introduced in this country on the 1921 Model A Deusenberg — a car which sported truly "hydraulic brakes" in a very real sense. The working fluid in the system was actually radiator coolant, water. A more satisfactory hydraulic system was brought out by Chrysler in 1924, and by the 1030s, most car manufacturers had adopted this type of brake activation.

The advantages of hydraulic brake are numerous and substantial when compared to the various devices for mechanical activation that had been used. Perhaps most important, you can pipe and hose hydraulic fluid anywhere without having to provide straight paths and clearances as you would for levers and rods. The most complex accesses and positions become easy to accommodate when you don't have to arrange room for mechanical motion. Then, too, hydraulic systems go a long way towards equalizing all four brakes — as long as the shoe mechanisms are not grossly out of adjustment. This is a far cry from the constant meddling that is necessary with the rods, bushings, collars, levers, pulleys, and the like in mechanical systems. When these devices are prone to binding and distortion, hydraulic fluid does not suffer this fault. The proportioning of brake application between front and rear brakes — it was soon discovered that because the front wheels bear most of a vehicle's weight in braking situations, they must do most of the braking — became simply a matter of selecting proper dimensions for the hydraulic cylinders and pistons in the system and, perhaps, providing a limiting valve, or valves, to control rear cylinder pressures. Finally, hydraulic systems are relatively cheap to construct and are very easy to maintain.

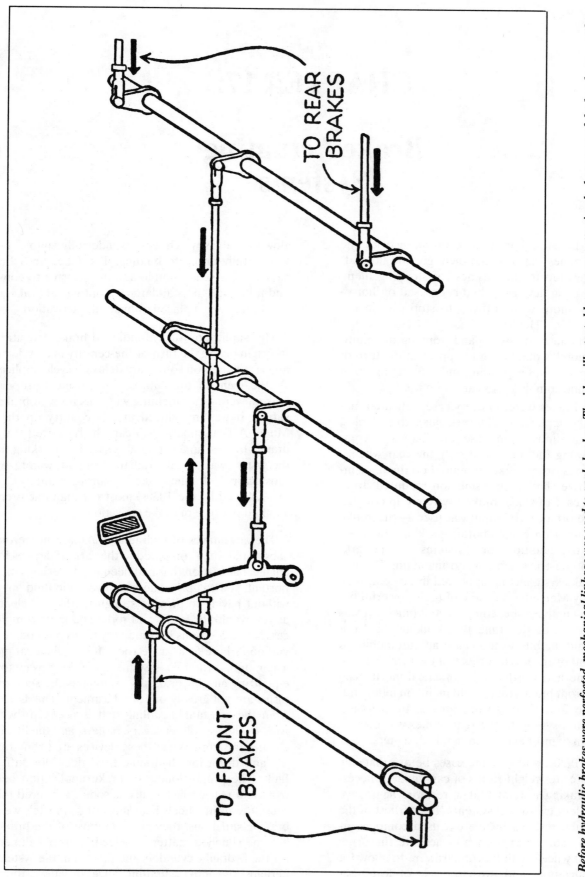

TO REAR BRAKES

TO FRONT BRAKES

Before hydraulic brakes were perfected, mechanical linkage was used to apply brakes. The idea, illustrated here, was pretty simple, but some of the hardware used to implement the idea got pretty "hairy."

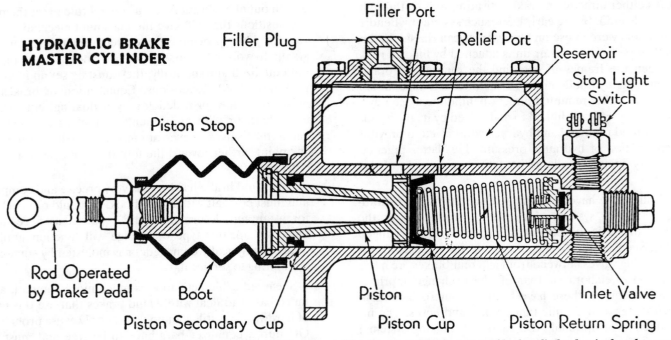

HYDRAULIC BRAKE MASTER CYLINDER

Filler Port · Filler Plug · Relief Port · Reservoir · Stop Light Switch · Piston Stop · Rod Operated by Brake Pedal · Boot · Piston Secondary Cup · Piston · Piston Cup · Inlet Valve · Piston Return Spring

Hydraulic brakes had many advantages over mechanically operated brakes. One disadvantage of hydraulic brakes is that they can fail for causes that are not apparent from an external inspection.

Okay, with all of these advantages there has to be something wrong — certainly Henry Ford thought that there was because he resisted hydraulic brakes into the late 1930s. What was wrong with hydraulic systems, for all of their great advantages, was and is that they are grievously vulnerable to complete and catastrophic failure. We're talking about an emergency in front of you, and your foot pushes almost effortlessly to the floor with no braking effect on your vehicle. Any breach in a single hydraulic system — leaking fittings, ruptured piston seals, rusted through or fatigued tubing, rotted hoses — any of these, and you will lose all four brakes. This applies to almost all collector cars. To eliminate this problem, Saab and Jaguar provided dual hydraulic systems on their cars starting in the 1950s, and such dual systems were required by law on new vehicles sold in the United States after 1966. Mechanically activated brakes may work badly when they are not properly maintained, but they do work. Neglect the inspection and maintenance of hydraulic brakes, and you will likely get a far more intimate view of another automobile or feature of the landscape than you had ever cared to. And hydraulic systems deteriorate from the day of manufacture. Often they do so internally and thus invisibly.

The vulnerability of hydraulic brakes has been recognized since their inception. A hydraulic system does, of course, have mechanical backup in the hand brake system, but this hardly provides adequate braking to stop a vehicle at speed in an emergency. On their premier car in 1950, Saab recognized this hazard and introduced "dual diagonal" hydraulic circuitry on their cars. It relied on two separate hydraulic systems to activate pairs of brakes in a diagonal pattern. At about that time, Jaguar had a similar system, "tandem brakes," that used separate hydraulic systems for front and rear brakes. In either system, if a hose ruptured or a line failed, you still had the

benefit of one front and one rear brake on opposite sides of the car, or of a front or rear pair of brakes, to stop the car. In 1966, the government of the United States made the requirement of separate and redundant hydraulic systems one of the first "safety" rules applied to passenger cars sold here. As these systems have developed since the 1960s, proportioning valves and pressure limiting valves have become accustomed parts of them, as well as warning lights that indicate a failure in one of the two hydraulic circuits.

While hydraulic brakes represent a usable and compact system that can be activated with reasonable pedal pressure and travel, without some sort of assistance, they may not apply enough braking pressure to stop a car within a suitable distances. The use of self-energizing ("servo" and "dual servo") shoe devices helps to solve this problem up to a point, but if you go too far down the self-energizing road, you get brakes that can lock up violently when applied at high speed. The infamous Midland "Steeldraulic" brakes of the 1930s are an example of this. The inherent performance limits of simple hydraulic brakes, taken together with the American public's assumed preference for "feather touch" braking, has resulted in the development of various mechanisms to provide "power assist" for braking purposes. Such efforts go back to Rolls-Royce in the 1920s, when that firm used clutched mechanical power from a transmission driven disc to enhance brake output. The French, always fascinated with the use of hydraulics, used engine pumped hydraulic fluid to activate their brakes on some cars, like the Citroen DS-19 — with the brake pedal being little more than a variable aperture hydraulic valve. The most common of these assist devices was, and is, the "HydroVac" type, that uses a vacuum reserve tank evacuated by engine manifold vacuum to activate a piston or diaphragm that enhances applied brake pressure. This works either directly on brake activating rods or through hydraulic fluid. By the early 1930s, such systems by Bendix and others were in use on heavy American classics in the form of piston-in-canister units attached by linkage rods between the frames of cars and the mechanical brake linkage. As hydraulic brakes came into use, vacuum assists were either mounted directly behind the master cylinder and physically linked to and valved by its push rod, or mounted remotely and hydraulically valved to provide amplification of hydraulic pressure. This latter practice was very common to large limousines and trucks of the 1950s.

While there have been many detail changes in hydraulic activation systems since their introduction in the 1920s, the basic concepts of their operation have changed little. Such additions as dual systems and the use of proportioning valves between front and rear brakes are more a matter of elaboration than of a basic change in principles. Of course, there have been vast improvements in such things as hydraulic fluids, lines, and hoses. The introduction of optional ABS (anti-lock braking systems) to American cars in the late 1960s and their subsequent digitalization and wide use by the 1990s represents a major improvement in braking effectiveness and safety. This innovation involves pulsing or modulating the hydraulic pressure to any wheel (or wheels) that decelerate(s) suddenly enough to skid. It produces both radically shorter straight-line stopping distances and increased steering control in most braking situations, and is probably the only basic change in automotive hydraulic braking systems in the last 50 years. Collector cars with hydraulic brake activation share a refreshingly high degree of *sameness* from car to car and decade to decade.

Mechanical Brakes

The operation and repair of mechanical brake activating systems is easy to understand but sometimes difficult to accomplish. The simple, two-wheel systems that operate only rear brakes involve single and double ("push-pull") rods, levers, cross shafts, and clevis or bearing joints. All of these items can be understood from inspection.

Usually, most of this linkage is keyed, splined, or flat-shafted into arbitrary relationships. Where adjustments are possible to the activating linkage of mechanical brakes, it is essential that they only be attempted if a problem is known to exist. There can be many variables in these systems, and each has an effect on the rest of the system. It is never advisable to dismantle one of these systems unless this is necessary to correct wear or misadjustment. If disassembly is attempted, the relationship of shafts to levers and clevis joints and to rods must be noted and reestablished. Adjusting the position of a lever on a shaft will affect the ratio of movement and applied force. It will also create specific dimensional change. Where levers, rods, or clevises are adjustable and have

gotten out of calibration, it is a general rule to set them in the positions that will give the maximum mechanical advantage while providing the correct dimensions for the system to work. Of course, when two sides of a system are not equalized automatically, they must be set up in identical ratios and dimensions. Equalization of brakes is most commonly provided for by a floating, equalizing lever/shaft, or with adjustments at the brake shoes or bands themselves. Never attempt to equalize brakes at any point farther toward the foot or hand activator than is necessary.

Perrot rod brake hardware is very precise and complex and must be dealt with by the book. It should be checked for wear and deformation and repaired as necessary. Once set up, this type of linkage will function until it wears, is physically damaged, or is molested by someone attempting to service it.

Sheathed cable activation is much more common and much easier to deal with. Hand brakes that use this type of hardware are still common, and rarely cause problems. Of course, equalizer bars have to be free and must be lubricated to this end. If a sheathed cable system does not have a provision for lubrication, it can and should be lubricated by spraying the cable entrance and the outside of the sheath with a good penetrating cable oil. This will keep it free and prevent internal corrosion. Cable systems that operate on pulleys require cleaning, lubrication of the pulleys and cables, and adjustment on a routine basis. Cable systems that terminate in a lever and shaft, with the shaft entering the brake backing plate, frequently have a provision for greasing this shaft. Be very careful here to use a minimum of grease because any excess can easily get on the brake shoe facings. When front brakes are operated by cables, it is imperative that interference between the cable sheaths and the front tires be made impossible. Sometimes, large circular rubber bumpers are attached to cable sheaths at the potential points of contact with the tires to this end. Most older cable systems can be greased directly with a fitting or by use of a cable lubricating device. Be sure to use a good quality grease with a rust inhibitor additive for this purpose. When new sheath cables are fabricated from bulk, it's a good idea to inject them with anti-seize lubricant as this will provide almost eternal lubrication and protection from corrosion.

The adjustment of cable systems is usually pretty straightforward. In most applications there is only one adjustment for shoe wear and cable stretch, and this adjustment usually has a self-locking nut or a double nut. A few systems that don't have an equalizing bar allow for individual adjustment of the cables on each side.

Hydraulic Brake Operation

The operation of hydraulic brakes is based on the simple fact that when you exert pressure in one place on an incompressible fluid that is contained in a closed system,

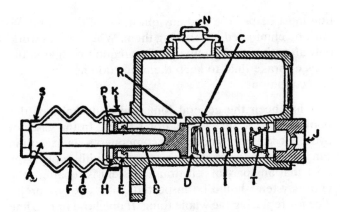

The compensating port ("C" in this diagram) is the key to master cylinder operation. It precisely controls the volume of the fluid in the system and makes up for expansion and contraction of the fluid. Be sure that this port is clear; they sometimes plug up.

it will almost instantly create an elevated and equal pressure in all parts of the system. In practice, this means that a piston (or pistons) in a "master cylinder" is pressed by a brake pedal, via linkage, and compresses the fluid in the master cylinder. The master cylinder is connected by brake lines and hoses to "wheel cylinders" so pressure applied at the master cylinder immediately becomes increased fluid pressure at the wheel cylinders. Pistons in the wheel cylinders are the only other parts of this closed system designed to move, so the pressure exerted on them causes them to move out in their bores.

Thus, as a master cylinder piston moves and displaces the brake fluid in its bore, there is a corresponding movement of the wheel cylinder pistons in their bores. Since they bear indirectly on the ends of the brake shoes, the shoes are moved. That movement brings them into contact with their brake drums.

Not only can an hydraulic system transmit and equalize fluid pressures, it can also proportion them. If, for example, a master cylinder pressurizes a system with front wheel cylinders that have twice the cross-sectional area of the rear wheel cylinders, there will be twice as much mechanical energy available from the front pistons for application of the brake shoes. Further fine-tuning of hydraulic systems can be accomplished with in-line metering, proportioning, and pressure limiting devices. These can limit, time, and sequence the operation of individual parts of the system. In a few rare applications, a restricting baffle is used between the two pistons in wheel cylinders so that one brake shoe gets full hydraulic activation before the other. When you get a feeling for hydraulic theory, you can figure out the reasons behind and functions of fine tuning devices, like this.

All but the earliest hydraulic brake systems use a "compensating port" design. This is necessary because the volume of fluid in a brake system changes minutely as the hydraulic fluid expands and contracts with temperature changes. If, for example, a closed hydraulic system made no provision for this change in fluid volume, an increase in temperature and a corresponding increase in fluid volume might tend to apply the brakes by displacing wheel

cylinder or caliper pistons. In the compensating port design, the brake pedal bears on a push rod that, in turn, bears on a double piston in the master cylinder. This piston has two soft sealing surfaces associated with it — the "primary cup" and the "secondary cup." The primary cup is responsible for pressurizing the closed hydraulic activation system, and the secondary cup seals the whole system from the atmosphere. The compensating port opens the hydraulic pressure system to the fluid reservoir at the completion of each braking cycle, and thus allows fluid adjustments that accommodate changes in fluid volume.

When the brake pedal is released, the forward edge of the primary cup comes to rest just behind the compensating port, which is a small hole in the top of the cylinder that leads to the fluid reservoir. When the brake is activated, the piston pushes the primary cup forward, displacing fluid through the compensating port until the primary cup has moved past the compensating port and the system is thus closed. Further movement of the pedal/piston/primary cup compresses the fluid in the master cylinder bore and exerts pressure through the lines and hoses on the other activating parts of the system. Each time the primary cup returns to rest and uncovers the compensating port, fluid flows to or from the reservoir to provide the correct volume in the working master cylinder bore. If the fluid expands or contracts, it can enter or leave that bore through the compensating port, as necessary.

There are a couple of other wrinkles necessary to make hydraulic brake systems work. One is that as brakes are released, the master cylinder piston is forced back rapidly by the spring that positions it, and it has the potential of creating negative pressure behind it in the system as it recedes. This would create a vacuum bubble that would invite air and moisture to enter. To prevent this, an intake port between the master cylinder bore and the fluid reservoir is provided just behind the rearmost position of the primary cup when it is at rest. The part of the piston that bears against the primary cup has several small holes drilled lengthwise around its periphery. When, as the primary cup and piston return rapidly to rest, the pressure ahead of the primary cup and piston goes below atmospheric pressure, fluid from the reservoir enters the master cylinder bore through the intake port and passes through the holes in the piston, around the primary cup, and into the area in front of the primary cup. This fluid is able to get past the primary cup to fill any vacuum because it is traveling in the opposite direction from the direction in which the cup seals pressure. This ability to prevent the buildup of excessive negative pressure in the hydraulics maintains the integrity of the system.

A second important wrinkle in all but the earliest hydraulic braking designs is the matter of residual pressure. This involves a spring-loaded or cup-type check valve at the output end of the master cylinder bore which maintains a constant pressure of about 12 pounds in the plumbing and hardware beyond the master cylinder. This pressure keeps the wheel cylinder cups expanded and in a state of readiness for brake application. The small pressure that this check valve retains in the entire hydraulic system beyond the master cylinder prevents anything from entering the system through the plumbing connections or wheel cylinder seals. On dual master cylinder units, the residual pressure check valves are positioned on the sides of the cylinders rather than in the ends of their bores.

The secondary cup, which is mounted on the back of the master cylinder piston, serves to align the piston and to seal the system from the outside atmosphere. It plays no part in pressurizing the brake fluid in the hydraulic system.

The master cylinder reservoir is usually part of the cylinder casting, but in some designs it is mounted above the cylinder and connected by a pipe or other means. In any case, the fluid reservoir must have the ability to give up and take on fluid without air locking as the operation of the master cylinder piston and its seals causes fluid to enter and exit through the intake and compensating ports. In older designs, this was a venting function and took place through a small hole drilled in the reservoir cap. More recent applications use a flexible diaphragm under the master cylinder filler cap that can move in and out easily to accommodate volume changes in the reservoir.

A major variation in the compensating port design was used by the British for several years after World War II. It used a mechanically tripped valve that unseated and opened the system to the reservoir at the beginning of each stroke. In this funky system, the master cylinder reservoir is at the end of the cylinder and the output port is in the middle.

Wheel cylinders, or calipers — also called "slave cylinders" — simply respond to the pressure produced by master cylinders. Most wheel cylinders have two opposed pistons with seals ahead of them and a spring to keep the pistons positioned against their brake shoe push rods. Some older designs use blind wheel cylinders with only one piston. This design is called "single acting." A few obscure systems use pairs of single acting cylinders, often on rear wheel brakes with a lever between the pistons to allow operation of hand brakes. There are many other obscure variations on the hydraulic braking theme.

Dual circuit master cylinders have more parts but operate on exactly the same principles as the single master cylinders outlined above. In most of these "tandem" designs, two separate pistons work in the same master cylinder bore, with the rear one bearing against the front one through the medium of a stiff coil spring. One or more seals are used to separate the two pistons. If one of the separate hydraulic subsystems loses its integrity, the brake push rod can still activate the other one.

Hydraulic System Diagnosis

Because the older hydraulic brake systems are single systems and have no backup in the event of failure — a hand brake is hardly an adequate backup — their opera-

tion must be perfect, and any questions of deterioration must be eliminated in servicing them. When brakes work only after they are "pumped up" or require regular additions of brake fluid to keep them functioning, they must be reconditioned.

It has been the general tone and philosophy of this book that "if it ain't broke, don't fix it." In the cases of hydraulic braking systems and components, an exception can and should be made to this tone and philosophy. Any time that any part of a hydraulic system is repaired, the entire system should be inspected, with a strong prejudice for replacing the whole thing. If one hose or one line or one wheel cylinder is leaking, then all hoses, all lines, and all wheel cylinders should be dealt with. Personally, I tend to go further than this. I don't believe in *repairing* the components of hydraulic systems; I believe in *restoring* entire systems. The usual cause of deterioration of any part is corrosion, or corrosion and wear. This factor will affect all parts in a system at different rates. However, if a wheel cylinder is leaking, it is a pretty good bet that the same corrosion that afflicts it has attacked the other wheel cylinders, the master cylinder and the lines, and even the metal reinforcing strands in the hoses. If you don't want to go the route of a complete overhaul when any single defect in hydraulics is encountered, at least *inspect* every component. But remember that dangerous deterioration of hydraulic systems is as likely to be internal as external, so even the most thorough inspection will probably miss critical faults. These faults can be deadly. Keep that in mind when you deal with hydraulics in braking systems.

Inspection of braking hydraulics should begin with the fluid in the master cylinder reservoir and at the slave cylinder bleeder nipples.

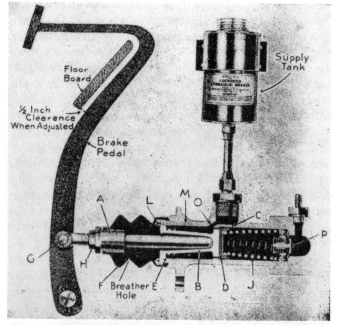

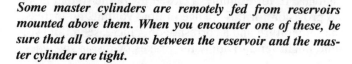

Some master cylinders are remotely fed from reservoirs mounted above them. When you encounter one of these, be sure that all connections between the reservoir and the master cylinder are tight.

If fluid is cloudy or brownish, it is a safe bet that it has been contaminated with moisture, and that internal corrosion in the system is underway. The master cylinder itself should be inspected for leaks with particular attention to any fluid leakage or corrosion that is concealed by the push rod boot. Brake operation should be checked for low pedal, spongy pedal, very high pedal, and sinking pedal. These faults indicate, respectively, fluid leaks in the system or leakage of the primary cup in the master cylinder, air in the system, improper push rod adjustment or improper assembly, or a bad primary cup seal or cylinder surface. Hoses should be inspected for cracks and seeping. Brake lines should be checked for external corrosion and for kinking. Either mandates replacement. Finally, the wheel cylinder boots should be pulled back and the cylinder ends inspected for fluid leakage and visible corrosion. Any of the above defects means a local repair of the problem area at the very least and probably reworking the entire system.

I realize that my suggestion, that any corrosion defect in a hydraulic system should be construed as grounds for refurbishing the whole system, sounds fanatical. Over the years, a couple of rapid approaches toward relatively fixed objects has bred this fanaticism, and this is one of the few forms of that condition that is healthy.

Some General Considerations in Hydraulic Brake Service

In addition to thoroughly inspecting hydraulic braking system components and having a general inclination to restore whole systems in the event of the discovery of defect in any component, you will do well to remember that any change in a friction system can affect the hydraulics. Installing new pads in disc calipers or new linings in drums will force pistons back into their bores where they are likely to have their seals in contact with pitted or otherwise deteriorated cylinder surfaces. This creates a tremendous tendency for calipers and wheel cylinders to leak a few thousand miles after new pad installation or relining. Consider this when you do work on a brake friction system. The advantages of reconditioning entire braking systems at one time are so great that piecemeal reconditioning should be viewed as substandard.

Before hydraulic parts are removed, it is a good idea to label them. Wheel cylinder assemblies should be marked in a way that identifies them as to location on a car. A numbering system will also serve you by making it possible to be sure that if you send cylinders out for sleeving, you can identify the ones that are returned as yours. A few years ago I had a problem with a major supplier of this service in this regard, and my numbering system made it possible to get my parts back from the location to which they had been erroneously returned by the provider.

There is no place in automotive restoration or repair that requires more cleanliness than hydraulic brake work.

This, of course, means that precautions must be taken to keep chips, abrasive grit, and flying smut off hydraulic parts prior to assembly. It also means that great care must be taken to avoid contamination by petroleum-based lubricants and solvents. Under no circumstances should metal or rubber parts be washed in petroleum-based solvents, and if contamination has already occurred, a thorough cleaning in methanol, ethanol, isopropyl alcohol, or in a chlorinated brake solvent is necessary. Petroleum based products cause hydraulic seals to swell and malfunction; very small amounts of contamination can do great damage. Sometimes this contamination is difficult to avoid, as is the case in one method of freeing stuck pistons from wheel cylinders, detailed later in this chapter, but these instances should be kept to a minimum, and complete follow-up cleaning with appropriate solvents must be carried out.

Some automobiles used OEM copper brake lines, and these lines are, in a strict sense, "authentic." Well, this is one place where authenticity should take a back seat to some sense of the preservation of human life. NEVER USE COPPER TUBING FOR BRAKE LINES. I don't know why some manufacturers saw fit to use copper lines as recently as the late 1940s and early 1950s for some parts of braking systems, but I do know that the practice was dangerous. Even super-strength copper alloys lack the toughness to withstand the repeated surges of hydraulic pressure that are common in brake systems. Copper line material will not flare properly for the mandatory "double flare" used in brake hydraulics, and it work hardens severely from road vibration over any long period. I have seen brake failures attributable to the use of copper lines, and this resulted in accidents that really didn't have to happen.

Many parts in an automobile are simply incapable of being misassembled. Suspension parts usually don't fit if they are assembled incorrectly, and if you hook up wiring incorrectly, the electrical components probably won't work. But the hydraulic components in brake systems are both subtly and endlessly susceptible to misassembly. Reversing wheel cylinder cups or getting the parts in a master cylinder out of order can be easy to do. The real problem is that a misassembled component may seem to work for a while, before the inevitable problems occur. There are three ways to confirm the order and orientation of parts in a master cylinder or in wheel cylinders. The logic of operation will make it clear why, for example, the flat side of a wheel cylinder seal always goes against the piston, or why the end of the master cylinder piston with peripheral holes drilled through it always faces the cylinder output end. A good diagram of the component that you are working on will also provide necessary assembly information. Finally, noting how assemblies came apart can usually be relied on to provide the key to reassembly, though this is the least certain of the three methods due to the possibility of misassembly in a previous rebuild.

Hydraulic systems are containment systems that are under continuous attack by corrosion from the inside and the outside. Every sealing part has a logic, and every

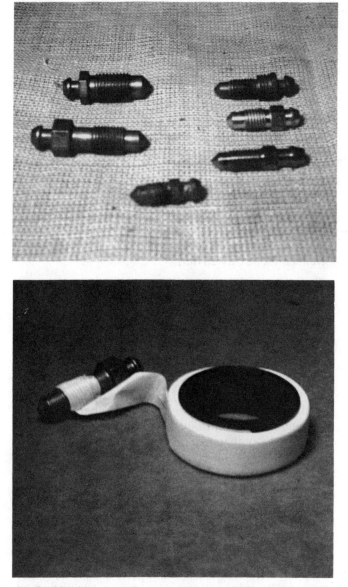

Brake bleeders come in many sizes and shapes. One thing that most of them have in common is that they are easy to snap off when they corrode into the threads that they screw into. A little PTFE ("Teflon") tape applied to their threads helps to prevent them from seizing and seals them to make vacuum bleeding easier.

junction has a reason that it seals. Think about this when you are reassembling a brake hydraulic system. If tapered pipe threads are used to create a seal, then nothing is needed to insure a seal beyond undamaged threads and adequate tightening. If, however, the threads at a junction are not tapered and there is no contact seat visible, it is likely that a seal is achieved by the use of a copper sealing washer. Flares, pipe threads, seats, and copper washers seal because they become slightly deformed and compressed when they are tightly assembled. Any visible physical damage to the surfaces of these parts will probably cause a leak. It is a good idea to routinely replace copper sealing washers, and to check all pipe threads for defects. A meaningful check of sealing surfaces means that you must understand the nature of each seal that is used in a system. Checking for leaks after completing assembly. is also a good idea, but it is no substitute for con-

sidering seal integrity at each junction as you go along.

Master and Wheel Cylinder Disassembly and Inspection

Master cylinders disassemble in a variety of ways. Some have one blind end and others have threaded end plugs and/or snap ring retained washers to keep everything inside. A few master cylinders and some wheel cylinders have stepped bores and use their two diameters for proportioning purposes. A good diagram or some experience will tell you how to get most of these apart. It is also good to remember that the internal parts of master cylinders, and of some wheel cylinders, are under considerable spring pressure so a means must be found of compressing their internal springs, while threaded plugs or snap rings are removed.

Usually, a dull Phillips screwdriver will perform this function admirably when pressed against the back end of the piston where the push rod would normally rest. Be sure to note the location and condition of sealing washers where threaded plugs are used to terminate master cylinders. Many tandem or dual master cylinders use small threaded stop plugs in the sides of cylinders to limit movement of the front piston. Be sure to remove such plugs before beginning disassembly. On single systems the residual pressure check valve will be found at the front end of the cylinder bore and should come out easily. On tandem cylinders these check valves are pressed or threaded into the cylinder output ports on the sides of the bores. If they are pressed in, they will have to be removed by catching them with the threads of a sheet metal screw and prying the head of the screw out.

Wheel cylinder pistons sometimes get stuck in their bores and can be very difficult to remove. When this situation is encountered, it is usually possible to blow them out with air pressure into a bunched rag. Be careful when you do this. You have to contain the pistons, and never eject them in a line where they can hit your body or wedge your fingers against something. They tend to pop out with enormous force. When air pressure is not enough, the car's hydraulic system can be used to force pistons out as long as the other cylinders are still in place and restrained or their lines capped. In extreme cases, I have used a grease gun to provide hydraulic force to remove badly stuck wheel cylinder pistons, but this is a last resort because it creates a petroleum contamination problem, and extensive cleanup must follow this procedure. Of course, any of these pressure methods will only release one piston. That solves the problem in single piston systems. For dual piston wheel cylinders, removal of one piston will allow you to remove the internal cylinder parts: cups, spreaders (if used) and springs. The opposite piston from the one that was removed by pressure can then be carefully tapped out of its bore with a brass drift that is padded on its sides to avoid hard contact with the cylinder walls.

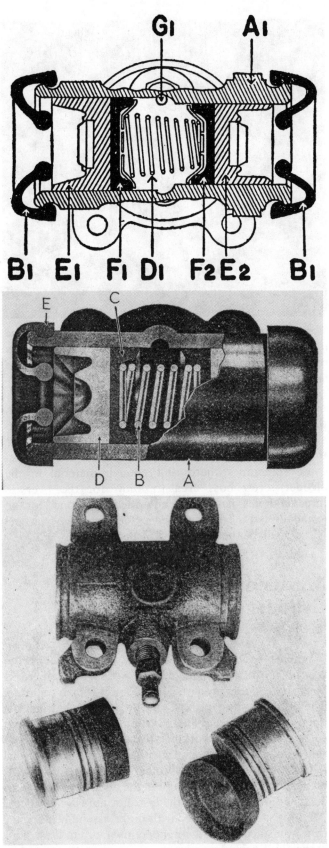

Many master and wheel cylinder kits contain new pistons and, of course, if the old pistons are scored, new pistons should be used. Otherwise, scored pistons can usually be successfully dressed with silica carbide sandpaper (400 to 600 grit) or, preferably, with fine glass bead (AH series). Cylinder walls may suffer either from scores or pits or both. These can sometimes be removed by honing with a brake cylinder hone. Generally, if a cylinder can be cleaned up and a piston-to-cylinder clearance of no more than 0.005 inch maintained, honing is an acceptable repair procedure. When honing is done, it should be held to the minimum material removal necessary to accomplish the job, and a good soap and water wash should follow the honing operation. Always lubricate hone stones with the type of brake fluid that will be installed in the finished system, and always use a very low speed drill to run the hone (800 to 1200 rpm). It is a good idea to follow up the material removal aspect of the honing procedure with a polishing operation. This is accomplished by wrapping your hone stones with a strip of 320 grit abrasive cloth, and running the hone in and out of the bore several times. Cleanup follows this step. Avoid a mirror-like cylinder finish, as it will deprive seal lips of adequate lubrication. Also, always make sure that the master cylinder intake and compensating ports have no projecting burrs that will damage delicate seal lips during installation or operation.

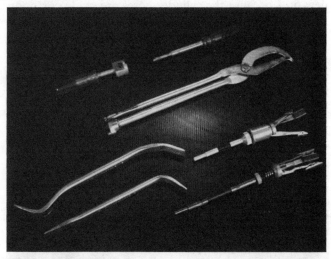

The brake "tool kit," pictured here, has many items that you will need to work on collector car brakes. Top left and right are two types of hold down spring tools. The big pliers below them is used to remove and install many different kinds of brake springs. Below that, and to the left, are star wheel adjusting tools. To the right of them are brake cylinder hones, the one on top is for disc caliper cylinders and the one below it is for regular slave cylinders.

Hydraulic wheel cylinders are pretty simple items. One thing that you should always remember about them is that unlike master cylinders, their pistons do not operate in a bath of hydraulic fluid because their seals are in front of them. This means that if fluid leaks past these seals it will tend to rust cylinder walls and score and corrode the pistons. Good rubber end boots that seal cylinder ends and pistons keep air from circulating near pistons and help to prevent this.

All honing operations should be followed by rigorous inspection of cylinder bores with an inspection light. If any pits or scores are left, or if there is more than 0.005 inch clearance between a cylinder and its piston(s), sleeving or replacement of the cylinder will be necessary because the seals will not work.

Cylinder sleeving is often cheaper than cylinder replacement, and if it is done in brass or stainless steel, it will produce an almost eternal working surface if the hydraulic fluid that is used is kept in good shape. This is because these materials, unlike original cast iron and aluminum cylinder surfaces, are not subject to the kinds of corrosion that will cause leakage. Brass is the most common sleeving material, and although this might seem a poor choice because of this metal's relative softness, it works very well if pistons are properly deburred. Remember, pistons run on a film of brake fluid and should never touch cylinder walls. If they are properly deburred and lubed for assembly, and if brake fluid is not allowed to transmit corrosion particles from other parts of the system into the master and wheel cylinders, cylinder to piston contact and wear will not occur for many years. Wheel cylinder pistons do not run on a film of lubricant or fluid other than what is put on them at the time of assembly. This is because their seals are on their inside ends. Always be sure to use a good film of brake assembly lubricant on these items when you install them.

The problem with honing brake cylinders is that it tends not to work in the long run. By the time you get visible pitting in cylinder walls, there will probably be invisible corrosion risers running into each pit's base through the intergranular structure of the casting metal. This is an ideal location for corrosion to restart after honing, and it frequently does. I vastly prefer properly sleeved master and wheel cylinders to honed items or new ores because the cylinder bores are made corrosion resistant by this process.

A final area of disassembly problems that you may encounter when you get into hydraulic systems is the business of stuck line jam nuts and bleeder nipples. If jam nuts round or split, they can be replaced. Bleeder nipples can sometimes be persuaded out with an air/impact wrench at a low setting. If an air wrench doesn't work, sometimes "tapping sockets" will work, but frequently a

These handy little repair nipples can sometimes be threaded into wheel cylinder and caliper bosses when you break off a nipple. You have to drill and retap to install these parts, and there isn't always enough material to allow this installation.

nipple will break, and removal will have to be pursued by drilling it out. There are some nifty brass nipple seats available that thread into an oversize hole and contain their own nipples. Don't depend on these, however, because sometimes there isn't enough material in the bleeder screw boss area to allow for the oversize threaded holes that have to be drilled and tapped for the installation of these repair items. Sometimes a new wheel cylinder will be the only practical answer.

Master and Wheel Cylinder Assembly

When reconditioned or new master and wheel cylinders and pistons are in hand, and *new* seals and other soft parts have been procured, reassembly can be started. There are two imperatives; get the parts in the right order, and to keep everything scrupulously clean. Be sure to provide a clean working surface, and be careful of things like the contamination that can fall out of your hair (if any) or off your clothing. Never store disassembled hydraulic brake parts out in the open where they can become contaminated with dust and abrasive residues. All parts should be coated with brake assembly lubricant (for non-silicone fluid intended use) or at least with brake fluid prior to assembly. Cups must be started in their bores carefully to avoid lip damage. A blunt plastic probe such as the handle of an artist's paint brush is handy for this purpose.

When a master cylinder is fully assembled, it should be "bench bled" by mounting the cylinder casting in a vise and running a line or hose from its output port(s) into its reservoir(s) and pumping fluid through it by depressing

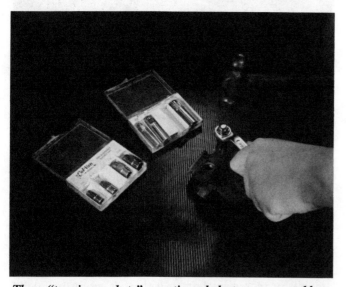

These "tapping sockets" sometimes help to remove stubborn hydraulic bleeder nipples without breaking them. The socket fits over the nipple, and you hammer on the socket as you turn the nipple and socket with a wrench. Sometimes the shock of hammering dislodges a stuck nipple. Other times, you break the nipple off anyway.

the piston with a metal rod. This will make bleeding the system in the car much easier later. The master cylinder boot should be examined for the presence of a small drain hole, and if this is found, it should be positioned downward when the boot is installed.

Be sure, before you install a master cylinder, that if it has an air vent in its reservoir cap, this vent is clear. If a diaphragm is used to seal the top of the reservoir, check it for tears, pinholes, or other defects. When the master cylinder is in place, its push rod should be adjusted for a little bit of clearance to the piston. If you don't provide clearance here, the primary cup lip may cover the compensating port with the possibility of hydraulic lock up. Too much clearance will produce low pedal. About one-eighth inch to one-quarter-inch is usually ideal, but check manufacturers' specifications for this factor. Wheel cylinders assemble in a straightforward way. Be sure to tighten them adequately but not excessively to brake backing plates.

Hydraulic Hoses and Tubing

If brake hoses are replaced, hydraulic hoses must be selected that are the right length and end configuration. Hoses that are too long can get mixed up with a car's tires when the wheels are turned or when an axle rebounds. The input ends of hydraulic hoses are secured by clips, nuts, or other devices to the chassis. These fasteners must be reused or preferably replaced with new hardware when hydraulic hoses are removed and replaced.

Brake lines can be purchased in prefabricated lengths with nuts and flares already assembled. They can also be fabricated from bulk materials which will make a neater job because you can cut it to correct lengths with no compromises. Whether reusing old lines — a bad practice — or using prefabs or making your own, be sure to carefully inspect any line that you are installing for damage to the double flare at its ends. Cracks here are common, so beware. If you do your own double flaring, be sure to ream and wire brush the naked end of the line before applying the first flare. A little brake fluid applied to the flaring mandrel will lubricate it and give you a much better job. Also, be sure to get the jam nuts in place before making your flares; they're easy to forget.

Always blow brake lines out with compressed air before you install them. If a line has to be threaded through a chassis, you should temporarily tape the end that is being threaded past obstructions to prevent contamination from entering it. Always locate brake lines away from hot engine and exhaust parts. Radiant heat can, in some cases, overheat brake fluid in lines and help cause it to boil. Installed lines should be inspected for kinks, damage to the anti-corrosion plating, nicks, and possible interference with any moving chassis parts. Any of these defects will require replacement or rerouting of the lines. Long runs of brake line must be clamped down to the chassis to prevent excessive vibration and work harden-

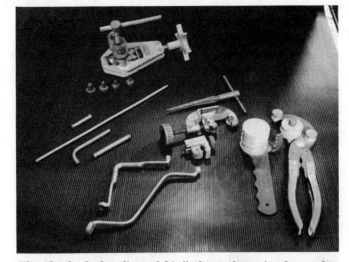

The "brake hydraulic tool kit," shown here, is about what you will need to fabricate new brake lines from bulk. On top is a tool for making double flare terminations on brake lines and several different sized mandrels for it. Below it and to the left are some pieces of brake line. To the right of them are a line reamer and two tubing cutters, the smaller one is great for working in tight quarters. In the right corner of the picture are two different devices for bending sharp curves in brake lines. These prevent the line from collapsing as you bend it. At the bottom left in the picture are two special bleeder wrenches so that you can bleed the hydraulic system when you have made new lines.

When you custom bend brake lines, it helps if you get the curves just right. This is easier to do if you hold one line gently in a vise as you bend the other line to its contours.

ing. Parts houses can often supply chassis clips for this purpose, when the originals have rusted and broken (almost always).

While brake lines can sometimes be bent by hand, it is better to use bending tools for this purpose. These tools are designed to prevent line kinking and collapse. It is usually easier to form brake lines prior to installing them using the old lines for patterns. Sometimes, however, this is not possible, as the lines must be bent-in-place to get by obstructions. If you are replacing factory brake lines, it is best to follow the original pattern, and not get too innovative in improving on factory engineering.

A Word(s) About Brake Fluids

Brake fluids have been made out of all sorts of things over the years from fish oils to phosphated diesters. Until recently, almost all of them have been hygroscopic, which means that they aggressively seek moisture from the atmosphere. Then contaminated fluid corrodes the internal parts of brake hydraulic systems. Most brake fluids have a disastrous effect on automotive finishes when they are spilled on them. For many years, the English had a predilection for using natural rubber seals and cups in their hydraulic braking systems. The conventional brake fluids available in the United States will swell and destroy these parts. American fluids used in English cars with old rubber seals must be designated as compatible with the English fluids: Girling "amber," "crimson," or "green" OEM fluids. Fluids sold in this country are typically designated by their boiling points, and were formerly described by an SAE grading system. More recently, DOT (Department of Transportation) numbers have become the prevalent standard for designating brake fluids. Presently, DOT 3 and DOT 4 conventional fluids are available, with DOT 4 having higher dry and wet boiling points.

In recent years, silicone brake fluids have become generally available, and these fluids are definitely an improvement on the older hydraulic fluids. These fluids are designated DOT 5, and have very high boiling points (wet, 500° Fahrenheit). They also resist thickening at low temperatures, which is one of the biggest problems with conventional brake fluids. The silicone fluids provide superior lip lubrication for seals, and are compatible with all seal compositions, including those in the troublesome English seals of the past. Best of all, the silicone based fluids are not hygroscopic, which means that they don't absorb moisture and lose their boiling resistance or become corrosive. They also don't damage automotive finishes.

With all of these advantages and only the disadvantage of a substantially higher price, I don't know why the purveyors of silicone fluids have frequently insisted on misrepresenting their capabilities. While these capabilities are great, silicone fluids cannot, as some sellers have suggested, be put in a system and forgotten forever. While they are not hygroscopic, they do *shed* moisture, and this will tend to pit and corrode brake parts internally. In relatively new systems this is not much of a problem because the master cylinder reservoirs are separated from atmospheric moisture by a diaphragm. In older systems with vent holes, minute amounts of moisture enter and are deposited in the brake system every time the brakes are operated. For this reason, silicone fluids installed in older cars must be changed every three or four years under normal conditions, and more often in some cases. While this falls short of the oft made promise of eternal life for these fluids, you will find that at the change interval mentioned above, there will be very little damage or deterioration of brake components.

When silicone fluid is installed, it is necessary to use an alcohol flush to completely remove the conventional brake fluid residues from the system that is to receive the silicone fluid. Pushing the old, conventional fluid out with new silicone fluid applied through the master cylinder is, in my opinion, sloppy and dangerous — despite the fact that some sellers of the silicone fluids endorse this practice.

Bleeding Hydraulic Brake Systems

Brake bleeding can be frustrating work. Bleeder nipples tend to stick and break, trapped air can be difficult to liberate, and spilled brake fluid can ruin finishes. Still, it's essential that this frustrating operation be done carefully and completely.

Brakes can be pressure bled by forcing brake fluid into the master cylinder reservoir under pressure and opening the wheel cylinder bleeders one at a time until all air has been expelled. The pressure tank needed to accomplish this is relatively cheap and simple, but so many different master cylinder filling configurations exist that the various adapters necessary to bleed the brakes on a variety of cars can be a problem.

Two-person bleeding is the old way. In this operation, one person pumps the brake pedal slowly and another cracks the bleeder nipples open slightly during the down strokes to allow air out of the system via a hose placed tightly over the bleeder nipple and routed into a jar with the end of the hose submerged in brake fluid. A bleeder hose with an automatic check valve ("one-man bleeder") can sometimes be used to replace the second person. In recent years, garages have begun to vacuum bleed brakes with hand or electric pumps. In this process, air, then fluid, is sucked through the bleeder nipple until clean, unaerated fluid emerges. Finally, some people bleed brakes by using a second person or a "one-man bleeder hose" at the wheel cylinders while they inject fluid into the master cylinder through the large fluid port in its reservoir with a special syringe that is sold for that purpose.

All of these methods work, and all of them require two cautions. One is not to attempt to reuse any fluid that you have already purged from a system. Such fluid is contaminated and must be discarded. The other caution is to keep the fluid in the master cylinder reservoir at a high enough level to prevent emptying the reservoir and allowing air to reenter the system. Some manufacturers recommend starting the bleeding procedure with the wheel cylinder that is farthest from the master cylinder and working to the closest one. Others recommend the opposite approach. I have always started with the farthest. The hardest air to get rid of in a system is the air that stands in a vertical section of brake pipe below the master cylinder. Persistence will help solve this problem, as will a few raps on the pipe to dislodge air bubbles adhered to its sides as you bleed the brakes. Disc calipers also tend to retain air bubbles and should be tapped

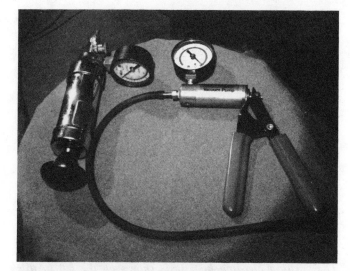

You'll need a jar, a hose, a bleeder wrench, and a confederate to bleed brakes the old way. The wheel setup for two-man bleeding is shown here. Your confederate pumps the brake pedal as you operate the bleeder wrench. Every once in a while someone should remember to refill the master cylinder reservoir as the bleeding continues.

lightly while they are being bled. When bleeders are frozen, never attempt to bleed a system by cracking the line nuts that feed the slave cylinders. This is sloppy and dangerous.

Always be sure to top off master cylinders after bleeding brake systems, and if silicone fluid has been installed, do something to alert mechanics and others to this fact. When using silicone fluids, be sure to pour them into master cylinder reservoirs slowly because if they are agitated excessively they tend to retain air bubbles that can then be pumped into the brake system. It is a nice touch to install rubber or plastic nipple caps over the bleeder nipple ends after bleeding a brake system. The completed brake system should be strongly activated by one person, while another looks for leaks at all junctions and connections. Be particularly careful to inspect areas where flared pipes go into junctions, as defects in the junction seats are common and will cause leaks. The hydraulic line connecting block, mounted on most rear axles, is one such place.

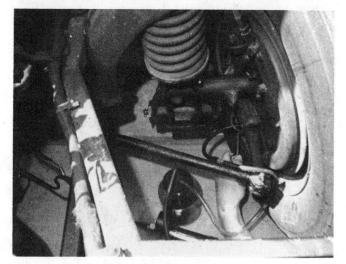

Vacuum bleeding can be accomplished with a hand pump and a receiving jar. The jar is plumbed to the bleeder nipple and then evacuated with the vacuum pump. Brake fluid flows into the jar. This is a one-man operation.

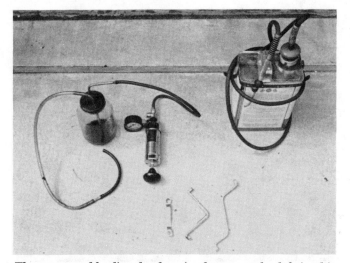

The vacuum bleeding hookup is shown on the left in this photo. On the right is a fluid pump in a one-gallon tin of brake fluid. This type of pump should not be used because it allows the fluid in the can to become contaminated with atmospheric moisture. Unless you go through a gallon of fluid a day, stick with one-pint cans, and keep their lids tightly secured when you are not pouring fluid out of them.

Brake Booster Operation and Service

The earliest brake boosters used leather-sealed vacuum pistons with crude valving to assist mechanical brake systems. Some of these vacuum cylinders required lubrication and some could be disassembled for repair. Many of these early units were sealed in a way that precludes repair. Later boosters used diaphragms that were acted on by engine vacuum and mounted directly behind mas-

ter cylinders. This type of unit can often be disassembled. Then its valves can be serviced or its diaphragms replaced. Many of these units are available on an exchange basis and there are specialty rebuilders out there who will do custom rebuilds. Owner rebuilds are also possible if you can get the necessary parts.

In service, brake boosters seldom fail. Usually what is taken for their failure is leaking vacuum plumbing leading to them or engine problems that resulted in low vacuum — vacuum that is too low to operate these units properly. When simple vacuum boosters do fail, the fault is usually in their valving, seals, or diaphragms. Many boosters have replaceable air inlet filters, and these should be checked and replaced periodically.

The simplest test of vacuum booster operation is to depress the brake pedal with steady pressure and then start a car's engine. If the pedal sinks farther to the floor under steady foot pressure when the engine is started, it means that the booster is doing its job. Never disassemble a working booster for any reason.

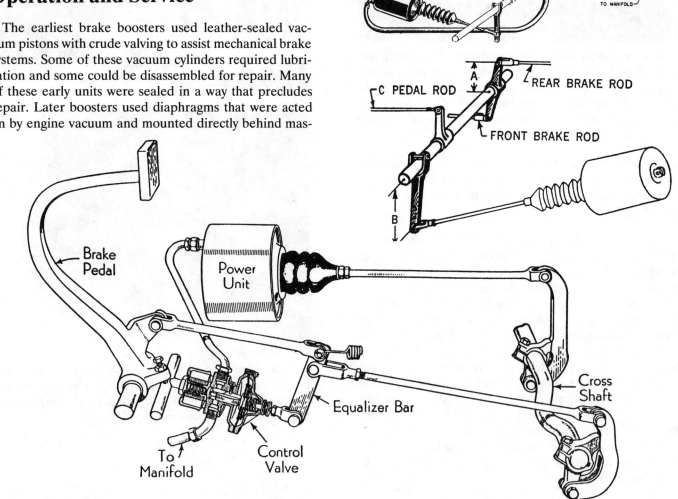

Early brake vacuum booster devices were connected to brake and valve linkage in a variety of ways. Some of these units are rebuildable and some are sealed and cannot be disassembled for restoration.

CHAPTER 18:

Chassis, Suspension, and Steering

Early automotive practice in chassis, suspension, and steering greatly resembled that in horse-drawn vehicles, bicycles, and steam traction engines — some of the progenitors of automobiles. In the very earliest days, this meant a wood, channel, or platform (spring leaf) chassis, full-elliptic springing, and either a steerable front axle or a kingpin/tie rod steered pair of front wheels. It is important to note that none of the forerunners of the automobile really provided the basis for automotive construction in these areas. Yet each had something to contribute to the concepts of automotive steering, suspension, and chassis construction.

Horse-drawn vehicles provided the concept of a frame supporting a body, and since the body design of some early automobiles was very similar to that of horse-drawn vehicles, these frames were somewhat appropriate. The problem was that this concept of framing was not designed to support and align the power drive components of the automobile. The springing of buggies and coaches did not comprehend the increased speeds available with automobiles, and the center pivoted axles of these very early vehicles worked well with a team of horses but were inadequate to the steering needs of self-propelled vehicles with *many* horsepower.

Bicycle frames provided an example of light, tubular construction, but this was mostly wasted on early automotive efforts because there was no simple technology for affixing the other components to a tubular framework. While bicycles did not incorporate much in the way of springing, they did provide the example of a king pin operated steering system, and with a little imagination and a lot of trial-and-error, automotive pioneers were able to join two such systems into the tie rod-steered systems that still prevail.

Steam traction engines — really locomotives without the need of tracks — provided the idea of a frame that could contain and align the power units necessary for self-propulsion. These cumbersome — and lovely — beasts operated at very low speeds, required a city block of planning to execute a mild turn or stop, and tended to be operated by individuals who could press 400 pounds without producing more than a minor puddle of sweat.

Taken altogether, then, the horse-drawn vehicle, bicycle, and steam traction engine provided the conceptual

bits and pieces for automotive frames, suspensions, and steering systems. But, of course, it took a lot of development to begin to make the bits and pieces fit into the working whole.

Frames

After evolving their frame design from horse-drawn vehicles, early American automobile manufacturers quickly settled on the use of ladder type channel frames, which remained the standard, with a few variations, until the advent of the unibody systems in low production by the 1930s and on the way to dominance after the 1960s. Engineering advances tended to modify the ladder frame into the X-frame and then modified the X-frame. There was also some experimentation with welding frames in place of riveting them. A few manufacturers, such as Franklin in this country and Morgan in England, continued to champion anachronisms like wood frames well after their obsolescence was obvious to everyone, but for the most part, the channel formed, riveted ladder and X-frame had become the standard practice by the 1930s. In addition to benefiting from years of development, these frames could be manufactured easily and efficiently by companies like A.O. Smith, and were both durable and relatively inexpensive to fabricate. Lighter frame forms, such as the backbone frame and box frame, found very little acceptance in the United States.

Early auto frames were, in many cases, also springs — a curious arrangement at best.

"Return with us now to those days of yesteryear...." It's all here, Delco lever action shocks, cable brakes, leaf springs, and drag link steering. What more could any car collector want?

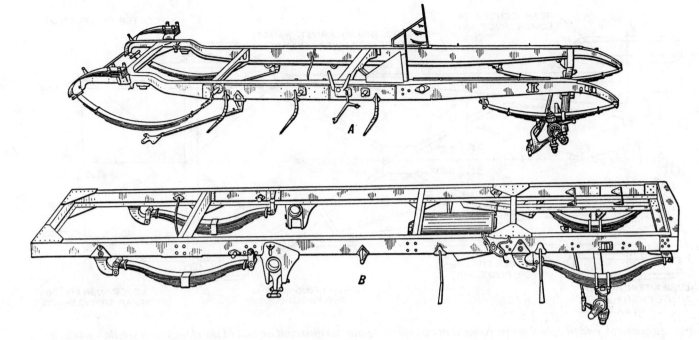

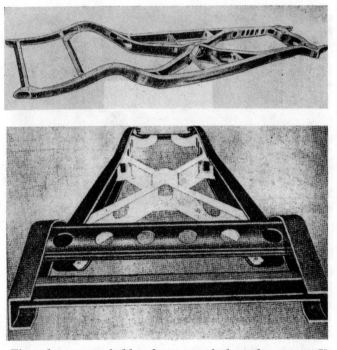

First there were ladder frames and then there were X-frames. Some of them were quite massive, but this didn't always stop them from cracking.

Some of the big Classics of the 1930s have frames with channels a foot deep and weights over 600 pounds. These units resemble battleship bulkheads and bridge girders and can operate with virtually no flexing. Most frames, however, allow for a certain amount of controlled flexing and are not meant to be absolutely rigid. The Model T Ford frame, for example, is a flimsy looking affair that has the appearance of tremendous inadequacy to rough roads and heavy loads. Of course, the metallurgy and simple design of the T frame are so good that few of these frames ever fractured. The battleship style frames, on the other hand, can fracture easily after years of operation. The problem of frame cracking was so prevalent

in early cars that Marmon even advertised that after delivering thousands of their Model 34 cars, only seven had been returned with cracked frames.

The structural defects in frames that a restorer is likely to encounter are: sagging, fracture, twisting, impact bending, and weld or fastener failure. In extreme cases with channel frames, and more frequently with welded box frames, it is possible to encounter corrosion damage so severe that it destroys structural integrity. Sagging primarily afflicts trucks that have been overloaded and passenger cars with advanced corrosion damage. There have been cars, like some early '50s Studebakers and some '60s Fords and Chevrolets, that routinely succumb to frame sag when they reach high mileages. If the sag was produced by overloading, it can be removed by applying counter-force on a frame straightening rack and "sistering" the sagged area(s) with additional structural material. Corrosion caused sags, and those in inherently weak frames can be dealt with by removal and splicing of the damaged areas. This is difficult work that requires careful measurement and a good deal of knowledge of the strains that act on a frame. For example, it does no good to splice a light piece into a frame and then weld it in the area of greatest stress. The weld will weaken the piece that you have added, and it will probably fail in the same way as the original frame did. It takes some careful consideration of the causes of the initial failure and some strategy to put strength where the failure originally occurred. It is frequently easier to find a replacement frame when sagging has occurred, or at least to replace the side rails completely. Welded box frames, favored by the British for many years, tend to corrode, weaken, and bend in critical areas. It is not uncommon to see some skillfully placed angle iron used to correct this problem on these cars.

Some British car specialists think that the inherent corrosion weakening problems of welded box frame cars are best dealt with by forcing oil into the box sections and

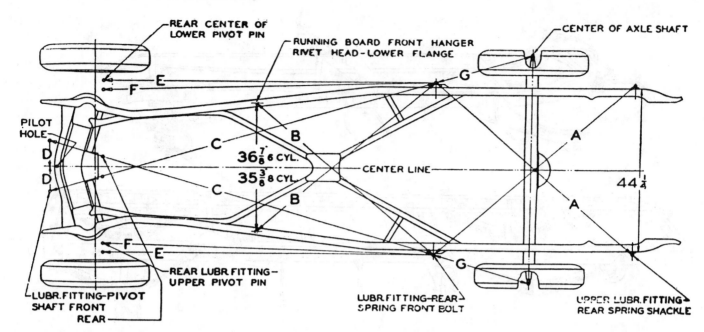

Frames are bilateral, and diagonal measurements across them should be consistent as should the elevation of similar points.

then draining it out on a fairly routine basis. If this sounds extreme, try the experience of welding patches to rapidly disappearing metal on this type of construction.

Twisted frames can usually be straightened on a frame rack. This involves using hydraulic pressure to force the components of the frame back into a semblance of their original alignment. When this is done to relieve twists or even to repair impact damage, any welds, rivets, or bolts that fasten the frame members together must be rigorously inspected for cracking, stretching, and hole deformation. It is generally a good idea to straighten frames cold when possible. Certainly most twisting, bending, and minor impact damage can be dealt with in this way. When more severe impact damage is encountered, it is permissible to use mild heat (1200° Fahrenheit or less) in conjunction with hammering and force to get things back to where they should be.

Any frame straightening operation should be guided by the fact that automobiles are constructed in a bilateral fashion, which means that the left and right sides are mirror images of each other in all important respects. In practice, this means that diagonal measurements on frames from distinctive points on each side should match. Altitude measurements to a (very flat) floor from similar points on each side should also be the same. Straight sections should, of course, be straight. Thus, unlike the situation with modern unibody cars which require a complex and expensive "body machine" and fixtures to correct damage, the older frames can be checked and put back to true with little more than a flat floor, a tape measure, and some long pieces of string — provided that you have the means of holding the frame and applying significant force where needed to straighten it.

Frames are held together with welds, bolts, rivets, or with combinations of these. Bolted frames are rare, and riveted frames are most common. I don't like rivets because there is no simple or certain way to determine how

Chassis damage can occur in unexpected places. This rear spring support has been damaged by flexing and corrosion.

tight they have remained in service. However, rivets should be checked for discernible looseness and frame members should be examined to see if they have left marks indicating a change in relationship to each other. Rivets can be tightened or replaced. When replacement is necessary, I prefer to use bolts and a locking compound. The bolt heads can be disguised to look like rivets if appearance is a problem. Cold riveting is possible but lacks the certainty of factory riveting. Bolts, of course, can be replaced easily, but be sure to use at least Grade 5 bolts to fasten frame members in any critical area. Old factory frame welding usually has the craftsmanlike appearance of work done by Ghengis Kahn's humblest servant. It may well be the worst welding that you will ever see, and the older it is, the more primitive the applied technology and resulting welds are likely to be. Even if frame welds show poor penetration, inclusions, and cracking (short of complete separation), they should be left alone. If structural integrity is in question, a rewelding operation must be undertaken. Such welding should always be done by stick or MIG methods and never with a torch. Do not over-weld a frame. Where welding was done in inch long beads, alternating with gaps, there was a reason for this, and repair should follow the same pattern, or new weaknesses can be introduced.

One common error that can produce frame fractures is to drill holes in a frame for what seem to be good reasons at the time. Avoid this practice because it can weaken a frame severely. If holes must be drilled, consider the problems of stress before you drill them in a way that will weaken a frame in a critical area. To restore a frame properly, you will have to get it very clean and examine it for fracture cracks. If any are found, repair them by welding.

Suspension Springs

There were a few unfortunate self-propelled vehicles built without springs, but the practice of springing had been firmly established in carriage and railroad usage before the advent of the automobile. Early automobile springing tended to follow buggy practice and consisted of two full-elliptic transverse springs. Gradually, this practice gave way to the use of four springs with two mounted fore and aft on each axle, and the full-elliptics were replaced by three-quarter-elliptics, and then by semi-elliptics. Henry Ford and a few others persisted in using transverse springs (why use four springs when two would do the job?), and the Ford and Lincoln lines were stuck with this archaic practice until two years after Henry's death. Some sophisticated transverse applications, such as the rear ends of modern Corvettes, have persisted to the present.

By the mid 1930s, independent front suspensions that used front coil springs had evolved into common use. Some manufacturers, like Buick, also applied coil/link

General Motors' famous "Knee Action" front suspensions were very popular from the late 1930s into the 1950s on most of GM's cars and on those of a few other makers.

systems to the rear. By the 1960s, Chrysler had introduced torsion bars (unwound coil springs) in this country in their front end suspensions. This practice gained popularity until the advent of Earl McPherson's wonderfully compact and efficient struts. By the 1970s McPherson's invention was being widely applied to rear suspensions (called Chapman struts after Colin Chapman who first applied them to rear suspensions), and the McPherson/Chapman setup is by now probably the most common form of suspension in use.

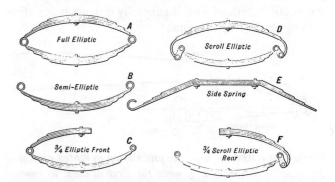

Years ago, when a mechanic went to trade school, he had to learn and remember the nomenclature for different springing arrangements. Most collector cars ride on "semi-elliptics," but earlier cars ride on all kinds of weird springs.

Most collector cars have leaf springs in the rear and either coil or leaf springs in the front. In most cases where leaf springs are used, a chassis is supported above its axles, but in some American cars and many British cars, it was common practice to hang the chassis under the springs ("underslung").

Springs succumb to breakage and loss of height or "arc." In either case, the best repair is spring replacement. Certainly a broken or sagged coil spring must be replaced because there is no repair or adjustment available. Sagged or broken leaf springs can theoretically be welded and recambered. I say "theoretically" because in actual practice such repairs tend to be short-lived.

An even worse repair practice is to substitute a coil spring or leaf spring that "sort of fits" for a damaged one. This is frequently done by people with a surplus of good intentions, optimism, and enthusiasm, but a notable lack of knowledge. In its worst form, this practice involves finding a leaf to replace a broken leaf in a multiple-element spring. With a little cutting and grinding, something can usually be made to fit. At best, this practice will result in unmatched springs with inconsistent rates. Such a condition produces a car with a suspension that is at war with itself. At worst, the replacement of one leaf of a spring with the wrong item will simply cause breakage of other leaves. Installing the wrong coil springs or torsion bars (beware of the difference between left and right torsion bars) will produce equally disastrous results. This is also true of installing spring "lifts" between the sagged coils of a spring. While this remedy may raise a vehicle back up to an approximation of its correct height, it will render the suspension ineffective and the steering dangerous. Spring breakage is the likely final outcome of this maneuver.

Sagged springs cause a car to ride too low and produce changes in the steering geometry and general handling characteristics of a car. New springs are really the only answer. If these are not available, it is frequently possible to have them made if data on the characteristics of the correct springs is available. Shop manuals usually give a method of measuring correct spring height in terms of some measurement from the vehicle to the floor. There should also be a tolerance for allowable spring sag, but if this is not stated, an inch is generally too much deviation in body height from original.

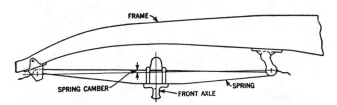

Rubber bumpers, such as the one shown mounted on top of the axle in this drawing, were the first attempt to control spring rebound. These bumpers are important, and you should make sure that they are in place on any car that you own.

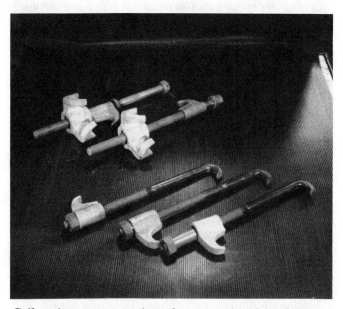

Coil springs can sometimes be removed without being restrained by spring compressors, but it is always a good idea to use them.

Spring removal is always a dangerous business, particularly in the case of coil springs. Not only must a car be well supported, but the energy in the springs must be released safely. Leaf springs will generally come off a car with a good set of jack stands, a good jack, and a clear-headed understanding of what you are doing. Coil springs can usually be dismantled this way, but, if possible, it is always best to use a good quality spring compressor. Some coil springs *must* be disassembled with a spring compressor.

Leaf springs require constant lubrication, or they will squeak and eventually bind up badly enough to deform

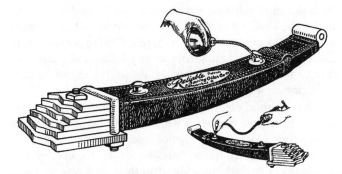

Most spring gaiters, whether leather or metal, tend to keep dirt and water in and lubrication out. The early gaiter pictured here provided for lubrication.

or break. Over the years, lubrication has been provided by a wide variety of methods. Early cars used heavy grease or oil impregnated canvas between their spring leaves. Later, Oilite buttons and rubber buttons were used, and plastics like polypropylene and mylar have also been used to separate and lubricate spring leaves. One of the best separators is zinc strips which are, I think, still used by some manufacturers on trucks. Many collector cars have spring "gaiters" or covers fashioned from anything from canvas and rubber to leather and sheet metal. These covers were designed to keep dirt and grit out and lubricants in, but in practice they seem to keep water in and to make it between difficult and impossible to get lubricants in.

My basic approach to leaf spring lubrication is to remove any covers, disassemble the springs, and spray them with a heavily graphited lubricant like SlipPlate. This lubricant is primarily designed for agricultural chains, sprockets, and machine glides, but it seems to work admirably on automotive springs. It inhibits rust and sticks tenaciously to spring surfaces without any undue affinity for dirt. Its appearance is charcoal gray. One of the areas where I tend to diverge from the strict observance of authenticity is in the matter of metal covers or permanently stitched leather gaiters for springs. If a spring cover isn't removed because to do so would destroy it, the springs under it will tend to deteriorate. Many metal covers have provisions for using a C-clamp-like lubricator tool to force lubricant into the leaves. This, however, does not force the water out that may have gotten under these covers and that tends to rust springs and make them squeak. In my estimation, most metal covers and stitched leather gaiters were removed soon after the cars equipped with them were delivered, and it is, therefore, not particularly inauthentic to run around without them. Laced leather covers are a different matter because they can be removed for "spring cleaning" and lubrication.

Leaf spring shackles and attachment points have been constructed over the years with everything from threaded bronze bushings to rubber insulators and on to no bushings at all. Where hard metal bushings are used, it is important that they be lubricated regularly with a good chassis grease and that new bushings and shackle bolts be fitted if any damage or wear has caused excessive clearance. Where rubber or plastic bushings are used, replace-

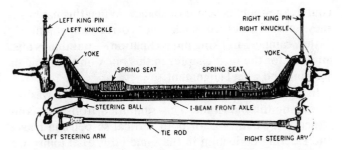

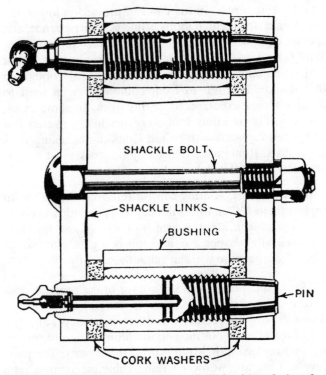

This spring shackle uses the "threaded" bushing design that was very popular for many years. This system works well as long as its gaskets seal out water.

ment is also the remedy for wear, damage, or deterioration. It is important that rubber and plastic spring shackle and attachment bushings not be lubricated with petroleum-based lubricants because these can soften and damage them. In fact, don't lubricate these bushings unless they squeak, and then only with a soap-based rubber lubricant or dressing.

Suspension Diagnosis and Repair

Rear suspensions on collector cars usually involve live axles and leaf springing. Such systems are almost endlessly durable. Some of these suspensions use Panhard rods to control lateral movement or stabilizer bars to control sway. Rear coil spring/link suspensions are less common, but there are still plenty of them out there. About the only vulnerable points in these suspensions, other than their springs and shackles, are any bushed pivot points, and these are usually easily paired with new bushings and bolts. A few collector cars use swing axle systems and fully independent rear suspensions. These are more difficult to maintain and restore as they use universal joints and more complex locating hardware than do simple live axles. Chapman strut rear ends also present special restoration problems, as struts contain "cartridges" or other internal components that must be repaired or exchanged when they wear out.

Front suspensions can be very simple or very complicated. The beam axle front ends that prevailed into the mid-1930s are simple and straightforward. Their chief maladies are king pin wear and beam distortion — the

Front beam axles don't cause much trouble if they don't get bent. You can adjust camber by using shims under the springs, but any other adjustments require bending the axle.

latter affects wheel alignment and will be discussed in the next chapter. King pin replacement procedures vary with type — ball, roller, or bushing, among others — but essentially involve replacing king pins and their bushings or bearings. This work usually requires the use of such specialized tools as a press and large reamers and should probably be left to someone with experience in this field. Correct shimming of king pin joints is something that you have to do by the book.

What *anyone* can accomplish is to check for king pin wear. This is done by jacking up the front end of a car until the wheels are off the ground and shaking them vertically. If there is discernible movement that is not in the wheel bearings, the king pins are worn to the point of needing replacement. Always observe appropriate safety precautions for a jacked car when you perform this test. Remember, too, that the early "Knee Action" or "unequal A-arm" front ends still used king pins that were and are susceptible to wear.

Beam axles are remarkably free of problems unless, of

Replacement king pins and bushings used to come in nice steel boxes like this one. If you see a box like this with the parts for your car, don't be bashful, buy it!

course, they get "bent out of shape." When this happens, they must be forced back into correct alignment — caster, camber, and king pin inclination — but that is also an issue for the next chapter in this book on the topic of steering and wheel alignment.

In the 1950s and 1960s, the venerable king pin was replaced by the ball joint. This simplified front end construction by allowing for both vertical suspension travel and steering deflection in the same joint. Ball joints are either bolted, riveted, pressed, or welded into their suspension arms, and are very susceptible to wear that necessitates replacement. These joints are frequently checked by the shaking procedure described for king pins — particularly when their soundness is being demonstrated by someone who is trying to sell you a car. This test will work on some suspensions where the coil spring is located between the two A-arms, or where torsion bars are used and the jacking is done on the lower A-arm and not the frame. However, when a coil spring is located in a "tower" above the top A-arm, a special wedging fixture must be placed between the upper A-arm and the chassis, and the car must then be jacked up from the frame or body pan.

Different ball joint and suspension designs have different checking procedures. A pry bar is used to check the style used on this car.

The object of all this is to "unload" the ball joints so that they can be checked for wear. Some systems tolerate more wear than others. Check the specifications for the car that you are working on in this regard. Many recently manufactured ball joints include wear indicators, which are pins that extend out of, or recede into, the ball joints when they are beyond their wear limits. Again, check a manual for the car that you are working on. Remember that in any ball joint system, one joint bears the car's weight, the "load" joint, and the other does not, the "follower" joint. The load joint will almost invariably wear out first, but be sure to check both joints because they are both susceptible to wear.

Ball joint replacement involves substantial disassembly of a front end, and it also involves releasing potentially lethal spring forces. In the cases of pressed-in joints, riveted joints, and welded joints, some skill, experience, and special equipment are necessary to effect replacement. While this work is not the most specialized area of front end repair and renovation, it is specialized enough so that it should be left to front end shops or at least to those who are experienced in this work. In some cases, bolted joints or joints that were originally riveted but have been replaced with bolted joints can be changed by generalists. Remember that ball joint work must be followed by a complete wheel alignment.

In most cases, A-arms will be removed for ball joint replacement. When this is done, it is a good idea to check and replace the inner A-arm bushings. These bushings are generally inexpensive, and this is a good time to replace them because you can get at them easily.

Many coil spring front ends have brake reaction rods and sway or "stabilizer" bars as part of their design. These frequently require bushing replacement, and this is just a matter of bolting and unbolting rods and removing and replacing their old, worn rubber parts. The parts involved are almost always remarkably inexpensive, and the improvement in steering control and ride stability that results from the replacement of these parts when they are worn is enormous.

Snubbers, Shock Absorbers, and Other Things That Prevent "Bump in the Night"

Shortly after someone noticed the advantages of springing automobile chassis from their axles, it was also noticed that without some added control the chassis tended to rebound violently and repeatedly when bumps in the road were encountered. The first attempt to limit this excessive and undesirable spring deflection involved rubber stop bumpers mounted between the springs and their axles. This not only prevented hard metal collisions when the springs fully compressed, but it also limited spring compression and, thus, the rebound. The rubber stop bumpers became a standard part of all suspensions and contributed mightily to chassis stability. However, the problem of excessive and unnecessary rebound was still there.

Early attempts to limit or damp this rebound included the Hartford patent friction shock, the Watson reel snubber, and various air-oil damping devices among others. By the late 1920s, hydraulic lever type shocks were gaining popularity, and by the late 1930s, the telescoping, hydraulic shock absorber had become common. There were, of course, variations on these themes — such as the complex Westinghouse air shock system and General Motors' Knee Action design. The latter incorporated a rebound limiting device in the A-arm of that particular suspension layout.

The Westinghouse air shock, shown here, was big, cumbersome, trouble-prone, and not very effective. But it was a great idea and it was the greatgranddaddy of all the modern computer controlled variable rate hydro-pneumatic suspensions.

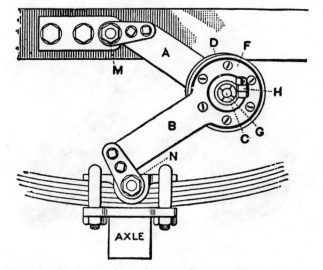

Friction shocks, such as the one illustrated here, were very prone to failure and really didn't work well when they did work. This design was quickly dropped in the early years of this century.

Devices like this "snubber" did little more than to control spring rebound when a bump was encountered. Snubbers operate like window shades — only in one direction.

Early friction shocks were temperamental when they got hot, wet, or wore, and they proved to be generally inadequate. Various reel type shocks, by the likes of Watson, Gabriel, and Lincoln (properly called "snubbers")

only prevented springs from unloading too rapidly because they only worked in one direction. True, effective, double acting shock absorption (in both directions) had to wait for the hydraulic units of the 1930s and after. Modern shocks of the tubular telescoping type are marvels of valving and temperature compensation and perform far better and more reliably than their predecessors.

Almost all early shocks are susceptible to rebuilding. The friction variety usually needs new flat springs and friction discs. The reel type almost invariably needs new canvas strapping and friction shoes. Sometimes they also need new graphite lubricators.

Early hydraulic lever shocks and more recent Armstrong (British) lever shocks sometimes need little more restoration than topping up with fluid, but sometimes they require extensive rebuilding to restore seals and piston or rotor clearances. All hydraulic shocks are prone to valve failure, and in the case of some of the later Knee Action shocks, this can involve three or more separate valving systems. Rebuild kits and instructions are available for some older shocks, but many will have to be sent to specialty rebuilders when their original performance needs to be restored.

British shocks must be filled with the correct fluid. This is almost invariably Armstrong Super Thin Shock Oil. Attempts to replace this fluid with its rumored equivalent, SAE 20 cycle fork oil, are to be discouraged. The original fluid is readily available from foreign car parts specialists and is relatively inexpensive. However, if you need much of it, the shocks you are filling probably need rebuilding. American lever action shocks should be filled with special shock or Knee Action fluids, which are the equivalent of some hydraulic "jack oils." Never use brake fluid or transmission fluid in this application. Permatex still makes a jack oil that works admirably in most American Knee Action and rotary hydraulic shocks. The same fluid can be used in the very few telescoping shocks that are refillable (Chrysler right after the war, for example).

Tubular, telescoping shocks were also compact and easy to locate, and are still the most common shock absorber configuration on the road today.

The lever action hydraulic shock (right) was a great improvement on snubbers and reel type shocks (left). As the second photo illustrates, they were also very easy to install on a variety of chassis designs.

Shocks should always be bench bled before installation. This almost invariably involves working the shock to its travel extremes in an upright position. A very small number of telescoping shocks are bled upside down. Check manufacturers' repair and replacement data on this point.

Chassis Lubrication

It is amazing how far suspension components will go if they are properly lubricated. Current practice is to specify molydisulfide, lithium, or aluminum complex-based greases for ball joints and a very high quality lithium-based grease for just about everything else. It is imperative that a high quality grease be used in these applications, and the cumulative cost of such grease is far less than the cost for a premature front end rebuild. I have used Lubriplate MoLith and 1200-2 greases for chassis application for years, and have found that these greases stand up to age, water, and pressure. There are other good greases, but whatever you load in your grease gun, this is no place to economize. Avoid using the price leader grease from your local discount house; it won't perform, and the repair costs will be significant. On older cars that specified heavy gear oils for chassis lubrication and used Alemite pin fittings, it is permissible and desirable to use modern greases. Of course, chassis that were lubed through oil cups must get oil of the specified weight. I would advise following manufacturers' recommendations on greasing intervals, but under no circumstances would I let the intervals exceed 2,000 miles or one year. Some recent cars have "grease bags," and have threaded plugs fitted where the grease fittings install. There is some mythology about not over-greasing these units to the point of running them almost dry. That may have been sound practice when they were new and the bags were intact, but by the time these cars enter the collector realm, it's a good idea to grease them sparingly but regularly. At least that keeps grease in the joints. The bags, which are really balloon seals, should be replaced when other work is done that requires their removal.

When I was taught to use a grease gun — yes, someone actually gave me instruction — it was alleged that grease should be applied only until you could see old grease begin to come out of a joint. Later, I figured out that this advice, given by the owner of the gas station where I worked, was incorrect. You should grease joints until a substantial amount of grease is pushed out and you see new grease escaping because you really want to purge the old, hardening grease. This advice should provide mirth for the fellows who manufacture and sell grease, but, nonetheless, it is sound. However, having given this advice, I hasten to add that the old grease that is exuded from the joints should be wiped off carefully and completely before it becomes a dirty mess. Grease fittings should always be wiped clean before a pressure gun is applied to them, or contamination from the road will be

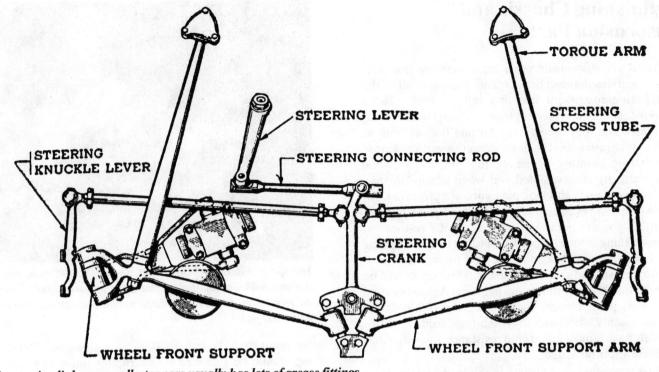

The steering linkage on collector cars usually has lots of grease fittings.

Grease joints that won't take grease at the 10,000 to 20,000 psi that most grease guns generate can sometimes be freed with an oil ram. This is a cheap tool that is configured as a piston in a cylinder. The other end of the piston is a hammer ram that extends out of the cylinder. You fill the cylinder with light oil, place its open end against any Zerk fitting (except a 90-degree Zerk which is easily broken), and hammer the piston against the oil. The force of the hammer blow seals the fitting to the end of the cylinder for an instant, and forces the oil into the fitting under enormous, instantaneous pressure. If this doesn't free a fitting or joint, the next and only step is disassembly. Heating fittings with a blow torch or propane torch to free them is futile and barbaric.

This oil ram is a very handy item to use if you encounter a plugged fitting or joint. It generates thousands of psi, and if it fails to dislodge solidified grease and dirt from a fitting or joint, disassembly is the only appeal.

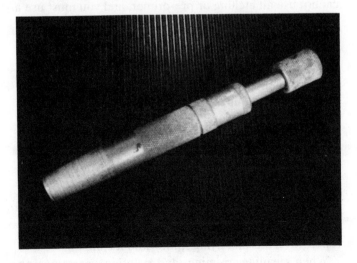

Refinishing Chassis and Suspension Parts

Chassis and suspension parts are among the few parts on automobiles that can benefit from the use of all of the sandblasting equipment that they sell out there. These components are heavy enough not to warp under abrasive blasts, and they are so irregular and thus difficult to clean that abrasive blasting is an attractive way to cleanse them before painting. However, this only works when these parts are disassembled and when sensitive areas, such as tie rod ends and king pin joints, are protected. All abrasive media residues must be removed prior to reassembly. If you are going the route of a total restoration and everything is apart, abrasive blasting or dip stripping is a very appropriate cleaning method for whole chassis and for chassis and suspension parts. Dipping should be followed quickly by priming and painting. A good enamel is the best paint choice. Avoid using the old asphaltic "chassis paints" because they tend to oxidize badly. Enamels have almost equal chip resistance and will maintain their luster far longer.

There is a movement abroad in the land to paint chassis and other parts of cars with Imron and other polyurethane enamels. This certainly gives them a beautifully shiny and totally inauthentic appearance, but these paints are certainly tough and can withstand chassis duty easily. I object to these paints on car bodies because they are totally inauthentic and look it. On the other hand, if you must go "high tech" in the area of paint, chassis and suspension parts are the best places to do this. I still object to the use of polyurethane finishes in these areas because it is difficult to remove and you may be creating a major problem for the next restorer — and there will always be a next restorer.

When abrasive blasting is used to clean a disassembled chassis or suspension parts, these must be primed within hours and painted within days. Priming alone will not stop rusting, and rusting of blasted surfaces occurs immediately. This problem is not as severe with dip cleaned parts because any good dip process involves a rust preventative phosphate coating as part of the final rinse. On blasted parts, primer is not enough protection. Now this may come as something of a shock to you people out there driving around in cars with enough primer spots to qualify them for a measles clinic, but *conventional primers aren't waterproof.* There are some epoxy primers on the market that are waterproof, but the sandable gray and red oxide primers that we all know and love are not. Point that out to the next vendor you see at a swap meet with a stack of freshly primed NORS (New Old Restored Stock) sheet metal parts.

When a car is not going to be disassembled for total restoration but there is a need to make everything look presentable, there are some half measures that will work on chassis and suspension parts. The first step is to totally degrease the area(s) to be dealt with. This can be done with a steam cleaner or high pressure washer. If a heavy-duty detergent is used in either of these devices, most of

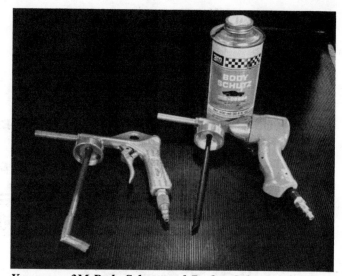

You spray 3M Body Schutz and Rocker Schutz right out of the can with one of the special guns pictured here. It produces a rough but resilient surface, and you can paint over it with body paint.

the paint should come off along with all grease. Degreasing should be followed with scraping and wire brushing any badly rusted spots and sanding deeply rusted areas. It is not necessary to remove all rust residues. You should then wipe everything down with a grease removing cleaner such as PrepSol (DuPont 3919S) or Pre-Kleeno (R-M 900). Enamel reducer will also work for this step, but be careful with whatever you use so that you don't spread grease around the surfaces that you are cleaning.

The areas to be painted should then be scuffed lightly with a 400 grit sandpaper or a fine Scotchbrite pad and blown off. You can then coat them with a pre-primer, primer, or conversion coating. If a pre-primer such as R-M's ZIP (834) is used, the paint adhesion will be superior but it will also be necessary to remove all traces of original paint and most traces of rust before application. If a metal conditioner like DuPont's Conversion Coating (224S) or R-M's Metal Conditioner (801) is used, you cannot use an etching or pre-primer, and you must use a conventional or epoxy primer before top coating. (The use of DuPont conversion coating [224S] requires use of DuPont Metal Conditioner — 5717S before the conversion coating is applied.)

It is also possible to go directly from the scuffing stage to priming without using metal conditioner, conversion coating, or pre-primer, but the paint adhesion will not be as good. The priming step should be followed by application of a good acrylic enamel, preferably with a hardener or curing agent. In areas of known and extreme road abrasion you can use a rubberized undercoating, such as 3M Body Schutz or Rocker Schutz, between the primer and the paint. This will give a wrinkled appearance, but will also produce a very resilient finish that will tend to repel gravel bits and flying smut without chipping.

When cleaning, priming, and painting operations on undercarriage components are completed, it is always good practice to grease all fittings and drive out any water that may have become lodged in the joints during steam cleaning or pressure washing.

CHAPTER 19

The Mysteries of Front Ends Made Almost Simple

I showed the first draft of this chapter to my favorite front end and frame man. He kept it for a couple of days, and when I stopped in to see him and discover his reaction to it, he looked at me with his head slightly cocked and very slowly and purposefully said, "I read 'er, and guess I didn't know half of that stuff. Ya know, it isn't really that complicated. All you gotta do is make the front wheels stand up straight." Well, it isn't quite that simple, either, but his point is well taken. The theory that governs front wheel alignment and steering geometry is pretty dense stuff. If you try to get into it too quickly, it will make your head hurt. You can know shockingly little of this abstruse theoretical stuff and still diagnose and correct many of the possible problems in these two systems. I don't recommend do-it-yourself front end restoration and alignment, but it will help you to commission this work if you understand the basic underlying theory on which it is based.

In the normal course of events, the average car restorer will never have occasion to do his own front end alignment and steering restoration work, beyond replacing worn bushings and joints, and maybe setting toe-in. Front end alignment should almost always be left to specialists who have the equipment, theoretical knowledge, and experience to do the job. While there is some old, portable front end equipment out there that can often be purchased for seductively low prices, I think that this capability makes little sense for individuals and shops operating at a level much below William Harrah in his heyday. However, it can be essential for restorers to understand front end alignment basics, just to get this work done correctly.

Front end alignment is fussy work which involves eight or more interrelated factors. It requires both experience and a feel for the theoretical aspects of the situation. I have seen inexperienced practitioners spend literally days trying to do something that a seasoned front end technician can accomplish in an hour. The example that I am referring to involved an attempt by a dealership to align the front end of a 1971 Saab that I owned. A whole day was spent on one of John Bean's newest optical racks. The problem got better and worse, but never disappeared. On the second day, after the service foreman embarrassingly failed to get the original complaint fixed without adding three or four other problems, and in complete frustration, the car was taken out on the road and shims were added and subtracted to get a "running fix." This didn't work either. Of course the then "new" front-wheel drive cars, like Saab, were much more critical in their alignment requirements than other (rear-wheel drive) cars, and the combination of an inexperienced technician and a misaligned rack produced a failure.

Success was attained in the way that success in alignment is almost always attained. The car was taken to a shop that was exclusively devoted to wheel alignment and frame work — every small to medium-sized city has one or more such shops — and the problem was routinely solved. That is because for such specialty shops, these problems are routine, and because it is a good bet that technicians who work exclusively on front end and frame alignment problems pretty well know this field and how to apply its solutions to the problems on your car. Remember, front end alignment is not an exact science. There is an element of judgment that mandates the use of the powers of observation, experience, and theory. If you find that a provider of this service is treating your problem like a big production, then go somewhere where it is treated routinely.

When you find one of the shops that specializes in alignment (they will typically have from two to fifteen racks) you may be in for a great surprise. Some of the equipment that they use is likely to be thirty years old (Bee-line, Bear, Hunter, and Bean are among the favorites) and is incredibly simple. You will almost never see the cumbersome optical equipment of the 1950s through the 1970s in use in these shops, and most of them have installed a minimum of the new digitalized laser and diode stuff, and only use it on four-wheel drive and four-wheel steer cars. The place where you will find the fancy stuff is at the dealerships, and you will usually, but not always, find the least competent front end technicians there, as well. The older equipment is without buttons and whistles and derives its readings from turntables and spirit levels on magnetic or clamp bases. These, in turn, derive their authority from gravity and from immutable laws of physics and geometry. This simple equipment requires the simplest calibration — namely a vertical post — and a flat floor to produce readings that are easily good to 1/10th of a degree. The fancy stuff at the dealerships that bounces signals off fixtures on a car's rear wheels to align the fronts needs constant and tricky calibration, among other things. The only advantage to using it on older cars is that it usually informs a mechanic where and how much to change shim and cam adjustments — something that any good front end technician would know without specific advice.

The one concession to modernity that most of the good front end shops that I know have made is to install a very simple and inexpensive optical device to read toe-in. This device has replaced the more original and quaint 1930s scribe markers in many, but not all shops. On the other hand, the up-to-date, computerized/laser stuff is often designed to be operated by very low paid recruits, fresh out of vocational schools. What it saves dealerships in wages, it probably returns tenfold in owner frustration from cars that don't track right, or scrub the edges off their tires. What the fancy computerized consoles excel in is producing a maze of mostly useless information about a car's alignment condition. I say "useless" because there aren't that many adjustments available on most cars, and the few that there are tend to affect each other as they are made. There are, in the nature of the thing, five angles and three factors that affect handling, steering, and tire wear patterns on older cars. Information beyond these factors is mostly useless, and often confusing.

Admittedly, modern front-wheel drive, four-wheel drive, four-wheel steer, and swing axle rear-wheel drive cars have become incredibly complex in the war to gain perfectly neutral steering at all speeds, and to eliminate the dreaded "torque steer." As a result, they may actually benefit from alignment on the computerized racks. Frankly, I don't pretend to understand these modern suspension and steering systems — neither do many of the best front end technicians whom I know.

But old car restorers are lucky. The cars that we collect, nurture, restore, and love tend to have beam axles or unequal A-arm ("double wishbone") front ends. If your tastes run to the modern, they might include cars with some early McPherson strut front ends, but not the new, tricky stuff. [You find that on "new cars."] The steering systems used on most collector cars respond favorably to no more than five alignment angle adjustments and three vehicle factors. This is the stuff that you were always vaguely aware of but didn't dare ask about for fear that someone might try to explain it to you. Tighten your seat belts.

Alignment Factors, Reasons, and Development

All alignment theory and practice flows from one simple purpose — to keep a vehicle's four wheels rotating with a minimum of slipping, scuffing, and dragging, no matter what amount of lock (turn) is applied to the front wheels. While it is impossible to completely eliminate slip, scuff, and drag in all driving situations, they can be reduced to low, and acceptable, levels.

Alignment theory, after the turn of the 20th century and up to the recent past, concentrated on five basic angles of the front wheel spindles and king pins to achieve the desired purpose. These are camber, caster, king pin inclination (KPI), toe-in, and toe-out-on-turns. We'll go into some details of these angles later, but to roughly describe them, picture an axle with king pins attached to it in perfectly vertical positions, and with wheels attached to spindles and pointing straight ahead. CAMBER involves leaning the wheels in toward each other at the top (negative) or out at the top (positive). CASTER involves inclining the tops of the king pins back, towards the rear of the car (positive) or forward (negative). King pin inclination (KPI) involves angling the king pin tops toward each other. This, of course, would cause the camber to go negative unless the KPI were accounted for in the construction of the spindle. KPI is a fact of front end construction, but is never adjustable and is rarely even measured. In double A-arm suspensions it is considered as a line between the centers of the two ball joints, or the angle of the king pin, if a king pin is used. If KPI is out of specification, it means that something is bent. TOE-IN involves angling the front or forward edges of the wheels toward each other — sort of pigeon toed — and TOE-OUT is the opposite, with the front edges of the wheels inclined away from each other. Finally, TOE-OUT-ON-TURNS is a nonadjustable feature that is built into the geometry of front end parallelogram and center steering

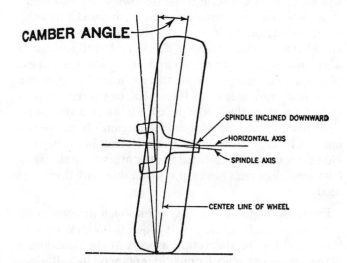

The CAMBER angle of a suspension is the deviation from vertical of a wheel with respect to the side of the car. Positive camber in a right side wheel is shown here.

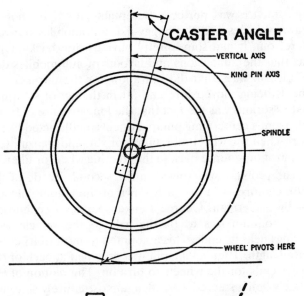

CASTER ANGLE

- VERTICAL AXIS
- KING PIN AXIS
- SPINDLE
- WHEEL PIVOTS HERE

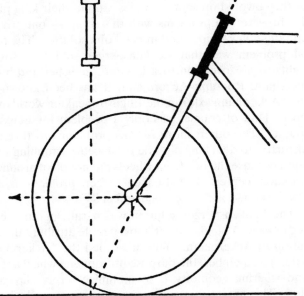

The CASTER angle of a suspension is the fore and aft deviation of the of the king pin or axis on which the wheel turns. If the top of the king pin or axis is inclined forward from vertical, the suspension is said to have positive caster.

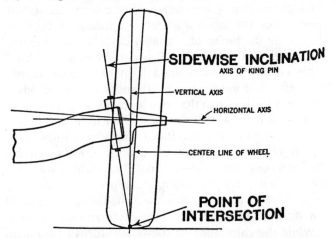

SIDEWISE INCLINATION
AXIS OF KING PIN

- VERTICAL AXIS
- HORIZONTAL AXIS
- CENTER LINE OF WHEEL

POINT OF INTERSECTION

KING PIN INCLINATION (KPI) is the angle of the kingpin or other axis on which a wheel turns from true vertical. KPI relates to camber, except that KPI is not settable and camber is.

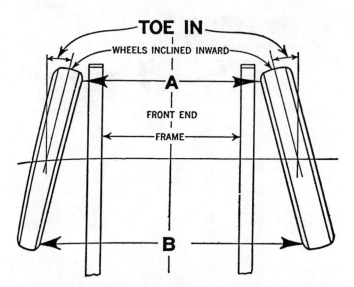

TOE IN
WHEELS INCLINED INWARD

A

FRONT END

FRAME

B

TOE-IN is the deviation from perfect horizontal parallelism of the front wheels. If the wheels point slightly towards each other this is called toe-in, but if they point out from each other the condition is called toe-out. Most suspensions call for a very slight amount of toe-in.

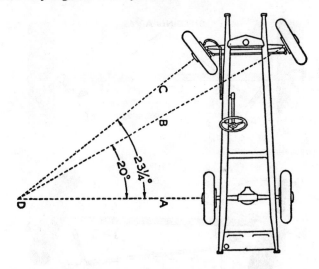

TOE-OUT-ON-TURNS is made necessary because the inner and outer front wheels in a turn describe different arcs with different radii. The inside wheel has to turn farther to avoid dragging and scrubbing.

linkage. It causes the inside wheel in a turn to turn a few degrees more than the outboard wheel. The reason for this will be explained shortly.

It is clear that there is a direct relationship between KPI and camber, but the other angles are also very interrelated. Any solution to a front end problem must take into account the fact that manipulation of any one of the five angles may require intervention in one or more of the adjustments for the others. The whole thing is a system and the parts are interrelated. That is where the application of experience and theory become necessary in front end work.

Numerous ways have been devised to make front end adjustments; some of them are truly obscure. The most common involve threaded sleeves, shims, cams, bolts-in-

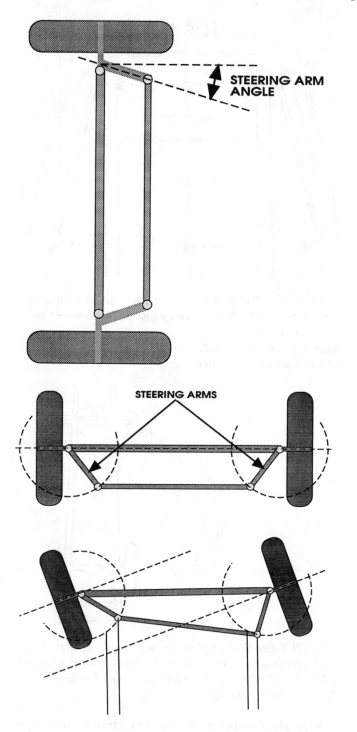

STEERING ARM ANGLE

STEERING ARMS

These three schematics show how Ackermann effect steering linkage works. The key is in the parallelogram structure of this system and the inclined side links.

slots, and adjustable struts. In the nature of the thing, it is common for manipulation of one adjustment to affect others. For example, shim adjusted double A-arm suspensions frequently utilize the same shim packs to adjust camber and caster. A change in one will affect the other, unless this tendency is accounted for in the first adjustment.

The earliest suspensions under wheeled vehicles involved the use of center pivot axles. Such axles had only one king pin at the center, and physically moved the wheels in fore and aft arcs in the act of steering. While this practice was perfectly acceptable for light, horse-drawn vehicles and the buggy-like automobiles derived therefrom, it had some pretty obvious drawbacks. One was that the dimensions and layouts of automobiles developed in ways that did not allow for the intrusion of wheels being moved fore and aft in the act of steering. Just as serious was the fact that the long expanse of front axle from a center king pin to a wheel spindle acted like a lever when the wheel hit a bump or rut, and transmitted an enormous jounce back to the steering wheel or tiller.

The problem was solved in the second decade of the 19th century — in the early dawn of the automobile age — by a German, George Lenkensperger. Lenkensperger's solution was to fix the axle to the vehicle with springs near its ends. This amounted to most of its crosswise length. Then a king pin was provided at each of the axle's ends for the wheels to turn on. The motion of the wheels being steered was, then, almost entirely sideways as they pivoted on short spindles around their king pins. There were two problems with this setup — one trivial, and the other serious and in need of a solution. The trivial problem was that Lenkensperger sold the British rights to his invention to a London publisher and book merchant, Rudolph Ackermann. It has been known as the "Ackermann axle" in the English speaking world ever since. This, of course, was only a problem for Lenkensperger. The other, more serious problem was that the uncorrected dual king pin axle produced a scrubbing situation because the two front wheels did not pivot around a common center. The Lenkensperger problem is, of course, known as "Ackermann effect."

The Lenkensperger solution was parallelogram steering linkage. You guessed it, most people attribute the solution to Ackermann. (Yup, it's called the "Ackermann axle.") Remember, the purpose of front end wheel angles and steering geometry is to minimize scrub, slip, and drag. This means that as a car rounds a curve, all wheels must be positioned as close as possible to exactly 90° to the direction of their travel, and oriented on circles radiating from a common center. This center was assumed until fairly recently to emanate from a line drawn through the rear wheel centers. To achieve such a common center, the inboard wheel on a turn must turn further — on the radius of a smaller circle — than the outboard wheel, or slipping will occur. In practice, this is achieved in the Ackermann axle by the use of steering geometry that automatically advances the inside wheel on a turn further than the outside wheel. With this provision, both front wheels are turned on radii that have a common center on a line drawn through the hubs of the rear wheels. As a point of interest, it is now known that the ideal common center is actually somewhat forward of the rear axle, due to certain phenomena involving centrifugal forces as a car rounds a turn. That's a fine point that neither Lenkensperger nor Ackermann appreciated.

While the calculation of toe-out-on-turns to compensate for Ackermann effect is complex, the actual hardware is very simple. By arranging the steering linkage in a parallelogram with the fore and aft connecting links canted in at the rear, the angular characteristics of turning levers can be used to advance the inside wheel farther than the outside wheel in a turn. Reference to the accompanying diagram should clarify how this works.

Unfortunately, the adoption of the Ackermann axle did not completely eliminate the problems that produce tire scrub and sideways slip in vehicles at speed. There still remained a "scrub radius" which is the distance between a line projecting a vehicle's weight onto the road and the actual contact patch of its tire. This "evil" radius tends to cause the steering spindle to act like a lever and transmit road shock back through the steering linkage. It also tends to put enormous force on the king pins and cause binding and hard steering. An American auto inventor and manufacturer, C. E. Duryea, considered these problems at the turn of the century and conjured up the idea of inclining the king pins, but not the wheels, outward at their tops to project a vehicle's weight closer to the center of the tire contact patch, and thus reduce the undesirable scrub radius. A more common solution was to actually camber the wheels out at their tops (positive camber) to bring their contact patches closer to the line of projected vehicle weight. As time went on, both of these ploys were used, along with wheels that offset a car's weight inward, and increasingly shorter spindles. Wider tires (balloon type) also helped in this effort to cancel scrub radius and made possible the successful application of four-wheel brakes. The problem here was that when brakes are added to the front wheels of a vehicle, the existence of any scrub radius will cause the vehicle to pull violently sideways if the brakes are even slightly out of adjustment. Four-wheel brakes, particularly non-hydraulic types that may have difficulty with force application equalization, require a scrub radius of nearly zero. Other innovations, like positive caster in combination with mild toe-in help to reduce scrub radius and its effects.

Ackermann steering linkage and various measures to eliminate scrub radius have come a long way towards reducing slip, scrub, and drag in automobile steering, but they have by no means completely eliminated these adverse factors. Despite theoretical perfection on paper, real world suspensions are subjected to a myriad of complex variables, like changing tire shape under varying loads and angles, vehicle wind resistance effects, varied road crown and bank, and so forth. It is hard to believe that these problems could ever be completely solved, though the advent of four-wheel steered cars with variable rear camber suggests that solutions to some of the classic suspension/steering dilemmas are "just around the corner."

Problems Requiring Wheel Alignment and Things To Look for Before Setting Alignment Angles

There are several obvious symptoms of a car's wheels being out of alignment, and a few that are subtle. The obvious ones are excessive and uneven tire wear or defor-

mation ("cupping"), the tendency for a car to pull to one side or the other when being driven on a flat road surface, a lack of stability that causes a car to "wander" about on the road, lunging into turns, failure of the steering wheel to return to center after a turn, or a tendency for it to violently snap back, etc. More subtle symptoms of misalignment sometimes involve a handling feel that is just not "right." I have owned cars that seemed to handle adequately, until I drove other examples of the same cars and found the handling much better or worse than the example that I owned. The change of half of a degree of caster can make this kind of difference in a car's handling feel, and there is generally some room in making front end settings to accommodate individual preferences, driving styles, and running conditions. For example, a car that is likely to be heavily loaded may need a bit of extra positive camber to compensate for the fact that running load can reduce actual camber. It is very important that a car owner communicate clearly and exactly what the problem(s) with a car is (are) and what kind of conditions the car is driven in. When I have alignment work done, I go a step further and stay with a car while the work is being done, so that I can "bug" the guy doing the work and make sure that it is done right.

No amount of alignment skill can compensate for worn or deformed suspension and steering parts. In any case the level hazard posed by these defects is intolerable. Oh yes, I know that the expedient of a bit of extra toe-in will seem to tighten up a front end with worn tie rod ends, but this a very temporary and unreliable fix. Certainly, before alignment work is attempted, things like worn or bent linkage, a sloppy steering box, bad ball joints, bad shocks, worn king pins, worn A-arm bushings, sagged front springs, etc. should be checked for and corrected as necessary. Unevenly worn tires will throw alignment settings off and make adjustment useless. Small things, like worn sway bar bushings or binding caused by excessive friction in some part of the suspension can create handling characteristics that are taken to have their origins in the suspension settings, but really don't. If the true causes of handling problems are not precisely determined, what follows will be a great deal of adjusting things, and readjusting things, to no useful end.

In any alignment proposition there are three issues that are as important as the wheel alignment angles themselves, and that must be settled before any measurement or adjustment of angles takes place. These are frame straightness, side-to-side wheelbase equality, and vehicle or spring height. If there is any evidence of frame misalignment or distortion, a frame must be measured laterally by taking diagonal measurements from similar points and comparing them. This is most easily done with fancy optical/laser/computerized/Captain Video equipment, but can also be done just as appropriately by dropping a plumb bob to the floor — it has to be a very level and smooth floor — and making chalk marks to represent the desired measurement points on the frame. A second critical pre-alignment check is that the distance between the front and rear wheels on each side of a car is the same. Recambered or mismatched springs, or incor-

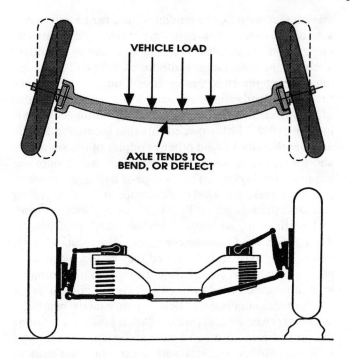

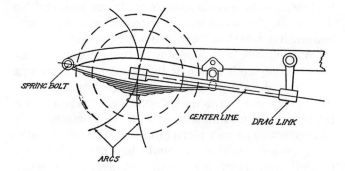

Drag link alignment is important in older collector cars. Misalignment can cause severe bump steer. This situation is found fairly often.

mon on older cars. Because modern independently suspended cars don't have the drag link setups used on older beam axle cars, many front end men don't have the experience to look for problems in this area — you may want to keep this potential problem in mind when having a beam axle system checked for wheel alignment.

Camber and King Pin Inclination

Historically, camber was the first alignment angle that received serious consideration. It was particularly important in early cars because no one had discovered the possibilities of KPI, and positive camber was the only known way to reduce the scrub radius. While modern cars utilize very little positive camber, they still carry enough to keep a vehicle's weight predominantly on the larger inner wheel bearings. In the days of leaf springs and beam axles, positive camber was included in front end designs, partially to offset the tendency of loaded axles to sag and produce the effect of negative camber. After the mid-1930s, the adoption of double A-arm front ends based on parallelogram geometry tended to keep load from effecting camber, and thus limited this factor. These modern suspensions often run on very little positive camber, and even zero camber under running load.

Camber is measured with the wheels pointed straight ahead on a flat floor or on alignment rack turntables. It is commonly measured off the machined surface of the spindle hub, but can also be measured from fixtures attached to a car's wheels. In either case, a spirit level device is the traditional method of measuring camber. Since camber and KPI are directly related, modern front end practice is sometimes to combine the two into a measurement called "included steering axis angle." Since KPI can not be adjusted, the term "included steering axis angle" really denotes what was traditionally referred to as camber in the sense of what is actually adjusted.

On cars with beam axles, the camber is not adjustable, except by bending the axle. Any shop that does much work on modern Ford Twin-I-Beam light truck front ends will have a nifty little hydraulic device for making this kind of adjustment. Camber should be equal on both

Overloading a beam axle will produce a dramatic camber change and really destroy a car's handling characteristics. Double A-arm suspensions are designed to maintain relatively stable camber throughout their travel, but some deviaation occurs. That's why sagged springs can cause handling problems in cars with this suspension design.

rect spring or axle mounting can create a dimensional error here, that for all the world will seem like an alignment problem in the front end. Finally, and most important, the height of coil springs must be measured at either the spring ends or by vehicle height and compared to data on the correct dimensions. This is so important that some manufacturers recommend using temporary alignment struts or braces to bring a vehicle up to correct height when alignment angles are set. If coil springs are sagged, most of the alignment settings that you make will be incorrect.

A final and often overlooked pre-alignment check involves drag link misalignment. On older cars with beam-type front axles, it is surprisingly common for a bent steering knuckle arm or sagged springs to cause drag link misalignment. This, in turn, can cause excessive and unpleasant road shock to be transmitted back from the suspension to the steering wheel. When drag link alignment is correct, the drag link shaft (or a line from the center of the pitman arm ball to the center of the steering knuckle arm ball) will intersect the front spring's front eye bolt at its center. On the few cars that have their front spring eye bolts at the backs of their springs and the shackles in front, the drag link should be aligned with the middle of the shackle. The steering knuckle ball end should be positioned roughly over the middle of the back of the width of the axle with the wheels pointed straight ahead, and the straight line distance from one end to the other of this curved part should be the same as from the pitman arm shaft center to ball center. Variation here means a bent steering knuckle arm — which is not all that uncom-

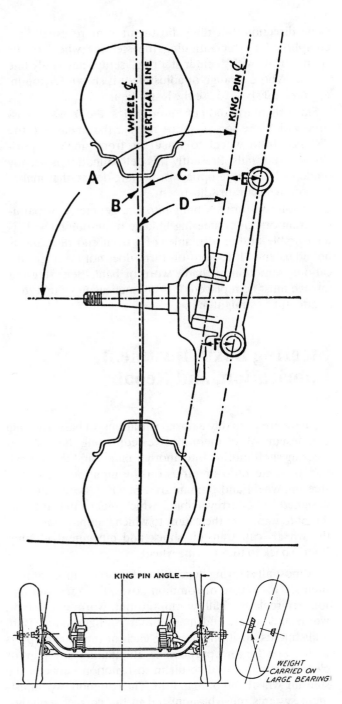

With the advent of independent front suspensions based on double wishbone hardware after the mid-1830s, cars were designed with just enough KPI to load their weight mostly on their (larger) inner wheel bearings. These diagrams show how it is possible to design KPI and camber to project a car's weight on a line near the center of the tire tread. This greatly reduces the undesirable scrub radius that would otherwise cause "bump steer."

front wheels, but in some independent front ends there is a slight provision for extra positive camber on the left wheel to compensate for the tendency of crowned roads to steer a car to the right, off the crown. A car will always pull to the side with more positive camber, so building some extra positive camber into the left wheel helps it climb road crown and keep a car going straight down the road.

Early A-arm suspensions used a variety of means to adjust camber, with shims behind the top A-arm mounting brackets and eccentric adjusters at the king pin ends being the most common approaches. Later, when ball joint suspensions came into common use, shims and bolts-in-slots, among other means, became the methods of choice to adjust camber.

KPI is usually in the range of 4 to 9 degrees and can be measured by using special equipment, but will never be incorrect unless a spindle or other major component is deformed. When this is suspected, KPI should be measured and appropriate action taken to replace bent parts.

It should be noted that although KPI cannot be adjusted, it does perform two important functions in front end design. I have already mentioned that the adoption of KPI added greatly to reducing the scrub radius of early automobiles and made possible the adoption of four-wheel brakes. Another desirable effect of KPI is that it causes the steering wheel to self-center in the straight ahead position. This is because when KPI is included in suspension design, steering the wheels off center causes the steering knuckles to raise the car slightly. While this rise is very slight, it does mean that the weight of the car bears — albeit at a tremendous mechanical disadvantage — to bring the wheels back to center position when they are turned out of that position. This produces directional stability and is one of the purposely employed design factors that keeps a car going straight.

Caster

Caster is the factor of tilting the tops of the king pins back (positive) or forward (negative) from a vertical axis. In the case of double A-arm suspensions, the king pin pivots, or a line through the ball joints is inclined forward (negative) or backward (positive) to produce caster. What all of this accomplishes is to project the vehicle's weight forward of, or behind, the tire contact patch. Projecting it forward produces a tire contact patch that is heavier in the direction that the wheels are turned. This, in turn, produces a factor called "self-aligning torque," which tends to straighten the wheel from the direction in which it has been turned. Boiled down to its nugget, this means that positive caster (king pin tops or axis back at the top) produces a tendency for the wheels to come back to center automatically. Bicycles use extreme positive caster to achieve self-centering, and that is why you often see brave and coordinated kids going down the road on bicycles without touching the handle bars. If too much positive caster is cranked into suspension settings, the wheels will tend to snap back too hard after making a turn, and the steering wheel will do the same. In some front end designs, king pin inclination has already been set to create directional stability and little or no positive caster is needed to bring the steering wheel back to center after a turn. This approach has the advantage of reducing any tendency for a wheel to self-center too violently. There are even some modern designs that use negative caster to reduce self-centering tendencies where KPI has been employed for this purpose.

Caster settings must be set correctly, or alignment problems from road wander and and wheel snap back, to the horrendous "caster shimmy" may result. Generally, the caster settings of both front wheels must be equal, although sometimes a slight variation of less than one half of one degree may be used to offset the tendency of cars to fall away from the crown of a road. Beam axles often used as much as 9 degrees of positive caster to keep wheels self-centered. Independent suspensions use much less caster than that.

If there is variation in caster between the wheels on a beam axle, the axle is bent and must be straightened. If both sides deviate from specification by the same amount, tapered shims can be used between the axle and springs to increase or reduce caster. Early double A-arm suspensions usually provided for caster adjustment via shims behind the upper control arm mountings, strut adjusters, pivot cams, etc. Some ball joint suspensions don't provide for caster adjustment at all, but require hydraulic ram tools used against the platform (unibody) sheet metal to make these adjustments.

Caster is measured by turning wheels through a total arc of 40 degrees (20 degrees in either direction off center) and measuring the difference in the deviation from vertical in that sweep. It is important to note that older equipment tended to work by measuring a greater arc, up to 60 degrees in some cases, and this equipment will not give correct readings for the now conventional 40 degree arc in which caster is measured. Minor variations in caster have a tremendous affect on the feel of a steering system and the directional stability of a car.

Toe-in

Toe-in was once considered to be related to camber, and manufacturers specified relatively large amounts of toe-in for that reason. Later it was discovered that this relationship does not really exist. Present theory holds that toe-in, or toe-out when a vehicle is steered straight ahead, will produce tire scrub — this reasoning appeals to common sense. A very small amount of toe-in, like 1/16 inch, is still specified for modern cars because this insures that the wheels will not toe out. The reasoning for this is that any looseness or wear in the steering linkage will be put under compression by toe-in and will, therefore, not result in toe-out. While toe-in produces scrubbing of the tires, toe-out will make for something worse — scrubbing, wander, and instability in the vehicle. On that basis, a little bit of toe-in is a good insurance policy against toe-out and its unpleasant consequences.

Toe is usually adjusted by means of two clamp sleeves on steering linkage tie rods. These should always be adjusted an equal amount in opposite directions to achieve an adjustment. On some cars the steering wheel is centered by moving both of the toe adjusting sleeves in the

same direction, but this adjustment is more usually accomplished by repositioning the steering wheel on its splines. Cars with "center steering" setups have only one sleeve. Where a range of adjustment is shown for toe-in, it is probably best to use the lesser figure.

Since the early days of automobiles, toe-in was measured with some sort of scribe marker that measured the distance from wheel to wheel or from similarly positioned tire treads. Presently this determination is usually made with a simple optical projecting device that makes for a more accurate adjustment.

Toe-out-on-turns is built into the geometry of parallelogram or center steering linkage of automobiles. It is measurable on the turntables of a front end rack, but is not adjustable. If toe-out-on-turns does not meet specifications, something is badly worn or bent. Bent steering linkage must be replaced. It is impractical and dangerous to attempt to straighten it.

Steering Box Adjustment, Lubrication, and Repair

There are probably a dozen variations on basic steering box design. All of them involve redirecting the plane of steering shaft motion into another plane, and the imposition of some ratio or ratios on the input/output of the steering wheel and pitman arm. Steering boxes are also designed to be "irreversible," which means that they attempt to minimize the extent to which bumping forces on the wheels can transmit shock and movement ("bump steer") back to the steering wheel.

Almost all steering boxes allow for two or more adjustments. This is true of common boxes, like rack and pinion, recirculating ball, worm and nut, worm and sector, worm and roller, and many other configurations. Both adjustments position and snug each of the moving parts in the box for the purpose of eliminating any play or clearance that would result in lost motion between the steering wheel and pitman arm. The common two adjustment systems must be adjusted in the correct sequence and often require the use of a small, accurate torque wrench to create a very mild preload on the bearings supporting the driving steering gear, or to measure small amounts of drag. The second stage of adjustment usually involves snugging the driven member of the system against the driving member and checking the system for binding throughout its range of motion. It is critical that during this adjustment the pitman arm be disconnected from the steering linkage so that the mesh of the steering gears can be sensed without interference. If the connection of the pitman arm must be broken at a splined joint, the relative positions of the components should be noted and marked so that it can be reestablished.

Power steering systems are divided into two types — the self-contained rotary type and the linkage type. Again, there is tremendous variation in the design of these units, from the early units pioneered by Pierce-

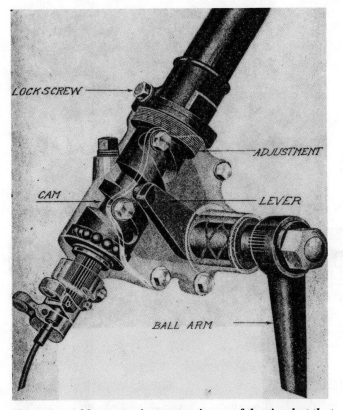

This cam and lever steering system is one of the simplest that there is. It isn't very durable compared to some more sophisticated systems, but it works. Keeping steering box seals in good condition and maintaining lubricant level and condition are important. Steering box adjustments are usually made with threaded rings or shims, and are critical to smooth operation and preventing damage to components.

Arrow and Revere, to modern systems. All of them use a torsion, or spool, valving device that operates pumped hydraulic pressure against a piston or baffle to assist steering. The pumps and steering units used to affect power steering are often rebuildable. When failure occurs, it is usually in the form of bad seals and valving components. Scored hydraulic parts are also a possibility. Power steering fluid should be periodically flushed and replaced and all hydraulic hoses in steering systems should be checked for signs of leakage and deterioration. If this occurs, replacement with new hoses is necessary.

Rotary and linkage power steering systems should only be replenished with power steering fluid. Some of them will tolerate automatic transmission fluid, but many will not. It is always best to use a specially formulated power steering fluid. Some linkage systems are externally valved and still need separate lubrication for their steering gear boxes. This lubrication is accomplished with the same lubricant used in conventional steering boxes — SAE 90 gear oil. Modern steering boxes will tolerate EP ("Extreme Pressure") lubricants, but older ones should be lubed with a non-EP mineral based oil. Some of these older units have felt seals that EP additives will destroy. NEVER use cup or chassis grease in a steering box. It will channel and fail to lubricate the pressure bearing surfaces on the gears and bearings. When you find grease in a steering box, it will usually have to be removed by disassembly. Sometimes if it isn't caked too densely, it can be thinned and siphoned out of the box by adding warmed SAE 80 gear oil to dissolve it.

The styling of cars like this 1958 Cadillac deVille four-door hardtop was controversial; some people found it shamefully gaudy. Say what you will about its styling, metal men loved its panels because they were so easy to work on. They were high crown or deeply curved panels, and that always makes body work easier. These panels were also made from very thick and soft metal, so they were easy to "ding out." There was also very good access to most of these surfaces from behind.

CHAPTER 20:

An Overview: The Physical Restoration and Refinishing of Collector Car Bodies

Please indulge me for a few pages while I tell a story.

A Matter of Perception

Many years ago, when I was old enough to have had my driver's license for a few years and had begun to take some of my father's classic cars to local meets in the vicinity of Bennington, Vermont, I had a startling experience. I had gone to a meet that was held in conjunction with a parade and other festivities, celebrating the bicentennial of a town in northeastern Massachusetts. The meet was poorly organized — things involving old cars were very informal in those days — and the bicentennial oversight committee had decided that there should be awards for the old cars but had no idea how to decide them. First they got the awards: a drop light from a local hardware store, a tow rope from an auto parts store, a soldering iron from an electrical shop, and a hundred bucks from somewhere. Then they hit on a unique "communitarian" way of judging the cars that participated.

After the parade, the cars were driven onto a huge field and lined up, side-by-side, in the random order they had arrived on the field. Then the cars were counted off in groups of three, and the owners in each group of three cars judged the cars in that group. The winners of this elimination were driven forward two car lengths, and new groups of three were counted off. Winners in this elimination were then driven forward, and so on, until my Lincoln and I reached the "finals." The other cars in the final group were a very badly restored Franklin Olympic 6 and a very nice Durant. As I remember, the mathematics of the thing worked out so that only the Franklin and my Lincoln arrived at the final selection, but to make the finals a decision of three — and thus reduce the possibility of a tie and an unseemly fist fight — the Durant had been selected by all of the residents of the next-to-last row, and promoted from there to the final selection.

The Durant was a nice job by the standards of that time and represented what we used to call "a good owner restoration." The Franklin was another matter. About the kindest thing that could be said about it was that its water pump wasn't leaking, and that was only because it had an air-cooled engine that didn't have a water pump. The car was a complete mess in every distinction and in every detail. The upholstery was beastly, crooked seams, stuffing bulging out, lumps, and so forth. The engine, when it finally started, belched out a cacophony of moans, knocks, wraps, and other noises of imminent self-destruction. The plating? There wasn't any; aluminum paint had replaced it. And the body and fenders had been hammered and filled with plastic to the point that it was hard to recognize that the thing was an automobile, much less a Franklin. Things were missing, obviously wrong parts were everywhere, lubricant seemed to be dripping from everywhere, even from places that don't normally contain oil.

Two related questions coursed through my mind. How had this thing, the Franklin, gotten here under its own faltering power, and why had it gotten to the finals? That question involved considerable self-interest because in those days, and particularly at my young age in those days, the hundred bucks part of the prize represented serious money. Enough money to plan any manner of frivolous fun, or even to contemplate a substantial automotive acquisition. As I said, the Franklin raised two interesting and nonessential questions; it was the Durant that had me mildly worried. Of course, it was absurd to be judging a mighty 12-cylinder Lincoln in the same competition class with a Model A-like Durant, but that detail had been overlooked by the oversight committee in the rush to "have some old cars at the celebration." On the other hand, the conceptual defects in the judging scheme seemed unimportant because the hundred bucks was cash.

Although I was young, I understood that one of the niceties of being a gentleman was not to vote for yourself in a competition, particularly with the voting so open to view. As I had the best restored car of the three and far-and-away the most interesting and impressive, I considered the pleasant fate of being selected by my colleagues to be all but inevitable. Since only gross misjudgment by my colleagues could result in any other outcome, I pretty much settled into the quandary of deciding between the several delightful alternatives that my newly acquired hundred bucks would make possible. The only cloud on the horizon was a nagging uneasiness about how poor the judgment had been that had promoted the Franklin to the final elimination, and some faint apprehension that a similar error could befall me in "the big one." No, the justice of my cause was too obvious. I dismissed my sense of nagging uneasiness and faint apprehension. Isn't it funny how easy it is to be overconfident in your father's car?

Of course, this story wouldn't be worth telling if my fortunes hadn't taken a severe turn for the worse at this point, and that is just what happened. A woman of about thirty, who had been hovering around the Franklin all afternoon, came over to me and the Durant owner and very earnestly asked for a moment in private with us. Her story was simple and compelling. Her father had begun to restore the Franklin years earlier, but had since contracted some disease of the nervous system. He had lost his job as a machinist, his sight was badly impaired, and his hand-eye coordination was all but nonexistent. Still he persisted in trying to restore the Franklin. It had become the most meaningful symbol in his shattered life, and he had come to derive his sense of self-worth as a human being from his engagement with it. Because of his deteriorated senses, he had no idea what a botch he had made of the car, and thought that he had done magnificent work. For reasons that are self-evident, no one of his acquaintance had informed him otherwise.

That afternoon his daughter had told this story to her father's competitors at each rung of the competition. Because he had voted for himself, he had won each round of the competition unanimously, up to that point. After she left, the Durant owner — who turned out to be something of a jerk — suggested to me that her story might be a clever deception; a ruse to grab the brass ring. He said that it should be "each man for himself." I told him that I would certainly vote for the Franklin and that he would inevitably lose by a two-to-one decision. I suggested that he drop it and vote for the Franklin.

Part of the strange judging format that we were using that day called for the members of each three-car group of owner-judges to examine the other cars in each group together, and to discuss the fine points of the thing. We started with the Franklin, and soon there was no doubt in my mind that the owner's daughter had been telling the truth about her father's condition and about the central role of the Franklin in his life. The poor fellow blindly and lovingly called our attention to each butchered detail of that miserable automobile so that nothing was missed. In addition to his other problems, the Franklin owner had very little knowledge of Franklins or of restoration. During the tour of his car he managed to point out several atrocities that he had committed against it that had

slipped past my cursory inspection. Of course, to him, these atrocities were ingenious implementations of breathtaking, new restoration techniques. What a mess. Muttering obscenities at fate, the Durant owner joined me and the Franklin owner and the award was unanimous to the Franklin.

There *is* a point to all of this. Different people see restoration, and particularly body restoration, differently, and the high standards that we are about to discuss are lost on many, if not most, people. I have seen the most miserable excuses for sheet metal work under paint applications that border on the criminal, which are held by the owners and craftsmen involved to be forms of perfection. And *these* people have no diagnosable maladies of perception. I have also seen — and this is important — work done to a standard that I cannot presently hope to duplicate. It is important because it is only when one recognizes one's limits that improvement is possible.

Expectations

Stepping back from the gross and slovenly that are all too common in "commercial" auto body and refinishing work, there are gradations of workmanship, up to and including the truly excellent. The distinctions can be subtle. The art of metal finishing involves, in its final stages, manipulations of surfaces by two- or three-thousandths of an inch. That may sound like precision beyond the necessities of utility, but the human eye can distinguish surface changes of this amount in small areas of sheet metal. Under certain conditions, a failure to hold surfaces to this fine standard can have visibly devastating results in the final product. Take the example of new cars, and this includes cars from the lowliest Toyota to the lordliest BMW. Have you ever noticed that the finishes on new cars are often terrible? There is a reason for that and it is instructive to examine it.

New cars are painted under conditions that are impossible to duplicate in refinish situations. The metal being painted is, or can be, completely free of defect and contamination. We are talking about freshly stamped and degreased metal. The air supply, primer, and paint are manufactured or provided to standards of consistency and purity that are unattainable in aftermarket refinishing situations. The paint application is often done by laser-guided robots, with a precision that no human being can hope to match. Ambient air in the paint area and in the air lines is absolutely clean and dry. The paint itself is usually a "reflow" system that literally flows again after its initial set, when it is subjected to oven temperatures of 160° Fahrenheit or more in huge bake ovens. This is completely different from the air dry finishes that are sold in the aftermarket where "what you see is pretty much what you get" after the first wet paint applications dry, except, of course, for the option of color sanding and "wheeling" a rough finish flat. Even though high heat drying would be desirable with air dry enamels, it is only possible to a limited extent because trimmed, upholstered, and wired interiors will not take much heat in a refinish situation.

So with all of these inherent advantages, why is contemporary factory paint so often so terrible? Why does it always contain levels of orange peel that no restorer would tolerate? The answer is simple. Today's car manufacturers have eliminated as much labor as possible from their production regimens. This means that die stamping has almost entirely been reduced to single station operations, which limits both panel design and panel quality. It means that panels and the dies that stamp them are designed so as to reduce expensive die maintenance, and this maintenance is held to an absolute minimum in the production of many cars. Finally, it means that there is little opportunity for handwork in the painting process so that inaccurately formed sheet metal somehow has to be made to look acceptable and to hide defects.

The answer is orange peel, purposely induced orange peel, to hide badly stamped sheet metal panels. This orange peel is guaranteed either in the basic paint chemistry that is used or by employing application standards that will cause it — like running spray gun head pressures of 70 pounds or more. The latter will guarantee ample orange peel to hide any manner of wavy panel fabrication. Sadly, the public has come to accept these citrus surfaces and little notice is taken of their essential ugliness. It is only in the early 1990s that new paints and new application technologies have combined with more accurate tolerances in sheet metal fit and finish standards to produce finishes that are sometimes as good as the old hand-rubbed factory finishes of many years ago. They call that "progress!"

Body and Refinish Standards Are Higher for Old Cars

The finishes on many of our collector cars were done to very high standards "at the factory." Early varnish finishes were applied with brushes and sanded and pumiced by hand to perfection. These finishes involved incredibly cumbersome sequences of application, baking, and sanding; and they often achieved the thickness of a dime. They were very expensive to apply. In fact, the old varnish systems created a bottleneck in auto production which had to be removed before the massive auto production figures of the late 1920s could become reality. The answer was the invention of nitro-cellulose lacquer ("Duco") by DuPont in 1923, and synthetic (alkyd) enamel in 1929. These early synthesized finishes were more durable than their predecessors and could be sprayed. The bottleneck was eliminated, and good, durable finishes became common to both cheap and expensive automobiles.

Then too, the bodies of middle-priced and upscale cars made in what we now think of as "the collector car era" were more meticulously and ruggedly constructed than are the bodies of many cars today. Panel thickness was once commonly 18 gauge or more, as opposed to the present practice of 22 gauge or less. Stampings were often done with more than a single draw, and a level of perfection was possible that is only beginning to again appear on a few cars today.

One of the effects of having cars leave the factory with good quality sheet metal and nearly perfectly applied finishes was and is that the quality of work in the repair sector tends to rise to match production quality. In the "old days" body men pounded out dents, welded tears, and generally dealt with metal in ways that involved skills and care way beyond the realm of contemporary body shops. In part, this was because bodies were easier to work on, due to the thicker, softer metal in them and better access to the backs of panels. Fenders were most often bolted on rather than welded on, and this made kinds of repair possible that are unthinkable today. Skills such as metal finishing and shrinking were commonly available, whereas they are hard to find in today's body shops. On the other hand, modern equipment and materials for repairing auto bodies and painting them have begun to close the quality gap in recent years.

In the 1950s polyester fillers, such as Bondo, mostly replaced lead fillers for the repair of auto bodies. These fillers, called "mud" in the trade, are still controversial, but they have been vastly improved in the last 35 years.

In the 1950s, the development of polyester ("plastic") body fillers ushered in an age of unskilled and shoddy work in place of the craftsmanship that had, in most cases, gone before. The "rough 'em out, smooth 'em up" school of Bondo artists came to dominate the field of crash repair. Gradually, but certainly, the public came to accept low quality sheet metal repair under badly applied finishes, which happened to match the basic appearance of OEM sheet metal and finishes. Is it any wonder that it is hard to find commercial body shops capable of doing work to restoration standards?

Let me cite an example of this problem. A few years ago, I was invited to the local unveiling of a new automotive paint product line by a very major paint manufacturer. I and several other of the guests that day were shocked at the amount of orange peel in the examples of this product that the manufacturer proudly displayed. In the course of the unveiling, the manufacturer's representative demonstrated the application of this isocyanate hardened acrylic enamel system. He achieved the same orange peel results in his application that were evident in the samples on display. I noted that his spray gun pressure indicated 85 psi at the wall regulator and 70 psi at the gun tailstock. When I suggested that this might be causing the orange peel, he laughed at me and said something to the effect of, "If you're so smart, let's see you do better." I took the challenge and reduced the air pressure to 45 pounds at the tail stock, after increasing the paint reduction from 125 percent to 180 percent. The result was far from great, but it was certainly a flatter paint application than the factory "rep" had been able to make. I had him, right? Wrong. He agreed that my application was flatter and better looking, but added that his application was far closer to new car factory standards. His point was that unless you were painting an entire car (a "complete") he had a better match to the rest of the panels in the average contemporary car. Unfortunately he was right, my smoother, flatter paint was the likely mismatch with the average new car. The standards of modern manufacture and aftermarket work do affect restoration in the very materials that are available...and sometimes unavailable.

Old Crafts and New Technologies

It is almost amusing that Detroit, following the lead of European and particularly Japanese manufacturers, is suddenly in a frenzy to improve "fit and finish," and to make, as the ad says, "quality Job #1." On all but the very cheapest American cars, fit and finish was always an important aspect of producing and marketing automobiles — and of repairing them. The lapses only began in the 1950s. But the new or reborn emphasis on fit and finish has one radically different aspect from what used to be called "quality." Whereas formerly quality was in part achieved by numerous manual operations requiring skill, coordination, and experienced craftsmen, the new emphasis on fit and finish is largely an outgrowth of statistical analysis and digital manipulation. It's all numbers. Take an example. Doors on cars used to fit because they were adjusted, either crudely or delicately, so that the jams and edges were even. Someone manually made them fit. Now they fit because the basic forming, jigging, and welding of the components involved is done by incredibly accurate machines. An avalanche of numerical data is crunched by computers and used to control complex and versatile machines that use feedback to constantly monitor and correct errors and mistakes. The result looks like craftsmanship in the old sense, but there is little skill or judgment involved at the production end. Now the skill and knowledge is applied almost solely in the engineering and specification.

In the repair sector a revolution of sorts is also taking place. The crude old frame racks are being replaced by three dimensional body/frame machines that can take a unibody that is twisted like a pretzel and move its distorted structure until everything fits precisely — and all of that is done without a single hammer blow. Or take the example of GMAW (Gas Metal Arc Welding, usually, and incorrectly called "MIG") welding. With one of these machines — which now realistically sell for less than $1,000 — and a good 0.023-inch wire, a virtually inexperienced operator can produce stronger and better-looking welds than could formerly be done by a master craftsman with the arcane art of "hammer welding." Skill in applying finishes has pretty much gone the way of chivalry since it is possible to apply modern finishes like catalyzed enamels and urethanes, and then color sand them and buff them. The results are not quite restoration quality, but they can be frighteningly good.

The field of body restoration cannot ignore the new technologies, but it must constantly evaluate them and their application to restoration work. Also, it is not desirable to embrace *all* of the new products and procedures that come along as, for example, several restorers found out when they tried a "revolutionary new" sprayable filler material a few years ago. It fell out and lawsuits followed.

The trick is to find an appropriate level of technology and to master its application. Some tools and skills haven't changed much for thousands of years. The dollies, spoons, picks and hammers used by metal men have their origins in the hand tools used by coppersmiths in the Middle East *millennia* ago when they formed pots, pans, and pitchers. This early repertoire was refined and expanded by tinsmiths and applied to the bodies of animal-drawn carriages in recent centuries. Body construction at first involved tacking sheet metal to a wooden frame and hammering it smooth. The technologies for such refinements as welding, filling, and painting gradually evolved, as did the expectation that the results of these crafts should look nice.

To my knowledge, the basis of good sheet metal work, metal finishing, has not changed in basic outline, or in many particulars, since the beginning of the age of the automobile. What has changed is our willingness to take the time to develop the skills to accomplish metal finishing. Without going into details here, metal finishing is the business of conforming sheet metal surfaces to their correct shapes by dollying, hammering, picking, and filing. Occasionally shrinking is required, and sometimes lead filling is necessary. Properly, most of this work is done with simple body hammers and dollies, and with a very clear understanding of the limits and capabilities of the material that this work involves — sheet metal. Sadly, contemporary body practice is too often to crudely pound out dents, often producing additional damage to the metal, and glob the results over with polyester body filler. Such repairs lack permanence and are usually visible to an experienced eye. Our discussion of sheet metal work in this book will not consider the use of the "rough 'em out, smooth 'em up" school of auto body work. It will also avoid the easy option of panel replacement that exists in modern body repair because that option is not often available to restorers.

Goals and Necessities

The need for safety is nowhere more crucial than in bodywork and refinishing. Like other aspects of automotive restoration, bodywork is laden with both obvious and hidden hazards. Eye, ear, lung, and skin protection fit into the *obvious* category, but there are also hazards that are subtle. The tin/lead filler used in body work tends to produce lead oxides at elevated temperatures, and this stuff is deadly to breath. Even the lead filings and dust that are generated in body work can penetrate human skin and produce lead poisoning. Some of the newer automotive finishes that are on the market are significantly more toxic than the older ones that they have replaced, and when you get into the isocyanate hardened paints, be sure to take label cautions *very* seriously.

One restoration goal that involves bodywork and refinishing and that is often botched is that of adopting a logical sequence of attack. My shop will soon be working on a Jaguar XK 150 that another restorer has already spent a fortune on; the body will be reworked and refinished. It will arrive here with all panels painted and repaired, and a nice white enamel finish in place. The only problem is that this car still has to be rewired, its interior has to be removed and replaced, and a complete mechanical restoration will have to be done. We anticipate repainting the car's exterior panels when we have finished all of that. The time and money already spent painting the car will have been wasted. Clearly, the sequence in which the original restorer of this car attempted to get the work done was wrong. While the debate over whether to do a car's interior before or after painting its panels can be a subtle one in the case of some body styles, it is generally most effective to make painting the last step. Certainly mechanical work should be completed before finish top coats are applied. The nature of what you are attempting to accomplish will dictate a logical sequence of attack, so figure out an approach. Don't just proceed at random.

Judgment in the abstract is easy to cultivate. The question "...what do you do when..." is always easier to answer as an exercise than when you have the stuff in your hands and you have to do something...quick. You have to work to develop judgment, and you must be vigilant to maintain its authority. It is amazing what atrocities are committed with body tools and refinish materials in the late hours of the night and in the wee hours of the morning.

Work habits fall into the same category as judgment — they only have value when they are not suspended in emergencies. Usually lapses of these two essentials of good work go together. In the end, good work habits controlled by sure judgment produce craftsmanship. There is no place in this proposition for luck, good or bad. When the time and trouble has been taken to learn to do something right, it should become a possession that is inalienable. At least don't alienate it yourself.

Permanence is the unseen component of quality body restoration. Of course, what is seen is important, but it is durability that is really the main issue. Of particular importance is corrosion resistance. Here, impeccable habits, such as neutralizing soldering fluxes and killing tallow residues (from leading) become paramount. Subtle errors in judgment, such as using lap welds instead of butt welds or brazing body joints instead of welding them, will limit durability and ruin your efforts before their time. Auto body paint is an unforgiving medium, and is particularly susceptible in magnifying little mistakes in what was done to the metal that lies below it. Small mistakes can come back and haunt you two years later. Have you ever had paint check, blister, peel, dull, crow's foot, etc.?

Up to this point, this discussion of body work and refinishing may have sounded pretty goody-goody, including as it has the topics of: safety, judgment, manual skills, etc. Bodywork/refinishing is not all that way because somewhere in good bodywork you will almost inevitably find the evidence of larceny, fraud, and deception. That's right, while body work is a matter of subtle appearances, it is performed with materials and skills that rarely yield absolute perfection. There is often need for trickery — real smoke and mirrors stuff. Some examples.

It can be difficult or impossible to match paint color exactly. If fenders and doors are assembled with a mismatch of "half a shade" (there really is no exact definition of a "shade") or more, the careful eye will sight along a door seam and the mouth that is attached to the same brain as the eye will mumble, "mismatch." The eye can make that distinction, and the mouth is frequently impossible to shut up. Of course, the eye *expects to see* a mismatch at the edge of a panel, so a parallel expanse of slightly mismatched panel edges will show it up like Rudolph the Red-Nosed Reindeer's schnaz at a New Jersey garden party. If, on the other hand, a slight mismatch is blended into a door or fender in a wavy line, the eye will never spot it because it will be mistaken for a phenomenon of varying light — maybe as a reflection off the ground or the projection of sunlight through a cloud. The eye pretty much sees what it expects to see, and that fact can be used to advantage to trick it into seeing what the metal man/painter/magician needs it to see. Judgment comes in when you restrain yourself from trying to hide a "two-shade mismatch" with tricks of the trade.

Okay, the fewer tricks, the better, but some are necessary. While it is important to shrink body metal into an approximation of its original lateral dimensions, some excess metal can be hidden in the high crown areas of body panels. If this kind of thing is not done, body work becomes endless.

There are certain realities of automobile construction that will both encourage and limit how much Houdini you can bring to what you are doing. Automobiles are basically bilateral, which means that their right and left sides are mirror opposites of each other. This would limit the variation that you could engage in from one side of a car to the other, but for the fact that cars are rarely parked in front of magnifying mirrors, and no one I know has perfected the business of seeing both sides of a car at once. Bodywork on both sides of a car should create a great similarity of features and dimensions, but absolute mirror image fidelity is not necessary and was rarely

Of all the hazards in body restoration work, lung hazards are among the most subtle and deadly. The breathing masks shown in the first photo have very specific and limited uses. The two dust masks on the left should only be used for sanding operations and never for protection when you are painting. The two masks on the right will adequately protect your lungs with some paints, but others will require an outside, pumped air supply. Be sure to consult manufacturers' recommendations on this issue. No protective filter will work when it is dirty or contaminated. It is important to change filters and pre-filters regularly on these devices. Old and new pre-filters are shown above and to the right of the mask in the second photograph. Old and new filters are shown below it and to the right.

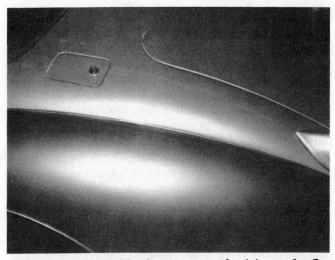

High crown panels, like these, are very forgiving and reflect light in ways that tend to hide rather than reveal defects in panel contours.

achieved on the premises of the factory or custom body builder anyway. Remember some of this before you go all out to measure and jig for the perfection of a panel contour that no one will ever notice because the only comparison is to the other side of a car.

Pitfalls and Worse

Let me mention a few of the thousands of things to avoid in this work. The first is buying a car that has had its bodywork butchered. While it can be difficult to tell how much Bondo and how many pop rivets and pieces of roofing tin lurk under shiny paint, some determination is possible. I would advise spending as much time as is necessary to make this determination because there is nothing worse than the queasy feeling that you get when you discover this kind of damage, "...Uh oh, someone's been here before."

Most auto body butchers will work in ways that tend to thicken body panels, but they must contour back at their ends where their cross sectional width is visible to meet their partners. When you see a panel that seems to fall away in the last few inches before its edge, watch out. Often, when a door panel has been built up excessively with filler, you will see the thickness at its vertical edges or you will see the panel fall away towards them in its final few inches.

Closely related to that kind of butcher work is the artistry that is sometimes practiced in creating modified and inauthenic bodies. Usually these are pretty easy to spot; touring cars don't often really look just like sedans below their beltlines, but some of this work is subtle. The fellows selling examples of it tend to have one thing in common — they sweat a lot.

Obviously, some materials, such as fiberglass bandages and pop rivets, should never be used in restoration work, but misusing proper materials can be just as destructive, and honest people sometimes do this. Here are two gen-

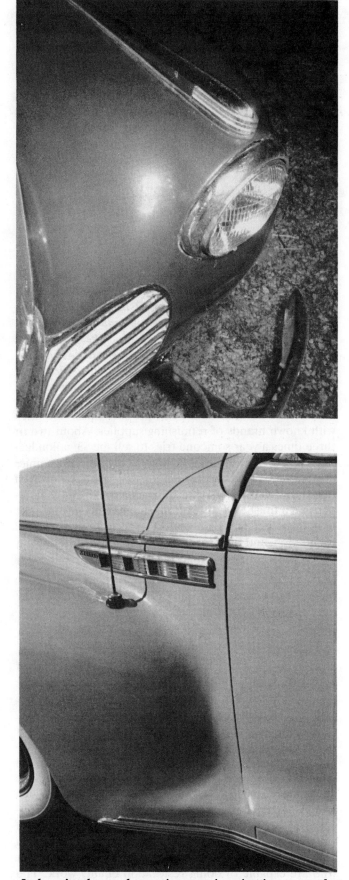

It doesn't take much experience or imagination to see that filler has been used excessively to hide damage in the two situations that are shown here. The panel contours are very uneven, and the panels certainly didn't leave the factory that way.

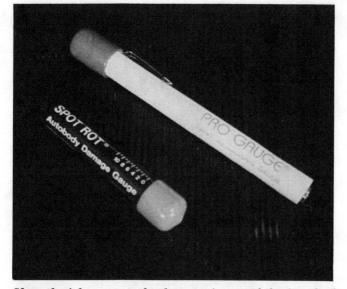

If you don't have an eye for the excessive use of plastic or lead filler, I highly recommend one of the inexpensive magnetic tools shown here. The Pro Gauge will indicate paint thickness and the use of small amounts of filler. The Spot Rot will reveal the use of excessive filler. I recommend these tools even if you do have a good eye for filler. They will confirm your best judgments, and they may surprise you on your worst!

eral "don'ts." Never mix paint product lines, and stick with known brands of refinishing supplies. About two or three times a year someone tries to sell me $3/gallon lacquer thinner put up in 55 gallon drums. The economics are attractive, but the results are invariably unlovely if this stuff is actually used to thin lacquer. Always remember that a finish will suffer from and magnify any mistake that lurks below its outermost aspect. Bodywork is a foundation, and filler, primer, and paint are built on it. A defect anywhere along that line will probably cause any finish to unravel like a cheap sweater.

Specialties

It is possible to do credible work in the areas of bodywork and refinishing with a minimal amount of equipment. What you attempt will depend mostly on the skills and conditions that you have acquired and created. If you are just starting out, you will find lacquer work easier because lacquer is a very forgiving finish and is almost endlessly susceptible to repair and rework. Unless you have substantially greater skills and a very dust-free environment, I would avoid a more difficult finish, such as alkyd enamel, which tends to be very intolerant of substandard application or poor application conditions. If you subcontract bodywork or paint work, you will find very few practitioners in the commercial repair sector who are capable of doing restoration quality work. You will also find restoration shops to be very expensive for this sort of work — they have to be to maintain quality. Materials, supplies, and equipment overhead are major expenses as is the labor of skilled craftsmen. For example, a set of air intake filters for our spray booth now

costs over $160, and a set will only stand in for two or three cars.

Some specialty work, such as striping — never with a wheel — have to go to specialists. I couldn't begin to develop these skills if my life depended on it, and I don't know many people who could. Other specialties, such as panel fabrication and welding, may involve combinations of skills and equipment that are impractical for the amateur restorer to acquire. On the other hand, they may not. I have learned to do "amazing things" with a small sheet metal brake, rawhide mallets, a shot bag, and a gas welding setup. The level of satisfaction that comes from some mastery of this work is enormous.

I have suggested that there are times when a smoke-and-mirrors approach to bodywork and refinishing is necessary, but there is also a basic, enforced honesty in bodywork. An inexperienced metal worker will not, with the aid of a $49.95 hammer and dolly starter kit and complete instructions for metal working, do Michelangelo-like metal finishing the first time out. With some practice, he may get acceptable results. Your basic Sears paint spray outfit, used in a dusty garage, will not produce good quality refinish work. But if you clean and vacuum that garage carefully, and use the Sears sprayer with skill, the results can be surprisingly good.

CHAPTER 21:

Sheet Metal Basics

Sheet metal work falls into the realms of manual arts and technical skills. The strategies for and operations of removing complex deformations from sheet metal body parts are so variable as to be an art. There is usually no *one* correct approach to such a complex task, and various approaches may produce virtually equal results. Of course, there are also numerous substandard or incorrect approaches which will hide original damage, while actually producing further damage. Because elements of judgment, efficiency, experience, and even inspiration are possible in this work, it borders on being an art. However, other aspects of sheet metal work, such as hammering, welding, and knowing the effects of heat on sheet metal, are highly technical and require a clear understanding of cause and effect before they can be properly understood and performed. These are really technical areas and can be demonstrated scientifically. The result of all of this is that good sheet metal work requires a study of the basic technical aspects, experience in the actual work, and imagination and ingenuity in approaching some of the more difficult problems posed by sheet metal repair.

There are several textbooks that deal with automotive sheet metal and refinish work generally, and devote one or more chapters to sheet metal repair in particular. Some of these books are fairly useful for beginners, but many of them are designed for use in conjunction with classroom instruction, and really don't work very well without it. While it is possible to approach some mechanical repair operations with "the book" open on a fender, this will never do for body restoration and refinishing. As well, classroom guides will tend to tell you just enough to make you dangerous and will often overlook much that is basic. That's the best of them. The worst of them tend to describe procedures, operations, and materials in a way that is completely and perfectly understandable as long as you understood these things *before* you read the descriptions of how to do them.

There are two books that really do provide useful insights into how to deal with various aspects of steel sheet metal repair. Unfortunately, one of them is too cursory for most people and the other is too detailed. However, if you are new to this work, you should have a look at both of them.

The Key to Metal Bumping by Frank T. Sargent was first issued in the late 1930s and was basically a user's guide to the body tools made by the Fairmont Forge company. Various revisions and editions followed the original issue, and by the third edition (1953) this book had become a pretty good treatise on the "Fairmont Method" of dealing with sheet metal repair, as well as including all sorts of helpful hints regarding welding and other skills. The basic premise of *The Key to Metal Bumping* is that there must be a method to straightening sheet metal — you don't just go in with a hammer and start banging out things that seem to be in. The method proposed involves distinguishing between permanently deformed metal and metal held out of place by permanently deformed metal. The prescription for repair is to analyze the order in which damage occurred during impact, and remove it in the reverse order. The book is a short one and leaves a lot unsaid, but it is a good basic guide to the field. At the time of its issue and revisions, it was almost revolutionary in proposing a method of analysis and plan of attack to confront sheet metal work. I would suggest that the proposed plan is useful, but not the only way to approach these problems. In any case, *The Key to Metal Bumping* is a good place to start the study of sheet metal work. It is also readily available from a number of old car hobby book sellers and from suppliers of body tools and supplies.

Automobile Sheet Metal Repair, by Robert L. Sargent (Chilton), and its newest revision, *Chilton's Mechanics Handbook, Volume 3: Autobody Sheet Metal Repair* is the most comprehensive general book that I know of on this subject. Whereas *The Key to Metal Bumping* makes this work sound wonderfully easy and simple, the Chilton book confounds the reader with the complexity of every aspect of the analysis and operations involved. It sure isn't bedtime reading, but if you take the time to read it and understand it, you will have a good grasp on the theory and the practice of this work. I recommend it highly.

One thing that you will get from reading these books, or the rest of this chapter, is the concept that sheet metal repair involves more than just beating or pushing out a dent. Beyond that, there are approaches that will efficiently yield a repair that looks good, is permanent, uses no or very little filler, and restores the basic integrity of a damaged panel. That, of course, is the object. But no matter how many articles, books, pamphlets, and videotapes you absorb on this topic, experience is still essen-

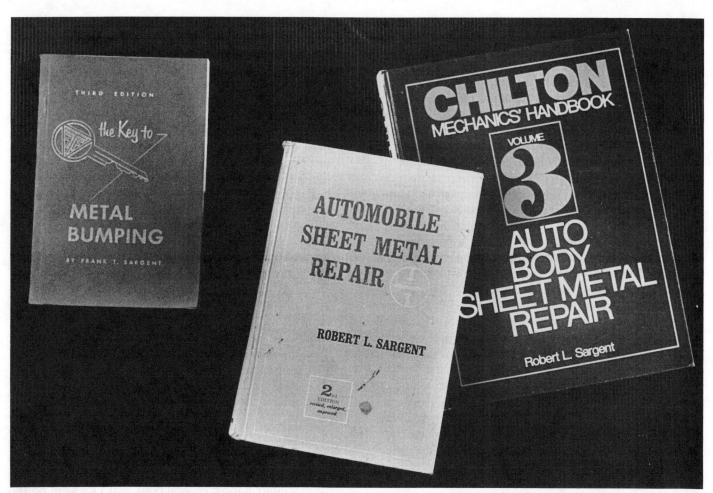

The three books, shown here, are the most important texts for the metal man. The one on the left evolved from a tool catalog and was the first systematic guide to auto body sheet metal work. The two on the right are really the same book in different issues. They offer a comprehensive understanding of auto body sheet metal work.

tial. NEVER attempt to do work like this solely on the basis of book knowledge. The best approach is to find some old body panels: doors, fenders, hoods, etc., and damage and repair them yourself to get the feel of the thing. Armed with a basic knowledge of the craft, you will learn more in five or six hours of experimentation with real sheet metal parts than you would have thought possible. I stress this point because I have seen body panels and whole cars ruined by people who thought that body work was as simple as skilled practitioners or glossy tool sales pamphlets make it look. It isn't. Scrap panels are cheap, but the repair damage you can do to a treasured car will be expensive to repair.

In addition to practicing on scrap panels during early learning, you can often try new or alternative strategies on them. Sometimes it's easy to approximately duplicate the actual damage in something that you are working on in scrap. You can then experiment to determine what the most effective repair strategy will be. Scrap panels also provide a wonderful inventory of formed metal sections for repair purposes. It's amazing how often you can find an area or part of a scrap panel that can be modified for a specific purpose that you have. This can save hours of work with rawhide mallets and shot bags.

There are lots of neat tricks in body work that can save time and promote quality, but there are also some very bad ones. In each case, it is important to know why something is supposed to work rather than just taking someone's word for it. Over the years, manufacturers have come up with many tools and materials that don't work at all or that work only to a limited extent or in limited situations. Take, for example, panel flanging tools. There are very few applications where these tools can be used appropriately and to advantage. Mostly they are used to save time and to reduce the skill required to fit panels properly for butt welding. When used improperly, these tools stop being a neat trick and become devices of destruction. In this case, either experience or common sense or both would guide you away from such uses.

Then there are the really dirty approaches that should *never* (as opposed to "almost never") be used. Drilling holes and using body hooks or welding studs to sheet metal to pull it when it could have been pounded out from behind come readily to mind. I realize that you will see so-called "professionals" doing this stuff and, in fact, I saw several examples of these and other barbaric "techniques" on display at this year's Automotive Service Industry Association show. That doesn't make them right for restoration work. Intuition and common sense should tell you which approaches are damaging and which are in the interests of the preservation of old automobiles.

One of the nice things about sheet metal work is that simple tools and simple approaches are often best suited to the needs of repair and restoration. Seemingly complex problems can often be subdivided into a series of simple problems and solved simply. While fancy clamping, pulling, pushing, and bumping tools are available, a few good hammers and dollies and the skill to use them will almost always provide the best basis for restoration repair work on sheet metal. This is not to argue against some of the sophisticated equipment and techniques out there, but just to state that knowledge and experience are always the starting points in this work, and that much of what passes for sophistication in the modern repair sector has very little application to old car restoration.

Sheet Metal: Composition, Fabrication, and Basic Characteristics

The sheet metal that is used for automobile panel fabrication, and for some panel support structures, is a highly evolved and complex series of alloys based in the steel family. Sheet steel uses several alloying components to achieve desirable characteristics. The most important of these is carbon, which is added to steel in concentrations of between one-quarter to three-quarters of one percent, usually near one-quarter percent for sheet metal. Because many operations are involved in converting a basic slab of raw steel into what we call sheet metal, the choice of characteristics that alloying is designed to accomplish must begin with these transformations in mind. Beyond that, automotive sheet metal has to be die formed into complex shapes, trimmed, and sometimes flanged. It also has to be weldable for attachment purposes in many cases. These needs dictate the specific constitution of the steel used in automobiles.

There are numerous technical terms used to define the physical characteristics of steels. These include elasticity, hardness, ductility, plasticity, yield strength, toughness, and so forth. Each of these terms, and several others that are available, has a specific meaning when used to describe steel. The descriptive terms that are of most interest to us are plasticity and elasticity. The first, plasticity, describes the ability of steel to be formed by pressure (dies) without tearing or otherwise failing. The second term, elasticity, involves the ability of steel to deform and subsequently spring back to its original shape without any change in that shape.

In both cases, the key phenomenon is the presence or absence of something called "work hardening." This phenomenon is of crucial interest to those who work with sheet metal. What is involved is the fact that as steel sheet is deformed (by die stamping, or accident impact, or by a repairman's hammer), its crystalline structure changes with the effect that it becomes harder and more resistant to further change. The classic example of this is a demonstration with a paper clip, which begins life as a piece of straight wire, and is then bent into its customary shape. Yet if you attempt to straighten one of the bends in a paper clip by grasping its straight sections half an inch back from a bend, and applying force in the reverse direction from which it was applied to make the bend, the wire will not straighten completely. Instead, the metal on either side of the original bend will ultimately deform before the bend is completely removed. Photos that accompany this chapter make this point with regard to a half-

This sequence of photographs describes a basic work hardening experiment in sheet metal. It illustrates how work hardening occurs, and what its effects are. The factor of work hardening is critical to auto body work and restoration because it limits how far you can move metal without annealing it. Here's how the experiment works and what the photos reveal:

1. The experiment involves a one-inch-wide strip of 22 gauge sheet metal. It will be deformed and straightened with a pair of sheet metal pliers.

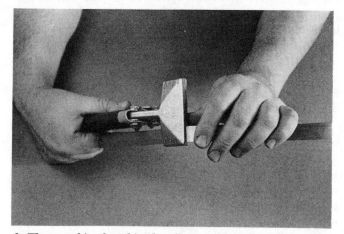

2. The metal is placed in the pliers and bent by hand as close to the pliers' jaws as possible.

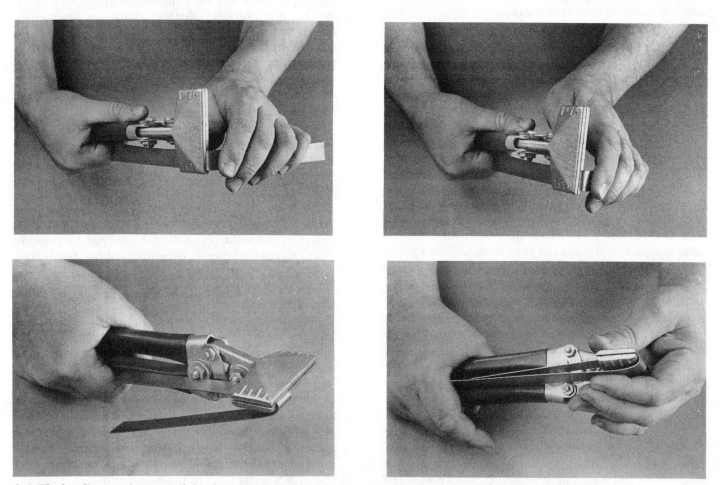

3-6. The bending continues until the sheet metal is bent back around the pliers' jaws as tightly as is possible by hand.

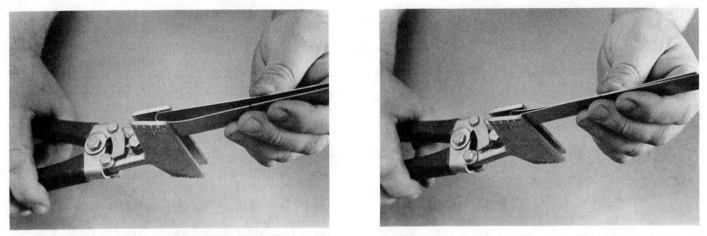

7 & 8. *Now the metal is gripped between the pliers' jaws and compressed slightly.*

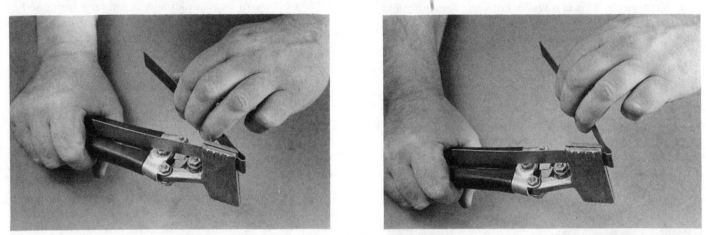

9 & 10. *The metal strip is now gripped in the pliers as close to the bend as possible, and an attempt is made to bend it back straight by hand.*

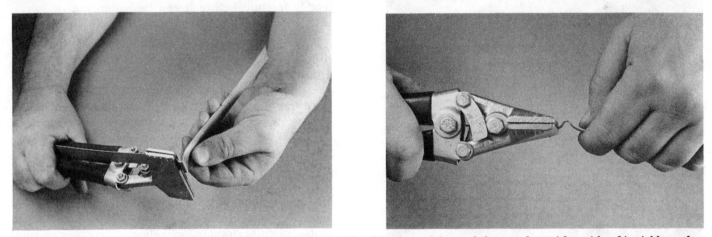

11 & 12. *You can see that the area of the first bend refuses to bend back straight, and the metal on either side of it yields to the reverse bending pressure first. This is because the original bend is work hardened and provides more resistance to bending than the unbent metal on either side of it.*

13. Without some further intervention, this is as straight as the author can get the steel strip with his hands and a pair of sheet metal pliers. This is a visibly dramatic demonstration of the work hardening phenomenon. It also is very similar to what happens when you attempt to hammer a crease out of a fender.

14 & 15. To really straighten this strip and overcome the work hardening in its bend, I would have to use mechanical force, as is shown here. That would tend to stretch the metal unless it is done very gently. Keep these characteristics of sheet metal in mind when you go to straighten out a ridge, V-channel, or buckle in a mild steel panel.

inch wide strip of 22 gauge body steel. What has happened in this example is that the original bend that I put in the strip of mild steel has work hardened it to the point that when I apply counter-pressure to it to remove the bend, I create two more deformations on either side of the original one. It is easier for the metal adjacent to the original bend to yield than it is for the metal in the original bend to yield because that metal has been work hardened by its deformation.

The phenomenon of work hardening is critical to the design and fabrication of sheet metal automobile panels. It is both a problem for and an asset to anyone who has to repair sheet metal. The asset is that the areas where dies have deformed sheet metal from its original flat state provide much of the panel strength necessary in body design. The problem is that when a panel must be straightened because of impact damage, it will have hardened in several places and in ways which may make it difficult to work with. It was hardened in the original stamping process of its manufacture. It has been further hardened by road vibration, which is particularly prevalent in configurations like pontoon fenders. Finally, the impact damage has further hardened it. Now it may be difficult or impossible to get the panel bumped back into shape without dealing with the work hardening of metal that is holding it in its deformed shape. Sometimes you can work around hardening by adopting a repair strategy that forces things back into place in spite of it. In the case of the infamous paper clip, it is possible to bend it almost back into a straight wire if the work hardened legs of the bend are supported close enough to the center of the bend during the reforming operation. In other cases, the effects of work hardening are so severe that the metal involved will readily fracture before it can be hammered or forced back into shape.

In these cases, heating the affected area to its "transformation" temperature is usually the best solution. This process is called "annealing." Auto body sheet metal will lose the effects of work hardening if it is heated to temperatures of about 1600° Fahrenheit and air cooled. The application of such heat allows the crystalline structure of the metal to rearrange itself in a way that undoes work hardening affects. The problem is that this solution will produce a panel or areas of a panel that have little of the hardness that was stamped into them originally. Since the original stamping was probably designed to induce work hardening into the panel in critical areas, as an element of its structural strength, annealing can create structural problems. Heating followed by water quenching is the most common solution to selectively softening metal in a way which maintains some of the original hardness of the original die stamped panel.

The die stamping process is a wonderful thing to behold in an automobile stamping plant. When you see it, you can appreciate the enormous forces at work when automobile panels are manufactured. In the stamping operation huge dies (108-inch long dies are pretty standard for large panels) that weigh many tons are forced together with sheet metal between them. The dies are often lubricated if they are the "deep draw" variety and the first action of their closing is for "binder rings" to clamp the metal at the edges before the dies deform it. If this was not done, metal would be pulled into the die and would wrinkle under the pressure of the closing die faces. Following the stamping process, trimming operations and often flanging operations occur. In almost every case, the areas of high deformation, such as creases that run the length of a panel, are put there to give the metal strength by purposely work hardening an area that bears stress or load. The sculpted and ridged sides of automobiles are usually as much accommodations to the needs of structural design as to the whimsies of styling. Of course, some areas of great deformation are there for the necessities of function, as, for example, the ends of a car that wrap around so that the car can end!

The die stamping operation produces three types of panel area, and infinite combinations of these three. The three basic types are: high crown, low crown, and reverse crown. The distinction between these three configurations of automotive sheet metal is critical in the repair of damaged automobile panels. "High crown" panels are those with a great deal of curvature in all directions. They have a rounded appearance and fall away from a point both north and south, east and west. These are, of course, panels that have been substantially deformed in the die stamping process. They are also usually much easier to work with than low crown panels because they have less tendency to buckle under heat, or when they are mildly stretched by impact and repair. When high crown panels are properly finished, they tend to reflect light in a way that is forgiving, even if their exact original curvatures are not retained in repair.

In contrast low crown panels have very little curvature to the north, south, east, and west. They may have curvature in one direction, like the top of a door or fender, where the format is usually a simple bend in one direction. The slab-sided doors on Lincoln Continentals in the early 1960s are another example of low crown panels. Low crown panels have little of the internal strength of high crown panels because they underwent very little deformation and work hardening in the die stamping process. Strength is often added to low crown panels by adding supports, or sometimes by forming them in the prestressed ("monocoque") construction that is occasionally borrowed from aircraft design for advanced automobile design. Low crown panels can be very hard to work with because if they are large, any stretching will make them buckle unless the extra lateral dimension of the panel can be chased to an edge or hidden in a high crown area somewhere. Otherwise, they have to be accurately shrunk when they are stretched, and this can be a very difficult repair procedure. A particularly common variant of this problem occurs in restoration work when cars with very flat doors have had these doors fill with water and rust out for a few inches along their bottoms. Any welding process that is used to section in new metal will produce some degree of heat distortion in the door skin, and this has to be painstakingly eliminated. When a four-door car is involved, the back doors usually have to have the same curves as the front doors. The door pairs on each side of

the car will have to reflect light in a way that indicates that the match is uniform. If this can't be done, I would suggest that the car always be parked in the middle of a large field or unlined parking lot, and away from anything distinctive that may reflect off of its sides and indicate the problem! Good luck.

Reverse crown panels are simply high crown panels in concave configurations. Reverse crown areas are sometimes found between fenders and trunks. Like high crown panels, they are usually easier to work with than low crown panels, but they often present problems of access that are unique.

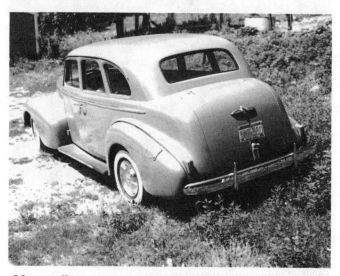

Many collector cars exhibit combinations of high and low crown panels. The roof, fenders, and rear body of this Buick are very high crowned but the doors are very low crown panels.

Obviously, most old car body panels are combinations of high and low crown areas with an occasional reverse crown thrown in. When a choice is available as to where to weld a patch seam or where small amounts of stretched metal should be relocated, high and reverse crown areas are good bets as long as they are not weakened by annealing or by changes in curvature in the process.

A final characteristic of auto body sheet metal that should be considered is its basic gauge or thickness. There are half a dozen gauge standards running around out there for wire and sheet steel, but automotive material is generally described by the "Manufacturers Standard Gauge for Sheet Steel" standard.

Automotive sheet metal once ran in the range of 18 gauge, which was forty-eight thousandths of an inch thick (actually 0.0478 inch). Twenty gauge became common in more recent times, and this meant 0.0359 inch thick metal — still a lot to work with in bumping and metal finishing. However, most recently, 22 gauge (0.0299 inch) has become common, and now 23 and 24 gauge (0.0269 inch and 0.0239 inch, respectively) have appeared on the scene under the euphemistic name, "high strength steel." This dreaded (by real metal men) and miserable stuff contributes slightly, I suppose, to lightening automobiles,

"MIG" welding has revolutionized some aspects of auto body work. The unit above cost nearly $2,000 in the early 1980s and is big and bulky. The welder on the right (late 1980s) cost less than half of that and is more compact and cheaper to run. This kind of welding is within the budgets and skill levels of many amateur restorers.

but carries with it a host of problems. The first is that the alloys used to make it are difficult to work with in repair situations because they are relatively hard and have very little elasticity — check out the decklids on some modern hatchbacks and note the dents and creases left by people's hands when they have been overenergetic in slamming them shut. These high strength steels are also so thin that they exhibit rust perforation problems alarmingly soon after manufacture in areas where salt and moisture are problems. The elaborate and highly advertised anti-corrosion treatments being applied and tooted by manufacturers are, in fact, necessitated by the thinness of the material from which their cars are fabricated. There is some hope, however, because some manufacturers have begun to *increase* panel thickness slightly on some of the newest cars.

The gauge of the metal that you are working with determines, in large part, the best repair approach. If, for example, at some future date someone decides to restore some of the econoboxes that graced our streets as new cars in the early 1980s, they had better locate a good supply of NOS body panels before they undertake these projects. Many contemporary panels are too thin and too hard to hammer straight if they are seriously deformed, and traditional metal finishing is out of the question because files tend to skate over them, or, if they do cut, they weaken the panels grievously or cut right through them. Even disk sanding them can be a hair-raising experience if you are not super careful.

The good news is that the thick, relatively soft metal in most collector cars is very susceptible to straightening, welding, and metal finishing. When some of the newer technologies, such as MIG (properly GNAW) welding, are applied to them, repair becomes so easy that it is permissible to listen to the radio while you are working. Basic hammer and dolly work, shrinking operations, and welding operations are attainable skills not the impossible dreams that they sometimes become when you attempt to apply them to most contemporary auto body sheet metal.

Acquired Characteristics in Old and Damaged Sheet Metal

The types of damage that can occur to collector car sheet metal are just about unlimited. The most common damages, by far, are corrosion damage and impact damage. Beyond this, each car that you work on is likely to exhibit some daring, new innovations in the field of possible sheet metal defect. Stress cracking occurs routinely in some areas of some cars. Wood-framed bodies often exhibit structural shifting that deforms sheet metal, and swelled framing wood can deform sheet metal in ways that are difficult to resolve. In cars with welded and spot-welded attachments, a combination of vibration and corrosion can cause things to break loose and move in ways that produce major messes.

Yet with all of these possibilities, the damage that I most dread is that done by people armed with minimum knowledge, bad attitude, heavy hammers, and the misconception that they are in the body repair business. When these types and their minions add an acetylene torch and pop riveter to their basic repertoire of chipped hammers and screw-tipped slide hammers, they become a definite menace to the welfare of sheet metal everywhere. It is sometimes difficult to fathom the degree of imbecility and resulting destruction that some of the Bondo artists have done to the panels of the poor automobiles that have had the misfortune to come under their hammers. Instead of carefully analyzing the nature of the damage in the panels that they deal with and repairing them in non-destructive ways, these people apply the heaviest hammers or biggest pry bars that they can wield against damaged areas, and literally bash things back toward their right places. In the process, they produce stretching, further deformation, and work hardening that are difficult to deal with later. When confronted with rust or torn metal, sectioning and welding are usually beyond their limited skill levels, so out come the flanging tools, brazing rods, and pop rivet tools. More damage occurs.

These guys buy plastic filler by the 55 gallon drum, and the only apparent limit to its use seems to be that on any car they deal with they never allow the weight of the filler to exceed the weight of the original automobile. Aside from the fact that this kind of work has a life expectancy of about six months to two years, it always produces severe problems when it has to be reworked by someone who wants to do it right. Okay, you've been warned. Also, as always, avoid seeing the world in stereotypes.

The two most common sheet metal damages, corrosion and impact damage, must be dealt with in very specific ways. Corrosion damage must be detected by inspection

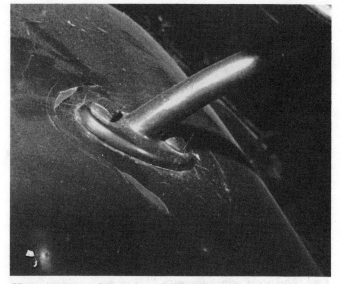

Here, stress cycles and probably minor impact have combined to cause damage. Corrosion has begun under fractured paint and added to the problems in this area.

The damage here is corrosion damage with maybe a little stress damage thrown in. This rust-out was probably initiated by the fender welting absorbing water and causing rusting of the metal near it. From there the rust continued on its own.

that involves physically picking and probing, in addition to visual inspection. This may seem brutal, but all kinds of corrosion can be lurking under seemingly sound paint. Certainly where paint has bubbled and blistered, there is good cause to suspect underlying damage, and a scratch awl is your best guide to its extent. Where body contours appear to be modified or where panels are an eighth of an inch thick or more, you will often find rust, fiberglass bandages, pop riveted roofing tin, and any manner of other mischief underneath. Flanged and brazed panel patches are also frequently found under bubbling paint. Sometimes, and this is almost a pleasant surprise, filler will be used to cover dents and other impact damage because the attempted repair involved difficult access to the back of a panel or the individual making the repair lacked the skill or commitment to bump the panel into correct contours. Alas, more often than not, a slide ham-

No doubt about it, this Aston Martin is the victim of impact damage. This car could be restored, but will probably be parted out.

A clumsy attempt to modify this fender has caused the failure here. This work was done with little or no consideration of the forces of vibration and corrosion that work on auto body panels.

mer and hardened screw, body hooks, or welded studs were used to pull dents out, and what lurks under the Bondo is serious corrosion damage made worse by the attempted repair.

The drift of all of this is that the only proper way to repair corrosion damage that perforates sheet metal is to weld in new metal, and the only proper way to deal with impact deformation is to beat it back out in ways that produce the least stretching and buckling of the metal. Sometimes, small amounts of filler are necessary, and when this is the case, body lead (actually an alloy of tin and lead which is now commonly available in a 30/70 ratio) is really the only way to go in restoration work.

In addition to the work hardening that occurs in body panels when they are stamped and later subjected to road vibration, there are several other changes in auto body sheet metal that occur when there is impact damage and the attempt to repair it. The most important of these is stretching. When a panel is severely deformed in an accident it is sometimes stretched. This means that the pressure exerted on it has caused it to become longer or wider or both. To do this it also has become thinner somewhere. Unfortunately, the act of straightening a deformed and stretched panel involves hammering its ridges and channels, either directly over a dolly block or adjacent to one. The result is often further stretching because the metal is further thinned when it is hammered on. Bad repairs invariably work harden and stretch metal, and this can be a hard combination to deal with in the context of a proper repair.

The opposite of stretching is "upsetting," which sometimes occurs in impact damage but more often is the result of a bad repair strategy. This phenomenon involves making the metal in a panel thicker and laterally smaller than it was originally. Hammering a bad buckle down directly over a dolly block can produce an upset because the metal may have no lateral place to go, with the result that the upset part of the panel becomes thicker and shorter than it was and than it must be to assume its cor-

rect original shape. Upsetting can be dealt with in a repair situation and is, in fact, sometimes induced on purpose to overcome the effects of stretching. In this case it is called "shrinking."

Impact Repair Approaches

Impact and corrosion damage are sometimes so severe that it is necessary to find replacement panels or to fabricate and section new metal into damaged areas. An example of a small panel fabrication and of section welding are shown and described in the photos and captions that accompany the text of the next chapter. Much of the body work that a restorer is likely to encounter involves minor crash damage — dents, scores, and the like. It is the complete removal of such damage that distinguishes a very well-restored car from one that looks like a near miss.

The most important aspect of repairing such damage is to understand the material that you are working with — sheet metal — and to have some general and specific no-

Sometimes new, NOS, and reproduction sheet metal parts can be found to replace collector car panels that are damaged beyond practical repair. Unfortunately, the replacements often require a great deal of rework to make them usable.

tions of how it got deformed and what kinds of repairs will be necessary to return it to its original shape with a minimum of distortion, stretching, and upsetting. Remember, a dolly block and hammer can be as or more destructive than the sequence that caused initial damage. You must proceed with a very definite plan of attack. Part of that plan should be based on the kind of known sheet metal theory that is described in this book and in the books mentioned at the beginning of this chapter. Another part of the plan will come from your experience gained from experimentation with scrap panels. The point is, when you swing a body hammer or decide where to begin to remove a dent or whether to work "on dolly" or "off dolly," your knowledge will guide you and your experience will give you an intuitive sense of what the results of a given procedure will be.

Prior to the publication of Fairmont Forge's *The Key to Metal Bumping* in 1939, such texts that existed in the field of body repair tended to be vague and to stress the black magic aspects of the craft. Sheet metal skills tended to be passed on by oral tradition, which meant that there were some awfully good practitioners and some who were pretty bad. *The Key to Metal Bumping* was a major contribution to the craft because it proposed a seemingly simple and very understandable format for sheet metal analysis and repair.

The nugget of the "Fairmont Method" was to logically distinguish between "direct" and "indirect" damage. Direct damage includes areas that have come into direct contact with an impacting object or objects. Indirect damage involves areas that are deformed and locked in by the forces of the direct damage but which were not actually hit directly. Most indirectly damaged areas will spring pretty much back into shape if the adjacent areas of direct damage are removed and the forces holding the indirectly damaged areas are thus released. Typically, briefcase-sized dents involve mostly indirect damage in terms of the amount of surface area affected. The Fair-

mont Method prescribes unlocking large expanses in sheet metal that are not deformed beyond their elastic limit by working only on those areas that are. A small "key" unlocks a big puzzle. The revelation of the Fairmont Method is that you don't have to get a big hammer and pound mindlessly on everything that seems to be pushed in or out in a process that inevitably stretches and work hardens the metal unnecessarily. Instead, inspection will indicate which areas involve direct damage and should, therefore, be dealt with first. In addition to inspection, the application of logic will yield an understanding of the sequence in which direct and indirect damage occurred. If direct damage is repaired in the reverse order that it occurred, most of the indirect damage will be released as you go along.

It all sounds simple, but in 1939 it probably had all of the impact of a major revelation because much of what had gone before in the official explanations of how to perform body work had involved incantation and witchcraft. As it turns out, it isn't all that simple because trying to determine exactly what order damage occurred in can be a proposition that will make your head hurt. It is always possible to construct a theory of the order in which damage occurred, but it is frequently the case that alternative theories are as good, or almost as good, as the preferred theory.

That's why more recent approaches to body damage analysis and repair strategy tend to pay more attention to what is there and less to how it got there. I tend to side with the latter approach but hasten to add that if you can determine the order of deformation of a particular damaged area, removing the constituents of the damage in the reverse order of their creation is always a good approach. It is not, however, a good idea to waste half a day theorizing about the order of creation of damage as this is not absolutely necessary information to have before you proceed with corrective measures.

In any theory of damage analysis and repair strategy, the damage itself is reduced to one or a combination of three possible constituent parts. These are V-channels, ridges, and buckles (also called "rolled buckles"). These three categories, and their almost infinite combinations, cover the field. Ridges are, as the name implies, areas of raised metal which stand out in a linear formation. V-channels are depressed areas formed into lines, or the opposite of ridges. Buckles are areas that are forced and locked into the metal by the wave form created in the metal in the original impact. Unlike ridges and V-channels, which are either results of direct damage or fairly gentle extensions from it, buckles are formed by the collapse of the metal when it is under pressure and literally has no alternative than to collapse. Buckles often involve substantial upsetting, which is not the case in ridges and V-channels.

When you recognize and understand the genesis of these three components of damage — ridges, V-channels, and buckles — you will be in a position to execute a strategy for their removal. In large part, this should unlock what are usually large areas of indirect damage. In a sense, the test of a good strategy is how *little* hammer and dolly work is necessary to remove damage. The analysis method works, because breaking damage into components and attacking these components logically represents an efficient attack on the causes of the problem. The alternative, to mindlessly attack the symptoms of damage, ends up as the "bigger hammer" approach and usually fails to recognize even such obvious components of damage as bent substructure. It substitutes damaging counter-force for intellect and skill, and it usually fails.

This sequence of photographs illustrates the Fairmont Forge approach to removing a fairly simple dent. The only tools used were hammers, dollies, body files and a disc sander.

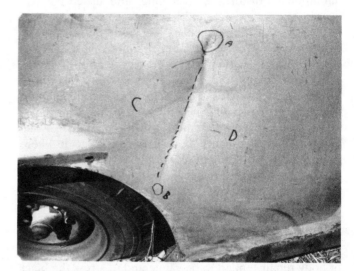

1. This fender "gotcha" is fairly deep. The situation is made worse by the fact that damage other than the main impact that caused the crease occurred either before or after it. Both ends of the crease have small buckles, particularly the top, which ends in the beginning of a high crown area. Little of this damage is direct. The depth of the impact has raised small ridges on either side of the obvious V-channel that is the basic element of this damage.

2. The first step that will be applied to repair this damage will be to unlock the metal in the buckles at "A" and "B." The buckle at "A" is much worse than the one at "B" because of the crown where "A" is located. Lines parallel to "A — B," centered on "C" and "D" represent the slightly ridged areas that will have to be hammered down to release the areas of indirect damage between "C" and "D." After this is done with a hammer-off-dolly approach, it will be necessary to rough out the V-channel between "A" and "B" somewhat.

3. A very little bit of hammer-against-spoon work on the buckles at either end of this damage has relieved them sufficiently to proceed with this repair.

4. Now, some roughing with a dolly from behind along the "A — B" crease, working from top to bottom, has sprung back much of the indirect damage.

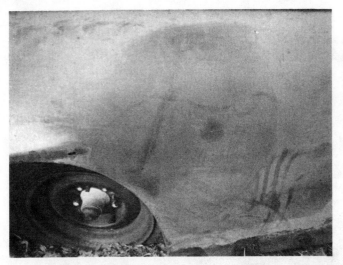

5. Some hammer-off-dolly work along the ridges at "C" and "D," with the dolly held firmly against the "A — B" line and worked from top to bottom, yields the result shown here. All of the indirect damage has sprung back and, except for a few low spots, everything is pretty much back to original contours.

6. Disc sanding reveals the exact locations of these low spots. The two worst are in the areas where the buckles were removed at the ends of the "A — B" crease. A few more are along the crease line, and the rest seem to be the results of other impacts, or, perhaps, of the hammering down of the ridges at "C" and "D."

7. A little bit of additional work with a pick hammer from behind and a little filing and sanding remove all of the remaining low spots.

8. When the damaged area and surrounding area are sanded and coated with a preservative, you can see that the damage no longer exists. Before this panel gets its final sanding before painting, it may require a very little bit of filler to perfect its surface and contour.

This absurdly sharp pick hammer can come in handy for carefully raising small areas of depressed sheet metal.

CHAPTER 22:

The Repair of Minor Impact Damage

The emphasis in this chapter is on the words *"repair"* and *"minor." Repair* must be emphasized because much that passes for repair is actually further damage, done in such a way that when it is covered up with "mud," it will give the short-term appearance of being repair. The proper object, of course, is to work for the long term and to create a repair that uses a minimum of filler, preferably lead, and that not only looks as though no repair has ever been made but also continues to look that way for a very long time. This means that the repaired area or areas must resist corrosion and metal displacement due to vibration as well or better than the rest of the panel to which the repair was made.

The term *"minor"* is emphasized for two reasons. The first is that when damage has progressed to the point where it is classed as "major impact damage" and a panel is buckled and distorted from several directions, it is beyond the competence of most shops to make effective repairs. Shops that employ specialists to do this sort of work can accomplish wonders, but the economics of the situation and the nature of the construction of most cars tend to work against this approach to most restoration projects. Certainly, damage that was repaired fairly routinely in the past is presently handled by panel replacement or by "totalling" a car.

Unless a car has very great value, the commercial proposition of building up a wreck for restoration purposes is almost always a bad proposition. An unwrecked car is a more expensive entry into car collecting, but the end result will almost always be more economically feasible and satisfying. I have seen many fenders that could *theoretically* be straightened, but that would require so much straightening, sectioning, shrinking, and other hand work that it is impractical to restore them when the cost and availability of replacement fenders in good condition is considered. This is not only true of panels that are badly crumpled from impact, but also of those that are badly rusted or which have been hammered and welded and brazed to the point that there isn't much usable metal left to work with.

The second reason that I emphasize *"minor* repair" in this chapter is that this is the most usual damage that will be encountered in collector cars. The usual proposition is the removal of a simple ding, dent, crease, or gouge. Such work is within the competence of many shops and, very probably, within the competence of many or most of the people reading this book. If, on the other hand, the damage in question is going to require the use of tensioning, heat, or a portable frame machine, it should only be attempted by those experienced in this work and equipped to do it. If the proposition is to turn a pretzel back into an automobile, consideration of new panels or of a very expert shop should be seriously pursued. As in so many other areas of automobile restoration, wisdom may be in knowing when to quit and what *not* to attempt. If someone wants to make a point regarding the limits of the art of the resurrection of sheet metal, it is best to let him do so on someone else's car and with his own or someone else's money.

Strategy for Removing Minor Damage

In the last chapter, reference was made to the "Fairmont Method" of sheet metal damage correction. This method involves careful analysis of specific damage and categorization of it into one or more of three distinct configurations: ridges, V-channels, and buckles and rolled buckles. As well, all areas of damage are distinguished as to *direct* and *indirect* damage, with the aim of working out direct damage in a way that releases indirect damage that may be locked into sheet metal. The "nugget" of the Fairmont Method is to remove damage in the reverse order in which it occurred. Most later theories of damage removal are not as completely concerned with the reverse order format and allow for other reasonable sequences of removal as long as they fit the logic of the situation.

The main item to remember is that there is nothing terribly mysterious about this business, and that a logical and orderly approach will cover most situations. Whatever approach to damage repair is pursued, the key will be careful analysis and adoption of a well-thought-out strategy to correct the damage. In a very few cases, genius is useful in this work, but I don't know much about that. The main point is that you must *think before you strike.*

Damage is caused by impact, and the removal of simple damage can almost always be accomplished by the use of carefully chosen impact. When tension, heat, and other extraordinary measures are required, the damage is no longer "simple." When you strike metal with a hammer or dolly or both, you must have reason to believe that it can, and will, move in the direction(s) that you want it to, and that it will do so without doing much else that makes the situation worse.

If your strategy for getting rid of a severe ridge is just to mindlessly pound it down with a hammer or dolly face, the result will be an uncontrolled upset, which amounts to further damage. The material that you are working with, sheet metal, is somewhat forgiving of mistakes, but it tends to get harder the more that you work it. If you make too many mistakes, it can become a very unforgiving medium. So when you hit a hammer blow, be sure that what you want to happen can and will happen. At first you will think a lot and hammer very little. That's fine. Later, your experience will enable you to know, almost intuitively, what will work and what will not work. Even the most experienced sheet metal man and certainly the novice will need more than a good plan of at-

tack. He will need to exercise powers of observation to see that the original plan is working or sometimes not working. When the latter is the case, he will have to modify the original plan to account for the unexpected results that have occurred before the plan is followed to the point of inflicting further damage.

Auto Body Hand Tools and Their Basic Uses

HAMMERS. Body hammers are specialized tools that have very specific uses. The most common body hammers are classified as: bumping hammers, picking hammers, or combination hammers. The latter have one crowned bumping face and one relatively sharp picking surface. The bumping face, or faces, of hammers are designed to move small areas of metal with overlapping impacts, either in conjunction with dolly blocks held on the other sides of the panels or without them. These hammers typically weigh from 12 to 16 ounces and have a crowned face or faces that measure from three-eighths of an inch to 1¼ inch across. The bumping face(s) of a ham-

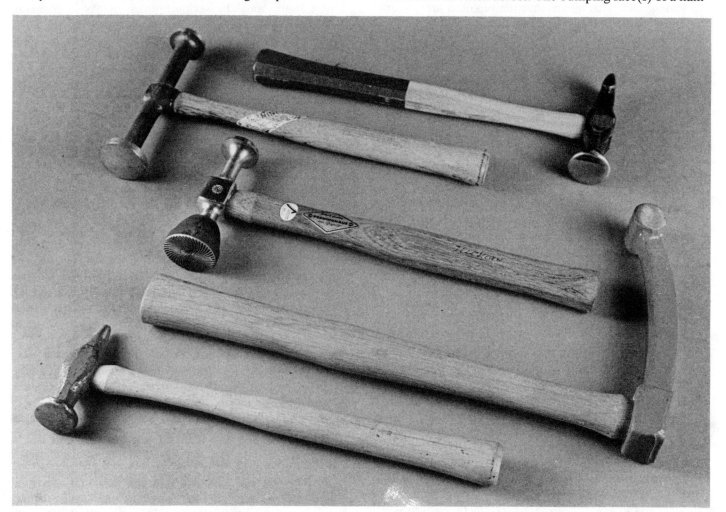

Body hammers come in many sizes and shapes for many purposes. On top is a high crown/flat pick combination hammer. Below it is a bumping hammer with large and small faces. Below that is a shrinking hammer. The next hammer is a fender dinging hammer used to push out damage from behind. Below that is a combination blunt pick and low crown dinging hammer.

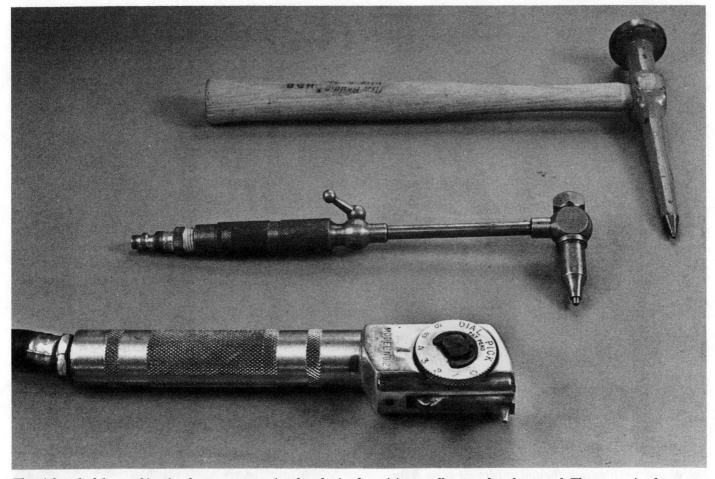

The pick end of the combination hammer on top is a handy size for raising small areas of sunken metal. The percussion hammer below that is driven by air and can be used like a pick hammer. Below that is a pneumatic, automatic picking hammer. The two air-driven picks come in handy when you have to persuade metal out in areas where there isn't enough room to swing a regular pick hammer.

mer is usually round, but there are some square faced hammers available for working evenly up to bends and edges. Small bumping hammer faces may be highly crowned and are used primarily for dinging off-dolly (just beyond the edge of a dolly held under and against the metal that you are hammering) or without a dolly. Larger, less crowned faces are generally used for dinging on-dolly. When striking a reverse crown panel or from the back of a crowned one, the hammer face must have slightly more crown than the area of the panel that is being struck.

The key to using bumping hammers is in knowing which one to use, where, and in what combination with or without dollies. It is also crucial to know how hard a blow to strike and the proper manner in which to strike it in widely varying situations. Generally, the best hammer blow is soft compared to that used in fields other than auto body, like carpentry or blacksmithing. Multiple, adjacent or overlapping hammer blows are the nugget of the thing. These blows are the opposite of the dead (no rebound) blows common to almost every other endeavor that involves a hammer. For most situations, the correct sheet metal blow is a rebounding, glancing slap that is generated primarily from the wrist, with the hammer held loosely enough to rebound smartly from each blow. In this work, forget what your father told you when he taught you to drive nails.

There are two simple cautions about the selection and care of body hammers. Buy good ones in the first place and never use them for anything but striking sheet metal. A good body hammer has a balance which allows it to be swung easily and to rebound crisply. Its face(s) must be kept polished and free of gauges or deep scratches otherwise it will damage sheet metal when it strikes it. I always do a little "custom contouring" with a grinder on the new hammers that I buy to get their crowns just the way that I want them. Hammers should be polished with a fine sandpaper to maintain the smoothness of their surfaces.

When a hammer is used directly on sheet metal, the selection of face size and crown is particularly important. A small bumping hammer face with a lot of crown will generate much higher local impact pressures than a large, less crowned one. When working on-dolly (striking metal with a dolly directly under the area that you are striking) or on a buckled area, a large, low crown hammer will be more forgiving than a small one because it will be less likely to compress and laterally stretch the metal. Some body men still use wooden, rawhide, or plastic mallets in situations like this.

Pick hammer faces are, as the name implies, radically pointed hammer faces. They are used to "lift" small areas of metal in the size range between a 25 ¢ piece, and the

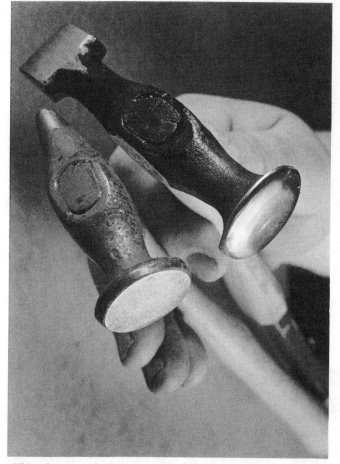

This photograph illustrates the different crowns of low crown and high crown hammers. Never use a hammer that has less crown than the metal that you are striking.

Cars like this XK-120 Jaguar have combinations of high and low crown panels. You'll need lots of different hammers to work on this one.

dimensionally smaller change that you can get for it. Very sharp pick hammers are intended for use on high crown areas. My experience is that the sharper ones are more useful if you use them with a little restraint. This is especially true when you use them on high crown panels. I find them much easier to control for fine work, but this is a matter of personal preference. A key to using a pick hammer effectively is not to try to do too much with it at one time and not to use it with too much force. An improper (usually overenthusiastic) pick hammer blow can make a real mess by creating reverse dimples and worse. On combination hammers that have one bumping face and one pick end, be ever vigilant not to allow the rebound of an enthusiastic bumping stroke to drive the pick end of the hammer back into some part of your body. It hurts.

DOLLIES. Dollies are the work horses of metal moving. They are really hammers without handles, or hand held anvils, depending on how you choose to use them. While a dolly block may look like a hunk of pig iron to the inexperienced eye, it is really a carefully evolved and highly complex tool. Dollies have several faces and working surfaces, which may involve several different crowns and combinations of crowns called "transitions." This variety of working surfaces is crucially important because in many applications you will have to match the crown of the dolly to the part of a panel that you are working on.

Like hammers, dollies will work best when they have a balance that allows you to easily strike with them and to use them as rebound tools. Both dollies and hammers reach their highest potential as tools when they are used in a way that allows their balance to create a natural rhythm as a worker manipulates them. In fact, there can be something wonderfully musical about the sight and sound of a good metal man working his craft — sometimes.

Dollies are often used as short, handleless hammers for roughing metal out in places where hammers would be impossible to swing. They are also used to back up metal that is being hammered on from the other side. In this

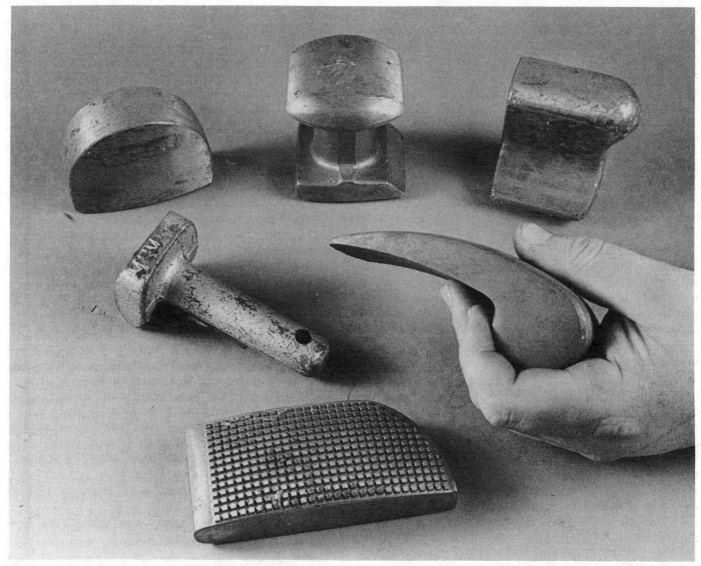

Dollies are really very complex and highly evolved tools. Each surface on a dolly has a specific use and purpose. The dolly in the bottom of this picture is a "shrinking" dolly.

Dollies are often used in combination with body hammers, but sometimes they are used alone.

Dollies are really just hand-held anvils when you use them to back up hammer work. You won't hand hold the item shown here, but it can be very useful in bodywork.

application, the dolly is sometimes held directly under the area where the hammer blows are being directed (hammering "on-dolly") or, more often, held adjacent to it. In this second mode ("off-dolly"), the dolly block is used in conjunction with a hammer to smooth out metal by knocking ridges down or bringing V-channels up. The tension of the dolly against the metal in the off-dolly mode is translated into a sharp rebound impact almost instantaneously after each hammer blow is struck on the other side. A combination of impacts is highly effective in moving metal back into the shape that it lost under the impact of an accident. While hammer on-dolly work is sometimes essential, the most impressive results in releasing indirectly damaged metal are usually achieved working off-dolly.

SPOONS. This class of body tools sometimes seems to include any impacting or anvil tool that isn't a hammer or dolly. Flat spoons are used to spread the impact of a hammer blow in such applications as hammering down bad ridges or buckles. Other types of spoons are small dolly-like anvils on handles, and still others have gentle curvatures that can be used to pry with or to back up hammer blows in hard-to-reach places.

BODY FILES. These specialized files are used in the final stages of metal finishing to level surfaces and to indicate low spots so that they can be "lifted" with a pick hammer or by other means. Minor high spots will be indicated or removed by filing. The use of body files requires experience and coordination. When properly used, a body file is pushed evenly and smoothly away from the operator in a mildly diagonal direction. It is also gently rocked from its front to its heel during the stroke. Never use a body file with the same rationale or motion that you use a wood rasp or bastard file — to remove a lot of material quickly. To do so would cause binding and gouging, which would serve no useful purpose. You can use a body file and pick hammers to perform the final stages of panel leveling, and this can be done with surprisingly little material removal. When lead filler is used, body files are the preferred method of shaping and removing excess material.

DISC SANDERS. These hand-held grinders are used to remove rust and paint and, like body files, for grinding metal to level it or to indicate where it has to be raised or lowered. The key to using a disc sander is to hold the disc as flat to the work piece as is practical — a 15° angle is about right, but this will take some practice — and to keep it constantly moving over a panel in slightly overlapping strokes. If the sander is kept in one place too long, it will remove too much material and become part of the problem rather than the solution. It is also easy to overheat a spot with a disc sander. This will become evident when a spot in the area that you are sanding turns red or a scorched hue of blue. On a seven-inch or nine-inch disc, at least one inch of cutting surface should be flexed into contact with the work piece. Small disc sanders (four inches and 4½ inches) have smaller contact rims with sheet metal. While the sander should be moved fast enough to prevent gouging and overheating, it should not be skated over the surface too quickly, or insufficient cut-

ting will take place and the result will be an uneven surface.

Many body shops begin sanding operations with a 24 grit abrasive (mountain boulders) and work up to finer grades. I have generally avoided using very course discs for paint removal. A DA (dual action) sander is slower but safer for this work. I prefer to use a 50 grit abrasive for leveling work. Many shops use a 36 grit abrasive for this purpose, but I find 50 is comfortably slow. Always use a closed coat abrasive when grinding is your purpose as opposed to paint removal. Generally, overlapping horizontal strokes will accommodate most work best, but it is permissible to use a vertical pattern for some grinding and indicating purposes. A disc sander is much faster and easier to use than a body file, but a properly used body file has a precision that I could never develop with a disc sander. Some body men use a disc sander to remove excess plastic and even lead filler, but I think that this is poor practice. Fillers are simply too soft compared to the surrounding sheet metal to be effectively leveled with a disc sander. In the case of lead filler, this practice is extremely dangerous because it puts a potentially lethal spray of minute lead particles into the air. These can be breathed, ingested, and absorbed through the skin.

OTHER BODYWORK TOOLS. As in every other area of restoration endeavors, there is an almost endless assortment of neat and wonderful tools and devices that may have substantial usefulness in bodywork. Even if they don't, they have an enormous potential for impressing everyone but your spouse, being borrowed endlessly, and leading to financial ruin. Bull's Eye picks have an enormous appeal, and pneumatically operated "power hammers" are terrifically useful for smoothing metals. If you get into sectioning and fabricating work, your tool *modus operandi* will soon outgrow using someone else's sheet metal brake, and your tool "wish list" will come to include a brake. Fabrication work will also require an assortment of rawhide, wood, or plastic mallets and a good shot bag. As you get further into this work, you will doubtless want an English wheel, a bead roller, and a shrinker-stretcher. All of this stuff can be useful if you have the skill to use it, but most restoration projects can be accomplished with simple hand tools like hammers, dollies, spoons, files, and a good disc sander.

In the photographs that accompany the text of this chapter, two relatively simple dents are shown through the processes of their removal. The text accompanying the pictures explains briefly what procedures were used and the rationales for and the tools used in these procedures. There are other ways to approach these simple dents, but the procedures that are outlined here are the simplest that I know of that will produce a high quality repair. The key sequence that is followed is analysis, roughing (where applicable), bumping, and metal finishing.

Each example of damage that you may encounter will present its own unique circumstances and dictate a preference for some particular strategies and procedures over others that are theoretically possible. One unifying theme will be that any appropriate procedure in metal

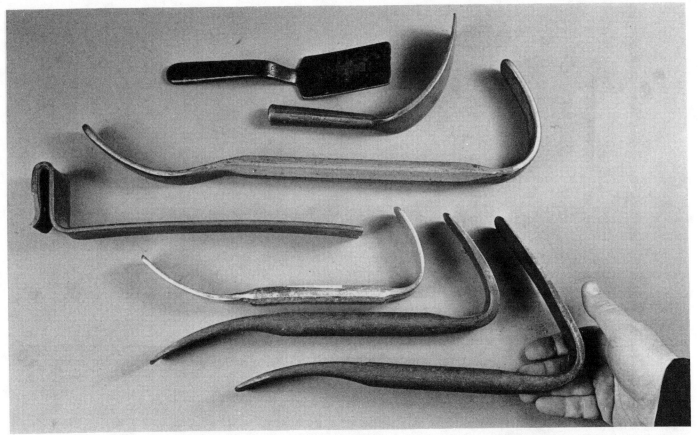

Body spoons are used to back up metal (like dollies, but where dollies won't fit), to pry out metal, and to spread hammer blows when they are hit against metal with hammers.

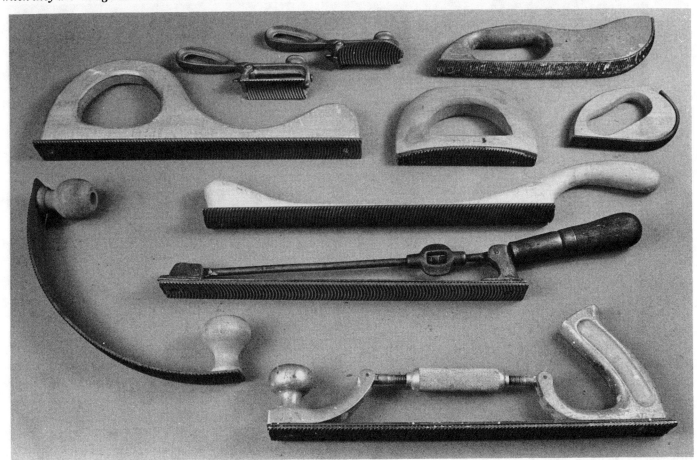

Body files come in a wide variety of shapes, sizes, and tooth patterns. These are among the most important tools in body work because they will help you to finely shape metal and to find high spots and low spots in it.

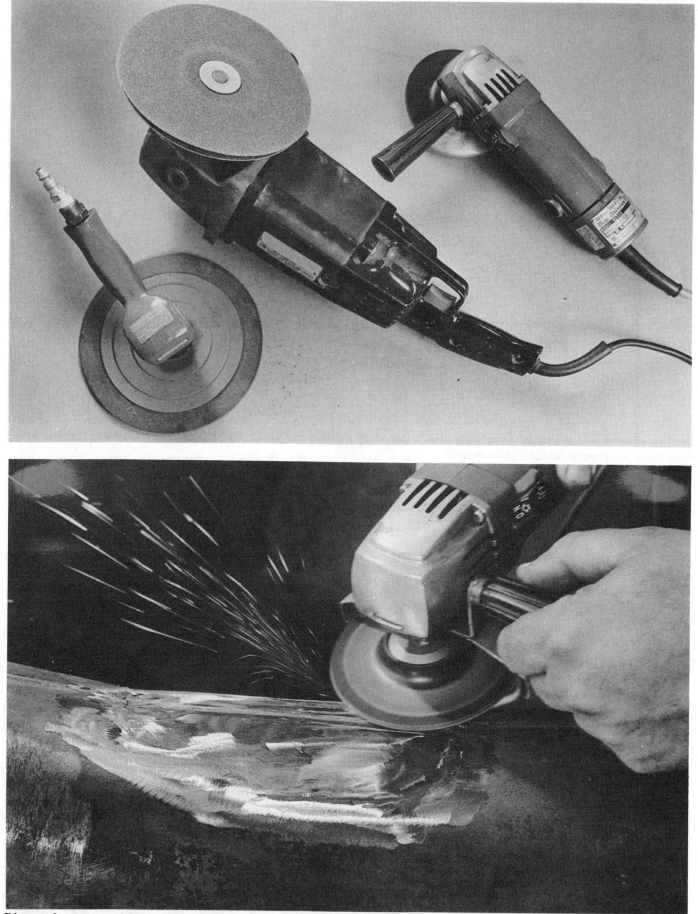

Disc sanders cut metal faster than files do, but they are neither as accurate nor as controllable for fine work. The sander on the left is air-driven, and the two on the right are electric. Always use disc sanders very carefully. You can do an enormous amount of damage with them if you don't.

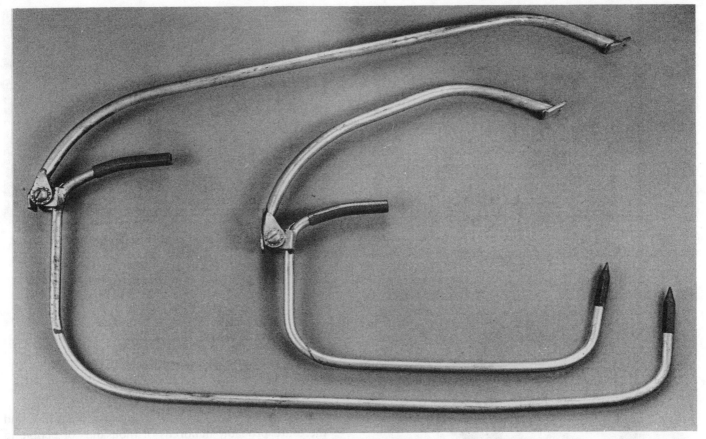

These Bull's Eye picks are used to reach behind a panel and push small depressions out. You place the target "V" where you want to raise metal and clamp the handle to swing the pick hammer at the target from behind. It really works!

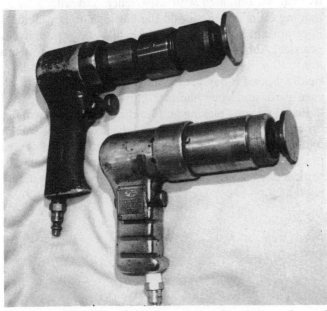

These power hammers are pretty violent, but they can be used to drive ridges out of severely damaged metal.

work will aim to work with the damaged metal in a way that unlocks as much indirect damage as possible by working on or near the direct damage. Thus buckles are worked on directly and early in any proper scheme of repair, and hammer off-dolly work is used extensively to level V-channels.

In every case, as the metal is struck, it is given a place to go that tends toward the desired final result. This is in distinction to the all too common body shop practice of reaching behind a severe dent and just bashing it out with a dolly along the line of the lowest V-channel. People who follow this unfortunate course of action create situations where there are so many distortions, stretches, and upsets in a panel that after they are done it would take expert applications of stretching, shrinking and sectioning, among other things, to bring the panel back to correct contours. Of course, people who would commit the first error are usually far from bashful about using torrents of "mud" to hide the results of their defective approach to basic sheet metal work.

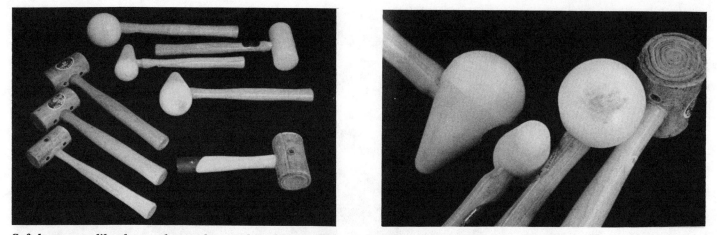

Soft hammers, like these polypropylene and rawhide mallets, work very well for straightening slightly deformed metal without stretching it. The more bodywork you do, the more you will come to use mallets instead of hammers.

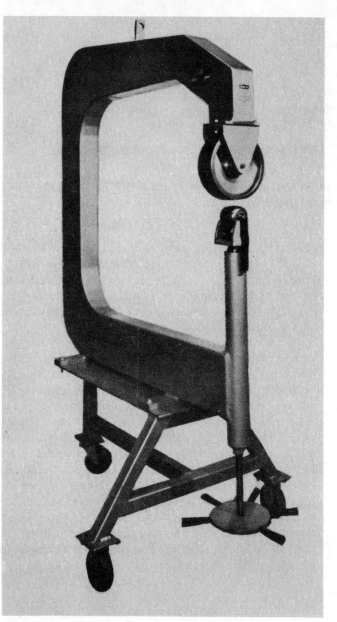

This English Wheel forms and stretches metal and is an incredibly versatile tool. Custom body builders used English Wheels to form the panels in many collector cars. An English Wheel costs thousands of dollars and requires great skill to use effectively.

Some Final Thoughts on Acquiring Bodywork Skills

Sheet metal work is not a mysterious black art, and there are probably hundreds of thousands of people in this country who have learned to use body tools properly and with very acceptable results. It takes basic knowledge, patience, imagination, and coordination. Most of this can be obtained with experience and with a bit of reading on or instruction in the basics. The key element in acquiring the necessary good habits and experience is practice. Almost anyone who seriously attempts to learn this craft will begin by using hammers too hard and too rigidly. Spend a day with some scrap panels from a salvage yard, and your hammer blows, your placement of dollies, and your picking and leveling techniques will improve almost miraculously. In the course of weeks, months, and years, many amateurs can become skilled practitioners of the sheet metal arts, even though this work is not the main pursuit of their lives. Have at it, and good luck.

MORE ▶

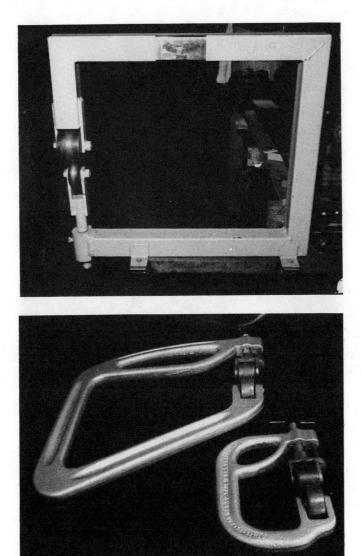

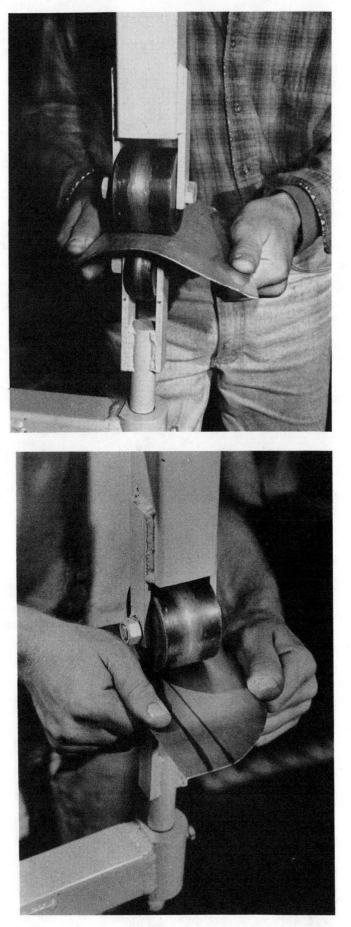

You could call these "poor men's English Wheels." They lack the size and precision of the real thing, but you can do a certain amount of forming and smoothing with them. The two cast devices are really fender smoothers from the 1920s and 1930s.

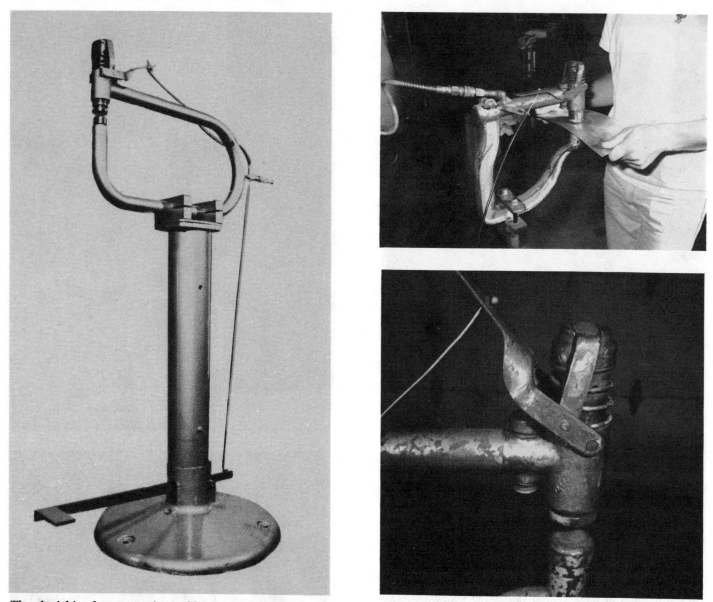

The plenishing hammers pictured here were designed to remove dents from the turret top cars of the late 1930s. They failed at that task because they stretched metal very badly. However, they are very useful for forming and smoothing metal. The first one shown is a modern reproduction of an old tool.

This bead roller is about the only effective way to put raised beads in sheet metal parts. It is very useful.

This combination sheet metal brake/slip roll/sheer works well for small projects in light gauge metal.

MORE ▶

Shot bags, like the two pictured here, are the best backup for most panel forming operations that you will have occasion to do with hammers and mallets.

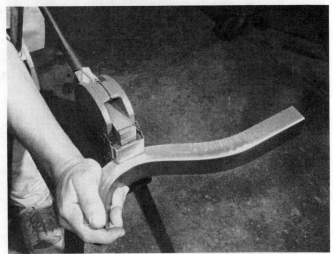

This shrinker/stretcher setup will allow you to make many items that are necessary in restoration sheet metal work. Window surrounds are hard to make without them.

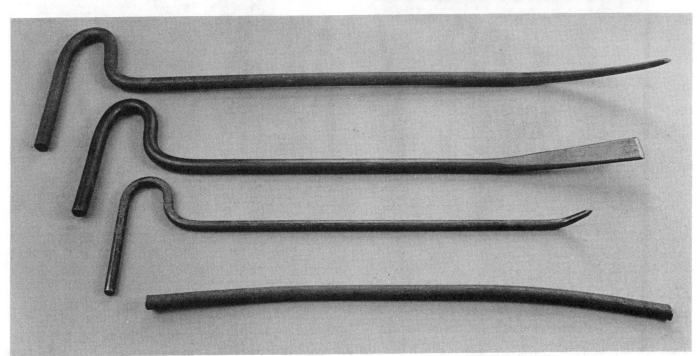

These pry bars are incredibly handy in bodywork. I haven't seen bars like these sold in this country for years, so if you see a set, try to buy them for your body tool collection.

MORE ▶

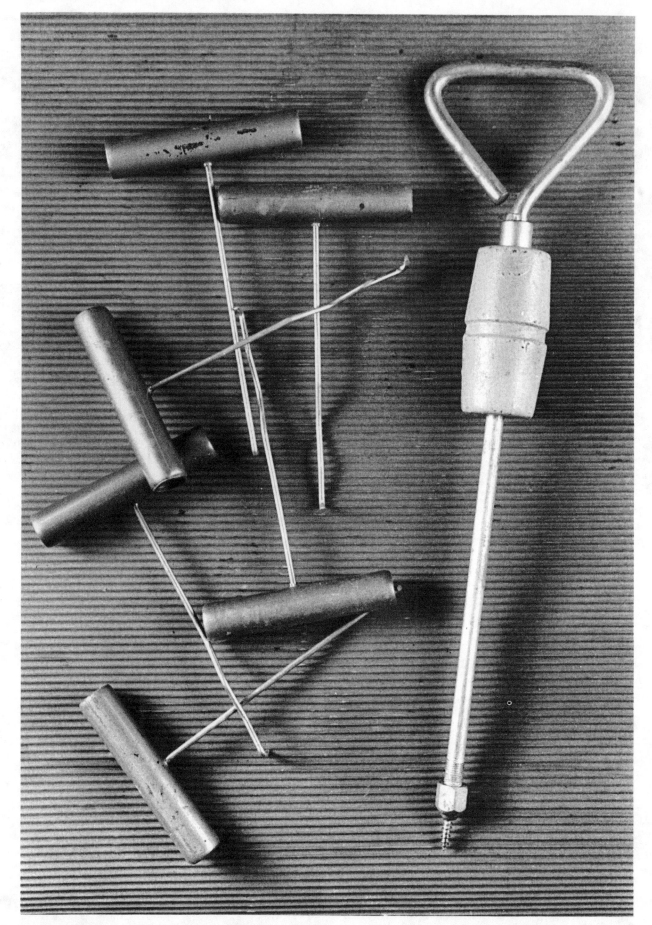

Tools like this "dent puller" (right) and these body hooks (left) are readily available in body shop supply stores and in hardware stores. I wouldn't say that they don't have a place in auto bodywork, but I will say that that place is not in restoration work. Using devices like these to pull out dents means drilling holes in sheet metal, and that should never be done in restoration work.

CHAPTER 23:

Shrinking and Stretching, Welding and Sectioning

Shrinking Metal

In an age when it is not unusual for body men to fill small dents with polyester dumdum, it never ceases to amaze me that there is still a great interest in the techniques of metal shrinking. The interest seems disproportionate to the need for this technique, but when metal is stretched, it is often necessary to shrink it and it is *always* desirable to do so. I have seen car bodies in restoration that looked as if they had some rare form of metal measles from the 200 or 300 shrink spots that graced their sides. Such applications are often done in excess. In the last few years, one seller of restoration aids has retailed serrated shrinking hammers, serrated shrinking dollies, mechanically activated shrinking hammers, slapping (shrinking) files, and finally, a "shrinking disc." It seems that restorers are interested in shrinking.

What perplexes me about all of this is that the basic technique of shrinking with an oxy-acetylene torch is both well-known and relatively easy to master. I cannot imagine why anyone would want to do this any other way, unless, of course, he didn't have a torch. In that case, it might be best to leave shrinking to someone who does have this equipment, but this does not rule out the possibility that some of the profusion of cold shrinking tools may even work. Certainly the good old torch shrinking technique works well. I think that it should be the first choice for this operation.

What shrinking involves is "upsetting" metal that has been stretched, and what that means, in practice, is that the metal will be made dimensionally thicker and laterally smaller (less long and wide) in a small area. The actual operation of creating the upset involves heating a small area of metal until it bulges slightly and hammering the bulge down. Because the colder metal at the boundaries of the heated area is harder than the metal in it, a hammer blow will force the heated area down and out. When it meets the unyielding boundary areas of cold metal, it will have no choice but to thicken. Surface area will be exchanged for thickness, and a "shrink" will be accomplished in a very small local area — say one-quarter inch to one-half inch across.

The purpose of shrinking is obviously to restore original contours to metal that has been deformed *and* stretched, either by impact in an accident or, as often, by the impact of a body man's hammer-on-dolly in a straightening operation. Identifying which bulges are stretched and which are simple deformations is part of the art or skill of metal shrinking. It is possible to overshrink metal and leave it under tension that is as counterproductive to restoring original contours as was the stretching that you were trying to remedy. One common mistake is to attempt to shrink all visible bulges in a panel. When a bulge that is simply metal locked in a rolled buckle is shrunk in a mistaken effort to put things right, it would have to be classified as further damage — although stretching it back will usually present few problems. All of this makes it imperative that any panel that is suspected of being stretched should be straightened *before* any shrinking operations are attempted. That is the only way to distinguish between real stretches and bulges that are not stretched. If you try to guess where the stretches are, and then shrink before you rough out and bump a panel, you are unlikely to be correct more than half of the time. Why gamble?

Another reason to straighten metal before you do any shrinking is that while the basic shrinking operation draws metal from all directions into an upset, the placement that you choose for your shrink spots can very precisely draw metal mostly from two directions. For example, if a gouge has stretched the metal in a panel, it is desirable to shrink metal at right angles to the gouge and not to draw the gouge in lengthwise. In practice, shrink zones of three-eighths inch to one-half inch in width by about two inches in length will prove adequate for shrinking most deep gouges. Note that gouges rarely produce stretching for their entire length. This is dictated by the nature of the kinds of impacts that create them, and the crowns of the panels where they usually occur. All of this depends, of course, on the severity of the impact, on the final configuration of the metal, and on damage to substructure that supports the damaged metal.

Terry Cowan's book, Auto Body Solder is the best source of information on the topic of using lead filler that I know of. It's short and to the point, but will tell you everything that you need to know to do this work.

Before any shrink operation is undertaken, the optimum location for shrink spots or zones must be determined. This is the most difficult part of the process. In almost all cases, the center of the stretched area should be the place to apply the shrink(s), but this is not always the case. As with any metal moving procedure, you have to determine what you want to accomplish and then construct a theory, or rely on experience, to determine that the action that you take will, in fact, cause the desired result. If you just "sort of" shrink somewhere in the vicinity of a stretch, the results will be at best inconsistent and at worst counterproductive.

The actual shrinking operation is remarkably uncomplicated. You simply heat a spot of three-eighths inch to one-half inch (larger spots are sometimes used) to bright red with a small tip on an oxy-acetylene torch. Always use a small tip. Somewhere between blue and bright red, the spot that you are heating will bulge out because local expansion of the heated metal is stopped by the unheated metal that surrounds it, and all that the heated metal can do to expand is to bulge out. At this point, put the torch *safely* aside, and with or without a dolly behind the spot, hit it flat against the surrounding metal with a large, low crown body hammer. Usually after this you will find a slightly depressed center and raised metal at the periphery of the heated and hammered area. The area should be worked flat or to the level of its terrain with a hammer-on-dolly. You do this by lowering the raised area that surrounds the depressed area of the shrink spot. Then you bring the depressed area up. Be sure to use a dolly with a crown which will allow you to flatten the metal around the shrink spot without interference with other areas of the surrounding panel.

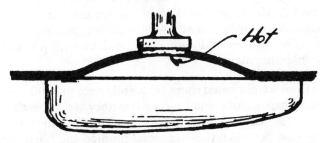

To shrink the bulge shown here, you heat a series of dime sized spots and hammer them back flat against the surrounding metal while they are still red hot. This "upsets" the metal, and excess lateral dimension is exchanged for thickness. The length and width of the area of the upset is decreased.

At this point in the metal shrinking operation, experience and judgment will dictate the next move. If it is apparent that overshrinking has occurred or will occur as the panel cools, it is possible to use the hammer and dolly to restretch the area slightly to prevent a final condition of overshrink. It is also possible to reduce the shrinking effect by quenching the shrunk area with a wet sponge while it is still hot. This "quenching" operation tends to reverse the shrink effect slightly. The point is you can fine tune the shrink at this point to fit the desired result.

That's all that there is to it. Shrinking isn't one of the black arts, but it does take some practice and experience to get a feel for when and where to shrink and how far to go with it. Mastery of conventional, oxy-acetylene shrinking should be a useful procedure for about as long as automobile bodies are constructed from sheet metal.

Sectioning: Cutting and Forming

At some point in many restorations, it is possible that body renovation will require the removal of parts of panels and the fabrication and attachment of replacement metal. This is necessary when parts of panels are so damaged by rust or impact or both that the existing metal in a panel cannot be salvaged. Cutting out the old metal is usually easy enough, and some simple shapes for "patch panels" are not difficult to fabricate. Others are. *Complex* panel fabrication is a highly specialized endeavor and should be left to those with experience in this field.

There are many ways to cut damaged sheet metal out of panels. You have a choice of shears, nibblers, saws,

The most common reason for sectioning in new metal is rust. The rust spot shown here is probably not bad enough to require the removal of metal, but if it progresses much further that can change. Note how the water dripping down the car's roof gutter has helped to cause this problem.

No question about it. New metal will have to be welded in, to repair this damage. The apparent cause of the damage is a badly done previous repair that left the back of the panel unprotected.

snips, grinders, and, most recently, plasma cutters. *Never* use an oxy-acetylene cutting torch for this purpose as it is much too hot and can cause metal to distort badly where cuts are made. Shears and nibblers are fast and easy to control, but because of the width of the cut that they produce, they can be difficult to use accurately. They can also be difficult to use in close quarters because they are often bulky, and they are not good at making cuts in sharp radius turns.

My preference in panel cutting tools is a saber saw with a sheet metal blade. This approach is slow, and sometimes there are access problems. A saber saw makes a very precise cut so the sacrifice in speed is probably worth it. The plasma cutters is a relatively new tool that cuts metal with a narrow stream of super hot air. They are still quite expensive, however, they cut very quickly and precisely and cause very little distortion in the metal adjacent to the cuts that they make. They are also capable of making very precise cuts. If you can afford one of

these devices, it is the premium way to cut out damaged sheet metal for sectioning.

When you cut metal out for sectioning, remember that you will have to fit new metal very closely to the cut line. For most welding techniques, the butt edges of the new and the old metal should be separated by about the thickness of a nickel. This means that you should design your removal of old metal to accommodate this close fit insofar as this is possible. The usual reason for metal removal is either very severe local impact damage or, more often, rust perforation. In either case, be sure to remove as much metal as is necessary to get past the damage and into good metal, but no more.

New metal for replacement purposes should have excellent fit-up in all dimensions, including thickness. Not only should the piece fit well into its lateral boundaries and thickness, but it should not have to be tacked into place under tension to make it match the contour of the panel that it is welded to. If pieces are fitted under tension with the surrounding metal holding them in place, it is likely that with time, vibration, and work hardening the whole panel will warp. Generally, a few extra minutes spent in perfecting fit-up and contour will save both time and quality in the final result.

Panel fabrication can be something that you can do with simple tools such as shot bags and wooden, rawhide, or plastic mallets; or it can require more substantial tools, such as a sheet metal brake, a shrinker/stretcher, a slip roll set, special anvils, a power hammer, or an English Wheel. Most of this stuff is beyond the sophistication of all but a few restoration shops. Yet many of us have access to a sheet metal brake and can acquire a good shot bag, set of mallets, and small wheeling machine. An amazing amount of forming can be done with just this simple equipment.

Even sophisticated shops frequently have to build complex shapes from small pieces that they weld together. Such fabricated shapes aren't very pleasing to look at in the raw, but when they are metal finished and filled, the results are quite acceptable. It is important to realize that it will be difficult or impossible for most of us to form complex shapes in metal without the expedient of welding subassemblies together. With a little planning and ingenuity you can replace a lot of expensive equipment, particularly when the need is only occasional. After some years of experimenting and acquiring sheet metal forming skills, I am often amazed at the fabrications of complex shapes that I am able to construct.

The hand and pneumatic nibblers on the left work well for removing damaged sheet metal from panels. Both are fairly usable in close quarters. The pneumatic and hand shears on the right can also do this work effectively.

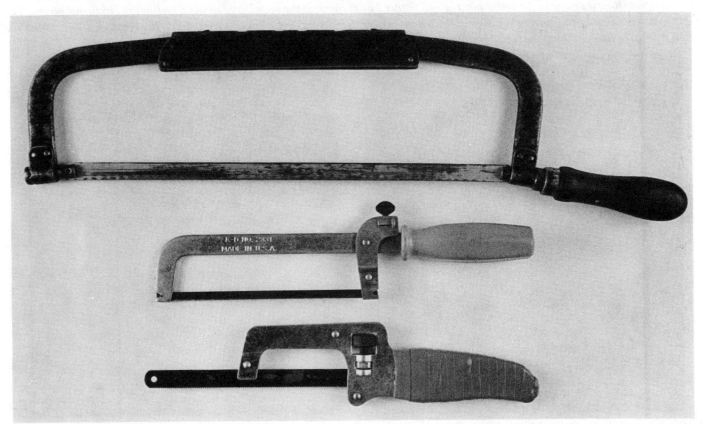

In some situations, hack saws are very handy for cutting out parts of panels. Note the hacksaw shown in the bottom of this photograph. It extends its blade so that you don't need much access to the back of a panel to use it.

The next twenty five photographs detail a sectioning repair to the fender of an early 1930's light car. More photos of this repair are shown later in this chapter, under the topic of welding, and the procedures for filling and metal finishing the fender patch area are shown in the next chapter. This section repair is typical of the minor sectioning work that is often required to restore old car bodies and fenders. Rust damage in the rolled bead of this fender has perforated the metal, and made a sectioning repair necessary. The damage was caused by impact to the edge of the fender, where the metal is rolled over a wire. Here, the restorer is examining the damaged area and checking the fender for flex, to see how weak it is. He does this by trying to bend it with his hands.

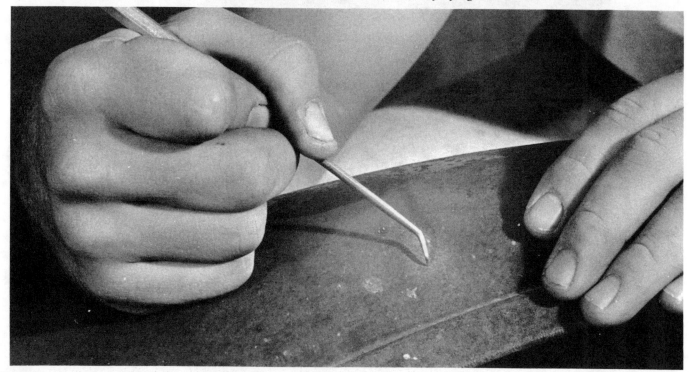

Suspicious areas, where rust-through may have occurred, are probed with a bent scribe to see if they go completely through the metal.

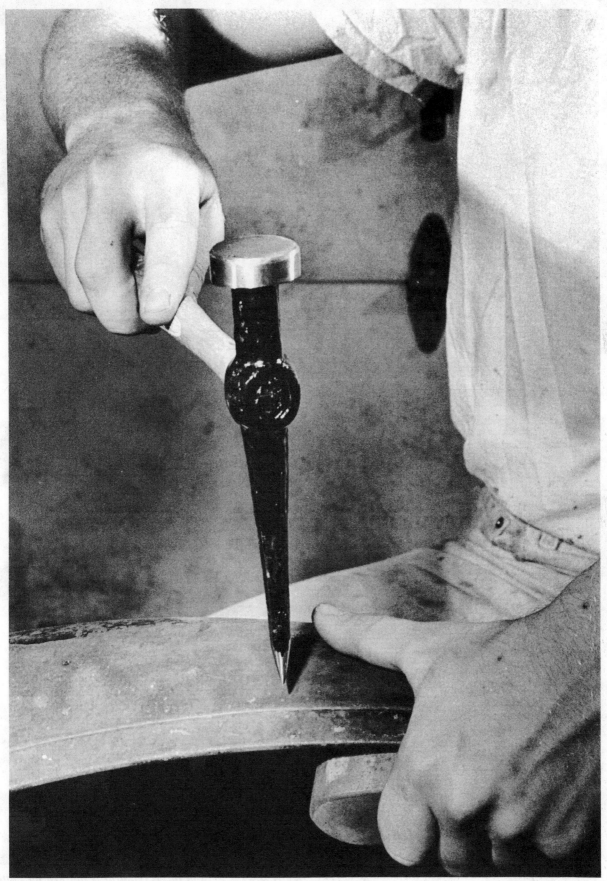

A sharp pick hammer is used to check for a pin hole near the fender bead. Note that the bead area is being backed up with a dolly to prevent the pick hammer from bending it.

Here, a suspected crack in the fender metal is revealed with a strong magnet and a sprinkling of iron powder.

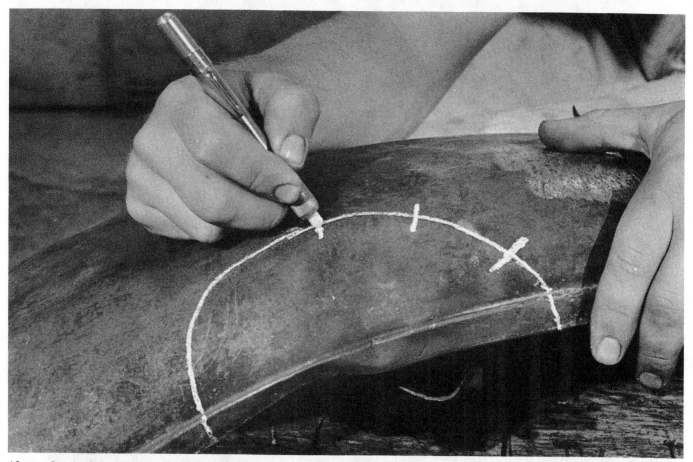

After a thorough inspection, the extent of the damage is fully known, and the area of metal removal is marked for cutting. The cross lines indicate where holes will be drilled for the "Cleco" type holders that will position and hold the patch piece while it is tack welded in.

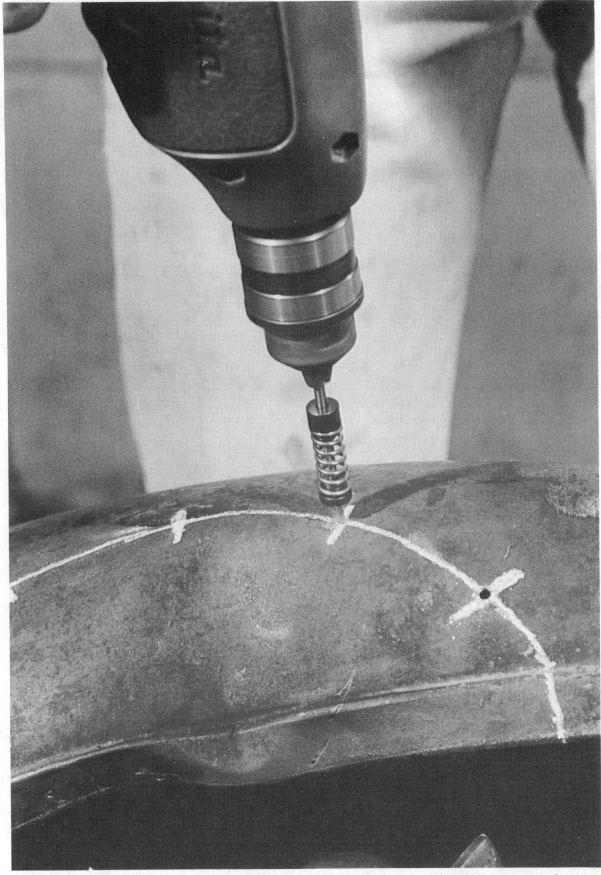

Holes are now drilled for the Cleco type holders. Backing plates will work with the Cleco type holders to position the new metal.

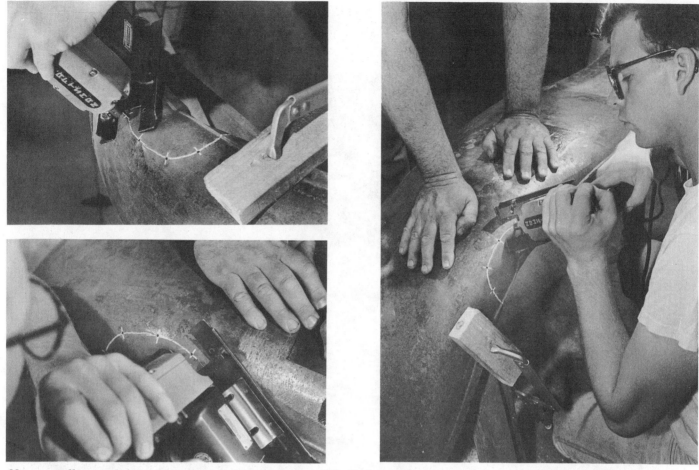

Now a scroll type saber saw is used to cut the old metal out. The blade in this saw can be turned with respect to the saw body. This makes positioning the saw much easier than it would otherwise be.

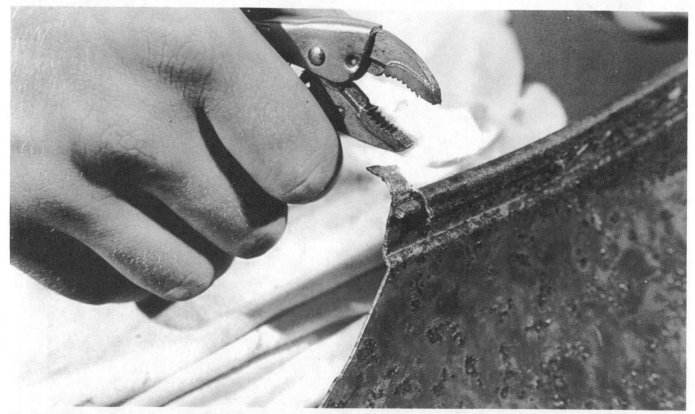

The metal in the fender has to be peeled back in the area of the fender bead wire, so that the wire in the patch can be welded to the old wire. This is necessary to maintain the strength of the fender. The metal that is peeled back was first scored with a hacksaw blade. Then a pair of locking pliers was used to roll it back and expose the wire.

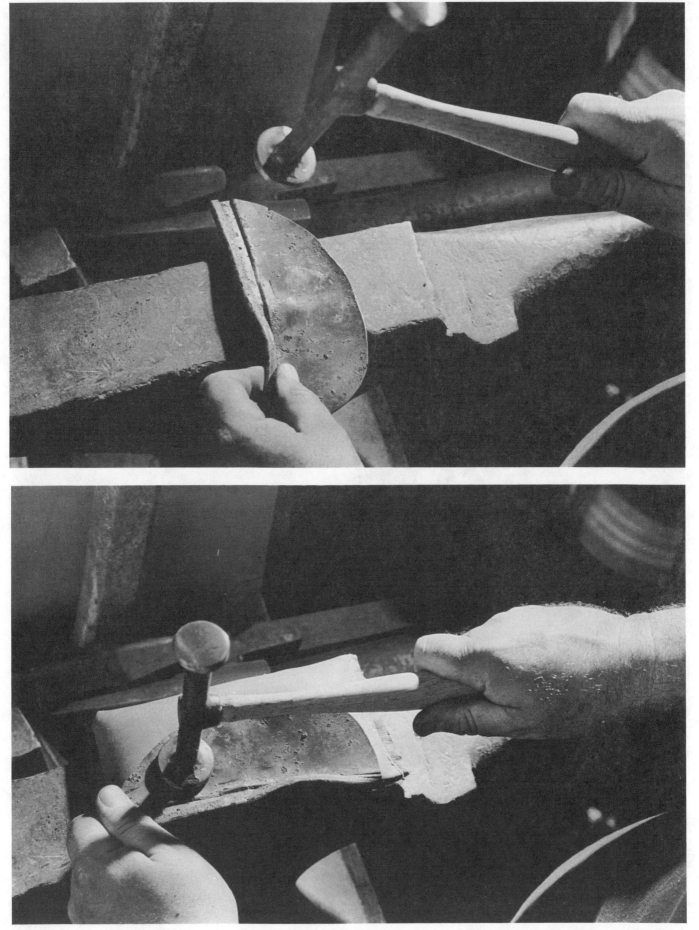

The old, damaged, section that was cut out is now straightened enough so that it can be used for a rough outline pattern for the new metal.

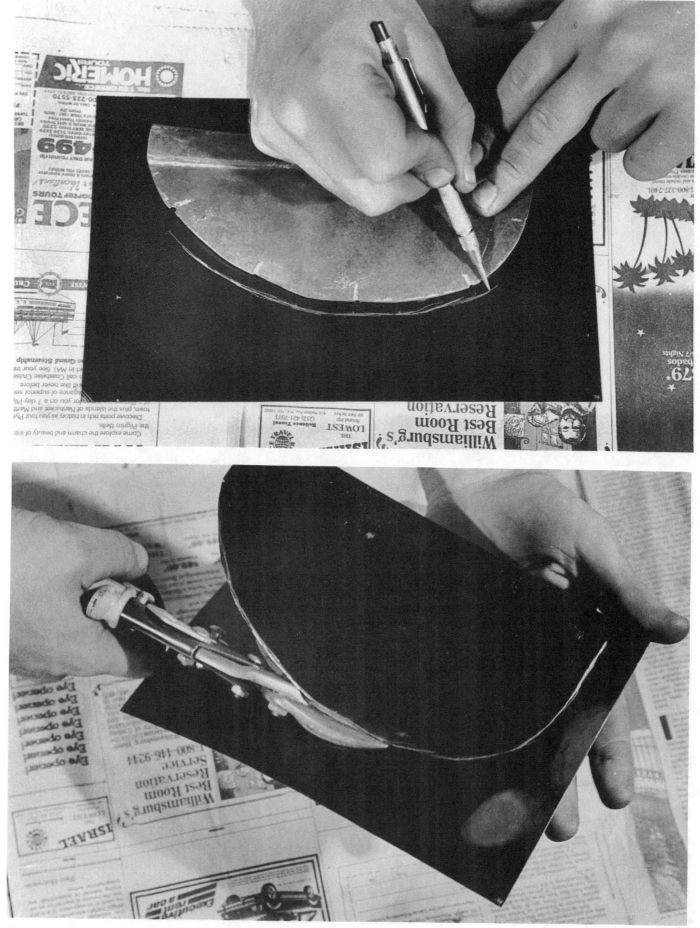

An oversize outline of the patch is scribed on a blued piece of 20 gauge mild sheet material, and the oversize piece is cut out with a pair of hand shears.

Now the patch piece is held against the fender cutout, and the location of the edge bead is marked on it with a felt tip marker. This position is confirmed from the other side of the fender.

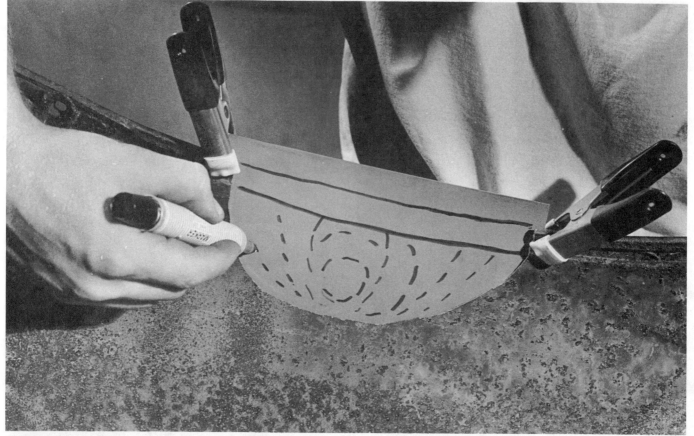

Depth and contour lines are marked, freehand, onto the patch piece to indicate the crown that it will need to match the metal in the fender.

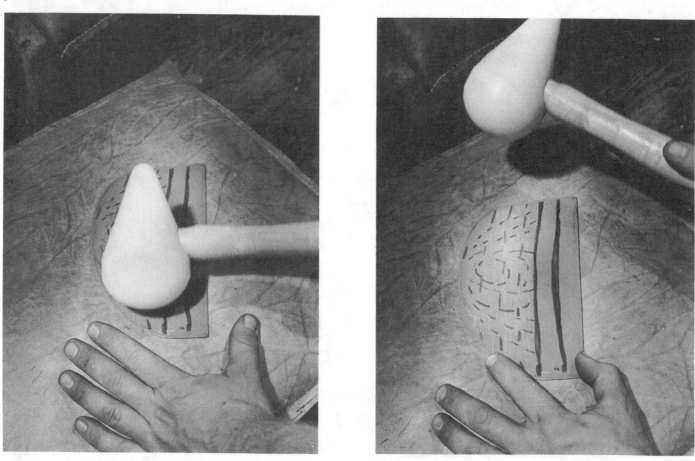

A polypropylene mallet is used to put the necessary crown into the patch piece. The patch piece is backed up with a shot bag for this procedure.

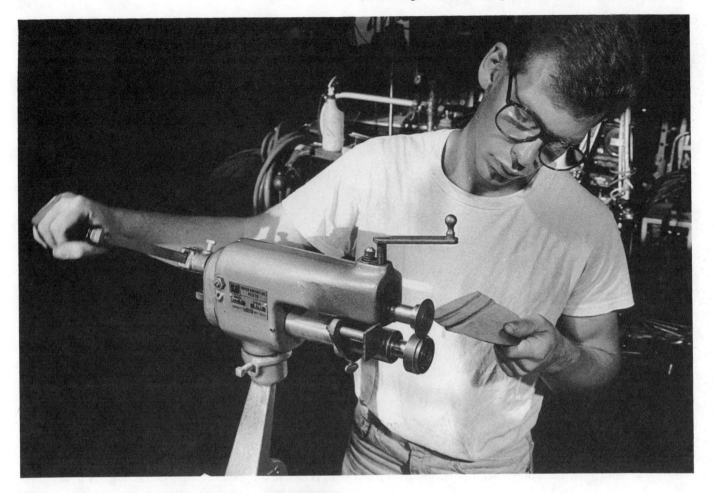

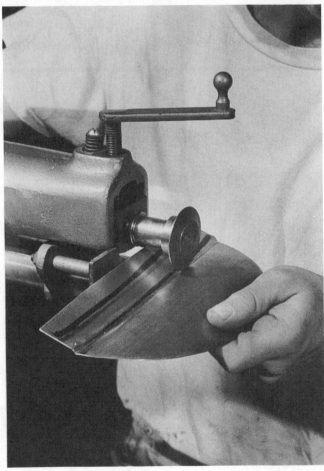

Now a bead rolling machine is used to impress the raised bead of the fender in the patch piece. The same machine bends the patch's edge over for the edge wire and seals it against the wire after the wire is installed.

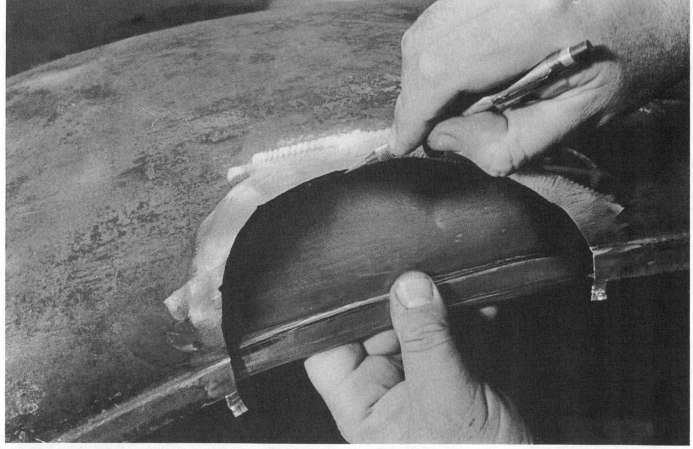

With the fender bead formed and the fender wire installed, the patch piece is held in the fender opening and scribed for a final trim and fit-up.

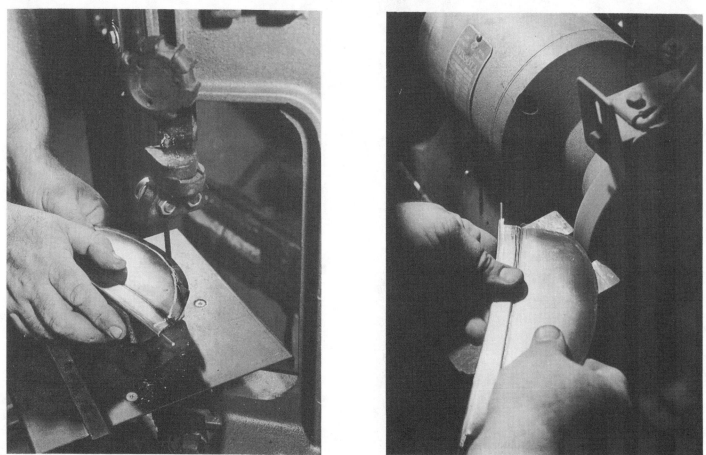

Now the patch panel is cut to the scribe line on a band saw and ground to fine tune its outline to the scribed mark.

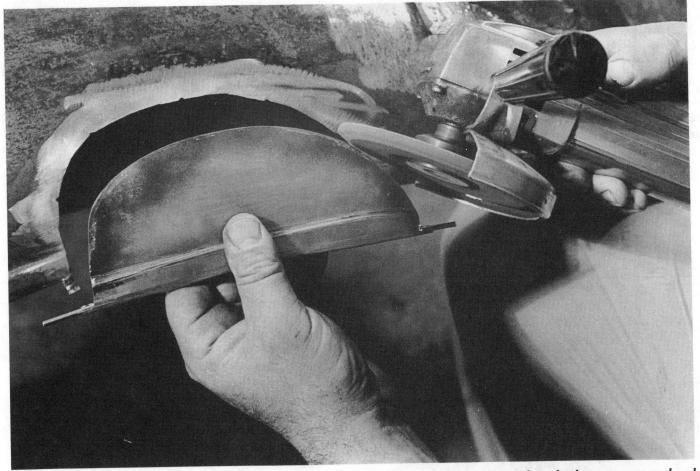

A final fitting of the patch panel to the fender cutout is done with a hand grinder. The fender and patch edges are compared and modified, until the fit is perfect. In this case, "perfect" means leaving about the thickness of a nickel between the patch and the fender cutout edges. This space will be necessary for the metal expansion that will be caused by the heat of welding the patch into the fender.

Some General Thoughts on Panel Attachment (Welding)

Welding is really the only way to attach panel patches. Over the years, everything from brazing to pop rivets and sheet metal screws has been used for this purpose, and over the years everything from brazing to pop rivets and sheet metal screws have failed in this application. In the last three decades, spot welding (resistance welding) has enjoyed some popularity for panel attachment and it has been one of the most dismal failures of all, except where it is used to replace attachments originally made in this manner. The problem common to all of these attachment methods is that the joint that results is a lap joint, and the repair must then hide that joint unless it is done in an area like a door jamb, which was originally formed with lap joints. When lap joints are used in areas that are flat and originally didn't have joints, a counterfeit contour must be used to replace the original contour of the panel in the area of the attachment. Also, no other method of attachment will have the strength that welding exhibits, and none of them are strong enough for the kind of service that should be inherent in restoration work. Finally, for various reasons, methods of panel attachment other than butt welding usually provide excellent places for corrosion to start or restart.

The trouble with welding sheet metal is that you have to know how to weld in general as a prerequisite. In addition, sheet metal is quirky and likes to warp and burn through when welding temperatures are applied to it. Hammer welding, which is welding followed by a stress relieving application of hammer-on-dolly, requires knowledge, experience, coordination, and planning. It is an attainable skill for many restorers but by no means for

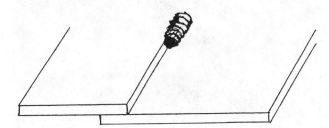

Sheet metal lap joints, like the one illustrated here, have several drawbacks. They thicken the metal in the joint area, and this must be hidden in an inauthentic contour, or behind the panel. They are also difficult to seal, and moisture sometimes attacks them from behind. As sheet metal vibrates in service, lap joints often end up as visible creases, because they can't flex like the sheet metal around them.

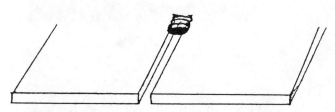

Butt welded joints, like the one in this illustration, are really the only way to go in restoration sheet metal work.

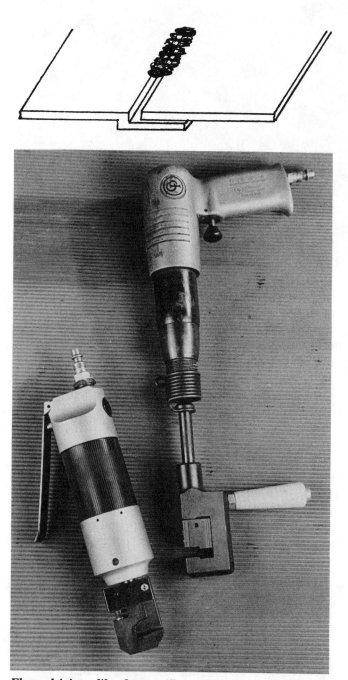

Flanged joints, like the one illustrated here, are made with tools like those in the photograph. The tool on the left is an air-over-hydraulic device that pinches and flanges the sheet metal at the edge of a panel. The flanging tool on the right is run directly off an air "zip" gun. Flanged joints have the same drawbacks as lap joints, and like lap joints, they are easy to fabricate.

all restorers. The expedient of brazing panel attachments has been used by some people because the heat involved is much less than that in welding, and the attendant problems are greatly reduced. The trouble is that braze welded joints lack sufficient strength for panel attachment, and capillary brazing involves the despised lap joint. By the way, when you encounter a brazed joint in sheet metal you may have a real problem because unless all traces of the braze are removed, you will never get a conventional weld to work.

If you don't want to invest the time in learning to hammer weld, you might consider joining the MIG Welding Revolution. While MIG welding has some small disadvantages when compared to hammer welding, they are minor and there are some very great advantages to MIG welding. This is because the heat involved is comparatively local, and distortion — the main enemy in panel welding — is reduced to a minor problem. Not the least of the advantages of MIG welding is that it is easy to learn — about half a day will do nicely for most people — and it is not absolutely necessary for someone to have the kind of metallurgical knowledge that is virtually required of a good gas welder. Then, too, in recent years the price of a usable wire feed (MIG) welder has come down thousands of dollars to as little as $600. Most MIG welds don't have the nice look of really good gas hammer welds, but the strength is there and usually the distortion isn't. When the finished weld is ground level and covered up, a good MIG weld will hold its own against a skillfully made gas weld.

There are several general rules for panel welding that apply equally to electric and gas weldments. One is that long reach Vise Grip type tools, clamps, Clecos, magnets and the like should be used to position pieces before making the tack welds that will hold them in place prior to final welding. Do not use sheet metal screws, pop rivets, and all the other substandard stuff that they sell for this purpose. With any welding technique, be sure to limit the distance that you attempt to weld at one time so that heat buildup can be minimized and distortion reduced. Sheet metal welds should be much flatter than welds in thicker materials. Near flush welds are usually best because welds that stand high above sheet metal surfaces will have to be ground flat anyway. You will always have to do some grinding, but it should be as little as possible.

Gas Welding and Brazing

The invention of the portable oxy-acetylene torch setup at the turn of the century provided a compact, reliable, and reasonably safe source of very high heat for cutting, forming, and joining metals. The flame produced by a "neutral" mixture of these two gasses is roughly 5850° Fahrenheit, with temperatures as high as 6300° Fahrenheit possible with an oxygen rich flame. One of the outstandingly useful characteristics of this flame involves its

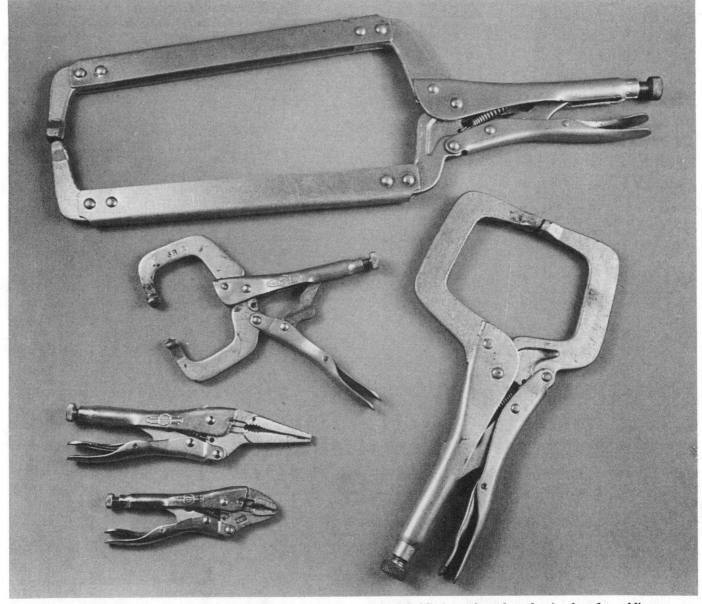

Locking pliers, like the ones shown here, are inexpensive and do a good job holding panels and patches in place for welding.

outer "envelope" which provides a relatively neutral or inert environment in which the rapid corrosion associated with ferrous metals at these temperatures does *not* take place. This envelope acts as a shield from atmospheric oxygen.

As the techniques of welding developed, people learned to move an oxy-acetylene flame along a seam of metals to be joined in a way that causes a "puddle" to flow along this joint. This puddle can be enhanced by the addition of filler rod to form a very strong joint of fused metals. For this reason, it is sometimes called a "fusion" weld, in distinction to soldering and brazing, which occur at much lower temperatures (typically under 800° Fahrenheit and 1100° to 1500° Fahrenheit, respectively) and involve some molecular commingling, but not actual fusion. The puddle used in gas welding is kept in the inert, outer flame envelope, with the hottest part of the flame, the inner cone, held some small distance from the surface of the puddle. The outer flame envelope prevents immediate oxidation (corrosion) of the weld and of the immediate area adjacent to it.

Unfortunately, gas welding produces considerable heat buildup in the areas adjacent to a weld, and distortion can easily be induced into the work. This distortion has to be worked out later in a time-consuming process. For this and other reasons, the technique of hammer or "forge" welding was developed for use on sheet metal, among other applications. In this technique, the operator welds a small length of a seam, between half an inch and an inch, and lays the torch aside. Very quickly, he hammers the hot weld between a hammer and a dolly, and quenches it with a wet rag or sponge. The effect is to relieve some of the stress that is inherent in the weld and surrounding area, and to limit the heat buildup and resulting distortion. It sounds simple, but it involves moving very swiftly and certainly and with a minimum of confusion. If you try this technique, you will find that such simple issues as finding a place to hang your still burning torch become critical because of the lack of time available for the whole operation before a weld cools.

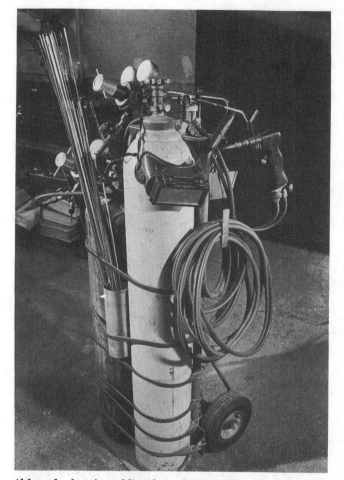

Although electric welding has almost replaced oxy-acetylene welding in commercial body shops in recent years, restoration work still benefits from gas welding in many situations.

The joints in sheet metal that are made with good hammer welding can be things of beauty, and the time needed to correct the distortion resulting from this welding technique may be worth the extra effort. However, I am not sure that MIG welding isn't a better bet if you haven't already mastered hammer welding. It's a matter of choice.

If you do decide to go the gas welding route, you will have to learn the basics of welding before you ever get near sheet metal. Foremost among these considerations is safety. Acetylene is inherently unstable and capable of violent spontaneous combustion. It must be treated with great caution. Pressurized oxygen can burn explosively in the presence of something as innocuous as engine oil, and must also be treated with considerable respect. The oxy-acetylene flame is almost unearthly hot and will do a better job on your flesh than most of the exotic weaponry in the latest Steven Spielberg sci-fi thriller.

There are a few things about gas welding that are subject to myth, rumor, and misconception. The first is that virtually all welding should be done with anything but a neutral flame. The neutral flame is the sharp, focused, unfeathered flame that you can adjust your torch to. The feathery flame is acetylene rich (carburizing) and the hissing pale blue one is oxygen rich (oxidizing). Always use a neutral flame when you weld sheet metal. The pro-

ponents of a mild carburizing flame for sheet metal welding tend to eat goulash before breakfast.

Most people who are inexperienced at gas welding sheet metal tend to use torch tips that are grossly oversized for the job at hand. The result is burn-through and distortion. The tips supplied with most welding outfits go from the mildly useful to the kinds of tips that would best be used on bridge girders and ship bulkheads. Before you attack sheet metal, be sure that you are using a sufficiently small tip. The key is keeping the heat very local to the weld. That avoids heat buildup and distortion.

When you torch weld sheet metal, be sure to use plenty of tack welds to hold things in place before you run a bead because surfaces will start to move as they get hot. Learn the technique of using the end of your filler rod to block heat from reaching sensitive edges. The key to success is torch technique and, in the case of sheet metal, this means forehand welding with tip angle, rate of travel, torch distance, and torch manipulation (weaving) techniques appropriate to the special requirements of sheet metal. Only practice will give you mastery of these critical details.

One very good habit to acquire in working with flame-generated heat is to control heat applications by moving the flame in and out from the work, not sideways. This is critical in some soldering applications but is also a good habit in welding. Unfortunately, it seems that most people's reflexes don't work this way, and you will have to cultivate this technique if you want to make it yours. Remember, when things look too hot, pull back, then adjust your rate of travel.

Finally, do not attempt to do too much welding with small oxy-acetylene tanks. Miniature acetylene tanks are okay for very small jobs, but if you attempt to withdraw gas from an acetylene cylinder at a rate of more than one-seventh of its capacity per hour, you will find that the tank will discharge the acetone that its acetylene is dissolved in, and you will have an awfully messy weld. For the same reason, when an acetylene tank is laid on its side in transit or for some other reason, it must be stood upright before it is used for at least the same amount of time (up to 24 hours) that it sat on its side. Otherwise it will discharge acetone.

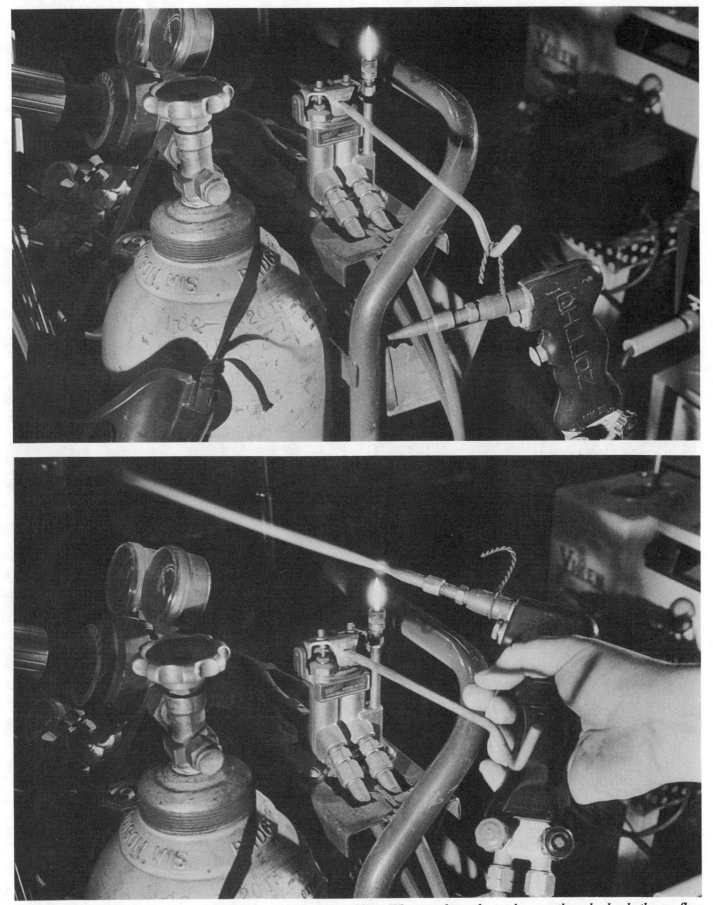

A "GasSaver" type valve is very useful when you do hammer welding. When you hang the torch up on the valve hook, the gas flow is stopped and the flame goes out. When you remove the torch handle from the hook, the gas flow is reestablished and the torch can be lit from the pilot light on the device. Without one of these valves, you will have trouble finding a place to safely stash your torch during the hammering and quenching phases of hammer welding.

Electric Welding

At about the same time that portable oxy-acetylene equipment was being perfected, electric welding became practical. In this technique, an electric arc (either AC or DC) is used to heat the area of a weld. Some electric techniques like TIG (Tungsten Inert Gas), carbon arc, and resistance ("spot") welding use nonconsumable electrodes and either weld by heat or heat and pressure. Some of these techniques require the addition of filler material from a rod. Other techniques, such as MIG and "stick," (Shielded Arc) welding always use a consumable electrode to add metal to weld.

From the 1920s on, stick welding became increasingly important in structural welding and was applied to sheet metal with some degree of success. While people did weld sheet metal with stick electrodes, and even did this with AC equipment, the results were often pretty terri-

ble, and the skill required was enormous. Massive improvements in alloys and fluxes, in the decades immediately before and after World War II, made stick welding a little more usable on sheet metal, but gas welding always seemed to be a better way to go. Enter the MIG welder.

Originally, wire feed welders were proposed only as a way to save the expense of wasted electrode stubs in conventional shielded arc welding. The idea was to feed a continuous wire into a weld and avoid these stubs. Feeding a wire electrode also made changing sticks in the middle of a weld unnecessary. The only problem was fluxing the weld. Stick welding relies on the powered flux that surrounds metal electrodes. This flux vaporizes at welding temperatures and, in part, turns into a shielding gas that protects a weld from atmospheric corrosion as it is being made and cools. A protective layer of slag, formed from elements in the flux, protects the weld during final cooling. With a continuous wire feed, fluxing did not seem possible because a coated wire could not be fed smoothly. The first solution was to use a flux cored wire, but this was expensive and hard to work with. A better

This modern stick welder has been fitted with a DC converter (top box) and is extremely useful for general purpose welding. Although sheet metal rod is still sold for welders like this one, the results with it are far inferior to what can be accomplished with a MIG welding system.

This is an older MIG welder and is rather heavy and bulky by today's standards. In MIG welding, wire speed is somewhat comparable to the amperage or "heat" setting on a stick welder, and the voltage adjustment is comparable to arc length in stick welding.

solution was to feed a shielding gas, like helium (and later argon and carbon dioxide blends, and later still just carbon dioxide) from the torch tip (properly, "electrode handle" or "gun") to shield the weld.

Very quickly, the application of wire feed gas shielded welding technology was applied to sheet metal fabrication and repair. Refinements in wire composition, gas blends, and feeding mechanisms occurred early in the development of MIG welding. Improvements in the electrical characteristics of the welding machine transformers quickly followed. Solid state controls and circuitry greatly reduced the sizes and weights of later MIG machines, and prices fell, accordingly. Features like "stitch timers," which turn the arc on and off automatically to reduce heat buildup in the welded areas, became standard features on many MIG welders instead of expensive add-ons.

In sum, the rapid development of MIG welders in the last decade has literally revolutionized body shop practice. Virtually every body shop has one or more of these welders, and the old oxy-acetylene torches are being relegated to dusty corners in many of these shops. MIG welding is cheap, fast, and effective. It requires far less skill than gas welding when sheet metal is involved. In the last few years, minimum wire sizes available for these units have been reduced from 0.035 inch to 0.030 inch and to 0.023 inch/0.025 inch. This thinner wire makes them capable of welding with even less heat and distortion. If you are contemplating getting involved in sheet metal welding, MIG is probably the way to go from now on.

The specific MIG format used on sheet metal is called "short arc," which involves burning off the end of the electrode in a "short" and then reestablishing the short as the wire feeds out of the gun and into the weld puddle. The cycle is repeated roughly 200 times a second. Other possible formats are globular transfer — globs of metal are transferred — and spray arc welding, which is a molecular transfer of metal. These last two formats are not used in sheet metal welding. Wire speed and voltage are

Better MIG welders allow you to set "burnback," and have settings for "stitch on" and "stitch off" timer control. The second knob down on this control panel is for setting a timer to make spot type welds.

The "spot" attachment for this welding gun is shown below it. MIG welders don't do real resistance welding, they approximate it by melting a spot in one piece of metal through, and into the sheet below it.

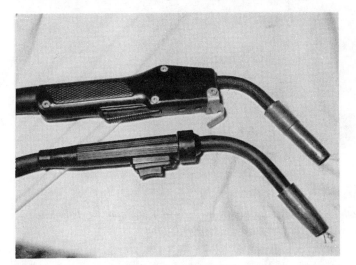

The "gun" or "torch" on a MIG welder feeds the wire out and energizes it. It also carries the shielding gas and the trigger signal. Some of the newer units allow setting voltage and wire speed from the gun handle.

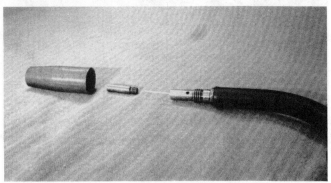

Welding wire in 0.023 inches is very fine, as you can see in this photograph of the disassembled end of a MIG gun that is fitted with this wire.

Spot welding was used in the production of many collectible cars. Modern unibody cars have upwards of 4,000 spot welds holding them together. The clamp type spot welder, shown here, does very nice work if you can gain access for its jaws.

adjusted in MIG welding to achieve a desirable arc. These adjustments are often made primarily from the sound of the arc as it occurs. An arc with a "frying egg" sound is usually ideal.

Control of the MIG welding arc is accomplished by adjusting voltage, which basically affects weld penetration and height, and wire speed, which basically relates to amperage and arc cycle frequency. Some of the newer units automatically adjust their voltages when wire speed is set, and many MIG welders have a "burnback" control that times the period that the electrode wire is energized after the gun trigger is released and the wire feed stops. This last adjustment is used to prevent the wire from sticking in the puddle when it freezes at the end of a welding application. "On" and "off" times can be set on welders with stitch controls. All MIG welders use direct current (DC).

Many MIG welders come with a spot attachment and spot timer. This setup allows you to make welds by heating through the top layer of metal into the underlying layer. This isn't as neat in appearance as a real resistance weld, but it can be very useful in restoration work.

Resistance or "spot" welders create a joint by applying very high amperages and fairly high pressures to the spot being welded. All of these involve mechanically or manually activated electrodes that are closed by levers or pneumatic devices. No filler materials are added. Resistance welding is extremely useful in reestablishing broken or corroded welds that were originally made with this technique.

Some welding modes, such as carbon arc welding, have become pretty much obsolete because other techniques outperform them in every application. Others, such as TIG welding, still excel in specific applications such as stainless steel and aluminum weldments where they outperform other techniques, but they have little general application beyond a few specialties. TIG welding produces very neat, low distortion welds in sheet steel but it is slow, the equipment for it is expensive, and it requires great skill to perform. MIG welding is, by the way, rapidly replacing TIG in many situations where aluminum must be welded.

One big caution that applies to all electric welding on automobiles is to be sure to disconnect the battery and alternator from a car before welding commences. Welding current surges can destroy alternator diodes and other solid state devices. They can also cause battery explosions, at least theoretically. For obvious reasons, never weld near gasoline tanks, hoses, lines, or other places where gasoline fumes can be ignited.

A recent development in arc welding has been the invention of safe and effective automatic self-dimming welding lenses. This type of device makes it so much easier to weld than a conventional helmet that I would recommend it to anyone who plans to do much electric welding.

This type of spot welder needs less access than the lever type, shown above. The blunt contact energizes the base metal, and the sharp contact makes the weld. You have to press hard with both contacts to make this kind of welding work.

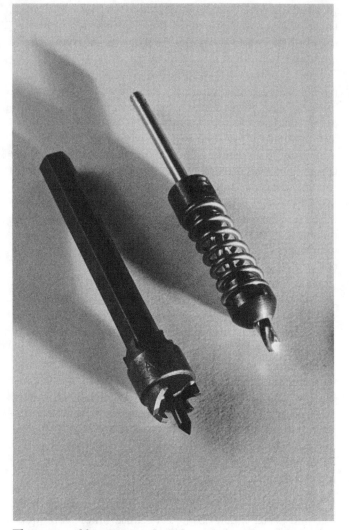

The spot weld cutter on the left, and the pilot drill on the right, are used together to remove old spot welds. First you drill a pilot hole in the center of the spot weld that you want to remove, and then you drill the weld out with the cutter. The cutters come in two or three sizes.

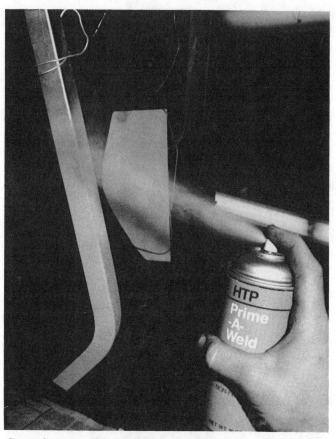

Several new products called "weld through primers" have recently come on the market. They are used to protect spot and MIG welds. You spray them on a weld area BEFORE you weld. This is very useful in protecting the overlaps in welded lap joints, where protection cannot be added after a weld is made, because there is no access to the area, and conventional rust proofing agents would interfere with the electrical conductivity that is necessary to make MIG and spot welds. Weld through primers survive the heat of welding and provide excellent protection.

Automatic, self-dimming welding lenses, like this one, allow you to see what you are doing through an undarkened lens. When you trigger an arc, the lens automatically dims in 1/500th of a second, or less. Both beginners and pros have given rave reviews to these new automatic lenses.

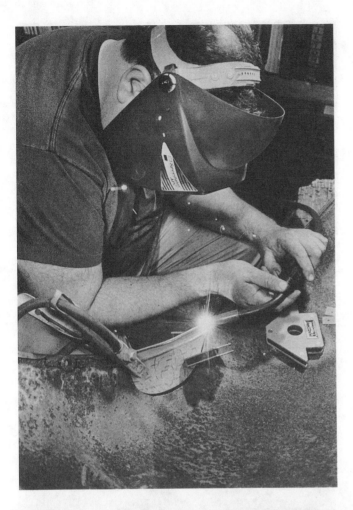

Now, back to our fender patching project. The next nine photos show the process and tools for welding the patch into the fender. The first step is to join the fender wire in the patch to the wire in the fender. This is done by MIG welding them. Note the welding magnet, below the torch, that is used to position the patch while the wires are welded together.

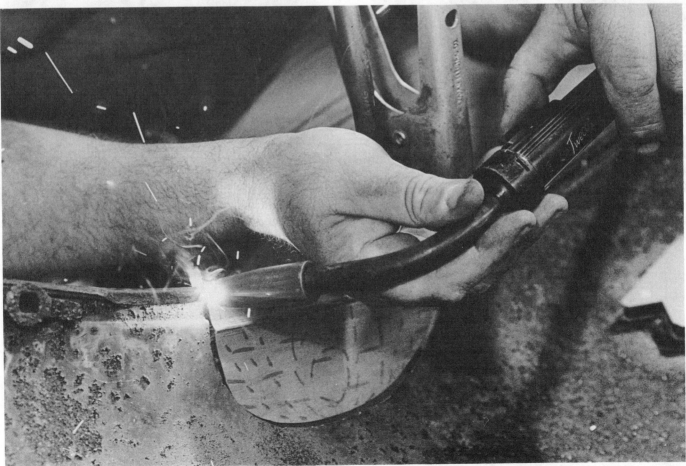

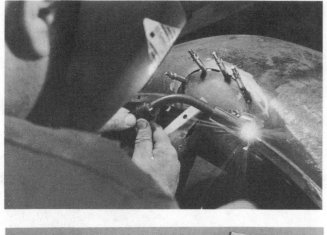

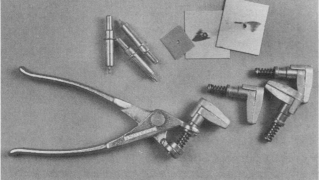

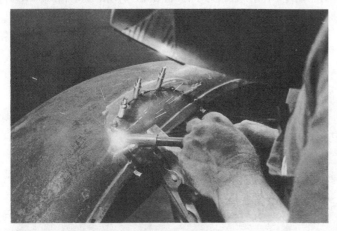

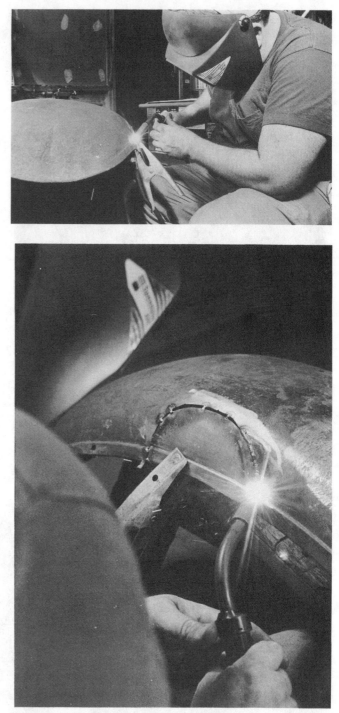

The patch is now positioned with Cleco type holders and backing plates, and tack welds are made along the seam. The holding system is also shown separately. The Cleco type fasteners help to hold things in position, and to maintain an ideal fit-up distance between the edges of the metal pieces.

Now a bead is run along the seam. Short sections are welded and cooled, by using the welder's stitch timer feature.

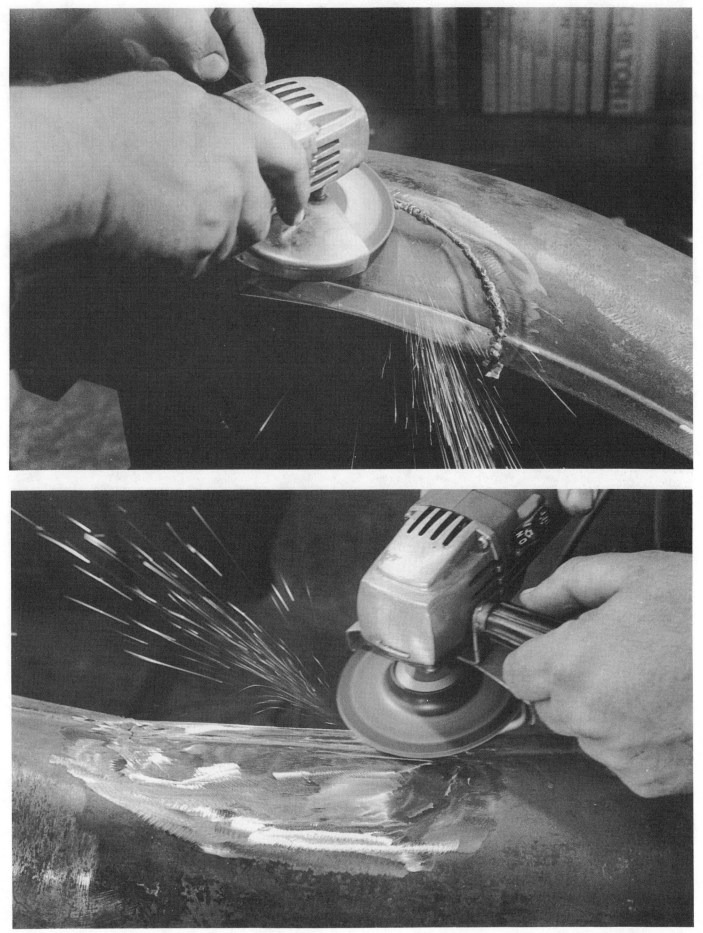

The final step in welding the patch panel in is to grind the weld bead flush with the panel. This is done with a small (4") body grinder.

This damage was once repaired with a polyester filler. The filler absorbed moisture and the damage continued to progress under it. Newer polyester fillers are said not to have this problem. Note that this filler was used near panel edges where it had little chance of success.

CHAPTER 24:

Auto Body Metal Preparation and Filling

Auto body repair and refinishing is a process that involves building step-by-step to a final result. If, at any step, there is a defect, this defect will often be carried into the final result. There are available fixes as you go along, but these frequently involve compromises of quality. For example, both body lead and polyester fillers are susceptible to pinholing. In either case, pinholes are usually a result of poor application technique. In either case, the pinholes can be filled with spot or glazing putty. This solves the immediate problem but frequently creates more problems down the line. Putties have a tendency to shrink and to trap solvents unless they are allowed to dry for extended periods. Since raw enthusiasm or production schedules usually get in the way of these extended drying times, the putty used to fill pin holes frequently lifts paint or falls in and creates noticeable depressions in the final painted surface. The point is, any mistake in building up to a final finish will usually come back to haunt you so there is a premium on not making mistakes as you build a finish. Body finishing may not look like precision work but it most definitely is.

Concepts in Body Filling

Ideally, there would never be any need to use body filler because metal would be bumped and metal finished to perfect contours without the use of any filling material. However, this is usually not practical. There are some dents which, because of their locations, cannot be completely bumped out. Usually this involves a lack of rear access. In other cases, welding and bumping have left minor lowered areas that cannot readily be metal finished by picking and filing. On newer cars, the sheet metal is so thin that there is literally not enough of it to file to a finish without weakening panels or actually cutting through them. In these cases, a little fill is an appropriate remedy.

It should be emphasized that the use of a little filler may be appropriate, but no matter what type of filler is used — lead or plastic — it is never appropriate to pile it up in half inch thick globs. There is always an alternative available to straighten the underlying metal better than that.

There are basically two classes of filler in common use and a few uncommon fillers. The only appropriate filler for most restoration work is lead. That may seem a flatfooted statement, but it is made on behalf of a flatfooted fact. Restoration work aims at preservation, permanence, and authenticity. Lead is the authentic repair for the period before the mid-1950s, and it is the only permanent repair filler. Plastic fillers were introduced in the mid-1950s, and quickly gained almost universal acceptance in the repair field. This was because they are cheap, fast to use, and require very little skill in application. They are also capable of producing a repair that is the equal of lead in finished appearance but not in permanence.

The problem is that every generation of plastic fillers has come with the promise that, unlike its predecessors, it is permanent and won't fall out or allow corrosion to start behind the filled areas. And with perfect regularity, each generation of polyester fillers has failed in these regards. While there has been general improvement in these fillers over the years, and while some of them are better than others, none of them seem to have the adhesive capabilities, inherent strength, or moisture sealing capabilities of body filling lead alloys. Some polyester fillers are junk, such as those that are thickened with talc, and these will start to self-destruct shortly after application. Others are formulated more carefully and use non-absorbing thickeners, such as granite spheres. If these are applied properly over well cleaned surfaces, they will last long enough to make respectable repairs. I doubt if any of them will last long enough for restoration work, and when plastic filler fails, it usually has allowed the original damage to progress to a much worse state than when the repair was made.

It is interesting to note that until fairly recently, the automobile companies still used lead to seal the seams on some top quality cars, and they often use lead to repair body damage that occurs on their assembly lines. In part,

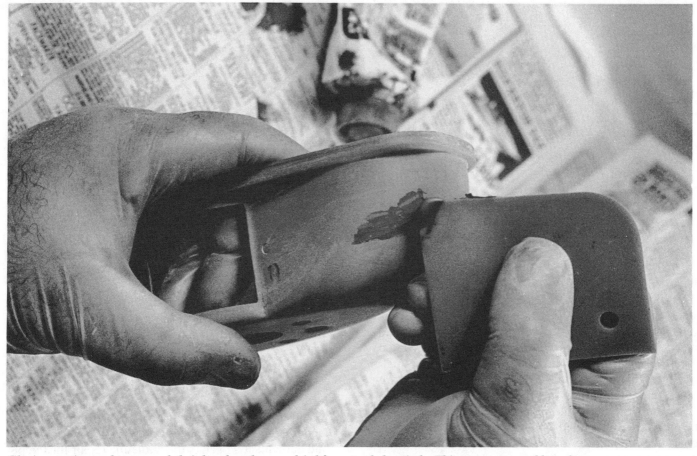

Glazing putties tend to gas and shrink unless they are dried for extended periods. This can cause problems later.

this is because of quality and, in part, it is because the time required for plastic filler to cure is not available in a manufacturing production schedule.

I cannot imagine a basis for claiming that plastic fillers are superior to lead in quality. The usual claims made for them involve material cost, overall labor cost, and skill level required for application. None of these claims would recommend them for restoration. It is true that virtually anyone can use plastic filler with little more instruction than is printed on the can, while lead work is nowhere near that easy. Yet lead work is an attainable skill for almost anyone who takes the time to understand the principles involved and to practice with the materials.

There are some fillers that are neither lead nor conventional polyester-based plastics. Some of these are epoxy resins that are filled with materials like aluminum powder. Most of these are comparatively expensive and, from what I have seen, they are marginally better than conventional, polyester-based fillers. Ditzler's highly regarded Alum-A-Lead, for example, used to fall out after five or more years of service, just as the cheaper polyesters did. Then there are the real exotics in the world of fillers, the sprayable polyesters. These achieved some unsavory notoriety a few years ago, when several restoration shops filed suits against one of the companies that manufactured this stuff. I have met people who swear by sprayable filler, and I have met really good body practitioners who use them in restoration work. At this point I would not recommend them or anything but lead alloys for body repair in almost all situations.

There are a few places where plastic fillers should be used in preference to lead. These should always be places where very little filler is needed and where the buildup can be kept to a minimum. The usual reason that plastic filler must be used is that framing wood, upholstery, or something else that will not tolerate the heat associated with tinning and leading is so close to the repair area as to make lead filling repairs impossible. In these cases, plastic can be used sparingly. However, plastic must never be used on edges or corners of panels because it lacks the necessary adhesion and structural strength for this kind of service.

Plastic must also never be used where it cannot be sealed from behind because all plastics are, to some degree, susceptible to absorbing moisture and causing rust and loss of adhesion. The practice of drilling holes in a panel and letting polyester filler ooze through them, to give it mechanical adhesion to the panel, will cause all kinds of problems unless the backside of such a repair is sealed against moisture. Even then, this is a sloppy and substandard practice.

Surface Preparation for Fillers

Whatever type of filler is used, surface preparation will be critical in achieving a successful bond. Welds in areas where fillers are to be used must be ground flat. Do not attempt to pile filler over a weld to hide it. The most

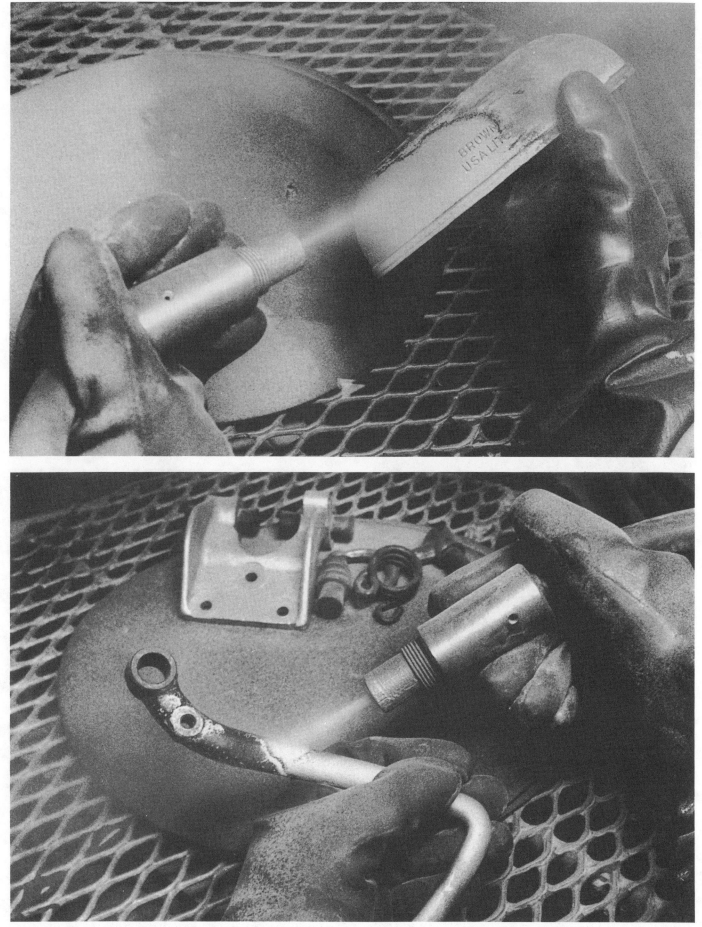

Abrasive blasting is very effective in removing paint, corrosion, and, particularly, deep rust pits. It works well on small parts like these but can cause warping in large panels unless special plastic beads or very fine mineral abrasives are used.

critical aspect of surface preparation involves getting the underlying metal absolutely clean. This means that all paint, rust, oil, silicone, loose galvanizing, etc. must be removed. If any of these contaminants is left on a sheet metal surface, the adhesion of coatings or filler will be adversely affected and corrosion is likely to start. The best way to clean panels in preparation for coating them or applying filler to them is to sand them, wire brush them, or very carefully blast them in deeply pitted areas. Metal that has been cleaned by dipping it in chemicals still needs to be cleaned before coating or filling. Since abrasive blasting has a great potential for warping sheet metal, it must be used very sparingly and very carefully. Blasting is very effective in dealing with porous areas, such as welds that will not yield their scale to wire brushing or sanding. If you do use blasting in areas where access prohibits other cleaning methods, be careful *not* to use aluminum oxide blasting media if leading is to follow — it will interfere with proper tinning. For some reason, aluminum oxide sandpaper does not cause this problem as badly as blasting with aluminum oxide media does.

One old practice was to use muriatic acid (HCL) to clean and etch metal in preparation for painting and as a tinning flux. This is a practice that has slipped into disuse, and properly so. It is difficult to clean up after that kind of an etch, and the acid fumes are dangerous. While there is something quaint about cutting the acid with zinc and all that, this is one "lost art" that should remain lost.

A spot blaster like this one is great for removing an occasional pitted area from a panel before you strip it with a disc sander or by other means.

One of the deadly enemies of filler and coating adhesion is silicone. Since this is a component in most auto waxes, it has to be removed from panels very thoroughly before they are coated or filled. Silicone and wax removers, such as Pre-Kleeno (R-M) and PrepSol (DuPont), should be used before paint is sanded off, or sanding will push silicone residues into the metal. It is also good practice to wipe down sanded bare metal with a silicone and wax remover before you tin for lead or apply plastic filler.

A 36 or 50 grit sandpaper will do nicely to provide a

surface for good filler adhesion. It is best to extend filler about two inches or more beyond the actual repair area so that it can be blended into the underlying metal. Always design your filling for minimum height. The glob-it-on-grind-it-off-later school has several drawbacks.

The Theory of Lead

The quality of tin/lead alloys — other alloying elements such as bismuth are sometimes used to supplement or replace tin — that makes them suitable for body fill is that they enjoy a "plastic" state for about 100 to 150 degrees Fahrenheit, in which they are neither liquid nor solid but have the consistency of a paste. Auto body tin/lead alloys typically begin to soften at 361° Fahrenheit and go liquid in the 450° to 500° Fahrenheit range, depending on the alloying proportions. These proportions in tin/lead body alloys vary from 10 percent tin to 60 percent tin, with greater tin content resulting in lower melting points. Interestingly, the alloys of tin and lead melt at lower temperatures than either of these metals does in its pure form. The best general purpose alloy is 30 percent tin and 70 percent lead. Alloys with more lead tend to be stronger but have more limited plastic ranges, and are, therefore, more difficult to work with. When structural strength is not the prime consideration, 30/70 body lead

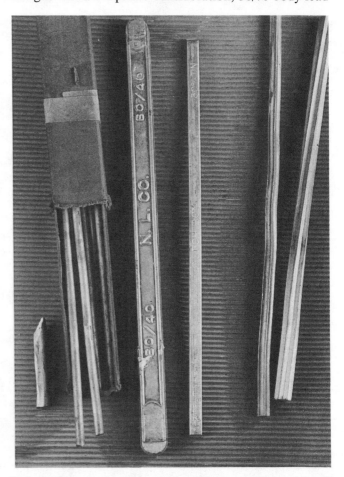

Body lead comes in many sizes, alloys, and shapes. Not all lead alloys are suitable for body work.

These old "lead guns" shoot molten lead. They were used with a "cold tinning" process to apply lead at very low temperatures. Modern body technicians would never use tools like these because the lead dust that they generate can be deadly.

is the best bet. It is important to note that not all "lead" is suitable for bodywork as, for example, plumber's lead, which is nearly pure lead and is wholly unsuitable for bodywork. The 20/80 and 10/90 tin/lead alloys are used to seal body seams and for other specialized purposes, but are not particularly suitable for general body filling.

Lead filling technology has been around for literally hundreds of years. The paraphernalia for applying body lead is simple and relatively inexpensive to acquire. It consists of a low temperature flame source (air/propane and air/acetylene work best), assorted hardwood paddles, and paddle lubricant (mutton tallow works best). While more exotic application methods such as "lead guns" have been used and innovations such as "cold tinning" once found considerable favor, these techniques have generally fallen into disuse because they were inherently dangerous and required great skill to get favorable results.

Success in applying body lead involves a certain amount of dexterity in torch and paddle manipulation, but above all, it involves close observation. If you carefully watch the lead you are working with, you will have ample indications of its changes of state from solid to paste to liquid. While lead doesn't give the obvious signals of color change and sparks that steel does when it is heated, it does give discernible signals that can be used to effectively gauge its state and to avoid working it too cold or overheating it. You have to watch carefully as a lead surface sags and shines when it is hot and frosts as it cools.

Tinning for Lead

Tinning means depositing a small amount of solder on a surface for an initial bond. When this has been done, lead can be built up over the tinned area. Tinning involves the use of a flux to allow solder to bond to aluminum or steel without corrosion. In this case, the flux acts as a cleaner to keep the metal from oxidizing at the temperatures that are needed for the initial bonding. Once the metal is tinned, there is no need for further fluxing because the solder coating from the tinning shields the underlying steel and thus prevents corrosion.

The key to tinning is to start with bright, shiny metal. It is tempting to try to bridge over a speck of hard-to-clean corrosion here and there, but it won't work. The object is not to remove *most* of the rust on a surface; it is to remove *all* of it. When a surface to be tinned is completely clean, it should be heated and fluxed. Only a flux designed for use under body lead should be used. There are many kinds of body lead flux available; the most common are fluids with zinc chloride dissolved in them and pastes that contain solder bits. Some of the older flux powders are also still available. The fluids are applied to hot metal

The first step in tinning panels for "leading" is to sand them clean and apply a good flux. The flux should fizzle and sputter off the heated panel. Always use a flux that is designed for tinning under body lead.

— hot enough to fizzle them as they are brushed on with a solder brush or wiped on with a rag — and a flame is played over the metal until 50/50 coil solder can be melted on the fluxed surface. When the solder melts, a thin coating is deposited and wiped gently over the surface. The wiping is done to spread the solder and to remove the flux debris and residues from it. The wiped, tinned area will have a clean and shiny appearance. If any flux beyond a trace is left at this point, it will embed in the lead when it is applied and cause problems later.

Soldering pastes contain minute bits of solder in a flux matrix. These pastes are applied much as the fluids are, except that they are heated after application and until they turn brown and melt on the surface being tinned. Then they are wiped. The pastes have the advantage of keeping surfaces cleaner than flux fluids because they bond solder to them just as the flux is cleaning them, without having to go to a second step to apply solder. Tinning pastes tend to be quite expensive.

The wiping operation in tinning must be vigorous enough to remove almost all flux residues, but not so vigorous as to remove the tinning solder and uncover the base metal. This would defeat the purpose of the tinning operation. While there are many theories and individual preferences regarding what solder to use for tinning, 50/50 has proven best for this purpose. *Never* use the shop trick of tinning with 50/50 *acid core* solder. This

This air/acetylene torch is ideal for tinning for lead and for applying lead.

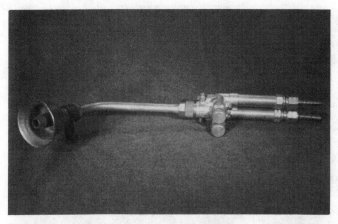

This natural gas/air torch is used in factory production to apply lead to exotic sports cars and other custom-built auto bodies.

malpractice was advocated at one time by trolls and gremlins who had body shops under drawbridges. It is a terrible practice that causes all sorts of problems because the corrosive flux continues to eat away at the base metal and solder after you complete your work.

The flame used in tinning and lead application work has to be a fairly mild flame with good neutral characteristics. Some people even use infrared heat lamps for this purpose; others use a propane torch, which is certainly adequate. I prefer to use an "air-acetylene" torch, which is relatively inexpensive and provides a calm, long, clean flame with very nice temperature gradations through its length. You can generate this flame either with a special torch that you run off an acetylene tank or with an inexpensive air-acetylene adapter tip that you slip over a regular oxy-acetylene torch tip. In the latter case, only acetylene gas is used. Tinning and leading with an oxy-acetylene torch and a carburizing flame is something like going after a house fly with a rowboat oar — it can be made to work after a fashion, but good results are difficult to achieve. The oxy-acetylene flame is simply too intensely hot and too closely graduated for lead work. It's use will frequently cause overheating and alloy separation, and it requires your complete attention just to manage the flame. In lead work there is plenty to do besides controlling the flame, so stick with a cooler flame that is easier to control.

The Practice of Applying Lead

After tinning, body lead is applied and shaped with a lubricated hardwood paddle. The same kind of torch that you used for tinning is used to supply the heat for lead application. Some lead men skip tinning with 50/50 coil solder or paste, and use 30/70 body lead to wipe on a tin coat. This practice saves very little time and will not produce the bond strength that tinning with 50/50 will. It's a practice that should be avoided.

Experience with lead is essential to gaining proficiency with it as leading is a matter of fine coordination and

precise judgments. There are a few rules that the beginner should note. It is much easier to apply lead to a horizontal surface than to a vertical one. Beginners, who usually have problems with overheating the lead and causing it to run and even to separate into its constituent metals, will find that applying lead to vertical surfaces is not unlike making water run uphill. For this reason, it is best to do leading when surfaces are horizontal. Sometimes it is not possible to arrange this, but if it can be arranged, it is all to the good.

Cleanliness is essential in leading. Any contamination that gets into the lead will cause problems later. The practice of working with charred or dirty paddles or in the presence of sanding debris is to be avoided. Always make sure that the lead bar that you are applying is as free from contamination as possible.

The most crucial element in applying lead is the control of temperature. If you overheat body lead, it will turn to liquid, separate into tin and lead, and run out or become unworkable. Separated body lead has little plastic state so it's virtually impossible to form it with a paddle. On the other hand, if you attempt to work lead too cold, it becomes grainy and crystallized and ultimately yields a result that is porous and weak. And, if all of that isn't enough, lead also tends to get funky if it is overworked, so you have to get things in shape quickly after you start to paddle your lead.

Temperature control is achieved by watching the lead surface carefully for the indications of change-of-state mentioned above. The trick is to tease the torch flame over the area that you are working on every five seconds or so, and then do your paddle forming between the flame applications. Remember that the paddle tends to cool the lead, and it is not good to work it right up to the point that it goes solid. If you work too long and allow too much cooling between flame applications, it will be difficult to heat the lead throughout its thickness without overheating the material close to the surface where the torch is played. Keep things well into a mushy state in the area that you are working on.

The best torch manipulation for temperature control is in and out. Human reflexes tend to cause one to move a torch to one side or the other when overheating occurs, but this only causes a "meltdown" someplace else. Learn to withdraw the torch from your work when heat is excessive and to bring it in when more heat is needed. The best situation when you apply lead is to kept it in a state like cold peanut butter, and to spread it at about that consistency.

Lead is usually sold in quarter-pound and half-pound sticks, and in one-pound and one-and-a-quarter-pound bars. There are also some odd shapes out there, like the wonderful "star bars" (they handle heat more evenly). I have found the half-pound sticks far easier to work with than the heavier bars. In practice, a stick is held in contact with the tinned panel and teased with a flame just above its contact with the panel until it softens. The object is to heat about the bottom three-quarters of the stick until it goes plastic and sticks to the tinned panel.

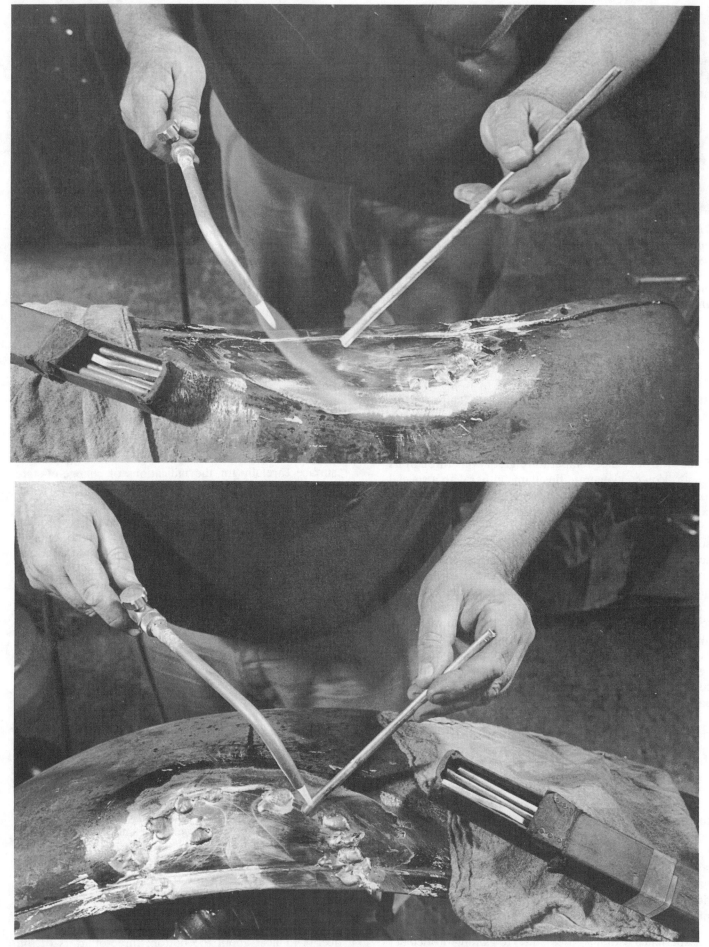

The process of "stubbing" lead sticks onto a panel takes some practice, but it's not difficult to master.

Then it can be twisted off with its stub adhered to the panel. When you see the stick begin to soften, push it in and give it a twist. Several of these three-quarter-inch-long deposits may be required to get enough lead in place to paddle into and fill depressions in the area that you are working on.

The tool used to form lead is a hardwood (usually maple) paddle that has been treated with a lubricant. The lubricant allows the paddle to glide over the lead without sticking or excessive charring. The paddle should be relubricated during use with refined mutton tallow or bee's wax. This is done by playing a torch flame over the solid lubricant and dipping the paddle working surface into the liquid lubricant that is melted. Tallow is far better than bee's wax because it is easier to clean later from the leaded panel. The same trolls and gremlins who used to tin with acid core solder also used to use motor oil as a lubricant for leading paddles. That was "way back when," at which time motor oils didn't have the detergent and other additive packages that they do today. Even then, motor oil was a poor choice of paddle lubricant because it was hard to cleanse ("kill" in the terminology of lead work), but with the present detergent additive packages in motor oils, it is impossible to kill this stuff. Refined mutton tallow is inexpensive and has advantages over all other possible lubricants that I have encountered.

One trick that you may find handy in lead work is to fabricate special paddles for working with special panel shapes. Commercially available paddles tend to be flat or convex. These are fine for work on flat, crowned, and mildly reverse crowned panels. However, if you are work-

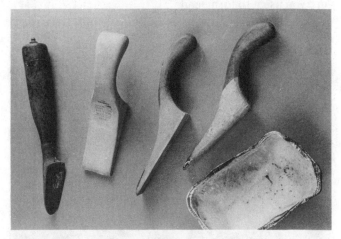

Good lead paddles, such as the three on the right, are inexpensive. The tin of refined mutton tallow (bottom right) will last a car restoration hobbyist for many years. The paddle on the left is about 60 years old. It's a metal paddle with a wooden handle. You were supposed to grease the paddle with a gun until the hollow handle was full. Then the grease dripped out of the hole in the heal of the paddle and lubricated your work. It is a terrible idea to use chassis grease to lubricate a paddle for lead work.

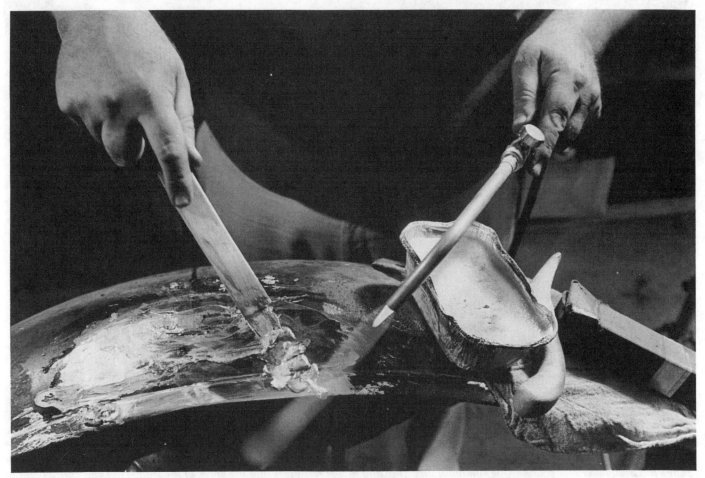

You play your flame over the lead as you paddle it. Temperature control is the key to successful lead work.

ing with a small diameter cylindrical shape, you will find a concave paddle invaluable. A good, dry maple board of about 1x2 inches can be filed and sanded into a variety of special shapes. It should be dipped in melted tallow before you use it to form lead.

If, for some reason, you are working with a fairly thick

A mush pot is the best way to apply lead when you have to apply it thickly. You paddle the lead right out of the pot and onto your work. However, applying lead thick is never a good idea.

lead application — a practice that should generally be avoided — you will find it difficult to make your torch heat penetrate the entire lead thickness. Sometimes even careful torch control won't accomplish this. When this happens, the lead can be grooved with the side edge of a paddle, heated, and then paddled back flat, as necessary. This is not a good situation because it usually involves overworking the lead, but it is sometimes necessary. A better approach to thick lead is to keep the lead in its plastic state in a mush pot or ladle and spoon it into place with your paddle. The use of a mush pot or ladle requires good manual skills and judgment, but it's sometimes the best approach.

While it is not necessary to quench lead, this is a good practice if the heat used in the tinning and lead application has caused any panel distortion. Quenching will tend to relieve this distortion and does no harm to the lead.

Some Body Solder "Don'ts"

Over the years the gremlins and trolls who had these body shops under the drawbridges developed some approaches to lead work that have not entirely disappeared from common usage. We can learn from their example

After you have completed applying body lead, you should "kill" it with with a good metal conditioner. Do this before and after you shape the lead, otherwise you may file contaminants (flux and tallow residues) into the pores of the lead. That can cause paint to lift later.

how *not* to do things.

In my opinion, lead is superior to plastic filler. However, when it is piled into dents or over very rough body work, its inherent superiority becomes meaningless. Don't feel that just because you are using lead instead of plastic that there is no limit to its usable depth.

Unlike plastic, which is best applied in progressive, thin layers, you should try to do all of your leading in one shot. Don't depress the center of a leaded area or gouge it to the point that more lead has to be added.

Don't work lead too hot or too cold. If you overheat it, you will probably lose the lead anyway. It will run off the panel and onto the floor. If you work it too cold, the lead will become granular and have poor strength and vibration resistance.

Don't overwork lead filler. It's like concrete; if you overwork it becomes brittle and funky.

DON'T ever disc sand a leaded repair. This won't work because even though lead is a metal, it is far too soft to disc sand, and you will gouge and depress it. The fact that it is a metal makes it easy to file because it is similar to the steel that it is adhered to and that borders it, but this advantage does not extend to disc sanding. More important, lead dust is highly toxic and can be absorbed through the skin or ingested. The body eliminates lead at such a slow rate that its effects tend to be cumulative, and lead poisoning is very unpleasant or deadly. There is no reason to disc sand lead, and if you do you will probably disappear, like the gremlins and trolls.

Finishing Lead

Finishing lead is relatively easy, particularly because it is a metal like the underlying panel. It should be shaped with a Vixen type body file of six, seven or eight teeth-per-inch configuration and finished with a finer Vixen type file. A mill file can also be used, depending on preference. The file should be slid away from you and sideways in a smooth, sweeping motion, and it should always be lifted for the return stroke. It is best to work from the toe of the file to its heel with a gentle rocking motion, and the file should always be glided lightly over the lead and steel, and not pushed into it. Always file from the outside of a leaded repair area toward its center to avoid depressing the center. Vixen type files are expensive, but they can be resharpened several times with a liquid hone (wet abrasive blast); besides, a slightly dull file seems to work better than a fresh, sharp one because it has less tendency to gouge the lead. New, freshly sharpened files can be lightly lubricated with turpentine, and they will glide nicely until they dull enough not to gouge. Turpentine is also an excellent preservative for body files.

The final contouring and smoothing of lead should be done with 50 and 80 grit open coat sandpaper mounted on a sanding board or wrapped around a body file or a flat paint stick. I prefer to use paint sticks for this work because if they are operated with fingertips, they give a

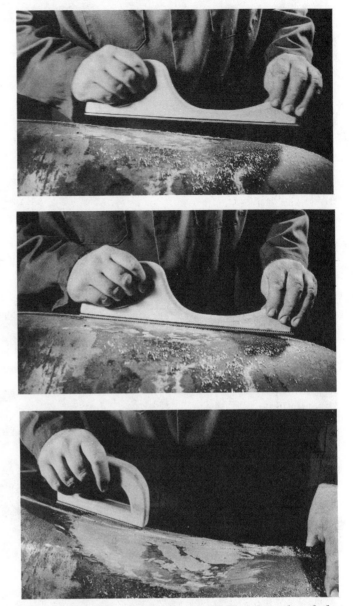

Successfully shaping lead with a body file takes a knack, but most people can develop this fairly quickly. The filing motion used is a sliding motion away from you and sideways. You should shift the weight on the file from its toe to its heel as you make your sweep.

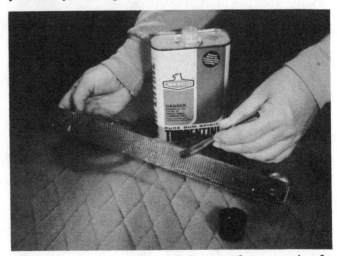

Turpentine is an excellent lubricant and preservative for body files.

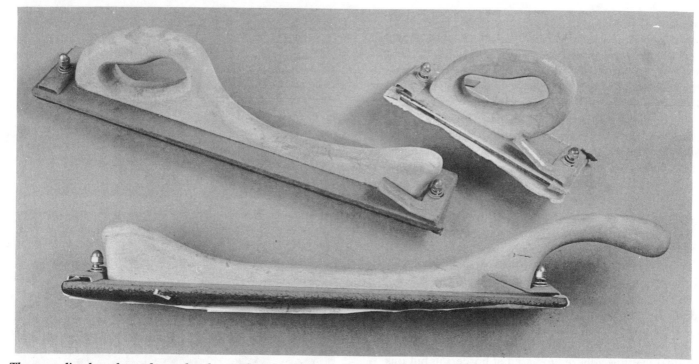

These sanding boards can be used to do very fine shaping, smoothing, and blending on panels that you have repaired with lead.

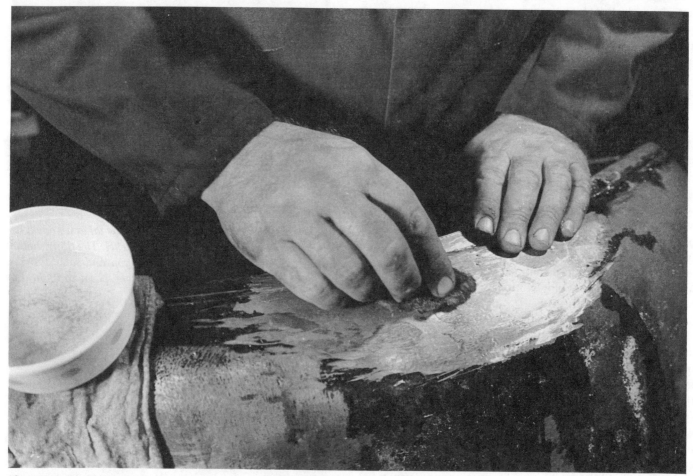

After you have finished shaping a lead repair, "kill" it again with a metal conditioner. The first "kill" should be before you file the lead.

very precise feel for the contours of the surfaces under them. Think about and feel what you are shaping while you file and sand lead filler because the feel that comes back to you is really a status report on the contour of the surface that you are working on.

The final step in lead finishing is to remove contaminants that can ruin the finish that you will build on top of your lead work. Tallow residues can be killed by scrubbing with Pre-Kleeno, PrepSol, and other similar solvents. Flux residues that may have worked up through the lead when it was paddled can be neutralized with vinegar, an ammonia and water solution, or a sodium bicarbonate and water mix. Killing the paddle lubricant and neutralizing flux residues may seem a fine point, but if these steps are not taken, you will probably regret it. One way to effectively neutralize both flux and tallow residues in the same operation is to treat leaded areas with a good metal conditioner. This type of product is offered by most major paint system manufacturers.

Plastic Fillers

Plastic filler is remarkably easy to use. Careful attention to the instructions on the can will tell you about all that you will need to know to carry you through. There are a few tricks to using plastic filler that I know, and there probably are several more that I don't know. One pitfall with plastic filler is that the plastic tends to separate in its can, and it should be stirred vigorously before the hardener (catalyst) is added to it. If this is not done, large wet spots that never dry may form in the catalyzed filler. Plastic filler should be mixed with its catalyst pretty much according to the manufacturer's recommended proportions. Exact analytical balance/micrometer measurements are not necessary, but if you get the mixing ratios too far off, the filler will never set or will set too fast. Mix this stuff well, as the tendency is not to mix it well enough. However, try to avoid too vigorous a mixing regimen that will trap air bubbles in the plastic, as this will later cause pinholing and other mischief later. It is important that plastic fillers be mixed on clean, non-contaminating surfaces. Glass and sheet metal are preferred for this purpose. Some people have mixed their plastic filler and catalyst on waxed cardboard, only to find that the wax gets into the filler and causes all sorts of problems. Others have found that unwaxed cardboard absorbs the polyester catalyst and throws the mixing proportions off.

Plastic is applied to panels with a putty knife or squeegee. It should be pushed into and along the panel to insure mechanical adhesion and to force air bubbles out of it. Several thin layers of plastic are always preferable to one thick one, and it is not a bad idea to lay down one very thin final coat, extra carefully, as a kind of seal coat. At normal room temperatures, plastic filler can be shaped with a "cheese grater" file after about 20 minutes, and it is best to accept this fact rather than to try to

shorten the cure time by over-catalyzing or by applying heat to the filler.

After plastic is grated into rough shape, it can immediately be coated with additional plastic filler to fill depressions or gouges from the first shaping operation. After a few hours — depending on temperature — the plastic can be finished with abrasive paper to bring it to final contour and smoothness before painting. Pneumatic "air files" work very well for this operation, as do orbital "jitterbug" sanders. Final sanding is done by hand with sanding blocks.

It should be remembered that because plastic fillers usually are not waterproof, they must be sealed on both sides of a repair soon after they are applied. People who drive around with their Bondo showing will find that it will absorb enough moisture to cause corrosion of the metal under the plastic. Then the rust expands and pushes the filler off the metal. This process can start before the filler is primed and painted. Then, after this is done, and at some later date, the whole repair can fall off the car. The same reasoning applies to plastic filler that is applied over holes drilled through a panel. Moisture can be absorbed through the holes and into the filler. Then rust will begin and deteriorate the repair.

And now a word about the use of fiberglass patches ("bandages") to cover rusted out sheet metal. "Don't."

Various Other Issues Involved in Surface Preparation and Filling

There is a certain logic involved in doing good work in the area of body surface preparation and filling. When this logic is followed and buttressed with careful observation, good work should come right along. For example, at every stage of this work, it is best to ask whether moisture will be able to somehow get at the underlying repair after it is finished. If the answer is "yes," something will have to be done to prevent this. Be careful not to do things such as plug drainage holes in the bottoms of doors. Don't take actions that require corrections later when this can be avoided. The best way to deal with a gouge in filler is not to make it in the first place. Don't count on the limited abilities of glazing and spot putties to get you out of trouble that you shouldn't have gotten into in the first place.

Always be ready to experiment with new techniques and new materials but confine most of your experimentation to your spouse's "everyday car" and save the "tried and true" stuff for restoration. Some great ideas pan out and some don't. For example, some years ago I experimented with filling under and behind the headlight brows and rocker panels of a car with a "non-shrinking, closed cell" urethane foam. I applied this foam to these body cavities after these rusted areas had been repaired. I reasoned that since the foam had a very minor shrink factor (0.5 percent) and could be injected into these areas, it might displace moisture that could condense in these body cavities. The fact that this foam is of a closed cell, non-absorbing nature made the proposition even better. So far it has worked, and if it works on about three more unloved cars and trucks for about 10 years each, I'll try it on a restoration project.

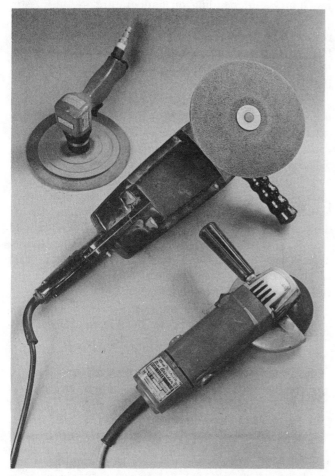

Disc sanding lead falls squarely into the "don't" category. It's dangerous because it creates airborne lead particles that are toxic. It also tends to gouge soft lead surfaces. Lead should only be shaped manually with files and sanding boards.

CHAPTER 25:

Automotive Refinishing, Part I

Paint used to be simple; we even called it "paint," and the act of applying it was simply called "painting." Now, of course, it is called "finish" and "refinishing," and you sometimes seem to need knowledge approaching the depth of a Ph.D. in organic chemistry to weave your way through the ever-increasing and confusing array of products recommended and mandated for successful results in refinishing.

Perhaps the most distressing aspect of the new finishes is that I find myself speaking authoritatively about the differences between acrylics and epoxies, or the effects of polyisocyanate hardeners or urethane cross linkers. Other people probably have the same problem. In point of fact, I have not the slightest idea of what these words really mean, but only some small sense of the observed characteristics of the different products that are called by these names. When you get into the intricacies of applying finishes with the new products, and the inevitable the "either or" decisions that have to be made, it all becomes mind-numbing.

How much simpler it was in the "old days." There was lacquer and there was enamel, and there were only a few very specific additives for these two paints. There were few or no problems of compatibility when these additives were used. Such application monstrosities as metallics and basecoat/clearcoat systems were pretty much reserved for the hot rod set, and you simply didn't encounter the difficult or impossible repair situations that "advances" in paint technology have made common today.

The old nitrocellulose lacquers are a case in point. They were almost absurdly easy to apply, and you could tolerate contamination in spraying them up to, and possibly including, walking on a freshly sprayed car. The trick was that the old lacquers were exceedingly hard and brittle and almost endlessly susceptible to being feathered out, spotted in, and sanded and compounded smooth. Virtually any mistake, or disaster, could be repaired easily or even compounded out without really repairing it at all.

The old, alkyd enamels, like Dulux and Super Max — they were often called "synthetic enamels" — were comparatively soft finishes. They were not difficult to apply, but it was understood that when they came out of tack

(dried to the point of no longer being vulnerable to landing dust contamination) what you saw was what you got. They could be repaired with some difficulty with lacquer, but, because they "gassed" unless they were baked at the time of application, it was difficult to recoat them until they had cured for six months to a year. These were very shiny and beautiful finishes, and their inherent softness gave them a great ruggedness as compared to the harder lacquers. The trouble was that they required a very clean spraying environment because when contamination landed in them before they came out of tack, it tended to produce craters. The idea of buffing (it was called "wheeling") enamel, or "color sanding" it, was virtually inconceivable. These enamels had to be applied in relatively wet coats, and they had a malignant tendency to "fish eye" if there was any grease under them. An early DuPont additive, FEE (Fish Eye Eliminator) gave some resistance to the dreaded fish eyes. Later, when silicone waxes became common, adding FEE to paint became a standard part of painting in some shops.

Both nitrocellulose lacquer and synthetic enamel are still very much available, and there is a small school of restoration purists which insists that cars painted in these finishes originally must be restored in them for the purposes of authenticity. These same purists will tend to wax lyrical about the "depth" of nitrocellulose lacquer, which is, indeed, one it its more desirable traits. The synthetic enamels are a bit harder to defend from the authenticity perspective because most cars that were painted in enamel were painted in a stoving enamel — a paint that was "reflowed" by oven baking it shortly after its factory application. This is virtually impossible to do in restoration. Still, contemporary synthetic enamels do approximate the appearances of these factory baked enamels and were a standard in the repair sector until the 1960s. They are even used today in commercial repair as "economy finishes" and in some restorations.

It should be noted that in their day, these older finishes were miracle finishes; much as the acrylics and urethanes were later to achieve this status. It is safe to say that if nitrocellulose lacquer had not been invented, automobile production as it came to exist in the 1920s and as it exists today would not have occurred. Prior to the introduction

Modern paint chemistry is extremely complex. Unless you do a lot of painting, you should stick with one product line to insure compatibility. We use BASF's R-M paints because we like the product and we like the local distributor.

of nitrocellulose lacquer in production in 1924, there were no sprayable finishes. The old varnishes had to be painstakingly applied by hand with a varnish brush or by dipping panels or flowing paint over them. It was not unusual for a factory varnish job to entail 40 or 50 labor-intensive steps, and to require more than a month for complete application. The old varnishes were truly beautiful, but the time and skill involved in applying them, smoothing them with sandpaper and pumice, and baking each coat made them expensive. Worse still, they were applied very thick, which meant that in many climates their life expectancy was little more than a year. The tendency for these thick finishes to crack, along with an equally disastrous tendency for them to oxidize ("chalk" in paint lingo) meant that about three years was the most that you could expect from such a finish. Add to all this a lack of resistance to chemical and petroleum stains and the fact that these varnished surfaces were very hard and brittle, and thus not very resistant to scratching and abrasion, and you can see why the auto industry was looking for something better by the 1920s.

Enter Duco, the first sprayable finish, in 1924. It revolutionized the business of painting and repainting cars. By today's standards it was an absurdly simple paint to compound because its binder basically involved dissolving cellulose (cotton fiber) in a solvent like acetone or toluene. Of course, there was more to it than that, and the production process for manufacturing nitrocellulose lacquers is one that involves a considerable hazard of fire and explosion unless it is carried out under very rigorous conditions.

The new nitrocellulose finishes of the mid-1920s could be sprayed on and dried in a few hours instead of a few weeks. This greatly reduced the cost of finishing cars and opened the bottleneck that the old varnishing operations had created in the logistics of mass-producing automobiles. By today's standards, nitrocellulose lacquer is a very fragile and undurable finish, but compared to the varnishes that preceded it, it was a miracle of durability.

Synthetic or alkyd resin enamels were introduced at the end of the 1920s and represented much more durable finishes than the nitrocellulose lacquers. They were also sprayable, and thus practical for production and repair. These enamels did not have the depth of lacquers, but they had greater gloss and did not have to be compounded to achieve final gloss. In fact, they could *not* be compounded until they had cured for months. The good side of that proposition was that they did not show the buffing marks that are almost always present in buffed lacquer finishes.

One distinction that should be made here is that the synthetic enamels were *softer* than the nitrocellulose lacquers and, as a consequence, they were more durable. It somewhat confounds common sense that a softer finish would be more durable than a harder one, but it is true. Here's why. Nitrocellulose lacquer, which is among the hardest finishes, is, for that reason, brittle and susceptible to chipping, cracking, and scratching. Softer paints, such as synthetic enamels (and later the acrylic lacquers and enamels, and later still, the polyurethanes), are much

Early automotive painting was done with varnish and brushes. Primers and paints had to be sanded and pumiced between coats. Dipping panels and flowing paint over them with a hose made production painting easier, but it was really the sprayable finishes of the 1920s (nitrocellulose lacquer and alkyd enamel) that finally removed the painting bottleneck in automobile production.

more resistant to any kind of flexing or abrasion damage *because* of their inherent softness. Softer, tougher paints are also less susceptible to being buffed or rubbed out because they tend to smear and burn when they are "wheeled." The new "hardened" or "catalyzed" enamels can be buffed — if anyone wants to.

By the mid-1950s, lacquers based on acrylic resins began to replace the less durable nitrocellulose lacquers. These new lacquers were not only more durable than the older ones, they also had less tendency to oxidize and to suffer abrasion damage. Part of this derived from the fact that they were softer than their predecessors, and part of it came from their improved resistance to the sun's ultraviolet rays. The first acrylic lacquers were sold by DuPont under the name "Lucite," but the other major automotive paint suppliers, Rinshed-Mason (R-M), Ditzler and Sherwin Williams, quickly followed with similar products of their own.

A few years later, in the early 1960s, acrylic-based enamels pioneered by Sherwin Williams began to replace the traditional alkyd enamels and provided the same kinds of advantages that acrylics had in the field of lacquers. Up to this point, the new acrylic products tended to resemble the older products in overall appearance but were vastly superior in durability. True, the nitrocellulose lacquers had more "depth" than the acrylics and some of the more translucent hues of the alkyd enamels seemed to have deeper gloss than their acrylic replacements, but, all told, the differences in appearance were minor. This comparison is made only between nonmetallic colors as modern metallic paints are so different from earlier nonmetallic paints in appearance. This is not to say that the older paints could not be mixed in metallic formats. What we call "metallic" was called Pearl Essence in the 1930s. Early Pearl Essence paints used a component manufactured from fish scales, but soon aluminum flakes replaced this quaint additive. Today, metallic effects are achieved by adding aluminum or titanium flakes to paint to create the metallic effect that is seen in almost every modern automotive finish. Whereas factory metallic finishes are the standard today, most of the old paints were nonmetallic, particularly where nitrocellulose lacquers and alkyd enamels were involved.

Paint developments after the 1960s included finishes that in no way resembled the older paints, except that they too were designed to cover metal. The aircraft and trucking industries provided the basis for the development of the super shiny, super tough (soft) polyurethane finishes, and for a myriad of urethane and isocyanate additives (called "crosslinkers" and "catalysts," respectively) to enhance the gloss and toughness of acrylic enamels and even of acrylic lacquers. The straight polyurethane enamels, such as Imron ("The Wet Look") and Durethane, have little chemical or physical resemblance to any previous finishes, and are, in my opinion, inauthentically shiny. The myriad of crosslinker, hardener, and gloss additive products that is presently available can also be used to make enamels buffable. Of course, a buffed enamel is an anomaly in restoration work because the traditional synthetic enamels could not be buffed out; they were too soft.

One trend that becomes obvious to anyone who follows the modern paint scene is that the enamels and their additive packages produce finishes that are harder and harder, and lacquers get softer and softer. In Europe and to a lesser extent in this country, manufacturers such as Kosmoski House of Kolor are developing super finishes like epoxy-acrylics that are difficult to distinguish in their characteristics in terms of the traditional distinction between enamels and lacquers.

The "official" distinction between enamels and lacquers is that lacquers form their films by simple evaporation of the solvents in them — the carriers (also called "vehicles" or "volatiles") that give them liquid form. Enamels, on the other hand, dry ("cure" or "set" in paint terminology) in a two-stage process. First the volatiles in their solvents evaporate, and then their "binders" oxidize or set through some other chemical reaction — which almost always involves oxidation of their binders by oxygen in the air. Lacquers can generally be dissolved in their solvents after they have dried. Enamels, on the other hand, cannot be dissolved with lacquer thinner or with the less aggressive enamel reducers after they have cured. This is the basis of a test to determine the nature of paint if it is unknown. If lacquer thinner will dissolve a dried finish, it is almost certainly a lacquer. If lacquer thinner will not dissolve a dried finish, it is probably an enamel.

Choosing Restoration Paint

In the past few years, the development of finishes has taken on a complexity that is almost awesome. It isn't just new products that relate to the new plastic automobile components or the new super durable finishes and clear coats. There are also so many additives for the older alkyd- and acrylic-based finishes that it is virtually impossible to keep up with them on a part-time basis in even one manufacturer's paint line. And there are four major lines, and some smaller ones, out there.

An example of this proliferation and complexity is R-M's old standby enamel, Super Max. This paint had been on the market long before I began painting cars 25 years ago, and was an alkyd enamel. Over the years R-M developed about half a dozen additives for Super Max. These imparted isocynate and urethane characteristics to this paint. More recently the label on Super Max indicates that it "contains acrylics," and a new R-M paint line, Limco, is sold as an alkyd enamel. R-M has also developed two new acrylic "super" enamels, Miracryl 2 and Diamont, and their parent company, BASF, owns the Glasurit line and sells its super enamels in this country and elsewhere. See what I mean about paint line proliferation and confusion?

A reasonable question that a restorer might ask is, "What is the best paint or line of paint products?" I don't know the answer. I used to be familiar with the DuPont and R-M lines — Ditzler finish systems were too complicated for me to understand, and I didn't like the service at the local Sherwin Williams' jobber. In recent years, it has been all that I can do to keep up with R-M finishes, and my familiarity with DuPont has slipped to a mild acquaintance. R-M, in turn, has exploded with new products since its sale by United Technologies to BASF of Germany. At this point, I would advise anyone who works occasionally with automotive finishes to find a good line of paint, with a good jobber behind it, and become as familiar with it as possible. There is a revolution going on in automotive finishes with the introduction of products like flex agents, elastomeric finishes, water borne primers, latex based paints, etc. It is also common wisdom in most cases not to mix paint product lines in the same job, because the complexity of the chemical reactions in modern paint products makes this risky. Finally, avoid the clever fads that come along, like using lacquer thinner to reduce enamel. The long term results of such ersatz innovations are generally pretty bad.

The Constituents of Automotive Finishes

Whatever the complexity of modern finishes, all paints and primers are still derived from three basic classes of components: pigments, binders, and solvents. Pigments are ground powders that, by their hues, particle sizes, and particle shapes impart characteristic colors to paints. Some paint experts believe that the pigment particles in paint tend to reinforce its film and make it stronger — much as gravel increases the strength of concrete aggregate. Pigment engineering in paints has improved in recent years with the introduction of more stable pigments and the use of ultraviolet shields (blue tints) to protect such traditionally vulnerable colors as reds.

The binders in paints are liquids that form paint films and bind the pigments in the film surfaces. Originally, the binders were made from natural entities, and particularly from rosins and natural oils such as tongue and linseed. Later, synthetic binders formed the basis of the alkyd enamels. More recently, man-made plastics, such as acrylics, polyurethanes, PVCs (polyvinylchlorides), and latexes have been used as the basis of paint binders. Most of the "improvement" in paint has come from the development of binders with improved adhesion, gloss, and durability characteristics.

The final component of all paints is some sort of vehicle or solvent that dissolves the binders (which have already dissolved the pigments) and allows them to be sprayed in atomized form from liquids. After spraying, the solvents evaporate and the paint film is formed. In the case of lacquers, the evaporation of the solvent (thinner) leaves a fully developed paint film and the process is complete. In the case of enamels, the evaporation of the solvent (reducer) triggers an oxidation or other reaction of the binders in the paint, which produces the final film. Of course, enamel takes much longer to dry than lacquer, and its reduction must be controlled more precisely than the thinning of lacquer.

There are, of course, exceptions to the simple paint componentry described above. Some of the new finishes use catalysts which cause their binders to set up almost completely, thus replacing oxidation by atmospheric air. Simple color pigments have now been supplemented with aluminum powder particles of different sizes, configurations, and coarsenesses to produce the metallics that prevail in contemporary automotive finishes. Finally, additives that the painter adds or that the factory has already added to the paint are used for a myriad of purposes, such as improving gloss, reducing tack time, improving chemical resistance, improving flow out, etc.

Needless to say, the original sprayable finishes — nitrocellulose lacquers — were marvels of simplicity because the binders were little more than cotton dissolved in solvents, and the solvents and pigments were also simple. After that, paint chemistry started to get much more complicated!

The Choice of Paint for Restoration

The choice of finishes for restoration work usually involves some level of compromise between authenticity and practicality. Early cars that were painted with varnish are not refinished in this material because cost, lack of availability, and extremely limited durability combine to make the use of original varnishes impossible. Instead, these cars are refinished in nitrocellulose and acrylic lacquers, which somewhat approximate the appearances of the original varnishes.

Cars originally finished in nitrocellulose lacquers are sometimes restored in these finishes. Although nitrocel-lulose lacquers came off the shelves of the major line automotive paint jobbers more than two decades ago, they are still readily available from several reputable specialty suppliers. Bill Hirsch's line of these paints is certainly as good or better than the original nitrocellulose finishes. The problem with using nitrocellulose paints is that their durability is very inferior to that of modern acrylic lacquers and their need for maintenance is constant. They scratch easily, and their surfaces oxidize quickly. On the good side, they are easy to feather sand and spot in — if you can match colors. That's a big "if" because some of the mixing colors for these paints have shelf lives of about six months, and the mixed paints tend to darken substantially after that. Saving some repair paint for a future emergency after you spray a car is usually futile, particularly if reds or browns are involved. And trying to match the presently available nitrocellulose paints by formula usually doesn't work; there just isn't that much control in their manufacture anymore. Hand or spectrometer matches are usually the best that you can do.

Some people, myself included, advocate using acrylic lacquers to replace nitrocellulose originals. I feel that the appearance of the acrylics is very close to that of original nitrocellulose finishes, and durability is much better. The ability to repair acrylic lacquer finishes is also very good. If you can find a paint chip for a standard color in a modern paint that is close to the original color that you are trying to duplicate, you are assured of being able to secure additional matching paint for repair or respray for years to come. And the major manufacturers control their color consistency rigorously, so a match should be easy. Remember, if you start with a nitrocellulose paint, there is no conversion possible of the formula for that paint to a modern acrylic finish.

Cars that were originally painted in baked enamels can still be refinished in "synthetic" or alkyd enamels. Paints of this type, like Ditzco and Dulux, are still somewhat available from major manufacturers. But this availability is limited and will doubtless end in the near future because there is a decreasing market for alkyd enamels. I have no particular objection to refinishing cars that were originally finished in synthetic enamels with acrylic enamels, and I have no objection to adding the best gloss and durability additives available to acrylic enamels to make them even better finishes. *But* I think that it is an act of barbarism to color sand and buff out acrylic enamels in restoration work. There is something so totally wrong about the appearance of the resulting finish that it makes me shiver. This is because the older enamels could not be buffed, and the whole point of using them was the gloss that they had *without* wheel marks. The fact that the hardeners available for acrylic enamels make it possible to buff them out does not mean that you should do this. The ultimate horror in this regard is the combination of orange peel and wheel marks that can be seen in many examples of contemporary body shop practice. That's okay on new cars, but it looks awful on old ones where this situation could never have existed when they were new. It should also be pointed out that when catalyzed acrylic enamels, such as Centari, Delstar, Acrylyd, Diamont, Ultra Base 7, etc. are used in conjunction with appropriate gloss additives, they produce beautiful finishes that air dry to an appearance that is very much like that of the old synthetic enamels. They are much easier to apply because they flow out more easily and they come out of tack faster.

Finally, we come to the modern exotic finishes such as basecoat/clearcoat systems, epoxy-acrylics, and polyurethanes. No one would argue that these are not inherently beautiful finishes, but they are totally and visibly inauthentic for most restoration purposes. They can be difficult to repair, and the problems of removing some of them will plague future restorers. All of this will probably rule out their use when the authentic restoration of old car bodies, chassis, and suspension parts is the issue.

If you have trouble distinguishing what the finish on your car is or was originally, you may be able to determine this from the paint plate on the car, by reference to the appropriate shop manual, or by consultation with a paint jobber who still has the manufacturer's color books for the period when the car was built. Generally, the finishes on lacquer painted cars can be dissolved in lacquer thinner. Thinner or reducer will not dissolve cured, air dried, or baked enamel. Before the mid-1950s, most cars, including Fords and Chryslers, were painted in baked enamel. The exceptions were GM and some of the independent automakers, who used nitrocellulose lacquer finishes on their cars. After the mid-1950s, acrylic lacquers steadily replaced nitrocellulose lacquers — you actually had to pay considerable extra for the option of a "Lucite" finish on a GM car in the mid and late 1950s. Ford, Chrysler, and some others experimented with "super" enamels in the late 1950s and early 1960s but generally went to acrylic enamels by the 1970s.

To sum up: In most cases, it is best to find a modern, nonmetallic color that closely approximates the original color that you want to use. If the original finish was a lacquer, an acrylic lacquer can be used, and if it was a synthetic enamel, an acrylic enamel can be used. If you want to go the route of absolute authenticity, nitrocellulose lacquers and alkyd enamels should be used, but durability will be sacrificed if this is done. And, of course, if one of the old enamels is used, don't attempt to buff it out unless it has been fortified with additives and crosslinkers that make this possible. I would advise against using clearcoat/basecoat systems in restoration work. They can be very beautiful, but they are inauthentic to all but the most recent cars and they can be very difficult to repair.

The Great "Bare Metal" Debate

"Of course, we went down to bare metal before we painted it." Sound familiar? It is always said with such commanding authority and such calm self-assurance that it makes you wonder why anyone would do anything else. But other approaches are possible and they are not necessarily "substandard." I have no objection to going down to bare metal. You have to when certain conditions are present. When substantial areas of a finish are breached and rust is coming through, it is necessary to take the whole finish to bare metal because the corrosion that can be seen is probably about to spring up in other places where it cannot yet be seen. When a finish is flaking and peeling or has defects like crow's feet that penetrate it, it is necessary to go down to bare metal before you refinish. But when a tough finish, such as factory baked enamel, has adhered to a car's panels for 25 or more years and shows no signs of defect or failure, it is emphatically *not necessary* to go down to bare metal, unless, of course, you like the sound of hearing yourself say, "Of course, we went down to bare metal when we painted it."

The point is, the adhesion achieved by some of the baked primers on factory fresh metal will be hard to equal if you take the car to bare metal and start over. When factory paint has been recoated one or more times in subsequent refinishings, it is a good idea to strip some or all of the later top coats away with a good DA sander or plastic blasting media to avoid ending up with a paint film that is too thick after you recoat. If you are using one of the new paints over an original factory primer or top coats, and particularly when you are using one of the new finishes with additives, it is often a good idea to use a sealer or sealing primer-surfacer as a barrier coat to prevent lifting and bleeding through, etc. R-M's water-born barrier coat primer is particularly useful for this purpose because it is incredibly neutral and will not lift any type of underlying paint or primer. It can also be used over air dry enamel that is still gassing.

What I think should be avoided is the business of sanding to bare metal just so you can say that you've been there. Any method of complete paint removal involves some hazards for a car's panels. Disc sanding can unnecessarily remove good metal if it is not done very carefully, and abrasive blasting often results in panel warping and other mischief if it is attempted without the benefit of one of the new plastic (type III) abrasives or the more exotic mineral abrasives. Chemical paint removers frequently leave residues in crevices that later cause paint to bubble and lift, and they can be messy to use. If paint must be completely removed to neutralize rust or to correct poor adhesion, then there is no choice but to use one of the common paint removal methods. Where a choice exists, evaluate the condition of the underlying primer on its merits and salvage it if it still has integrity.

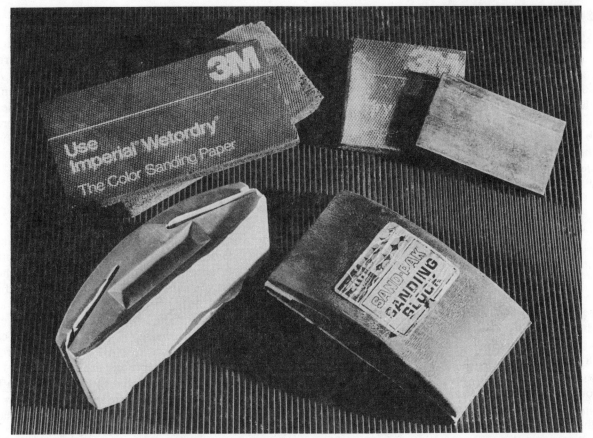

No matter how "high tech" modern finishes get, careful surface preparation and contour sanding will probably always be the basis of achieving great results with sprayed automotive finishes.

You can remove top coats from old, baked primers and preserve the primers by gently using the DA and orbital action sanders shown here to selectively strip the top coats off them. It's slow work but it's usually worth the effort to preserve original primers if they are in good shape.

Primers — The Foundation of Any Refinishing Endeavor

The old primers that were available for refinishing were made with nitrocellulose binders and were wonderfully sandable due to their hardness. They weren't very durable because they were very brittle, but if the thickness of their applications was kept at reasonable levels, they soldiered on under paint for extended tours of duty. They did not have the "fast build" of modern primer-surfacers because they were blended with fairly low levels of solids. At recommended thinning, they were comparatively watery, which is probably why they were such good primers.

There are only two ways that a primer can bond to a base metal — mechanically and chemically. The old primers, with the exception of the (then) exotic zinc chromate based primers, achieved adhesion purely by mechanical bonding. What this means is that primer infiltrates the nooks, crannies, and crevices of sanded base metal in a way that mechanically locks the primer to that jagged terrain.

The trouble with the old primers — from a modern body shop practice point of view — is that they were sprayed thin and didn't build fast enough to do much filling without many applications and a lot of dry ("flash") time between applications. With the introduction of modern acrylic paints, a revolution in primers occurred. It gave us "fast build" or "high solid content" primers (now called "primer-surfacers") based on acrylic binders. These primers saved time, and the less brittle acrylic binders added a certain durability to them. I have never thought that the mechanical adhesion of these thicker primers is as good as that of the older, thinner primers. Their very thickness prevents them from interlocking effectively with the topography of base metals. Read on; this story has a happy ending.

In the last decade, the major paint companies have introduced "etching" primers (usually based on zinc phosphate additives and one-part or two-part epoxy binders). These are truly miraculous primers that bond to base metal like nothing available before ever did. The secret is that they are thin, tough, and chemically reactive with steel, aluminum and galvanizing. This produces chemical bonds *and* mechanical bonds. My experience with R-M's zinc phosphate primer, "Zip" (product 834), leads me to believe that its bond to metal will probably survive anything short of a nuclear detonation at ground zero. This class of primers (I would tend to call them "pre-primers" because they are not sandable and should have conventional acrylic based primer-surfacers applied over them for filling and sanding) is so good on steel, aluminum, and galvanizing that it is foolish to paint a car in restoration without them if a bare metal substratum surface is involved.

Unlike the old zinc chromate primers, which were available for aluminum and even steel, the new zinc phosphate primers are relatively inexpensive and are very easy to apply. It is best to apply them thinly, and you must not cut into them when you sand or you will have a terrible mess. But the adhesion of these new etching primers is out of this world. Because these reactive primers are designed to react with base metals, you must *not* use a conversion coating or metal conditioner when you use them. I give them five stars on a four-star scale. They're that good. They are also waterproof so the problem of moisture getting through primer before you apply top coats is eliminated.

You should use a good, sandable acrylic primer-surfacer over etching primers. This will give you a surface to sand. It is also a good idea to change primer colors (red to gray, or gray to red) after the first coat of primer-surfacer has been sprayed on an etching primer. That first "guide coat" of primer-surfacer will warn you to back off when you get near to cutting into the etching primer as you sand the primer-surfacer. Avoid using the "quick and dirty" non-sanding primers, such as Corlar, because restoration work will always involve sanding primer coats to get a good, smooth, properly contoured surface for top coats to build on. A few nitrocellulose primers are still available and are probably the best sanding primers you can get, but their durability suffers from their hardness, and the better acrylic primers produce very sandable surfaces. There's more discussion about how to sand primers in the next chapter.

Facilities and Equipment

The facilities and equipment required for refinishing are pretty straightforward. You will need a good environment to spray in, a good source of clean, dry, non-pulsating air, and a good spray gun. Depending on the climate where you live and the nature of the construction of your workplace, and maybe your skill in negotiating, this setup will cost you anywhere from $600 to $25,000. Let's take the components of a good spraying environment and setup, one at a time.

An adequate environment for spraying means a clean area where you can severely curtail or eliminate dust fall, and where you can force enough air through to provide a minimum of one air change every minute or so. Such an area must be well-lighted and absolutely separated from any open flame or source of ignition spark. Control of temperature must be reasonably constant, and humidity control is highly desirable. Most of this suggests a spray booth or something very close to it. Yet very credible spraying can be done in a clean, force ventilated area of a garage *if* dust can be kept out of it and if the floor can be kept wet to suppress dust. In some climates, winter spraying means the use of a huge furnace ("air makeup unit") to provide ignition free, warm incoming air to replace the air that is extracted by ventilating fans. Take heart because there are some body shops that do credible work and have spray booths (mandated by state and local regulations), but that tend not to use them because of the

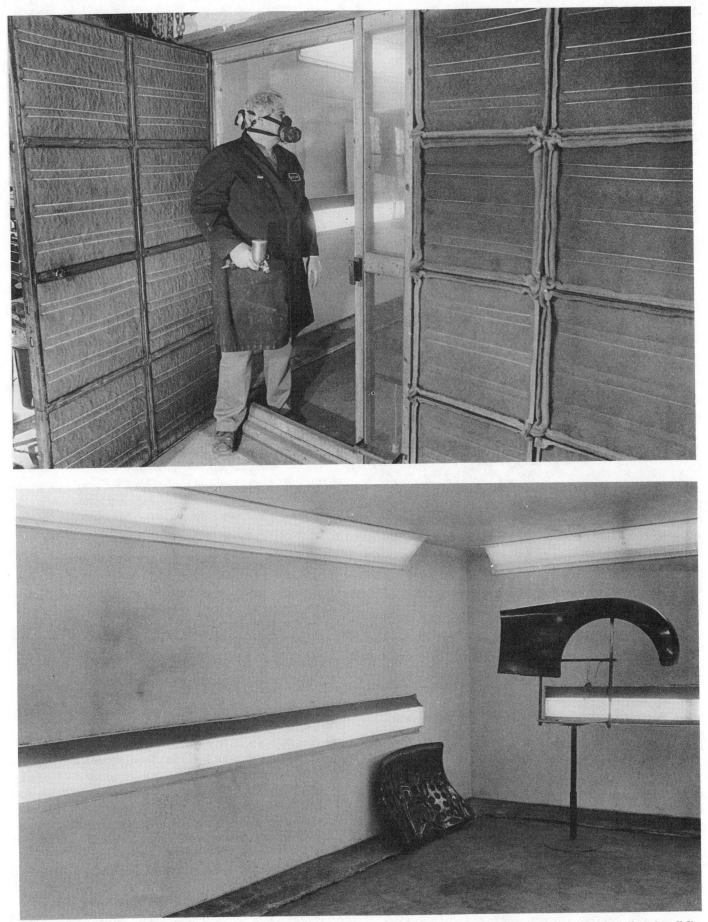

This not particularly modern spray booth is home-built. It uses the latest "sticky filter" technology and is dustproof and well lit. The air change interval is about 45 seconds. Some of the new high tech, down draft spray booths with conditioned air go for more than $40,000. But that's production painting stuff. Old car restorers can easily make do with much less sophisticated facilities.

difficult logistics of moving cars in and out of them. Instead, at 4:00 p.m. every day, they hose down the floor and spray everything in sight. What they don't directly spray, they usually hit with enough overspray so that they might as well have sprayed it directly. There's a lot of cleanup in these propositions! Anyway, this reality points to the possibility of spraying without a spray booth and saving between the $600 and $40,000 that a contemporary spray booth costs. An important item that some good spray booths provide is adequate light. This is critically important as it is impossible to do good work when you cannot see what you are doing. Any usable spray environment must have adequate light.

You'll need six or seven SCFM (Standard Cubic Feet Per Minute) of clean, dry air to spray cars — more if you choose to use one of the marvelous new low overspray HVLP (High Volume Low Pressure) spray guns. For conventional spray equipment, this translates into at least a two-horsepower compressor with at least a 20-gallon tank. A five-horse, two-stage job with a 60- or 80-gallon tank will serve you much better and will comfortably handle HVLP spray guns. Don't try to spray restoration finishes with a one-horsepower compressor with a 12-gallon air tank. It will probably add so much oil, water, grunge, and air pulsation to your spray air that it will be all but impossible to do high quality work.

This five-horsepower compressor is about the minimum air pump that will give you really good spray air. Smaller compressors can be made to do the job, but the results are sometimes ragged.

Compressors used for painting should have their tanks drained daily, and they should be connected to one or more air filters or "transformers." The "coalescing" filters offered by Hankenson, LeMan, Balston, Van Air, and other manufacturers are highly recommended. Since silicone contamination is one of the deadly enemies of good refinishing — it causes fish eyes — it is highly recommended that a compressor oil be used that is free of silicones. Most industrial grade compressor oils use silicone foam suppressants, which accounts for a lot of the trouble that body shops have with fish eyes — they come with the spray air. Be sure to use a compressor oil that

This air transformer and coalescing filter setup used to provide adequate air filtration for spraying the old paints. Modern finishes are much less tolerant of air contamination and moisture, and you should figure on a desiccant, deliquescent, or refrigeration air purifying system if you expect to do really top quality work.

does not include a silicone foam suppressant because some compressor oil will inevitably get past any compressor's rings and into your air. The best filters may not be able to completely remove this silicone.

In addition to clean and dry air, adequate and consistent pressure is critically important in the application of modern paint systems. Air pressure that is too low will cause inadequate atomization of paint, which results in orange peel and other paint problems. Air pressure that is too high will cause solvents to evaporate too rapidly and before the paint hits the target. In enamels this can cause orange peel as the high velocity air and solvent disrupt the curing process of the coats under the one that you are spraying. Never rely on your compressor's air pressure gauge or on your transformer air pressure gauge for accurate indications of the air pressure at your gun. An inexpensive tailstock regulator and gauge will tell you exactly what the air pressure is entering your gun and allow you to effectively regulate it. Air pressure for spraying should be kept within paint manufacturers' recommended limits. Good painters generally favor the low to middle range of these recommended spray pressures.

Painters used to be divided on the merits of Binks

For many professional painters, the Binks 7 spray gun (right) was the reigning champion of lacquer guns. The (counterfeit) Eclipse touch-up gun on the left was preferred by many painters for spotting in finishes to repair damage. More modern spray guns have replaced these old standbys but they are still very good and very usable guns.

(models 7 and 62) and DeVilbiss spray guns. A few favored Marsten, Sharpe, and the wonderful but strange Bendix Sicmo (now greatly improved and sold under the Croix name) guns. In recent years, Japanese and Taiwanese copies of the Binks 7 and other "classic" guns have proliferated. I have used the copies and I own examples of the originals. I think that the originals are better but hardly enough better to justify the price difference between as little as $25 for the copies, and over $150 for the originals. If your use is occasional, the copies should do nicely. The wonderful new HVLP spray guns by Binks, DeVillbis, Mattson, Croix, Accuspray, Sharpe and a few others will set you back between $400 and $1,000 a copy.

Until recently, almost all good automotive refinishing spray guns used a siphon principal to draw paint into their air streams. More recently, many painters have been experimenting with gravity-fed guns and pressure-fed guns (HVLP), and with two-quart, belt-hung pressure feed pots to feed their conventional guns. I think that all of these innovations offer advantages to painters — in some cases, major advantages.

Air-driven stirring attachments for spray gun paint cups are nice if you are going to spray a lot of cars, but are hardly necessary for occasional general automotive painting. Gun heaters and the use of "hot" lacquer and enamel should be discouraged for safety reasons. By "hot," I refer to the old technique of spraying lacquer and enamel at 160° Fahrenheit to reduce overspray and economize on thinner and reducer. HVLP equipment will accomplish the same purpose and will not involve the fire and health hazards that are inherent in spraying finishes at elevated temperatures. It is a good idea to raise the temperature of the paint that you spray from 20° to 30° Fahrenheit above the ambient temperature in your spray environment because this is the range of the drop in spray temperature that occurs from atomization and

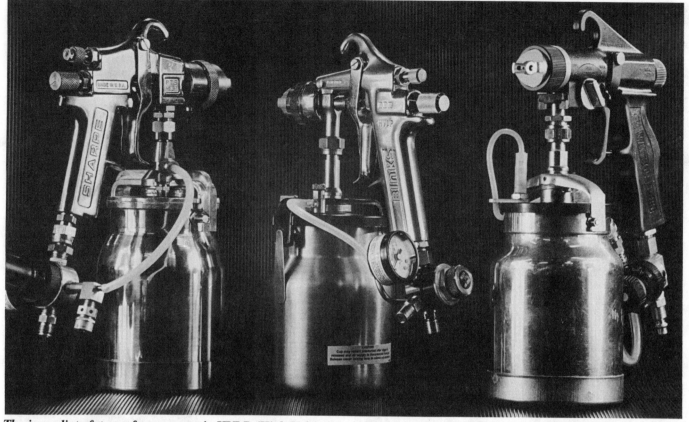

The immediate future of spray guns is HVLP (High Volume Low Pressure). The guns in this photo (left to right) are Sharpe, Binks, and Mattson HVLP guns. They are better than any of the older, non-HVLP guns, and some of those were very good. HVLP guns use a lot of compressed air but they do a great job atomizing paint, and they produce much less overspray than conventional guns. That means a healthier spray environment and less pollution from painting.

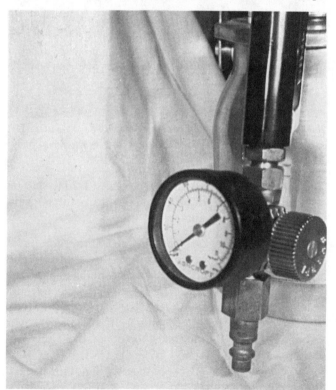

An inexpensive tailstock air pressure regulator, such as the one shown here, can be very helpful in maintaining consistent air pressure. These "cheater" valves help to address the issue of air pressure drop in the long hoses that feed air to spray guns.

Here's an important painting tip. No matter how well you apply pre-primers, primers, and top coats, your sheet metal will always be vulnerable to attack from its backside. Always use the best products that you can find to protect these areas, or nasty rust will come right through your panels.

evaporation of the solvents between your gun and your target. Heating paint beyond this point is hazardous and is ill-advised.

The latest thing in industrial painting is electrostatic attraction. Surely some high-buck restoration shop will advertise this innovation in the near future, but it is beyond what is necessary to do very good work.

CHAPTER 26:

Automotive Refinishing, Part II

There is something almost athletic about automotive refinishing when it is compared to most other aspects of restoration endeavors. It's not only that you have to be alert to move smartly around a car when you paint it, you will also have to call up knowledge, skill, coordination, and experience to do this work well. Unlike mechanical restoration work, where you can sort of poke away at things at your own pace, painting tends to impose its own schedules on you. Frequently, several things have to happen at the same time or in a very close sequence. With today's complex painting systems, the need for precision is great. There can be times when you may want to push the "panic button" as sags, runs, or other disasters occur. This is normal for beginners, but when you get the gist of the thing, the disasters should be small and infrequent. Painting simply requires a disciplined approach to the work and the ability to deal with special problems as they arise. The more you paint and the more different materials and systems you paint with, the easier it gets. When it becomes natural, you can go after perfection.

The simplest prescription against panic is to attend to the details as you go along. This doesn't entirely preclude the possibility of local disasters such as contamination getting into a freshly painted area, but at least it raises the odds in your favor and helps to rule out careless mistakes — the ones that you can avoid. In painting, the trouble that you don't get into is the trouble that you don't have to get out of.

Various and Assorted Matters of Strategy

The war of restoration refinishing is won or lost on the battlefield of small details. Small early mistakes can mushroom into catastrophic events if you don't perspire over the small details. Take, for example, the matter of the contamination of paint from the surface below it. It is always best to wash a car or repair area with detergent and water, and to rinse it thoroughly with water before you paint it. You follow this wash by wiping down the surface with a special wax and silicone remover *before*

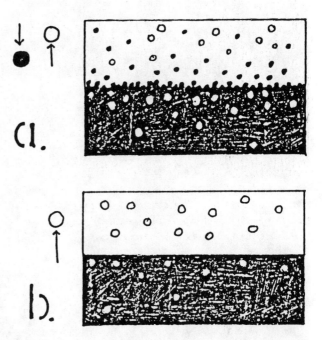

With enamels (a), each coat intermingles with the one below it, and this means that problems in one coat tend to create problems in the next one. Lacquer coats (b) don't intermingle that way and are easier to repair if you have a problem when you spray them.

sanding and painting it. Finally, after sanding and before priming or painting, you do a final wipe-down with wax and silicone remover.

If this regimen is followed and each step is invested with an adequate amount of washing and the use of clean wiping rags or towels, there should be no contamination problem in your priming and painting. If, however, contaminants, like silicone, are not removed in the initial wipe-down with solvent, they will be sanded into the old finish and can come back to cause fish eyes in the primer and in the finish. This can be a very difficult problem to deal with when you are spraying a car, and it would have been better to have prevented the problem with a thorough initial washing so that it could truly be "the trouble *you didn't* get into."

Solvent cleaners such as PrepSol (Dupont) and Pre-Kleeno (R-M) are designed to remove all of the contami-

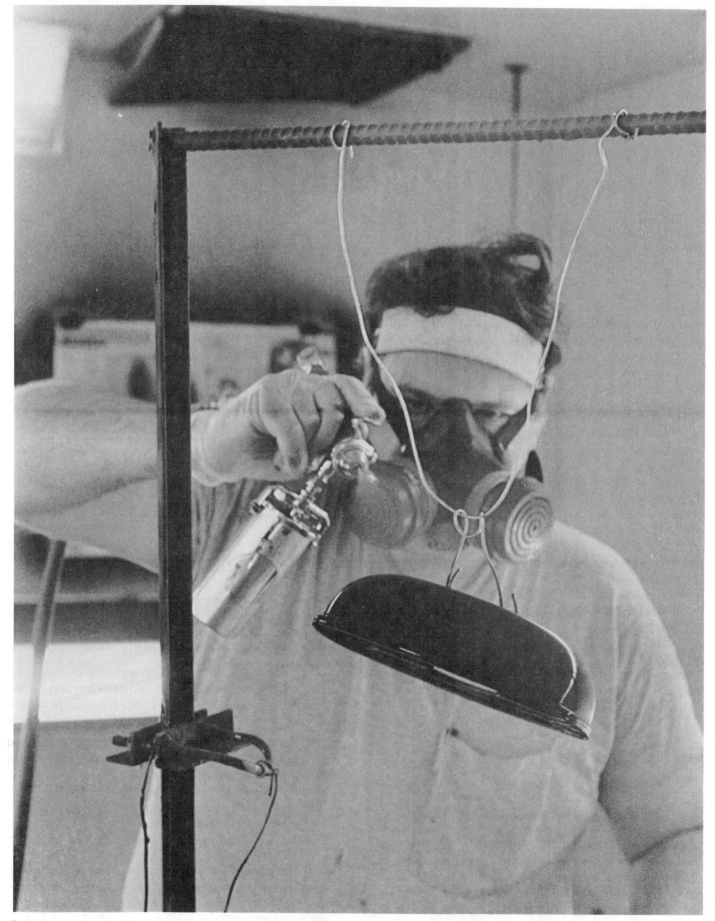

Painting involves building a finish from metal or from undercoats. What you get in the end depends largely on the things that you did before you applied the top coats.

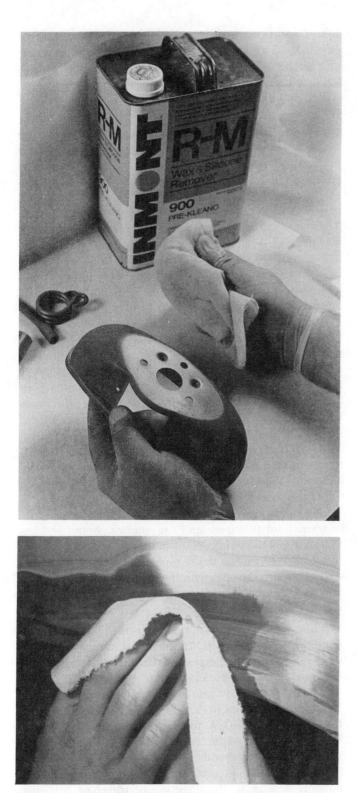

This stone damage is pretty severe. It could be spotted in, chip-by-chip, but it is probably easier and better to paint the whole lower body or maybe the whole car.

Often the number of these areas will dictate sanding the whole car or panel to bare metal. If this is not the case, you must feather edge sand each defect. There can be a great temptation to try to talk yourself out of a few minor spots ("it'll never show"), but this will come back to haunt you later. At best, it will look terrible to leave defects that come through and show in your freshly painted surface; at worst, the paint will tend to lift off underlying finish areas that are not properly sanded, primed, and leveled.

Or take the matter of cut-throughs. Sometimes the best of us on the best of days sands through primer and down to shiny metal. "Oh, c'mon, how can a little spot like that hurt? What? Dirty a clean spray gun just to prime that little spot? And then have to wait and wait for the primer to dry. Then sand it. Then clean the gun. Then you are back where you started. How much can it hurt to paint over it? After all, there's primer all around it."

Well, you will always lose in the long run if you try to paint over cut-throughs without repriming. The deities of painting know where every cut-through is, and they always couple with the demons of rust to make sure that the most innocent of these raises a rust bubble no smaller than your thumb nail. Don't mess with the paint deities and the rust demons or "you'll be sorry."

And while we are on the unpleasant topic of cut-throughs, it should be mentioned that whenever you encounter a rust spot or nick, it must be sanded to bare metal. Whenever you encounter a cut-through it must be sanded to a feather edge. Both of these defects should be treated with a one-part or two-part metal conditioner/conversion coating system and primed before painting.

Do fenders really have to come off to paint a car? Isn't there a strategy to avoid this? Well, if the paint is in basically good condition and the fender seams are factory filled (almost always associated with welded-on fenders), you can sometimes get away with not removing fenders. But the fender seams are always suspect and must be inspected closely for pending trouble. If, on the other hand,

Whether you are painting a taillight housing, spotting in a fender, or painting a whole car, be sure to wipe down the areas that you will paint with a good cleaning solvent just before you spray.

nants that tend to disrupt paint. They also soften underlying finishes to promote the adhesion of succeeding coats of finish or primer. They should always be used on any surface that has sat for more than 24 hours since the previous coat of primer or paint was applied.

Sometimes you will have occasion to paint a surface that has numerous chips, rust spots, and other defects.

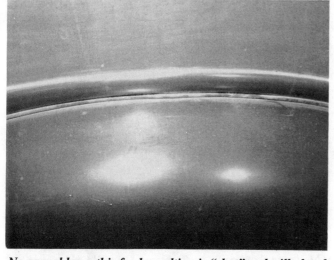

No appeal here; this fender welting is "shot" and will absorb moisture and ruin the paint and metal adjacent to it. The fenders on this car have to come off to paint the car.

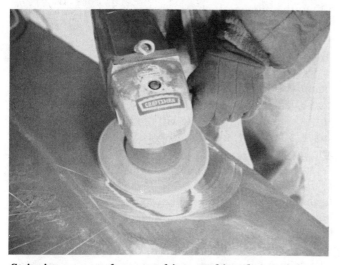

Stripping a car to bare metal is something that most restorers would like to avoid, but sometimes it's necessary.

the construction of a car involves the use of fender welting on fenders that are bolted to body panels, *you must remove the fenders before you paint.* There is no way to paint up to fender welting, nor should you waste much time trying to find one. By the time paint is defective, the welting will be defective, either where it is visible or in the seam where it can't be seen. It must be replaced when a car is painted.

It is possible to paint up to trim, and there are some tricks to accomplish this that are noted later in this chapter. However, if it is at all possible to remove trim before you paint, it is always desirable to do this. All kinds of contamination and frequently rust lurk behind old trim. The only time that you shouldn't remove trim before you paint is when trim cannot be replaced, and removal entails the likelihood of destroying it.

Sometimes, restoration work involves spot repair. This, of course, only applies if you are lucky enough to have a collector car with only one spot or area or a few spots or areas that need attention. Some colors and some paints are so difficult to match that refinishing a whole car be-

comes necessary, even for the repair of only a spot or panel. More often you can make a spot or panel repair that will be indistinguishable from the rest of the car. But you need a good underlying strategy and a whole lot of skill to pull this off.

The most obvious gremlin lurking out there in these situations is the matter of color match. There are so many reasons that paint can be mismatched that it amazes me that it ever actually matches. The paint that you are trying to match by formula may have been off in the first place, or the paint that you are matching it with may be off color. This is usually the result of mixing error. Then, too, the existing paint may have faded since the car was painted. When formula matching fails or cannot be attempted for lack of a valid, original formula or materials, you go to spectrometer matching (very limited availability) or hand matching (limited availability). Matches attempted with the handy-dandy little "tint" kits that are offered by paint manufacturers usually produce a color that is, well, recognizable as the one that you are trying to match — no more. Real hand matches are the province of strange, old men who live in the back rooms of a very few paint supply stores. I think that these individuals are kept under lock and key because their talents are so rare and useful that they dare not be let out into the sunlight. I know that our own favorite little-old-can-match-any-color-perfectly-for-twenty-five- bucks-plus-the-cost-of-the-paint-man lives in a city almost 100 miles from here, and I am glad to drive the distance and pay the $25 every time I need a color match.

One sure way to miss a color match is to buy your paint at some joint that uses apes for counter people and lets the apes mix the paint. You can usually spot these joints in advance of buying badly mixed paint from them. It's easy. They are the ones with the messy mixing equipment and the counter-people who say, "ya know, ya know," a lot.

When you are trying to spot paint in or paint only one panel on a car, the best strategy is to make your blend where the eye doesn't expect to see it. This is because, for the most part, the human eye sees what it expects to see or wants to see. Have you ever seen lightning strike up? Of course not. Things fall out of the sky, and you expect that. Lightning strikes down from the heavens, right? Wrong! Ninety-plus percent of all visible lightning strikes upward from the ground to the sky, and, in any case, it all happens so fast that the unaided human eye could not possibly determine the direction of travel of lightning. But it always *seems* to strike down because that's the way it *should* go and that's what you *expect* to see. That is, until you read this.

Let's apply this concept of expectation and perception to auto body work. If your idea of panel painting is to paint only a door, a hood, or a fender, then your color match will have to be absolutely perfect and that is unlikely. If the door, hood, or fender that you paint is just a little bit off the shade that it has to match in the surrounding panels, your eye will instantly detect the problem at the panel edges. If, on the other hand, you run the blend line in an irregular fashion into the adjacent pan-

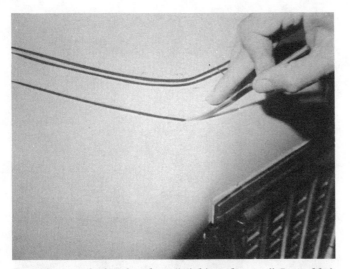

Sometimes painting involves "tricking the eye." I wouldn't blend a spot repair at the pin stripes on this car, but the horizontal/vertical foldover just below it would be a good place to hide a slight color mismatch if it occurred.

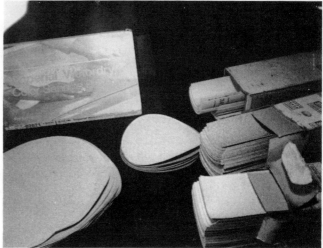

Sanding backups and abrasives come in very wide variety. Some work better than others for specific jobs.

els, your eye (any eye) will not notice it because a color change of that sort could be caused by any number of optical and lighting variations. In the same vein, if you blend paint near a point where a panel has a near 90° bend or intersects trim, your eye will have trouble detecting the blend and mismatch because it expects lighting variations to produce color change in such areas. All of this amounts to a necessary kind of trickery that can be employed to hide slight mismatches. It is a good insurance policy even if you achieve a near perfect match. That's because no match is or will ever remain perfect. Remember, even if they initially match, old paint and fresh paint will tend towards a mismatch as they age. This is because they are aging from different starting points and they lack perfect chemical identities and environmental histories.

One sure tip-off to a spot repair is a failure to level the repair area. Remember, when you spot in paint, you have to bring the area that you have sanded and feather edged back up to level, or it will stand out like the proverbial "sore thumb." Panel surface variations of as little as 0.003 inch or 0.004 inch can be seen easily, particularly if they occur in a small enough area.

A very good strategy in blending a panel or spot repair is to use a mist coating of uniforming finish to melt overspray into the underlying paint. This involves a very fast shuffle or the use of two spray guns. It sounds like a real potato race, but with some practice it will come naturally. Major paint manufacturers provide detailed instructions and materials for this strategy.

Sanding

Sanding is a subtle art. If it is not done correctly, the deficit will show through any amount of good paint that you may apply. Mostly, good sanding involves good manual techniques, attention to detail, and clean habits.

The choice of abrasive is important. Silica carbide sandpaper is best for sanding paint and primer, and aluminum oxide-based papers are best for sanding metal. When paint is sanded, a wet technique with a "wet-or-dry" type paper is usually best — though some painters advocate dry sanding in some situations. Never sand with your bare fingers or the pressure points on them will put ridges into what you are sanding. Machine sanding is okay for rough work, such as scuffing with a DA sander, but finishing work must be done by hand.

If you try to strip paint with such boulder-type abrasives as 24 grit or 36 grit, you will have scratches to fill that require excessive effort or filler. It's okay to use this stuff where you know that you will be using filler over it and it gives the filler something to hang on to, but I wouldn't use it on sheet metal that is only going to be primed and painted. To strip paint in that situation, 80 and 100 grit abrasives are plenty rough enough. Because good restoration work is not vitally concerned with production schedules, it is best to use sanding grits for rough work in the 80 to 100 range, certainly never less than 50. At each sanding stage, a grit must be chosen that is capable of removing the scratches caused by the last grit that was used. This removal must be complete and efficient. It

Modern sanding abrasives are infinitely better than the ones used when many collectible cars were built. The grits are more consistent and there are some very fine grits available these days.

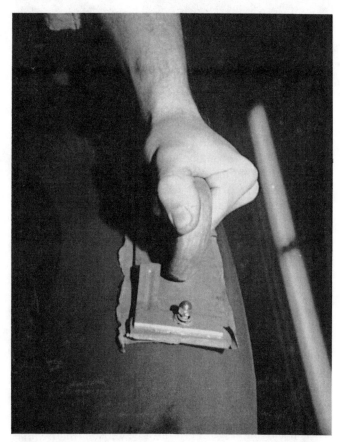

Always back sandpaper up with a board, foam pad or hard pad. Otherwise you will sand finger ridges into your work.

may take three or four grits to get from 80 or 100 to 400 or 600. If you try to abbreviate this process, you will either take more time than necessary to produce a satisfactory result, or you will produce an unsatisfactory result.

Because sanding is based on the averaging tendency of random patterns, make sure that your patterns are random. Straight line sanding is best, but be sure to vary the contact patch of sandpaper and panel to avoid ridging paint or primer. Use a foam or hard rubber sanding block or pad to back your abrasive paper. Inspect your work regularly by wiping it clean with a damp rag or sponge, and then go on to the next (finer) grit. When you change grits, be sure to change backing pads and sanding water, and be sure to clean up completely after each grit. Failure to do this will produce abrasive cross contamination, and you will put isolated scratches of the previous, coarser grit into the work that you are now doing with a finer grit.

Parallel, lengthwise strokes work best for most sanding. Circular strokes have some application in feather edging but generally should be avoided when you do general sanding. An occasional wipe of Ivory soap across your wet-or-dry sandpaper will make it last much longer and will give you a better feel for the surface that you are wet sanding. Never use white gas or any other volatile solvent to wet sand.

Raised edges or corners are a particular hazard when you are sanding — they like to cut through. You can

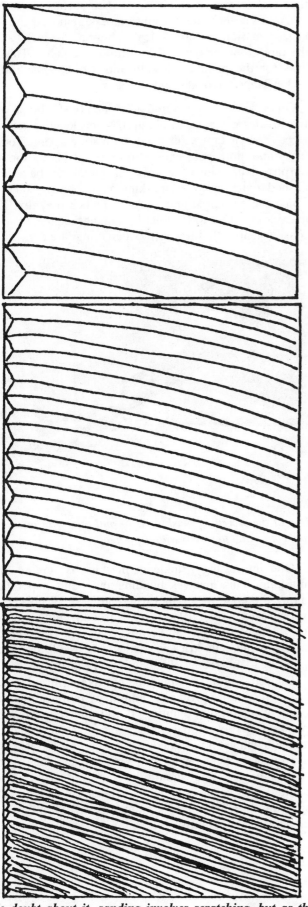

This 36 grit sanding disc will remove finishes fast, but you can do a lot of damage to metal with it. I prefer tamer grits for paint removal, say in the 80 to 100 range.

avoid this by spending less time on these troublesome areas and more on flatter areas. Ultimately, the best leveling with sandpaper is done in the early stages of sanding with a board sander. One neat trick in the final stages of leveling the primer under a finish is to wrap a paint mixing stick in sand paper and run it down the surface under three fingers. This will give you a very fine feel for what is underneath. Never try to determine surface level with your bare hand on any painted surface. If you do this on primer, you will contaminate it and, in any case, you will not get a good idea of surface condition because of the friction drag of your fingers. A rag under your fingers tips changes the whole picture and will expose every defect in a surface.

One way to determine primer film thickness and how close you are to cut-through disaster as you sand is to use a "guide coat" of primer. This involves changing primer colors after the first or second coat. When your sanding takes you to the color change, you know how close you are to what is under the primer.

Masking

Masking a car does not involve the subtlety that sanding does, but errors in masking tend to be obvious and ugly. The first issue is tape. There must be 50 or more manufacturers of masking tape, and the major supplier of the stuff, 3M, must have 50 different grades of it. It is important to use a good grade of masking tape, one that is intended for body masking. Stick with known brands of tape. Masking paper comes in many variations of quality and effectiveness. You tend to get what you pay for. Cheap masking paper or, heaven forbid, newspaper used for masking tends to let paint bleed through — this is particularly true when the paper lays down flat against the surface of the masked area. When acrylic lacquer is used, newspaper will shed its ink just from the solvent vapors that contact it.

For masking tricky, curved areas, 3M has special mask-

No doubt about it, sanding involves scratching, but as the scratches become finer, a surface becomes smoother. That's why you work from coarse abrasives to fine abrasives when you sand.

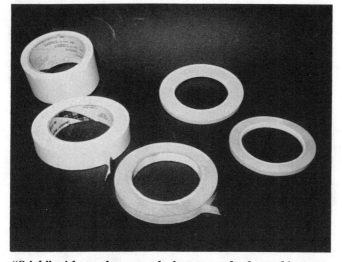

"Stick" with good tape and always use fresh masking tape. The two rolls of tape on the right are 3M's Fine Line and Plastic Tape, in 1/16-inch widths. They are great for making sharp corners.

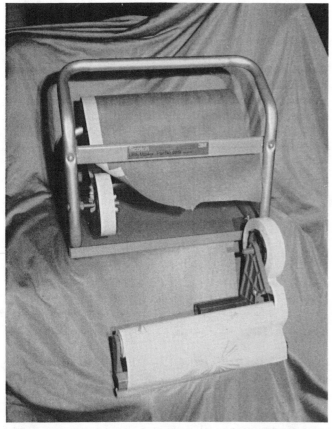

These "maskers" automatically apply tape to the edges of masking paper. They save time and are inexpensive to own.

ing tapes called "Free Line" (218) and "Plastic Tape" (471). Both of these will flex far more than conventional masking tape, and Scotch Plastic Tape can be bent in very sharp radius turns. It's just great for precision masking finicky trim. Both tapes come in widths from 1/16 inch to 3/4 inch. They are quite expensive. The trick in applying any masking tape is to pull it under tension around curves and force it into conformity smoothly. Don't pull tape too tight or it will fight its way back by losing adhesion.

When you mask rubber parts, be sure to clean them first with solvent as adhesion to their surfaces is uncertain if this is not done. If trim cannot be removed and you have to mask it, be sure to leave about a 1/32 inch gap in the tape from the base of the trim to the panel. This allows for the paint to flow in and avoids some rather "sticky" tape removal problems later.

On occasion, you will find a 3/4-inch bristle brush with the bristles cut back to about 1/2-inch length useful to force masking tape against what you are masking. Toothpicks and clothespin ends also come in handy for this purpose. Really intricate work can sometimes be accomplished with spray-on masking compounds, some of which can be scored and peeled off when they dry. This marvelous stuff is water soluble, and masked areas can be coaxed clean with water spray when things are dry.

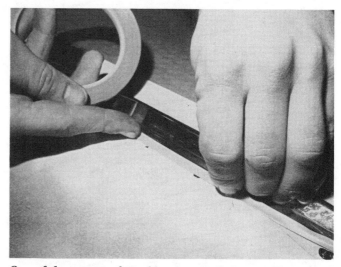

One of the secrets of masking is to pull tape with one hand and conform it to panels with the other.

One interesting wrinkle in masking is "crease line" masking. This involves bending tape and paper back along the edge of a panel to create a small pocket. As spray reaches the pocket it tends to eddy and produce a very nice blend that can be mist-coated or compounded into a panel. This trick is particularly usable if you are painting to metal edge that bends very sharply.

The removal of masking tape has likely caused the expression of more profanity than many more difficult aspects of restoration painting. If you pull tape when the paint on a panel is too wet, the paint will string and creep and you will get a rough edge. If you pull it too late, you are likely to peel paint back with the tape and get a ragged edge. Tape should be removed from panels painted with lacquers and acrylic lacquers an hour after spraying and from panels painted in alkyd and acrylic enamels after six hours.

The Great "24 Hand Rubbed Coats of Lacquer" Fallacy — Paint Film Thickness

For some reason, mostly ignorance, there is a notion abroad in the land that a pile of paint half an inch thick is somehow desirable in restoration painting. It is supposed to have visible "depth." While it is technically possible to

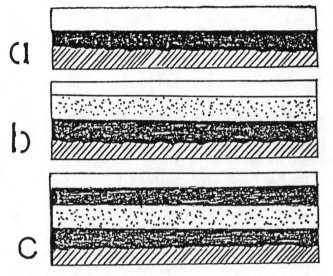

Modern paint systems are sandwiches. Figure "a" shows a simple primer and top coat sandwich. Figure "b" adds a clearcoat to the sandwich. By the time you get to "c," you have a club sandwich. Now you have an etching primer, a sanding primer, top coats, and clearcoats. Keep all of this in mind when you try to keep total finish thickness to eight or nine mils!

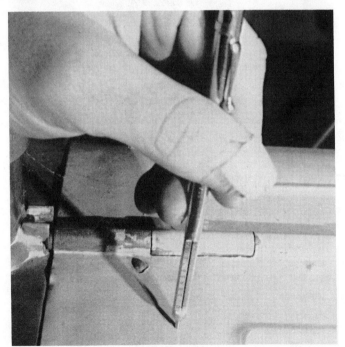

A paint thickness gauge, such as this old Tinsley gauge, will tell you pretty accurately how much paint there is on a panel. It's good information to have before you plan your strategy for refinishing.

stack 20 or more coats of paint onto an auto body, it is most clearly and distinctly *not* desirable to do so. It doesn't add to the appearance of the poor car that has to burden under this load, and it produces a finish that is not long destined for this world. One of the main causes of paint failure is that the thermal expansion characteristics of paint and its limited ductility combine to cause paint to fracture over extended periods. The thicker paint is, the greater the chances of thermal cycle failure. As paints get older and harder, they become increasingly vulnerable to this kind of failure.

In the days of the old, nitrocellulose lacquers, there was a factor of abrasion and chalking that meant that these paints had to be compounded fairly regularly to remove surface scratches and oxidized material. Each compounding or polishing removed paint and, eventually, you would cut through the finish. This situation suggested to some that a thick initial finish would be serviceable for a longer time. This was marginally true — up to the point that the paint cracked from its overly thick application.

In any case, modern acrylic-based paints, and particularly modern catalyzed enamels, are so tough and resistant to oxidation that it is hardly necessary to polish or compound them to maintain their luster. This means that a more durable, thinner application will survive the envi-

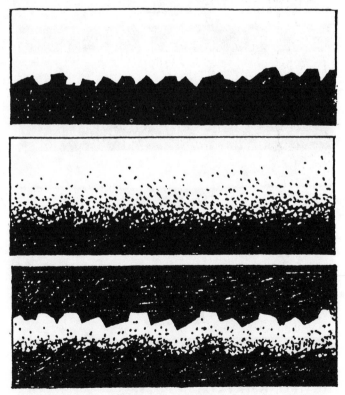

One of the basic strategic choices that you have to make in refinishing is what factor you will use to insure paint adhesion to metal and to undercoats. Mechanical adhesion (top) is okay and was the basis of paint adhesion for many years. The chemical adhesion of metal conditioners (middle graphic) was added to new cars by Ford many years ago. It was called "phosphatizing," and it is also available for refinishing. Modern etching primers (bottom graphic) provide for both mechanical and chemical adhesion.

ronment better. There is no reason to pile up acrylics and there is every reason not to. Modern catalyzed enamel systems will produce good results in as little as two coats, and there are painters who advocate holding their application to this level. Acrylic lacquers can be held to four or five coats with very acceptable results. Because restoration involves a more permanent proposition than simple repair, I would suggest spraying enamel in four or five coat applications and spraying acrylic lacquers in six to eight single-coat thicknesses or three or four double coats. In the case of enamels, the coats should be full and wet after the first coat, which is usually medium. In any case, the total thickness of paint on a car should not exceed 0.007 inch to 0.009 inch (seven to nine "mils"), and less than this may well be better. It is important that in observing this limit, the total film thickness be considered. This includes underlying paint and primer, sealers, primer surfacers, and, of course, the paint that you add.

The nonsense about "24 hand rubbed coats of lacquer" means that time and money have been wasted and quality has been compromised. At best, it means that paint has been used where lead or primer-surfacer should have been used for filling. At worst, it means that a very fragile and short-lived finish has been produced.

One place where unnecessary paint often accumulates is in priming. I have seen primer applied so thick that it must have taken 10 wet coats to produce the accumulation. Primer is not a substitute for body work. Rather than pile it up, use a guide coat to keep it honest.

Putties — A Matter of a Shady Reputation

You remember in high school there were some people who seemed okay, but who had "bad reputations" for cutting up. Often they reformed their ways but the reputations lingered. Spot and glazing putties are like that. They have terrible reputations and are often assumed to be guilty of causing any problem that occurs in a finish. Actually, these materials are not bad in themselves. They are just endlessly misused, and they get blamed when it is the practitioner on the other end of the squeegee who should take the rap.

Putty has its obvious limitations. It is not body filler and is much too brittle and shrinkable to use for that purpose. It also has very little "holdout," which means that

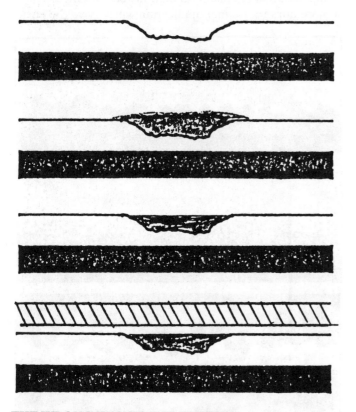

THE WRONG WAY TO USE PUTTIES

(a) Shows damage in primer coat to be repaired with putty.

(b) Damage has been filled with spot putty, but putty was not allowed to dry thoroughly.

(c) The putty was sanded level with the panel but continued to dry.

(d) The putty dried completely after it was painted and it sank below the surface of the panel, pulling the paint in with it. The result was an ugly depression in the finish.

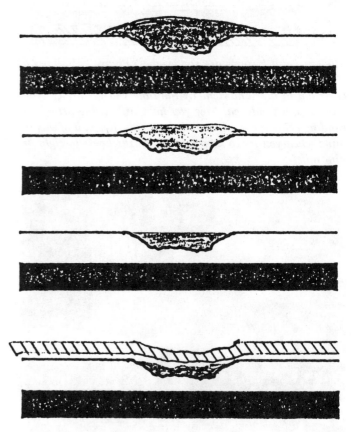

THE RIGHT WAY TO USE PUTTIES

(a) This time, enough putty was applied to the defect to provide for shrinkage.

(b) The putty was allowed enough time to dry and to completely shrink before it was sanded level with the panel.

(c) Then it was sanded level, but it didn't continue to shrink.

(d) The paint applied over the putty remained level with the panel.

This sequence of photographs shows the application of glazing putty to fill some minor sand scratches in the primer on a taillight housing. In this case, the putty was applied and wet sanded. Then the part was sprayed with a sealer and "denubbed" with a Scotchbrite pad. Sealing is one way to guarantee that there will be no sand scratches in a finish. Note the use of surgical gloves to protect the primer from skin oils.

top coat finishes tend to sink into it. Still, it can be used effectively to fill deep scratches and pinholes up to about 0.040 inch, provided that two cautions are observed. First, putty must be allowed to dry completely before it is coated over, or it will gas and shrink in a way that destroys anything that you try to put over it. Second, its holdout is so poor that it requires covering with a sealer or primer-sealer before you can attempt to paint color coats over it. Dry times with putty can be up to a day or two if you elect the maximum depth of 0.040 inch. Glaz-

ing putty differs from spot putty only in that the former is compounded with 80 percent solids and the latter contains 90 percent solids. Putties are designed to dry as rapidly as possible, given their thickness. Many of them are still compounded in the format of nitrocellulose lacquers with extremely high solids content.

Spray Guns

The choice of spray gun is an important aspect of finishing. Some guns are of questionable quality and some are very good. Different guns have different characteristics that make them work better or worse in varying situations. The nozzle and air cap setup for a good enamel gun will probably not work well with lacquer. Guns with sharp cutoff patterns have applications where guns with softer pattern edges do not, and *vice versa*. Ultimately, you will need different guns for different applications, but, in the interim, the different specification fluid tips and air caps that are available from most manufacturers for their guns will cover a range of applications with a single gun. Always use fluid tips and air caps that are designed for the purposes that you are pursuing.

Spray guns come in an astounding variety of sizes, designs, and qualities. A general purpose gun (right) and a spotting gun (left) are shown here.

In the hierarchy of spray guns, the lowly primer gun is at the bottom. Primer is highly abrasive to the insides of spray guns and very difficult to clean out completely. It is good practice to demote your worst gun to this fate and, when it is too shabby for even that, bury it decently.

The wings on a spray gun air cap are generally used in a horizontal position, which produces a spray pattern that is vertical. However, for some jobs it is very advantageous to turn the wings to a vertical position and to use a horizontal pattern. One problem that used to routinely afflict spray guns was that their cup vents dripped. Every siphon gun has to have an air vent in the lid that allows air in to replace the paint that is evacuated from the gun cup. This, of course, *only* pertains to siphon-fed guns. Air vents used to be an ever-present hazard to good painting because when you tilted a gun down to paint a horizontal surface such as a hood or roof, paint dripped out of the vent onto the surface that you were painting. About 15 years ago dripless cups by Binks and Marsten arrived on the scene. This type of cup has now pretty much replaced

The latest thing in car spraying is HVLP (High Volume Low Pressure) guns. They use low atomizing pressure and produce very little overspray. The gun on the left is the HVLP type, and the one on the right is conventional. Note the huge "fan" holes in the air cap on the HVLP gun.

Other than the introduction of HVLP spraying in recent years, spray guns changed remarkably little from the late 1930s to the 1980s.

the old "drippers." That is almost entirely good, except that the dripless air vents require a little extra attention when you clean a gun. Extra attention should also be paid to the cup gasket when you clean a gun because paint that lurks there can ruin color matches. Guns should never be stored with the cup lid secured tightly on the cup gasket. Leave the lid-securing handle or lever just slightly tightened beyond contact. This saves lid gaskets.

It is important that spray guns be cleaned scrupulously and thoroughly after each use. Never put off cleaning a gun that has been used until the next day. Acrylic lacquer thinner or gun cleaner is the best solvent for this purpose, and repeated shaking, wiping, and spraying of solvent are the best ways to clean a gun. When your gun is almost completely clean, you can loosen its air cap a few threads

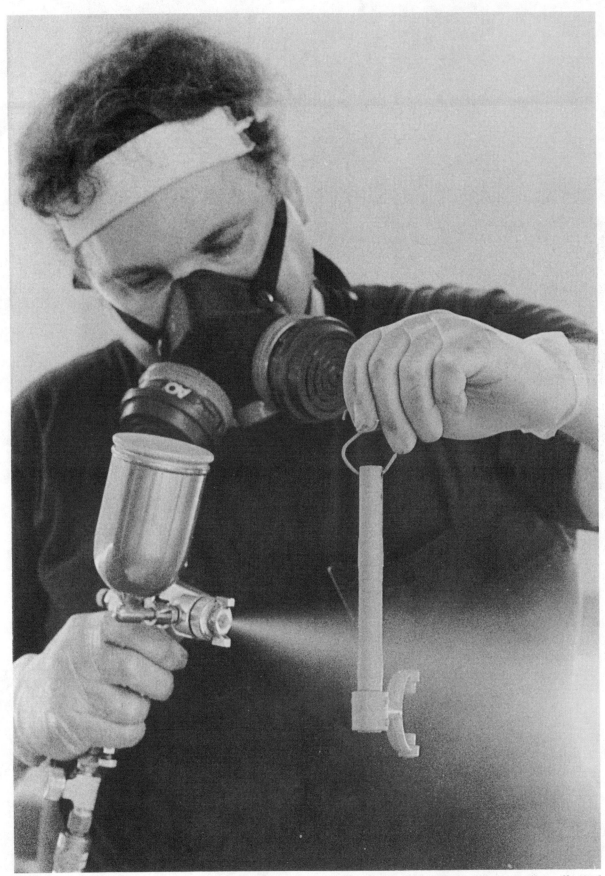

This gravity type gun is ideal for painting small to medium-sized parts and panels. Its pattern is too small to effectively paint a whole car.

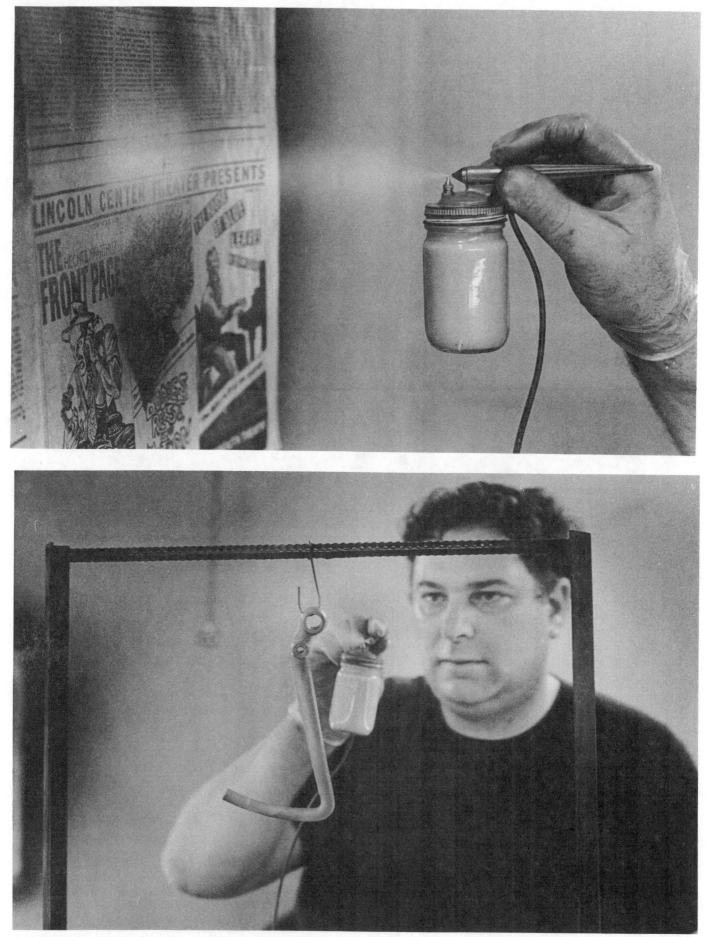

An inexpensive gun, such as this one, can be very handy for spraying the intricacies of small parts. The only trouble is it has a round spray pattern, and that can take some getting used to.

After you finish using and cleaning a spray gun, always lubricate its shafts with light oil where they enter its packings.

Adjusting a spray gun takes some practice. First you set the pattern (top knob), then you set the material flow to fill the pattern that you have set (bottom knob).

and hold a rag over the gun tip. Then spray out some solvent to force air and solvent down through the gun.

Never immerse a gun in solvent, and avoid the automatic gun cleaning devices that tend to do this unless you have a modern gun with packings that are designed to take this kind of cleaning. The problem with immersion is that the gun packings will be wetted and dried out to the point where they won't work. The outside of a gun can be cleaned with a bristle brush and solvent. After cleaning, the packings on a gun's air and material needles should be lubricated with a drop of light oil and tightened only finger tight. Finally, it is important not to lay a gun on its side before it is cleaned. This can cause paint to run back into air passages and plug your gun. Be particularly careful if you are using catalyzed enamels or polyurethane paints because they have the potential of setting up and ruining a gun if they are not cleaned out of it during the period of their "pot lives."

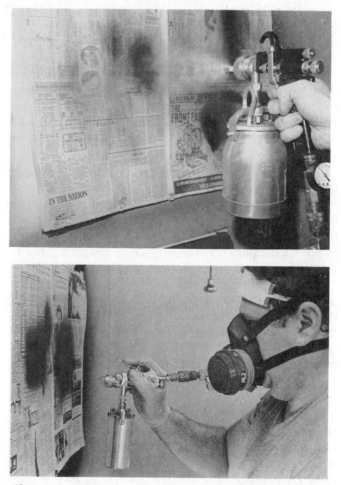

Spray Guns: Adjustment and Technique

It is important to always remember the goals of spray painting and to create conditions that naturally lead to the fulfillment of these goals. They are to spray in a way that causes paint to flow out in a uniform coat that has no runs or sags and that has minimum effects from overspray. Part of success in the attainment of these goals involves the choice of paint, thinner, retarder, and additives. Part of it involves gun adjustment and technique. What you do with a spray gun can usually make the products you are using work or not work.

There are basically five factors that you can control on a gun. These affect the amount of paint deposited, its format, and the shape of the deposit pattern. The first factor is air pressure, which controls the degree to which a gun atomizes paint. The thicker the paint is, the more

Always spray a test pattern with your gun before you attempt to spray a part or panel. And always remember that if you spray your test pattern on paper, you will have to allow for the difference between paper and a panel and account for that difference. Paper absorbs the solvents in paint so paint is less likely to sag or run on paper than on a panel.

air pressure you will need for complete atomization. Yet the more air pressure you use, the more likely it is that the most volatile fractions of the paint/solvent mix will evaporate before paint reaches a panel. This can result in

All of these test spray patterns are usable for particular purposes. The one on the far right is very balanced and will produce a smooth finish.

several problems because the paint mix becomes unbalanced. Orange peel is among the problems that can be caused by excessive spray air pressure. Every manufacturer recommends a pressure range for each of their products, and it pays to follow these recommendations. Generally, the lowest pressure that will adequately atomize a paint is best. Gun air pressure should always be measured and fine-tuned with a tailstock gauge and adjustment.

The second gun adjustment is the "fan," "pattern," or "spreader." This controls the amount of free air routed through a gun's air cap wings to squash the pattern from round into an oblong shape. The adjustment of this factor changes the spray pattern from a circle to an increasingly long, thin shape. A full-bodied oval shape is best. When fan pressure is too high, you begin to get a pattern that looks like two circles. The best way to set the fan is to "flood" a test sheet with paint by triggering your gun until paint runs out of the pattern that you are spraying. This is done with the pattern set horizontally. The paint should run out of the pattern evenly and not more strongly at the ends or in the middle. With sufficient experience, it is possible to skip this test and set your gun's fan air adjustment by the achieved shape of the pattern on a test sheet.

When the desired spray pattern has been tuned in, the material control adjustment (which is really a trigger stop) is manipulated to "fill the pattern." This simply means that you adjust the rate of material flow until paint is deposited at the rate that you want when the gun is moved at the speed and distance from the panel that you are going to use. The gun will operate best when it is moved at a speed of roughly one foot per second and is held at a distance of six inches to 10 inches from a panel. Lacquers work best with a gun distance of six inches to eight inches, and enamels are generally sprayed at distances of eight inches to l0 inches. HVLP spray guns reduce these distances somewhat.

Clearly, these adjustments are closely interrelated. Air pressure, material flow, gun speed, and gun distance all affect the amount of paint deposited in one place. Pat-

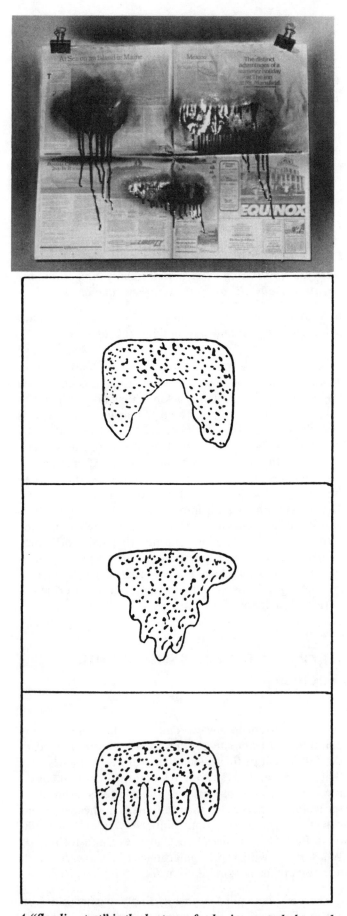

A "flooding test" is the best way for beginners to balance the pattern (fan) and material adjustments on spray guns. In the graphic, the adjustment that sprayed the bottom flooding test pattern is the right one to use.

tern format and paint reduction also affect this, as does the amount of overlap between succeeding gun strokes. But remember the goal — to achieve flow-out without runs or sags and with minimum overspray. The interrelated factors affecting paint deposit are all aimed at this relatively simple purpose. Your experience is the only guide that you can go by. To some extent, lacquers, and to a great extent enamels, require a bit of faith to achieve flow out. Paints do not land on panels in a flowed out condition. Some enamels may take minutes to achieve this; others take only seconds. You have to spray enough faith with your paint to know that flow-out will occur. Of course, if you spray too dry, you will not get paint to flow out, but if you try to spray wet enough to get instant flow-out, you will get sags and runs in a finish. Experience and faith are needed. Lacquers are less of a problem in this regard because they are sprayed very thin (125 reduction is pretty much standard) and are harder to make run or sag. Lacquer solvents are also much more volatile than those used with enamels, so when you are spraying lacquer, what you see while you are spraying is pretty much what you will get when the paint dries.

Paint manufacturers like to specify the kinds of coats that are best for the applications of their various products. Such terms as dust coat, dry coat, fog coat, mist coat, medium coat, light coat, heavy coat, full coat, etc. abound on paint cans and on paint data sheets. For the most part, these terms are self-explanatory, and advice of this type from a manufacturer should always be followed.

Sometimes you have to adjust your paint thinning or reduction after you mix paint. You can't cover all contingencies with spray gun and air pressure adjustments. This paint was mixed to its manufacturer's instructions but was too thick to spray with this gun. Thinner had to be added to the paint in the gun and mixed with it to make things work.

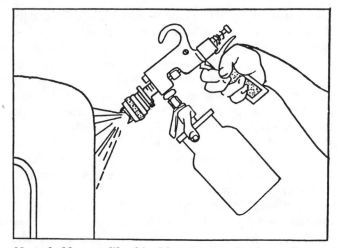

Never hold a gun like this. It's not perpendicular to the panel and will produce very thick paint at the top of its pattern and very thin paint at the bottom.

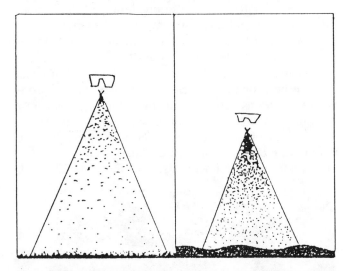

If you hold a spray gun too far from a panel (left) you will get dry, flaky paint (lacquer) or orange peel (enamel). If you hold the gun too close to a panel (right), you'll get thick, sagging, running paint.

For most spraying with automotive finishes, a 50 percent overlap left-to-right and return right-to-left spray pattern is used.

There are a few terms that are not obvious. "Double coats" involve a rapid application of two coats. These are frequently achieved by repeating each gun stroke. "Cross coating" means applying a second coat — usually immediately — at right angles to the first coat. This is one of

the times that you will want to adjust the air cap wings on your gun for a pattern at right angles to the one used in applying the previous coat. "Mist" coats and "fog" coats are very light coats with minimum deposit. Fog coats usually involve very high atomization with abnormally high gun air pressures and large gun-to-panel distances. These coats are used to lay a base for some enamels and sometimes to spray special primers such as zinc phosphate and zinc chromate. Mist coating can be used to melt-in overspray from lacquer and acrylic enamels that are used in spot and in some panel repairs. In this approach you use over-thinned or over-reduced materials.

The use of "banding" coats is an old trick. This involves gun passes that outline a panel at its edges before it is sprayed in the usual half overlap, horizontal strokes. "Triggering" is the business of stopping the paint and air

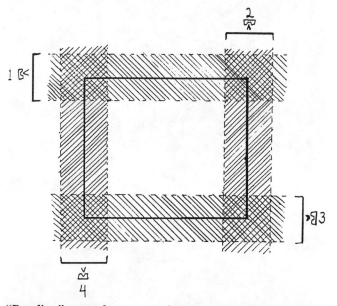

"Banding" a panel means applying coats of paint around the edges of the panel before you spray it for real. It's an old trick and a good one. After the banding coats are sprayed, you spray the panel in a conventional 50 percent overlap, left-to-right, etc., way.

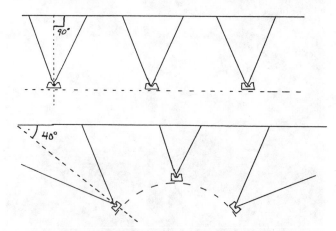

Always keep your spray gun at 90° to a panel as you move it along. That way you will deposit paint evenly on the panel (top graphic). If you "fan your gun," you will deposit paint unevenly and make a terrible mess. Fanning a gun can be a difficult habit to break.

flow from your gun at the end of each stroke, and then starting it again on the reverse pass. If this is not done, you will tend to get excessive paint buildup at the ends of your gun strokes as you reverse the gun, and you will promote unnecessary overspray.

One of the most pervasive errors made by novice painters is to "fan" a spray gun or move it with a combination of arm travel and wrist twist. Good, steady arm travel is fine. You should hold your spray gun as perpendicular as possible to panels. Excessive wrist twist or "fanning" a gun changes its angle to a panel. As the angle goes to either side of 90°, the effective distance from the gun to the panel increases and uneven paint application results. I have a tendency to fan a spray gun, and I have to periodically cure it with an Ace-type bandage around my wrist when I spray.

Never try to paint by continuing gun strokes into areas that you can't see in the vain hope that if you don't change any gun factors (speed, overlap, target distance, etc.), the paint will flow out all right. This is a gamble that you can easily lose.

Those Dreaded Sand Scratches

Sand scratch swelling can be a very persistent problem for some painters — you certainly see enough of it on restored cars! Unlike defects such as blushing and fish eying, which are easily preventable with good habits and judgments, sand scratch swelling is a problem that sometimes seems to defy the exercise of good paint practice. It is caused by solvent residues and vapors lingering in the bases of scratches in underlying coats and coming back to swell top coats. The cheap and easy solution to this problem is to always use sealer over primer or over sanded finishes that are being recoated. Sometimes sealers *are* necessary, but the most effective sealers are the non-sanding types, and these produce an inferior base for the application of top coats. Correctly sanded primer is always the best base upon which to build a finish.

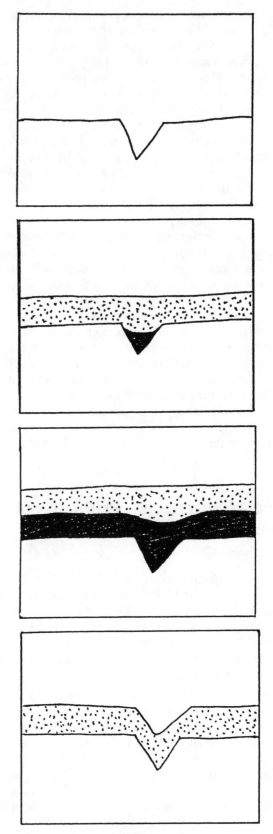

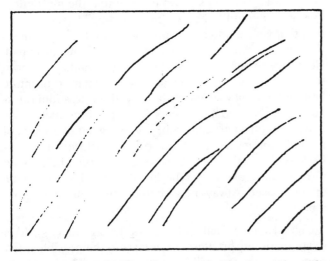

Sand scratches are those fine scratch-like depressions that can sometimes be seen in finishes.

This is how sand scratch swelling occurs.

(a) A scratch is left in an undercoat.

(b) The solvent from a top coat lingers in the bottom of the scratch and is trapped there when the top coat dries.

(c) The solvent works through the top coat, and the top coat falls into the depression left by it.

(d) When the solvent completely evaporates, the top coat follows the contour of the scratch as it fills it.

The good alternative to sealers to prevent sand scratch swelling is to eliminate the scratches themselves. This is done by avoiding sand paper grit cross contamination and by using carefully graduated sandpaper grits up to 600 grit. Some people advocate using some of the relatively new "ultra" type sandpapers (1200, 1500, 1800 grit and higher), or even compounding primer to guarantee removal of all scratches that could cause sand scratch swelling. Compounding is advocated particularly for use around feather edges where sand scratches can lurk and are hard to see in primer. I think that compounding is beyond the needs of these situations, and if an oil-based compound is used, the cleanup presents problems. Adequately sanded primer, say 600 grit, should not produce sand scratch swelling and should not usually need sealing. Some argue that compounding or the use of ultrafine grits of sandpaper guarantees that there will be no sand scratches that can swell. Others, myself included, believe that these practices leave surfaces with too little "tooth" for adequate adhesion of top coats. I have never seen sand scratch swelling where primer was carefully and completely sanded with uncontaminated 600 grit paper. Finer grit sanding and the use of sealers seems unnecessary to me if you are top coating fresh primers. You can do a lot to prevent sand scratch swelling when you paint by making your first gun passes as fog coats and by allowing adequate drying times, flash times, or setup times between coats throughout the priming and painting process.

Special Situations, Problems of Compatibility, and Sealers

Beginning painters often ask, "Is it lacquer that you can't put over enamel, or the other way around?" In fact, things aren't that simple. I wish they were. The rules of paint compatibility are complex, and as the variety of paints and additives has increased, these rules have become more complex. There *are a few* simple statements that can be made about paint compatibility.

Fresh, uncatalyzed enamels that were not force dried cannot be recoated for a year after they are sprayed unless some exotic coating, such as water-born primer/barrier coat, is used over them. The same can be true of uncatalyzed acrylic enamel. Paint that is chalked, cracked, or crumbly cannot be made the basis of any top coat system no matter what "miracle" sealer is used. Such defective paint must be removed and a new base built up before you paint.

Almost any kind of paint can be applied over any other, but it is almost always best to use a sealer when color coats are sprayed over anything but a primer, primer-surfacer, or primer-sealer. In the case of acrylic lacquers over enamels, a sealer will enhance adhesion. In the case of painting over nitrocellulose and acrylic lacquers, it will promote holdout and prevent fading or sinking in. There are sealers designed for top coating with lacquer and

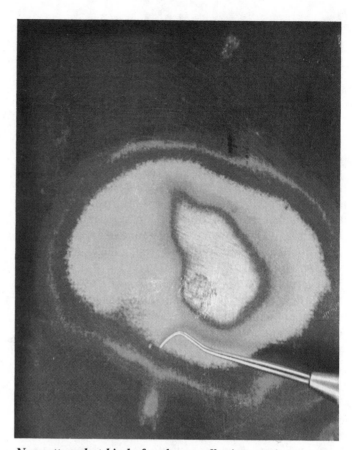

No matter what kind of sealer or adhesion coating you use, you just can't make crumbly, flaky paint the basis for building a finish. The second coat down in this feather edge crumbles when you touch it. It will have to be sanded off.

sealers designed for top coating with enamel. This distinction must be observed. It is also critical that an enamel based sealer or primer never be "sandwiched" between a lacquer base and lacquer top coats. Virtually any other combination can be made to work well if an appropriate sealer is used. Of course, all of this requires that the final, combined film thickness of the old paint and the new paint is kept at a reasonable level; 0.007 inch to 0.009 inch is about as much paint as you should have in a finish.

When sealers are used, it turns out that the most effective of them tend to be the "non-sanding" types, and the best that you can do to smooth them out after spraying is to knock the "nubs" off them with a fine Scotchbrite pad. Never try to sand these sealers. The advantage of non-sanding sealers is that they are more certain to promote holdout, and they accomplish this with far less film thickness than the sandable sealers. If overall film thickness is a problem on a particular job, you may want to use one of the non-sanding sealers. Some primer-surfacers have limited sealing abilities; this depends on their type: nitrocellulose-based, acrylic lacquer-based, or synthetic enamel-based. Always be sure to use the right sealer for a job.

The advent of such additives as flex agents has added to compatibility problems or at least to the possible questions that a painter will have about them. The best solution is to deal with a good jobber who has the informa-

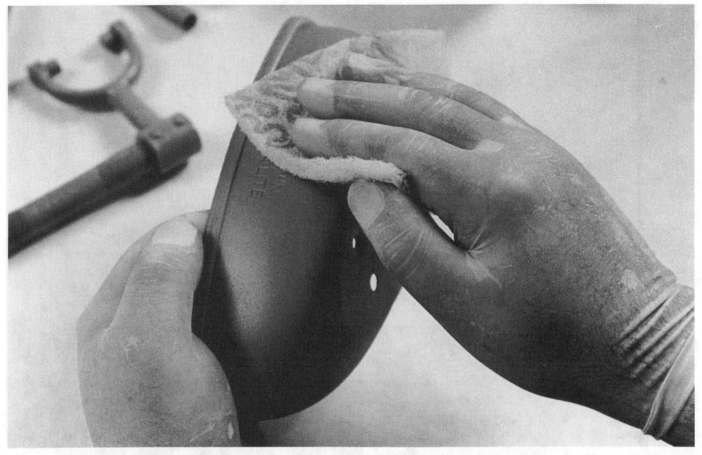

This item was sealed to prevent sand scratch swelling. A fine Scotchbrite pad can be used to knock the nubs off the sealer, but you cannot sand it. That's a problem with most sealers.

tion that you are likely to need or who can talk to someone in the manufacturer's home office or regional office to get this information. Most of the major paint companies provide very good technical support for their products.

General Admonitions

There are some general warnings and recommendations that are contained in or on virtually every refinishing shop manual, paint data sheet, and paint can label. I think the reason these warnings are repeated so often is because there are people out there who still ignore them. Let's sample a few.

Mix paints thoroughly. To do less is to cause color match problems or even film problems. Paints that have sat for a long time should be stirred with a paddle and then shaken on a paint shaker. This will free the "glup" that has settled on the bottom of the can so that it can be shaken into solution. Never use paint if everything in the can cannot be mixed into solution. Paints should also be mixed thoroughly with their thinners and reducers. You can't overmix solvents and paints, but it is easy to undermix them. Paint will settle in a spray gun cup as you spray so be sure to swirl it periodically or mix it with a stick if it has sat in your gun for very long. An automatic stirring cup eliminates this problem. Some paints cannot be shaken due to aeration, and this prohibition must be observed when it is stated in instructions. Other paints need to have their additives poured into them slowly and with minimum air inclusions. Always observe instructions regarding minimum "gel" times for some paint additives, and never spray catalyzed or two-part paint systems after or even near the ends of their "pot lives."

Paint must be handled in a clean environment. Be careful at every stage of handling paint to avoid contaminating it. Always blow off the jambs on paint can friction lids *before* you open them so that contaminants lodged there don't fall into the paint. Always use clean vessels to receive paints and to mix them in, and always use clean spray equipment. Paint should be strained through a gauze filter on its way to your gun cup, and your gun should be outfitted with an in-cup filter.

Don't touch primed surfaces with your bare hands. Skin oils can never be sufficiently removed from your hands to avoid contamination. The best policy is to clean an about-to-be-painted surface with a cleaning solvent or with fast enamel reducer. The surface should then be wiped with a tack rag and blown off with the air-only-trigger-position on your gun. If cracks or crevices such as door seams are involved in the area that you are painting, always blow them out with an air gun before painting.

Don't let your enthusiasm or boredom get in the way of allowing adequate flash times (lacquer) or setup times (enamel) between the succeeding coats that you spray. Lacquers benefit from intervals between coats that are a bit

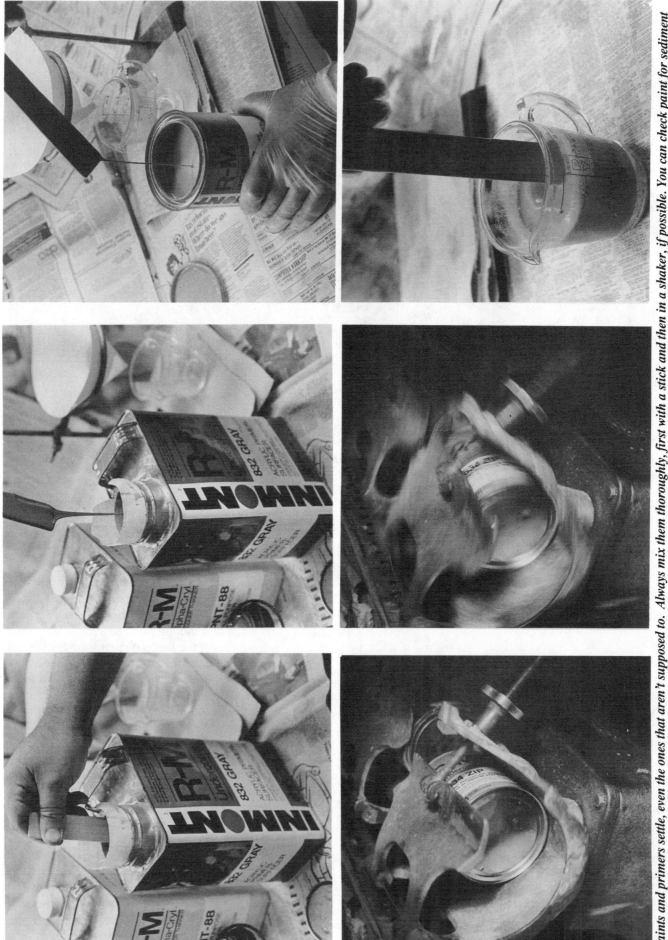

Paints and primers settle, even the ones that aren't supposed to. Always mix them thoroughly, first with a stick and then in a shaker, if possible. You can check paint for sediment by probing the bottom of the can with a mixing stick. After paints are thinned or reduced, they still need to be stirred to keep their solids in suspension. Keep mixing things as you go.

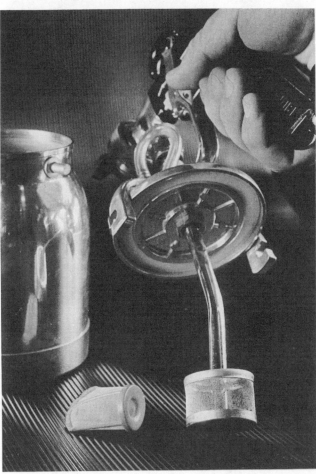

First filter your paint or primer when you pour it out of the can. Then filter it again after you have thinned or reduced it when you pour it into your paint cup. Then, if possible, fit the pickup tube on your spray gun with a small filter to add a final guarantee of paint purity.

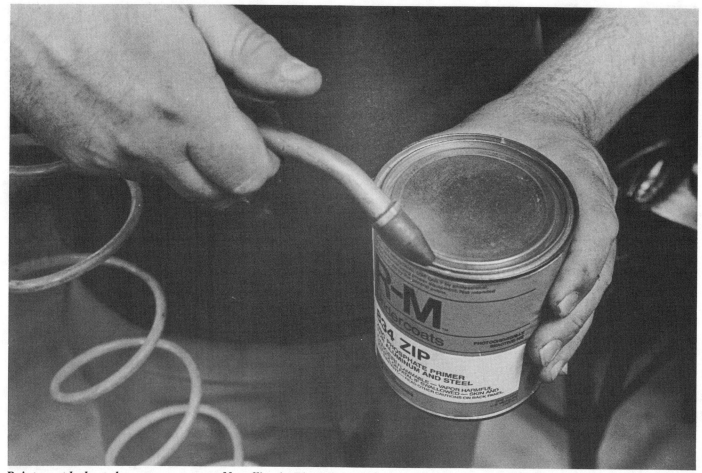

Paint must be kept clean at every stage of handling it. Blowing friction can lid seams out before you open the cans is just common sense.

longer than their apparent flash times, and enamels need from l0 to 30 minutes of setup time before recoating. If you abbreviate these times, you are likely to have problems with trapped solvents in lacquer and runs, sags, or excessive orange peel in enamels. Primers are best sprayed in fairly wet coats for maximum adhesion, but this means that they need decent flash times and then some between coats.

Follow manufacturers' recommended mixing ratios for thinners and reducers for specified shop conditions. You can't make "medium" reducer or thinner work in all shop conditions and it's foolish to try. In very hot and humid conditions, retarders *may* allow you to spray lacquers and acrylic enamels without blushing and other defects. Don't count on it!

Tricks of the Trade

There must be hundreds or thousands of little tricks that make painting easier and better. There are also plenty of pretty bad tricks, but these usually look like what they are, unacceptable short cuts. Just watching an experienced painter (best done with one's mouth firmly set in a closed position) can provide a wealth of ideas on good ways to do things.

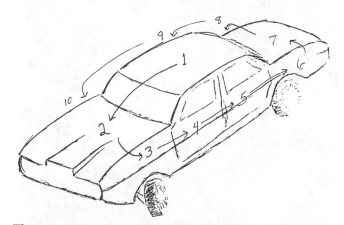

There are several strategies for painting a complete car. Be sure that you have one in mind that will work before you begin this job.

When complete cars are being painted, it's crucial that you adopt an approach to proceed from panel to panel in a way that minimizes overspray problems. There are three or more panel sequences that experienced painters use. The adoption of a particular pattern depends on the venting characteristics of the spray booth or area that you are working in and the nature of the car that you are painting. Just working from front to back or *vice versa* is almost never the best approach. This is a situation that requires some thought and planning.

When you work with a new paint and particularly with some of the new enamels, it's a good idea to experiment on a primed panel. You can't get a good sense of how paint will flow if all you do is spray it on the paper that you use to set your gun pattern. Paper tends to absorb the solvents in paint spray and it will give you a false indication of the potential for sags and runs with a new paint.

Color matching, and particularly metallic color matching, depends mostly on the paint tint. It also depends on gun air pressure, speed of travel, material setting, fluid tip and air cap choice, paint thinning, and coat wetness and overlap.

A surprising amount of color adjustment can be accomplished by varying the factors that affect the wetness of the coat that you are applying.

When you spray paint to fill and level a feather-edged area, the practice of "feathering" the gun trigger can be invaluable. This involves working the gun trigger deeper where you want more paint and backing it off as you come to the feather edge. This will give you more paint where you want it, in the low spots. Feathering a gun takes some practice, but it is a skill worth developing.

Sometimes, despite your best efforts, an area catches too much paint and you get a sag or run. Keep a cool head and don't despair...yet. Your pinky, thumb, or forefinger can be educated to make a quick cleanup repair. Later, when the paint has set up, some pretty dry gun passes, followed by some wet ones, will make the damage done by your finger virtually disappear. When you use an "educated finger" for this maneuver, you still have to be careful of overspray and careful not to get the paint film too thick in the repaired area.

Melting in overspray can save a lot of hand work on lacquers and enamels. To do this, a uniforming solvent or a retarder mixed with thinner or reducer is used in a mist coat. The mist coat is radically over-thinned with only about 10 percent paint in the mix. Different manufacturers have different approaches to mist coating for blending, and these should be followed. This kind of operation can make quite a difference in the overall results that you get in a "paint job."

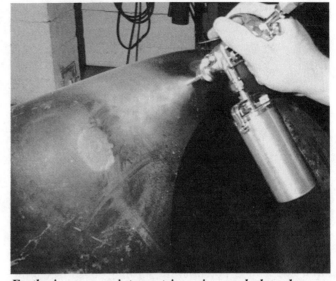

Feathering your paint gun trigger is a real plus when you have to level paint in areas like this feather-edged spot repair.

Some "tricks of the trade" are little habits that promote cleanliness in handling paint and equipment. The practice of blowing out the lid interfaces of friction cans has already been mentioned. It is a little habit that prevents a lot of contamination. It isn't a bad idea to tape paint can lids with masking tape when you store paint to keep dirt out. Taping the inside of a paint can rim to form a pouring spout that keeps paint out of the can top groove is a good practice.

Surgical gloves are great for protecting your hands from paint and solvents and for protecting panels from the oils in your skin.

One trick that is always a benefit is to know the complete line or system that you are painting with. Additives such as FEE (fish eye eliminator) and retarder that are designed to correct painting problems should not be used just because they are there. It is always better not to use

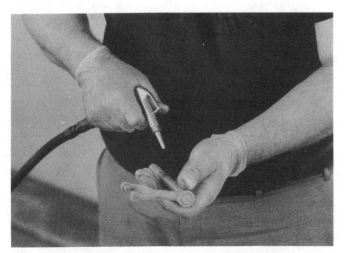

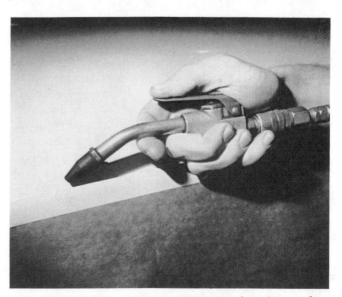

Always blow off parts and panels in your final approach to spraying them. This will drive sanding residues out of crevices so they won't end up in your paint.

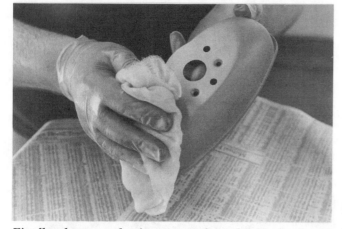 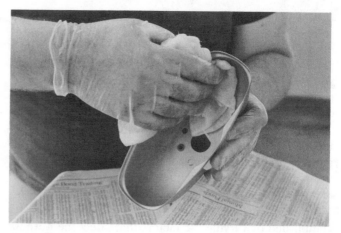

Finally, always gently wipe parts and panels with a tack rag before you spray them.

them if possible. If conditions call for them, you have to know about their potential for solving problems. On the other hand, performance additives, such as gloss additives, often improve paint quality.

Always remember that proficiency in refinishing includes dealing with the unexpected, quickly and effectively — as if you expected it.

CHAPTER 27:

Automotive Refinishing, Part III; After the Paint Dries

Most of our experience is, of course, with dried or cured paint. Refinishing an old car is a complex, time-consuming, and expensive proposition, and most of our efforts are necessarily directed to making existing paint work. Sometimes this is paint that we have recently sprayed and that needs further work to produce an acceptable finish. At other times, it is possible to work with an older, existing finish in a way that allows us to improve its appearance to the point that it becomes acceptable. Occasionally, the problems of an existing finish or of a new finish are so great that the only practical approach is to refinish. All of these situations differ from those discussed in the previous two chapters because they involve existing finishes. Finally, after a finish has dried, it must be maintained and sometimes repaired if it is to have a reasonable service life.

Compounding and Polishing

Old, oxidized, or stained finishes and new, unleveled, rough ones require polishing to achieve a smooth and attractive luster. Compounding and polishing are essentially the same operation except that compounding involves coarser abrasives than polishing. Both compounding and polishing level painted surfaces by abrading or "scratching" them very minutely. While it may sound strange to consider scratching a surface to polish it, this is the nugget of virtually all polishing processes. The key is in the size of the abrasives that are used and the sizes of the scratches that they make. Just as 300 or 400 grit abrasives will visibly scratch and dull a finish, abrasives in the 1500 grit and above range will polish it. In the latter case, the scratches are so fine and closely spaced that they produce the optical effect of gloss and luster. That is, until you look at them under a microscope; then they look like what they are, scratches!

Compounding is the first step and polishing is the second step in bringing full luster to a rough finish. Finishes that are already pretty level do not need to be com-

pounded, and you can go directly to polishing. Both of these processes can be accomplished either by hand or with a machine. Hand compounding and polishing have the advantages of vastly reducing the risk of cutting through a finish on edges or at styling reliefs. Hand compounding and polishing often produce fewer objectionable swirl marks than machine compounding and polishing because they can be performed in relatively straight lines as opposed to the circular motions characteristic of machine polishing. The main problem that some people have with hand compounding is that it represents a variant of the human experience known as "WORK" and even "hard, dull WORK." Machine compounding and polishing are also "work," but never "WORK." While I prefer the appearance of a hand-compounded and polished finish, the amount of effort required to level and polish lacquer or catalyzed enamel finishes by hand can be considerable in some cases. It all depends on what you start with.

Not all finishes can be compounded or even polished. Lacquers and acrylic lacquers dry in a way that invariably leaves a surface that will be improved by polishing and/or compounding and polishing. Catalyzed urethane and cured or hardened alkyd enamels can be polished with fine abrasives, and this should give them an added gloss. Alkyd enamels cannot be polished until they have aged for six months or a year. I consider polishing any kind of enamel an to be an unnecessary and inappropriate step in restoration work. This is, of course, a personal opinion and goes against a lot of modern restoration practice. I think that if these enamels are properly applied in an appropriately dust-free environment, they will achieve a natural gloss that I find far more attractive and authentic than the one which includes the swirl marks that accompany polishing.

The abrasives used in compound and polish are made from anything from tripoli to pumice, talc, and synthetic abrasives. Hand polishes and compounds generally use oils for their bases, and machine compounds and polishes usually have water bases. Compounds and polishes come in many different grades, depending on how aggressively

This equipment buffs and polishes finishes. It can be used to bring out the best in the paint that you spray or on old finishes, but there are limits to what you can do with buffing and polishing.

you need to remove surface films and decayed paint to level a finish, and how fine you want the abrasives for your final polishing to be. As in any abrasive finishing operation, you move to progressively finer grits to produce a glossier and more highly polished result. When working with enamels, you begin with finer abrasives than those used initially on lacquers. Both machine and hand abrasives are designed to break up into ever finer particles as polishing with them progresses and the final stages of shine are achieved. Abrasives designed for machine application tend to break up faster than those designed for hand application. Machine compounds also tend to dry (evaporate their solvents) faster than hand compounds because of their different bases. In general, use hand abrasives for hand compounding and polishing and machine abrasives when you use a machine for this work.

It should also be noted that there is a tremendous difference in the quality of various brands of compounds and polishes. The ones sold in body shop supply stores and marked "for professional use" invariably produce better results than the cut-rate stuff sold in discount stores. The professional stuff doesn't come in neat little $1.29 tins, so if you want good quality compounds and polishes, be prepared to spend more than that. In working with polishes and compounds, employ the least abrasion and surface removal that will get the job done. In the case of old finishes with deep scratches or of new ones with excessive orange peel, a fairly course grade of compound or even a preliminary "color sanding" with a 600 grit abrasive paper, followed by smoothing with 1200, 1500, 1800, or even 2200 grit abrasive paper, may be necessary for the initial leveling. Recent developments in coated abrasive technology have produced papers that are much finer than those that were available just a few years ago. Some of these are consistently higher than the old 1200 grit papers and are not just made up of particles that *average* to a stated grade. While these new papers can be used to do terrific leveling work, they should only be used when it is absolutely necessary to remove quite a bit of material for leveling purposes. They are very expensive.

One unfortunate tendency that has crept into the practice of some body shops and even some restoration shops is the business of applying finishes, particularly catalyzed enamels, badly and in grossly contaminated environments. This dirty application is then routinely followed by color sanding to level the finish and machine compounding and polishing to give it gloss. This approach produces superficially attractive results, but close inspection will still indicate the sins of unevenness and contamination in the paint. The options of color sanding and wheeling a finish can be valuable, but they should never become a routine part of refinishing with any material, particularly catalyzed enamel.

It is also important to understand that, just as some finishes, such as uncatalyzed acrylic enamel, cannot really be effectively polished right after they are applied, there are other limits to what can be done after the fact with abrasives and finishes. Acrylic lacquers, for example,

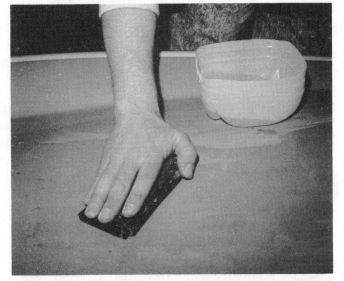

New, much finer abrasive papers and catalyzed enamels have made it possible to do something that you never could do in the past — polish and buff enamel. I'm not sure that restorers want to use this option.

require some form of polishing after application, but if you attempt to do this too soon, you will dull and ruin the surface that you are working on. Sometimes, older finishes that have chalked (oxidized) can be saved with compounds and/or polishes, but sometimes they are deteriorated to the point that they can no longer be polished.

Whether a hand or machine application of compound or polish is being attempted, it is important to mix the compound thoroughly before you commence compounding. In hand compounding and polishing, the abrasive is applied to a soft damp pad or wad of rag, and the surface is rubbed in straight lines. Apply only enough compound to do the area that you are working on, and confine this area to about the size of a car door or less. As the surface begins to polish and the abrasive breaks up, your rubbing strokes will encounter less resistance; you will feel this happen. At this point, you can ease up the pressure on your applicator. Finally, the mostly dried compound should be buffed with a clean cloth and very little pressure. A second clean cloth can be used to advantage for a final buff.

While it is much more difficult to cut through a finish in a hand operation than in a machine operation, it is possible. This is particularly true when the rougher grades of compound are employed. Course compound is also a hazard when it is used on older finishes where you really don't know how much color coat there is left to compound or polish. Anytime you compound or polish, be particularly careful of raised edges, crease lines, and other places where a panel bends sharply. Not only does the pressure from hand and particularly from machine polishing tend to concentrate in such places, but the finish is thinner there to begin with, and consequently, it is easier to cut through it. Be careful....

Machine compounding and polishing is much faster than comparable hand operations. A tufted wheel or a "bonnet" is used with paste type abrasives, and a lamb's wool bonnet is used with liquid polishes or with very fine

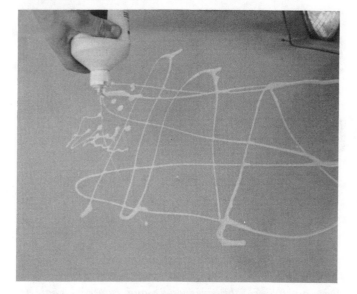

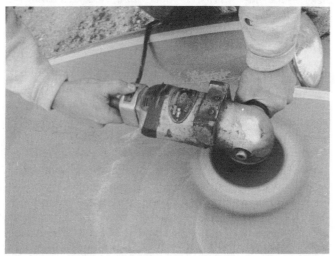

Spreading liquid compounds and polishes on panels before you power buff them is easy...and fun, but the actual buffing operation has to be done very carefully or you will burn or cut through a finish.

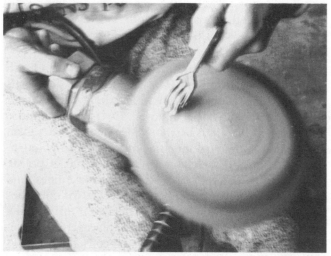

As a bonnet gets clogged with paint and spent abrasives, you can clean it with this special tool.

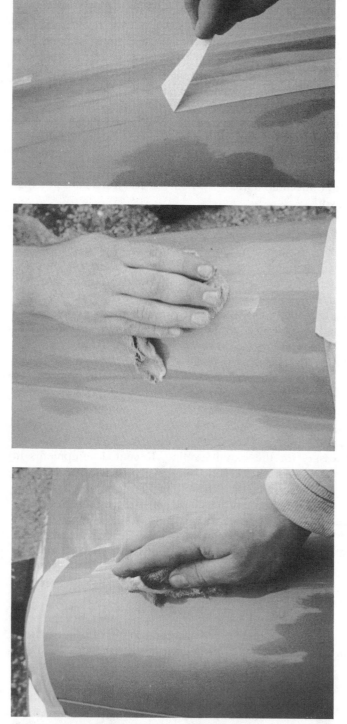

You have to protect edges and styling lines when you power compound or polish, otherwise you may cut through the paint at these points. One way to protect these areas is to tape over them and then hand compound and/or polish them later.

paste type abrasives. There are several other, new polishing head configurations on the market. Effective polishing machines operate at around 2,000 rpm or less, so you should avoid using the faster hand-held machines that are really designed for grinding. Excessive speed or pressure will either cut through paint or burn it. Good wheel polishing is done with only moderate pressure, and you must keep the wheel moving at all times to avoid burning or cutting through a finish. As you polish, a bonnet will tend to clog with paint and spent abrasive, and it must periodically be cleaned by running a cleaning tool over it to remove the clogs.

In machine polishing, abrasive is applied to a surface that is being polished and the machine is moved first horizontally back and forth with overlapping strokes over a small area. The machine is then moved vertically up and down with overlapping strokes over the same area. The edge of the pad or bonnet should be lifted slightly, about one-half inch, in the direction that the wheel is being moved, either horizontally or vertically. Do not continue to polish after the liquid lubricant in the abrasive has evaporated or you will damage the finish. Also, do not attempt to work too large an area at one time. A door or fender will be about right.

Machine compounding and polishing can produce dramatically favorable results, but it is also very possible to produce burns, scorches, and cut-throughs with surprising ease. Edges and bends in panels exacerbate these problems, and such areas should be avoided when you wheel panels. If it is difficult to avoid these areas with a wheel, it is best to tape them with masking tape to prevent problems. After machine polishing is complete, you can remove the tape and do the vulnerable areas by hand. It is almost never possible to get safely into every painted surface on a car with a wheel, and some hand work is generally necessary. Caution is the byword here because it is a terrible feeling to have to repair a *new* finish that has been damaged by cutting through it or burning its paint with a polishing wheel. It should also be noted that polishing wheels throw off fine airborne abrasives in considerable quantity and with great velocity. It is necessary to wear goggles and a respirator or dust shield when operating one of these machines.

Spot Repairs to Damaged Finishes

The ability to spot repair a finish is often utilized in restoration practice when damage is confined to one or to a few small areas. The objectives of spot repair are to produce a finish that blends into the panel being repaired and that matches it in gloss, color, texture, and level. While spot repairs can be made with finishes other than acrylic lacquer, this is certainly the easiest modern finish to work with in this way, and it usually produces very acceptable results in spot refinishing.

Spot refinishing generally follows the outline given for panel and overall refinishing stated in the last two chapters on refinishing in this book, except, of course, that

there is the additional problem of blending the edges of the repair area into the old finish. The first step in spotting in work is to wash the panel where the repair will be made. Do this well beyond the edges of the repair area. Wash with water and mild detergent, and then rinse thoroughly with clean water. This should be followed by a solvent wash with a silicone and oil removing solvent. The repair area should then be sanded down as far as is necessary.

If a paint defect was the reason for the repair, it must be sanded to bare metal or to primer if it is intact. If there is rust or if metal repair was necessary, the sanding must

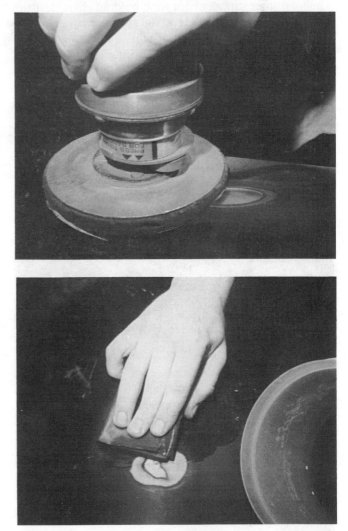

When you do spot repairs and panel blends, you have to feather edge the places where an old finish meets a new one. This graphic shows a feather edge that has been sanded to make a spot repair. The next step will be to fill the depression and level it to the paint in the surrounding area.

Feather edges can be machine sanded or hand sanded. I like to start with a DA sander and then finish by hand with a foam backup pad.

go to bare metal in the repair area. When bare metal is exposed, it should be treated with metal conditioner. Then the excess conditioner must be wiped off the surrounding finish with a damp cloth. If you are simply repairing a scratch or similar superficial defect, you should sand far enough to prevent excessive film thickness when the color coats have been applied. The total thickness of paint and primer should not exceed eight or nine mils, in any case. There are various devices for measuring paint thickness, such as the magnetic Tinsley Gauges or some very fancy electronic gear. Generally, with some experience, you can tell by sight and feel how much paint is on a panel when you sand through it to bare metal in one spot.

Whether bare metal or primer remains after sanding, the edge of the repair area must be feather sanded so that it *gradually* comes up to the level of the areas beyond the repair area. There are wiping "lacquer dissolving" solvents available to feather lacquer finished surfaces for this purpose, but these tend to produce an inferior result to sanding feather edges and should only be used on very small spots, if at all.

Surfaces well beyond a feather edge sanded area should be masked to avoid deposits of overspray. If there is bare metal in the repair area, it should be primed. Then a primer surfacer with good holdout characteristics should be used to fill and level the entire repair area. The technique of feathering a spray gun — releasing the trigger partially and applying less paint on the feathered edges of a repair area — can be utilized to great advantage in this work. Be sure to allow adequate flash times for primer-surfacers and for the color coats that come later. Remember that drying paint shrinks roughly 50 percent from its wet state.

Some refinishing practitioners advocate compounding the feathered edges of a repair area before spraying primer-surfacer. Hand compounding is best if this procedure is followed, but machine compounding can be used and is advocated by some painters. I have never found compounding necessary at this point, but prefer to do

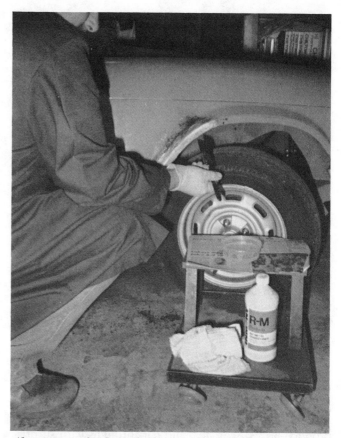

Always treat feather edged spot repairs with a good metal conditioner when you have sanded to bare metal.

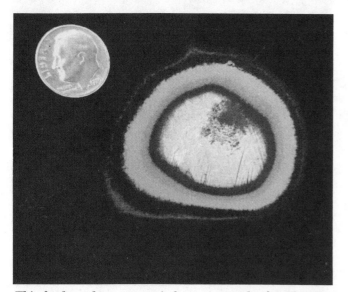

This feather edge spot repair has uncovered a festering rust spot (2:00 o'clock position). All rust will have to be removed from this spot before a finish can be built on it.

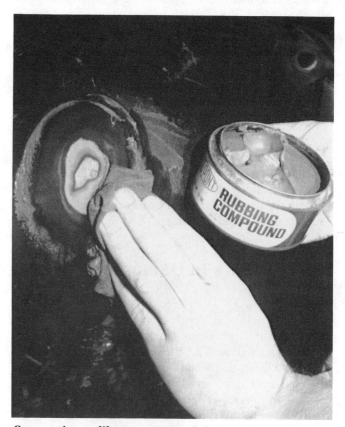

Some painters like to compound feather edges to remove scratches in dark primer coats that can be difficult to see and eradicate. I think that this practice is unnecessary and that the same purpose can be accomplished with fine abrasive paper wet sanding.

careful sanding with uncontaminated 600 grit paper. In either case, the area should be cleaned with water and then with solvent prior to applying primer-surfacer to it. It is generally recommended that a cleaning solvent be used for this purpose, but I have found that these solvents tend to soften the primer and can produce several problems later. A fast enamel reducer is almost ideal for this solvent cleanup. After the primer-surfacer that was applied to the repair area has dried adequately, the area should be block sanded or board sanded to level the repair area with the surrounding panel surface. This area should then be cleaned with a solvent cleaner or fast enamel reducer after it has been washed down with water. You are now ready to apply color coats.

If the repair is to be made with acrylic lacquer, a two-gun technique will serve best. The basic proposition here is to cover the repair area with as many color coats as are necessary to achieve hiding of the primer and to blend the edges of the repaired area into the existing finish. When hiding is achieved, a mist coat of highly thinned color (five percent color) is applied with the second gun to the edges of the repair area. This mist coat will blend these edges into the surrounding finish. A product like DuPont's Uniforming Finish is ideal for this purpose, but, of course, this should only be used with DuPont systems. Other manufacturers have special products or special procedures with conventional thinners and reducers to accomplish the same result. While it is generally effective to follow color coating with a blender coat, sometimes more than one blender coat is necessary and sometimes it is necessary to alternate color coats with blender coats around the edges of paint that is spotted in after applying a second color coat.

It is much more difficult to effect spot repairs with enamels but it is possible, and with some finishes it is necessary to do this to get a texture and gloss match. Enamels are used in roughly the same way that lacquers are for spotting in, except that straight retarder is usually the solvent used in the blender (mist) coat. The blender coat is sprayed over the edges of the repair and it is sprayed very dry, and only *after* the color coats, never between them. The blending process with enamels is almost a fog coating process.

When the repaired finish is thoroughly dry, it should be compounded well beyond the repair area to remove any overspray and to blend it into adjacent areas that were masked during the repair. If everything was done properly, a repair can be made that is indistinguishable from its surroundings. Remember, body shops accomplish such repairs with metallic colors every day, and compared to the problems encountered in that proposition, spotting in solid colors can be kid's stuff.

There are some points that will help you to make successful spot repairs. The first is that this is demanding work, and it is important to strenuously observe all of the general cautions of good paint practice regarding cleanliness, paint mixing, solvent choice, gun technique, and the like. It is also important to choose the boundaries of your spot repair area carefully so that the contours of panels will work to your advantage and not against you. If, for example, your chosen boundaries end at panel edges, it will be much more difficult to make a repair that does not show. It is also important to remember that while it is possible, by rigorous attention to detail, to control the leveling of a repair area, its gloss and the quality of its blend into the surrounding areas, you will have great difficulty controlling its color match. Good paint mixing and careful attention to gun technique will help get a good color match, but if the repair paint does not match the surrounding panel, there is very little adjustment possible with gun technique alone that will save the situation. The use of a factory tinting kit may help. One thing that you should do is to raise your masking barrier and check the color match after you have sprayed two or three color coats. Color adjustment can be made at this point with the final color coats as necessary.

One of the surest ways to ruin a spot repair is to neglect to provide adequate flash times as you go along with primer and color coats. This factor should be watched carefully.

Very Minor (Brush) Repairs

Automobile manufacturers sell and people buy little bottles of "repair" or "touch-up" paint that allegedly can be used to repair modern automotive finishes. This has been going on for at least 50 years. Business must be pretty brisk because all kinds of aftermarket manufacturers also sell little bottles of this stuff. Actually, there isn't anything particularly wrong with what is in the bottles, but it is what is *not* printed on the bottle that can get you into trouble. Now remember that these are small bottles, about the size of a Magic Marker, and there isn't room to print much on their sides. Generally, the instructions suggest that it is important to shake the bottle until the agitator ball can be heard, and for some discreet period after that. Then the instructions often seem to trail off into vagueness and only generally hint at application technique.

Armed with these bottles, people attempt to cover little rust spots and nicks with the handy-dandy little nail polish-type brushes that are included in the lids of the bottles. You see people performing this repair ritual in their driveways with every expectation that they have preserved the finishes of their cars. Often the touch-up paint is applied over rust and even over the moisture that is left from washing the cars. The prime time for such repairs is in the fall to protect finishes from the ravages of winter. Of course rust just continues to fester under this kind of ill-conceived repair. Apparently the well-meaning people who indulge in this fix-up-fantasy don't realize that the thumb nail-sized bubbles in the paint on their cars often originate in tiny nicks that were repaired this way. They just go on buying the bottles of touch-up paint and performing their touch-up ritual every year.

It is possible to make quick and reasonably effective

brush repairs to small (one-quarter-inch in diameter or less) breaches in finishes, but it takes more than a dab of paint out of a bottle.

Proper brush repairs can be an effective, temporary repair technique. To be durable and look good, you still must follow the logic and sequences of proper refinishing. This begins with removing *all* rust from the area to be repaired.

A dental pick can be very handy for this purpose, particularly where rust has gotten into the pores of metal and produced pitting. The area should then be sanded and feather edged. Since the object of brush repairs is to keep the repair area small, the feathering can be done with a lacquer dissolving feather edging solvent if lacquer is the finish being applied. Otherwise, you can rotate a piece of 320 or 400 grit sandpaper under the tip of your finger to produce shiny metal and a feather edge at the repair site. The bare metal should then be treated with metal conditioner, and the excess wiped off surrounding paint with a damp cloth. The repair area should then be primed and filled by brushing in coats of primer-surfacer until it is roughly level with the rest of the finish. The primer-surfacer can be applied with either a small artist's brush or a striping brush. It can also be air brushed through a one-eighth-inch round aperture in a 3x5-inch card. The air brush and card technique produces the best repair, but you have to vibrate the card mask slightly as you shoot to blur the edges of the spray. This can be something like patting your head and rubbing your tummy at the same time; some people can do it naturally and other people have trouble with it. Whatever technique is used to apply the primer-surfacer, it should be allowed to dry thoroughly between coats. The characteristic shrink of primer-surfacer of 50 percent from a wet condition to a dry one should leave room for color coats and keep them roughly level with the panel when they dry.

When the primer-surfacer has flashed and dried, it should be sanded lightly with 600 grit sandpaper. This type of repair will rarely produce perfect leveling and is really a stopgap measure to arrest corrosion and further deterioration of a finish and to produce a reasonably attractive surface. If you try to achieve a perfect level, you can easily sand through the primer-surfacer, so settle for a reasonably level surface with a little depth left for filling with the color coats. The next step is to brush the color onto the repair in about four coats. It should then be allowed to dry thoroughly. The repair area is then compounded to blend it into the surrounding paint. Acrylic lacquer works best for this type of repair and should be mixed relatively thin with about five percent to 10 percent retarder included to help it flow out. Don't try to brush more paint in when the preceding coats are tacky and stringy.

While brush repair is far from a perfect repair technique, it is a reasonable maintenance technique for finishes that would otherwise deteriorate from stone chips and other paint film defects. It has the integrity to confront the problems of corrosion, and if this kind of repair is carefully leveled, it will have a reasonably attractive appearance.

Paint Defects — What Went Wrong?

Back in the 1950s when automotive finishes were done in either nitrocellulose lacquer or alkyd enamel, there were very few special problems in normal painting situations. One problem that did plague painters was the problem of fish eyes. Remember, many shops were using war surplus and prewar vintage equipment, and some of those compressors had to have their oil checked very regularly because their rings were tired and they leaked oil. Since rebuilding a compressor was a bothersome prospect and the down time was a real problem, some other solution seemed desirable.

DuPont introduced what may well have been the first paint film additive. It was supposed to suppress fish eye and was called FEE (fish eye eliminator). It came in a squirt bottle. One squirt per pint paint cup seemed to smooth out paint almost miraculously — like oil on troubled water. Of course, miracles were simpler in those days. Some of those compressors were fuming oil pretty badly, and one squirt of FEE seemed to help, but it didn't always do the job. Now it seemed that if one squirt would help, two squirts would be twice as good. Three, four, and five squirts followed as we got used to those miracles in the postwar world.

The trouble was that finishes that were applied with gobs of FEE — the other manufacturers quickly mar-

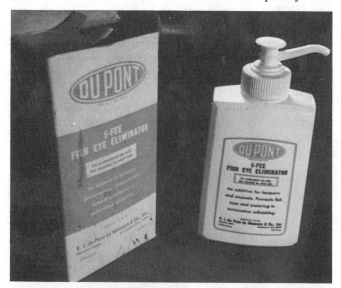

FEE (fish eye eliminator) was a big topic in the 1950s when DuPont introduced it. It was a very early paint film additive that was supposed to suppress fish eyes. It did and we all loved it. Many of us made using too much of it part of our routines. A couple of years later, we found out what the drawbacks of this silicone additive were. From then on, most painters followed the directions on the FEE package very carefully.

keted their own versions of the stuff — tended to craze and crack a year-and-a-half down the road. Of course, you had yourself to blame for this problem because it was caused by purposely disregarding the instructions that came with this product. Worse yet, since FEE and its clones were designed to suppress fish eyes by literally saturating the paint with silicone (to change its surface tension characteristics), it became very difficult to refinish cars that had had all of this free silicone embedded in their finishes. And this was exactly what happened when massive amounts of the stuff were squirted into paint.

In today's world of numerous and complex paint additives, the chances of additive-induced defects are infinitely greater. I suppose that is part of the price that has to be paid for finishes that are inherently better than the finishes of 30 years ago.

The surprising thing is that most defects in paint can be traced to fairly basic application problems and errors. There is an enormous commonality of causes for a varied list of paint defects, and it is not often necessary to look for exotic causes. Such simple problems as contamination, inappropriate gun technique, and failure to allow adequate flash times and setup times for finishes can cause a multitude of paint defects. The list that follows is not an exhaustive list of defects, nor do the causes given for each defect constitute a complete list of possible causes. I have concentrated on the most prevalent and obvious paint defects and the most common and correctable causes. Various refinishing textbooks and paint shop manuals can be referred to as needed for some of the more exotic paint defects and their causes.

In the following discussion of paint problems, the corrective measure to be taken for each problem should be assumed to be to reverse the cause of the problem. If, for example, the cause of a problem is stated to be inadequate air pressure, the appropriate correction is to increase the air pressure. Where the corrective action required for a problem involves a factor other than reversing the cause, as, for example, the use of a sealer to prevent bleeding, the appropriate corrective action will be stated specifically. Finally, where the factor of "gun technique" is stated as a possible cause of a problem, this is meant to include gun fan and material adjustments, tailstock air pressure regulation, distance from the panel, speed of the pass, and correct gun stroke technique.

RUNS AND SAGS. This problem afflicts novice painters as they attempt to find the territory between causing this defect and spraying too dry. The most usual causes of runs and sags are gun technique and a failure to allow sufficient flash (lacquer) and setup (enamel) times for underlying paint coats. The use of solvents that are too slow for shop conditions and of air pressure that is too low are also often implicated in runs and sags. Be particularly careful when you spray very dark colors that you can see what you are spraying and adjust your gun pass speed appropriately to avoid runs and sags.

COLOR MATCHING PROBLEMS. The paint itself is the usual culprit in color match problems, and it is a good idea to spray a sample of any paint that has to color match so that adjustments to the paint itself can be made

(Artwork courtesy Joseph W. Joseph.)

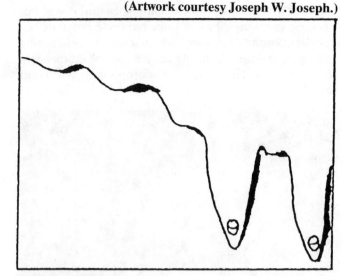

"RUNS AND SAGS"

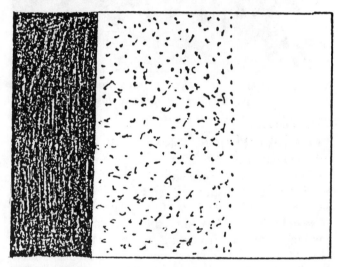

"BLEEDING"

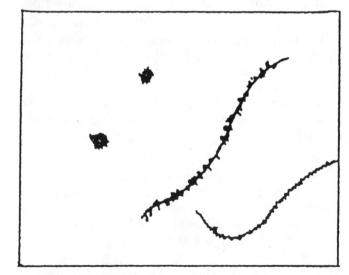

"CONTAMINATION"

before you commit to a bad match. The factors involved in gun technique can make a difference in paint color, even with solid colors. Finally, a failure of top coats to completely hide underlying paint coats can result in color match problems. Complete hiding may require more paint or the use of a sealer under top coats.

BLEEDING. This problem can involve any color, but it is most pronounced when some red undercoats are being over-coated. It involves a top coat solvent penetrating underlying paint and causing the color to bleed through. When bleeding is a problem, an appropriate sealer has to be used.

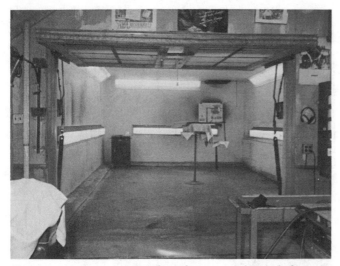

Keeping your spray area clean by vacuuming it before you spray and wetting its floor to suppress dust will help keep contamination out of your paint.

CONTAMINATION. This is an ever-present threat. Contamination on the surface that you are painting, of the room that you are painting in, or of the air or the paint that you are spraying can cause a whole range of problems from cratering to fish eying and lifting. Surfaces to be painted should be solvent cleaned, blown off, and tack wiped before coating. The spray area should be cleaned with a vacuum cleaner and the floor watered down to suppress dust. A painting area must have adequate ventilation, but such ventilation must not draw dust and grit into the area where painting is done. The air supply for painting must be filtered clean of solid and liquid contaminants. Paint must be handled carefully and filtered into clean vessels when it is measured and mixed. Spray equipment must be kept completely clean and should always be cleaned immediately after use. Be sure to clean spray gun lid gaskets and anti-drip tubes completely.

ORANGE PEEL. Some orange peel is normal in enamels and it is somewhat inherent in the nature of how enamels dry. The equivalent of orange peel in lacquer is a roughness that can be compounded out and, in fact, lacquers are compounded and polished level and glossy as standard operating procedure. Orange peel in enamels can be limited by using the correct solvent for shop conditions, sticking to manufacturers' recommended levels of reduction, and following recommendations on air pressure. Correct air pressure is essential to spraying enamels as very low air pressure produces orange peel by producing inadequate atomization of the paint and excessive air pressure tends to disrupt underlying coats and to evaporate solvents before the paint can hit the panel. Good gun technique and adequate setup times also

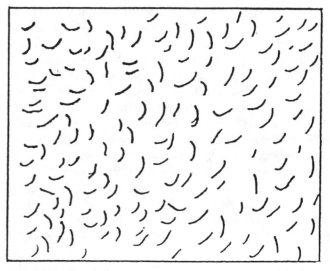

"ORANGE PEEL"

greatly influence the occurrence of orange peel. Remember that some cars were originally painted with large amounts of orange peel, and it is not desirable to eliminate this defect to the point that you create a mismatch with OEM paint in the process. Of course, if you are painting an entire car, you have a chance to improve on the OEM finish.

"BLUSHING"

BLUSHING. This defect is manifested as a cloudiness in color coats and is caused by moisture (humidity) getting into a paint film. The use of too fast a solvent for conditions can cause this defect. This is particularly true on humid days. If it is possible to schedule painting at times that allow you to avoid very humid conditions, this is desirable. Using appropriately slow solvents and even additions of retarder for hot, humid shop conditions should prevent blushing. Sometimes a mist coating with a slow solvent heavily laced with retarder will reverse blushing if you get to it quickly before it dries completely.

FISH EYES. These are small defects where newly applied paint pulls away from small areas and refuses to adhere to them and coat them. They are always caused by wax, oil, or silicone contamination. The best insurance against fish eyes is to carefully wash the area to be

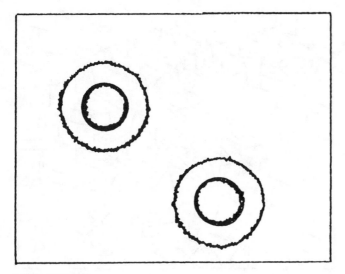

"FISH EYES"

painted with mild detergent and water and then to wipe it down with an oil and silicone removing solvent before sanding. It should be rewiped with this solvent after it is sanded and just before it is painted. Fish eye eliminating additives will suppress fish eyes, but because they do this by saturating paint with silicone, it can cause problems later when another refinish is attempted. In fact, the fish eye problems that you encounter on a previously refinished car may well be due to the excessive use of this additive at the time of the previous refinish.

In some shops, airborne silicone can be pulled into a paint area by ventilation fans that pick up wax debris from cars waxed with silicone waxes in adjacent areas. Some silicones get into painting air supplies because this substance is used as a foam suppressant in most industrial oils, and these oils are commonly used to lubricate air compressors.

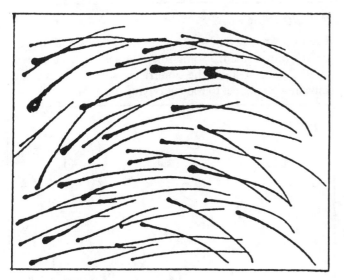

"SAND SCRATCH SWELLING"

SAND SCRATCH SWELLING. This defect produces very small scratch patterns in fresh paint and results from solvent trapped in the bottoms and sides of the grooves left by abrasives. Careful washing between the use of different grits of sandpaper, to avoid abrasive cross-contamination, and final sanding with grits in the range

of 600 should eliminate most of this problem. The use of ultra grades of sandpaper or rubbing compound on vulnerable areas like feather edges is also highly effective. However, this last practice may produce long- range adhesion problems by not leaving enough tooth in the primer for really good adhesion. A final protection against sand scratch swelling involves using an appropriate sealer to prevent the solvent in top coats from penetrating what is under them.

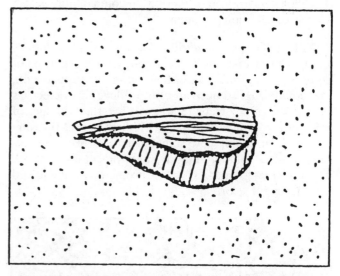

"ADHESION PROBLEMS — PEELING AND LIFTING"

Lifting is one of the ugliest paint failures of all because it is usually very easy to avoid.

ADHESION PROBLEMS — PEELING AND LIFTING. This type of problem may not manifest itself immediately, but it's pretty common because there are so many possible causes for it. Painting over uncured enamel is a common cause of paint lifting and peeling, as are compatibility problems between top coats and their bases. Even when sealers are used, if they are the wrong types for the top coats involved, they will not prevent lifting. Too thick an application or accumulation of paint will cause adhesion problems in the long run, as will the use of incompatible solvents for the paint systems being used. Painting over an unscuffed surface can result in lifting, and painting over oil and other contamination, such as rust, will quickly cause paint to lift. Sandwiching an enamel primer or color coat between lacquer coats will produce lifting at a later date, and failure to provide adequate flash times for lacquers can cause lifting. Sometimes softening an underlying finish with a pre-clean solvent will allow top coat solvents to slightly penetrate it and will provide for better adhesion. Condensation trapped under top coats or primer can expand in warm conditions and cause a finish to lift and peel. This usually first shows up as blisters. Additive incompatibility is also a cause of adhesion problems.

DULLING. This condition involves a gradual loss of gloss or luster in a finish. It is frequently caused by compounding or polishing a finish too soon after application. Inadequate flash times can also produce this defect, as can the use of incorrect additives or incorrect dosages of appropriate additives. Improper reduction and thinning can result in dulling, and sometimes these problems are caused by a "holdout" failure when the color coats sink into underlying paint. This last problem can be solved with the use of a correct sealer.

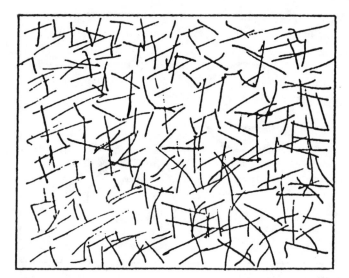

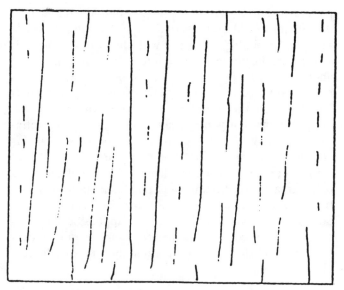

"CHECKING"

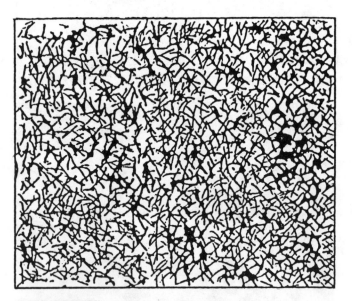

"WRINKLING"

WRINKLING. This defect involves enamels and can have many of the same causes as adhesion problems. It can also be caused by a rapid change in shop temperature conditions in the early cure stage of enamel or by the use of the wrong solvents for shop conditions. Wrinkling often results from additive incompatibility, piling on too many thick, wet coats, or force drying a finish too soon after application and while the solvents are still very present. Low air pressure and surface contamination of underlying surfaces can also cause wrinkling.

CHECKING, CRAZING, AND CRACKING. This kind of stress defect in paint surfaces usually takes some time to show up and is frequently brought out by extreme temperatures. Paint films that are too thick are frequently the cause of cracking defects, and compatibility problems of top coats and undercoats are also often implicated. Additive compatibility problems can cause this

"MICRO-CRACKING"

type of defect, as can inadequate flash times and incompletely mixed paint. Sometimes cracking occurs in a paint surface because the underlying surface cracks and transmits the defect to the overlaying top coats.

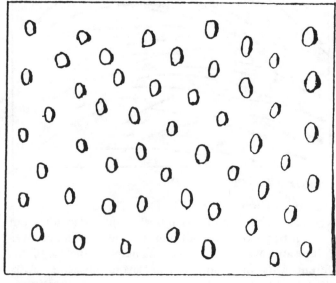

"BLISTERS"

BLISTERS. These nasty little pinhead-sized bumps are usually caused by humidity or moisture trapped under a paint surface. Blisters can be a result of weather conditions (high humidity) at the time the paint was applied. Moisture in your spray air supply or moisture residues from wet sanding that were not removed prior to color coating can also cause blisters.

OVERSPRAY. This defect can, of course, be controlled with proper masking. It can also be compounded out. In enamels, excessive overspray can result from the use of the wrong reducer. Gun technique is also an issue in overspray. The new HVLP spray equipment pretty much eliminates any overspray problems.

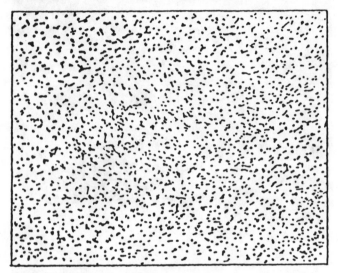

"DRY SPRAY"

DRY SPRAY. This problem can afflict lacquers and enamels and results from the use of the wrong solvent or of an inappropriate gun technique. Any gun technique and air pressure combination should be chosen to atomize a finish and apply it without runs or sags but also in a way that will cause it to flow out smoothly.

SINKING TOP COAT AROUND A FEATHER EDGE. This is the tendency for paint to sink into a feather edged area around a repair and to produce a dull halo effect. The use of a primer-surfacer with good hold-out characteristics should prevent this problem from occurring.

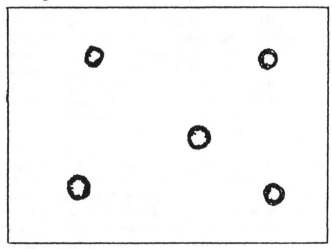

"PINHOLING"

PINHOLING. These little pin-sized rascals in top coats are caused by inadequate flash times with lacquers, by spraying with your gun close to a panel, or by piling paint on too thick and too wet. This type of defect is caused by trapped solvents under paint that was applied too fast or too thick or both.

SINKING. This problem involves the application of paint over incompletely cured body filler or over incompletely dried putty. Both of these substances shrink as they dry, and if they are painted over before they have fully cured or dried, a finish will tend to sink with them.

DRY SPOTS. This is a problem that is usually created by the use of under-thinned or under-reduced paints or by the use of poorly manufactured solvents. Air pressure that is too high will also cause this defect, particularly in lacquers.

"WET SPOTS"

WET SPOTS. This defect involves paint that never dries but always remains tacky. It can be caused by paint contamination, surface contamination, incompatible paint and thinner or reducer, or cold or poorly ventilated drying conditions. Failure to allow undercoats to dry before recoating can also cause this problem.

Finish Maintenance

Automotive finishes are under constant and vicious attack by road dirt, acid rain, industrial soot, flying stones, road salt, humidity, insects, pesticides, and sunlight — to name just a few of the hazards out there. The question naturally arises, "What can be done to protect finishes and prolong their service lives?"

The simplest maintenance of automotive finishes is to wash them regularly with a mild detergent and cold or lukewarm water. Avoid washing a car in direct sunlight and be sure to flush off loose grit with a hose before sponging or wiping a finish. If you don't do this, you will abrade a car's finish when you wash it. Always flush the underside of a car with water when you wash it.

If at all possible, try to use soft water when you wash a car to avoid spotting its paint with the minerals dissolved in hard water. Never wash a car with hot water — it stresses the paint. Always dry a car with a chamois or soft towel after it is washed, and never allow it to air dry without wiping. Any washing process involves rubbing the finish of a car and removes some paint in that process. There is always a very real possibility of scratching a finish when it is being washed. Be sure that sponges, brushes, and towels used in washing and drying are free from grit that could scratch a finish. Belt buckles can be real finish destroyers when you are washing a car.

Proper maintenance of automotive finishes requires that small breaches in paint be repaired, as outlined earlier in this chapter, and this should be done as quickly as possible, certainly before corrosion can penetrate deeply into the metal. Modern paints tend to be very resistant to oxidation compared to their predecessors, but at some point any finish will chalk, and the appearance of oxidation — usually visible as a slight clouding and roughening of a finish's surface in its initial stages — should be compounded and/or polished out.

There are two schools of thought about waxes and about the new super "sealants" that have been on the market for the last decade. One school holds that waxes do little to protect finishes and, because most modern waxes contain abrasives and chemical paint softeners, they tend to deteriorate a finish in the long run. Almost all modern waxes, and particularly the sealants, contain silicones and these get into crevices and later make refinishing difficult. The anti-wax school holds that modern finishes are so inherently tough that they do not benefit from the application of waxes, and that while the appearance of water beading on a freshly waxed hood is a satisfying sight, wax does little to protect a finish. The other school of thought holds that waxes seal and protect paint and even enhance its ability to resist scratching and chemical damage.

I have attended to this question with almost incessant meditation and prayer — it requires no less — and have come to the conclusion that waxing a properly applied modern finish is pointless. There is no significant protection available from waxing, and the abrasion and softening of finishes caused by most waxes is undeniable. If you enjoy waxing a car, I think that you should continue to enjoy this activity, but the probability is that you are doing it for yourself and not for your car. The gloss-enhancing effects of wax are very temporary at best. Certainly wax should not be applied over fresh finishes as it will interfere with their "breathing" and, thus, with their complete drying or curing. Sometimes, cars are waxed after refinishing to remove swirl marks that were induced by hand or machine polishing. There are several products on the market, such as Liquid Ebony and Final Finish, that give freshly painted cars a gloss and temporarily subdue swirl marks without interfering with the drying or curing of a fresh finish. Every time I feel the urge to wax a car, freshly painted or not, I reach for one of these pseudo waxes and use it.

On cars finished with nitrocellulose lacquers or in cases of deteriorated acrylic finishes, waxing probably does help. In these cases, a wax system should be used that has an abrasive polish as a first step and a pure carnauba wax for the second part. This avoids the chemical softeners and silicones that are common to the one-step waxes that are the basis of the waxing controversy.

Areas like this inner fender should be taken to bare metal, painted, and undercoated. Note that the factory was kind enough to leave this area in raw metal below the horizontal paint line that is visible.

Since much of the rust that deteriorates finishes originates from the undersides of panels, there is the idea that sealing a car with undercoating and sealing its trim with paraffin-based sprays will retard body deterioration. I think that this is true if the application of undercoating is very carefully done and if a non-hardening, paraffin-based undercoating is used. The old, asphaltic undercoatings ruined many cars because they hardened and cracked, and in that state they tended to attract moisture to metal by capillary action. They then held moisture against metal, and that helped to rust the metal. Similarly, I have seen modern paraffin-based undercoatings that were so casually applied that rust that might not have otherwise started, occurred at the edge of the application. I have yet to see undercoating stick to the undersides or backsides of panels on a car that was not relatively new when it was undercoated. Steam cleaning an old car will not help in this regard. Undercoating a rusting surface is probably pointless and maybe even counterproductive. It is also critical that if undercoating is used in car doors and other areas that have drainage holes, these holes not be plugged with the undercoating.

One of the greatest contributions that you can make to the survival of the finish on a collector car is good storage. Storage outside in the sun is, of course, bad for paint, upholstery, rubber, etc. Yet storage in a musty, dank garage is just as damaging in other ways. The height of bad storage is to put a car under a plastic sheet so that the plastic (usually polypropylene) can scratch and abrade the finish it contacts. Plastic sheets also tend to trap moisture and keep cars in near rain forest conditions. Car covers, tarps, and the like usually do more harm than good by trapping moisture. I have seen cars ruined by this kind of storage over prolonged periods. I use simple bed sheets to cover cars in storage. Any cover should be at least "breathable," or it should keep moisture entirely away from a car. The Omnibag storage system completely seals a car from moisture in a heavy plastic bag and uses a desiccant that can be periodically dried to keep the moisture level in the bag at desert levels. This system works.

Concrete floors look as if they should be waterproof, but in an untreated state, concrete is a substance that constantly passes and releases moisture that can attack the underside of a car. Putting foamed styrene sheets or polypropylene sheets under concrete before it is poured can help limit this problem. There are also sealants that can be applied over clean concrete that will greatly reduce its ability to release moisture. Putting a four or six mil polypropylene sheet, such as Visqueen, *under* a car in storage can help a lot, but, of course, moisture that the concrete releases still comes around the sides of the car. Good ventilation is your best bet, and this can be arranged in most storage buildings without having to resort to forced draft ventilation.

This approved safety can is a good place to deposit used paint towels and rags because they can spontaneously combust under certain conditions. I hope that your restoration efforts proceed on "full" as you enjoy our wonderful hobby.

About the Author

Matt Joseph was born in December 1944 in New York City and grew up there and in Bennington, Vermont. He attended Deerfield Academy and the University of Chicago and did graduate work at the University of Wisconsin-Madison in American history. He is married and has three children, ages 12, 21, and 25.

Matt has taught college classes on five campuses of the University of Wisconsin System and was employed as an assistant professor of history and program coordinator at U.W.-Extension from 1971 through 1983. He continues to teach classes in the U.W. system on an *ad hoc* basis.

Joseph's passion for automobiles and automotive history dates from the 1950s when he began collecting and restoring cars. His particular marque interests are early Lincolns and postwar Aston Martins.

Since 1983, he has published over 200 feature articles on a wide variety of auto-related topics in several automotive, consumer, and general periodicals and newspapers. Matt is a contributing editor of *Skinned Knuckles* magazine and has written monthly articles on car restoration there for the last seven years. He also contributes a monthly column to *Cars & Parts* magazine, and is an associate editor of that magazine.

The author has served on the board of directors of the Society of Automotive Historians, Inc. and chaired that group's publications awards committee from 1981 through 1989. In 1989 he was elected to a two-year term as president of the society, after which he was elected to a three-year term on the SAH board. He is a former board member and past president of the Wisconsin Chapter of the SAH. He is also a member of 14 other automobile and automotive history organizations.

Joseph has addressed numerous groups on varied automotive topics. He has worked as an industry consultant and has provided consulting services to corporate and government clients on various aspects of automotive design, marketing, purchasing, and policy.

Following his full-time employment as a professor at the University of Wisconsin, Matt became involved in public radio. He co-hosts a weekly program, "About Cars," on the 12-station Wisconsin Public Radio Ideas Network.

In addition to his writing and speaking activities, Matt has sold the rights to automotive inventions and owns and operates a small automotive consulting enterprise, MATTCO — Martinsville Antique Transportation Technologies Company — located in south-central Wisconsin near Madison.

About the Photographer

Joseph W. Jackson III was born in Madison, Wisconsin in 1943. "My mother saved the first drawing I made in kindergarten. It was a car. Well, at least it had wheels." Joe graduated from Madison West High School in 1961 and was drafted into the Army in 1964 where he served two years as an operating room technician. This included a tour of duty in Vietnam.

Joe always appreciated art and design and used a box camera that was given to him as a junior high student. He improved his darkroom skills at the U.S.O. Club photo lab in Saigon, where his Vietnamese instructor knew no more than 10 words of English. Joe's first full-time job was with the *Mason City Globe Gazette* in Mason City, Iowa.

Joe returned to Madison in 1975 as a staff photographer with the *Wisconsin State Journal.* He has won awards in Iowa and Wisconsin, and his photographs have been published nationally on several occasions.

"I met [Matt Joseph] after many years of listening to him on Wsconsin Public Radio. I used to plan my days around his radio program," Joe says.

"I partly agreed to do photographs for this book to learn more about cars, but partly to learn more about Matt. Often we would stop in the middle of a 'shoot' as Matt would march me to the blackboard in his shop for some chalktalk.

"My first car was a 1932 Chevy. It is a sincere hope to someday have another of those beautiful 1920s-1930s cars."

Jackson, a fourth generation Madisonian, resides with his wife and two daughters in Madison.

UNIQUE AUTOMOTIVE REFERENCES